D0744638

Other books in the series

Glen Dudbridge The *Hsi-yu Chi:* A Study of Antecedents to the
Sixteenth-Century Chinese Novel
Stephen Fitzgerald China and the Overseas Chinese: A Study of Peking's
Changing Policy, 1949–70
Christopher Howe Wage Patterns and Wage Policy in Modern China,
1919–1972
Ray Huang Taxation and Government Finance in Sixteenth-Century
Ming China
Diana Lary Region and Nation: The Kwangsi Clique in Chinese Politics,
1925–37
Chi-yun Chen Hsün Yüeh (A.D. 148–209): The Life and Reflection of an Early
Medieval Confucian
David R. Knechtges The Han Rhapsody: A Study of the *Fu* of Yang Hsiung
(53 B.C.–A.D. 18)
J. Y. Wong Yeh Ming-ch'en: Viceroy of Liang Kuang (1852–8)
Li-li Ch'en Master Tung's Western Chamber Romance
(*Tung hsi-hsiang chu-kung-tiao*): A Chinese *Chantefable*
Donald Holzman Poetry and Politics: The Life and Works of Juan Chi
(A.D. 210–63)
C. A. Curwen Taiping Rebel: The Deposition of Li Hsiu-ch'eng
Patricia Buckley Ebrey The Aristocratic Families of Early Imperial China:
A Case Study of the Po-ling Ts'ui Family
Hilary J. Beattie Land and Lineage in China: A Study of Tung-ch'eng County,
Anhwei, in the Ming and Ch'ing Dynasties
William T. Graham, Jr. 'The Lament for the South': Yü Hsin's
Ai Chiang-nan fu
Hans Bielenstein The Bureaucracy of Han Times
Michael J. Godley The Mandarin-Capitalists from Nanyang: Overseas Chinese
Enterprise in the Modernisation of China, 1893–1911
Charles Backus The Nan-chao Kingdom and T'ang China's
Southwestern Frontier
A. R. Davis T'ao Yüan-ming (A.D. 365–427): His Works and Their Meaning
Victor H. Mair Tun-huang Popular Narratives
Ira E. Kasoff The Thought of Chang Tsai (1020–1077)
Ronald C. Egan The Literary Works of Ou-yang Hsiu (1007–1072)
Stanley Weinstein Buddhism Under the T'ang
Robert P. Hymes Statesmen and Gentlemen: The Elite of Fu-Chou, Chiang-hsi,
in Northern and Southern Sung
David McMullen State and Scholars in T'ang China
Arthur Waldron The Great Wall of China
Hugh R. Clark Community, Trade, and Networks: Southern Fujian Province
from the Third to the Thirteenth Century
Denis Twitchett The Writing of Offical History Under the T'ang
J. D. Schmidt Stone Lake: The Poetry of Fan Chenda (1126–1193)
Brian E. McKnight Law and Order in Sung China
Jo-shui Chen Liu Tsung-yuan and Intellectual Change in T'ang China, 773–819
Tim Wright Coal Mining in China's Economy and Society, 1895–1937

Cambridge Studies in Chinese History, Literature, and Institutions
General Editor   Denis Twitchett

SHEN PAO-CHEN AND CHINA'S MODERNIZATION IN THE NINETEENTH CENTURY

沈文肅公真像

Shen Pao-chen and
China's Modernization
in the Nineteenth Century

David Pong
University of Delaware

CAMBRIDGE
UNIVERSITY PRESS

Published by the Press Syndicate of the University of Cambridge
The Pitt Building, Trumpington Street, Cambridge CB2 1RP
40 West 20th Street, New York, NY 10011-4211, USA
10 Stamford Road, Oakleigh, Melbourne 3166, Australia

First published 1994

Printed in the United States of America

Library of Congress Cataloging-in-Publication Data
Pong, David, 1939–
Shen Pao-chen and China's modernization in the nineteenth century/
David Pong.
p.   cm. – (Cambridge studies in Chinese history, literature,
and institutions)
Includes bibliographical references and index.
ISBN 0-521-44163-3
1. Shen, Pao-chen, 1820–1879.   2. China – History – Self-
strengthening movement, 1861–1895.   3. Statesmen – China –
Biography.
I. Title.   II. Series.
DS763.63.S53P66   1993
951′.03 – dc20   92-36630
CIP

A catalog record for this book is available from the British Library.

ISBN 0-521-44163-3 hardback

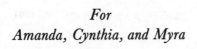

For
Amanda, Cynthia, and Myra

Contents

List of maps, tables, and figure		page x
Acknowledgements		xi
A note on spelling		xv
Abbreviations used in the notes		xvi
Introduction		1
The Ch'ing Restoration		2
The potential for change		11
The subject at hand		17
A question of terms		21
1	**Early years**	24
	Family background and childhood	25
	Marriage and family life	30
	Official of the central government, 1847–55	32
	Conclusions	44
2	**Local official in Kiangsi, 1856–1859**	47
	Tseng Kuo-fan's assistant, January to May 1856	47
	The defence of Kuang-hsin: an act of supreme loyalty	49
	Circuit intendant with two masters	53
	Conclusions	55
3	**Governor of Kiangsi, 1862–1865**	57
	The governor's powers and responsibilities	60
	Civil administration	62
	Military affairs and the dispute with Tseng Kuo-fan over military funds	73
4	**First encounters with foreigners**	87
	The Nanchang antimissionary incident	87
	Foreign affairs and the Confucian polity	98

The end of the first phase of Shen's career: looking
    forwards and backwards   103

5 Director-general of the Foochow Navy Yard   107
Origins of the Foochow Navy Yard   109
Characteristics of the Foochow Navy Yard   112
Shen as first director-general   124
Implications for Shen's political career   129

**6 The Foochow Navy Yard: early developments,
1866–1867**   134
Tso's legacy: a 'five-year plan' begun with a skeleton staff   135
Shen's assumption of office at Ma-wei   140
Chinese opposition   144
Local British and French reactions   153
Conclusions   158

**7 The Foochow Navy Yard: administration and
personnel**   161
Shen and his Chinese staff   162
Discord between the French directors and consular
    interference   176
Chinese and Europeans: harmony at all costs   190
Conclusions   198

**8 The Foochow Navy Yard: building and training
programmes**   203
Construction of the Navy Yard   205
Building a Chinese flotilla   217
Training new naval personnel   225
Conclusions   240

9 The Foochow Navy Yard: financial crises   245
Initial financial arrangements   246
Steamship maintenance and financial crisis   249
Sung Chin and the debate on closing the Navy Yard   254
Continuing financial problems, 1873–5   260
Conclusions   266

**10 The next steps in defence modernization: Ma-wei
and beyond**   272
The command of the Ma-wei vessels   273
Fuel for Ma-wei and China's first modern coal mine   284
Promoting the study of science among China's elite   289

Modernizing China's defence capabilities and erecting the
  first telegraph line 291
Conclusions 295

11 Towards a plan for self-strengthening 299
The way of self-strengthening 301
Towards a stronger and richer China 304

Conclusion 315

Glossary of Chinese characters 338
Bibliography 342
Index 361

Maps, tables, and figure

Maps

1 South-East China   *page* xviii
2 Plan of the Foochow Navy Yard   204

Tables

1 An attempted reconstruction of the revenue of Kiangsi
   province, 1860–4   77
2 Military expenditure of Kiangsi province, 1860–4   79
3 Steamship construction schedule at the Foochow Navy Yard,
   1868–77   219
4 Steamships built at the Foochow Navy Yard during Shen
   Pao-chen's time   220
5 Cost of steamships produced at the Foochow Navy Yard   261

Figure

1 Comparison of the income and maintenance costs for
   steamships retained by the Foochow Navy Yard   250

Acknowledgements

Over the years, I have incurred debts to many. I owe G. William Beasley, Denis C. Twitchett, Wang Erh-min, and Kwang-ching Liu much of what I know about modern Chinese history. The last, in addition, was indefatigable in his constructive criticism of two versions of my manuscript. John K. Fairbank, Ian Nish, Kuo T'ing-i, and a host of his colleagues at the Academia Sinica, too, have been my mentors, and all, at one point or another, helped as only the best of friends would. As one who has spent his entire teaching career in a university without a graduate program in East Asian studies, I have grown to rely on and, yes, exploit the good nature of many of my peers. Jack Gerson, Marianne Bastid-Bruguière, and Hao Yen-p'ing were among the first to read my Ph.D. dissertation and give valuable comments. Successive revisions of the manuscript, necessitated partly by the periodic availability of new, significant archival and other source materials, benefited from the critical contributions of Jane Leonard, Willard J. Peterson, and Tim Wright, who all read substantial portions of the manuscript. They will no doubt recognize traces of their extensive comments in this book. Chapters that were presented as papers during my three years at the Australian National University benefited from the lively seminars there, whose regular participants included Wang Gungwu, Lo Hui-min, Joe Moore, John Fincher, Antonia Finnane, and the late Jennifer Cushman.

Given that my study required working with difficult sources, I would like to mention Wang Erh-min once more, for he has taught me so much about Ch'ing institutions and how to read Ch'ing documents. Similarly, D. C. Lau, at one time a colleague at the School of Oriental and African Studies (S.O.A.S.), showed me the way to better translation. For their invaluable assistance at the French archives and with the rendering of numerous difficult passages into English, I am indebted to Caroline

Phillips Mustill, Frances Bazela Katsuura, and F. de Burgh Whyte. For the much-improved prose of this study, credit goes to the copy editor, Mary Racine. It goes without saying, however, that the flaws in style and content are entirely mine.

Studying the varied career of Shen Pao-chen required the use of a broad range of primary sources scattered around the world. Locating these materials alone was a daunting task. In this, however, I had the good fortune of friends and colleagues who not only drew my attention to these valuable materials but in some cases selflessly supplied me with copies. Thus, from Marianne Bastid-Bruguière I obtained a copy of Giquel's diary; from Shen Tsu-hsing of Taipei, Shen's unpublished memorials and the 'Chia-p'u' of his family; from Lin Qingyuan of Foochow, some of Shen's unpublished letters; from F. E. Elliott of Saltash, Cornwall, the private papers of James Carroll; and from Lai Chi-kong, a copy of Li Hung-chang's letters to Ting Jih-ch'ang, newly published.

The helpfulness, good humour, and patience of archivists, curators, and librarians everywhere I went should not go unmentioned. I extend my thanks especially to John Lust of S.O.A.S.; M. Audouy, conservateur en chef des Archives de Ministère de la Marine at Château de Vincennes; Y. S. Chan and Sydney Wang, respectively, of the Australian National University Library and the Australian National Library; Lai Shu-tim of the University of Hong Kong; Eugene Wu of the Harvard-Yenching Library; and Margaret Wang and Vivian Chou of the University of Delaware Library. In addition, I benefited from the assistance of countless women and men who staffed the numerous research collections I had the good fortune to visit. Other than the institutions already mentioned, these include the Public Record Office, the University of London Library, the British Museum (now the British Library), the National Maritime Museum at Greenwich, the Cambridge University Library, the Archives de la Ministère des Affaires Etrangères, the Fu Ssu-nien Library, the Institute of Modern History Archives at the Academia Sinica, the National Palace Museum of Taipei, the Taiwan Provincial Museum, the Taiwan Provincial Library, the Tainan Provincial Museum, the Toyo Bunko, the Fujian Provincial Library, the U.S. National Archives, the Library of Congress, and the libraries at Columbia, Princeton, and Hawaii universities.

Parts of this study are drawn from works previously published. Though they appear here revised and updated, I am nonetheless grateful to the following for permission to use these materials: *Modern Asian Studies*, the *Journal of Asian Studies*, the *Journal of the Institute of Chinese Studies of the Chinese University of Hong Kong*, and *Papers on Far Eastern History*.

The long years that I have taken to complete this book have required great personal sacrifice by those around me. Yet they have been patient, forbearing, and loving. My wife, Barbara, has been supportive throughout. And our children have been a source of spiritual uplift when I was down. I wish I could write enough books to dedicate one to each of them!

A note on spelling

This book uses the Wade–Giles system for transliterating Chinese names and terms. For the spelling of place names, the *Chinese Postal Atlas* has been used as a guide. However, where the latter is inadequate in distinguishing a town or a region from an administrative unit of the same name, the administrative units have been rendered according to the Wade–Giles system. For example:

Chinese Postal Atlas	*Wade–Giles system*
Taiwan (island)	T'ai-wan (prefecture or circuit, depending on the suffix or context)
Kiukiang (town, treaty port)	Chiu-chiang (prefecture)

This convention enables the reader to identify, for instance, the Chiu-chiang component in the Kuang-Jao-Chiu-Nan circuit in Kiangsi province.

Abbreviations used
in the notes

CHTC	*Chiang-hsi t'ung-chih* (Gazetteer of Kiangsi province)
CTSM	*T'ung-chih chia-hsü Jih-ping ch'in-T'ai shih-mo* (The complete account of the Japanese invasion of Taiwan in 1874)
FCTC	*Fu-chien t'ung-chih* (Gazetteer of Fukien province)
FCTC : LCH	*Fu-chien t'ung-chih lieh-chuan hsüan* (Selections from the biographical section of *Fu-chien t'ung-chih*)
FO	Great Britain, Foreign Office Archives
HFT	*Hai-fang tang* (Facsimile of the maritime defence file)
IWSM	*Ch'ou-pan i-wu shih-mo* (The complete account of our management of barbarian affairs)
LKI	Liu K'un-i, *Liu K'un-i i-chi* (Collected works of Liu K'un-i)
LWCK	Li Hung-chang, *Li Wen-chung kung ch'üan-chi* (The complete works of Li Hung-chang)
MAE	France, Ministère des Affaires Etrangères
MHHC	*Min-Hou hsien-chih* (Gazetteer of Min and Hou-kuan districts)
MM	France, Ministère de la Marine
NCH	*North-China Herald and Supreme Court and Consular Gazette*
SCTI	*Tao Hsien T'ung Kuang ssu-ch'ao tsou-i* (Memorials from the Tao-kuang, Hsien-feng, T'ung-chih, and Kuang-hsü reigns)
Shih-lu	*Ta-Ch'ing li-ch'ao shih-lu* (Veritable records for the successive reigns of the Ch'ing dynasty)
SWSK	Shen Pao-chen, *Shen Wen-su kung cheng-shu* (The political works of Shen Pao-chen)
TWCK	Tseng Kuo-fan, *Tseng Wen-cheng kung ch'üanchi* (The complete works of Tseng Kuo-fan)
TWHK	Tso Tsung-t'ang, *Tso Wen-hsiang kung ch'üan-chi* (The complete works of Tso Tsung-t'ang)

TWTC   *T'ai-wan t'ung-chih* (Gazetteer of T'ai-wan)
TY:CHCW   China, Tsungli Yamen Archives: Chiang-hsi chiao-wu
           (Missionary affairs in Kiangsi)
TY:'O'   China, Tsungli Yamen Archives: 'O' (Russian file)
YCT   China, National Palace Museum Archives: Yüeh-che tang
           (Monthly compilation of memorials for the State History
           Office in the Ch'ing dynasty)
YWYT   *Yang-wu yün-tung* (the *yang-wu* movement)

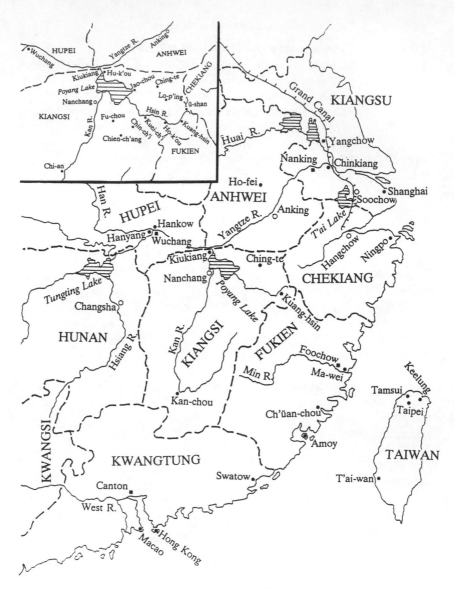

Map 1. South-East China

Introduction

In the middle decades of the nineteenth century, the viability of the Ch'ing dynasty was severely tested. Massive internal uprisings, defeat in two foreign wars, and continued external threats could have toppled the two-century-old Manchu ruling house. Only the timely emergence of 'a galaxy of extraordinarily able officials' saved it from extinction.[1] They put down the rebellions, worked hard at reconstruction, attempted to upgrade the bureaucracy, and tried to restore the old order. To block further imperialist inroads, they adopted aspects of Western diplomatic practices and military technology. By dint of dedication and effort, these men tried to bring about a dynastic revival – the Ch'ing Restoration – and prolonged the life of the dynasty by half a century.

This book is about one of those 'extraordinary able officials' whose life and career were an integral part of the late Ch'ing experience. This man was Shen Pao-chen (1820–79), who began his journey to the top of Ch'ing officialdom after passing the civil service examinations. At the relatively young age of forty-one (1862), he was already the governor of an important province in the rich Yangtze valley. Then, in 1867, abandoning the security of high office and the chance for an early promotion to the rank of governor-general, he accepted the leadership of China's first fully fledged modern naval dockyard and held that position for more than eight years. His career closed with a four-year term as governor-general of Liang Kiang, which comprised the key provinces of Kiangsu, Anhwei, and Kiangsi. He was thus a pivotal person of the period; his public life touched almost all of the important aspects of the Ch'ing Restoration. But before we can begin discussing the man, we

---

1 Mary C. Wright, *The Last Stand of Chinese Conservatism: The T'ung-chih Restoration, 1862–1874*, second printing (Stanford, Calif., 1962), p. 312. Unless otherwise stated, all references to this work are to the second printing.

1

must take stock of our inherited understanding of the Restoration itself and to examine the potential for change in late Ch'ing China.

The Ch'ing Restoration

No discussion of the Ch'ing Restoration would be complete without reference to Mary Wright's magisterial work, first published in 1957.[2] In it she argues that the Restoration was essentially a conservative movement; its thrust was to revamp and revitalize the old Confucian order. The cultivation of and search for good, moral men in government and the restoration of the agrarian economy were central to the entire effort. There were innovations, however. They involved, on a limited scale, improvement of the traditional armed forces, including some use and manufacture of Western arms, and new means for handling foreign affairs. The military undertakings are subsumed by scholars under the rubric 'Self-strengthening Movement' (*tzu-ch'iang yün-tung*), and those associated with the use of Western methods or technology are known as *yang-wu* (literally, Western matters or Western affairs). But these innovations were promoted or tolerated only because they were deemed necessary for preserving the old order, not its modernization. Thus, even though the Western powers, under the 'Co-operative Policy', created a favourable international environment for China's modernization, the Restoration leaders could not halt the dynastic decline. By the time the Co-operative Policy was discarded in 1869 and 1870 (the rejection of the Alcock Convention and the Tientsin Massacre), all the signs of failure had become, or were soon to become, apparent. Wright therefore concludes that the requirements of Confucian stability were not compatible with the demands of modernization. The Restoration was doomed to failure.

That the Restoration failed is not in question – the degree of the failure is. Most of the controversies among historians, however, focus on the causes of failure. In recent years, Wright's central thesis that Confucianism was incompatible with modernization has been challenged. Wang Erh-min, for example, contends that Confucianism and Western learning, especially Western science and technology, were not at all incompatible: some scholars of the early nineteenth century were quite receptive to Western scientific ideas, and a few even applauded Western political institutions.[3] Other historians also conclude that Confucian

---

2 Ibid.
3 Wang Erh-min, 'Ju-chia ch'uan-t'ung yü chin-tai Chung-Hsi ssu-ch'ao chih hui-t'ung', *Hsin-ya hsüeh-shu chi-k'an*, no. 2 (1979), 163–78.

values were not in themselves an obstacle to change and, in some cases, were an adequate basis for the formulation of new ideas.[4]

In the realm of implementation, Kwang-ching Liu points out some real successes – there had been a 'reassertion of the essential features of the Ch'ing polity ... [and] despite certain necessary adjustments, the inherited institutions persisted'.[5] There were failures, he admits, but what really prevented the Restoration from developing into a more effective reform movement was the opposition of the high authorities. The flexibility granted the officials by the throne during the Taiping era was quickly replaced by a return to rigid adherence to rules and regulations.[6]

As the debate continues, our attention is also drawn to the ideology and self-interests of specific elite groups, the role of the gentry and of the various strata of government, the throne, the powerful provincial leaders (regionalism), institutional inertia, the impact of imperialism, and the strengths and weaknesses of the traditional economy.

On the ideology and self-interests of elite groups, Jonathan Ocko argues that a key to understanding the Restoration lies in the way reform-minded scholar-officials analysed and dealt with the problems of government.[7] These officials, informed by the School of Practical Statecraft (*ching-shih*), clung for too long to the preconceived notion that effective government depended largely on administrative measures and the selection of moral men. They failed to get at the root of China's problems – the social inequities among the traditional elites. They ignored both the personal ambitions of the nonofficial scholar-gentry class and its desire for reform, especially in improving local government. The two groups thus competed as much as they co-operated, particularly in the areas of tax collection and local control. A weak imperial institution, represented by a boy-emperor and his regents led by Prince Kung and

4 Lü Shih-ch'iang, 'Feng Kuei-fen ti cheng-chih ssu-hsiang', *Chung-hua wen-hua fu-hsing yüeh-k'an*, 4.2 (February 1971), 1–8; Liu Kwang-ching, 'Nineteenth-Century China: The Disintegration of the Old Order and the Impact of the West', in Ping-ti Ho and Tang Tsou, eds., *China in Crisis* (Chicago, 1968), vol. 1, book 1, p. 142; Albert Feuerwerker, 'Economic Aspects of Reform', and Saundra Sturdevant, 'Imperialism, Sovereignty, and Self-strengthening: A Reassessment of the 1870's', both in Paul A. Cohen and John E. Schrecker, eds., *Reform in Nineteenth-century China* (Cambridge, Mass., 1976), pp. 36 and 67; Shannon R. Brown, 'The Ewo Filature: A Study in the Transfer of Technology to China in the 19th Century', *Technology and Culture*, 20.3 (July 1979), 550–68.

5 Kwang-ching Liu, 'The Ch'ing Restoration', in John K. Fairbank, ed., The Cambridge History of China, vol. 10, *Late Ch'ing, 1800–1911*, part 1 (Cambridge, 1978), pp. 477–8.

6 Ibid. The Restoration failed particularly to improve the quality of local government.

7 Jonathan K. Ocko, *Bureaucratic Reform in Provincial China: Ting Jih-ch'ang in Restoration Kiangsu, 1867–1870* (Cambridge, Mass., 1983).

the Empress Dowager Tz'u-hsi, was in no position to provide direction or support to either group for innovative change. Ocko thus lays the blame on the self-interests as well as a fatal blind spot in the intellectual heritage of the reforming officials.

Inevitably, different sociopolitical groups perceived the Restoration differently and chose their course of action accordingly. For instance, the gentry of Soochow, in James Polachek's view, simply used the Restoration as an opportunity to seize power from the local government. The resulting conflict then largely nullified the effort of dynastic revival.[8] Yet the study of the gentry's activism does not always yield a bleak picture. Philip Kuhn, for example, acknowledges the growing power of the gentry during and after the Taiping era, but stresses that the local elite were, at the same time, brought into the formal structure of local government at the expense of rapacious clerks and runners. Such a development, in fact, was quite in tune with the Restoration objective of revitalizing local government.[9]

The growth of powerful regional leaders is yet another evil often attributed to the Restoration. It originated in the exigencies created by the Taiping Rebellion, which had led to the growth of mercenary armies (*yung-ying*) commanded by actual or would-be provincial officials. They recruited their troops from their own provinces and drew their financial support, though with imperial approval, largely from the regions in which they operated. With provincial revenue and the commercial transit duties (the likin) under their control, these high officials gained great, even autonomous power.[10] Since the bulk of the Restoration leaders came from among their ranks, and since many of them vigorously promoted such *yang-wu* enterprises as arsenals and shipyards as part of their Restoration effort, it is not hard to conjure up a picture in which personal or regional power was the ultimate concern.

The growth of 'regionalism', as this phenomenon is called, has been analysed by Franz Michael and Stanley Spector. They stress in particular the personal loyalty the regional leaders commanded of their military and civilian staff. As a result, these powerful men, even as they were

8 James Polachek, 'Gentry Hegemony: Soochow in the T''ung-chih Restoration', in Frederic Wakeman, Jr., and Carolyn Grant, eds., *Conflict and Control in Late Imperial China* (Berkeley and Los Angeles, 1975), pp. 211–56.

9 Philip A. Kuhn, *Rebellion and Its Enemies in Late Imperial China: Militarization and Social Structure, 1796–1864* (Cambridge, Mass., 1970), and idem, 'Local Self-Government under the Republic: Problems of Control, Autonomy, and Mobilization', in Wakeman and Grant, eds., *Conflict and Control*, pp. 265–8.

10 Lo Yü-tung, *Chung-kuo li-chin shih* (Shanghai, 1936), vol. 1, pp. 84–6. Control over these resources was facilitated by the power of the governors-general and governors to appoint financial managers from among large pools of expectant officials. The latter were thus beholden to the high officials for their preferment.

shifted from province to province, never lost control over their sub-ordinates and the resources at their disposal. Michael further argues that these regional leaders, once installed in power, did not dissolve their political or military organizations at the end of the rebellions, which were the raison d'être of their existence. He asserts that, as regionalism undermined central control, there was no real dynastic Restoration.[11]

Michael and Spector's thesis has been challenged by Kwang-ching Liu, Wang Erh-min, and myself. By taking a closer look at how decisions and political appointments were made, how a large number of 'regional' armies were disbanded in the mid-1860s and the remaining troops were financed and moved about, and how disputes were resolved, we have found that these so-called regionalists were far more loyal to the Ch'ing court and the latter far more in control of provincial affairs than Michael and Spector have alleged.[12]

According to some, this rebuttal has won the day.[13] But according to Stephen MacKinnon, in the redistribution of power in the late Ch'ing, there emerged 'three simultaneously expanding and overlapping nodes of power', namely, the central government, the provincial leaders, and the local elites at the subdistrict level. None expanded at the expense of the others.[14] Be that as it may, the regionalism thesis still has its following, kept alive largely by historians of twentieth-century China, who find in it a plausible explanation for the rise of warlordism after 1916.[15]

11 Stanley Spector, *Li Hung-chang and the Huai Army: A Study in Nineteenth-Century Chinese Regionalism* (Seattle, Wash., 1964). The introduction, entitled 'Regionalism in Nineteenth-Century China', is by Franz Michael. The first major works to argue along this line were those of Lo Erh-kang and P'eng Yü-hsin. Lo, 'Ch'ing-chi ping wei chiang-yu ti ch'i-yüan', *Chung-kuo she-hui ching-chi shih chi-k'an*, 5.2 (June 1937), 235–50; P'eng, 'Ch'ing-mo chung-yang yü ko-sheng ts'ai-cheng kuan-hsi', *She-hui-k'o-hsüeh tsa-chih*, 9.1 (June 1947), 83–110. Both have been reprinted in *Chung-kuo chin-tai-shih lun-ts'ung*, 2d ser., vol. 5: *Cheng-chih*, comp. Li Ting-i, Pao Tsun-p'eng, and Wu Hsiang-hsiang (Taipei, 1963), pp. 85–100 and 3–46, respectively. Future references are to the reprint edition.

12 David Pong, 'The Income and Military Expenditure of Kiangsi Province in the Last Years (1860–1864) of the Taiping Rebellion', *Journal of Asian Studies*, 26.1 (November 1966), 49–66; Wang Erh-min, *Huai-chün chih* (Taipei, 1967), esp. pp. 376–86; Kwang-ching Liu, 'The Limits of Regional Power in the Late Ch'ing Period: A Reappraisal', *Tsing Hua hsüeh-pao*, new ser., 10.2 (July 1974), 176–207 [in Chinese] and 207–23 [in English].

13 Thomas L. Kennedy, 'Self-Strengthening: An Analysis Based on Some Recent Writings', *Ch'ing-shih wen-t'i*, 3.1 (November 1974), 5–6.

14 Stephen R. MacKinnon, *Power and Politics in Late Imperial China: Yuan Shi-kai in Beijing and Tianjin, 1901–1908* (Berkeley and Los Angeles, 1980), pp. 5–10.

15 See, e.g., James E. Sheridan, *Chinese Warlord: The Career of Feng Yü-hsiang* (Stanford, Calif., 1966), pp. 1–9, and Diana Lary, *Region and Nation: The Kwangsi Clique in Chinese Politics, 1925–1937* (Cambridge, 1974), pp. 1–17. Although both trace the origins of modern regionalism to the mid-nineteenth century, both emphasize that twentieth-century warlordism was not a direct descendant of the regionalism of the Taiping

A major obstacle to understanding the phenomenon of regionalism is its frequent confusion with provincialism and other levels of local interests. Regionalism, as just defined, was not an accepted norm in the traditional state. There was always opposition to it, ideologically and politically. The so-called regional leaders discussed by Michael were never fully able to take over the provinces they 'occupied'. Provincial officials continued to be appointed from Peking, and they had as much to gain (or lose) by aligning themselves with the 'regional' leaders as with local interests, which often resisted the extractive alien 'regional' regimes. Provincialism, in fact, was a far more prevalent form of political power with which all men with regional pretensions must contend. And, in contrast to regionalism, provincialism was a perennial feature of the Chinese state. Though not encouraged (certainly when it became excessive), it was nevertheless condoned by the imperial government.

The power structure within a province was complex. Local interests (at the district or prefectural level) were frequently at odds with larger provincial interests. And ambitious or energetic governors-general and governors could too easily be misconstrued as harbouring regional desires. Thus, in this study, I distinguish regionalism from provincialism, localized interests, and the personal ambitions of high provincial officials.

Assuming, for the sake of argument, that regionalism was a widespread phenomenon, its impact has still to be determined. Within the framework of the traditional political order, which the Restoration tried to revive, regionalism was ultimately antidynastic, as Michael and Spector suggest. Yet as an expression of the desire for greater regional or personal power, regionalism could accommodate, and even welcome, most forms of *yang-wu* undertakings, which were an integral part, and, some would argue, a more progressive part, of the Restoration. In this regard, the view can be sustained that regionalism, despite its antidynastic appearance, in fact provided the mechanism by which local leaders could go beyond the limits of change imposed by the central government. Greater successes on the part of the regional leaders in their *yang-wu* enterprises could well have reversed dynastic decline. The question is, why did they not achieve more?

Developing his argument mainly from Mary Wright's ideas and to a lesser degree from Michael and Spector's, John Rawlinson contends that

era. In a later work, Sheridan clearly states: 'The regional army leaders [of the nineteenth century] used their armies on behalf of the monarchy. More than that, they were personally subject to the authority of the monarchy. (The political–military machines they created did not flourish into the twentieth century and then overthrow the monarchy, as is sometimes suggested.)' See his *China in Disintegration: The Republican Era in Chinese History, 1912–1949* (New York, 1975), p. 37.

it was traditional institutions, based on Confucian ideology, that gave the Restoration and *yang-wu* movement their essential character and limited their achievements. Thus, China's tardy and inadequate response to the Western challenge, such as the failure to develop a national navy, as opposed to a number of competing provincial squadrons, can be directly traced to a weak imperial institution and strong regional loyalties.[16] Rawlinson thus implies that regionalism both promoted and hindered *yang-wu* modernization.

Adopting a broader perspective, Thomas Kennedy tries to strike a balance between internal and external forces which influenced *yang-wu* modernization. China's modern ordnance industry, he argues, was an institutional innovation which ushered in a new era of mass production. It could have served as the foundation of a light industry but for the semicolonial environment in which it emerged. The financial troubles of the arsenals and the poor quality of the foreign technicians were partly attributable to the nature of the Western presence. The Chinese, for their part, managed the arsenals as they would have a bureau in the traditional government, resulting in corruption and inefficiency. Poor imperial leadership as well as the lack of co-ordination among provincial officials complete the list of reasons for what went wrong.[17]

The impact of imperialism, all too briefly and obliquely discussed by Kennedy, is more systematically addressed by L. A. Bereznii and Frances Moulder. The former, a Marxist scholar, stresses the deleterious effects of imperialism: it was economically exploitative as well as politically, socially, and psychologically damaging. The imperialists, by supporting the Ch'ing regime and 'reactionary elements' such as Tseng Kuo-fan and Li Hung-chang, inhibited progress. China's failure and Japan's success in modernizing their countries were directly related to their different degrees of exposure to imperialist exploitation.[18]

Moulder, in contrast, adopts the world-system approach. She argues that the traditional societies of China and Japan were essentially similar. Institutional or cultural factors therefore cannot explain their failure or success. Rather, China's failure should be understood in terms of its higher level of incorporation into the world economy (and therefore greater Western encroachment). By bringing about the Opium Wars the

16 John L. Rawlinson, *China's Struggle for Naval Development, 1839–1895* (Cambridge, Mass., 1967), pp. 198–204.
17 Thomas L. Kennedy, *The Arms of Kiangnan: Modernization in the Chinese Ordnance Industry, 1860–1895* (Boulder, Colo., 1978), pp. 150–60.
18 L. A. Bereznii, 'A Critique of American Bourgeois Historiography on China: Problems of Social Development in the Nineteenth and Early Twentieth Centuries', an unauthorized digest of the book by the same title [in Russian; Leningrad, 1968] (Cambridge, Mass., 1969).

West also caused much economic and social dislocation. Large-scale rebellions resulted. All contributed to the dismantling of the state apparatus, leading to the rise of regionalism (à la Spector). Incorporation also severely reduced the central government's capacity to finance, among other things, modern enterprises.[19]

In recent years in post-Mao China, there has been a revival of scholarly interest in the *yang-wu* movement. Previously, the prevailing view of the movement was negative: it was seen as a plot by the feudal elites – the Ch'ing officials – to shore up their power. They collaborated with Western capitalists, exploited the people, and sold out Chinese interests. Although by introducing modern industries they broke the ground for Chinese capitalism, they also hindered capitalistic developments and hastened the growth of semicolonialism. Feudal control and semicolonial exploitation severely deformed the native capitalism, and it remained uncorrected until after 1949.[20]

Since 1978 the discussion has been far more open and lively. Though some scholars still adhere to the established view, more are seeing the *yang-wu* movement in a relatively favourable light. The latter argue, for example, that it was simply a product of the time. As such, it promoted the development of capitalism. The leaders of the movement, despite their class origins and intentions, introduced modern industries, produced new ideas, trained new talents, and created an environment in which a working class could emerge. In consequence, their efforts slowed rather than abetted the growth of semicolonialism. The movement nevertheless failed because of imperialism and the bureaucratic vices associated with the management of its enterprises.[21]

---

19 Frances V. Moulder, *Japan, China, and the Modern World Economy: Toward a Reinterpretation of East Asian Development, ca. 1600 to ca. 1918* (Cambridge, 1977). According to Stephen C. Thomas, the adverse effect of imperialism on Chinese industrial development did not become serious until the 1890s. See his *Foreign Intervention and China's Industrial Development, 1870–1911* (Boulder, Colo., 1984).

20 Mou An-shih, *Yang-wu yün-tung* (Shanghai, 1961), and *Yang-wu yün-tung*, by the editorial group of the Chung-kuo chin-tai-shih ts'ung-shu [Modern Chinese history] series (Shanghai, 1973).

21 The picture painted here is a composite one only. The actual debate contains many shades of interpretation even among those who see some progressive elements in the *yang-wu* movement. *Chung-kuo li-shih-hsüeh nien-chien*, ed. Chung-kuo shih-hsüeh-hui (Peking, Annual). See volumes for 1979 (pp. 157–67), 1981 (pp. 84–93), 1982 (pp. 93–9), 1983 (pp. 84–90), and 1984 (pp. 105–13) (there seems to have been no publication for the year 1980); *Chi-lin ta-hsüeh she-hui k'o-hsüeh lun-ts'ung*, 1980, no. 2: *Yang-wu yün-tung t'ao-lun chuan-chi*, ed. Chi-lin ta-hsüeh she-hui k'o-hsüeh hsüeh-pao pien-chi-pu (Chi-lin, 1981); Huang I-feng, *Chung-kuo chin-tai ching-chi-shih lun-wen-chi* (Yangchow, 1981), pp. 182–376; Chang Kuo-hui, *Yang-wu yün-tung yü Chung-kuo chin-tai ch'i-yeh* (Peking, 1979); Huang I-feng and Chiang To, 'Ch'ung p'ing yang-wu yün-tung', *Li-shih yen-chiu*, 1979.2, 58–70; and Hsü T'ai-lai, 'Yeh p'ing yang-wu yün-tung',

Scholars in China, unlike their counterparts elsewhere, have to live with the consequences of the *yang-wu* movement. Its failure may well have had much to do with post-1949 developments. Chinese discussion on the subject is more impassioned than it is in the West and, given the Marxian historical framework, more preoccupied with the function of the *yang-wu* movement in China's development from feudalism to semifeudalism and semicolonialism and to bureaucratic capitalism. It is therefore critical for historians in China to determine the class origins of the *yang-wu* movement, its phases of development over thirty-five years, its internal contradictions, the role it played in the penetration of Western capitalism and the attendant problems of technological transfer, and its contribution to the emergence of national capitalism – in brief, whether it was moving along with or was opposed to the currents of history, whether it was progressive or reactionary.

The outlandish terminology belies the many areas of common ground shared by Chinese and non-Chinese historians alike. 'Feudalism', for instance, encompasses such concerns as the nature of the traditional order and its ideological foundation; 'semicolonialism' deals with the nature and impact of imperialism; and 'bureaucratic capitalism' entails the manner of government or official intervention in industrial and economic affairs. Nevertheless, Chinese scholars seem less concerned with the role of the central government, especially that of the imperial institution. It is generally assumed that the throne, the central government, and the bureaucrats belonged to the same class and were, therefore, a single historical force.

We have already alluded to the negative role of the central government. Dwight Perkins regards the fault of the central government as one of omission rather than commission. What made it so helpless, he observes, was a lack of money.[22] My recent work shows, in contrast, that the court at Peking squandered an opportunity to create an imperial navy largely because of its reluctance to change the system of public financing, though insufficient funds were also a factor.[23] The subject certainly bears further investigation.

ibid., 1980.4, 19–36. The last two are quite representative of the tone of the debate in the late 1970s and the early 1980s.

22 Dwight H. Perkins, 'Government as an Obstacle to Industrialization: The Case of Nineteenth-Century China', *Journal of Economic History*, 27.4 (December 1967), 478–92. More recently, Madeleine Zelin has shown that at least in early Ch'ing the ability of the central government to introduce reforms was hamstrung by a lack of means rather than a lack of vision or will. Zelin, *The Magistrate's Tael: Rationalizing Fiscal Reform in Eighteenth-century China* (Berkeley and Los Angeles, 1984).

23 David Pong, 'Keeping the Foochow Navy Yard Afloat: Government Finance and China's Early Modern Defence Industry, 1866–75', *Modern Asian Studies*, 21.1 (February 1987), 121–52.

As regards the impact of the economy on the Restoration, no comprehensive picture has yet emerged. In broad terms, it appears certain that the economy, as reflected by the standard of living, had changed little from the Ming to the late Ch'ing. Yet the devastation of the midcentury rebellions was immense, a situation with which the Restorationists had to contend.[24]

A depressed rural economy with diminished tax yields undoubtedly undercut the government's ability to function. But the loss was more than compensated for by two new taxes: customs duties on foreign trade and likin on domestic trade. In fact, the size of the Ch'ing economy as well as that of government revenue, in relation to its population, may have reached new heights in the post-Taiping era. The question is, who controlled these resources and directed their use?

Albert Feuerwerker's recent study suggests that in the late Ch'ing there existed the potential for savings but the government, even in normal times, did not penetrate deeply enough into society to tap those resources or manage the people's economic life. It lacked both the facilities and the political power to do so. The several Restoration leaders who advocated government intervention to bring about economic development ran into stiff opposition from the local elites. The latter were either ideologically averse to change or disinclined to bear the economic burden of development.[25] Feuerwerker thus shifts the blame for the failure of the Restoration away from imperialism and back to the internal weakness of the Ch'ing system.

The achievement of the Restoration (including its *yang-wu* component) has been characterized in divergent ways, ranging from near success to mere illusion. Whatever the judgement, it remains a significant and critical phase in modern Chinese history. Nevertheless, many questions remain unanswered. For example, the influence of the local elite on administrative reform has received some scholarly treatment, but what was the relationship between the increasingly powerful gentry and *yang-wu* enterprises? And if regionalism was indeed the driving force behind many *yang-wu* undertakings, did it not also hinder, inhibit, or distort *yang-wu* modernization? The distinction between regionalism and provincialism having been clarified, how should it affect our understanding of the Restoration?

Concerning the throne, adequate evidence is seldom evinced to demon-

24 Dwight H. Perkins, *Agricultural Development in China (1368–1968)* (Chicago, 1969), pp. 28–9, 186–9.
25 Albert Feuerwerker, 'Economic Trends in the Late Ch'ing Empire, 1870–1911', in John K. Fairbank and Kwang-ching Liu, eds., The Cambridge History of China, vol. 11, *Late Ch'ing, 1800–1911*, part 2 (Cambridge, 1980), pp. 59–61, 65, 67–8.

strate its negative impact on the Restoration. The part played by the central government and the conservatives, also frequently alluded to, is even less well documented. The impact of imperialism could certainly bear further investigation. We particularly need to look at the so-called Co-operative Policy at all levels. Finally, if we do possess some overall picture of China's economy in the second half of the nineteenth century, we certainly need to know more about the way it affected the Restoration in its multifaceted operation, and how successfully the leading officials altered the administration of financial matters to suit their needs.

Undoubtedly, the tone of our enquiry has been dominated by the indisputable fact that, at a point still to be determined, the Restoration failed. We have concentrated too much on the negative. Would a more open-ended enquiry yield a different picture of traditional China? If, indeed, we see new strengths in the *ancien régime*, would it not lead us to a fresh assessment of why the Restoration met with failure?

This study on the life and career of Shen Pao-chen (up to 1875) intends to shed new light on some of these questions. But before we begin, we must turn to another issue: the potential for change in traditional China.

The potential for change

Until recent decades, the prevailing image of old China in the West was one of stagnation. Things hardly ever changed, or they changed mainly in cycles. This view was shared by a wide spectrum of scholars, from Hegel and Marx to Spengler and Toynbee. It was also held by those who dealt with or shaped policies towards China. The traditional Chinese historians, who habitually saw their own past in cyclical terms, reinforced this perception.

In the past fifty years or so, Western as well as Chinese and Japanese historians have begun to see patterns of change in China's past. Among them there exists a strong predilection for analysing Chinese history in terms of stages of development, an approach that would render Chinese history comprehensible in a global context. They focus on pivotal changes between vast expanses of time. For instance, Karl A. Wittfogel sees a single period (that of the 'Complex' Hydraulic Society) lasting from about the third century B.C. to the nineteenth century. For Naito Konan and the Kyoto school of Chinese studies, the 'autocratic' stage ran from the mid-T'ang (c. 800 A.D.) to the 1830s or 1840s. And for many Marxist historians in China, the 'feudal' stage spanned nearly three thousand years, from early Chou (1027 B.C.) to the Opium War (1839–42)! Although this extended period is often divided into phases, each

11

The School of Empirical Research, known also as Han Learning, was a break-away of seventeenth-century Sung and Ming Confucianism. Critical of the latter's preoccupation with metaphysics, it called for the rediscovery of true Confucian principles through solidly grounded study of the classics (*shih-hsüeh*) and for the prudent application of those principles in action (*shih-hsing*). This School, unfortunately, quickly divorced itself from Confucian sociomoral concerns and turned almost exclusively to textual and philological studies.

But Confucianism, being concerned primarily with 'setting the world in order', could not tolerate such a divorce for long, certainly not in a time of crisis. So towards the end of the eighteenth century, when government inefficiency and corruption reached new heights, reaction set in. Scholars of both Sung and Han Learning began to revive the sociopolitical emphasis of Confucianism. An eclectic approach to the study or application of Confucianism also gained a following. Contrary to Joseph Levenson's assertion that this eclectic trend emerged only as a Chinese response to the challenge of a genuine alternative from the West,[32] it is now clear that the movement appeared much earlier as a response to a Chinese problem.

At the same time, there was a resurgence of an old approach to 'setting the world in order'. This was the so-called New Text School. While accepting the importance of self-cultivation in managing the affairs of this world – the original premise of Sung and Han Learning – the School insisted on the primacy of institutional renovations. By further insisting that the true Confucian man (*chün-tzu*) be prepared to make great personal sacrifices in serving the state, its leaders injected a new zealousness into their beliefs.[33] The stage was thus set in the early decades of the nineteenth century for the rise of the School of Practical Statecraft (*ching-shih*), one that advocated pragmatism in government and was not afraid to urge institutional readjustments. Under its influence, eclectic scholarship broadened to include Legalist concepts, notably the notion of wealth and power (*fu-ch'iang*) as a legitimate goal of the state.

By this time, eclecticism had affected scholars of all stripes. For example, Tseng Kuo-fan, who was usually identified with Sung Learning, had no compunction in adopting concepts from Han Learning or even the Legalist School.[34] And both Kung Tzu-chen and Wei Yüan, key

---

32 Joseph R. Levenson, *Confucian China and Its Modern Fate: A Trilogy* (Berkeley and Los Angeles, 1968), vol. 1, p. 50.
33 Frederic Wakeman, Jr., *History and Will: Philosophical Perspectives of Mao Tse-tung's Thought* (Berkeley and Los Angeles, 1973), pp. 101–14.
34 David Pong, 'The Vocabulary of Change: Reformist Ideas of the 1860s and 1870s', in

figures in the School of Practical Statecraft, were also scholars of the New Text School. Though not all New Text scholars were committed to reform, one would have been hard-put to claim 'membership' in the School of Practical Statecraft without such a commitment. After all, the School's very existence depended on its deep concern for political applicability. There was clearly a political awakening among sections of the literati at the turn of the nineteenth century.

What kind of change or reform did they advocate in the pre–Opium War era, before the Western threat firmly entered their consciousness? They began with the self. Early in the nineteenth century, when lamenting the superficiality of bureaucratic behaviour, the Practical Statecraft scholar-official Kung Tzu-chen tried to restore administrative vitality by instilling a sense of shame among the literati – an old Confucian approach.[35] 'If the scholars know no shame', he insisted, 'then the entire country will be disgraced'. If, however, they acquired a sense of shame, they would strive for regeneration, first of the self and then of the world around them.[36] From this humanistic desire to rectify social ills, Kung and his *ching-shih* associates explored a wide range of ideas and methods.

Among the early Statecraft proponents, Wei Yüan was probably the most familiar to the reformers of the post-Taiping era. His ideas on administration and reform can therefore serve as a bench-mark against which the achievements of Restoration officials are to be measured.[37] For the modern historian, Wei's idea that 'change was inevitable and inexorable . . . natural and good' is at once significant and appealing. It allowed him to see historical development in a linear fashion. But this

David Pong and Edmund S. K. Fung, eds., *Ideal and Reality: Social and Political Change in Modern China, 1860–1949* (Lanham, Md.: 1985), pp. 25–61. In the 1860s, Tseng called for *pien-fa* (reform) and *shang-chan* (commercial warfare); both had Legalist connotations. See also Thomas A. Metzger, *The Internal Organization of Ch'ing Bureaucracy: Legal, Normative, and Communication Aspects* (Cambridge, Mass., 1973), pp. 26–27, esp. note 8, and Shen Chen Han-yin, 'Tseng Kuo-fan', pp. 72–3.

35 'Great is the use of shame to man. . . . If a man is not ashamed of being inferior to other men, how will he ever become their equal?' *Mencius*, trans. D. C. Lau (Harmondsworth, 1970), 7.A.8, p. 183.

36 Ch'ien Mu, *Chung-kuo chin-san-pai-nien hsüeh-shu-shih* (Shanghai, 1937), vol. 2, pp. 533–54. The quotation comes from p. 533.

37 I am indebted to the following scholars and their works for the materials appearing in the next paragraphs: Peter Mitchell, 'The Limits of Reformism: Wei Yüan's Reaction to Western Intrusion', *Modern Asian Studies*, 6.2 (April 1972), 175–204; Feng Yu-lan, 'Wei Yüan ti ssu-hsiang', in Shang-hai Jen-min ch'u-pan-she, eds., *Chung-kuo chin-tai ssu-hsiang-shih lun-wen-chi* (Shanghai, 1958), pp. 11–25; Jane Leonard, *Wei Yuan and China's Rediscovery of the Maritime World* (Cambridge, Mass., 1984), pp. 12–31; and idem, 'Chinese Overlordship and Western Penetration in Maritime Asia: A Late Ch'ing Reappraisal of Chinese Maritime Relations', *Modern Asian Studies*, 6.2 (April 1972), 151–74.

seemingly progressive view had its limitations: it had no vision of what might be awaiting humankind at the end of the process, and thus was unable to provide direction for contemporary action. So political activities were still confined largely to correcting administrative ills or human inadequacies: restoring moral government rather than directing legislative or administrative reforms towards building a new Jerusalem.

Nevertheless, Wei's thoughts were often unorthodox. Like his *ching-shih* associates, he insisted that government be judged by usefulness and practicality. From this utilitarian position, the idea emerged that it was legitimate for the government to strive for profit (*li*). Profitability for the general public, rather than the Son of Heaven, was to be the key link between heaven and man. In government, this meant wealth and power (*fu-ch'iang*) for the state, a statistical approach to economic planning, and greater freedom for merchants and official utilization of their services, especially for transporting tribute grain. In the geopolitical sphere, Wei advocated internal colonization, especially of important border regions, and an aggressive diplomacy, backed by modern naval power, to reassert Chinese overlordship in South-East Asia to check Western expansion. Thus, to restore Confucian government, which was at once moral and effective, he envisaged a more caring and intervening approach, though he might not have been cognizant of its consequence – a larger bureaucracy.

Wei's ideas were not thoroughly modern. His failure to envision a better society for the future was directly related to an inability to visualize an expanding economy and therefore an unwillingness to think in terms of basic changes. So the orthodox Confucian belief – that government by virtuous men was far more important than new laws and institutions – continued to make sense.

These shortcomings notwithstanding, Peter Mitchell argues that Wei 'represented a more flexible attitude toward traditional thought', whereas 'the reversion to unreconstructed Confucianism in the aftermath of the Taiping shock doomed the later synthesis of Western and native thought'.[38] Mitchell has thus stood Mary Wright on her head. Wright maintains that it was the Restoration statesmen who 'had a far more dynamic conception of change'.[39]

Were the Restorationists truly backward looking? Was the 'reversion to unreconstructed Confucianism' really so thorough and widespread as to preclude any genuine synthesis of Western and Chinese thought? Or was it the Restoration leaders who possessed the more modern concept

38 Mitchell, 'Limits of Reformism', p. 204.
39 Wright, *Last Stand*, p. 63.

of change? Again, an examination of Shen Pao-chen's career will contribute to the answer.

The subject at hand

The history of late Ch'ing reform can be divided into four distinct but overlapping stages. The first belonged to the early *ching-shih*, or practical statecrafters. The second, in the decades that flanked the First Opium War (1839–42), belonged to those reform-minded scholar-officials who also began to probe the nature of the Western threat and seek solutions for its containment. The third was the dynastic Restoration, whose collapse led to the drive for sweeping structural and institutional changes in the 1890s, the fourth and final stage in our typology.

This brief, schematic overview of late Ch'ing reform is not intended to shed light on the complex character of each of the stages and their relationships. It is presented here at the outset in order to place Shen Pao-chen in a historical context. The stages of reform will be discussed more fully in the Conclusion when we assess Shen's place in modern Chinese history.

Shen was a key figure in the third stage of late Ch'ing reform. His life and career can be divided conveniently into three phases. The first covers his formative years, his first appointments as a junior official, in Peking and in the country, and his rapid rise during the Taiping Rebellion, culminating in his governorship of Kiangsi province in 1862–5. The second revolves around his director-generalship of the Foochow Navy Yard in 1866–75. This phase also includes two tours of duty on Taiwan in 1874 and 1875, defending that island against the invading Japanese and developing it as a new frontier of the Ch'ing empire. The last phase encompasses his tenure as governor-general of Liang Kiang, from late 1875 until he died in office in December 1879.

Whereas all three phases lend themselves to individual studies, common threads also run through Shen's entire life and career. However, to address a specific set of questions, this study restricts itself to the first two phases. The last phase must be left to a future endeavour.

The questions central to this book are the following: Why did an official as successful as Shen at the end of the Taiping era decide to dedicate himself to *yang-wu*, as the head of the Foochow Navy Yard? Given the terrible reputation former bureaucrats had as managers of modern enterprises, was Shen's bureaucratic past a serious obstacle to sound management? And bearing in mind the controversy over the Restoration leaders' ability to synthesize Western and Chinese thought, did Shen's adherence to Confucian values stand in the way of effectively

17

directing *yang-wu* enterprises, developing a modern navy, and, on a personal level, imbibing Western science and technology? Further, how did Shen's experience at the Foochow Navy Yard in turn affect his view of China and its established order? In sum, through a better understanding of Shen, we want to know what the chances were of late Ch'ing China transforming itself into a 'modern' state, one that could improve internal stability and the general quality of life, increase government services, and at least begin to slow down and eventually stop imperialist encroachments.

Although this study ends with Shen's departure from Foochow in 1875, four years before his death, it is largely biographical. As such, it has two purposes other than elucidating the issues raised in the preceding paragraph. First, it attempts to examine Shen's life in the broader social and political context. Second, it tries to probe his inner thoughts, as much as the sources allow. We wonder why he criticized the emperor, telling him to study and what to study, why he rejoiced at the predicament of the French missionary when the latter was attacked by a Chinese mob, or why he headed a demonstration of the gentry to prevent the departure of the governor-general from his home province. Perhaps the biggest question of all concerns why he, an extremely successful provincial governor, abandoned the security of his job and opted for a risky career as the head of a novel but controversial modern naval dockyard, and why he then pursued this new career with dogged devotion. Was he, deep down, a bloody-minded Legalist in pursuit of modern guns and gunboats? Was his earlier Confucian moralism a sham? Or was he a special kind of Confucian? This last question takes us back to one of the central concerns of this book: did Shen's attachment to Confucian values hinder or help him? To shed light on these questions, I shall attempt an analysis of his early and formative years that is of much greater depth than any hitherto accorded a mid-nineteenth-century figure. In the process, I shall relate his actions to the development of his political outlook, which, in turn, I shall examine in the context of the Confucian reform tradition discussed earlier.

Shen was not among the most powerful men of his time. During the T'ung-chih reign there were, in Peking, the duad of Prince Kung and Wen-hsiang and, in the provinces, the triumvirate of Tseng Kuo-fan, Tso Tsung-t'ang, and Li Hung-chang. Each of these men had a greater say and left a deeper imprint on national affairs than Shen. The study of Shen is nonetheless important for two reasons. First, in terms of power and influence, he was more representative of the bulk of high provincial officials. Second, his career was marked by a unique phenomenon: when he took charge of the Foochow Navy Yard in 1867 he became the highest-ranking official in the late Ch'ing who had ever assumed *full-time and personal* direction of a modern defence industry.[40] We certainly need to know why he chose such a career change but, in the light of what has been said about the failure of the Restoration, we also need to understand how a leader of his calibre could affect the chances of success of a modern enterprise. And in more concrete terms, we need to know whether it mattered that he was once a well-connected and successful provincial governor.

Much of our conventional wisdom about late Ch'ing politics and *yang-wu* undertakings is derived from our knowledge of Li Hung-chang. There is no doubt that after 1872, with the death of Tseng Kuo-fan and with Tso Tsung-t'ang deeply immersed in the affairs of the North-West frontier region, Li was the most dominant territorial official of the empire. Naturally, he has received the lion's share of modern scholarly attention. His career was the only one of that era to have been examined by two full-length studies: one by Stanley Spector and the other by Li Shou-k'ung.[41] Valuable though these studies are, they inevitably lead to a lopsided view of the Restoration. As noted, to see post-Taiping history as a development of regional power is a direct result of 'overconcentration' on Li. Of course, two full-length studies cannot be justly described as 'overconcentration', except to underscore the fact that other key officials of the period have been left unstudied in a small academic field. The only exceptions are one book each on Ting Jih-ch'ang, Tso Tsung-t'ang, and Shen Pao-chen, which have already shown us new ways of looking at the Restoration.[42] It is my hope that this study, too, will make a contribution.

Writing a biography requires the support of other biographies, which, as noted, are in short supply. Even the corpus of secondary works by modern scholars on the middle decades of the nineteenth century is quite small. Any attempt at putting an individual in a wider context will prove difficult. Whereas in most fields of history one could turn to secondary materials for basic information, one must, in the present instance, frequently fall back on traditional Chinese materials.

Confucius taught that it was man who played the pivotal role in creating and preserving order. Even with the later injection of the idea

---

40 A number of directors-general after Shen were governors-general or Tartar generals, but they held the post concurrently. Ch'ien Shih-fu, comp., *Ch'ing-chi hsin-she chih-kuan nien-piao* (Peking, 1961), pp. 72–3.

41 Spector, *Li Hung-chang*, and Li Shou-k'ung, *Li Hung-chang chuan* (Taipei, 1978).

42 Lü Shih-ch'iang, *Ting Jih-ch'ang yü tzu-ch'iang yün-tung* (Taipei, 1972); Tung Ts'ai-shih, *Tso Tsung-t'ang p'ing-chuan* (Peking, 1984); Lin Ch'ung-yung, *Shen Pao-chen yü Fu-chou ch'uan-cheng* (Taipei, 1987).

that heaven was an active agent, Confucianism continued to insist, up to at least the end of the nineteenth century, that it was human actions that invited heavenly intervention. So individuals whose lives were judged to have had an impact on the sociopolitical order were awarded a central place in Chinese history and record keeping. The resulting biographical accounts thus became a reservoir of historical lessons; they tend to be pedagogical, moralistic, and stereotypical. As Denis Twitchett observes, they present enormous difficulties for the modern historian who tries to populate traditional China with live personalities.[43]

Nonetheless, other forms of primary sources are plentiful. The collected papers, letters, diaries, and chronologies (*nien-p'u*) of numerous nineteenth-century figures are still extant. Compilations of official reports (memorials) on special topics have been made since late Ch'ing times. Of interest are those put together by research institutes on both sides of the Taiwan Strait from the 1950s on. There are, in addition, treaty port newspapers (Chinese and English), missionary publications, private papers, and public archives around the world. Further, after decades of labour, the Ch'ing government archives in the Palace Museum in Taipei have become fully accessible. Those on the mainland are also becoming increasingly available.

Under normal circumstances, an individual's collected works are the logical place to begin the study of a political leader. Shen's collected works, however, were hastily put together and published within a year of his death. Compiled by a provincial governor who had worked under him for a mere four years in a city two hundred kilometres away, they contain only a small portion of his memorials.[44] None of his correspondence or any other forms of writing, such as poems, diary, or letters, which might give us a glimpse of his inner thoughts, have been included. In my attempt to assemble as full a picture as possible of Shen, I have had to draw more heavily than usual upon widely scattered materials such as those listed in the preceding paragraph. On top of these, I have been fortunate enough to locate a number of private papers and unpublished manuscripts, already described in the Acknowledgements.

---

43 Denis Twitchett, 'Problems of Chinese Biography', in Arthur F. Wright and Denis Twitchett, eds., *Confucian Personalities* (Stanford, Calif., 1962), pp. 24–39.
44 *Shen Wen-su kung cheng-shu* (hereafter, *SWSK*; The Political works of Shen Pao-chen) was compiled under the direction of Wu Yüan-ping, governor of Kiangsu, 1874–81. Wu's seat of government was at Soochow, Shen's at Nanking. The *SWSK* was published at the end of 1880. It contains a mere 337 memorials covering the eighteen-year period from 1862 to 1879.

A question of terms

In the course of my research, I have come to understand several late Ch'ing phenomena in a different light. The conventional terms for describing them are no longer satisfactory. They call for redefinition to show how Shen and numerous leading figures of the time understood and used them. Redefinition would thus lead to greater analytical clarity.

The first concerns the Restoration, commonly called the 'T'ung-chih Restoration' because the generally accepted dates for it mark the beginning and the end of the T'ung-chih reign, 1861–74. Mary Wright adopts these dates, although she also cautions us that 'historic periods rarely begin or end on particular days'.[45] Nevertheless, this caveat does not adequately deal with the real question: when did the Restoration begin and end?

Elsewhere I have briefly addressed this issue, suggesting that restoration efforts continued throughout the 1870s. While any one of a number of crises in that period could well have signalled the end of an era of reform and reconstruction, such events as the rejection of the Alcock Convention (1869), the Tientsin Massacre (1870), the Japanese invasion of Taiwan and the death of the T'ung-chih emperor (1874), and the Margary Affair (1875) in fact raised consciousness of the Chinese and spurred them on to further endeavours. Moreover, because the Restoration was not a movement proclaimed by or associated exclusively with the reigning monarch, none of the Restoration officials considered their efforts terminated by the passing of the emperor. The era came to an end only when the momentum of reform was checked by the ascendency of Confucian fundamentalism (*ch'ing-i*, or pure discussion) at the close of the 1870s and the early 1880s.[46] I am therefore particularly gratified by a more recent discussion of this issue by Paul Cohen, although he argues that, as late as the 1890s, there were still Chinese who would adhere to restorationist methods and solutions.[47]

It could be suggested that the term 'T'ung-chih Restoration' is still useful because it started (even if it did not end) in the T'ung-chih reign. But closer examination of the sources indicates that the restoration of civil government, local control, economic rehabilitation, military reform,

---

45 Both this quotation and the characterization of Wright's argument come from her *Last Stand*, p. 299.
46 David Pong, 'The Vocabulary of Change: Reformism in the 1860s and 1870s', Paper presented at the workshop 'China in Transformation, 1860–1949', Australian National University, 24–25 October 1981. See also Shen Yü-ch'ing, *T'ao-yüan chi* (n.p., 1920), p. 221.
47 Cohen, *Discovering History in China*, p. 28.

as well as tax reductions and reforms – all critical elements of the T'ung-chih administration – were begun, and in some cases, well under way in the middle and late 1850s.[48] However, because the Restoration began with individual and largely uncoordinated efforts, it was not recognized as a restoration until collective results were clearly discernible, in the late 1860s. Throughout this book, I use 'T'ung-chih Restoration' only when citing or paraphrasing other people's works. Otherwise, for the sake of historical accuracy and to reflect the perspective of the leading officials of the 1860s and 1870s, I adopt the term 'the Restoration' or 'the Ch'ing Restoration', which, to reiterate, lasted from the mid-1850s to at least the mid-1880s.

From this discussion it can be deduced that the Restoration encompassed both reconstruction and reform. Several types of reform can be distinguished.[49] They range from minor adjustments to major remodeling and even the creation of new institutions and practices. Of the institutions and practices created, those introduced from the West were the most conspicuous. They included Western diplomatic practices, technology for the defence industry and other support industries, military training, and commercial practices. The business of bringing them to China, adapting them to local conditions, and using or practising them were called *yang-wu*, sometimes awkwardly rendered as 'foreign matters' or 'foreign affairs'. Since neither of these translations is satisfactory, we shall retain the Chinese term.

Although *yang-wu* began as part of the Restoration, it outlived the rest of the Restoration efforts by perhaps a decade or more, lasting as it did until 1894–1895, when the Chinese were routed in a war with Japan. And because it was concerned exclusively with things foreign, it frequently appeared to have a life of its own. It often impinged on the traditional order in ways different from those brought about by reforms in the civil administration.

Our last term, 'self-strengthening' (*tzu-ch'iang*), is also the most problematic. Virtually all modern scholars outside the People's Republic of China use it to describe the military reforms and modernization in the post-1860 period. Mary Wright's usage is quite representative. It is true

48 See, e.g., Hu Lin-i's memorials of 12 May 1855 (HF 5/3/27), 29 December 1866 (HF 6/12/3), 12 Novermber 1857 (HF 7/9/26), 29 November 1857 (HF 7/10/14), and 20 January 1858 (HF 7/12/6), in Hu Lin-i, *Hu Lin-i chi* (Taipei, 1957), pp. 1, 8–11, 15–19, and Hsia Nai, 'T'ai-p'ing t'ien-kuo ch'ien-hou Ch'ang-chiang ko-sheng chih t'ien-fu wen-t'i', *Tsing Hua hsüeh-pao*, 10.2 (April 1935), 409–74; reprinted in *Chung-kuo chin-tai-shih lun-tsung*, 2d ser. (Taipei, 1958), vol. 2, pp. 145–204. See also Liu Kwang-ching, 'The Ch'ing Restoration', in Fairbank, ed., *Late Ch'ing, 1800–1911*, p. 477.
49 James T. C. Liu, 'The Variety of Political Reforms in Chinese History: A Simplified Typology', in Cohen and Schrecker, eds., *Reform*, pp. 9–13.

that some Restoration leaders like Prince Kung and Li Hung-chang frequently employed this term to mean improving China's military strength.[50] But throughout Chinese history, 'self-strengthening' had always had a broad meaning, embracing both military and nonmilitary activities. In the Restoration era, it was used by conservatives and progressives alike. In its original Confucian context, and on a personal level, 'self-strengthening' referred essentially to character building, to acquiring personal or inner strength through self-improvement. It was primarily in this sense that the conservatives understood it. When employed to describe collective efforts, however, it could have a military connotation as well. For example, in the middle of the thirteenth century, when asked by the Southern Sung emperor (Li-tsung) about border defence, the minister Tung Huai replied, 'When a country is faced with an enemy, the best strategy is self-strengthening.... If we are self-strengthened, then the others will fear us and we will not be overawed by them'.[51] What exactly Tung meant by 'self-strengthening' remains unclear. The sources indicate that he devoted himself both to restoring sound government and to training troops. It is therefore interesting that a number of nineteenth-century Restoration leaders did employ the term to call attention to the need for both good government and military strength. Among them were Tseng Kuo-fan, Tso Tsung-t'ang, Shen Pao-chen, and Ting Jih-ch'ang. Consequently, in the minds of these officials, 'self-strengthening' and 'restoration' were, for all intents and purposes, coterminous.[52]

Because 'self-strengthening' does have a military connotation and some nineteenth-century leaders used it frequently in a military sense, the term is often employed by modern scholars as a substitute or alternative for *yang-wu*. Hence, we have a 'Self-strengthening Movement' and a *yang-wu* 'movement', both referring to the same phenomenon. This can be quite confusing because, in reality, not all *yang-wu* undertakings were military-related. Yet to use 'self-strengthening' to refer to military matters or 'foreign affairs' is too restrictive – it meant different things to different people.

50 *Ch'ou-pan i-wu shih-mo* (hereafter, *IWSM*) (Peiping, 1930); see *HF*, 72:11.
51 *Sung-shih*, comp. T'o-t'o et al. (Beijing, 1977), 18.12428–32 (*chüan* 414).
52 'Self-strengthening' is discussed more fully in David Pong, 'The Vocabulary of Change: Reformist Ideas of the 1860s and 1870s'. On Tso Tsung-tang's use of the term, see *IWSM*, TC 42:48b. In my view, Lü Shih-ch'iang uses the term 'self-strengthening' correctly in his book *Ting Jih-ch'ang*. Scholars in the People's Republic of China do not use the term 'self-strengthening movement' at all. Instead, they use *yang-wu yün-tung* (foreign matters movement).

1
Early years

The city of Foochow, the capital of Fukien, was divided into two administrative halves by a major thoroughfare, with the Min district in the east
and Hou-kuan in the west. But if the city were divided according to the
character of its sectors, a northern quarter of government and religious
buildings, straddling the two administrative districts, could be easily
distinguished. In many ways, Foochow was just another southern Chinese
city with its eleven-kilometre wall enclosing the various wards, each with
its narrow and dirty streets, badly paved with blocks of granite. In size,
it was a little bigger than Canton, but the affluence and lustre of the
latter were lacking. The city wall, in fact, enclosed a considerable amount
of wasteland. Foochow, however, was not without its charms. Its Curiosity
Street displayed merchandise ranging from antiques and fine lacquer-
wares to exquisitely executed rice-paper flowers. Three wooded hills rose
above the horizon of the city, which also boasted many banyan trees
in its public areas. The Chinese called it the Banyan City. But one
inescapable feature of this provincial capital was the large number of
officials among its six hundred thousand inhabitants and the space
dedicated to government offices. Learning, and its close tie with office,
was given expression by the academies and the examination halls, one
with ten thousand cells. Foochow had traditionally produced more than
its fair share of scholars and officials, both in the province and in the
empire.[1] It was here on the west side of the city (Hou-kuan) that Shen
Pao-chen was born into a family of the gentry class on 20 March 1820.

1 William F. Mayers, N. B. Dennys, and Charles King, *The Treaty Ports of China and Japan*
(London, 1867), pp. 274–81; *Ch'ing-shih*, comp. Ch'ing-shih pien-tsuan wei-yüan-hui
(Taipei, 1961), vol. 2, p. 959; Henry N. Shore, *The Flight of the Lapwing: A Naval Officer's
Jottings in China, Formosa, and Japan* (London, 1881), p. 93; Ho Ping-ti, *The Ladder of Success
in Imperial China: Aspects of Social Mobility, 1368–1911* (New York, 1962), pp. 246–51.

Family background and childhood

The Shen clan originally hailed from Honan. It moved to Chekiang as the Sung dynasty retreated to the south in the face of the Mongol conquest. Although it was not among the more prominent lineages of the empire, it had produced a long line of degree- and office-holders since Sung times. In 1734 a branch of the clan moved to Fukien and settled in Hou-kuan. Shen Pao-chen belonged to the fifth generation of this branch.[2]

In an area well known for its scholars and scholar-officials, the Shens quickly established themselves as part of the local elite. The eldest son of each of the first three generations, down to Shen Pao-chen's grandfather, had served as private assistants (*mu-yu*) to local officials, excelling in managing granaries, the salt monopoly, and financial affairs. Yet despite ample opportunities for graft, they remained honest men. None became rich. Some had to pawn their belongings to pay for their children's education. They were also caring towards others. Shen Pao-chen's grandfather, Ta-ch'üan (1754–1812), always tried to persuade landlords to keep their rent low wherever he went. And his respect for education was such that he even forced a neighbouring child to go to school by beating him in front of his mother and then personally escorting him to his teacher.[3]

Little is known of Ta-ch'üan's influence on the education of his second son, T'ing-feng (1787–1870), who was to become Shen Pao-chen's father – T'ing-feng having been adopted by an uncle who had no heir of his own. Nevertheless, Ting-feng received a good education and earned the *ling-sheng* degree by passing the prefectural triennial examination with flying colours at an early age. That immediately guaranteed his gentry status at the top 0.25 per cent of the empire's population.[4] When he came of age (i.e., twenty according to Ch'ing statutes), he studied the classics with Wu Lan-sun, a metropolitan graduate (*chin-shih*) of 1808 from the Min district side of Foochow. Impressed by his scholarship, Wu appointed him libationer (*chi-chiu*), a ceremonial post otherwise reserved

---

2 Shen Tsan-ch'ing, comp., 'Wu-lin Shen-shih ch'ien Min pen-chi chia-p'u' (n.p., 1933). Unpaginated; page numbers given in this manuscript are my own. See pp. 1–12, 59–67, 180–94. The other half of the lineage remained at Hangchow and was massacred by the Taipings. A copy of the 'Chia-p'u' is in the possession of Mr. Shen Tsu-hsing, Taipei, Taiwan. I am grateful to him for the use of this manuscript. See also Li Yüantu, *T'ien-yüeh shan-kuan wen-ch'ao* (n.p., Kuang-hsü period), 14:9.
3 Lin Ch'ung-yung, *Shen*, pp. 1–9; *Fu-chien t'ung-chih lieh-chuan hsüan* (hereafter, *FCTC:LCH*) (Taipei, 1964), pp. 332–3.
4 Shen Tsan-ch'ing, 'Chia-p'u', p. 63. On the size of *sheng-yüan*, see Chang Chung-li, *The Chinese Gentry: Studies on Their Role in Nineteenth-century Chinese Society* (Seattle, Wash., 1955), pp. 97–141.

for an elderly scholar. It is said that Lin Tse-hsü (1785–1850), who was then a mere personal staff member (*mu-yu*) at the provincial governor's yamen, saw T'ing-feng's essays and so admired them that he gave him the hand of his younger, eighteen-year-old sister. Later, Lin invited T'ing-feng to join his personal staff, presumably after 1820, when he earned his first territorial appointment.[5] In view of Lin's subsequent rise to national prominence and the high esteem accorded him long after his death, these associations were to be of great importance to the Shen family.

In the meantime, however, T'ing-feng produced a family of considerable size. Eight children were born, although only six remained in the family. Perhaps because of the demands involved in raising a family, T'ing-feng did not pass the provincial (*chü-jen*) examination until the age of forty-five. Worse still, he failed the metropolitan examination no less than three times before giving up trying after 1844, by which time he was already fifty-seven. Without a *chin-shih* degree, it was virtually impossible to enter the imperial bureaucracy. Nevertheless, he became a scholar of some repute and was able to support his growing family by teaching (conducted at home), which, apart from the family land, was his main source of income.[6]

Shen Pao-chen was thus born into a gentry family of modest means. His first years were spent in relative poverty. To save money, the family moved from a small dwelling in the north of the city to a rented one-room house in a secluded area. There, they were frequently burgled. Despite the hardship, the family was known for its charity, which, it was commonly believed, would bring its members good fortune in times to come.[7]

Conditions were hardly favourable for bringing up children. Both the first son and the first daughter born to the family died in infancy,

---

5 *Fu-chien t'ung-chih* (1922; hereafter, *FCTC*), 'ju-hsing chuan': 26, and 'lieh-nü chuan, mu-i': 24b; *FCTC:LCH*, p. 333; *Min-Hou hsien-chih* (1933; hereafter, *MHHC*), 93:6b; Lin Ch'ung-yung, *Lin Tse-hsü chuan* (Taipei, 1967), p. 8. All references to age have been converted to the Western style of reckoning.

6 *FCTC:LCH*, pp. 333–6; Shen Tsan-ch'ing, 'Chia-p'u', pp. 61–71; Lin Ch'ung-yung, *Shen*, p. 11. T'ing-feng's income from teaching must have been modest: he taught only about thirty students in his entire career. Since he did not possess the *chü-jen* degree before 1832, the fees he commanded could not have been high, although the situation might have improved somewhat thereafter. By that time, his family had become quite large and Shen was already in his teens. Most likely, then, his earnings were in the lower bracket of the teaching profession – around 200 taels a year. To this, one must add the so-called respect fees from students, which varied considerably from case to case. On the gentry's income from teaching, see Chang Chung-li, *The Income of the Chinese Gentry* (Seattle, Wash., 1962), pp. 92–102.

7 *FCTC*, 'lieh-nü chuan, mu-i': 25a–b; *MHHC*, 93:6b–7.

although the third child, a girl, survived. Shen Pao-chen, born fourth, thus enjoyed whatever benefits the family could afford that were normally given to the eldest son of a Chinese family. He was joined by another baby boy the following year. The youngest son, who was later adopted by a paternal uncle, was not born until 1826. There were as well four other girls, whose order of birth is not known.[8]

The size of the family caused material privation and poor health. Shen, in his childhood, suffered from frail health and nyctophobia – a fear of darkness.[9] In his adult life, he was plagued by a number of ailments, including eye, back, and leg problems, probably some form of insomnia, and dropsy, which caused his death at the age of fifty-nine.[10]

Financial difficulties, however, did not stand in the way of the children's education. At the age of three, Shen, in spite of his fragile health, was given daily lessons by his mother, who, on top of the usual chores, copied all of his study materials in her own fair hand. The teachings of Confucianism were carefully transmitted, and the belief that true courage and will could come only from loyalty (*chung*) and filial piety (*hsiao*) was also strongly inculcated into his thinking. Because of his understanding of these Confucian virtues, it was claimed, Shen was cured of his nyctophobia.[11]

Little is known of Shen's formal education. It presumably followed one or more of the normal paths for educating a young gentry scholar, at a local school, under a private tutor (*shu-shih*), or under his father. Shen was certainly familiar with what his father taught to his students at home. Decades later, when writing his father's biography, he recalled that the subjects included the Confucian classics, the histories, the literary

8 Shen Tsan-ch'ing, 'Chia-p'u', pp. 13–14, 64, 71–2; Yang Yen-chieh, 'Shen Pao-chen chia-shih jo-kan shih-shih k'ao-pien', *Shih-hsüeh yüeh k'an*, 158 (November 1905), 110. Shen Pao-chen's second brother, Ch'i (1821–59), was a *pa-kung-sheng* recommended to take the metropolitan examination. The youngest brother, Hui-tsung (1826–93), was a *chü-jen* of 1859 and was district examiner for several places. All of Shen's sisters married well – their husbands were either degree- or office-holders. Worthy of note here is Wu Chung-hsiang (d. 1891), also of Hou-kuan, who was destined to become one of Shen's right-hand men in the 1860s and 1870s.
9 See note 7. Shen's childhood nyctophobia was probably a well-known fact in his time. His political opponents claimed that this phobia harassed him throughout his life, especially towards the end. According to them, it was the apparitions of those who died unjustly at his hands that caused his tragic death in 1879. Ko Hsü-ts'un, *Ch'ing-tai ming-jen i-shih* (Shanghai, 1933), 16:12a. The story is probably groundless. Similar stories were told of officials who had, for one reason or another, taken the lives of many in the course of their career. Shen himself used one such story to warn other officials against unnecessary deaths caused by public work projects. Shen Pao-chen, *Chü-kuan kuei-nieh* (n.p., 1863), 1:93b–94.
10 *SWSK*, 3:110b, 5:70, 6:74–5, 7:45–46b, 56–7, 77–8, 126a–b; Arthur Davenport to Thomas Wade, 23 December 1879, in FO 228/633, no. 4.
11 See note 7.

arts, wise sayings through the ages, and the family instructions of Liu Tsung-yüan (773–819). Liu was a famous T'ang prose master and a practical reformer who stressed the value of antiquity as a source of principle rather than a rigid model for mindless adoption in subsequent ages. The biography also suggests that Shen had had frequent discussions with his father. One such occasion, which he remembered with feeling, was a long exposition by his father on the *Book of Rites* and the *Commentary of Tso Ch'iu-ming on the Spring and Autumn Annals (Tso chuan)*, punctuated by Shen's own searching questions.[12]

Apart from teaching, T'ing-feng was closely associated with the Ao-feng Shu-yüan, or Academy, the premier institution of learning in the province, and was among the four local scholars most admired by at least one principal lecturer there. But the Ao-feng Academy was more than a reputable scholarly institution. Founded in 1707 by Governor Chang Po-hsing, it was intended as a centre for reviving the values of Sung and Ming Confucianism for practical application. It thus reflected the trend towards 'substantial learning' (*shih-hsüeh*) discussed in the Introduction. Chang was a reformer, distinguishing himself in water control, famine relief, and fighting superstition. The Academy had a long roster of eminent scholars and reformers as its lecturers and directors. Successive editions of the province's gazetteer were compiled under their direction.[13] T'ing-feng's association with the Academy thus reflected the predilection of his own scholarship and reformist bent, an important part of Shen's intellectual upbringing.

Another person who greatly influenced the young Shen was his uncle, Lin Tse-hsü, easily the most distinguished man in his family. Between 1824 and 1830, Lin spent long stretches of time at Foochow, mourning the deaths of his parents. Although Shen was barely ten years of age when Lin resumed his career in 1830, the latter's presence could not but have made a deep impression on him. His Confucian upbringing as well as the predisposition of Chinese parents to hold up successful relatives as role models made sure of that. At the same time, Lin and his wife saw admirable qualities in the young Shen, and in 1832, they decided to betroth their second daughter to him.[14]

12 For Shen's biography of his father, see *FCTC:LCH*, pp. 332–6. On Liu Tsung-yüan, see Michael T. Dalby, 'Court Politics in Late T'ang Times', in Denis Twitchett, ed., The Cambridge History of China, vol. 3: *Sui and T'ang China, 589–906*, part 1 (Cambridge, 1979), pp. 601–6.

13 *FCTC:LCH*, p. 333; *MHHC*, 33:1a–b; Arthur W. Hummel, ed., *Eminent Chinese of the Ch'ing Period* (Washington, D.C., 1943), pp. 51–2, 81–2, 97–9, 440–1, 571–2, 646–7.

14 Lin Ch'ung-yung, 'Lin Ching-jen yü ch'iyüan hsüeh-shu', *Chung-yang yen-chiu-yüan chin-tai-shih yen-chiu-so chi-k'an*, 7 (June 1978), pp. 287–8, and his *Lin*, p. 8. References to Lin Tsehsü in the next two paragraphs come from the latter work, pp. 55–177.

For the next five years, Lin was governor of Kiangsu. Allegedly, Shen was brought into his service at Soochow, but our evidence indicates otherwise. Lin's absence, however, did not preclude his having an interest in the intellectual growth of his future son-in-law, whose essays he read from time to time. Shen could not have escaped Lin's influence either. The care with which Lin handled reports from his subordinates was already well known in the family: Lin always responded to these reports personally, taking care to register his own comments before returning them. But Shen learned also that the attentiveness was not an end in itself; it was as well a means to gain a more intimate knowledge of the officials so that even the poor and honest, if able, would be noticed.[15]

More important, Lin was already a prominent reformer by the early 1830s, having established a name in water control, famine relief, as well as salt administration and judicial matters. His integrity earned him the sobriquet 'Lin, the Clear Sky' (Lin Ch'ing-t'ien). His close association with such established statecraft reformers as Kung Tzu-chen and Wei Yüan was also well known. In Kiangsu, Lin added opium suppression to his long list of reformist activities. All of this Shen learned through family discussions.[16]

At the age of seventeen (1837), Shen received instruction from Lin Ch'ang-i, a close friend of Lin Tse-hsü and Wei Yüan. Lin was an authority on the *Three Ritual Classics* (the *San-li*), comprising the *Institutes of Chou*, the *Chou Rituals*, and the *Book of Rites* (*Chou li, Yi li*, and *Li chi*), works that became a source of reformist ideas because of their emphasis on institutions and regulations in government. His contemporaries called him a 'modern-day Ku Yen-wu' because of his practical reformist bent. Lin was also a patriot whose hatred of the British after the Opium War was such that he named his study 'The Eagle-Shooting Loft', a pun for 'The English-Shooting Loft', since both 'eagle' and 'English' are pronounced 'ying' in Chinese.[17]

In sum, during his childhood and adolescence, Shen was given a 'liberal' Confucian education. He was tutored not only in the classics

---

15 Hsü I-t'ang, *Ch'ing-tai mi-shih, ch'u-chi* (Taipei, 1953), p. 108; Shen Yü-ch'ing, *T'ao-yüan-chi*, pp. 124–5; Lin Ch'ung-yung, *Lin*, pp. 8, 50–1; and idem, *Shen*, p. 42.

16 Lin Ch'ung-yung, *Lin*, pp. 88, 108; Chang Hsin-pao, *Commissioner Lin and the Opium War* (Cambridge, Mass., 1964), p. 122; Wang Chia-chien, *Wei Yüan nien-p'u* (Taipei, 1967), p. 53.

17 *Ch'ing-shih lieh-chuan*, 73:50; Lin Ch'ung-yung, *Shen*, p. 42; idem, 'Lin Ching-jen', p. 289. On the *Ritual Classics* as a source of reformist thought, see Kung-chuan Hsiao, *A History of Chinese Political Thought*, trans. F. W. Mote (Princeton, N. J., 1979), vol. 1, pp. 114–16, 182–93. See also *Li chi* (Book of rites), trans. James Legge, ed. with an introduction by Ch'u Chai and Winberg Chai (New York, 1967), vol. 1, pp. lxxiii–lxxx; and Wakeman, *History and Will*, pp. 101–2.

that prepared him for the civil service examinations, but also in a wide variety of works that formed part of the 'pharmacopoeia' of practical reformers. His association with his teacher, Lin Ch'ang-i, and his uncle, Lin Tse-hsü, not to mention the influence of his father, must have instilled in him a strong sense of loyalty, integrity, and patriotism. At a time when most young scholars could ill afford to wander from the prescribed texts for the civil service examinations until their entry into the bureaucracy had been assured,[18] Shen was exposed to a variety of enriching experiences. Of course, he studied for the civil service examinations, too, and in 1839, at the age of nineteen, he, along with his teacher, earned the *chü-jen* degree. Shen was placed third.

Marriage and family life

The year in which Shen passed the provincial examination he married Lin P'u-ch'ing (1821–73), Lin Tse-hsü's second daughter, who was also his first cousin. As Shen later recalled, his relationship with P'u-ch'ing began in early childhood when Lin Tse-hsü brought his family back to Foochow in 1824–30 to mourn his mother's and then his father's death. This extended sojourn brought the Lin and the Shen families even closer together, their vast differences in wealth and status notwithstanding. And P'u-ch'ing, by the time she was five or six, was said to have developed a special fondness for Shen even though she was constantly surrounded by cousins and playmates from wealthier families.[19]

Since Shen and his bride had been playmates from an early age, their union was untypical of most traditional marriages, which so often involved total strangers. This special relationship could well explain P'u-ch'ing's devotion as a wife and as an assistant to Shen in his later career. Familiarity with the Shen family also enabled her to adapt to the life-style of a much poorer family. But it was not until her encounter with a pawn ticket – her first with such a document – that she realized the extent of the Shen family's financial plight: her mother-in-law had just pawned her own garment for money to buy food. From then on, according to Shen, she devoted herself even more to pleasing her parents-in-law. The fact that her mother-in-law, the oft-dreaded figure in a traditional

18 David S. Nivison, 'Protest Against Conventions and Conventions of Protest', in Arthur F. Wright, ed., *The Confucian Persuasion* (Stanford, Calif., 1960), pp. 177–201.
19 Unless otherwise stated, sources for this section are *Ch'ing-shih*, vol. 7, pp. 5521–2; *FCTC*, 'lieh-nü chuan, jen-chih', 3:11b–12b; *MHHC*, 95:2; Shen Tsan-ch'ing, 'Chia-p'u', pp. 13–14, 18–25, 68–71; Shen Yü-ch'ing, *T'ao-yüan chi*, pp. 30, 169; Huang Chun, *Hua-sui-jen-sheng an chih-i ch'üan-pien*, ed. Hsü Yen-p'ien and Su T'ung-ping (Hong Kong, 1979), p. 30; Lin Ch'ing-yung, 'Lin Ching-jen', pp. 287–90.

Chinese family, was also her aunt made for an affectionate relationship between the two.

The first years of married life were hard. P'u-ch'ing had to do most of the housework while Shen prepared for the metropolitan examination, which he failed in 1840, 1841, and 1845 before succeeding in 1847.[20] To help finance his trips to Peking and his sojourn there in 1844–7, P'u-ch'ing, in an act reminiscent of her mother-in-law's pawning a garment, sold some jewels from her dowry. As Shen said later, although his family eventually prospered, the beginning was hard.

Because P'u-ch'ing was well educated by the Lin family – she was a literary figure in her own right – she also dedicated herself to educating her children. After Shen had started an official career, she helped him prepare his papers and handled all his confidential documents. Further, she often tried to correct, through gentle persuasion, one of Shen's major character defects – his narrow-mindedness and irritability – although by Shen's own admission, she did not succeed. And despite her having to raise altogether five sons and five daughters, she continued to assist him in his work until her death in 1873, at the age of fifty-three.

When Shen finally established himself as an official, he took a concubine in the late 1840s or the early 1850s and a second in the 1860s. They each bore him a son and a daughter.[21]

In 1847 Shen acquired the much coveted *chin-shih* degree, at age twenty-seven. During the preceding years of study, much disaster had fallen upon the country. Needless to say, many people were outraged by the Opium War. Its effect on Shen's teacher, Lin Ch'ang-i, has been noted. Its impact on Shen was probably equally profound. The fact that the two spent some time together in Peking ensured that Shen did not escape the fury his former teacher felt. Moreover, the war and its aftermath affected Shen and his family in a tangible way. For waging what was considered a righteous war against opium, his father-in-law was disgraced and banished. After the war, his home-town, Foochow, was opened as a treaty port. The local leaders of the gentry were incensed by the fact that, of all the southern coastal provinces, Fukien alone had to open two treaty ports; they thought the opening of Amoy was more than adequate. Then, when the British arrived, they occupied the Kingfisher-Gathering Temple (Chi-ts'ui ssu) on Black Rock Hill (Wu-shih shan). The Black Rock Hill and its several religious buildings were an area frequented by the people of Foochow, especially on festive

---

20 Lin Ch'ung-yung, *Shen*, pp. 24, 85–6. The examinations in 1841 and 1845 were *en-shih* (special examinations).
21 *Ch'ing-shih*, vol. 6, p. 4796; Li Yüan-tu, *T'ien-yüeh shan-kuan*, 14:9; *Ch'ing-shih lieh-chuan*, comp. Ch'ing-shih kuan (Shanghai, 1928), 53:35.

occasions. Back in 1821, Lin Tse-hsü had had the hill's most beloved structure, the Kingfisher-Gathering Temple, restored. Its occupation therefore aroused much local opposition. Eventually, in 1850, Lin, at the head of a delegation of gentry, effected the British evacuation.[22]

Shen was deeply influenced by the events of the Opium War era and particularly by Lin, whose deeds he often retold for the benefit of his children.[23] His own patriotism and unswerving determination to wipe out opium smoking and production in his later years may have stemmed from opinions formed at this time.[24] His subsequent dedication to reform and the introduction of Western military and naval technology may also have been influenced by Lin, who, during and after the Opium War, became one of the earliest advocates of this type of 'modernization'.[25] Although Shen and Lin had few opportunities to meet after the war, Lin's activities and political papers, which Shen later compiled for publication,[26] must have had a profound effect on the young scholar.

Official of the central government, 1847–55

At the metropolitan examination of 1847 Shen came in forty-second among the 231 successful candidates. Since the top three were given the *chin-shih* degree of the first rank, Shen was placed thirty-ninth in the second rank. In consequence, he was given the title of 'bachelor' (*shu-chi-shih*) and dispatched to the Department of Study (Shu-ch'ang-kuan) of the Hanlin Academy for further study. Shen commenced his duties after a brief visit to Foochow to bring his family to the imperial capital. As he left, his father urged him to apply himself to practical learning (*yu-yung chih hsüeh*).[27]

Because the civil service examinations emphasized style rather than

22 Lin Ch'ung-yung, *Lin*, pp. 60, 615–16.
23 Lin Ch'ung-yung, *Shen*, p. 48.
24 Li Yüan-tu, *T'ien-yüeh shan-kuan*, 14:15b.
25 Gideon Ch'en, *Lin Tse-hsü: Pioneer Promoter of the Adoption of Western Means of Maritime Defense in China* (Peiping, 1934). Lin's influence on the thinking of some of his contemporaries was considerable. An example is Tso Tsung-t'ang, whose ideas were deeply influenced by Lin's writings and by a memorable interview with him in 1849 – the only occasion on which these two great men met. Gideon Ch'en, *Tso Tsung-t'ang: Pioneer Promoter of the Modern Dockyard and the Woollen Mill in China* (Peiping, 1938), pp. 2–3.
26 The *Lin Wen-chung kung cheng-shu* (Political works of Lin Tse-hsü), published in 1876, was compiled by Lin Ju-chou and Shen. *Hai-fang tang* (hereafter, *HFT*), comp. Chung-yang yen-chiu-yüan chin-tai-shih yen-chiu-so (Taipei, 1957), II, 469. Lin made only brief visits to Foochow between changes of posts before his exile to Ili. Lin Ch'ung-yung, *Lin*, p. 623.
27 Unless otherwise stated, information on Shen comes from the following works: *Ch'ing-shih lieh-chuan*, 53:35; *Ch'ing-shih*, vol. 6, p. 4769; Li Yüan-tu, *T'ien-yüeh shan-kuan*, 14:9; Lin Ch'ung-yung, *Shen*, pp. 85–8.

substance, the successful candidates would need further training before official appointment. Lower-ranked graduates were sent to the Six Boards or other offices for practical training. Higher-ranked ones like Shen were given considerable freedom as they furthered their studies at the Hanlin Academy, making use of the vast reference library and other resources there.[28]

Having done well in the examinations set at the end of the third year of study (1850), Shen was made a compiler of the second class (*pien-hsiu*, rank 7a), also in the Hanlin Academy. There, he worked on source materials for compiling the history of the reigning dynasty. A prestigious appointment in itself, it was a critical step towards a promising career later in life, for those who did less well would end up with a junior metropolitan appointment or a district magistracy. For the moment, preparation for high office continued as Shen was promoted one year later to a proof-readership (*tsuan-hsiu*) in the Printing Office and Bookbindery at the Throne Hall (Wu-ying-tien Hsiu-shu-ch'u), which prepared books for the court. He was thus able to further acquaint himself with the principles and practice of government affairs. Then, in June 1852, at a special examination for Hanlin scholars below the rank of reader (*shih-tu hsüeh-shih*, rank 4b), Shen did well enough to be in the second of four grades into which candidates were divided. This soon resulted in his appointment as associate examiner (*t'ung-k'ao kuan*) at the Chihli provincial examination in September.

Examiners were judged according to how fairly they graded the examinations and therefore how successful they were in picking out the truly talented. Shen apparently did his job well. In 1853 he was duly recommended for a censorial post, and in June 1854 he was appointed one of the six supervisory censors of the Kiangnan circuit (*Chiang-nan tao chien-ch'a yü-shih*, rank 5b), which covered Kiangsu and Anhwei. It was an important appointment, for these two provinces not only were among the richest in the empire but, in 1854, were also being bitterly contested by the Taipings. Besides, the Kiangnan supervisory censors also had the general responsibility of keeping a watchful eye on certain currency, granary, and tribute grain matters, all of which were of vital concern during the Taiping War.[29] Only three of Shen's censorial memorials

---

28 Adam Lui Yuen-chung, 'The Practical Training of Government Officials under the Early Ch'ing, 1644–1795', *Asia Major*, 16. 1–2 (1971), 87; Lin Ch'ung-yung, *Lin*, p. 46.

29 Normally, two censors were assigned to each province. Because of their importance, Kiangsu and Anhwei (making up the Kiangnan circuit) had six between them, each charged with special responsibilities. Shen's responsibilities are not known. Chang Chin-chien, *Chung-kuo wen-kuan chih-tu shih* (Taipei, 1955), pp. 222–3; *Ch'ing-shih*, vol. 2, p. 1371.

have survived, but they dealt with some of the most critical issues of the time. They also underscored his zeal for reform and his espousal of Confucian principles. They are therefore treated here in some detail.[30]

Attacking the government's inflationary policy

The unexpectedly rapid success of the Taiping rebels in the early 1850s ruthlessly exposed the weaknesses of the ailing dynasty. Among these was the monetary system. Troubled already by repeated shortages of copper since around 1800, the system virtually broke down in 1853 when rebels completely cut off supplies from Yunnan. Rising military expenditures then forced Peking to successive debasements of the copper coinage and the issuing of paper notes with minimal backing.[31] Confusion reigned while counterfeiting got out of hand.[32] At the same time, the debased coins, especially those of the highest denominations, met with increasing popular resistance.[33]

The paper money was equally unpopular, for although the notes were theoretically redeemable, redemption was made as difficult as possible lest their purpose be defeated. In the market-place, the value of the notes soon dropped by half. To keep the notes (and the debased coins) in circulation, the government resorted to paying certain categories of its

30 I have analysed these memorials in greater detail in 'Dynastic Crisis and Censorial Response: Shen Pao-chen in 1854', *Journal of the Institute of Chinese Studies*, 5.2 (1972), 455–76. The memorials are also published for the first time as appendices in this article. They come from Shen Pao-ch'en's unpublished political works: 'Hsien Wen-su kung cheng-shu hsü-pien', comp. Shen K'o (1889). Since the Palace Archives at the National Palace Museum in Taipei have become accessible, I have found a copy of the second memorial, dated 18 July 1854. It is identical to the one in 'Hsien Wen-su kung' except that it also carries an imperial rescript, instructing the Board of War to give Shen's proposals a thorough discussion. Republic of China, Palace Archives (Kung-chung tang), HF 005604. Lin Ch'ung-yung, unaware of my article, has also examined these memorials in great detail. His interpretation differs from mine, and in my view he exaggerates Shen's role and influence. Lin Ch'ung-yung *Shen*, pp. 121–93.

31 For general information on the Hsien-feng inflation see Jerome Ch'en, 'The Hsien-feng Inflation', *Bulletin of the School of Oriental and African Studies*, 21 (1958), 578–86; Frank H. H. King, *Money and Monetary Policy in China, 1845–1895* (Cambridge, Mass., 1965), chaps. 5 and 6; T'an Pi-an, 'Ch'ing chung–yeh chih huo-pi kai-ke yün-tung', *Shuo-wen yüeh-k'an*, 4 (May 1933), reprinted Li Ting-i, Pao Tsun-p'eng, and Wu Hsiang-hsiang, eds., *Chung-kuo chin-tai-shih lun-ts'ung*, 2d ser., vol. 3: *Ts'ai-cheng ching-chi* (Taipei, 1958), pp. 38–48; Yang Tuan-liu, *Ch'ing-tai huo-pi chin-yung shih-kao* (Peking, 1962), chap. 3.

32 See, e.g., Tsai-ch'üan's memorial of 16 July 1854 (HF 4.6.22) in *Ta-Ch'ing li-ch'ao shih-lu* (hereafter, *Shih-lu*) (Mukden, 1937), HF 134:9b–10b. Punitive edicts against counterfeiting were promulgated at frequent intervals, but they went unheeded. In one instance, in August 1854, the scoundrels at T'ung-chou were so brazen that they set up a furnace for counterfeiting in the midst of a bustling market in broad daylight. The local officials, frightened by their numbers, dared not even investigate. *Shih-lu*, HF 136:5b–6.

33 Jerome Ch'en, 'Hsien-feng Inflation', p. 584.

civil and military personnel in fixed proportions of paper money, standard coins, and 'big coins' – the debased coins.[34]

These inflationary measures undoubtedly harmed the people, hurt the government's credibility, and, vitiated by counterfeiting, caused economic chaos. The withdrawal of the most objectionable 'big coins' failed to solve the problem. Shen therefore strongly denounced the government's ill-conceived policy.[35] As he underscored, currency debasement could not take care of the government's long-term financial difficulties. On the contrary, it would benefit the counterfeiters, who could use their bad coins to buy silver, the more stable medium of exchange in the bimetallic system, and so exhaust the government's reserves and further undermine its fiscal stability.

More important, Shen took a holistic view of the matter: debasement not only caused suffering among the common people and demoralization among the troops, but also undercut the government's revenue base and would eventually affect the quality of local government.[36] Although he was naïve in fearing that a large number of peasants would leave farming for counterfeiting (thus ruining the government's revenue and bringing about poor government), he was nonetheless perceptive in showing how debasement affected various types of commoners. For example, the merchants, who dealt mostly in large coins (with a lower copper content), would have a hard time doing business with country folks who, being used to small-denomination coins of higher copper content, were bound to view the 'big coins' with disfavour. Debasement, in effect, had created a two-tier copper coinage that seriously inhibited the flow of rural produce to the towns and cities. A decline in trade would then create further social discontent and unrest, compounding the problem already at hand.

The circulation of debased copper coins had caused other forms of hardship as well. As Shen pointed out, because taxes were assessed in silver and paid in copper coins, debasement of the latter was in effect a disguised form of tax increase. He therefore suggested that in the metropolitan and surrounding areas where taxes were collected in money, the copper–silver exchange rate be fixed at 2,000 cash to the tael. In this

34 King, *Money*, pp. 150–1, 153–5; T'an Pi-an, 'Huo-pi kai-ke', pp. 46–7; Yang Tuan-liu, *Ch'ing-tai huo-pi*, pp. 107–11.
35 Pong, 'Dynastic Crisis', app. A.
36 The Bannermen were already badly paid. Their pay, set according to the seventeenth-century cost of living, had not been adjusted despite inflation (40–100%) and increased family size. Nor were there additional positions for the larger number of Bannermen. Michael's introduction to Spector, *Li*, p. xxxiii.

way, the taxpayers would feel the benefits of what amounted to a tax reduction while the government would be more certain of its revenue.

Shen was less critical of the paper money. These government notes were unpopular only because they were not redeemable. Once made redeemable, they would gain acceptance and restore popular faith in the government. But true to his strong Confucian leanings, he maintained that, in dealing with the empire's finances, the monetary system was only of secondary importance, whereas grain and clothing were the root of it all. He therefore recommended that the land and poll tax (*ti-ting*) and tribute grain (*ts'ao-che*) be partly collected in kind. While the Peking-bound portion of the revenue should still be collected in silver (to facilitate transportation), the portion kept in the provinces should be levied 80 to 90 per cent in copper cash and the remainder in kind (unhusked grain and textiles). With this reform, the people would be better able to pay their taxes, while the storage of grain and textiles in the provinces would sustain the local population in the face of rebel attacks.

Shen was not alone in opposing these inflationary measures, but most objections were mild. The majority of the provincial officials showed their disapproval by simply going slow in introducing the new currencies or by stressing popular rejection. Few were prepared, as Shen was, to make jarring criticisms and propose solutions. One exception was Wang Mao-yin (1798–1865), the junior vice-president of the Board of Revenue and a central figure of the Hsien-feng financial reforms.[37] Our focus of concern does not warrant a detailed analysis of Wang's criticism. Suffice it to say here that both his criticism and solutions were based more on financial and fiscal considerations than were Shen's, as would be expected of a person in his position. Thus, while Wang was troubled by the unbridled inflation that the debased currencies had brought, Shen attacked wholesale the basis for debasement.[38]

Indeed, Shen's remedies combined Confucian idealism with the naïveté of a young censor: they aimed at preserving social order and promoting administrative benevolence without taking into consideration the practicality of such measures in an age of rebellion and social turmoil. Collecting

---

37 For the role played by Wang, see Wu Han, 'Wang Mao-yin yü Hsien-feng shih-tai ti hsin pi-chih', *Chung-kuo she-hui ching-chi shih chi-k'an*, 6.1 (June 1939), reprinted in Li Ting-i, Pao Tsun-p'eng, and Wu Hsiang-hsiang, eds., *Chung-kuo chin-tai-shih lun-ts'ung*, 2d ser., vol. 3: *Ts'ai-cheng ching-chi* (Taipei, 1958), pp. 49–70; King, *Money*, chap. 6.

38 Frank King writes: 'The question debated in Peking during 1853 and 1854 was not whether the measures they were adopting were potentially disruptive and inflationary – the officials knew they were – but exactly how far they could go, how much they could get away with'. *Money*, p. 152. Shen must have been the odd man out among the dissenters.

taxes in kind at a time when transportation had been so seriously disrupted was unrealistic. His call to halt currency debasement and make paper notes redeemable also failed to provide real solutions to the government's financial plight. To be fair, though, no one else had the answer either, not until the effectiveness of the likin transit tax became apparent later.

The significance of Shen's memorial, then, lies in the audacity with which he attacked a policy over whose adoption the deeply troubled government had little choice. His criticism was principled, but impolitic. This might have invited political disaster in view of the fact that Wang Mao-yin had already been removed from the Board of Revenue in April 1854 partly because of his troublesome memorial.[39] Shen was more fortunate – his strong criticism went unpunished, for censors, too, could be penalized for their outspokenness, notwithstanding their theoretical immunity.[40]

Military reorganization

Shen's second memorial dealt with organizational problems in the war against the rebels. It is well known that long before the Taiping Rebellion both the Banner and the Green Standard forces had lost their vigour.[41] Yet in the early 1850s, the gentry-led armies which eventually proved effective against the rebels had barely been organized, and the central government had no alternative but to entrust its fate to the hands of the existing, decrepit forces.

At the local level, two major problems arose. The first concerned the command of local defence forces, the militia (*t'uan-lien*). In south China in the Opium War era, a model of militia organization emerged which, from the government's viewpoint, conceded too much power to the

39 Ibid., p. 155; Yang Tuan-liu, *Ch'ing-tai huo-pi*, pp. 97, 111–12. Wang was transferred to the Board of War. Although policy disagreement was a major factor in Wang's transfer, I am inclined to think that the main reason was his awkward personal relations with his senior colleagues at the Board of Revenue, notably the senior vice-president, Ch'i Sui-tsao. After all, Wang's view on monetary matters was known before he was made junior vice-president of the board. Besides, he was merely transferred, not demoted (as one might have expected), and within seven months he was promoted to senior vice-president of the Board of War. Ibid., pp. 107, 111; Wu Han, 'Wang Mao-yin', p. 67; *Shih-lu*, HF 149:21b.

40 Despite theoretical immunity, outspoken censors had been punished from time to time in the Ch'ing period. This point will be discussed later. See T'ang Chi-ho, 'Ch'ing-tai k'o-tao chih ch'eng-chi', *Chung-shan wen-hua chiao-yü-kuan chi-k'an*, 2 (1935), 521, and idem, 'Ch'ing-tai k'o-tao-kuan chih kung-wu kuang-hsi', *Hsin she-hui k'o-hsüeh chi-k'an*, 1.2 (1934), 211.

41 Spector, *Li*, pp. xxxii–xxxv.

gentry.[42] Therefore, in 1853 the government promoted its own formula for militia organization, placing these forces under civil officials – the magistrates. Although this model eventually became the most influential,[43] the government's assumption that the civil officials could be just as effective militia commanders as were gentrymen was by no means proven, certainly not in 1854 or the years immediately following.[44]

The second problem was how to tackle the large and fast-moving Taiping forces. In late 1852 the court had reluctantly granted *t'uan-lien* leadership to trustworthy high-ranking officials who happened to be on leave in their native places. Out of this arrangement emerged the Hunan Army of Tseng Kuo-fan (1811–72).[45] But Tseng's new army, though mobile, was too centralized to suit local defence needs. Meanwhile, the Taipings continued on their rampage through the country. Appalled by such conditions, Shen, whose censorial duties covered the lower Yangtze area, the main theatre of the anti-Taiping campaign, wrote an inspired memorial on how to render the traditional military forces more effective.[46]

As Shen saw it, the main flaws in the Ch'ing military system were the lack of co-ordination among the commanders at the top and poorly defined responsibilities among local defence leaders. Poor co-ordination had led many commanders to pour their troops into places of rebel concentration, leaving adjacent areas inadequately protected. Thus, as one town was recovered, others fell. And a handful of rebels could easily tie down several commanders at any given time. Shen's remedy was to tighten the chain of command at the top, put the provincial commander-in-chief or even a court-appointed general (*ta-shuai*) in charge of overall strategy, and make the brigade-generals (*tsung-ping*) responsible for guarding the key locations as well as dispatching reinforcements and strike units.

Shen regarded confusion among local military leaders as even more critical, for much could be saved only if the local forces could hold out long enough for reinforcements to arrive. But even the most dedicated prefects and magistrates failed to do just this, for although they were responsible for local defence, they controlled only the irregular forces or mercenaries (*yung*), not the regular troops (*kuan-ping*), who had their own officers. In the event of a military emergency, confusion reigned,

---

42 Frederic Wakeman, Jr., *Strangers at the Gate: Social Disorder in South China, 1839–1861* (Berkeley and Los Angeles, 1966), and Kuhn, *Rebellion*, pp. 50–7, 142–5.

43 Ibid., pp. 57–8.

44 For example, in 1855–6, eight of the thirteen prefectural capitals and more than fifty hsien in Kiangsi fell into rebel hands in rapid succession. Pong, 'Income', p. 51.

45 Kuhn, *Rebellion*, pp. 135–52.

46 Pong, 'Dynastic Crisis', app. B.

especially when outside troops were also involved. The military and civilian authorities distrusted each other; neither would take orders from the other. They competed with one another whenever easy victories were expected. But no one would assume responsibility in the face of a strong rebel onslaught. Rivalry and suspicion also permeated the ranks. And the soldiers' tendency to bully and prey on the commoners further strained an already sour military–civilian relationship.

Shen's proposed remedy shows a readiness to advocate institutional change and, in the best tradition of Confucian and statecraft scholarship, to draw inspiration from historical precedents. So to improve military training and operation, to promote co-ordination among the commanding officers, and to curb their proclivity for evading responsibility, he called for an adaptive revival of the Han practice whereby local troops were placed under local officials. Thus, officers from the first captains (*tu-ssu*) down would be led by prefects, and those from the lieutenants (*ch'ien-tsung*) down would be subordinated to magistrates. In return, the local people would provide financial support for the soldiers. Mutual dependence meant that the soldiers would be prepared to protect the commoners not only from rebels but also from thieves and bandits. When these changes were combined with a revival of the *pao-chia* (mutual responsibility) system, local defence would be so improved that outside forces would rarely be called in even in a military emergency. This in itself would be no small blessing, for outside troops were as troublesome as they were useful.

Shen's diagnosis of the military organization in 1854 was not entirely original, though strikingly perceptive. The Ch'ing military system, with two distinctly separate armed services (the Banner and Green Standard forces) and poor relations between the military and the civil bureaucracy, was designed to prevent the concentration of power, not to ensure battle-worthiness. In the early 1850s, military effectiveness was found more often in personal armies (*ch'in-ping*), such as that organized by Hu Lin-i (1812–61), but the government understandably viewed such armies with disfavour.[47] Even Tseng Kuo-fan's Hunan Army, which had Peking's blessing and was increasingly successful, was not regarded as universally desirable. By 1854, the rise of Tseng was watched with fear and suspicion in some quarters in the imperial capital (as discussed later). The cautious central government still preferred the Banner and Green Standard forces, the mercenaries (*yung*), and the gentry-led militia, deployed independently or in motley combination. Shen's solution, therefore, had much to recommend it, for it clarified the chain of command, defined responsibilities

47 Kuhn, *Rebellion*, pp. 117–35.

for each level of the now more highly co-ordinated military–civilian hierarchy, and promoted better soldier–commoner relations.

Some of the proposed reforms, however, were unrealistic. The military establishment, for one, could hardly be expected to embrace any attempt at breaking up its chain of command or subordinating its officers to civil officials. This latter proposal, which was likely to encourage localism, would also draw opposition from the central government. Moreover, how could it be assumed that civil officials could both train and lead troops? The Confucian model of a civil official, to be sure, was that of a man who, armed with high principles, could attend to all facets of government. But such ideal officials rarely existed, as testified by Tseng Kuo-fan's later complaint that civil officials capable of commanding troops were hard to find.[48] Finally, given the exigencies of the time, Shen's proposals would have taken far too long to materialize on a large scale. Thus, the Board of War, when ordered by the Hsien-feng emperor to evaluate these proposals, took no action on them.[49]

Shen's solutions, if at times idealistic, were nevertheless based on sound analysis. Lei Hai-tsung (1902–62), an authority on the military tradition and culture of China and one who, writing in the mid-1930s, had also to deal with a country plagued by civil strife and foreign threat, agreed with Shen's diagnosis to a remarkable degree when he said that the loss of the ancient identity of soldiers and people, institutionalized in the militia, was at the source of China's military decline since Han times.[50] And Shen, despite his failure to effect institutional changes in 1854, later demonstrated that some of his ideas were practicable, at least at the local level. In 1856, he, as prefect of Kuang-hsin, Kiangsi, promoted military leadership among the local officials and successfully frustrated rebel onslaughts (see Chapter 2).

The strategy of October 1854

Shen's third memorial dealt with situational issues: strategic options in late 1854. So far the government was forced to be on the defensive in the

48 Tseng Kuo-fan, *Tseng Wen-cheng kung ch'üan-chi* (hereafter, *TWCK*) (Taipei, 1952), vol. 9, 'Letters', pp. 37–8.
49 Li Yüan-tu, *T'ien-yüeh shan-kuan*, 14:9.
50 Lei Hai-tsung, 'Chung-kuo ti ping', *She-hui k'o-hsüeh tsa-chih*, 1.1 (1935), 1–47, and idem, 'Wu-ping ti wen-hua,' ibid., 1.4 (1936), 1005–39. For a discussion of Lei's ideas, see Kuhn, *Rebellion*, pp. 10–13. Dr. Michael Godley of Monash University suggested in a seminar at the Australian National University, in the summer of 1979, that Lei had fascist leanings. If so, his political views might have influenced his scholarship and his desire to militarize the civilian population. However, the identity of soldier and peasant was an ancient Chinese ideal. Shen had never in his entire career intended to militarize either the people or the gentry elite.

Taiping War. As Shen had pointed out, even defence was poorly organized. In October 1854, however, despair gave way to hope. On the 14th of that month, Tseng Kuo-fan's army, after three days of general assault, took the twin city of Wuhan (Wuchang and Hankow), the capital of Hupei.[51] At that time, the city, which had been in rebel hands for four months, was strategically the most important along the Yangtze. Had the Taipings been able to defend it as well as they had Hu-k'ou (Kiangsi) and Anking (Anhwei) downstream, they would have been able to threaten any of the Yangtze provinces and also maintain a vital supply line all the way to Nanking. Wuhan's recapture was therefore the first major victory for the dynasty, ushering in a new phase of the war.

'This huge victory is quite beyond Our expectations', exclaimed the emperor. So delighted was he that Tseng was immediately awarded the button of the second rank, granted the right to wear the single-eyed peacock feather, and, to cap it all, appointed acting governor of Hupei. Tseng was then ordered to deliberate with Yang P'ei, the governor-general of Hu Kuang, on measures to rid the province of rebels and to begin its rehabilitation.[52]

This assignment would tie down Tseng in Hupei indefinitely. Meanwhile the momentum of his campaign and the morale of his troops would dissipate. A superior strategy would be to ride the crest of this first major victory, continue the campaign downstream, and secure the Yangtze before turning to the rehabilitation of Hupei. This, in fact, was Shen's thought. He therefore opposed Tseng's territorial appointment and urged the emperor to change his plan.[53]

Unbeknownst to Shen, Tseng, for different reasons, had already declined the appointment of acting governor.[54] Then in a second memorial Tseng stressed that he was still mourning his mother's death and would breach Confucian protocol by formally assuming a resident office away from home. He therefore proposed to return the acting governor's seal and lead his troops down the Yangtze.[55]

Before this second memorial reached Peking, however, the court had already changed its mind. The acting governorship was withdrawn and, instead, Tseng was awarded the brevet of vice-president of the Board of War. He was then ordered to prepare for the defence of Hupei and the campaign downstream.[56] Although Shen's proposal reached the court

51 Kuo T'ing-i, comp., *Chin-tai Chung-kuo shih-shih jih-chih* (Taipei, 1963), vol. 1, p. 221; W. J. Hail, *Tseng Kuo-fan and the Taiping Rebellion* (New Haven, Conn., 1927), pp. 169–72.
52 Edicts of 26 October 1854 in *Shih-lu*, HF 144:18–20b, 20b–21.
53 For the text of Shen's memorial, see Pong, 'Dynastic Crisis', app. C.
54 *Shih-lu*, HF 144:10b–11.
55 *TWCK*, vol. 2, 'Memorials', pp. 84–5.
56 Ibid., vol. 1, 'nien-p'u', p. 32; *Shih-lu*, HF 145:3b.

before Tseng's second memorial (internal evidence suggests this), it did not critically influence imperial policy, for a policy change was already under way. So in commenting on Shen's memorial, the Hsien-feng emperor wrote, 'The Court has already foreseen this', rather than the usual 'Noted' (*chih-tao-liao*).[57] What really changed the mood in Peking was the growing fear that the new military leaders, if given regular provincial posts, would gain too much power and control over local revenues.[58] In Tseng's case, the court was caught between those who wanted to make ues of his new-found talent as military leader and those who wished to curb his growing power. Eventually, it was the advocates of the latter cause, headed by the powerful grand councillor Ch'i Chün-tsao, who held sway; Tseng was instructed to pursue the Taipings down the river (but with inadequate logistic support!).[59]

This policy change had two major beneficial effects on Shen's career. By inadvertently lending support to the new policy, he had given that policy, the outcome of a factional struggle at court, a semblance of 'public support', which a censor supposedly represented. And because his assessment of the military situation was also in accord with Tseng Kuo-fan's, the latter took note of him, admired his insightfulness, and soon became his patron.

In theory the censor performed an important regulatory function in government. In practice, however, a censorial appointment was little more than a brief and routine interlude in a bureaucrat's career, at best a training period for higher positions.[60] Yet Shen's memorials show that he took his job seriously. Admittedly, they constituted only a small proportion of what he must have written as a censor; they nevertheless demonstrate a readiness to exercise his censorial privilege to criticize and influence major policy issues.[61] Although the memorials on the Hsien-feng inflation and on military strategy represent a post facto criticism of government policies, all three memorials contained substantive proposals,

---

57 Li Yüan-tu, *T'ien-yüeh shan-kuan*, 14:9.
58 Spector, *Li*, p. xl.
59 Hsiao I-shan, *Ch'ing-tai t'ung-shih* (Taipei, 1963), vol. 3, pp. 411–12.
60 T'ang Chi-ho, 'Ch'ing-tai k'o-tao-kuan chih kung-wu', p. 211.
61 In Ch'ing times, censors were required to meet certain quotas. In times of crisis, they were also expected to memorialize more frequently. We have some indication, for the T'ang and the Ming periods, of the voluminous output of censors, particularly in critical times. For example, during the T'ang, Po Chü-i was allotted two hundred sheets of paper per month for memorials. However, for the Ch'ing period, few censorial memorials have been preserved. While fortunate in having three of Shen's memorials, we are mindful that our samples are small. Wu Han, 'Wang Mao-yin', p. 50; Eugene Feifel, *Po Chü-i as a Censor* (The Hague, 1961), p. 32; Charles O. Hucker, *The Censorial System of Ming China* (Stanford, Calif., 1966), pp. 232, 323 n. 8; T'ang Chi-ho, 'Ch'ing-tai k'o-tao chih ch'eng-chi', p. 518.

unmistakably intended to help shape policies. While the exigencies of the time could well explain the urge to take part in policy-making,[62] these memorials do provide full testimony to the convictions, vigour, and initiative that characterized Shen's entire career.

In the first two memorials Shen betrayed a number of idealistic traits. Chang Hao, in studying the political application of Neo-Confucianism, distinguishes two approaches adopted by scholar-officials: moral idealism (normative approach) and practical statesmanship (*ching-shih*). The former maintained that the moral order could be realized only by one's successful striving for sagehood. The latter, while retaining all the Confucian moral values, insisted that government must also take the environment into account.[63] The normative approach is most clearly visible in Shen's second memorial, in which he argued that a more Confucian state could be brought about only by officials of high principles who were given charge of all aspects of local government, including the military. His model was the Three Ages (San-tai: Hsia, Shang, and Chou), upheld by Confucian idealists as the paradigm of moral order. In this mythical era of perfect order there was no separation between the soldier and the farmer, the commander and the official.

But Shen, like the Liu Tsung-yüan he studied in his youth, did not adhere rigidly to the ways of the ancients. He took note of the world in which he lived and spoke of institutional adjustments (*pien-t'ung*) for the benefit of all. He thus argued that even the most virtuous and able officials would be rendered helpless if the inflationary measures were left unchecked – a heresy in the eyes of the Confucian fundamentalists. Further, he accepted the 'modern' instrument of paper money, as long as it was redeemable, predicating his argument primarily on material benefits (*li*) and profits (the same character, *li*). Here, Shen leaned towards the practical statecraft persuasion.

Ultimately, Shen's central concern was benevolent government: no government should lose sight of the people's well-being, whether it was trying to keep its budget balanced or attempting to keep the rebels at bay. It was this concern that enabled him to move with apparent ease (and without the nagging awareness of the contradiction) between the two Neo-Confucian approaches to government.

In insisting on the revival of Confucian values, however, Shen had in effect pointed up the gap between reality and ideal in the Ch'ing state –

---

62 Hucker (*Censorial System*, p. 177) makes the interesting observation that, in the chaotic era of 1620–7, the Ming censors spoke out more often as individuals than as institutional representatives of the censorate and behaved predominantly as shapers of policy.

63 Chang Hao, 'On the *Ching-shih* Ideal in Neo-Confucianism', *Ch'ing-shih wen-t'i*, 3.1 (November 1974), 36–61.

a serious indictment of imperial policies. He thus ran the risk of punishment, for the Ch'ing system tended to favour the impeaching rather than the remonstrative role of the censor. Further, although in theory a censor was empowered to criticize on the basis of hearsay, to better protect his source of information, he could be penalized for having relied on doubtful or false information.[64] Nevertheless, in spite of the treacherous grounds on which an outspoken censor must tread, Shen's memorial on inflation – the most critical of all three and one clearly directed at an imperial policy – went unpunished. His memorial on military reorganization, though critical, was directed at a general situation. Its perceptiveness and relevancy drew imperial notice, and the Board of War was ordered to give it a full review. But it was his memorial on military strategy, a nonideological issue and one not critical of Ch'ing institutions, that endeared him to the throne. So, shortly thereafter, he was recommended for a prefectural appointment; meanwhile, in July 1855, he was made chief censor of the Kweichow circuit.[65] This is hardly surprising because good censors were hard to find,[66] and despite his readiness to criticize, Shen was a good and loyal censor.

Conclusions

Though Shen grew up in a family of limited means, the strong scholarly background of his parents assured him of a sound education. Close ties with Lin Tse-hsü's family were also important. Up to the time he left for Peking for the metropolitan examination, the greatest single influence on his intellectual and moral development coming out of these family ties was probably Lin himself. The latter's impeccable personal and public life, his perseverance and determination, commitment to the ideas of the School of Practical Statecraft, his reformist zeal and patriotism, all of which were already widely known, could not but have reinforced the educational and character-building efforts of Shen's parents and teachers. Later, Shen used Lin as a model when instructing his own children.[67]

In fact, Chinese historians often regard Shen as a 'moral successor' to Lin.[68] Their in-law relationship is invariably recorded in all of Shen's biographies, whereas Shen's father is sometimes not even mentioned. In many cases, Shen's biography is placed in the same group of biographies

---

64 Chang Chin-chien, *Chung-kuo wen-kuan*, pp. 236–7; T'ang Chi-ho, 'Ch'ing-tai k'o-tao-kuan chih kung-wu', p. 211.
65 *Ch'ing-shih lieh-chuan*, 53:35.
66 T'ang Chi-ho, 'Ch'ing-tai k'o-tao-kuan chih jen-yung', *She-hui k'o-hsüeh ts'ung-k'an*, 1.2 (November 1934), 155–8; Hucker, *Censorial System*, pp. 57–8.
67 Shen Yü-ch'ing, *T'ao-yüan chi*, p. 125.
68 See, e.g., Lin Ch'ung-yung, *Shen*, p. 45.

as Lin's. Because collections of biographies were traditionally meant to be read and judged as a corporate account of exemplary lives from a given period, the message is unmistakably clear.[69] While the answer to whether Shen can indeed be viewed as Lin's 'moral successor' must be deferred for the moment, we should bear the question in mind as we examine his life and career.

The close relationship with the Lin family calls attention to the beneficial effect it might have had on Shen's early career. Available evidence suggests that the effect was small. Although Shen's career as a metropolitan official began after Lin's political rehabilitation in 1845, his various appointments and promotions were routine. In fact, the most important factor in his early career was his failure to attain the first grade in the *chin-shih* examination, which precluded all chances of attaining a high metropolitan office. Nevertheless, being Lin's son-in-law was not an advantage that could be easily discounted. A quarter of a century later, opponents of Shen's reforms took note of his family connections and, partly for that reason, avoided a personal attack on him.[70] But then one can always read too much into these connections for, in terms of the success of his career, Shen certainly did much better than Lin's own sons. As evident in his performance as censor, it was his courageous and, to some extent, perceptive memorials that earned him his promotions and, ultimately, the patronage of Tseng Kuo-fan.

In his capacity as censor, Shen, like his colleagues, was expected to uphold orthodoxy and conformity without the benefit of any administrative experience. It is natural that his memorials betrayed a great deal of idealism, 'undigested' Confucian learning, and naïveté, his early exposure to reformist thinking and Lin Tse-hsü's influence notwithstanding. Since censors were supposed to be the 'ears and eyes' of the throne – an important form of stewardship – Shen later viewed with horror the immaturity of his ideas expressed in 1854.[71] But did he abandon his idealism as he mellowed? More important, from 1856 on, as he changed from being a 'guardian of mores and polity' (a censor) to being one of 'those who will be found guilty' (a territorial official),[72] his ideological

69 Twitchett, 'Problems of Chinese Biography', pp. 32–3. Even in a recent biographical compilation, Shen's biography was placed immediately after Lin's. *Fu-chien li-tai ming-jen chuan-lüeh*, comp. Fu-chien shih-fan ta-hsüeh li-shih hsi (Foochow, 1987), pp. 170–92.

70 *Yang-wu yün-tung* (hereafter, *YWYT*), comp. Chung-kuo k'o-hsüeh-yüan chin-tai-shih yen-chiu-so shih-liao pien-chi-shih (Shanghai, 1961), vol. 1, p. 130. See also David Pong, 'Shen Pao-chen and the Great Policy Debate of 1874–1875', *Ch'ing-chi tzu-ch'iang yün-tung yen-t'ao-hui lun-wen-chi* (Taipei, 1988), pp. 215–21.

71 *IWSM*, TC 53:27.

72 Charles O. Hucker, *The Traditional Chinese State in Ming Times (1368–1644)* (Tucson, Ariz., 1961), p. 51; Etienne Balazs, *Political Theory and Administrative Reality in Traditional China* (London, 1965), p. 58.

commitments were to be subjected to severe tests. Was he, then, able to maintain a healthy balance between idealism and the harsh realities of the bureaucratic world? These are some of the questions we shall attempt to answer.

Finally, during the seven years or so in the metropolitan area (1847–54), Shen must have come into contact with numerous junior officials like himself. We cannot preclude, for instance, an association with the reformer-thinker Feng Kuei-fen, who had once been Lin Tse-hsü's favorite disciple.[73] A number of these men certainly became his lifelong friends and close colleagues. Liang Ming-ch'ien, his right-hand man at the Foochow Navy Yard after 1866, is a case in point.[74] Not a few had also earned the *chin-shih* degree the same year he had (1847). They were therefore his *t'ung-nien* (lit., same-year graduates). Among these were Li Hung-chang, Li Tsung-hsi, Ho Ching, Ma Hsin-i, and Kuo Sung-tao.[75] Li Hung-chang and Shen also had the same examiner.[76] Under the Ch'ing, after the examinations were over, the results known, and the examiners identified, the candidates and their examiners were expected to develop a kind of teacher–disciple or patron–client relationship.[77] As 'disciples' of the same 'teacher', Shen and Li could well have developed strong ties. On the other hand, the significance of *t'ung-nien* relationships can be exaggerated. Some of the men just mentioned became Shen's political enemies later on. But where common interests existed, *t'ung-nien* relationships could assume great importance. Mutual consultation and support among Shen, Kuo, and Li Hung-chang proved valuable in their later careers.

---

73 Lin Ch'ung-yung, *Shen*, p. 170. Feng was in Peking from late 1848 to sometime in 1850. Hummel, *Eminent Chinese*, vol. 1, pp. 241–2.

74 Shen Pao-chen, *Yeh-shih chai sheng-kao* (n.d., n.p.), p. 28.

75 *Tao Hsien T'ung Kuang ming-jen shou-cha* (Shanghai, 1924), part 1, *ts'e* 3 (unpaginated); *Ming Ch'ing li-k'o chin-shih t'i-ming pei-lu* (Taipei, 1969), vol. 4, pp. 2517–28; Ts'ai Kuan-lo, *Ch'ing-tai ch'i-pai ming-jen chuan* (Shanghai, 1937), vol. 1, p. 406.

76 Li Hung-chang, *Li Wen-chung kung ch'üan-chi* (hereafter, *LWCK*) (Nanking, 1905), 'Letters', 5:37.

77 Lin Ch'ung-yung, *Lin*, p. 42.

2
Local official in Kiangsi, 1856–1859

Within a short span of six years, from 1856 to 1862, Shen rose from prefect (rank 4b) to provincial governor (rank 2b), despite a two-and-a-half-year self-imposed retirement (July 1859 to January 1862). His rise was truly meteoric; never again would he enjoy such a rapid series of promotions. The exigencies of the time and the patronage of Tseng Kuo-fan, who was himself being catapulted to high office in this period, were contributing factors. But his transformation from a regional to a national figure was entirely the result of his own achievements. In this chapter, we shall first examine his brief service under Tseng, which happened quite by accident, and then his exploits as a local official in the Taiping War.

Tseng Kuo-fan's assistant, January to May 1856

In January 1856 Shen found himself journeying towards northern Kiangsi to take up his first territorial appointment as the prefect of Chiu-chiang, a key prefecture along the Yangtze.[1] But as Kiukiang, the prefectural seat, had been in rebel hands since February 1853, Shen, on arrival in the area, decided to proceed to Nan-k'ang, thirty kilometres to the south, to discuss matters with Tseng Kuo-fan at his headquarters. In the course of their conversation, Tseng warmly recalled Shen's memorial of October 1854 on military strategy and strongly urged Shen to join his personal staff.[2]

Shen's assistance was especially desirable at this time because Tseng was facing an extremely grim military situation. The optimism that his recovery of Wuchang brought in 1854 had dissipated. The Taipings were

1 *MHHC*, 93:7.   2 Shen Yü-ch'ing, *T'ao-yüan chi*, p. 30.

47

now firmly established at their capital at Nanking. And their capture of Hankow and Han-yang for the fourth time and Wuchang for the third in early 1855 once again gave them control over the most important stretch of the Yangtze, from Hankow down to Nanking and beyond.[3] The repeated reverses Tseng sustained quickly turned him into a laughing-stock among the gentry and officials of Kiangsi who were singularly uncooperative. Isolated from other provinces, Tseng suffered from inadequate supplies as well.[4] Meanwhile, local rebels surging forth from Kwangtung and Kwangsi in the south further aggravated the situation. The only supply line open to Tseng was in north-eastern Kiangsi, through Kuang-hsin into Chekiang. As William J. Hail puts it, he was practically a 'prisoner at Nanchang', the provincial capital.[5] As a result, his management of military affairs came under heavy fire from censors, and in February 1856, the emperor addressed a reproving enquiry to him.[6]

Little is known of Shen's activities in Tseng's camp. He probably served as a military adviser in view of Tseng's admiration of his previous discussion on military strategy. Yet it was unlikely that he formally became Tseng's personal assistant (*mu-yu*).[7] After all, he was still officially the prefect of Chiu-chiang and as such was on the government's payroll, not Tseng's. Besides, since the prefectural city, Kiukiang, was still in rebel hands, he expected a comparable appointment elsewhere. In fact,

---

3 The Taipings took Hankow and Han-yang on 23 February 1855 and Wuchang on 3 April. The last two were not recaptured by Ch'ing forces until 18 December 1856. Franz Michael, in collaboration with Chung-li Chang, *The Taiping Rebellion: History and Documents* (Seattle, Wash., 1966), vol. 1, pp. 93, 95, 104; Kuo T'ing-i, *Chin-tai Chung-kuo shih-shih*, vol. 1, pp. 228–9, 235–6, 253.

4 Chien Yu-wen, *T'ai-p'ing t'ien-kuo ch'üan-shih* (Hong Kong, 1962), vol. 1, pp. 1144–5. On 28 February 1856 Tseng memorialized that he had 11,000 troops in Kiangsi supported by a monthly allocation of 60,000 taels, which came from tribute grain, 'contributions', and salt tax. Because of the rebels, he maintained, all these sources of revenue were ruined. *TWCK*, vol. 3, 'Memorials', p. 187.

5 Ibid., p. 191; Hail, *Tseng*, pp. 183–4.

6 Ibid., p. 194; *TWCK*, vol. 3, 'Memorials', pp. 183, 187.

7 Spector (*Li*, p. 19) states that Shen was Tseng's personal assistant, but the source cited does not support this. Li Ting-fang's *Tseng Kuo-fan chi-ch'i mu-fu jen-wu* (Kwei-yang, 1946), which gives great details on this subject, does not mention Shen. Nor is Shen described as Tseng's *mu-yu* in two later studies: Kenneth E. Folsom, *Friends, Guests, and Colleagues: The mu-fu System in the Late Ch'ing Period* (Berkeley and Los Angeles, 1968), pp. 72–5, and Jonathan Porter, *Tseng Kuo-fan's Private Bureaucracy* (Berkeley and Los Angeles, 1972). The only source which lends some credence to Spector's contention is a poem dedicated jointly to Shen and Tseng by Shen's fourth son. Shen Yü-ch'ing, *T'ao-yüan chi*, p. 30. The author might have exaggerated the relationship between his father and Tseng in an attempt to minimize criticism of the two great men, who later engaged in a bitter policy dispute (see Chapter 3).

this materialized soon after, in April, when a vacancy became available at Kuang-hsin prefecture. Shen assumed his new office in May.[8]

Shen's service under Tseng, though brief, had great impact on his later career. Tseng was a key figure of this period. Both his position and his scholarship attracted to him many scholars, tacticians, military commanders, and later on, mathematicians and 'experts' on foreign affairs.[9] Many became influential subsequently. Service under Tseng thus provided Shen with a wide circle of well-placed friends, several of whom worked closely with him in his later career: Kuo Sung-tao, Kuo K'un-tao, Chou K'ai-hsi, Li Han-chang, Li Yüan-tu, Chou T'eng-hu, and Hsia Hsieh, to name just a few.[10] Not all of them served Tseng in the first half of 1856. Nevertheless, the esprit de corps among Tseng's followers was a factor to be reckoned with.

The defence of Kuang-hsin: an act of supreme loyalty

Shen's appointment as the prefect of Kuang-hsin was itself an indication of his growing importance. *The Complete List of Officials of the Ch'ing Empire* (*Ta-Ch'ing chin-shen ch'üan-shu*) describes the job of the Kuang-hsin prefect as a very important one. And the prefecture, thanks to its strategic

8 *Chiu-chiang fu-chih* (n.p., 1873), 5:33, 6:33b.
9 Folsom, *The mu-fu System*, pp. 73–7.
10 Kuo Sung-tao (1818–91), a native of Hunan, was known for his scholarship and was China's first minister to England. Although Kuo did not always agree with Shen on specific issues, he always acted as a friendly critic. On broad matters of policy, however, the two were often in agreement, lending each other their support. There was also much mutual admiration. When Shen left the Foochow Navy Yard in late 1875, he recommended Kuo to succeed him as director-general. Kuo K'un-tao (1823–82), brother of Sung-tao, had a less brilliant career, but was extremely important to Tseng Kuo fan, and after 1860 also to Tso Tsung-t'ang, in managing military supplies for their armies. In doing this, he worked closely with Shen. *Pa hsien shou-cha* (Shanghai, 1935), pp. 128–30; *Ch'ing-shih*, vol. 6, p. 4945. Chou K'ai-hsi (1827–71), like the Kuo brothers, was a native of Hunan. During the early 1860s, he was a close associate of Tso Tsung-t'ang and later became Shen's right-hand man in the Foochow Navy Yard. Li Han-chang (1821–99), the elder brother of Hung-chang, was a circuit intendant in charge of a section of the Kiangsi likin administration during Shen's governorship. Li Yüan-tu, another Hunanese, commanded some of Tseng Kuo-fan's troops and co-operated closely with Shen in military matters in 1857–8. Shen's relationship with Chou T'eng-hu (1816–62) is obscure, but both Chou and his father were close friends of Lin Tse-hsü, Shen's father-in-law. Chou was known for his scholarship and wealth of ideas and, at least on one occasion, wrote Shen a lengthy discourse on salt administration when Shen was prefect of Chiu-chiang. T'ien Pu-shan, comp., *K'un-ling Chou-shih chia chi* (Ch'i-nan, 1924), pp. 1, 3b–10; Morohashi Tetsuji, comp., *Dai Kanwa jiten* (Tokyo, 1955), vol. 2, p. 949; *Ch'ing-shih*, vol. 6, p. 4832; Sheng K'ang, comp., *Huang-ch'ao ching-shih-wen hsü-pien* (Wu-chin, Kiangsu, 1897), 52:75. Hsia Hsieh, a native of Anhwei, was an expectant magistrate of Nan-ch'ang hsien when Shen was governor of Kiangsi and gave the most detailed eye-witness account of the Nanchang antimissionary riot. Paul A. Cohen, *China and Christianity* (Cambridge, Mass., 1963), p. 88.

location, was classified as troublesome, wearisome, and difficult. The only compensation for Shen was the relatively high salary of 2,800 taels per annum.[11]

The timing of the appointment, however, was unpropitious. In mid-1856 Tseng Kuo-fan was still effectively encircled in northern Kiangsi but for a precarious life-line along the Kiangsi–Chekiang corridor in which Kuang-hsin was located. It was therefore expected that the Taipings would soon want to seize control of this line. Earlier, in January, Ho Kuei-ch'ing (governor of Chekiang) and Lien Ch'ao-lun (Kiangsi provincial director of education and *t'uan-lien* commissioner) had expressed concern over the safety of Kuang-hsin. So vital was this prefecture and its surrounding area that Lo Tse-nan, Tseng's right-hand man in the Hunan Army, was ordered to leave the siege of Wu-han for its defence.[12] Lo was too late, but he managed to recapture the prefectural seat two days after it had fallen to the rebels in early February. For a while, pressure on Kuang-hsin abated as Taiping forces were recalled to raise the siege of Nanking. But this breathing space was soon cut short as threats loomed in the south from April on.[13] Kuang-hsin was once again in danger.

For all the importance Tseng Kuo-fan attached to the security of Kuang-hsin, he was unable to spare troops for its defence.[14] And despite the relief expedition led by Lo Tse-nan in February, the defence of the area had been shouldered by Lien Ch'ao-lun for nearly a year under extremely trying conditions. According to Lien, the provincial mercenary (*yung*) units, the only troops that could be relied upon, were grossly outnumbered: their sixteen thousand men had to take on seventy thousand local rebels and Taipings. Worse still, the units were not under a single command. They typically competed with one another for rewards in the event of a victory but, in the event of a defeat, shied away from responsibility. He therefore urged that they be reorganized into three or four large brigades of four thousand to five thousand men each.[15] The court, probably fearful of further concentration of military power, did not heed his advice.

However, when Shen took over Kuang-hsin prefecture, he embraced

---

11 *Ta-Ch'ing chin-shen ch'üan-shu*, Spring 1857 ed., *ts'e* 2:64b. On the difference in importance between a local official position in an out-of-the-way place and that in a difficult locality, see Balazs, *Political Theory*, pp. 55–6.
12 Memorials of Lien and Ho, received 18 and 19 January 1856. *Shih-lu*, HF 186:10 and 187:4a–b, respectively.
13 Chien Yu-wen, *T'ai-p'ing t'ien-kuo*, vol. 2, pp. 1145–6, 1178, 1185, 1889.
14 Tseng's memorial, 5 April and 24 May 1856 in *TWCK*, vol. 3, 'Memorials', pp. 194, 205.
15 Ibid., p. 228; *Ch'ing-shih*, vol. 6, p. 4828.

Lien's ideas. After all, they were very similar in spirit to his own proposals presented to the throne not quite two years earlier. Both favoured a more centralized military organization. But, as prefect, all that was within Shen's power was to improve co-ordination among the militia leaders in the seven counties under his jurisdiction. To further increase his defensive strength, he had to mobilize the gentry leaders to intensify troop recruitment and training.[16] Co-operation with Lien, of course, continued. Details are no longer available, but their combined efforts soon led to the recovery of Chin-ch'i and Chien-ch'ang, strategic towns guarding the southern approaches to Shen's own prefecture.[17] Things were looking up, but not for long.

Meanwhile, members of a central Kiangsi secret society, the Pien-ch'ien Hui, threw in their lot with the Taipings. They entered Kuang-hsin prefectural territory in late August and, on 2 September, took the district seat of Kuei-ch'i, the first of many towns to fall. The newly trained mercenaries failed to put up an adequate resistance.[18]

At this juncture, Shen and Lien were recruiting and collecting military supplies some fifty kilometres away. On learning of Kuei-ch'i's collapse on 3 September, they at once set out for Kuang-hsin and, at the same time, appealed to Brigade General Jao T'ing-hsüan for help. At the time, Jao, who was charged by the Chekiang authorities to defend their end of the Kiangsi–Chekiang corridor, was stationed at Yü-shan, fifty kilometres upstream on River Hsin (Hsin-chiang).[19]

At Kuang-hsin pandemonium reigned. With only four hundred men left for its defence and Shen still away, most officials and yamen servants took flight. The city was literally deserted. But Shen's wife, Lin P'u-ch'ing, refused to flee and, of her own accord, wrote a letter in blood drawn from her finger beseeching Jao to send reinforcements. In the letter she vowed that she would wait for Shen's return, and together they would defend the city until death as a gesture of gratitude for the emperor's bounteous favours.[20] Lin was not driven by martyrdom, for she really wanted to save Kuang-hsin, hence her appeal to Jao's common sense: if Kuang-hsin fell, Jao's own base at Yü-shan would become

16 *Kuang-hsin fu-chih*, comp. Li Shu-fan et al. (1873), 5:33.
17 *Ch'ing-shih*, vol. 6, p. 4828.
18 Chien Yu-wen, *T'ai-p'ing t'ien-kuo*, vol. 2, pp. 1189–90. The Pien-ch'ien Hui was based in an area around Chien-ch'ang and Chi-an in central Kiangsi. Not much is known about its activities or organization.
19 *Kuang-hsin fu-chih*, 6:33b–34; *Ch'ing-shih*, vol. 6, p. 4695; Chien Yu-wen, *T'ai-p'ing t'ien-kuo*, vol. 2, p. 1190.
20 *Ch'ing-shih*, vol. 7, pp. 5521–2. The literary style of this dispatch is highly praised by Liang I-chen, *Ch'ing-tai fu-nü wen-hsüeh shih* (Taipei, 1958), pp. 245–57, which reproduces the entire text.

indefensible. She knew he would come. Touched by Lin's plea and moved by strategic considerations, Jao mobilized his forces.[21] But alas, his boats were held up by low waters on the Hsin. All hope of saving the prefectural capital would have been dashed had there not been heavy rain on the 6th, enabling Jao and his 2,100 men to reach Kuang-hsin on the 7th. Several bloody but indecisive engagements ensued, but on the 11th, the beleaguered city was under heavy attack by a sizeable Taiping reinforcement. Desperation, however, brought out the best of the besieged. With the yamen virtually depleted of officials, clerks, and domestic servants, Lin P'u-ch'ing took upon herself the duties they normally performed: she did clerical work, kept accounts, handled the soldiers' pay, and even cooked for the troops. Shen, for his part, devoted himself to defence, while Lien Ch'ao-lun donated his salary to help pay the troops. Thanks to the sheer determination of Jao's troops and the inspiration given them by Shen, Lin, and Lien, the siege was raised on the 13th, which, according to the lunar calendar, was also Lin's birthday.[22]

The successful defence of Kuang-hsin was a godsend for Tseng Kuo-fan, for at stake was not only the integrity of his sole supply line but also his leadership, which had been seriously questioned. Although he had previously contended that his resources could not be extended to the Kuang-hsin area, the court had no intention of leaving the safety of such a strategic area solely in the hands of Lien. When it was first threatened in early September, the throne expressed displeasure at Tseng's evasion of responsibility.[23] Thus, the success of Shen and Lien had saved Tseng from further embarrassments, of which he had seen too many in his Kiangsi days. But perhaps because he felt that the throne's displeasure

21 Jao and the Shens were natives of Hou-kuan. Although they had never met, Jao was certainly aware of Shen's relationship with the late Lin Tse-hsü, the most prominent public figure from Hou-kuan within memory. Besides, as a loyal commander (died in action, 1861), Jao could well have been moved by the sincerity, loyalty, and sense of sacrifice conveyed by Lin P'u-ch'ing's plea. Shih Shu-i, comp., *Ch'ing-tai kuei-ko shih-jen cheng-lüeh* (Shanghai, 1922), 10:8b; Shen Pao-chen, *Yeh-shih chai*, 10b–11. For a biography of Jao, see *MHHC*, 68:22b–24. According to the *Kuang-hsin fu-chih* (5:34b–35) and several later accounts, Jao's decision was influenced by a sense of personal loyalty and duty because he had once served under Lin Tse-hsü. Shen's son, however, denied the existence of such an association. His contention is also supported by Lin Ch'ung-yung's exhaustive research. Shen Yü-ch'ing, *T'ao-yüan chi*, p. 215; Lin Ch'ung-yung, 'Lin Ching-jen', pp. 297–304.
22 On Lin P'u-ch'ing's activities in this crisis, see her biography in *FCTC*, 'lieh-nü chuan', 3:11b–12. Since this biography was written by Shen Pao-chen himself, one may suspect some embellishment and partiality. A brief reference to Lin's role in Tseng Kuo-fan's memorial, however, confirms the general nature of her contribution. Tseng's memorial was not based on Shen's report, but on someone else's, probably Lien Ch'ao-lun's. On Jao and Lien, see *Ch'ing-shih*, vol. 6, p. 4828.
23 Edict. 23 September 1856. *Shih-lu*, HF 205:25a–b.

at him had been abetted by Lien's memorials, Tseng deliberatly glossed over Lien's contribution and singled out Shen as the hero of the day.[24]

Shen's feat looked all the more impressive when one considers the many officials who abandoned their posts in less threatening situations. In the course of 1856, eight out of fourteen prefectural cities and fifty-three of the seventy-five district townships in Kiangsi fell largely because the officials merely put up a half-hearted resistance or fled before the enemies appeared. The loss of Kuei-ch'i, mentioned earlier, was one such case of extreme negligence and irresponsibility. At the time, its defence was in the hands of a certain Shih Ching-fen, who, on hearing that a township in a neighbouring prefecture was in danger, took his best two thousand men to its rescue. He missed his enemies, who then took his own inadequately protected Kuei-ch'i. Instead of returning to help defend his prefecture, he quietly retired to his home-town, leaving his troops with neither a leader nor provisions.[25]

As Tseng Kuo-fan put it, territories were lost not because the rebels were strong but because resistance was wanting. This was an exaggeration, perhaps, but it was nevertheless against the background of rampant negligence and cowardice that Shen's defence of Kuang-hsin was judged. So as Tseng sought orders from Peking to punish delinquent officials, he praised Shen for having given full expression to Confucian principles (*shen-ming ta-i*). Shen's name was duly registered for promotion on the strength of his recommendation.[26]

Circuit intendant with two masters

In June 1857, after only thirteen months of service as a prefect, Shen was appointed the taotai of Kuang-Jao-Chiu-Nan circuit in northern Kiangsi, comprising the prefectures of Kuang-hsin, Jao-chou, Chiu-chiang, and Nan-k'ang. Since Kiukiang, the seat of the office, was still in rebel hands, he directed his activities from Kuang-hsin. By this time the general situation for the dynasty had improved; in consequence, the function of Kuang-hsin also changed. Just as reinforcements from Hunan and Hupei had reopened lines of communication with other parts of the empire, the bloody power struggles among the Taiping leaders since the latter part of 1856 had seriously weakened the rebels. So despite Tseng Kuo-fan's temporary retirement in February to mourn his father's death,

---

24 *TWCK*, vol. 3, 'Memorials', pp. 234–5.
25 Shih was dismissed for his negligence. Li Yüan-tu, *T'ien-yüeh shan-kuan*, 18:13; *Shih-lu*, HF 207:10–11.
26 *TWCK*, vol. 3, 'Memorials', pp. 213, 234–5; edict, 4 October 1856, in *Shih-lu*, HF 207:12b.

the rebels in north-eastern Kiangsi were forced to retreat towards Anhwei and Chekiang.[27] Kuang-hsin now became one of the bases where anti-Taiping campaigns would be organized.

To speed up the military effort, Tseng cut short his mourning and returned to Anhwei and Chekiang in July 1858. On his way, he had a meeting with Shen and Li Yüan-tu near Kuang-hsin on 14 September. Li was Tseng's confidant and a commander of the Hunan Army who had recently joined Jao T'ing-hsüan as the protector of the Kiangsi–Chekiang corridor. At the meeting it was decided that Li should rejoin Tseng while Shen should take over his troops for the defence of the Kuang-hsin area.[28] Soon after Tseng left, he gave Shen further responsibilities. First, Shen was to seek out talented men and report to him. Then he put Shen in charge of the military supplies for his Hunanese troops.[29] Thus, in less than three years after their first meeting, Tseng was prepared to entrust Shen with a very vital role not only in the defence of the Kiangsi–Chekiang corridor but also in his overall military operations. By accepting these responsibilities, however, Shen had become an official with two masters – Tseng and the Kiangsi provincial authorities.

Little is known of Shen's relations with Tseng during this period. In all probability he was more or less able to meet Tseng's demands for military supplies, for despite sporadic shortages, there was no complaint from Tseng.[30] But Shen's close link with Tseng strained his relationship with the Kiangsi provincial administration because of competing interests and the long-standing rivalry between Tseng and the Kiangsi authorities. Besides, Governor Ch'i-ling was also jealous of Shen's ability.[31] For these reasons, Shen tendered his resignation in March 1859 on grounds of ill-health.[32] His request was denied. But three months later, with the recapture of Kiukiang, he was able to move back to his official residence there, thus avoiding further awkwardness.[33] Then, in July, with the

27 Chien Yu-wen, *T'ai-p'ing t'ien-kuo*, vol. 3, pp. 1593–7.
28 Ibid., pp. 1626, 1629; Wang Erh-min, 'Tseng Kuo-fan yü Li Yüan-tu', *Ku-kung wen-hsien*, 3.3 (June 1972), 3, 16 n. 14; Ts'ai Kuan-lo, *Ch'ing-tai ch'i-pai ming-jen*, vol. 2, p. 992; *Ch'ing-shih*, vol. 6, pp. 4695–6, 4884.
29 *TWCK*, vol. 9, 'Letters', pp. 35–6; *TWCK*, vol. 3, 'Memorials', p. 291.
30 Liu T'ieh-leng, comp., *Ch'ing-tai erh-pai chia chün-cheng ming-tu hui-pien* (Shanghai, 1926), 17:10; *T'ao-feng-lou ts'ang ming-hsien shou-cha* (1930), unpaginated, *ts'e* 4, Shen's letters of HF 9.2.12 and 9.2.26 (16 and 30 March 1859, respectively).
31 Li Huan, *Pao-wei chai lei-kao* (1891), 95:21.
32 Tseng Kuo-fan to Hu Lin-i, 4 February 1859 in *TWCK*, vol. 9, 'Letters', p. 38; Shen to Ch'i-ling, 30 March 1859, in *T'ao-feng-lou, ts'e* 4, HF 9.2.26; Shen to Kuo K'un-tao, no date, in *Pa hsien shou-cha*, pp. 128–30.
33 Permission for this removal seems to have been secured by the middle of April, but Shen remained at Kuang-hsin at least until mid-June. *T'ao-feng-lou, ts'e* 4, Shen's letters

death of his only surviving brother, he had to retire to his native Hou-kuan to look after his aged parents.[34]

Conclusions

Shen's administration in the Kuang-hsin area represents an important turning point in his early career. Although he had difficulties with the governor, he worked well with Tseng Kuo-fan, won his confidence, and was able to establish useful connections with local officials. Among these officials was Grain Intendant Li Huan (1827–91), an able and honest official. Li, like Tseng, came from Hunan and, despite his position in the Kiangsi bureaucracy, was willing and able to co-operate closely with Shen to meet Tseng's needs.[35] He was later to serve as Shen's right-hand man.

We know little of Shen as a civil official, although contemporary accounts indicate that he implemented, with some success, some of the high ideals he propounded as a censor in 1854. All describe him as benevolent but firm and fair, which is also in agreement with our understanding of his later career. As one with the additional responsibility of protecting the Kiangsi–Chekiang corridor, he was dearly remembered by the local people for his defence and measures for suppressing banditry. Plauditory remarks in contemporary and local records were not always perfunctorily made. No other civil or military officials were similarly eulogized in the 1873 edition of the Kuang-hsin gazetteer, even though it was compiled at a time when Shen, as director-general of the Foochow Navy Yard, was regarded by some as having strayed from the path of a traditional Confucian official.[36]

In terms of his career, the defence of Kuang-hsin in 1856 was the most important event in this period. Even without Tseng Kuo-fan's partisan report, Shen stood out as a person of valour, dedication, self-sacrifice, and loyalty. While official commendations of this kind were made partly for their propaganda value so that others would have someone to emulate – an important consideration at the time – there is no doubt that the local people admired him and were grateful to him. It is said that when he left in 1859 thousands of people and local leaders begged him to stay. A few

of HF 9.3.11 and 9.5.13 (13 April, 13 June 1859); Tseng's memorial, 26 June, in *TWCK*, vol. 3, 'Memorials', p. 316.

34 Li Yüan-tu, *T'ien-yüeh shan-kuan*, 14:10; Li Huan, *Pao-wei chai*, 95:21; Shen Tsan-ch'ing, 'Chia-p'u', p. 71.

35 Hummel, *Eminent Chinese*, vol. 1, pp. 458–9; Li Huan, *Pao-wei chai*, 1:1–4; *Chiang-hsi t'ung-chih* (1880; hereafter, *CHTC*), 16:31.

36 Li Yüan-tu, *T'ien-yüeh shan-kuan*, 14:10, 18:14; Li Huan, *Pao-wei chai*, 95:20b–21; *Kuang-hsin fu-chih*, 6:33b–34.

months after he died (1879), people from the seven districts of Kuang-hsin honoured him with a memorial temple.[37]

The defence of Kuang-hsin, in fact, had turned Shen into an instant legend, a paragon of all the Confucian virtues found only in the greatest scholar-officials. Illustrated and romanticized accounts of the incident were widely circulated; less flamboyant narratives continued to appear in official and private writings long after the Ch'ing dynasty had vanished.[38] It gave him national stature and helped him in his career. His actions, because of the virtues they were purported to represent, along with his connection with Lin Tse-hsü, moral and physical, also shielded him from many a conservative attack later on.

Shen's military exploits in this period also gained him two valuable friends. After the successful defence of Kuang-hsin, he and Jao T'ing-hsüan became sworn brothers. The close co-operation between him and Li Yüan-tu, a valuable aide of Tseng Kuo-fan's, also resulted in friendship and mutual admiration, which they sealed by the marriage of Shen's second son to Li's third daughter.[39] Although Jao's subsequent decline and early death had no effect on Shen's later career, Li's support, as we shall see, contributed to his re-emergence from self-imposed retirement in early 1862.

Because of his achievements, national fame, and familiarity with the Kuang-hsin area, Shen was repeatedly urged throughout 1860 and 1861 by high officials both in and out of Kiangsi to give up his retirement and return to active service. And no sooner had he yielded to the pleadings of Tseng Kuo-fan and others than, quite unexpectedly, he was appointed the governor of Kiangsi in early 1862.

---

37 *Shih-lu*, KH 116:9a–b; *North-China Herald and Supreme Court and Consular Gazette* (hereafter, *NCH*), 28 October 1880. In 1884 the gentry of Kuang-hsin wished to honour Shen's wife also in this temple. An edict of 23 July 1884 granted their request. P'an Wei's memorial, KH 10.6.2 (23 July 1884), in China, National Palace Museum, Taipei, Palace Archives: Yüeh-che tang (hereafter, YCT), KH 10/6 *shang*.

38 Lin Ch'ung-yung, 'Lin Ching-jen', pp. 293–304.

39 Shen Yü-ch'ing, *T'ao-yüan chi*, pp. 206–7, 214–15. On Li's relationship with Tseng, see Wang Erh-min, 'Tseng Kuo-fan', pp. 1–21, and Porter, *Tseng*, pp. 34, 76.

3

Governor of Kiangsi, 1862–1865

Shen's appointment as governor of Kiangsi was directly related to the collapse of the regular Ch'ing forces at Nanking in May 1860. Faced with a bleak situation, the imperial court now had to rely even more on such new forces as Tseng Kuo-fan's Hunan Army; high provincial officials were also granted greater freedom of action. Thus, on 8 June, Tseng was appointed acting governor-general of the Liang Kiang provinces: Kiangsu, Anhwei, and Kiangsi. Then, on 23 August, he was made governor-general and concurrently the imperial commissioner in charge of military affairs in these provinces. Three months later, he was elevated to a position of authority unprecedented for a territorial official since the dynasty consolidated its power in the 1670s. An edict of 30 November put the military affairs of the four provinces of Kiangsu, Anhwei, Kiangsi, and Chekiang under his direction. 'All the governors and generals of these four provinces are to be placed under his control', the edict declared.[1] Thus, Tseng was no longer the 'guest' of these provinces, as he used to grudgingly describe himself, but the 'master' who, potentially, could channel their resources into an all-out effort to put down the Taipings.[2]

Tseng, on his own, had already begun work on a general strategy for the suppression of the rebels before these new powers were showered on him. From 30 May to 9 June, he held a series of conferences with Hu Lin-i, Tso Tsung-t'ang, Li Hung-chang, Li Han-chang and Li Yüan-tu. Recognizing the critical shortage of able men, they decided that Shen Pao-chen should be recalled for active service.[3] With Shen's return,

1 *TWCK*, vol. 3, 'Memorials', pp. 350, 435.
2 Wang Erh-min, *Huai-chün*, pp. 26–7.
3 Li Yüan-tu, because of his in-law relationship with Shen, was asked to persuade Shen. *TWCK*, vol. 9, 'Letters', pp. 55–6.

Tseng could divide his troops into three 'routes', the first two of which he would lead in an anti-Taiping offensive. The third was to remain in north-eastern Kiangsi under the joint leadership of Li Yüan-tu, Shen Pao-chen, and Jao T'ing-hsüan, who, together, had worked wonders before.[4] The scheme was to protect Kiangsi, his main source of revenue, as well as Hunan, his native province and recruiting ground, in support of a march towards the Taiping capital at Nanking.[5]

In Kiangsi, too, a sombre mood prevailed after the government troops were routed at Nanking. There, Yü-k'o, the new governor, and Li Huan, the acting treasurer, also urged Shen to return. Yü-k'o particularly wanted to put him in charge of the Kiangsi–Chekiang corridor, even if it meant removing the incumbent.[6] Given Shen's past association with this area, it was a sound idea. Tseng Kuo-fan obviously thought so, for Shen's return to Kuang-hsin would, even if only temporarily, also give help to Li Yüan-tu, who, in Tseng's opinion, had trouble managing his subordinates.[7] Shen, however, was determined to tend to his parents at his native Hou-kuan.

Then on 21 June, Tseng and Hu Lin-i independently sought an imperial injunction to secure Shen's return. Hu suggested a provincial treasurership (rank 2b) or judgeship (rank 3a) for him, even though hitherto he had served only two years as a circuit intendant (rank 4a). Hu then intimated to Tseng that the Kiangsi treasurership would be particularly appropriate, given Shen's past service in that province.[8] Perhaps feeling that Hu's proposal would have given Shen too much too soon, the throne favoured Tseng's idea and ordered Shen to return to Kuang-hsin. Once again, Shen declined,[9] but expressed a willingness to work for Tseng as a personal assistant (*mu-yu*) if he were allowed to visit his parents once a year.[10]

Other high officials, too, wanted to see Shen resume active service. For example, Grand Councillor Wen-hsiang, whose power soared after the Second Opium War, recommended him for a 'substantive post'. Then Vice-President Sung Chin of the Board of Works, as if to echo Hu Lin-i's

4 Ibid., p. 54.
5 *TWCK*, vol. 3, 'Memorials', pp. 332–3; Pong, 'Income', p. 64.
6 Li Huan, *Pao-wei chai*, 53:1–2b. Li also wrote Tseng on 5 July 1860 recommending Shen's return to Kiangsi. Ibid., 15b–16.
7 *TWCK*, vol. 9, 'Letters', p. 58.
8 *TWCK*, vol. 3, 'Memorials', p. 332; Hu Lin-i, *Hu Wen-chung kung i-chi* (1867), 'Memorials', 27:8; 'Letters', 72:3.
9 Soon after, Shen was appointed taotai for southern Kiangsi and then was ordered to organize the militia of the entire province. Shen declined both appointments because of his aged parents. *FCTC*, 'lieh-chuan', 39:39.
10 *Pa hsien shou-cha*, p. 9.

proposal, recommended him for a provincial treasurership.[11] Finally, in late 1861, some eighteen months after the first attempts to bring him out of retirement, the court instructed him to go to Tseng Kuo-fan's camp 'to await appointment'.[12] At about the same time, it ordered Tseng to look into the ability of the incumbent governors of Kiangsu and Chekiang.[13] Although the court might not have intended Shen for the governorship of either province, such an office was not entirely out of the question as the dynasty grew increasingly desperate for capable men. Tseng, however, preferred Li Hung-chang for the Kiangsu post because Li was a more gifted military leader.[14] Then, on 17 January 1862, while Shen was en route to Tseng's camp in southern Anhwei, the emperor appointed him governor of Kiangsi (rank 2b).[15] He was then forty-one years of age.

Thus, Shen, who had served altogether less than four years as a prefect and a taotai, was now, after a two-and-a-half-year furlough, catapulted into high office. A tour as provincial judge or treasurer before a gubernatorial appointment would have been more in tune with established practices. Was his meteoric rise the result of Tseng Kuo-fan's patronage? His brief service under Tseng in 1856 undoubtedly helped; at least Tseng and his colleagues had had first-hand knowledge of him. All but one of the key figures at the crucial meetings in May–June 1860 were Tseng's *mu-yu*. Yet, it was Wen-hsiang, Sung Chin, and Hu Lin-i, who had few or no connections with Shen, who recommended him for high-level appointments. Of the three, only Hu was remotely associated with Shen; he had been a prefect in Kweichow during Lin Tse-hsü's governorship.[16] Shen's rapid promotion to governor, therefore, owed less to patronage than to his proven ability, his reputation, especially that derived from his legendary defence of Kuang-hsin, and the exigencies of the time. Whatever the reason, all who had a hand in his ascendency also had high expectations of him, not the least of whom was Tseng, who had had such difficulties with Kiangsi officials.

In Tseng's scheme, Kiangsi was the first province behind the front line. As the main source of his supplies, its security had to be coupled with an effective internal administration. In order to meet his needs the new governor must be able to win the allegiance of the provincial

11 *Ch'ing-shih*, vol. 6, pp. 4627, 4823–4.
12 *SWSK*, 1:3.
13 *TWCK*, vol. 3, 'Memorials', pp. 436–7.
14 Hsüeh Fu-ch'eng, 'Shu Ho-fei po-hsiang Li-kung yung Hu p'ing Wu', in Tso Shun-sheng, comp., *Chung-kuo chin-pai-nien shih tzu-liao ch'u-pien* (Shanghai, 1931–3), p. 164; Folsom, *The mu-fu System*, p. 86.
15 *SWSK*, 1:1.
16 Lin Ch'ung-yung, *Lin*, pp. 610–11.

officials and elite and to convince them that their interests would be best served by fulfilling their obligations to Tseng and, therefore, ultimately to the throne. The moment Shen stepped into his new shoes, he recognized these to be his main tasks and vowed that he would give his very best in the service of the empire and abide by the principle of loyalty and filial piety (*chung-hsiao*).[17]

But the principle of loyalty and filial piety, a conceptual unity in Confucian thought, in fact encompassed a wide range of competing loyalties. Loyalty to such high principles as popular welfare and administrative integrity, and loyalty to such temporal powers as the throne, other government authorities, and the gentry, were not always easily reconciled.[18] Already, in 1854, Shen had to defend the well-being of the common people against an imperial policy of inflation. Later, as taotai, he was awkwardly caught between the contending but legitimate interests of Tseng Kuo-fan and Kiangsi province. Then he had been a servant of two masters; now he was, in theory, one of the two masters. But was a governor really a master of his province? Before attempting an answer, we need to examine first the power and responsibilities of the governor. Only then can we evaluate the key features of Shen's administration, his perception of the needs of his province, and the success with which he met those needs in the face of Tseng's demand for military funds.

The governor's powers and responsibilities

In broad terms, the primary function of a provincial governor was to oversee the officials, maintain justice, collect taxes, promote popular welfare, eradicate evil or corrupt practices, and, in Confucian parlance, soothe and pacify the masses.[19] These were onerous duties to which the governor and his staff could not attend in person. It was the local officials, particularly the district magistrates, who actually dealt with these matters among the people.[20] Yet, as Shen deeply believed, an energetic governor could induce good government down to the local levels, and his legislative powers could reinforce his personal vigour. In this sense, the governor could justly be held responsible for the well-being of his province.[21]

17 *SWSK*, 1:1b–2, 3, 9–10.
18 Albert Feuerwerker's comments on Kwang-ching Liu, 'Nineteenth-Century China', in Ping-ti Ho and Tang Tsou, *China in Crisis*, vol. 1, book 1, pp. 179–93.
19 Unless otherwise stated, information in the following paragraphs is drawn from Fu Tsung-mou, *Ch'ing-tai tu-fu chih-tu* (Taipei, 1963), passim. The manner in which the function of the governor is analysed is mine.
20 John R. Watt, *The District Magistrate in Late Imperial China* (New York, 1972), pp. 11–22.
21 Shen Pao-chen, *Chü-kuan kuei-nieh*, 2:1b–3.

The governor's authority over his subordinates was considerable. He personally conducted the periodic examination of the provincial treasurer and the judical commissioner, the highest officials under him. While he had to rely on the reports of other officials on the lesser men in the bureaucracy, he could gain direct information by a tour of the province. Rewards or punishment might then follow. Further, he could nominate candidates for certain categories of official positions. Nevertheless, all personnel changes were subject to approval by the central government, which was by no means pro forma. Any departure from established rules or practices could be challenged, and the governor, like all officials, could be impeached for serious misdemeanours.

In theory, the ultimate objective of government was to improve the people's livelihood, by, for example, promoting agriculture, and to nourish their moral well-being. In practice, as Shen understood, a governor's concern for the economic conditions of the people as well as the need for fairness and justice might run afoul of government demands for revenue.[22] This was no mere financial matter, for his ability to carry out government policies greatly depended on the loyalty and support of his people.

Nourishing popular morality was a task as intangible as it was difficult to implement. The conventional method was to uphold state orthodoxy and to promote Confucian learning, especially among the scholar-gentry class, so that they could serve as models. Official rectitude, including the governor's own, was believed to have a similar effect. Even if both the objective and the method reflected what we may consider Confucian idealism, Shen argued that they could contribute to a more orderly society and a less corrupt bureaucracy.[23]

Where the power of persuasion and the judicial process failed, the governor could resort to the use of force. The provincial Green Standard Army, which functioned essentially as a constabulary, was at his disposal. For larger disturbances, he had recourse to the governor's brigade (*fu-piao*), which numbered between one thousand and two thousand men. In the case of Kiangsi, the governor's military responsibility was greater because he also doubled as the provincial commander-in-chief, although the forces under his command were much smaller than those in most neighbouring provinces.[24] Major uprisings could be overcome only with the help of outside reinforcements.

Since the opening of the Yangtze and the interior to foreign travel and

---

22 Ibid.
23 Ibid., 1:38, 100b–101; 2:24b–25.
24 The Green Standard Army in Kiangsi had 12,500 men; that in Kiangsu, 38,100; Anhwei, 9,400; Hunan, 27,100; and Kwangtung, 46,800. *Ch'ing-shih*, vol. 3, p. 1632.

shipping in 1860, the governor of Kiangsi had also to deal with foreign affairs. Shen's management of them will be analysed in the next chapter.

The administration of a province was often complicated by the relations between the governor and the governor-general. While these two officials were by and large equal under most circumstances, the governor of Kiangsi was to some extent subordinate to the governor-general of Liang Kiang. And when it came to matters of importance, the imprimatur of the latter was essential.[25] Yet the distances separating Nanking, the seat of the governor-general, from Nanchang, the capital of Kiangsi, gave the governor a modicum of autonomy.[26] But then, in the early 1860s, the vast powers vested in Tseng Kuo-fan and the location of his headquarters in nearby southern Anhwei significantly increased his ability to intervene in Kiangsi's affairs. So as we study Shen's governorship, we shall focus also on the potential rivalry between him and his patron as well as their competition for scarce resources.

Civil administration

Even as military affairs occupied the empire's leaders, Shen continued to stress the primacy of civil administration in provincial government. In one sense, his approach can be viewed as a rationalization of the stark reality. As the forces of Tseng Kuo-fan and Tso Tsung-t'ang moved progressively towards Nanking, his already inadequately defended province would become even more vulnerable. Yet Kiangsi's straitened finances and its huge commitments to support Tseng and Tso ruled out any significant military build-up. Shen's solution therefore was to improve the quality of government. If the local officials were carefully chosen and the sufferings of the people relieved, he reasoned, then at least the province would be able to rebuild its strength and increase its financial resources for military purposes. For now, Kiangsi could afford only to improve its existing forces without additional expenses – by careful selection of army personnel and cultivation of military leadership.[27]

But Shen was not guided merely by expediency, for he was deeply convinced of the fundamental importance of civil administration. This vital matter had long occupied his mind and had resulted in the publication in 1863 of his *Chü-kuan kuei-nieh* (Precepts for office-holders). In it he

25 H. S. Brunnert, and V. V. Hagelstrom, *Present Day Political Organization of China* (Shanghai, 1912), nos. 820, 821, 821A.
26 Because of Kiangsi's distance from Nanking, it was suggested in 1830 that the province be detached from Liang Kiang. The issue was debated at court but was rejected. *Ch'ing-ch'ao hsü wen-hsien t'ung-kao*, comp. Liu Chin-tsao et al. (Shanghai, 1936), 132:8914.
27 Shen's memorial of 11 April 1862. *SWSK*, 1:9b–10.

stressed the primacy of service: 'He who takes up office for a day must do a day's worth of good deeds', for compared with the gentryman and commoner, 'the official's power to do good is unlimited'. To serve well, however, an official must be incorrupt, diligent, cautious in decision making and personnel matters, and 'constantly aware that one has fallen short of expectations'. In this work and elsewhere, Shen reiterated the conventional wisdom that the prefects and the magistrates were the cogs in the Confucian bureaucratic wheel, the 'father and mother officials' who were in the position to do the greatest good, and harm, to the people.[28]

Shen further argued that, in a world torn by civil disorder, a good prefect was worth more than a good general, for it was the prefect's benevolent government that could nip troubles in the bud, whereas military force could deal only with the symptoms of popular discontent.[29] This was good preventive medicine, but conditions did not always permit such an approach. For even as the dynasty's fortune improved from 1862 on, Kiangsi was still subjected to frequent threats. As Shen soon found out, he had little time and a difficult task before him.

Dealing with local officials

In looking at the government of a province, Shen considered all offices important, each designed for a specific function. And true to his Confucian belief, he stressed the importance of selecting capable men (*jen-ts'ai*, lit., men of talent) for office, but as one experienced in local government, he also believed in placing them in positions commensurate with their ability. In line with his views on government, he considered this specially critical when it came to choosing local officials, for only the virtuous among them could bring peace to the people.[30] Thus, within months of his governorship, he had the prefects of Chi-an and Nan-k'ang exchange their posts, despite objections from the Board of Personnel. The reason had to do with ability and suitability. The prefect of Chi-an, while understanding, careful, and dutiful, was unable to cope with either the negligent officials or the feuds, clan wars, tax resistance, and ruffians who dominated the yamen. Chi-an was notorious as the province's most difficult prefecture to govern even in the best of times. In contrast, the prefect of Nan-k'ang, sincere, incorruptible, intelligent, and resolute, was

28 Passim, but see esp. 1:15ab, 22ab, 30, 36b–37, 71.
29 Ibid., 52b; *CHTC*, 128:40.
30 *SWSK*, 1:1b, 52a–b; Shen Pao-chen, *Chü-kuan kuei-nieh*, 2:1–23, 24a–b. Shen subscribed in particular to the instructions given to local officials by the great late Ming scholar-official Kao P'an-lung (1562–1626).

by far the most outstanding prefect in the province; he had more talent than was required to govern a small, uncomplicated prefecture. In terms of Confucian virtues, little separated the two; there was, however, a huge gap between their abilities. Utterly convinced that the exchange of offices would produce salutary results, Shen went ahead without approval from Peking. Local records indicate that conditions in Chi-an improved markedly.[31]

Confucian dogmatists, of course, would insist that virtue and talent were synonymous. Shen, pragmatic but unorthodox, saw their distinction clearly and effected personnel changes accordingly. But such administrative measures were of limited application. As he recognized, the main task of the governor still lay in the handling of the incompetent and the delinquent.

Long years of war had brought deterioration to local government. The supervision of local officials had slackened, and many cases of negligence and timidity went unnoticed. (A case of officials failing to control bad elements among the gentry will be discussed later.) In addition, the government, needing to sell titles and offices to raise military funds, had brought into the civil service many who were plainly incompetent. Some had difficulties handling even the simplest documents. So at the risk of jeopardizing the government's fund-raising efforts, Shen rid the bureaucracy of such men. At the first annual evaluation of some of his subordinates in early 1863, he retired six of these officials.[32] As a censor noted, Shen and Tso Tsung-t'ang were among the few who made good use of this type of measure to ensure good government.[33]

Official corruption was a perennial problem, especially since the late eighteenth century. Although Kiangsi was not particularly notorious for its rapacious officials or its oppressive gentry, who might have colluded with them,[34] whatever official misdemeanours that existed were exacerbated by wartime conditions. As vast amounts of money and material were raised for the war effort, many could not resist the temptation to line their own pockets. For instance, a magistrate kept 2,000 taels out of a 3,000-tael donation from a gentryman and, when discovered, falsely claimed that the money was to be sent to Tso Tsung-t'ang's army in

---

31 Shen K'o, 'Hsien Wen-su kung', pp. 18–19; *SWSK*, 1:52–3; China, National Palace Museum Archives, Taipei: Kung-chung tang (palace archives), TC 017764; *CHTC*, 130:44b. This last source, which predates Shen's incumbency, confirmed the problems of Chi-an. See 'chüan shou', part 3:10a–b.
32 Memorial of Lü Hsü-ch'eng, TC 2.1.22 (11 March 1863). YCT, TC 2/1 *hsia*.
33 *Ch'ing-ch'ao hsü wen-hsien t'ung-kao*, 93:8531b.
34 Hsiao Kung-chuan, *Rural China: Imperial Control in the Nineteenth Century* (Seattle, Wash., 1960), p. 432.

Chekiang. 'In order to induce respect for Imperial regulations . . . and to make an example of those who are avaricious', Shen dealt with the case firmly. The magistrate was dismissed and barred from future appointments. His rapacious underlings were also severely punished.[35]

During Shen's governorship, officials found guilty of one kind of misdemeanour or another were said to have been many and the penalty inflicted on them severe. As Tseng Kuo-fan once remarked, '[Shen], for all his modesty, is harsh in handling administrative matters; he will surely prove a match for his father-in-law [Lin Tse-hsü] in the future'.[36] Treasurer Li Huan, who thought highly of Shen as a governor, was critical of the hastiness and severity with which he dealt with delinquent officials during his early days in office. According to Li, popular complaints were often taken at face value and punishment meted out without thorough investigation. Shen became more careful later on, thanks to Li's advice.[37]

Ironically, Shen's disciplinarian approach was a reason for both Tseng Kuo-fan's initial appreciation of him and then a bitter dispute between the two. During the first years of their relationship, Tseng had nothing but respect for Shen's judgement on personnel matters, inviting him on several occasions to criticize his own staff.[38] However, after two years in office, Shen became critical of Tseng's employment of men dismissed from Kiangsi. As Censor Hua Chu-san explained, Shen, in governing a province, had to maintain high standards for his officials, whereas Tseng, in directing a large campaign, had to use every man of ability, though some may have been lacking in rectitude.[39] Tseng was not unaware of the problem. In 1859, four years before his dispute with Shen, he had argued that, in managing civil and military affairs, different standards had to be applied.[40] But now, with his influence in Kiangsi so dependent on the men he had placed there, his more tolerant approach conflicted with Shen's demand for a disciplined bureaucracy.

Shen, on the whole, was not given to acrimony. He worked well with those he held in high regard and was never hesitant to show appreciation for the meritorious.[41] As we shall see, many of his financial measures

35 *SWSK*, 1:41–2.
36 *CHTC*, 128:40; Li Huan, *Pao-wei chai*, 78:9a–b. The quote comes from *I-wen ts'ung-chi* (Taipei, 1978), vol. 16, p. 6.
37 Li Huan, *Pao-wei chai*, 78:9–10b.
38 Tseng to Shen, 1860, in *TWCK*, vol. 9, 'Letters', p. 58.
39 Hua's memorial as summarized in Shen's of 30 December 1863. *SWSK*, 2:72a–b.
40 Tseng explained his argument in a letter to Hu Lin-i in 1859 that 'in civil administration, there is a routine, and it is possible to establish the rules before seeking the persons [for office]; in military affairs, there is no regularity, and one should first look for the men, and then set up the rules'. *TWCK*, vol. 9, 'Letters', p. 38.
41 *SWSK*, 1:89a–b, 2:54; Shen K'o, 'Hsien Wen-su kung', 29–30.

could not have been carried out without the ready and valuable assistance of Li Huan.[42] Nor should his dismissal of men originally recommended by Tseng be viewed as a struggle for power, for he was mindful not to let junior officials be used as pawns in a dispute between high officials. However, a man of responsibility should not try to please everyone, for fairness and justice would suffer.[43] Our records show that he did not discriminate when it came to reward and punishment.

Though never slow in resorting to disciplinary measures, Shen did not abandon the Confucian belief in the power of persuasion. He strove to promote better government by setting a personal example. It was said that he, at the end of his incumbency, left with the same personal belongings as those with which he came. He also went to great lengths to eschew nepotism, and when Li Yüan-tu, his close friend as well as his son's father-in-law, recommended a relative to him, he sent the gentleman away with a sum of money.[44]

In the last analysis, one of the governor's greatest challenges was to secure active local official support for his policies, especially ones that did not bring tangible advantages to the officials. As one imbued with Confucian values, Shen abhorred the practice of female infanticide and its implications for family life. But his attempt to stamp out the evil totally failed to elicit any enthusiasm from the officials. For all the care he took to print and distribute appeals and regulations, all written in a clear and simple style to reach the larger public, his efforts came to nought. The officials, when instructed to submit reports on the state of the reform, colluded with the gentry and presented false claims. Nothing was changed.[45]

Handling the gentry

The importance of the gentry in local government need hardly be stressed. Their co-operation was critical to such local services as tax collection, waterworks, charity, and granary maintenance. In providing these services, gentrymen acquired vast privileges, which they often abused.[46] For an official, winning the co-operation of the gentry and, at the same time, containing their excesses was crucial in achieving order and efficiency.

---

42 *SWSK*, 1:15.

43 Shen Pao-chen, *Chü-kuan kuei-nieh*, 1:20b, 28.

44 Shen Yü-ch'ing, *T'ao-yüan chi*, p. 218; Hsü I-t'ang, *Ch'ing-tai mi-shih*, p. 109.

45 Memorial of Wang Pang-hsi, dated KH 4.2.30 (2 April 1878), in YCT KH4/2, *ts'e* 4; *Tao Hsien T'ung Kuang ssu-ch'ao tsou-i* (hereafter, *SCTI*) (Taipei, 1970), vol. 9, p. 4177.

46 See, e.g., Chang Chung-li, *The Chinese Gentry*; Ch'ü T'ung-tsu, *Local Government in China Under the Ch'ing* (Cambridge, Mass., 1962); Hsiao, *Rural China*.

In general, except for the most flagrant offences, cases of delinquency among the gentry were dealt with at the prefectural level or below. However, a few cases were sufficiently serious as to require Shen's attention, shedding light on his handling of criminal gentry.

In 1862 and 1863 'several hundred thousand' farming households in Ch'ing-chiang district, central Kiangsi, were ruined by successive floods. The floods could not have been avoided entirely, but the damage could have been reduced if the gentry leaders upstream had not repeatedly defied orders from the prefect and the magistrate and tampered with the river dike to save their own land. Official orders to have the dike repaired and for the instigators to surrender were also ignored. The victims then appealed to Shen, who ordered the prefect to arrest the culprits and repair the dike. The latter, afraid of the consequences, took no action. Another flood came. This time Shen called up troops: five hundred men and a fleet of war junks. The offending gentrymen were arrested and punished, and several were summarily executed.[47] Clearly, when the abuses of the gentry got out of hand, Shen was prepared to take strong measures.

In the Ch'ing-chiang case, their excesses were abetted by official ineptitude and cowardice. As Hsiao Kung-chuan's study on rural control shows, competent officials were usually able to keep the gentry in their place; only the incompetent and corrupt contributed to their delinquency. Shen said as much and insisted that those who frittered away their time must not go unpunished. He thus had the names and records of the offending prefect and magistrate sent to the Board of Personnel for deliberation and punishment.[48]

Punishing delinquent gentrymen, like using force against rebels, was a corrective, not a preventive. In Shen's opinion, the ultimate answer to local peace and stability rested on restoring traditional qualities to the local elite, whose moral fibre had been eroded by years of war. Opportunism had become rampant. To revive a proper sense of value, Shen sought public honours for scholars of outstanding character, scholarship, and integrity. Prefectural examinations, suspended for nearly a decade, were resumed in 1863. Thus, at the local level, Shen restored the regular route to office and influence that was more likely to attract worthy aspirants. Finally, officials and civilians who had demonstrated unquestionable courage, dedication, and probity were publicly honoured. Shen believed that if men with these qualities were singled out for praise, the common people would look up to them as paragons of virtue. If the

47 *SWSK*, 2:38–40b.   48 Hsiao, *Rural China*, p. 433; *SWSK*, 2:40a–b.

same set of values was widely accepted, social and political harmony would return.[49]

If Shen's approach seems idealistic, bear in mind that public honours and examination degrees, let alone office-holding, had always brought substantial benefits. And when tempted, the gentry-scholars could be induced to give the dynasty their allegiance and support, thus helping to restore order at the local level. So Confucian idealism notwithstanding, Shen's measures could actually help revive and strengthen the symbiotic relationship between the state and the local elites. Moreover, informed by Mencius, Shen was keenly aware that these measures alone could not restore popular allegiance and faith in the government unless the people's material needs were attended to as well.[50] This task he took upon himself almost as soon as he assumed office.

The government's purse and the people's needs

War and devastation had greatly complicated Kiangsi's financial affairs. General impoverishment tended to breed social disorder and reduced the population's ability to pay taxes or support the government's soaring military expenditure. Similar conditions in Hunan and Hupei had prompted key officials there to launch a 'tax reduction movement' in the mid-1850s.[51] In Kiangsi, the first steps towards tax reduction (really a surcharge reduction) were taken by Tseng Kuo-fan in 1861, before Shen's time. Tseng's aim was to control corruption, lessen the taxpayers' burden, and thereby increase their capacity to make 'contributions' *directly* to his military efforts. The real beneficiaries of the reform, therefore, were the landowning taxpayers, not the rent-paying tenants. Although the rhetoric suggested that the benefits would somehow trickle down to the lower strata of society, there were no assurances to this effect. Nor was there a guarantee that the reform would satisfy the malcontents.

In concrete terms, Tseng's scheme called for fixing the land and poll tax (*ti-ting*) at 2,400 cash per tael of assessed tax and the commuted tribute grain (*ts'ao-che*) at 3,000 cash per tan (100 catties). Both were much lower than existing rates. And they included all surcharges, thus barring illegal exactions by officials and gentry when assessing or collecting

49 *SWSK*, 1:55–6, 89a–b; 2:58a–b; 3:81–2.
50 A well-known passage from the *Mencius* reads: '[In the constitution of a state] the people rank the highest, the spirits of land and grain come next, and the ruler counts the least'. William Theodore De Bary, Wing-tsit Chan, and Burton Watson, eds., *Sources of Chinese Tradition* (New York, 1960), p. 110.
51 Unless otherwise stated, the source of information in this and the next three paragraphs is Hsia Nai, 'T'ai-p'ing t'ien-kuo', pp. 146, 165, 171–81.

taxes. Then, to wipe out all regional inequalities, the new rates were to be uniformly applied throughout the province. In Kuang-hsin, which had the highest surcharges in Kiangsi, the new rates amounted to a fourfold reduction in tax payment. To further enable the people to contribute to his campaign and the province to absorb the drastic revenue cuts without hurting its level of operation, Tseng also wrote off all the province's tax arrears in a single stroke.[52]

Back in 1854 Shen had advocated fixing the tax rate as a means to cut illegal impositions and a disincentive to tax evasion. The virtues of low levies, extolled by his grandfather, seem to have impressed him from an early age (see Chapter 1). Therefore, Tseng's reform, including the rather dubious assumption that surcharge reduction would eventually benefit the nontaxpaying commoners, appealed to him. He did, however, see two serious flaws in Tseng's scheme. First, the uniform tax rate disregarded regional variations; it also did not allow for extra expenses incurred by collecting taxes from distant areas. Second, levying taxes in copper cash, which had a low exchange rate against the silver tael at the time, would further reduce government revenue. Tseng readily concurred, for no sooner had the tax reform been introduced than he realized that it had given away too much. So after discussion with Treasurer Li Huan, Tseng and Shen modified the scheme in mid-1862. Taxes were once again assessed and collected in silver at the official exchange rate of 1,600 cash to the tael. The rate of the land tax (2,400 cash) thus became 1.5 taels for every tael of assessed tax and that for the tribute grain (3,000 cash) was commuted at 1.9 taels per tan. In Kuang-hsin prefecture, however, tribute grain was commuted at the rate of 3 taels per tan because of its 'favoured' conditions.[53] Shen's revised scheme thus raised the tax level somewhat, but the overall impact of the reform was still a very sizeable reduction for the taxpayers.

With the tax rates fixed, government revenue became more predictable. As a result Shen was able to institute a crude system of budgeting for the entire province, allowing adequate funds for administrative purposes at each level, so that local officials would not have to worry about shortages or to resort to excessive exactions.[54] It was by far his most innovative measure, reflecting a practical statecraft (*ching-shih*) emphasis on financial administration.

52 *TWCK*, vol. 4, 'Memorials', pp. 495, 500–1.
53 Li Huan, *Pao-wei chai*, 11:2; Shen to Tseng, 14 May 1862 (TC 1.4.16) in *T'ao-feng-lou, ts'e* 4; *TWCK*, vol. 4, 'Memorials', p. 500; Hsia Nai, 'T'ai-p'ing t'ien-kuo', pp. 162–4, 178–81.
54 The problems Shen attempted to tackle had been the bane of Ch'ing public finance since the K'ang-hsi reign (see Zelin, *Magistrate's Tael*). No detail of his budgetary system has survived. According to Liu Ping-chang, governor of Kiangsi in 1875–8, the

Together, the tax reduction and budget systems were expected to save the taxpayers more than 1,000,000,000 cash (roughly 600,000 taels) in surcharges a year and yet provide the government with 300,000 taels for military purposes. As Shen wrote to Tseng, 'Both the government and the people will profit by it'.[55] But the reform suffered two setbacks almost immediately. First, the Kuang-hsin taxpayers protested against the discriminatory rates and, bound by Tseng's initial promise of a uniform system, Shen had to back down, despite his influence on the local leaders there. Then the price of silver unexpectedly fell, causing a drop in revenue (though benefiting the taxpayers). So in 1864 Tseng and Shen decided to collect taxes in copper coins again, and no debased coins were accepted. To insulate the government from future exchange rate fluctuations, they adopted a new flexible policy: henceforth, the currency for tax payment was to be determined on a yearly basis.[56]

The tax and budget systems Shen had helped devise remained largely unaltered for the next several decades. After the initial flaws had been removed, the tax reduction scheme brought huge savings to the taxpaying population. Thus, in 1865 the provincial government collected more than a million taels less in surcharges than in the pre-1862 period, and this sum was equal to nearly half of the land and poll tax and commuted tribute grain levied that year. No wonder that Liu K'un-i, Shen's successor, applauded the scheme for having benefited both the government and 'the people'.[57] Even as late as 1878, the conservative ideologue Huang T'i-fang praised Tseng and Shen for their tax policy, which, among other benefits, also reduced official corruption (although some illegal exactions did creep back into the system). Both men, he said, were 'just

disbursement per 1.9 taels of tribute grain commutation and per 1.5 taels of land and poll tax levied was as follows:

	Tribute grain commutation (taels)	Land and poll tax (taels)
For Peking	1.3	1.1
For Kiangsi provincial administration	0.2	0.1
For administrative expenses from provincial treasury down to districts	0.4	0.3

Liu's memorial, KH 4.3.25 (27 April 1878). YCT, KH 4/3 *hsia*.
55 Li Huan, *Pao-wei chai*, 11:4; Shen to Tseng Kuo-fan, 14 May 1862 (TC 1.2.16), in *Tao-feng-lou*, *ts'e* 4.
56 Liu Ping-chang's memorial, KH 4.3.25 (27 April 1878) in YCT, KH 4/3 *hsia*. For the approximate date of the depreciation of the tael, see *SWSK*, 2:4b.
57 *IWSM*, TC 41:47b.

and loyal in serving the empire; they really understand the business of government'.[58]

Although the tax reduction benefited the taxpayers, its success in inducing larger 'contributions' to military funds remains uncertain. Whatever fresh 'contributions' there were, they went primarily, if not entirely, to the local militia and perhaps also the several thousand mercenaries (*yung*) that Shen recruited in late 1862 and early 1863 (discussed later). As far as can be ascertained, little went to Tseng Kuo-fan, which was the original intention.

As governor, Shen had not only to meet the needs of the provincial government and take care of popular welfare but also to deal with the competing demands of his province vis-à-vis those of the central government. During the early 1860s the court at Peking repeatedly attempted to tap the resources of Kiangsi and other lower Yangtze provinces to replenish its depleted treasury and granaries. One such attempt was to suspend those portions of official salary and government compensations which, in recent years, had been paid in government notes. This order, in effect, would cut official salaries and military pay by 20 per cent. For the families of those who died in war, it would mean a total cancellation of compensations, half of which were paid in government notes; the other half, paid in silver, had long been suspended. Besides inflicting further hardship on the widows and orphans of those who had died for the dynasty, the measure would increase demoralization in the bureaucracy and the army. Shen therefore adamantly opposed the court's policy. Instead, he proposed retrenchment and, in an act reminiscent of his long-standing hostility towards nonredeemable paper money, abolished the bureau for issuing government notes in Kiangsi![59] It was an understandable move but hardly an appropriate response to Peking's appeal for funds.

In order to restock its granaries, the central government was persistent in demanding that the provinces send their grain tribute in kind. But with vast stretches of its waterways either blocked or under constant threat of rebel or bandit attacks, shipping grain to Peking was an unrealistic solution. Most important, the huge cost would immediately increase the taxpayers' burden, nullifying the benefits of the tax reform and alienating the people from the officials. Fortunately for Kiangsi, Shen's objections prevailed.[60]

Overall, Shen was an energetic governor. He maintained high standards in judging the behavior of bureaucrats and gentry and was not afraid to

58 *SCTI*, vol. 8, pp. 3503–4. On the return of some illegal exactions, see Hsia Nai, 'T'ai-p'ing t'ien-kuo', p. 200.
59 *SWSK*, 2:4–5, 55a–b.   60 Ibid., 56–57b.

use his disciplinary powers. Yet he was also a caring governor who defended the widowed, the orphaned, and the newly born, although he failed to see the need for broad socioeconomic changes which alone could have dealt successfully with the evil of female infanticide. His handling of the tax reduction scheme reveals initiative and leadership, while his budgeting system suggests imagination and a willingness to make institutional changes. It also shows an ability to work both with his colleagues in Kiangsi and with Tseng Kuo-fan, despite his difficulties with Tseng later.

The provincial government's inability to make itself felt at the lowest levels was Shen's greatest failing – hence, his abortive campaign against female infanticide. Perhaps preoccupation with the province's defence precluded a more active role in the campaign. But most certainly, the failure is attributable to the built-in weaknesses of Ch'ing local government for which Shen could not be held responsible. It is true that he did not try to improve that system, but he did make full use of the mechanisms that system provided, as when he dealt with delinquent officials and gentry. In contrast to his successor, Liu K'un-i, who sought to maintain order by being indulgent to all, Shen disciplined the undesirable elements, whose support he did not seek. On his administration and energetic style, Li Huan had this to say: 'Because Shen takes everything upon himself, all aspects [of the government] are looking up'.[61] On balance, then, Shen was an effective governor, firm but caring, and as a result he was both popular and respected. Leaders of the gentry continued to call for his return months after his incumbency ended.[62] In the modern history of Kiangsi, it can be said that the Restoration there began with him.

Shen was also a strong governor, always prepared to challenge the court whenever its directives threatened his programme for Kiangsi's rehabilitation. It was his belief that the well-being of the people was the very reason for the government's existence. Without it, popular allegiance to the throne would diminish; it must therefore be given priority over the short-term, though urgent, needs of the central government.[63] In resisting Peking's demands for remitting tribute grain in kind or suspending the

61 Li Huan, *Pao-wei chai*, 75:9. See also *CHTC*, 128:40. For more details on Shen's diligence and attentiveness, see Lin Ch'ung-yung, *Shen*, p. 49. On a comparison between Liu and Shen, see Li Kuo-ch'i, 'T'ung-chih chung-hsing shih-ch'i Liu K'un-i tsai Chiang-hsi hsün-fu jen-nei ti piao-hsien', *Li-shih hsüeh-pao*, 1 (January 1973), 241–6.

62 *Shih-lu*, TC 141:6–7.

63 *SWSK*, 2:4b, 56b; Shen Pao-chen, *Chü-kuan kuei-nieh*, 1:37b. A major reason for tax reduction was to appeal to popular support and counteract the Taiping economic programmes. Hsia Nai, 'T'ai-p'ing t'ien-kuo', pp. 163–4.

payment of salaries or compensations, he was not hoarding Kiangsi's resources. In fact, compared with other governors, Shen had consistently provided the court with the most detailed financial reports. Thus, as Tseng Kuo-fan observed, Shen was not disloyal; he was simply making the best of an impossible situation.[64]

Nonetheless, Shen's perspective on popular welfare had it limitations. What he had failed or refused to see was the inherently conflicting economic interests between the scholar-gentry class, which many of his financial and administrative policies favoured, and the masses of the people, which these measures largely ignored. It was a myopic assumption that the benefits of such reform as tax reduction would eventually trickle down to the poor, nontaxpaying populace. But this assumption was not openly challenged until later in the century. In terms of the objectives of the Ch'ing state at the time, Shen's measures still had a great deal to recommend them.

Realpolitik also demanded that the interests of the gentry be heard, for war and the fear of social disorder had greatly increased the government's dependence on the local elite. In consequence, the officials' authority over them suffered. Shen was certainly powerless against the gentry of Kuang-shin when he, having first cut their taxes by a huge margin, tried to increase the rate again to meet expenses. Thus, although the power of the governor, vis-à-vis Peking's, had grown in this period, his control over the gentry had suffered a setback.

Military affairs and the dispute with Tseng Kuo-fan over military funds

As mentioned, part of Tseng's grand scheme of mid-1860 was to turn Kiangsi into his main source of military supplies. Steps were soon taken to control a portion of the province's tribute grain and, with certain exceptions, its entire likin. The exceptions were five likin stations located in northern and north-eastern Kiangsi; the excise from three of them was set aside for Tso Tsung-t'ang's new army, and that from the other two for the river fleets of P'eng Yü-lin, a commander under Tseng, and Liu Yü-hsün, a prominent native of Nanchang.[65] To further his control over

---

64 *TWCK*, vol. 4, 'Memorials', pp. 606–7. Provinces affected by rebellion could not possibly produce full financial reports. However, many used the turbulence of the time as a pretext for sketchy reports to cover up official corruption. By contrast, Shen kept very full records, enabling his successor, Liu K'un-i, to submit relatively detailed reports soon afterwards. P'eng Tse-i, *Shih-chiu-shih-chi hou-pan-ch'i ti Chung-kuo ts'ai-cheng yü ching-chi* (Peking, 1983), pp. 123–9, 135–7.

65 The likin stations set aside for Tso were Ho-k'ou chen, Ching-te chen, and Lo-p'ing, and those for the fleets of P'eng and Liu were Wu-ch'eng and Hu-k'ou. *TWCK*, vol. 4, 'Memorials', pp. 521–2; *CHTC*, 87:25. On P'eng, see Hummel, *Eminent Chinese*, vol. 2,

Kiangsi's likin administration, he wrenched the Likin Bureau from the provincial treasurer, who was already in charge of the commissariat for his army. The likin administration was then divided into two regions, north and south, and placed respectively under the direction of Li Huan, then Kiangsi's grain intendant, and Li Han-chang, the elder brother of Hung-chang. Both had served under him; Li Huan was also a fellow Hunanese. In exchange for these extensive powers over Kiangsi's finances, he undertook to protect the province from the Taipings.[66]

As his troops moved progressively away from Kiangsi in the direction of Nanking, Tseng could not fulfil his part of the bargain. Already, in late 1861, he had to appeal repeatedly to Tso Tsung-t'ang to help protect Kiangsi from his position in Chekiang. Tseng, of course, was aware of the limited forces at Tso's disposal, but he had no choice.[67] Consequently, northern and eastern Kiangsi were ravaged time and again by desperate rebel rumps driven from Anhwei and Chekiang, although the Taipings posed no major threats to the province until early 1863.[68]

Under these circumstances, Shen, who was also the provincial commander-in-chief, had to strengthen Kiangsi's own defence. No sooner had he taken up office in the spring of 1862 than he had to go to the Kuang-hsin area to organize a defence of the key Kiangsi-Chekiang and Kiangsi-Anhwei supply lines. With limited funds, however, he decided not to recruit more mercenaries (*yung*). But when he turned to the militia, he also realized how divided they had become since the days when he, as prefect of Kuang-hsin, was able to forge some semblance of unity among them. His only option was to 'strengthen the walls and clear the countryside' (*chien-pi ch'ing-yeh*), a proven method in local defence. The scheme called for the construction of strongholds at strategic locations so that, in the event of an attack, people in nearby villages could take their belongings and seek refuge in them, thus depriving the rebels of recruits and provisions. The advantage of this method, Shen averred, was that it would work with the existing militia. He then donated 1,000 taels towards the construction of such strongholds and urged the local leaders to do the same. Meanwhile he also tried to improve the co-operation between the local forces and Tso Tsung-t'ang's Hunanese

pp. 617–20; on Liu, see *CHTC*, 140:47b–48, and *Nan-ch'ang fu-chih* (1873), 'chüan shou':2.
66 *CHTC*, 87:24b–25; *TWCK*, vol. 3, 'Memorials', pp. 332–3, 337; vol. 4, 'Memorials', p. 521; *SWSK*, 3:1b–2, 3.
67 Tseng to Li Huan, c. December 1861. Tseng Kuo-fan, *Tseng Kuo-fan wei-k'an hsin-kao*, comp. Chiang Shih-yung (Peking, 1959), p. 4.
68 *SWSK*, 1:5a–b; *Kuang-hsin fu-chih*, 5:38; Tseng to Liu Yü-hsun, Winter 1863, in Tseng Kuo-fan, *Wei-k'an hsin-kao*, p. 196.

Table 1. *An attempted reconstruction of the revenue of Kiangsi province, 1860–4 (in taels to the nearest thousand)*

Year	Tribute grain	Land tax	Ch'ang-shui (Kiukiang only)	Customs duties	Likin
1860	700,000	750,000	—[a]	—	Jan.–June 438,000 July
1861	700,000	750,000	—[a]	—	|
1862	700,000	750,000	—[a]	—	7,960,000 (1,990,000
1863	700,000	750,000	120,000	428,000	per annum)
1864	700,000	750,000?	330,000	377,000	August
Subtotal	3,500,000	3,750,000	450,000	805,000	8,398,000
Grand total: 16,903,000					

[a] An unknown amount of boat likin (*ch'uan-li*).
Sources: SWSK, 1:34a–b; *CHTC*, 87:7b–9b; *Parliamentary Papers of the House of Commons*, 1865, vol. 53, [3489] (China, no. 1), 'Foreign Customs Establishment in China', pp. 148, 172; *LKI*, vol. 1, 'Memorials', 5:185–6, 6:219; Pong, 'Income', pp. 54, 56.

that is, duties on shops, the sale of farm animals, wine, boat building, and the leather industry, which amounted to 91,623 taels a year.[76] During the Taiping period, receipts from all categories drastically declined,[77] as one would expect, but they were augmented by two new items – the likin[78] and, after the beginning of 1863, customs duties from the treaty port of Kiukiang.[79] According to my calculation, the income of Kiangsi for the period from 1860 to 1864 was approximately 16,903,000 taels (Table 1).[80]

76 Liu K'un-i, *Liu K'un-i i-chi* (hereafter, *LKI*) (Peking, 1959), vol. 1, 'Memorials', 2:44–5; 3:98; *CHTC*, 83:7b–8; 87:8b–9, 17.
77 For example, the Kan-chou *ch'ang-shui* dropped by half to 36,819 taels in the period from 10 November 1859 to 28 October 1860. Li Huan, *Pao-wei chai*, 4:23a–b.
78 For an analysis of the history and receipts of Kiangsi's likin, see Pong, 'Income', pp. 57–8.
79 Kiukiang was officially opened as a treaty port on 8 March 1861, and in December an office of supervision was established, but not for the collection of duties. It was not until the end of 1862 that the customs house there began to operate. Great Britain, *Parliamentary Papers of the House of Commons*, 1865, vol. 38 [3509] (China, no. 1), 'Foreign Customs Establishment in China', p. 6; *HFT*, I, 137.
80 For source and methods used for the calculation, see Pong, 'Income', pp. 51–9. The figure here is slightly higher due to an inadvertent omission in my article of a likin receipt of 438,000 taels for the period from January to July 1860.

In the years 1860–2 the revenue of Kiangsi came mainly from the land tax and, before July 1860, also from part of the likin. The tribute grain had already been earmarked, half for Peking and half for Tseng Kuo-fan. From the land tax, monies were drawn for the provincial administration, the army and the mercenaries, as well as the army of neighbouring Chekiang.[81] Yet the land tax receipt of 62,500 taels a month could not support even the provincial army, which had a monthly budget of 200,000 taels. Therefore, in July 1862 Li Huan, now provincial treasurer, requested partial exemptions of the tribute grain for 1860 and 1861 because of military disturbances and floods in the province. The case was genuine enough; troop payment was eight to nine months in arrears at this time. The tribute grain for 1862 and 1864 was again not sent to Peking, and there is no evidence that it was delivered in 1863 either.[82]

These measures were paralleled by steps to recapture revenues previously transferred to Tseng Kuo-fan. When Tseng took over the military affairs of Kiangnan, his military expenditure rose from 200,000 taels to about 300,000 taels a month. Later, this soared to more than 500,000 taels a month as his army grew to a force of eighty thousand strong.[83] Part of his financial support came from Hunan and, from mid-1862, also from Kwangtung's likin.[84] Although Kwangtung's contribution was substantial, its delivery was irregular. Thus, even as Kiangsi began to cut back is support, it remained Tseng's main source of financial aid.[85]

The progressive withholding of aid to Tseng eventually caused a bitter dispute between him and Shen. From the time he set foot in Kiangsi, Tseng had always had to contend with a hostile gentry and administration there. The placement of his men in its government and his constant and increasing demands for funds aggravated the ill-feeling. But above all else, it was the unfulfilled expectations of what Kiangsi could contribute financially to his that brought matters to a head. The origins of these problems predated Shen's governorship. The question is, could Shen have changed the situation and averted a rupture with Tseng?

In Tseng's original plan made in mid-1860, Kiangsi was to transmit to him 140,000 taels of likin per month. Over a period of fifty months, from

---

81 *SWSK*, 1:34–5. I have no other evidence that the land tax was used by the army of Chekiang.
82 *TWCK*, vol. 4, 'Memorials', p. 495; *SWSK*, 1:35; *LKI*, vol. 1, 'Memorials', 3:85.
83 *TWCK*, vol. 3, 'Memorials', p. 358; vol. 4, 'Memorials', pp. 579–80. By late 1863, Tseng's army had grown to 120,000 men. Tseng Kuo-fan, *Wei-k'an hsin-kao*, p. 195.
84 *TWCK*, vol. 4, 'Memorials', p.550; *SWSK*, 1:35.
85 Tseng to T'ang Hsün-fang, Spring 1863, in Tseng Kuo-fan, *Wei-k'an hsin-kao*, p. 143. Kwangtung contributed a total of 1,200,000 taels of its likin to Tseng's campaign. *LKI*, vol. 1, 'Memorials', 6:219.

Table 2. *Military expenditure of Kiangsi province, 1860–4*
(in taels to the nearest thousand)

Expenditure	Kiangsi army and civil administration	Pao Ch'ao's army	Tseng Kuo-fan's army	P'eng Yü-lin's fleet	Lay–Osborn Flotilla
Tribute grain			760,000		
Land tax *Ch'ang-shui*	9,540,000				
Customs duties					80,000
Likin[a]		750,000	6,150,000	1,060,000	
Other	—[b]		560,000[c]		
Subtotal	9,540,000	750,000	7,470,000	1,060,000	80,000
Grand total: 18,900,000					

[a] Over the years, 450,000 taels of likin were also sent to Shensi, Kansu, and other places, but the dates are not known. See *LKI*, vol. 1, 'Memorials', 6:219.
[b] Between 1853 and 1864 the gentry and commoners of Kiangsi contributed more than 3,670,000 taels towards the local militia. Ibid., 4:195–6.
[c] This sum was subsidized by funds from the grain intendant's treasury. Ibid., 3:85.
Sources: LKI, vol. 1, 'Memorials', 3:87–8, 6:219; *TWCK*, vol. 4, 'Memorials', 579–80, 634; *HFT*, I, 167, 264–5; Pong, 'Income', p. 61.

June 1860 to August 1864, this would have given him a total of 7,000,000 taels.[86] When the province was free from rebel harassments in 1862, he expected the likin receipts to at least double. But this never materialized. In fact, from the start, remittances fell short of the target, sometimes by more than half. Over the fifty-month period, however, Kiangsi managed to send him 6,150,000 taels of likin, an average of 123,000 taels a month. Although, in terms of his original plan, this represented only a 12 per cent shortfall, it was a far cry from the fast-growing revenue he had expected (Table 2).[87]

By contrast, the river fleets of P'eng Yü-lin and Liu Yü-hsün, which were entitled to 20,000 taels of Kiangsi's likin per month, or 1,000,000

86 This amount was erroneously presented as 12 million taels in my article, 'Income', p. 61. It more closely reflects Tseng's expectations than Kiangsi's commitment.
87 *TWCK*, vol. 4, 'Memorials', pp. 358, 521–2; *LKI*, vol. 1, 'Memorials', 6:219. For source and methods used in computing the figures in this paragraph, see Pong, 'Income', pp. 57–62.

taels for the same fifty-month period, seem to have received their monies in full.[88] But what really outraged Tseng was the fast-growing yield from the three likin stations set aside for Tso Tsung-t'ang. Although figures are not available, Tso reported that 'the governor of Kiangsi is most concerned with funds for my troops; deliveries are never short'.[89] The reasons for the preferential treatment are not hard to find. The river fleets of P'eng and Liu were of more immediate importance to the defence of Kiangsi. Moreover, Liu was a prominent leader of the Kiangsi gentry. Similarly, Tso's forces were crucial to the security of the Kiangsi–Chekiang corridor, of which the all-important Kuang-hsin area was a part.[90] It comes as little surprise that Tseng soon became disenchanted with Treasurer Li Huan and his management of the Kiangsi Likin Bureau. In November 1862, he asked the throne for an investigation.[91]

In August 1860 when the shortfall in Kiangsi's likin was already evident, Tseng, with imperial approval, had started to tap the province's tribute grain commutation to the tune of 50,000 taels per month. The money was duly sent from September 1860 to January 1862, when it was reduced to 40,000 taels a month. Then in October 1862 remittances stopped as rebels threatened the province. Likin apart, about 1,320,000 taels were sent to Tseng in the years 1860–4, of which 760,000 taels came from tribute grain and the remainder from funds taken out of the grain intendant's treasury (*tao-k'u*).[92]

In fairness to Shen, it should be noted that he had resisted pressure to build up Kiangsi's armed forces for as long as he could. And when extra military funds were needed, he first turned to the Peking-bound tribute grain, not revenues promised to Tseng. Withholding funds from Tseng

88 Liu K'un-i reported in 1865 that a total of 2,120,000 taels had been transferred to the fleets during the years 1856–64. We assume that approximately half of this amount, or 1,060,000 taels, was remitted in the period in question. *LKI*, vol. 1, 'Memorials', 6:219.
89 *TWCK*, vol. 4 'Memorials', pp. 521–2; W. L. Bales, *Tso Tsung-t'ang: Soldier and Statesman of Old China* (Shanghai, 1937), p. 128. The quote comes from Tso Tsung-t'ang, *Tso Wen-hsiang kung ch'üan-chi* (n.p., 1890; hereafter, *TWHK*), 'Memorials', 4:21b.
90 The different treatments Tseng and Tso received may have contributed to their personal conflict later. *TWHK*, 'Memorials', 6:38a–b, 46.
91 *TWCK*, vol. 4, 'Memorials', pp. 521–2. Li attributed the problem to the difficulty in finding enough honest gentrymen to manage the likin stations. Although impeached, he seems to have held no grudge against Tseng, and the likin administration suffered no disruption. Li, however, did try to avoid further conflict with Tseng by remaining aloof from him. Li Huan to Tso Tsung-t'ang, 28 October 1862, to Tseng, 26 January 1863, and to Li Hung-chang, 30 January 1863, in Li Huan, *Pao-wei chai*, 74:2b–3; 76:2–5b, 8–9; 79:5a–b; and Hummel, *Eminent Chinese*, vol. 1, p. 458.
92 *TWCK*, vol. 3, 'Memorials', p. 358, vol. 4, 'Memorials', pp. 579–80, 634; Tseng Kuo-fan, *Wei-k'an hsin-kao*, p. 96. The term *tao-k'u* can also refer to the treasury of the salt taotai or the military-administrative taotai. In the present context, it refers to the treasury of the grain intendant. *LKI*, vol. 1, 'Memorials', 3:85.

was a last resort: Tseng's troops had simply moved too far away to defend Kiangsi. At that point, even Li Huan, who had served Tseng so well before, now agreed that there must be priorities in managing military funds,[93] implying that the security of Kiangsi should be given precedence. Kiangsi's official and gentry were jubilant, but Tseng was irate.[94]

With the low likin receipts and the withdrawal of commuted tribute grain, Tseng's deficit shot up. His troops now received only 40 per cent of their pay, 20 per cent less than before, and payment was eight to fifteen months behind. According to him, desertion due to inadequate pay now occurred for the first time in his nine years of fighting. So in June 1863, he turned to the customs duties of Kiukiang, requesting a monthly remittance of 30,000 taels. But only a single payment of 15,000 taels was made. In the following month Shen obtained imperial permission to keep the money when Tseng passed on the cost of the troops he had sent to defend north-eastern Kiangsi.[95] However, according to Chao Lieh-wen, a personal assistant (*mu-yu*) of Tseng's, Shen held back the money because he resented that the first payment was made without his approval. Chao also alleged that Shen had unwisely listened to the counsel of self-seeking underlings. Whatever the case may be, Tseng felt obliged to return the 15,000 taels.[96] It appears that the Kiukiang customs was encountering real financial difficulties, however, for it soon failed to provide funds for the Lay–Osborn Flotilla.[97]

The situation was most unsatisfactory for Tseng. Matters were finally brought to a head in early 1864 when Shen, threatened by an invasion of desperate rebels fleeing from Kiangsu and Chekiang, kept all of the likin for internal use. To make matters worse, he did so without consulting

93 *SWSK*, 1:27b, 30; Li to Tso Tsung-t'ang, 28 October 1862, in Li Huan, *Pao-wei chai*, 74:2b–3.
94 Tseng Kuo-fan, *Wei-k'an hsin-kao*, p. 96; *LWCK*, 'Letters', 2:27b. Li Huan, having just been impeached by Tseng, strongly opposed Shen's measure for fear that Tseng might accuse him of conspiring with Shen. After the event, however, Li was pleased that Kiangsi's treasury was augmented by at least 600,000 taels, which he claimed was badly needed. Li Huan, *Pao-wei chai*, 84:1–3, and Li's letters to Liu Chan-yen, 10 November 1862, to Li Yüan-tu, 20 November 1862, to Tso Tsung-t'ang, 15 February 1863, in ibid., 74:11a–b, 15b; 76:13a–b.
95 *TWCK*, vol. 4, 'Memorials', p. 580, 645; *SWSK*, 2:22a–b.
96 Chao Lieh-wen, *Neng-ching-chü jih-chi* (Taipei, n.d.), pp. 1313–14 (entry for 17 April 1864); Tseng Kuo-fan, *Wei-k'an hsin-kao*, p. 214.
97 According to Shen, Kiukiang did not have the capacity to raise 30,000 taels for buying the flotilla. However, during 1860–2 Shanghai had collected 81,484 taels on export-bound Kiangsi silk. He therefore suggested that Kiangsi's contribution be taken out of this fund, but the idea was turned down by both the Tsungli Yamen and the Board of Revenue. As for the 10,000-tael monthly contribution towards the flotilla's operation, Shen was willing to take it out of Kiukiang's customs duties, but he made it clear that this extra burden had deprived the Hunanese troops of badly needed funds. *HFT*, I, 162b, 167a–b, 200a–b, 227–9b.

Tseng, as he should have done, perhaps in retaliation for Tseng's unilateral action earlier. Tseng was indignant and sternly reminded Shen that

as the governor-general of Liang Kiang and the imperial commissioner, I am empowered to appropriate all of Kiangsi's revenue . . . let alone likin, the use of which was specifically approved by the throne. . . . It should not be regarded as financial assistance or can it be called [funds] raised by a neighbouring province on my behalf. If Kiangsi regards me as a 'guest' on whose behalf [it raises money] then where is the territory from which I am entitled to raise the funds?[98]

He then berated Shen for being impertinent as an official and inconsiderate as a colleague and his protégé.

A running feud over personnel policies made matters worse. It will be recalled that Tseng had earlier placed a number of his associates in Kiangsi's likin administration. As they worked at close quarters with the provincial officials and became entangled in their politics, Shen refused to tolerate it.[99] It is probable that these men were among those disciplined and dismissed by Shen and then later re-employed by Tseng (as described earlier). But this was just another irritant in an already strained relationship.

The battle for military funds, of course, concerned provincial self-interest. After all, the issue was over Kiangsi's revenue. But Kiangsi's challenge to Tseng's authority was by no means unique, for it had to do with the larger question of how power and resources should be shared in the empire. Even Hunan, Tseng's home province, begrudged the constant siphoning of its resources to his army, although nobody dared voice any objection.[100] The situation in Kiangsi arose because funds were simply insufficient to meet the needs of both parties. As Li Huan observed, even had Tseng and Shen been harmonious, the problem of funding would still have arisen.[101] From 1860 to the end of July 1864, Kiangsi had a combined civil and military expenditure of 9,540,000 taels and an accumulated debt of 1,290,000 taels.[102] As noted, its defence was weak and its troops not paid in full. Tseng argued, however, that Kiangsi was better off than other provinces, for its troops received 80 per cent of their

98 Huang Chun, *Hua-sui-jen-sheng*, pp. 55–6; *TWCK*, vol. 4, 'Memorials', pp. 634–6.
99 Chao Lieh-wen, *Neng-ching-chü*, pp. 1313–14 (entry for 17 April 1864).
100 When Tseng established his headquarters at Anking he created the Eastern Campaign Bureau, in addition to the Likin Bureau, especially for directing funds from Hunan. He began by taxing merchants in Hunan's capital on an experimental basis. Everybody complained but no one dared raise his voice openly, although there was talk of showing resistance by closing shops. Li Huan, *Pao-wei chai*, 96:23a–b.
101 Li Huan to Li Han-chang, 2 November 1862, in ibid., 74:7b.
102 The debt was incurred in these ways: first, arrears in troop payment; second, funds advanced by the provincial treasury against future tax revenue; and third, money borrowed from local authorities during local military emergencies. *LKI*, vol. 1, 'Memorials', 3:87–8.

pay and their payment was less than five months in arrears (Shen had claimed eight to nine months in October 1862).[103] On the basis of this argument, Tseng accused Shen and his province of wilful discrimination.

When resources were scarce, the question of priorities assumed great importance. In Shen's view, the primary duty of a governor was to protect his province and look after its people; a well-governed and secure Kiangsi would contribute more to restoring peace and order than would channelling an ever-increasing proportion of its resources to the front line. Since both he and Tseng were committed to a low land tax rate, his only alternative for raising money was to increase likin charges, but that would inflict greater hardship on the people. The best approach, then, was not to raise more money but to arrive at a set of balanced spending priorities.[104] As Li Huan remarked, it would not be impossible to please Tseng if one were prepared to exploit the people, but if an official cared only for the troops and neglected the people's welfare, then neither would be looked after properly. In the present case, Shen's interests and those of Kiangsi's officials and gentry struck a harmonious chord. Li thus praised Shen for his foresight, sense of balance, and courage in adopting the correct priorities.[105] Nevertheless, Shen was willing as a compromise to share the likin with Tseng. That was in May 1864. With the fall of Nanking in July and the subsequent capture of the main Taiping rump, military expenses were no longer a serious issue, and on 20 September Tseng relinquished his claim to the other half of Kiangsi's likin.[106]

In all, Kiangsi provided 7,470,000 taels for Tseng, constituting some 30 per cent of his total military outlay, or more than 44 per cent of Kiangsi's revenue. In the same period, Kiangsi kept only 9,500,000 taels for its own civil and military purposes (see Tables 1 and 2). Despite Tseng's misgivings, then, Kiangsi's contribution to his success was considerable.

But as the dust raised by the financial dispute was just about to settle, another complication arose. After capturing Nanking, Tseng reported in July and August that Hung Hsiu-ch'üan, the rebel leader, had poisoned himself and that his heir, Hung Fu, had either burned himself or was killed in the confusion of the defeat.[107] Tseng's report, however, was contradicted by Tso Tsung-t'ang's, whose intelligence revealed that Hung Fu had actually escaped.[108] Tso was proved correct when Shen's forces

---

103 *SWSK*, 1:33b–34.   104 Ibid., 3:2–3b.
105 Li to Fan T'i-heng, 25 November 1862, in Li Huan, *Pao-wei chai*, 75:1–2.
106 *SWSK*, 3:1–3b; *TWCK*, vol. 4, 'Memorials', pp. 682–3.
107 Tseng's memorials, 26 July, 8 August 1864. *TWCK*, vol. 4, 'Memorials', pp. 657, 659.
108 *Shih-lu*, TC 118:1a–b.

finally tracked down the Taiping heir and captured him in October. Thus, unintentionally, Shen had made Tseng look quite foolish. Nevertheless, for their role in the Taiping War, both were generously rewarded by the throne. Tseng was made marquis of the first class and Shen was given the hereditary title *ch'ing-ch'e tu-yü* of the first class,[109] respectively the second and the sixth among the nine hereditary ranks.

In the Taiping era, Tseng had surrounded himself with many able men. But because of the magnitude of his task, he had come to expect superhuman efforts and results from them, even when resources were scarce. Their failure often led to bitter disappointment, followed by impeachment or recrimination. Among these men were Li Yüan-tu, Li Huan, Tso Tsung-t'ang, and Shen.[110]

In the dispute between Tseng and Shen, their differences were exacerbated by weaknesses in the power structure. Earlier we noted that the authority of the Liang Kiang governor-general and that of the Kiangsi governor were delicately balanced. The appointment of Tseng as governor-general upset this balance. Not only were his headquarters at Anking close enough for him to interfere with the affairs of Kiangsi, his concurrent position as imperial commissioner gave him both the power and the legitimacy to interfere. But the edict which vested him with this authority did not in any way divest the Kiangsi governor of his power or, even more important, exonerate him from those areas of responsibility affected by the new arrangement. This contradictory arrangement created problems not only for these two men but for Kiangsi's officials as well. As Li Huan discovered, it had become very difficult to serve two masters at once, despite his strong ties to Tseng earlier.[111] Under these circumstances, effective administration had to depend to an undesirable degree on the persons involved, and especially on their perception of their responsibility and authority. Yü-k'o, Shen's predecessor, was compliant with Tseng's

---

109 *SWSK*, 3:107a–b, 115.
110 On Li Yüan-tu, see Porter, *Tseng*, pp. 50–1; Hummel, *Eminent Chinese*, vol. 1, pp. 497–8; Wang Erh-min, *Ch'ing-chih chün-shih shih lun-chi* (Taipei, 1980), pp. 207–44. Tseng later confessed to the throne that he had allowed his personal disappointment to affect unduly his attack on Li and expressed the wish that the court would instruct a high official to make appropriate recommendations in Li's behalf. Tseng's memorial of TC 3.8.21 (21 September 1864) in YCT, TC 3/8 *chung*. Li Hung-chang also bitterly fought with Tseng over what he considered excessively harsh treatment of Li Yüan-tu. Li Shou-k'ung, *Li*, p. 29. On Li Huan, see Hummel, *Eminent Chinese*, vol. 1, p. 458. On Tso, see *I-wen ts'ung-chi*, vol. 10, pp. 173–87; Wu Ju-lun, *Wu T'ung-ch'eng shih-wen chi* (1904), 'Wen-chi', 2:69a, 73b–74a. Both these works stress that the Tseng–Tso split originated with their divergent views on Li Yüan-tu and their conflicting memorials on the fate of the young Taiping king after the fall of Nanking. The importance of military finances and their respective relations with Kiangsi have been overlooked.
111 Li Huan to Li Hung-chang, 4 May 1862, to Ch'ien Ying-p'u, 29 January 1863, in Li Huan, *Pao-wei chai*, 69:5; 76:7b–8.

wishes, enabling Tseng to exert greater control over Kiangsi's affairs. But then Yü-k'o had neither ability nor initiative and was duly impeached and demoted. It is therefore ironic that Shen, Tseng's own choice, should have turned out to be capable, vigorous, and too inclined to take the initiative to serve Tseng's purposes.[112]

The personality of the two men clashed as well. On the darker side, Tseng was described as quick-tempered, peevish, ready to find faults with others, and slow to forgive,[113] whereas Shen was said to have been ferocious in temper, self-important, and narrow-minded.[114] These flaws were no doubt exaggerated or unjustly levelled at both by their critics and were probably less apposite than the fact that both were equally strong in character. Their loyalty to the throne and dedication to their duties and ideals were not in question.[115] As Li Hung-chang observed, the conflict arose only because both men were eager to assume responsibility.[116] When two closely ranked officials with hazily defined authority had to act on and respond to divergent circumstances and competing demands, differences were likely to emerge. Sharing a common, anti-Taiping objective was not enough to smooth over disagreements on specific issues. Both men recognized the dilemma, but neither was willing to give in.

During the dispute, Shen derived strength from his competence and popularity as a governor with deep roots in the province. Still, he did owe his gubernatorial office to Tseng's patronage, a fact Tseng would not allow anyone to forget.[117] The falling out was thus a source of embarrassment for Shen. So as his respiratory troubles worsened in the early winter of 1863, he tendered his resignation, although it was widely believed that he wanted to end his difficulties with Tseng by removing himself from the region.[118] The throne turned down his resignation and instead granted him a four-month extended leave (October 1863 to January 1864). But because of fresh military emergencies, he returned to office on 13 November 1863.[119]

---

112 Ibid., 76:7b; *Ch'ing-shih*, vol. 6, pp. 4646, 4824.
113 Shen Yü-ch'ing, *T'ao-yüan chi*, p. 30; Shen Sun-yü, 'Shen Wen-su Kung i-shih k'ao-cheng', *Tung-fang tsa-chih*, 44.10 (October 1948), 39–40; Hsü K'o, comp., *Ch'ing-pai lei-ch'ao* (1928), 34:77.
114 Ko Hsü-ts'un, *Ming-jen i-shih*, p. 310; Tseng Kuo-fan, *Wei-k'an hsin-kao*, p. 376; Chao Lieh-wen, *Neng-ching-chü*, entry for TC 6.5.18 (19 June 1867).
115 Censor Hua Chu-san's memorial as summarized in Shen's memorial, 30 December 1863, in *SWSK*, 2:72b.
116 Li Hung-chang to Li Huan, 15 March 1863, in *LWCK*, 'Letters', 3:7.
117 Tseng Kuo-fan, *Wei-k'an hsin-kao*, pp. 391–2.
118 *SWSK*, 2:59–60; *TWHK*, 'Letters', 6:37.
119 Ibid., 6:50b; Li Hung-chang to Tseng, 15 October 1863, in *LWCH*, 'Letters', 4:10b; *SWSK*, 2:72, 73b.

A year later, Shen resubmitted his resignation, this time to return to his native Hou-kuan to tend to his aged parents. Back in early 1862 when he reluctantly agreed to resume public service, he had indicated a desire to seek retirement the moment the Taipings were defeated. That time had come. Besides, his mother had been seriously ill for months and he was the only surviving son.[120] Nevertheless, Li Hung-chang, still thinking that he wanted to leave office because of disagreements with Tseng, urged the latter to reconcile with him. Shen, Li argued, should not be allowed to go at a time when the empire so desperately needed capable leaders. The throne, too, fearing that his service would be lost for too long, granted him only a three-month leave of absence with the proviso that, once his mother's health began to improve, he should cut short his leave and return to Kiangsi.[121]

Shen was insistent, however, although he repeatedly delayed his departure as rebels, defeated elsewhere, poured into Kiangsi. His dedication to the defence of his province immediately drew imperial approbation lauding him as 'one who loves his country as he loves his family'.[122] Then, all of a sudden, everything became irrelevant when his mother died (March 1865)[123] and he returned post-haste to Hou-kuan.

Shen's relationship with Tseng was thus left unresolved. The dispute had been bitter and intense, and many leading officials feared the split would seriously weaken the dynastic cause.[124] It also gave Shen the reputation of being difficult to get along with.[125] Many years would pass before he and Tseng would begin to patch up their differences.[126] By that time, however, the situation that had once brought them together was no longer attainable.

---

120 Li Yüan-tu, *T'ien-yüeh shan-kuan*, 14:12; *SWSK*, 1:4a−b, 3:110a−b. Shen's second brother died in 1859, and his youngest brother had been adopted by his uncle. Shen Tsan-ch'ing, 'Chia-p'u', pp. 14, 64−5, 71−2.

121 Li to Tseng, 4 April 1865, in *LWCK*, 'Letters', 6:14a−b; *Shih-lu*, TC 130:14−15, 132:34a−b.

122 Ibid., 131:6b−8.

123 Shen Tsan-ch'ing, 'Chia-p'u', p. 64.

124 Li Hung-chang to Li Huan, 15 March 1863, in *LWCK*, 'Letters', 3:7; *SWSK*, 2:72a−b; *Ch'ing-shih*, vol. 4, pp. 4834−5.

125 Ting Jih-ch'ang's memorial, 5 July 1879, in *YWYT*, vol. 2, p. 391.

126 For some years Tseng and Shen refused to write to each other, although they had resumed a working relationship by 1871 at the latest. Tseng Kuo-fan, *Wei-k'an hsin-kao*, p. 376; Tseng Kuo-fan et al., *Chin-tai shih-tai-chia ch'ih-tu* (Taipei, 1971), p. 64. For two dramatized accounts of the occasion on which Tseng was brought round to reconcile with Shen, see Hsü K'o, comp., *Ch'ing-pai lei-ch'ao*, 34:77; Huang Chun, *Hua-sui-jen-sheng*, p. 109.

4

First encounters with foreigners

In the management of foreign affairs, Shen's education and experience could provide little guidance. Nor was he aided by a bureaucracy familiar with these matters. As yet undeveloped was an administrative apparatus that could deal with issues arising from the opening of the province to foreign trade, travel, and evangelization. And while the freshly signed Treaty of Tientsin (1858) and Convention of Peking (1860) helped define the overall nature of China's foreign relations, their provisions were extremely unfavourable to the Chinese. Thus, as the foreigners attempted to maximize their privileges by interpreting the treaties liberally, the Chinese tried to curb foreign encroachments and influence by a more literal reading of the treaties. Nonetheless, because the central government often failed to provide a detailed interpretation of the treaties as they might be applied in concrete situations, much was left to the devices of individual local officials.

Influenced by his teacher, his father-in-law, and *ching-shih* scholars such as Wei Yüan, Shen was troubled by China's deteriorating international position, especially since its defeat in 1860.[1] But up to 1862 he had had no contact with foreigners or foreign affairs. Since he later emerged as a leading manager and promoter of modernizing (*yang-wu*) enterprises, and many features typical of his later career can be traced back to ideas formulated in the early 1860s, his conduct of foreign relations deserves analysis.

The Nanchang antimissionary incident

During Shen's governorship, a single event dominated the foreign affairs of Kiangsi: the Nanchang antimissionary incident comprising a series of

---

1 Ko Shih-chün, comp., *Huang-ch'ao ching-shih-wen hsü-pien* (Shanghai, 1888), 101:10b–11.

demonstrations and riots that began in mid-March 1862.[2] Though the first violent anti-Catholic outbreak in the province in the era of the new treaties, it was not an isolated incident. Historically, Kiangsi ranked alongside Hunan, Hupei, and Chekiang as the most promising mission fields. And despite a period of decline after 1784, Chinese converts grew in number again from about 1830. By 1846 there were enough of them for the province to be made a vicariate separate from Chekiang. In 1856, their number reached nine thousand.[3] In the Kiukiang–Nanchang area, where there was a concentration of converts, conflicts and persecutions occurred. In 1855 a church outside Nanchang was destroyed, and in its place a Dragon-king temple was erected. In 1860 Kiangsi was among the few provinces that implemented a persecution edict that had been promulgated the previous December.[4] There was a tradition of anti-Catholicism in the province.

After 1860, tensions between the Catholics and the Chinese intensified as the missionaries now came with broad privileges. They could reclaim previously confiscated properties and rent or buy land and build on them as they saw fit.[5] The prospect of a Catholic revival was as alluring to the missionaries as it was repulsive to the bulk of the Chinese. Meanwhile the Chinese officials were torn between an obligation to protect the missionaries and a duty to defend Chinese interests, especially their traditional values and social structure. This was the situation that awaited Shen in early 1862.

The story begins in late 1861 with the arrival at Kiukiang of Antoine

2 There already exists an excellent study of the Nanchang incident by Paul Cohen from the point of view of gentry leadership and antiforeignism (*China and Christianity*, pp. 88–94, 96–107). This chapter focuses on Shen's attitude and policy towards popular antiforeign movements, Roman Catholicism, the Chinese government, and the French minister at Peking.

3 Arnold H. Rowbotham, *Missionary and Mandarin: The Jesuits at the Court of China* (Berkeley and Los Angeles, 1942), pp. 114, 201, 208–9, 211; Kenneth S. Latourette, *A History of Christian Missions in China* (London, 1929), pp. 321, 323; Joseph de Moidrey, *La hiérarchie catholique en Chine, en Corée, et au Japon (1307–1914)* (Variétés sinologiques, no. 38; Shanghai, 1914), p. 99; Evariste-Regis Huc, *The Chinese Empire: Forming a Sequel to the Work Entitled 'Recollections of a Journey Through Tartary and Thibet'* (London, 1855), p. 385. Huc claimed that there were ten thousand converts in the early 1850s. In any event, Latourette shows that the number had grown to about twelve thousand in 1875 and slightly more than thirteen thousand by 1885.

4 Hsia Hsieh, *Chung-Hsi chi-shih* (1865), 21:1b–2; Latourette, *A History*, p. 306.

5 *Chiao-wu chi-lüeh*, published by order of Chou Fu (Variétés sinologiques, no. 47; Shanghai, 1917), pp. 48–50. The clause granting the right to rent and buy land was inserted into the Chinese text of the Peking Convention by fraud. Since it was absent in the French version, the sole legal text, the interpolation had no legal standing. The Chinese did not protest, probably because they were ignorant of the fraud at first and, later, for fear of indignity. There is no evidence that at the time of the Nanching incident, the Chinese were aware of the fraud, which therefore had no bearing on their actions.

Anot, a French Lazarist recently appointed the *provicaire* of Kiangsi. He was accompanied by a Chinese assistant, Fang An-chih, and six others. Both Anot and Fang had had at least seventeen years of mission experience in China. Their objective was to proceed to Nanchang to negotiate for the return of confiscated Catholic properties and to expand the church on Temple Lane (Miao hsiang), about three kilometres south of the city. To prepare the way for Anot, Fang was first dispatched to the provincial capital; he was also to establish a new orphanage. On arrival, he was met by Hisa Hsieh, an expectant magistrate of Nan-ch'ang district, and Chang Kuo-ching, a gentry leader and a former acting prefect in Fukien. Fang soon bought a house on Chopsticks Lane (K'uai-tzu hsiang) for the orphanage, taking in thirteen girls, aged five to twelve, with five house mothers and two sisters. All were natives of Kiangsi.[6]

On 17 January 1862 Anot reached Nanchang. Governor Yü-k'o, uncertain of the protocol for receiving missionaries, consulted Hsia Hsieh. Not wishing to precipitate an incident, they treated the missionary generously as if he were a foreign consul. Anot then left, only to return in early February. Presumably dissatisfied with the status accorded him during his initial visit, he now added to his visiting card the presumptuous inscription 'acting on behalf of the minister plenipotentiary'. Just as Hsia was about to urge Yü-k'o to decline reception, the latter had already arranged a full-dress welcome customarily reserved for a governor or governor-general. The people and gentry of Nanchang, already startled by this excessive honour, then became inflamed when Anot requested that the newly won proclamation of toleration for Christianity be widely promulgated. Worse still, they mistook him for the missionary expelled for illegally hiding in the church on Temple Lane some twenty years earlier. The public became more indignant as a result.[7]

---

6 *IWSM*, TC 5:4b–5b; Hisa Hsieh, *Chung-Hsi*, 21:2a–b, 3b–4. Born in 1814, Anot became a Lazarist in 1838 and was ordained four years later. He arrived at Macao in 1843, but little is known of his activities until he was made *provicaire* of Kiangsi in 1860. He held that post for five years. He died in 1893, at Fou-chou fu, Kiangsi. P. J. van den Brandt, *Les Lazaristes en Chine, 1697–1935: Notes biographiques* (Peiping, 1936), p. 48; Moidrey, *La hiérarchie*, p. 101. Fang An-chih had served the church as early as 1844, when he was sent to work at Ting-hai, Chekiang. Within a year he was expelled by the local people for converting temples into churches. The French refused to deliver Fang to the Chinese authorities for trial and threatened to send warships to China, but they did withdraw Fang and others from Ting-hai. FO 682/325/4 (17J); *IWSM*, HF 5:19–21b. Fang has been variously described as a native of Fukien, Nan-hai (Kwangtung), and Fu-chou prefecture (Kiangsi).

7 Hsia Hsieh, *Chung-Hsi*, 21:3–4. The governor was Wu Wen-yung, who held office from 1841 to 1848, and the missionary expelled was one Tai-li-ch'ao (unidentified). *CHTC*, 16:26, 28; *Ch'ing-shih*, vol. 6, p. 4666.

Soon after, in the first half of March, two vehemently anti-Christian manifestos appeared in Nanchang. Written by gentrymen from neighbouring Hunan, they inveighed against both missionaries and converts for breaking traditions and violating filial piety, for promiscuous deeds and such vile acts as sucking the semen of young boys and extracting the menstrual discharge of women. They were also inculpated as spies for their fellow Christian Taipings. These manifestos, printed in 'tens of thousands' overnight by two prominent local gentrymen, were widely circulated and displayed.[8] The charges confirmed in the mind of the public the suspicion they had about Anot's activities, and especially the secrecy with which his followers guarded the orphanage and its inmates.[9] Besides, there was a genuine fear that the converts would collude with the 'Christian' Taipings to take Nanchang.[10]

Just at this juncture, thousands of gentry-scholars gathered at the provincial capital, getting ready for the civil service examinations. Words about Anot's activities spread quickly among the candidates – self-appointed guardians of Confucian values – and hostility towards the Christians reached a fevered pitch. Sensing trouble, the missionary requested an investigation with a view to punishing those responsible for printing and distributing the Hunan manifestos. But Governor Yü-k'o, who had been so accommodating towards Anot, had already left, and Li Huan, the acting governor, would rather leave things as they were until the new governor, Shen Pao-chen, arrived. However, when Shen took office on 15 March, he also refused to meet Anot.[11]

The Christians and their enemies were thus left to themselves. On 17 March, in midafternoon, Wang Pi-ta, the prefect of Nan-ch'ang, and Sun Chia-to, the magistrate, told Hsia Hsieh that anonymous circulars had been distributed calling on the people to destroy the church on Temple Lane the following noon. The immediate cause seems to have been the Christians' refusal to return a girl at the orphanage to an examination candidate for a sum of money. Just as the three officials, Wang, Sun, and Hsia, were trying to prevent any untoward incident, the

---

8 Hsia Hsieh, *Chung-Hsi*, 21:4a–b. Because of the obscenities therein, Shen did not present them to the throne. Instead, copies were sent to the Tsungli Yamen. *SWSK*, 1:8b; China, Tsungli Yamen Archives, Taipei, Chiang-hsi Chiao-wu (hereafter, TY: CHCW), pp. 2040–9. For their contents, see Cohen, *China and Christianity*, pp. 89–91.

9 For details, see Cohen, *China and Christianity*, p. 91. It should also be noted that traditional Chinese orphanages were for much younger children. When girls from five to twelve were taken in, suspicion was bound to grow. *SWSK*, 1:7, 19b.

10 *IWSM*, TC 12:33b–34. The Taipings had posed serious threats to Kiangsi only a few months earlier. *TWCK*, vol. 4, 'Memorials', p. 495.

11 *SWSK*, 1:7a–b; Hsia Hsieh, *Chung-Hsi*, 21:4a–b. Shen arrived at Nanchang on 13 March and officially assumed duty two days later. Li Huan, *Pao-wei chai*, 1:13–14b.

orphanage was destroyed; Anot and Fang An-chih luckily had escaped. Before anything could be done, dozens of shops and houses belonging to native converts were also demolished. It was getting dark, the city gates were closed, and the mob dispersed.[12]

Hsia and Chang Kuo-ching then reported the incident to Shen, and the latter was quoted as having said:

The barbarians have for a long time been doing what they want with us; they never expect our people to take action in revenge. Even though we, ourselves, must shoulder the responsibility for mismanaging [this affair], I hope no arrests will be made.[13]

In that same night, Anot's boat and the Temple Lane church were also wrecked. The orphans, however, were taken safely by local officials to Fu-chou, a hundred kilometres away. Meanwhile Anot also escaped to Fu-chou, staying with a native Christian on the way. On that account, the convert's house, and several others, were also razed. Later, Anot fled to Kiukiang and thence to Peking, to seek indemnification through the French minister.[14]

Shen was certainly remiss in managing the incident up to this point. Though not responsible for the origins of the riots, he could still have taken measures to avert mob violence. A call on the gentry leaders to observe the treaties while expressing a pesonal sympathy with their anti-Catholic sentiments could well have calmed their fury. He could also have tried negotiating with Anot, although the latter's demand for celebrity treatment remained a serious obstacle. For Shen, who had become governor only two days earlier, an unduly lavish reception of the missionary would have gravely undermined his authority and prestige and set a dangerous precedent. To be fair, however, the difficulties arose only because the treaties failed to specify the diplomatic status of missionaries and the procedures for them to lodge complaints.[15] Be that as it may,

---

12 Hsia Hsieh, *Chung-Hsi*, 21:4b–5; *SWSK*, 1:7b, 19b.
13 Hsia Hsieh, *Chung-Hsi*, 21:5a–b. The translation is based on Cohen's. A slightly different translation is offered by Alexander Michie, *Missionaries in China* (London, 1891). Shen's statement is corroborated by Kuo Sung-tao in a letter to Tseng Kuo-fan, in Kuo, *Yang-chih shu-wu i-chi* (1892), 10:17b.
14 *SWSK*, 1:7b–8; Hsia Hsieh, *Chung-Hsi*, 21:5b–6.
15 Alexander Michie, a prominent merchant on the China coast after 1853 and a special correspondent of the *Times* at Tientsin between 1883 and 1894, points out that the 'Trade Regulations' of the treaties were far more elaborate than the provisions for religious tolerance. 'If such precautions were necessary with regard to a matter so clear and intelligible as commerce, how much more was it necessary to provide for the operations of religious propagandism respecting which it was quite certain that there was no common intelligence between the parties!' Michie, *China and Christianity* (Boston, 1900), p. 153.

Shen deliberately avoided meeting the missionary. Instead, he announced at the end of the first day of rioting that no arrests were to be made, thus purposefully allowing the antimissionary riots to run their course.

Now with damage done to the properties of the church and its followers, some action had to be taken. Besides, the British consul at Kiukiang, probably at the urging of Anot, also warned that the French would be bringing in gunboats to seek redress.[16] Shen therefore ordered the local officials to investigate the matter, while he reported the incident to the Tsungli Yamen in late March or early April and to the throne on 11 April. As it turned out, this early communication to Peking was a clever move, for the initial protests from the French minister, based on information from the Chinese, were mild.[17]

Shen's timely reports gained the Chinese temporary relief but failed to mitigate the basic dilemma: how to appease both the Chinese people and the French. So the Grand Council gave Shen a rather contradictory order: not to alienate the French further or lose the confidence of the Chinese people when seeking a settlement. The Tsungli Yamen also urged Shen to repair all damages promptly and to be more accommodating generally, reminding him that the French (and British) were giving the Chinese valuable military assistance against the Taipings at Shanghai and Ningpo.[18] At the same time, it presented to the French a grim picture of China's internal situation to gain time for Shen and to explain why a settlement could not have been more expeditious.[19]

From late April to early June Shen went to the Kuang-hsin area to build up its defence. Meanwhile investigations at Nanchang continued but with little result. Whether Shen wanted to delay proceedings remains uncertain, but it was clear by early June that he was not about to bow to French diplomatic pressure, even if his tactics might cause embarrassment to the central government. The following excerpt from his 'progress report' bears this out:

The suspicion of the stupid people developed into anger, and they became of one mind [in opposing the Christians]. Without giving [the matter] due consideration,

16 *SWSK*, 1:8. Anot approached the British consul at Kiukiang a number of times in the hope that he, who was about to leave for Shanghai, would lodge a complaint on his behalf. Li Huan to Shen, 27 April 1862, in Li, *Pao-wei chai*, 68:14b.
17 Tsungli Yamen to French minister, TC 1.3.18 (16 April 1862), and French minister to Tsungli Yamen, TC 1.3.23 (21 April 1862), in TY:CHCW, p. 2049–50; *SWSK*, 1:7–8b.
18 *IWSM*, TC 5:29a–b, 6:49b, 11:17, 12:49a–b; Tsungli Yamen to Shen, TC 1.3.28 (26 April 1862), in TY:CHCW, p. 2053.
19 The Yamen also told the French that it had dispatched secret investigators to Kiangsi to make sure that nothing was withheld from Peking and that delinquent officials would be punished. I have no further evidence to support the Yamen's claim. Tsungli Yamen to French minister, TC 1.3.26 (24 April 1862), in TY:CHCW, p. 2051.

they [blindly] followed one another. When news of investigation and arrests came, not only did the culprits remain silent, but even the onlookers present at the scene [of the riots] were also unable to tell who were the instigators and who committed [the crimes]. . . . [We] have been employing all kinds of methods but still have no clues.[20]

Liu Yü-hsün and Hsia T'ing-chü, the two gentry leaders responsible earlier for reprinting the Hunan antimissionary literature, were not implicated. Liu, a breveted provincial judge of Kansu, was a powerful gentry leader who, as noted in Chapter 3, was in command of Kiangsi's naval force. Hsia was once a Hanlin academician and currently a lecturer at the Kiangsi Academy (Yü-chang shu-yüan) in Nanchang. According to Hsia Hsieh, he was the only man who could have prevented the incident on 17 March.[21] Both were influential figures who otherwise rendered valuable service to the province. It is understandable that Shen, still new to his office, should have avoided disclosing their identity. But it should also be stressed that he, true to his words that no arrests be made, did not implicate anybody at all, high or low.

Shen's action could only have invited further antimissionary adventures. And indeed, Hsia T'ing-chü soon presented to him as proof of the missionary's crimes a collection of bones, some dried blood, and a copper tube, all said to have come from the orphanage. Allegedly, the dried blood had been refined from the bone marrow of children and the copper tube was for gouging eyes. As the bones belonged to adults, Shen disregarded them but insisted on forwarding the other items to the Tsungli Yamen so that the French minister could clarify their uses, 'to allay popular suspicion'. Then, in an attempt to turn the treaties to China's advantage, he added that, whatever the nature of these objects, the treaties still did not provide for the churches to keep orphans. He then submitted himself for punishment for failing to take precautions before the incident, to put the culprits behind bars, and for mismanaging the whole affair.[22]

To Shen's mind, the antimissionary incident was symptomatic of the problems China was facing. The Second Opium War had already outraged the people, and to make matters worse, the treaties that brought it to a

---

20 Memorial of 8 June 1862, in *SWSK*, 1:20b.
21 Miao Ch'üan-sun, comp., *Hsü pei-chuan chi* (1893), 37:21b–22; *CHTC*, 140:47b–48; Li Yüan-tu *T'ien-yüeh shan-kuan*, 14:11. Liu's high standing is also reflected in his role as a compiler of the *Nan-ch'ang hsien-chih* (1870). On Hsia, see Hsia Hsieh, *Chung-Hsi*, 21:4b–5.
22 Shen's memorial of 8 June 1862, in *SWSK*, 1:19b–20 (the quotation comes from this source); Shen to Tsungli Yamen, TC 1.5.10 (6 June 1862), in TY:CHCW, p. 2055.

close favoured the Chinese Christians. As these converts became more jubilant and arrogant, popular hostility towards them grew. Under these circumstances, any official attempt to appease the Christians, such as repairing their damaged properties, would only arouse greater hatred from the other Chinese. However, Shen reasoned, if he were severely punished, the foreigners would desist from making more demands and the Chinese, seeing that an example had been made of a high official, would also refrain from violence.[23]

Shen's solution was unacceptable even to those who approved of his uncompromising stance, for it would only put the Tsungli Yamen in an awkward position and undermine the authority of China's government and its officials. But seeing that Shen was not ready to treat with the French, the Yamen tried a semiofficial approach: Shen was to send a deputy (*wei-yüan*) secretly to see Anot, offer him a sum of money, and persuade him to build another church 'in a quieter place'. Secrecy was stressed so that the wrath of the people would not be provoked. To bring Shen around to its position, the Yamen once again stressed the importance of the French military aid. Shen received these instructions in mid-July, but did not send Hsia Hsieh to see Anot (then at Kiukiang) until September. In any event, the missionary refused to see Hsia and soon left for Peking, presumably to bring pressure to bear on Count Michel Kleczkowski, the French minister.[24]

Meanwhile, Kleczkowski grew impatient.[25] He had threatened to call up the gunboats if the local officials remained recalcitrant. But the Yamen, instead of heeding his threat, raised the question of the 'dried blood' and copper tube and asked for an explanation. Though an explanation was given – the 'dried blood' came from wine and the tube was for percolating coffee – Kleczkowski was incensed by the Yamen's stratagem and for the first time named Shen, as well as Tseng Kuo-fan, as chief instigators of the anti-Catholic activities.[26] It was in this frame of mind, and egged on by Anot (now in Peking), that Kleczkowski presented

23 Shen to Tsungli Yamen, TC 1.5.29 (25 June 1862), in TY:CHCW, pp. 2060–2; Hsia Hsieh, *Chung-Hsi*, 21:4.
24 Li Huan to Shen (at Kuang-hsin), 10 and 19 May 1862, in Li Huan, *Pao-wei chai*, 69:6a–b, 14b–15b; Tsungli Yamen to Shen, TC 1.6.5 (1 July 1862), Shen to Tsungli Yamen, TC 1.9.11 (2 November 1862), and Tsungli Yamen to Shen, TC 1.9.22 (13 November 1862) in TY:CHCW, pp. 2062–6, 2105–6.
25 Kleczkowski's impatience was probably aggravated by the tardy settlement of two other antimissionary outbreaks in Hunan and Kweichow. For these other incidents, see Cohen, *China and Christianity*, pp. 94–107, 113–23.
26 Kleczkowski to Tsungli Yamen, TC 1.7.26 (21 August 1862), Tsungli Yamen to Kleczkowski, TC 1.8.10 (3 September 1862), and Kleczkowski to Tsungli Yamen, TC 1.8.25 (18 September 1862), in TY:CHCW, pp. 2068, 2077–8, 2088–90, respectively.

a list of stringent demands in October, threatening to proceed to Nanchang with gunboats if they were not met.[27]

The first set of demands provided that Anot be assured a safe return to Nanchang. On the way he was to be personally received by Tseng Kuo-fan at Anking, escorted to Nanchang, and received by Shen within two days of arrival. A proclamation drafted by the French was then to be posted alongside the 1862 edict of toleration at four places in the city of Nanchang for a period of one month. The second set of demands dealt with reparations, totalling 70,000 taels. On top of that, the Catholics were to be given a communal orphanage outside the city to make up for the loss of the one on Chopsticks Lane. Finally, for Anot's personal suffering, the church was to be granted a plot of land, about fifteen mou (nearly one hectare) in size, in the city of Kiukiang.[28]

Kleczkowski backed up his demands with a personal attack on Shen, accusing him, though not by name, of being intransigent, of conniving with local leaders to disseminate the anti-Christian handbills, and of 'hating our country [France] as he hates the English'. A personal and hospitable reception of Anot by Shen was therefore imperative.[29]

Thanks to the outbreak of several other antimissionary incidents, the Peking government's diplomatic position weakened, especially as it later admitted that the Chinese were in the wrong. Besides, a joint Sino-French defence of Ningpo was under negotiation. Since the French had expressed a willingness to place their forces under Chinese direction – a significant consideration in terms of Chinese sovereignty – the court at Peking wanted to avoid a rupture. Yet it had to be delicate in seeking compliance from the provinces, for they were governed by men of unquestionable loyalty whose dignity and authority must not be impaired if they were to remain effective in a rebel-ridden empire. Thus, the Grand Council and the Tsungli Yamen could do no better than forward the French demands to Shen, enjoining him to reach a fair agreement with the French expeditiously.[30]

No quick settlement came, however, for even as Shen was discussing the French demands with the gentry leaders, rumours that the inflammatory proclamation of the French had to be posted in five days provoked fresh demonstrations. Emotions became highly charged. Li Huan was accosted by almost a hundred persons every time he stepped out of the

---

27 *IWSM*, TC 9:32b, 19b.
28 Ibid., 9:20b–26b. The French proclamation dwells on the French military assistance against the Taipings, the virtues of the Catholic faith, and the distorted views of that faith held by the Chinese.
29 Ibid., 9:32–33b.
30 Ibid., 11:16b–17b, 9:20b, 21a–b.

yamen, all clamouring for an explanation. Meanwhile anti-Christian notices appeared everywhere, detailing the crimes of Anot and Fang An-chih in the vein of the Hunanese literature. They urged rejection of all demands for compensation because China needed the scarce resources for the suppression of rebels. They further threatened Anot's life if he dared return and called upon the people to execute all who followed his evil ways. After the officials explained that the French proclamation would not be posted until after Anot's return, popular outcry abated a little. Nevertheless, there remained strong opposition to the transfer of properties to the missionary. Li Huan therefore recommended that Anot be persuaded to build his church one hundred li (sixty kilometres) from the city so that it would not attract unwelcome attention.[31]

To sound out popular opinion and ferret out the antimissionary leaders, Shen had his trusted friends, disguised as travelling merchants, talk to the people. Their findings revealed a widespread animosity towards the Christians and a predisposition among the public to believe in the propaganda of the anti-Christian notices. The people also resented the success of the converts in acquiring shops and land, which they attributed to missionary help and protection. The fear that the Christians were traitors and spies of the Taipings, though unfounded, further fuelled anti-Christian sentiments. Finally, Shen found that the people were extremely cynical about the government's concern for them. The officials and gentry, they said, would not resist the missionary's demands because they were too interested in their own careers to risk causing a crisis.[32]

For Shen, a Confucian conservative in the sense that he attached great importance to popular trust in government, the central message of the findings was this: there was a crisis in confidence. To restore the people's faith in the officials and the gentry and to preserve the national polity (*kuo-t'i*), he insisted on a strong policy:

[The French] use such threatening words ... because we are not satisfying their demands. ... [But] how can we be frightened by these [words]? In my opinion, the art of controlling the barbarians certainly should not be too forceful; nor should it be submissive. If we accede to every one of their demands on account of their threats, then there will be no end to their aggression. In the end, there will not be room left even for ourselves. Since ancient times, there has not been a case in which thoughtless entreaty for peace was not followed by immediate failure.[33]

31 Ibid., 12:26b–28b, 34–5. Li Huan to Shen, November/December 1862, in Li Huan, *Pao-wei chai*, 12:10b–12. For a translation of the anti-Christian notice, see Paul A. Cohen, 'The Hunan-Kiangsi Anti-Missionary Incidents of 1862', *Papers on China*, 12 (1958), 20.
32 *IWSM*, TC 12:33–4. For a translation, see Cohen, 'Hunan-Kiangsi', pp. 21–2.
33 *IWSM*, TC 12:30a–b.

Thereupon Shen rejected all the major French demands. First, popular hostility towards Anot, he said, precluded the establishment of a residence and personal reception for him at Nanchang. Second, it was beyond his power to hand over ownership of the orphanage outside the city because it was communal property. Finally, against the French claim of 70,000 taels for damages, he offered 5,000.[34] He then explained the solution he was about to propose. The propagation of the Christian faith, like the growth of Buddhism in China, would take a long time. In Shanghai, where there had been a longer period of exposure, Christianity was beginning to take root. But to force the pace of propagation was to flirt with disaster, as in the case of Hunan and Kiangsi. Shen therefore insisted that Anot's return be at least postponed. Again, he begged for personal punishment for mismanaging the case.[35]

So in late January 1863, two months after the French had served their demands, repeated instructions from the throne and the Tsungli Yamen pressing for an early settlement could not prevail upon Shen to modify his stance.[36] The Yamen was thus forced to by-pass him in reaching an accord with Kleczkowski, whereby Anot was to be given an escort for his return journey from Peking to Nanchang. Local officials were ordered to provide hospitality along the way. An edict further instructed Shen to receive the missionary in person.[37]

Around March, when news of Anot's return broke, the people of Nanchang once again became agitated. To avert further incidents, Shen tried hard to persuade Anot to stay at Kiukiang for negotiations, offering to hand over the indemnity there and then, but Anot refused.[38] Instead, he went to Anking to seek support from Tseng Kuo-fan. Tseng treated him hospitably. But on 3 April, while Anot was on his way to Anking, posters appeared in Nanchang again calling on the people to 'act as

---

34 Ibid., 12:31–3.
35 Ibid., 12:28–9.
36 The French demands were sent from Peking on 17 October 1862. Shen's memorial responding to the French demands left Nanchang on 23 January 1863. *SWSK*, 1:48–51. For the edict and the Yamen's communications, see *IWSM*, TC 11:16b–17b; Tsungli Yamen to Shen, TC 1.10.11 (2 December 1862), TC 1.11.5 (25 December 1862), TC 1.12.9 (27 January 1863), TC 1.12.11 (29 January 1863), in TY:CHCW, pp. 2106, 2107, 2114, 2116.
37 Kleczkowski to Tsungli Yamen, TC 1.12.5 (23 January 1863), and Tsungli Yamen to Shen, TC 1.12.18 (5 February 1863), in TY:CHCW, pp. 2112, 2140; *IWSM*, TC 12:46b–48, 49a–b.
38 The size of the indemnity Shen offered is unclear. Available evidence suggests that it was not the 70,000 taels the French demanded but the 5,000 that Shen had earlier considered fair reparations for the damages. Shen to Kuan-wen (governor-general of Hu Kuang), TC 2.2.22 (9 April 1863), in TY:CHCW, p. 2159.

planned'. As the officials could not calm down the people,[39] a hostile atmosphere awaited Anot's return.

Undaunted, Anot approached Nanchang on 27 May, and Shen, despite previous protestations, had had arrangements made for his residence and reception. The next day, Shen dispatched officials to keep the people under control, but when their orders went unheeded, he took no further action. So when a yamen runner was sent to 'prepare' for Anot's entry to the city, he was stoned by a noisy crowd as he got near the missionary's boat. Anot, sensing danger, quickly left for Kiukiang. The mob, too angry to disperse, turned on the local converts, blaming them for luring the missionary back, and had six of their shops levelled before the day ended.[40]

The fifteen-month struggle finally took its toll on Anot. He was now ready to negotiate at Kiukiang and, moreover, yield to the bulk of Chinese demands: he agreed to abandon both the orphanage and the church in Nanchang and build a new church and orphanage in an 'out-of-the-way' place; the inflammatory French toleration proclamation was to be replaced by a milder version drafted by the Chinese; reparations were reduced from 70,000 to 17,000 taels. These terms were later endorsed by the two governments in question.[41]

Foreign affairs and the Confucian polity

The settlement was a huge diplomatic victory for Shen, the fruit of his persistent refusal to yield under pressure from the French as well as his own government. By letting the people express their antimissionary sentiments with few restraints, he was able to reject most of the French demands. And although he had to pay a larger indemnity than his original offer, Anot had to make a much bigger concession. Then, soon after the settlement, Shen established his own orphanage on Chopsticks Lane, the very same street from which the Catholics had been ousted. It

39 Tseng to Tsungli Yamen, TC 2.2.29 (16 April 1863), and Shen's memorial of TC 2.5.15 (30 June 1863), in TY:CHCW, pp. 2163, 2168; *IWSM*, TC 15:3b–4.
40 *IWSM*, TC 16:18–19. Anot and Kleczkowski accused Shen of planting his soldiers among the crowd, whence they stoned the yamen runner and threatened Anot's boat. Shen categorically denied the charge, arguing that it was unlikely that his soldiers would attack a yamen runner; besides, even had there been soldiers in the mob, they would not have been in uniform, and therefore the French could not have identified them. Kleczkowski to Tsungli Yamen, TC 2.5.26 (11 July 1863), Yamen to Kleczkowski, TC 2.5.30 (15 July 1863), and Shen to Tsungli Yamen, TC 2.8.8. (20 September 1863), in TY:CHCW, pp. 2171–2, 2173, 2181.
41 Shen's memorial, TC 2.7.5 (18 August 1863), in TY:CHCW, pp. 2178–9. Kleczkowski had indicated earlier that he would endorse whatever terms Anot found acceptable. *IWSM*, TC 9:32b.

was funded by a personal donation, gifts from the gentry, and a small levy from the merchants.[42] This smart move, capping a diplomatic triumph, firmly established him as the champion of the people, a significant feat for a first-time governor in an era in which popular trust in government had been badly shaken.

No further antimissionary outbreaks occurred for the remaining twenty months or so of Shen's office. Anot's removal from the provincial capital, the hotbed of activism among the gentry, was a factor. The French, on their part, wanted to improve their relations with the Chinese, enhance their international prestige, and make a success of the joint Franco-Chinese military operations against the Taipings.[43] Nevertheless, in mid-1863, no one could have predicted peaceful international relations in Kiangsi. Shen's intransigence could well have led to a breach with the French, as Tseng Kuo-fan and Li Hung-chang observed.[44] Why, then, did Shen persist in pursuing such a potentially dangerous course?

In 1871, Wang K'ai-yün, scholar and one-time secretary under Grand Secretary Su-shun (d. 1861), remarked that Shen was known for his antiforeignism in his early career.[45] Li Huan, reminiscing on the incident some twenty years later, claimed that the whole affair, involving antimissionary violence elsewhere, was directed by Shen; the conspiracy collapsed because the governor of Hunan, where two such incidents had flared up, was afraid of the consequences.[46] As treasurer under Shen, Li was privy to Shen's policy, but to speak of him as the leader of a major conspiracy seems fantastic and is not supported by evidence. Two factors coloured Li's opinion. First, he and Shen had become estranged since the mid-1860s because Shen had chosen to promote the introduction of Western science and technology to China, whereas Li adamantly opposed it.[47]

---

42 *CHTC*, 94:4a–b.
43 During the 1860s the French generally desired smooth relations and regarded the 'Co-operative Policy' as the most satisfactory formula for dealing with the Chinese. In a communication to the Tsungli Yamen, Kleczkowski emphasized the four centuries of amicable relations between the two countries and especially the role played by the French in the Taiping War. His willingness to delegate full negotiating powers to Anot almost immediately after serving the Chinese his stringent demands can be read as an opening for some concessions without loss of honour. Wright, *Last Stand*, pp. 21–37, esp. pp. 33–4; *IWSM*, TC 9:29b–33.
44 Tseng to Tsungli Yamen, February/March 1863, in Tseng Kuo-fan, *Wei-k'an hsin-kao*, p. 135; Kuo Sung-tao, *Yang-chih shu-wu*, 10:17b–18b.
45 Chin Liang, comp., *Chin-shih jen-wu chih* (Taipei, 1955), p. 157.
46 Wang K'ai-yün, *Hsiang-ch'i lou jih-chi* (1928), 11:44a–b. The governor was Mao Hung-pin.
47 Li argued that such 'gimmicks' as steamships, mechanized mining, and telegraphy would cause widespread unemployment and disrupt administrative procedure. In 1867 he ardently supported Wo-jen's objection to adding mathematics to the T'ung-wen Kuan's curriculum. Both he and Wang K'ai-yün regarded Shen as an opportunist

Second, Li's remark was made in the presence of Wang K'ai-yün, a fellow Hunanese and critic of Shen. Be that as it may, Shen's initial reaction to the incident was intensely vengeful, and he remained intractable throughout. Without doubt, Shen was opposed to Western expansion in China, but other considerations entered into the picture as well.

In 1862–3 Shen, in addition to the antimissionary incident, was involved in a number of difficulties arising from the growing Western presence in Kiangsi. On 17 March 1862, that first day of violence against Anot in Nanchang, a fight broke out between the British and the Chinese at Kiukiang. In the course of opening the city as a treaty port, the British had been given a concession of 9.2 hectares (150 mou) just outside the city. But the area handed over to them was actually smaller. A fracas followed in which a Chinese was shot at and another wounded by a metal instrument. A British officer was also hit by a stone. On receiving a report of the incident, Shen, realizing that the Chinese were in the wrong and that the British had willingly given medical treatment to the wounded Chinese, promptly authorized the transfer of the full concession area and declared the case closed.[48]

Shen also demonstrated fairness and speed when dealing with the salt smuggling cases in which Americans were involved. In each instance, negligent officials allowed the foreigners and their Chinese accomplices to escape, some after having successfully sold their cargo. Subsequent investigations and enquiries addressed to the U.S. consul produced no results. Under these circumstances, Shen could do no better than order the culprits' arrest. The negligent Chinese officials, however, were impeached and later punished.[49]

Under normal circumstances, foreign affairs were not a major concern in Kiangsi, and the boom in the Yangtze trade in the early 1860s largely by-passed its short riverine shores.[50] Nonetheless, Shen never neglected the foreign affairs of his province. Kiangsi's quarterly reports on foreign relations, compared with those from other provinces, were exemplary.[51] They also attest to the vigour with which he and his subordinates, especially the taotai of Kiukiang, adhered to the treaties, using them to curtail further foreign encroachments.[52] Yet as we have just seen, Shen's

when Shen accepted the directorship of the Foochow Navy Yard in 1867. Li Huan, *Pao-wei chai*, 95:20b–21b, 96:4b–17b, 98:20b–23; Chin Liang, *Chin-shih jen-wu*, p. 157.

48 *IWSM*, TC 5:30–31b.

49 *SWSK*, 1:85–88b; *Chung-Mei kuan-hsi shih-liao: T'ung-chih ch'ao*, comp. Kuo T'ing-i et al. (Nankang, 1968), vol. 1, pp. 44–9, 72–4, 101–3, 136–8, 213.

50 Britten Dean, *China and Great Britain: The Diplomacy of Commercial Relations, 1860–1864* (Cambridge, Mass., 1974), pp. 101–2.

51 See, e.g., *Chung-Mei kuan-hsi*, pp. 123–4, 302.

52 P. J. Hughes to Thomas Wade, 11 October 1864, 10 June 1865, in FO 228/371,

observance of the treaties was executed with reason and a co-operative spirit. The intransigence he manifested in the antimissionary case had to do with the serious threats it posed: Anot's unwarranted claim to high diplomatic status, the break-up of the moral and social fibre of Chinese society by Roman Catholicism, and the backing of that enterprise by a foreign power. Writing in 1867, Shen had this to say:

[Foreign] trade and the netting of profits are what human feelings can still tolerate, but heterodox doctrines and perverse behaviour make both man and god indignant. Nevertheless, the religions practised [by the Westerners] differ from each other. The Protestant religion esteems as its guiding principle purity of conduct, and although [its conception of] right and wrong runs counter to that of the sages, it can still be treated on a par with Buddhism and Taoism. The Catholic religion, however, takes in the scum and filth and perpetrates all sorts [of evil], providing a haven for fleeing culprits and constantly making trouble for the local authorities. In appearance it is [concerned only] with propagating the faith; in reality it harbours sinister motives. The upright literati and law-abiding subjects, being overcome with anger and hatred, resort to acts of violence and killing. Seizing upon these occasions to start trouble, the French invariably cause us in turn to be at a loss for words [in defence]. Their entire store of energy is brought to bear on these [matters].[53]

In Shen's thinking, these threats to both the integrity of China's foreign relations and the fabric of its society could not be easily contained by treaty provisions. Extraordinary measures were called for, even at great risks. Recalling his reactions some thirteen years later, he remarked:

In 1862, during the Kiangsi missionary case, it cannot be said that the French protest was not loud, and yet I dared not waver in the slightest degree. [Today,] I still cringe when I think back on this. If we consider ourselves in the wrong in every instance, it is like placing oneself in a losing position before a fight. Even [with the great courage and strength of the two ancient heroes,] Meng Pen and Hsia Yü, can we save the day?[54]

So in battling the evils of Catholicism, Shen, in this rare moment of his life, found that the end justified the means. Indeed, he saw in

ff. 76–81 and 228/393, no. 8, respectively; and Tsungli Yamen to Shen and to Hsüeh Huan, 2 and 7 December 1862, in *Chung-Mei kuan-hsi*, pp. 47 and 49, respectively. Shen and his officials were certainly advised by the Tsungli Yamen to use the treaties to restrain foreigners. Although the British never complained about Shen, they were singularly critical of Taotai Ts'ai Chin-ch'ing of Kiukiang, accusing him of being uncooperative, 'wanting in straightforwardness', and malicious towards foreigners. Hughes to Bruce, 1 August 1863, in FO 228/352, no. 19.

53 Memorial of 16 December 1867, in *IWSM*, TC 53:7. The translation is based on Paul Cohen's in his *China and Christianity*, p. 200.

54 Shen to Tsungli Yamen, 14 August 1875, in *HFT*, IV, 191a.

Catholicism so serious a threat that he even helped perpetuate the sinister folklore about its evil practices. When a reasonable explanation was given by Kleczkowski for the 'dried blood' and copper tube found in the orphanage, Shen did not pass it on to allay popular suspicion, as he had promised. Thus, Tseng Kuo-fan, when dealing with the Tientsin Massacre of 1870, in which a dozen Catholic nuns and priests were killed, accused Shen and other officials of failure to clear the Catholic church of these calumnious tales; they were therefore in some way responsible for subsequent antimissionary outbreaks.[55]

Shen's conduct can also be understood in another, wider context. As noted, he regarded the people's well-being and the preservation of traditional values essential to restoring social harmony; Roman Catholicism, as a faith and as a temporal power, undermined it. Furthermore, opposition to Catholicism could also galvanize communal unity in an age of disorder. In traditional China, thanks to the unequal distribution of wealth and power, social tensions had always been great, and social harmony precarious even in the best of times. It was a problem far beyond the power of a single official to solve. Yet opposition to an easily identified external enemy provided exactly the kind of opportunity that even a handful of officials could exploit to bring back some semblance of social harmony. Shen's refusal to punish any of the culprits, of whatever social origins, must therefore be seen as an effort to restore social cohesion and harmony as well. The following comments by Kuo Sung-tao in his letter to Tseng Kuo-fan, dated 12 July 1862, provide important clues for our interpretation:

Recently, I was at Changsha, [Hunan,] and heard of the case in which French missions in Kiangsi were destroyed. Shen Pao-chen, assuming responsibility, even went as far as to say that this was a gratifying result of two hundred years of nurturing the scholar-gentry. I am perplexed by this. Generally speaking, in our twenty years of managing barbarian affairs, we began by deceiving the foreigners, and in the end, they succeeded in riding roughshod over us. The root of the matter lies in our ignorance of what is reasonable. The empire is confused, and the people stir up each other's anger. . . . The *Tso chuan* says, 'Only propriety (*li*) can put an end to disorder'. Why are we placing ourselves in a position of impropriety so as to encourage disorder and fan its flames? . . . The gentleman never stoops to following the wishes of the stupid people for the sake of making a name. Consequently, the law always prevails and the people are well disciplined. This I would like to convey to Shen Pao-chen, but seeing that the whole country is in a state of drunkenness, a few worthless words [from me] will have little effect. Should you [Tseng Kuo-fan], administering over the Wu provinces

---

55 *TWCK*, vol. 5, 'Memorials', pp. 917–18. Tseng certainly had a point here irrespective of his personal relations with Shen.

[Kiangsi, Anhwei, and Kiangsu], mismanage this affair, more troubles will come, and [I] fear that [you] may lose your authority and dignity, and at the same time fail to find a satisfactory way to deal with the foreigners.[56]

Kuo's remarks point up not only the importance of the gentry's leadership in the antimissionary movement but also the popular resentment against all forms of foreign inroads. While Kuo insisted that the authorities detach themselves from the ignorant masses, Shen argued that the gap between the two must be bridged. He could not have done otherwise, being sensitive to the popular allegation that the officials and gentry had been too accommodating towards the missionary and his followers, allowing them to exploit and bully innocent pepole.[57] A few years later, he stressed that, in an extremely unfavourable international setting, the Chinese still had one option: 'If the people of the provinces are united and the territorial officials benevolent, we can still arouse their anger and sense of loyalty so that there will be no mistake as to the identity of our common enemy'.[58] Therefore, in dealing with the Nanchang incident, he was insistent that the terms of settlement be acceptable to both the government and the people. He was not, as Kuo Sung-tao claimed, 'following the wishes of the stupid people for the sake of making a name'. Rather, he was exploiting the common antagonism towards Catholicism and its propagators to underscore oneness between the government and the governed.[59]

The end of the first phase of Shen's career: looking forwards and backwards

As Shen left for his native Hou-kuan in the spring of 1865 to mourn his mother's death, the first phase of his career came to a close. From his earliest extant writings, we can conclude that Shen's approach to government was akin to that of the *ching-shih* (practical statecraft) scholar-officials. The zeal for rectifying mistaken policies, reforming ineffective institutions, and finding new ways to deal with new situations, which was so characteristic of his father-in-law, distinguished his career as a territorial official. The motivating force behind this reformist zeal

---

56 Kuo Sung-tao, *Yang-chih shu-wu*, 10:17b–18b.
57 *IWSM*, TC 12:33–4; Shen to Tsungli Yamen, 20 September 1863, in TY:CHCW, pp. 2180–1.
58 *IWSM*, TC 53:1b.
59 Chiang T'ing-fu (T. F. Tsiang), comp., *Chin-tai Chung-kuo wai-chiao shih-liao chi-yao* (Shanghai, 1932–4), vol. 2, p. 70; Li Shih-yüeh, 'Chia-wu chan-cheng ch'ien san-shih nien chien fan yang-chiao yün-tung', *Li-shih yen-chiu*, 6.5 (1958), 1–15; Li Huan, *Pao-wei chai*, 69:15.

originated, of course, from his overwhelming concern for the governed, both on paper in 1854 and in action after 1856. He was resolute in opposing policies and pressure from Peking if he considered them un-Confucian or impractical. He was diligent in his efforts at improving official performance and nurturing traditional values among the gentry. Yet he was always firm, to a fault, in dealing with the misuse of power by officials and the gentry, a major source of disorder. If these policies and administrative measures can be loosely described as elements of Confucian values, we can say that Shen was deeply committed to these values.

In the handling of government affairs, ideals had to be modified to suit actual conditions. Caught between the Confucian belief in the power of persuasion and the need for administrative fiat in government, Shen often erred on the side of severity in punishing delinquent officials and 'bad' gentry. In balancing the interests of the government and the governed, at least in one important instance – tax reduction – he mistook the well-being of the gentry for popular welfare. And in the interests of preserving social harmony and protecting the moral fibre of Chinese society from undesirable foreign influences, he was indulgent towards the 'good' gentry even as they incited mob violence. Despite these faults, Shen never sacrificed his ideals.

In dealing with other government authorities, Shen proved himself a strong and independent official. He did not vacillate in the face of powerful pressures from the French and from the central government in the Nanchang antimissionary case. He stood firm against Tseng Kuo-fan over the question of military funds. He also held off for a considerable length of time the demands of the gentry for a military build-up until Kiangsi was in serious danger. Shen was one who, having once made up his mind, would not change easily. As he realized, and his wife agreed, he could be inflexible.[60]

By the early 1860s, the Western presence in the Chinese world was a reality. A minor irritant at best, this foreign presence, with its multifarious manifestations, was often seen as a threat to the Confucian society. Shen undoubtedly reacted strongly against many forms of outside intrusion, but he was not blind to the advantages of certain foreign devices. He was quick to realize the positive uses of the treaties to curb foreign inroads: in 1862 he tried to limit the missionary's influence by citing the treaties, and in 1863 his lieutenant at the Kiukiang customs confiscated a steamship from U.S. merchants who had violated trade regulations. The steamer, with a Western captain and engineer hired from Shanghai, was

60 Lin Ch'ung-yung, 'Lin Ching-jen', p. 290.

then used to patrol Kiangsi's waters on the Yangtze. For a time, it was the only steamer that had come into Chinese hands through confiscation.[61]

Once the treaties were seen as a new means of defence, the question arose as to what needed defending. In handling the Nanchang incident and the smuggling cases, Shen revealed a concern for China's administrative autonomy, but nowhere was this more clearly exhibited than in his opposition to the hiring of foreign steamers to transport tribute grain. The idea was mooted in early 1862 by Shen Chao-lin, the acting governor-general of Shensi and Kansu, to replenish the depleted granaries in Peking. As noted in Chapter 3, Shen had objected to sending the tribute in kind because rebellion had rendered it unsafe. Now the use of steamships posed new problems as well: the hired steamers could easily evade Chinese patrols, and the foreigners, untrustworthy as they were, could use them for smuggling, carrying their personal merchandise, or supplying the rebels. Moreover, and perhaps mindful of the history of the Imperial Maritime Customs Service, he feared that the foreigners, once entrenched in the carrying trade, would oust the Chinese from the business altogether. Shen therefore preferred buying steamers for the purpose, but doubted the foreigners' willingness to sell vessels in sound condition to the Chinese. Further – and here he practically predicted the outcome of the ill-fated Lay–Osborn Flotilla – he argued that even if the Chinese bought the boats, they would still have to fly foreign colours and employ foreign sailors. Very soon the Chinese would lose control over the whole matter. To send the tribute in commuted form was still the best answer, he contended. As for the granaries in Peking, foreign merchants and steamers should be encouraged to bring rice from South-East Asia. For every load of rice carried, they would bring in one less of opium. This was a naïve assumption, no doubt, but Shen certainly thought this was one way the country's economic interests as well as the people's livelihood (*kuo-chi min-sheng*) could be taken care of.[62]

In Shen's mind, China's administrative autonomy and territorial integrity were closely linked. Thus, on whether foreigners should be

---

61 *Chung-Mei kuan-hsi*, pp. 101–3; *HFT*, I, 709–25.
62 *SWSK*, 1:24–6. Shen also presented several other objections which are not pertinent to our present discussion: lack of storage, an absence of loading and unloading facilities at Kiukiang and Tientsin for large quantities of grain shipped at the same time, and the danger of Taiping attacks. The idea of letting foreign merchants ship grain to Peking was not new. Its merits had been discussed by Hsüeh Huan and the Tsungli Yamen in 1861. *IWSM*, HF 71:10b–11, 72:6a–b. Later, in 1864, Shen proposed hiring steamers to ship grain from Taiwan to his native Fukien to strengthen its defence. Presumably, the routes between Taiwan and the mainland were not subject to the same kinds of dangers and abuses as those between Kiangsi and Peking, although one cannot preclude Shen's partiality to his province as a factor. Shen Pao-chen, *Yeh-shih chai*, 6b.

allowed to introduce telegraphic communication and railways, he had this to say:

The foreigners' steamers, being faster than China's courier system, have already severely impeded our government operations. If permitted to set up telegraph lines as well, they would be in a position [to transmit information] over vast distances in just a few moments, [further weakening our control over government business]. Still less can we be sure that they will not fabricate unfounded reports in the newspapers to startle us. As for railways, they are even more threatening. The levelling of naturally strategic mountains and rivers is bound to bring catastrophes in the future, while the destruction of people's homes and graves will surely bring about immediate disputes.[63]

The implications of this passage and Shen's discourse on hiring foreign steamers for transporting grain are extremely significant; they show that he, despite his conduct during the Nanchang incident, was not blindly antiforeign. On the contrary, he was fully aware of the advantages of such Western contraptions as steamships, telegraph lines, and railways. But he was even more acutely aware of the danger of these modern amenities when not placed under Chinese control. The unhappy experience with the Lay–Osborn Flotilla could only have reinforced this anxiety about foreign domination.[64] In short, in Shen's thinking in the early 1860s, we find elements of patriotism, which, to no small degree, account for his subsequent pursuit of *yang-wu* 'modernization'.

The question remains, could a Ch'ing bureaucrat deeply immersed in Confucian values be effective as a 'modernizer'? And could Shen's overwhelming concern for the governed be easily reconciled with the demands of modernization? Much of the rest of this book will focus on these questions.

63 Shen to Tsungli Yamen, 29 March 1865. *HFT*, IV, 10.
64 There is, as far as I know, no extant documentation on Shen's personal reaction to the Lay–Osborn fiasco. For a general discussion of the subject and Chinese reaction to the unwelcome prospect of continued foreign domination over a flotilla they had purchased, see Rawlinson, *China's Struggle*, pp. 25–7.

5

Director-general of the Foochow Navy Yard

The news of Shen's mother's death reached Peking in April 1865. The throne immediately realized that Shen, 'being by nature pure and sincere', was likely to request a full three-year mourning. The throne, however, was reluctant to grant such a leave; an effective and popular governor should not be allowed so long an absence in an era of postrebellion reconstruction. So it instructed him 'to turn his filial piety into an expression of loyalty', observe an abbreviated mourning of a hundred days, and then return to Kiangsi as an acting governor. This last injunction was in fact a hint that a higher or more prestigious post was in the offing, inserted perhaps as an incentive for Shen to follow orders.[1]

Shen, however, was persistent. Despite a decree summoning him back to Kiangsi to deal with a mutiny of demobilized troops in May, he insisted on a full mourning. The throne finally acceded to his pleas.[2]

Thus, at age forty-five Shen was prepared to settle down to a period of quiet life, tending his ailing, seventy-seven-year-old father. Further, after a hectic tour of office in Kiangsi, he was more than happy to spend time with his family, now comprising a wife, a concubine, six sons, perhaps an equal number of daughters, and some grandchildren.[3] It was at this time that he established the Chih-yüan t'ang (Hall for the Realization of Lofty Aspirations) for educating his children and young relatives.

---

1 *Shih-lu*, TC 134:5a–b. The edict ordering Shen to return to Kiangsi as *acting* governor was issued on 19 April 1865. Since no one had yet been named to fill the governorship, Shen could have continued as governor after the hundred days of mourning. The fact that he was not to do so indicates that the court had something else in mind for him. Eventually, three days after the throne permitted Shen to observe the full mourning, Liu K'un-i was named his successor. Ibid., TC 139:38b–39; Kuo T'ing-i, *Chin-tai Chung-kuo shih-shih*, vol. 1, p. 467.

2 *Shih-lu*, 131:30–1, 138:7b–9, 139:38b–39.

3 *YWYT*, vol. 5, p. 16; *SWSK*, 3:110b; Shen Tsan-ch'ing, 'Chia-p'u', pp. 69–71, 74–5.

Modelling it on Lin Tse-hsü's Ch'in-she (Family Association), the Chih-yüan t'ang held regular meetings in which the youngsters were given instruction and taught the various forms of literary composition.[4] Shen kept his life so private that he did not venture a single step into an official's yamen.[5]

Then, in October 1866, half-way into his mourning period, Shen mobilized more than a hundred local gentrymen to petition the high provincial authorities and the central government to delay Governor-General Tso Tsung-t'ang's departure from Foochow: Tso had just been appointed governor-general of Shensi and Kansu to suppress the Muslim rebels there. Shen, despite his age, was the most prominent member of the local gentry, and given his deep concern with public affairs, it is surprising that he had stayed away from the public eye for so long. But the circumstances that led to his 'activism' were special; they had little to do with the interests of the gentry class.

For some months past, Tso had been negotiating intensively with two French naval officers for establishing a modern naval dockyard and academy on the Min, downstream from Foochow. His departure would seriously jeopardize the undertaking unless a capable man could be found to give the strong leadership this novel venture needed. Tso had thought all along that the navy yard should have its own, independent administrative head and, with his imminent departure, he turned to Shen, Fukien's most prominent gentryman, and recommended him for the job. But Shen, worried about the fate of the proposed project, strongly urged that Tso be permitted to stay at least until the foreign technicians and engineers had arrived and the establishment of the navy yard was well under way.[6]

From the court's viewpoint, Tso's services were urgently needed in the North-West and, not fully understanding Tso's intent or the magnitude of the navy yard project, it readily accepted his recommendation of Shen as head of the new naval establishment. Besides, the throne welcomed the idea of Shen's early return to public service.[7] After all, what could be more appropriate than having a local gentryman performing a local task while in mourning, just as so many militia commissioners had done in the Taiping War? As a result of this imperial decision, Shen became deeply immersed in the management of one of China's biggest modernizing enterprises for the next eight years (1867–75), joining the ranks of that

---

4 Shen Yü-ch'ing, *T'ao-yüan chi*, p. 233; Lin Ch'ung-yung, *Lin*, pp. 614–15.
5 *SWSK*, 4:1a–b.
6 *IWSM*, TC 45:17b–19.
7 Even after Liu K'un-i had been made governor of Kiangsi, the court continued its attempt to shorten Shen's mourning. *Shih-lu*, TC 141:6–7.

handful of Ch'ing officials who led China into a period of what may be called 'defence modernization'.

Origins of the Foochow Navy Yard

Among a small number of progressive officials, there had been a long-standing concern for China's ability to defend itself against foreign encroachment. But their attempts at casting modern guns and building steamships since the Opium War had been sporadic. It took another defeat at the hands of the Anglo-French forces in 1860 before the need for modern military technology was more profoundly felt. This new political awakening has been studied elsewhere;[8] suffice it to say here that Tso Tsung-t'ang's desire to create a modern navy was given an opportunity in 1866 when he was ordered by the throne to discuss the empire's future policies as proposed by Robert Hart and Thomas Wade. Hart was the inspector-general of the Imperial Maritime Customs, and Wade the Chinese secretary of the British Legation. Their memoranda, couched in critical and arrogant terms, would have been rejected by the Chinese in better times. But having lost two foreign wars and having barely escaped destruction by rebellions, the Ch'ing court felt compelled to consult its key officials. Tso seized the opportunity and on 25 June 1866 proposed the establishment of a naval dockyard.[9]

Interestingly, neither Hart nor Wade mentioned warship construction in their memoranda. While Hart proposed building steamships for commercial purposes, Wade referred to naval training only briefly.[10] Tso's proposal was therefore an attempt to realize a scheme he had been

8 For the ideas on and early experiments in defence modernization, see Wang Erh-min, *Ch'ing-chi ping-kung-yeh ti hsing-ch'i* (Nankang, 1963), pp. 21–72; Lü Shih-ch'iang, *Chung-kuo tsao-ch'i ti lun-ch'uan ching-ying* (Nankang, 1962), pp. 1–56; Chang Yü-fa, 'Fu-chou ch'uan-ch'ang chih k'ai-ch'ang chi ch'i ch'u-ch'i fa-chan (1866–1875)', *Chung-yang yen-chiu-yüan Chin-tai-shih yen-chiu-so chi-k'an*, 2 (1971), 178–80; Rawlinson, *China's Struggle*, pp. 19–40; Lin Ch'ing-yüan, *Fu-chien ch'uan-cheng-chü shih-kao* (Foochow, 1986), pp. 1–6; Shen Ch'uan-ching, *Fu-chou ch'uan-cheng-chü* (Ch'eng-tu, 1987), pp. 13–29.

9 *IWSM*, TC 40:10b–36. Tso's response to the Hart–Wade memoranda came in two memorials, both dated 25 June 1866. The first deals with issues raised in the memoranda; the proposal for a navy yard appears only towards the end. The second deals exclusively with the navy yard, spelling out the reasons and laying down the details involved in its creation. *TWHK*, 'Memorials', 18:12b–13; *HFT*, II, 5–9b.

10 Gideon Ch'en states that the Hart–Wade memoranda included a proposal for the purchase of foreign steamers. See his *Tso*, p. 18. Steven Leibo claims that they suggested the use of foreign *naval* technology. See his *Transferring Technology to China: Prosper Giquel and the Self-strengthening Movement* (China Research Monograph, Center for Chinese Studies, University of California, Berkeley, 1985), p. 75. I find no such references in the memoranda. When Hart discussed steamers, he used the term *tsao-ch'uan* (building [steam]ships).

cherishing for at least three years. In March 1863, when discussing the problems of piracy, he suggested to the Tsungli Yamen that China should learn to build steamships as a long-term defence policy.[11] Thus, his interest in steamships from the very beginning was a naval one, and although he was also aware of their commercial application, his concern in subsequent years remained essentially unaltered.

The first concrete step was taken in 1864, after Tso had recaptured Hangchow from the Taipings on 1 April. Recognizing Tso's interest in acquiring Western machines for a variety of *yang-wu* projects, the French, who had already established a foothold in Ningpo and Foochow as well as a close relationship with Tso, offered to sell him their shipyard at Ningpo. At first, Tso was pleased with the prospect of having at his disposal a modern shipyard where four gunboats had been built. However, on learning that the facilities could be used to build hulls, but not engines, propellers, or cannons, he changed his mind. Proceeding on his own, he had a Chinese artisan manufacture a prototype – a two-seater, which he tried out on Hangchow's famous West Lake around September or October. The boat was disappointingly slow.[12]

Undaunted, Tso showed the boat to the two Frenchmen with whom he had close associations: Paul-Alexandre Neveue d'Aiguebelle (1831–75), a first lieutenant of the French navy and commander of the Franco-Chinese Ever-Triumphant Army, and Prosper François Marie Giquel (1835–86), commissioner of customs at Ningpo, a founder of the said Franco-Chinese force, and a lieutenant on leave from the French navy. Giquel's reaction was polite, but behind the backs of the Chinese, he referred to the boat as 'a toy'. It appears that both men were initially cool towards Tso's request for help in building a naval dockyard, but with the disbanding of the Ever-Triumphant Army close at hand, they had their future to consider. According to Léon Médard, who later

---

11 *TWHK*, 'Letters', 6:10. See also *HFT*, II, 52.
12 *TWHK*, 'Memorials', 18:5b–6; Prosper Marie Giquel, Diary, entries for 7 and 15 June 1864. I am most grateful to Madame d'Ussel, Giquel's granddaughter, for permission to use this diary and to Marianne Bastid-Bruguière for a typescript of it, since the original is handwritten and difficult to read. A substantial portion of the diary has been translated by Steven A. Leibo and Debbie Weston, with an introduction and brief annotations by Leibo under the title *A Journal of the Chinese Civil War, 1864* (Honolulu, 1985). Since my study was largely completed before the diary's publication, my references are to the entries in the typescript.

Ningpo was the 'birthplace' of the Franco-Chinese Ever-Triumphant Army (Ch'ang-chieh chün) and where Giquel served as commissioner of customs. The commissioner of customs at Foochow was also a Frenchman, Eugène Herman de Méritens, who was also very interested in acquiring modern machinery on Tso's behalf. Hosea Ballou Morse, *The International Relations of the Chinese Empire* (London, 1910–18), vol. 2, pp. 78–9; *TWHK*, 'Letters', 19b–21b, 21b–22b.

taught at the Navy Yard School, d'Aiguebelle wished to return to the French navy whereas Giquel was keen on co-operating with Tso, seeing in it a chance for rapid advancement. D'Aiguebelle was soon persuaded by Giquel. Besides, he was already engaged in earnest discussions with Tso about purchasing machinery, especially a minting machine, and the hiring of French artisans. With the prospect of French technical help, Tso's interest grew: he was still under the impression that the minting machine and the shipbuilding machine were one and the same, or at least one could produce the other. By November 1864, broad agreements had been reached, but before the final arrangments could be made d'Aiguebelle left for Japan suddenly while Tso had to move his campaign into Fukien on the 26th.[13]

On returning to China, d'Aiguebelle paused only briefly before leaving for France, whence he sent Tso, via Giquel, plans and drawings of a dockyard and steamships. When he came back in late 1865, he was ready to finalize the arrangement, but the project had to be shelved once more as Tso took his campaign into Kwangtung in early 1866. Nonetheless, by the time Tso proposed the founding of a navy yard, only the final details had to be worked out.[14]

In establishing the navy yard, Tso had the support of several provincial officials, including Chiang I-li, the provincial treasurer of Chekiang and a fellow Hunanese, with whom he worked closely. According to Chiang, he co-operated with Tso in the West Lake experiment in 1864. As information from d'Aiguebelle began to arrive, Tso also shared his thoughts with Ma Hsin-i, Chekiang's governor, and Ying-kuei, the Tartar general of Foochow.[15] Up to this point, only the high officials in Tso's viceroyalty of Fukien and Chekiang were consulted, but officials in Kwangtung were soon involved when Chiang was made its governor in April 1866. On the way to his new post, Chiang was most impressed by

---

13 *TWHK*, 'Memorials', 18:5b–6, 'Letters', 7:21b–22; Giquel, Diary, entry for 14 October. In a number of places, the typescript of the diary has proved to be more complete and accurate than the translation by Leibo and Weston. For example, the date of the present entry is mistakenly cited as 16 October. Leibo and Weston also misread *joujou* (toy) as *jonque* (junk), which is hardly appropriate for describing a two-seater. Léon Médard, 'Note confidentielle sur l'Arsenal', dated 1898, in France, Ministère de la Marine (hereafter, MM), BB4 1556 17/5/54. On Tso's campaign, see Kuo T'ing-i, *Chin-tai Chung-kuo shih-shih*, vol. 1, p. 458.

14 *TWHK*, 'Memorials', 18:6a–b; *HFT*, II, 30; Kuo T'ing-i, *Chin-tai Chung-kuo shih-shih*, vol. 1, pp. 474–5.

15 Tso to Chiang, TC 4/6/-(23 July–20 August 1865), in *TWHK*, 'Letters', 7:63b; *TWHK*, 'Memorials', 18:3; *HFT*, II, 23b. Unlike Chiang, Ma apparently had no close relationship with Tso. *Ch'ing-shih*, vol. 4, pp. 4738–9, 4849–50; Ts'ai Kuan-lo, *Ch'ing-tai ch'i-pai ming-jen*, vol. 1, pp. 343–6, vol. 2, pp. 1066–70; Hummel, *Eminent Chinese*, vol. 2, pp. 554–5.

the British fleet in Hong Kong and became even more committed to the idea of a modern Chinese navy. Jui-lin (d. 1874), governor-general of Liang Kwang and Chiang's superior, was soon brought over to his views. Chiang and Ma then agreed to pool their financial resources with Tso's for building a navy yard.[16]

Tso had laid his groundwork well, and when he submitted his proposal for a navy yard and academy in June 1866, the throne readily approved it. That the imperial advisers took no more than two to three days to consider the matter strongly suggests that the court had already come to terms with the need for some form of modern naval defence.[17] This, of course, is not to downplay the opposition, to which we shall return in later chapters, but it should be borne in mind that by 1864 Tseng Kuo-fan and Li Hung-chang had already created a number of small arsenals. In that same year, Prince Kung also strongly supported Li's plan for a substantial arsenal at Shanghai, complete with shipbuilding facilities.[18] Besides, Tso had been in communication with the Tsungli Yamen specifically on the subject of a dockyard since early 1863. The throne's approval, though unusually expeditious, comes as little surprise.

Characteristics of the Foochow Navy Yard

In founding a navy yard and academy, Tso's motive had been patriotic, based on a deep concern for the security of the Ch'ing empire.[19] His fierce hatred of the British, the leading predators in China, is well known. He even resented the authors of the Hart–Wade memoranda simply because they were British: 'Their outrageous and arrogant words are enough to make anyone's hair stand on end!'[20] Hatred alone was not enough to prod any Ch'ing official towards defence modernization. In Tso's case, hatred was combined with a new political awareness dating back to the beginning of the First Opium War (1839), when he started to read everything on the maritime countries written since T'ang and Sung times. He particularly admired Wei Yüan and Kung Tzu-chen for their ideas on practical statecraft (*ching-shih*) and Lin Tse-hsü for his unimpeachable sense of right and wrong.[21] From the works of these men,

16 *YWYT*, vol. 5, pp. 11–13.
17 Tso's proposal was dispatched on 25 June, and the edict approving it came nineteen days later, on 14 July. *HFT*, II, 10. It took at least fifteen days for a dispatch from Foochow to reach Peking.
18 Wang Erh-min, *Ch'ing-chi ping-kung-yeh*, pp. 78–9.
19 Sinclair to Alcock, 23 November 1866. FO 228/408, no. 54.
20 *IWSM*, TC 42:46. See also Gideon Ch'en, *Tso*, pp. 1–2, and Wright, *Last Stand*, p. 266n.
21 *TWHK*, 'Memorials', 18:5b; Li Shih-yüeh, 'Ts'ung yang-wu, wei-hsin tao tzu-ch'an chieh-chi ke-ming', *Li-shih yen-chiu*, 1980.1, 32. In his memorial of 13 May 1872 Tso also

Tso gained a new geopolitical awareness and a sense of urgency, which informed his patriotism.

Tso's patriotism was infused with a combative and competitive spirit. Not only must China keep abreast of the Japanese, who had had a head start in learning steamship construction, it must also wrench the leadership of naval development from the Western powers so that they could not abuse the Chinese.[22] On this Wei Yüan had already pointed the way: China must learn the skills of the Westerners, hire their artisans and navigators to teach the Chinese, and develop a modern navy capable of engaging its enemies on the high seas.[23] It was this idea that inspired Tso and accounted for the character of the Foochow Navy Yard.

At its inception, the Foochow Navy Yard was designed as a comprehensive industrial complex for the triple purpose of shipbuilding, learning how to manufacture and operate marine engines, and navigational and naval training. An ultimate objective, and a very important one, was China's technological independence. As a Western reporter observed, Tso's navy yard was different from other defence establishments, thanks to its well-planned programme of instruction aimed at the eventual replacement of foreign management.[24] This objective was spelled out by Tso with striking clarity in those parts of his memorial of 25 June 1866 specific to the establishment of a naval dockyard and academy. When translated into concrete form, the Foochow Navy Yard, as described by Giquel, was

an assemblage of yards and workshops devoted to ship-building, and having, as an accompaniment, a metal-working forge constructed for the rolling of iron into bars and plates. The object contemplated in establishing it, was to supply the Chinese with a naval service for the purposes of war and transport, and to give the native pupils instruction, so as to enable them to construct and work the fleet of steamships; and, finally, to utilize the metallic wealth, especially in iron, which the province of Fohkien possesses.[25]

The inclusion of an iron-rolling plant – a necessity because of the absence of a modern iron industry in China – and schools comparable to colleges of marine engineering and naval training in Europe, in intent if

cited in abbreviated form Wei Yüan's famous dictum: 'Learn the superior techniques of the barbarians in order to control the barbarians'. *IWSM*, TC 86:4.

22 *TWHK*, 'Memorials', 18:4a–b.

23 Lü Liang-hai, 'Wei Yüan hsiang Hsi-fang hsüeh-hsi wen-t'i ti t'an-t'ao', *Chin-tai-shih yen-chiu*, 1980.2, 239–47.

24 Anon., 'The Chinese Arsenals and Armaments', *Cornhill Magazine*, December 1872, p. 698.

25 Prosper Giquel, *The Foochow Arsenal and Its Results: From the Commencement in 1867, to the end of the Foreign Directorate, on the 16th February, 1874*, trans. H. Lang (Shanghai, 1874), p. 9.

not in the level of instruction, led a Western observer to conclude that the Navy Yard was truly a unique establishment on the China coast.[26]

The Foochow establishment, therefore, defies accurate description by a single term. It was not an 'arsenal', a term commonly used by Westerners at the time. Nor was it simply a 'shipyard', as the Chinese term *ch'uan-ch'ang* implies. The name 'Foochow Navy Yard', which we adopt, is also inadequate.[27] For this terminological problem, we have only the far-sightedness of Tso and his French aides to blame.

Another feature of the Foochow Navy Yard was its naval character, which, oddly enough, has been a matter of some misunderstanding. Wang Hsin-chung, Gideon Ch'en, and several recent scholars maintain that Tso's aim was to create not only a modern navy but also a merchant marine to compete with foreign shipping firms.[28] Their argument is based largely on a general introductory remark in Tso's memorial of 25 June, which reads:

Since foreign ships were permitted to carry away northern goods to be sold in the various ports, the prices of commodities in North China have soared sky-high. The great merchants of Kiangsu and Chekiang, who used to make sea transport their business, when they go north to purchase merchandise, have to bear higher cost and increased prices. When they return south, the cost of transportation is high and speed slow and they cannot reduce prices in order to compete with foreign merchants. As time goes on, expenses have increased, and they suffer heavy losses. Gradually, business will have to cease.... If this depression is allowed to continue ... the boats may, due to disuse, decay. At present, sea transport in Kiangsu and Chekiang is experiencing a shortage of ships; and the grain tribute administration is placed in a very precarious position. There is no alternative but to establish immediately a dockyard to construct steamships.[29]

Towards the end of the memorial, Tso summarizes:

When the steamships are completed, the administration of grain transport will be prosperous, the military administration improved, the merchants' distress

---

26 Anon., 'The Chinese Arsenals', p. 698.
27 I am simply following the pioneering work of Knight Biggerstaff, *The Earliest Modern Government Schools in China* (Ithaca, N.Y., 1961).
28 Wang Hsin-chung, 'Fu-chou ch'uan-ch'ang chih yen-ko', *Tsing Hua hsüeh-pao*, vol. 8 (December 1932), 10–11; Gideon Ch'en, *Tso*, pp. 19–21. Among recent scholars, Chang Yü-fa does not discuss this issue, and Lin Ch'ing-yüan and Shen Ch'uan-ching follow Wang's line despite their more detailed treatment. Chang, 'Fu-chou ch'uan-ch'ang'; Lin, *Fu-chien ch'uan-cheng*, pp. 10–14; Shen, *Fu-chou ch'uan-cheng*, pp. 42–3.
29 *TWHK*, 'Memorials', 18:1b. The translation is based on Teng Ssu-yü and John K. Fairbank, *China's Response to the West: A Documentary Survey, 1839–1923* (Cambridge, Mass., 1954), p. 82, and Gideon Ch'en, *Tso*, p. 20, with modification.

relieved, and the customs duties greatly increased. The temporary cost will produce profit for many generations.[30]

Whereas Ch'en claims that Tso stressed naval and commercial development equally, Wang and others concede that the commercial objective was secondary. They misinterpret the spirit of Tso's historic document.

This misunderstanding can be explained. First, Tso's concern was with the introduction of a novel undertaking of huge proportions. It was clearly to his advantage to be inclusive, listing all the advantages of the steamship without making a fine distinction between naval and commercial vessels, in an attempt to gain wider support. Second, Tso himself might not have been fully aware of the differences between the various types of vessels; in one breath he spoke of using the same ships for tribute grain transport and commercial and naval deployment.[31] Third, Tso was an energetic administrator deeply imbued with the Confucian ideal of benevolent government. To him, a modern defence industry was only one aspect of 'self-strengthening', for the security of China was but a means to a larger end: the reconstruction of a war-torn empire. Further, the navy yard was to be not only a new means of defence but also the opening wedge for commercial shipping and general industrialization. Other measures, ranging from the cultivation of Fukienese scholarship to the promotion of silk and cotton manufacture to clothe the poor, completed his programme for postwar revival.[32] If his memorial is read in the context of his overall concerns, we can understand why he, in discussing the steamship, drifted back and forth between the general and the specific. When dwelling on the general, he was writing more as an essayist, or even a visionary, a role he rather enjoyed playing when elaborating on things considered above the head of his contemporaries. As Giquel once remarked, Tso loved to talk.[33] But when it came to specifics, he left no doubt as to the kind of ships he wanted built:

Your minister humbly believes that if we desire to prevent harm from the sea and, at the same time, to receive its advantages, we must reorganize our navy; if we wish to reorganize our navy, we must establish a plant, to . . . build steamships.[34]

---

30 *TWHK*, 'Memorial', 18:5. Translation adapted from Teng and Fairbank, *China's Response*, p. 83.

31 *HFT*, II, 7.

32 Tso to Yang Ch'ang-chün (provincial treasurer of Chekiang), c. July 1866, in *TWHK*, 'Letters', 8:50b–51. On Tso's use of the term 'self-strengthening', see *IWSM*, TC 42:48b.

33 Giquel, Diary, entry of 15 June 1864.

34 Translation by Teng and Fairbank, *China's Response*, p. 82. Chinese text: *TWHK*, 'Memorials', 18:2. Tso also said that the navy, expensive though it may be, was a means to put an end to all future war indemnities, which were certain to be more

And on the practical matter of training and command, he had this to say:

When we decide upon an agreement [with the foreigners], we must first settle clearly with them that they shall teach us shipbuilding as well as navigation. When the ships are built, [the Chinese] shall accompany them to sail the oceans and visit the ports. Those who are thoroughly acquainted with [the art of navigation] and are capable of captaining a ship, irrespective of whether they are soldiers or persons of any description, shall be given military commissions. . . . They will be given command of the water forces.[35]

In the introduction of advanced technologies to a technologically backward country, the following phenomenon is often encountered. The native promoters are prone to believe in or make exaggerated claims for a range of applications much greater than the machines can actually perform. In Tso's case, a belief in the versatility of the steam-powered warship is clearly evident. The eventual arrangement provided for the building of ships capable of carrying various quantities of grain, 240 to 280 tons (3,000 to 4,000 tan) for the smaller ones and 600 tons (10,000 tan) for the larger ones. Nevertheless, Tso emphasized, all vessels were to be constructed in the style of men-of-war.[36] The plan, then, called for the construction of gunboats and naval transports, not merchantmen.

The last of the important characteristics of the Foochow Navy Yard has been a matter of debate. Western observers on the China coast often asserted that Tso's intent was essentially to counterbalance or challenge the power of Tseng Kuo-fan and Li Hung-chang, who had earlier founded the Kiangnan Arsenal and Shipyard at Shanghai. The *Cornhill Magazine* claimed in 1872, without availing itself of the benefit of hindsight, that 'the foundation of the most extensive and costly of the three existing arsenals was due in the first place not to any far-reaching designs, but rather to a spirit of rivalry between two Chinese officials . . . Li Hung-chang . . . and Tso Tsung-t'ang', each of whom, 'eager to outdo if possible the exploits of his celebrated rival', established 'an arsenal similar to that already in successful working order at Nanking [*sic*]'.[37] But the writer

costly. Ibid., 18:5. In a letter aimed at the British audience, he proudly claimed that the purpose of the shipbuilding programme was to suppress piracy. But as Chang I-li had written, 'piracy suppression' was also a code word for taking on a foreign aggressor. Tso to Charles Carroll, acting British vice-consul at Foochow, enclosed in Carroll to Alcock, 15 September 1866, in FO 228/408, no. 38; Chang to Tsungli Yamen, 18 August 1866, in HFT, II, 11.

35 *TWHK*, 'Memorials', 18:3a–b.
36 'Des propositions d'exécution', MM BB4/1555 17/5/1, and Tso's memorial of 11 December 1866, *TWHK*, 'Memorials', 20:62b–63.
37 Anon., 'Chinese Arsenals', p. 697.

then pointed to the unique objective of the Foochow Navy Yard – to achieve technological independence[38] – thus acknowledging the primacy of Tso's patriotic, not petty political, motives.

In a similar vein, but along very different lines, the *North-China Herald* stated that 'Tso Tsung-t'ang was considered to be rather a rival of Li Hung-chang's; and when the arsenal at Foochow was commenced under his auspices, people hinted that he had been instigated from Peking to establish it as a counterenterprise to the one which was so particularly under Li's control in Kiangsu'.[39] However, without convincing evidence, this view, though subscribed to by some later writers, and even modern scholars, remains speculative.[40]

One cannot discount personal rivalry completely. The protracted Taiping War had strained the relationships of many leaders who were once close associates. In the early 1860s, Tso, like Shen, had become estranged from Tseng Kuo-fan, his patron. His relations with Li had also turned sour. Disagreement over public policies, like disputes over resources, had often become entangled with personal feelings (see the following section). Yet one cannot dismiss the genuine convictions that motivated these men. All of them had developed ideas about self-streng-thening and defence modernization before personal conflicts separated them. To say that the Foochow Navy Yard was primarily the product of rivalry or a power struggle is to deny the historical existence of the Restoration, that sum total of individual efforts to save the Ch'ing empire from internal collapse and external threats.

Of course, the court at Peking was not above playing one group of officials against another and, in the present instance, using Tso to break up the Tseng–Li monopoly on the modern armament industry. This certainly helps explain the ready imperial approval given to Tso's navy yard. But if curbing the power of Tseng and Li was a matter of high priority, it seems odd that the court should so soon dispatch Tso to the North-West, before planning for the navy yard was complete. And though the court might fear a Tseng–Li monopoly, an intensified rivalry could prove equally detrimental and not to be encouraged. Besides, leading members of the Grand Council at the time saw the need for defence modernization. It was they who called on *all* the high officials of the coastal and Yangtze provinces to make concrete proposals when responding to the Wade–Hart memoranda.[41] This was the spirit of the

38 Ibid., p. 698.
39 *NCH*, 11 April 1872.
40 Alicia Little, *Li Hung-chang: His Life and Times* (London, 1903), p. 53; and Spector, *Li*, p. 173.
41 Edict of 1 April 1866 in *IWSM*, TC 40:12–13b.

Restoration and the *yang-wu* movement. The fact that few other than Tso took advantage of this opportunity to initiate programmes is also one of the tragedies in this early phase of China's modern development.

Personal rivalry apart, did the establishment of the Foochow Navy Yard contribute to the growth of regional power in late Ch'ing China? Did Tso intend it to bolster a personal satrapy or genuinely to strengthen the empire's defence? We showed earlier that Tso's motive was patriotic. Here we shall explore the question further by retracing the steps he took in preparing the proposal for a navy yard and see whether he manoeuvred to enhance his personal power either vis-à-vis the throne or his rivals.

Tso's proposal was prompted by the Wade–Hart memoranda. From the time he was ordered to respond to them until the time he made the proposal, he had fully two months in which to canvass his colleagues. We have no evidence that he did. Of the ten officials instructed to discuss the memoranda, only two other than Tso favoured steamship building. One was Ch'ung-hou, commissioner of trade for the northern ports, and the other was Liu K'un-i, governor of Kiangsi.[42] Neither was particularly close to Tso. Tso's own protégé, Chiang I-li, who had shared his interest in steamships and, until recently, had served under him as treasurer of Chekiang, was noncommittal because his new superior, Governor-General Jui-lin of Liang Kwang, was unenthusiastic. Meanwhile, Ma Hsin-i, Tso's subordinate and governor of Chekiang, failed to mention the subject completely.[43] Tseng Kuo-fan, Li Hung-chang, and Kuo Sung-tao, all known to have favoured China's buying or building its own steamships, did not memorialize.[44] It is thus clear that Tso, when making the proposal for a navy yard, did not conspire with his colleagues for personal ends.

Tso, of course, had discussed the matter with a number of officials, particularly those in the Fukien, Chekiang, and Kwangtung region. As his memorial of 25 June openly admits:

---

42 *IWSM*, TC 41:26b–30, 43–50b.

43 Ibid., 42:58b–65b; 45:44b–54.

44 Though Tseng and Li were preoccupied with the Nien rebels at the time, their silence is hard to explain. Nevertheless, Tseng had previously favoured building steamships while Li leaned towards purchasing. *HFT*, III, 27–28a, 33–4; Lü Shih-ch'iang, *Chung-kuo tsao-ch'i ti lun-ch'uan*, pp. 148–53; idem, *Ting*, pp. 175–6; Thomas L. Kennedy, 'Industrial Metamorphosis in the Self-Strengthening Movement: Li Hung-chang and the Kiangnan Shipbuilding Program', *Journal of the Institute of Chinese Studies*, 4.1 (1971), 208–9. On Kuo's view, see Kuo T'ing-i, K. Y. Yin, and Lu Pao-ch'ien, comp., *Kuo Sung-t'ao hsien-sheng nien-p'u* (Taipei, 1971), vol. 1, p. 327. Kuo had just been removed from the governorship of Kwangtung and therefore did not respond. Besides, he was still smarting from Tso's failure to come to his rescue in his struggle with Kwangtung officials, despite the fact that the two were related through marriage. The relationship between

Your minister has, by correspondence, consulted Ma Hsin-i, the governor of Chekiang, and Chiang I-li, the newly appoined governor of Kwangtung. Both regarded this [construction of a shipyard] as urgent and are willing to get together some funds in order to make it a success. . . . If Fukien, Chekiang, and Kwangtung make a co-operative effort over a period of five years, an expenditure of several millions [taels] is not beyond our capacity.[45]

On the surface, this passage lends weight to Stanley Spector's assertion that the Foochow enterprise 'was supported by the central government and southern provincial leaders in an effort to counter the growing power of the Li-Tseng clique'.[46] But the issues are not so clear-cut for, at this point, support from Kwangtung was far from certain. Furthermore, at this stage of the discussion, the number of participating provinces and, to a lesser extent, the location of the proposed navy yard, were still open questions. Regarding provincial participation, there were three possible options: one involved the majority if not all of the coastal provinces, a second envisaged a co-operative effort by Fukien, Chekiang, and Kwangtung, as Tso alluded to earlier, and a third called for a solely Fukienese undertaking. Thus, even as late as the end of July or early August, Chiang I-li was still able to discuss this matter with the Tsungli Yamen in an open-ended manner:

Your minister, on a previous occasion travelling through Fukien, had a thorough discussion with Governor-General Tso Tsung-t'ang and intended to set up metal plants for shipbuilding in provinces along the coast. . . . All the provinces, irrespective of territorial boundaries, will pool resources for this enterprise. . . . Your minister has also consulted, in detail, Governor-General Jui-lin, who absolutely agreed to the idea. We therefore intend to write this instant to Tso Tsung-t'ang about the matter. Whether we are building the plant in Fukien or in Kwangtung, we hope to produce a foolproof plan. . . . As soon as we receive a reply from Tso Tsung-t'ang we will memorialize for its execution.[47]

Jui-lin, whose initial reactions to the naval project were distinctly cool, had now changed his mind, partly because of Chiang's persuasion and partly because of the interprovincial concept. His support, however, was important. Like Ma Hsin-i, he had no close ties with Tso and, as a governor-general, had no need to curry Tso's favour. With his support and Chiang's proposal, the first public support from outside Tso's provinces, the idea of an interprovincial venture suddenly came alive, and Peking promptly instructed him and Chiang to write to Tso and make a

them was also tarnished by their differences over military supplies. *Ch'ing-shih*, vol. 4, p. 4944; Hsiao I-shan, *Ch'ing-tai t'ung-shih*, vol. 3, p. 815; Kuo T'ing-i, *Kuo*, vol. 1, p. 328.
45 *HFT*, II, 6b–8.   46 Spector, *Li*, p. 173.   47 *HFT*, II, 12.

joint effort. The court thus reversed its earlier decision, which approved a purely Fukienese navy yard.[48] We have no further information on what went on between Tso and Chiang until October, when the interprovincial concept assumed a more concrete form. By this time the site at Ma-wei (Mamoi), below the city of Foochow, had been confirmed and the contracts with the Frenchmen signed; only the question of funding and staffing had to be worked out. On the subject of finances, Tso wrote to Chiang:

The establishment of the shipyard bureau, dockyard, employment of European mechanics, the setting up of a school, etc., will require expenses in the region of Tls. 400,000. For this, Fukien alone shall be responsible. Thereafter, we shall need Tls. 40,000 per month for salary, provisions, labour, and material. . . . Fukien will be responsible for [Tls.] 20,000, Kwangtung, 10,000, and Chekiang, 10,000.[49]

Because of the location of the navy yard, the bulk of the financial burden naturally fell on Fukien. Chiang I-li, who had pondered other sites, now conceded, correctly, that Ma-wei was more suitable than Whampoa on the Pearl River. Further, since he thought Tso had already acquired nearly half the machinery, it was only fitting that Tso should take the pioneering step in building the shipyard with Kwangtung's financial support.[50]

Chiang was Tso's protégé. That he should yield to Tso on the matter of location is to be expected. Besides, the choice of site had never been a truly open question. Since at least the closing months of 1865 Tso had assumed that the navy yard would be located in the vicinity of Foochow.[51] And his personal ambition need not even enter into consideration. Under Ch'ing practices, it would have been unthinkable for him to establish a navy yard outside his territorial jurisdiction. The choice of Foochow, or, more precisely, Ma-wei, was also based on other factors. First, it was strategically located, guarding the approach to the provincial capital. Second, the depth of the Min at that point was adequate for

---

48 *YWYT*, vol. 5, p. 13. The new edict, dated 17 August 1866, superseded that of 14 July. It is highly unlikely that Chiang would have had the chance to see the edict of 14 July before he dispatched his memorial in late July or early August. It is almost certain, however, that he would have seen a copy of Tso's memorial of 25 June from either Tso himself or a government gazette. Chiang was thus reacting and giving support to Tso but, looking at the matter from Kwangtung, he envisaged a more substantial form of interprovincial co-operation.

49 *TWHK*, 'Letters', 8:56; *YWYT*, vol. 5, pp. 445–6.

50 Chiang to Tsungli Yamen, 24 November 1866, in *HFT*, II, 23. According to *Kuo-ying Chao-shang-chü ch'i-shih-wu chou-nien chi-nien-k'an* (Shanghai, 1947), the river channel at Ma-wei is superior to that at Whampoa (pp. 179–90).

51 Giquel, Diary, entry for Monday, 14 January 1866 (the 14th was actually a Sunday).

vessels the dockyard was designed to build, although Giquel wished that it were deeper, to accommodate future needs.[52] Most important, Ma-wei was close to Tso's seat of political power.[53] Proximity would not only facilitate control but also ensure the Navy Yard's very existence and survival. In view of the decentralized nature of the traditional state, Ma-wei was a reasonable choice and need not be construed as an expression of regional power.

Finally, the manner in which the Navy Yard was financed underscored its multiprovincial character. The financial support from the three provinces came from their maritime customs receipts, a part of the imperial revenue. The Navy Yard was therefore in effect supported by a 'national' fund, and as such, it was as imperial a project as could be expected. As Halliday Macartney remarked, and his opinion is valuable because of his long association with Li Hung-chang's arsenals, the Navy Yard was 'more imperial than any of the rest'.[54] This imperial character was strengthened by the fact that Shen Pao-chen, the first director-general, and his successors were all appointed by Peking. I shall return to this subject in the next section.

Unfortunately, as management procedures evolved, the Navy Yard was transformed increasingly into a provincial enterprise. Despite Kwangtung's contribution to its operating funds, the Cantonese officials did not seek nor were they given even a modicum of influence. All financial matters were handled by Fukien and Chekiang officials resident at Foochow. At the suggestion of Tso Tsung-t'ang, policy matters were to be left in the hands of the Foochow Tartar general, the governor-general of Fukien and Chekiang, and the Fukien governor, while the provincial treasurer of Fukien was to assist in carrying out their decisions.[55]

52 In public, Giquel did not express any reservation about the Min at Ma-wei, although he did state its limits. Giquel, *Foochow Arsenal*, p. 9. In his Diary (entry for 14 January 1866) he expressed his wish that conditions were better: 'But the real jewel of the colony [Saigon] is unquestionably the Donnai River. How happy we should be if the Foochow River [Min] were its equal, and how much more beautiful would be the prospect offered by the Arsenal which we are going to build. We should be able to build at once for an unlimited future, sure of not being limited in the size of our ships by the lack of depth and navigational dangers!' (trans. by Frances de Burgh Whyte). According to E. Frandon, French vice-consul at Foochow in the 1880s and 1890s, Giquel's choice was a site in the San-sha Bay, north of the Min estuary. Obviously, that would be too far for Tso's political purposes. Frandon to Pichon, 28 June 1898, in MM BB4 1556 406/1/197.
53 Giquel, *Foochow Arsenal*, pp. 9–10. In Fukien, Amoy had a deeper harbour channel, but Amoy was too far to be run effectively from Foochow. On harbour conditions, see *Kuo-ying Chao-shang-chü*, pp. 179–90.
54 Macartney to Alfred Hippisley, 20 March 1876, cited in Demetrius Boulger, *The Life of Sir Halliday Macartney* (London, 1908), p. 250.
55 *HFT*, II, 21b.

Even the provincial interests of Chekiang were represented only in the rather dubious form of the governor-general. This organizational arrangement was set up towards the very end of October 1866, apparently for the administrative convenience of the authorities at Foochow.

The next streamlining effort was made by Tartar General Ying-kuei about three weeks later. Considering that all three provinces were contributing funds both to the Kansu campaign and to the Navy Yard, he thought it more convenient if Kwangtung and Chekiang each sent an additional 10,000 taels to Kansu on behalf of Fukien, which would then be entirely responsible for the Navy Yard's monthly expenditure of Tls. 40,000.[56] Much could be said in favour of such an arrangement; it would prevent insufficient or tardy remittances so typical of interprovincial transactions under the Ch'ing. Thus, for the sake of efficiency and the security of funds, Kwangtung and Chekiang's already tenuous link with the Foochow Navy Yard was sacrificed.[57]

While the interprovincial ideal nearly materialized in the autumn of 1866, it soon fizzled out. It is curious that Chiang I-li supported the idea of a multiprovincial project so vociferously at first. The prospect of Foochow-built steamships engaging in transport and pirate suppression in participating provinces was certainly a consideration.[58] For this expectation, Tso Tsung-t'ang must be held responsible. In his memorial of 25 June, Tso did hint, ever so vaguely, at a fleet that would serve the whole empire. To the Tsungli Yamen he also spoke of training people from all the maritime provinces in navigation so that they could sail the ships.[59] But none of the documents that dealt specifically with the organization of the Navy Yard referred to such a scheme. The Foochow authorities, for their part, were less than generous in sharing their control of the Navy Yard. So, by November, Chiang had come to accept the inevitable: Kwantung would still contribute funds but would have no influence over it. Only after the Fukien experiment had demonstrated its worth would Kwangtung launch its own naval project. 'For the moment', he remarked, 'the most urgent task for Kwangtung is to strengthen popular trust and support and to select and train its troops. . . . We must first have a means of securing internal peace before we can be adequate in resisting foreign threats'.[60]

The interprovincial concept had not been properly grasped and Tso,

---

56 Ibid., 29.
57 Steven Leibo, citing my earlier work and misinterpreting it, states that 'the interprovincial funding project was never carried out'. *Transferring Technology*, p. 77.
58 *HFT*, II, 11.
59 Letter of October 1866 in *TWHK*, 'Letters', 8:55b–56.
60 Chiang to Tsungli Yamen, 24 November 1866, in *HFT*, II, 23b–24.

at least, should share the blame. On the other hand, given his imminent departure, it is understandable that he should place his close associates in positions critical to the Navy Yard's survival. Besides, he had to contend with local vested interests in Fukien, which were not always compatible with his own. After all, the new enterprise was a potential source of patronage and peculation for the high officials of the province. Personal gains might have moved some to support the reorganization of the Navy Yard's funding arrangement just mentioned. So, step by step, by intent or by default, the Navy Yard acquired a more provincial character. Meanwhile, the court at Peking, never sure of its own position on the matter, gave its blessing at every turn.

In the last analysis, truly co-operative projects were alien to the Ch'ing administrative system. The traditional model of interprovincial undertakings, such as the case of military aid examined in Chapter 3, was clumsy, slow, unreliable, and, above all, dysfunctional. Each province dealt directly with Peking more than with neighbouring provinces. In the process, needless misunderstandings, disputes, and personal conflicts arose. The Grain Tribute System and the Salt Administration were, of course, multiprovincial operations, but were too diffuse and loosely organized to function as corporate wholes.[61] Such loosely organized entities lent themselves easily to the court's manipulation, but they also impeded the central government's ability to mobilize them effectively. For a modern industry such as the Foochow Navy Yard to be truly interprovincial or imperial, it was necessary for Chekiang and Kwangtung to have permanent representation at Foochow, making corporate decisions and interacting responsively with the central government. In a political system that lacked the wherewithal to intervene in local governments on a regular basis, such a restructuring of the central–provincial relationship was inevitably viewed in negative terms – as the rise of regional power. The court's behaviour gave every indication that, as it accepted the necessity of modern defence undertakings, it preferred to see these new sources of power accrue to individual leaders or provinces rather than to a confederation of them. Consequently, although the Foochow Navy Yard was more imperial than the other arsenals, it still suffered from a heavy provincial colouration. And when Shen Pao-chen became its director-general, he dealt directly and almost exclusively with the high officials at Foochow and Peking.

---

61 Harold C. Hinton, *The Grain Tribute System of China (1845–1911)* (Cambridge, Mass., 1956), pp. 2–6; S. A. M. Adshead, *The Modernization of the Chinese Salt Administration, 1900–1920* (Cambridge, Mass., 1970), pp. 1–38.

Shen as first director-general

On 25 September 1866 the throne ordered Tso Tsung-t'ang to proceed immediately to the North-West to direct the campaign against the Muslim rebels there.[62] The uprising, which began in 1862, had by now spread from eastern Shensi to most of Sinkiang and was soon to embroil the Ch'ing with the British and the Russians. Early attempts at suppressing these fierce, though divided, central Asians had failed miserably.[63] It was under these desperate circumstances that Tso was instructed to go directly to his new post, omitting the usual audience at Peking. To replace Tso as governor-general of Fukien and Chekiang, the throne picked Wu T'ang (1814–76), the director-general of grain transport.[64]

The imperial injunctions, which reached Foochow on 14 October,[65] came at an inopportune time, for Tso was deeply immersed in drawing up the final plans for the Navy Yard with d'Aiguebelle, who had just returned from Annam (5 October). What was even more unfortunate was the court's failure to consider the future of the Navy Yard when choosing Tso's successor. Wu T'ang was simply expected to take charge of it, regardless of his attitude towards such an unusual undertaking.[66] Whatever the court's intent, it was contrary to Tso's plan.

Even before his transfer, Tso had been thinking along the lines of a full-time director-general (*tsung-li ch'uan-cheng*) appointed from Peking who would take exclusive charge of the Navy Yard for an extended term and would increasingly benefit from his experience in management and production. A governor-general or Tartar general, because of his many responsibilities and the frequency of transfer, would not have done as well.[67] Besides, Wu T'ang had never shown any support for *yang-wu* or defence modernization and, on a personal level, Tso may also have resented his relationship with Tseng Kuo-fan, who had more than once recommended him for honours and promotion for his role in suppressing the Nien.[68] Tso therefore decided to look elsewhere. To that

---

62 *TWHK*, 'Memorials', 18:69; *Shih-lu*, TC 183:5–6.
63 Immanuel C. Y. Hsü, *The Ili Crisis: A Study of Sino-Russian Diplomacy, 1871–1881* (London, 1965), chap. 1.
64 Two edicts of 25 September 1866, in *Shih-lu*, TC 183:5–6b.
65 *TWHK*, 'Memorials', 19:26b–27. Urgency notwithstanding, the edict took twenty days to arrive, making it one of the slowest deliveries on record. On the time taken for an edict to reach Fukien, see J. K. Fairbank and Teng Ssu-yü, *Ch'ing Administration: Three Studies* (Cambridge, Mass., 1961), pp. 32–3.
66 Edict of 4 November 1866, in *Shih-lu*, TC 185:24–5.
67 *HFT*, II, 18, 21.
68 See Wu's biography in Ts'ai Kuan-lo, *Ch'ing-tai ch'i-pai ming-jen*, pp. 417–22. Wu was a native of Hsü-i district, Anhwei. He acquired the *chü-jen* degree in 1835 but failed the metropolitan examinations three times. He began his career as a district magistrate in

end, he begged to be allowed to stay at Foochow for at least another month.[69]

Since events had taken an unexpected turn, Tso argued, there was not sufficient time to wait for an appointee to be sent from Peking. So after consulting Ying-kuei and Hsü Tsung-kan, the governor of Fukien, he chose Shen Pao-chen. But after thrice visiting Shen at his home and doing some hard persuading, Tso failed to secure Shen's acceptance.[70]

Meanwhile, Shen felt that the magnitude of the Navy Yard project and the complexities involved in its establishment were such that it was absolutely necessary for Tso to delay his departure. Even more important, because Tso had been so personally involved in its creation, if he were allowed to leave prematurely, the project would collapse. Shen therefore mobilized more than a hundred of the most progressive elements in the Foochow gentry and petitioned for a postponement of Tso's departure, at least until the Navy Yard had begun to take shape and the European engineers had arrived.[71] This, of course, would mean much more than the extra month or so that Tso had requested. The upshot of Shen's effort was an edict (17 November) ordering Tso to manage the Navy Yard's affairs jointly with Ying-kuei and Shen. They were to be joined by Wu T'ang when he arrived.[72] Thus, Shen, having declined Tso's invitation and then led a campaign to delay his departure, had unwittingly drawn imperial attention upon himself. Some form of involvement now seemed unavoidable.

For Tso, this makeshift arrangement would not do; he still wanted a full-time imperial appointee. As a matter of fact, even before the latest edict reached Foochow, he had decided to seek an imperial order to effect Shen's appointment. Meanwhile, Shen, perhaps out of respect for Tso's sincerity and persistence, agreed to take charge of the Navy Yard if ordered by the throne, but would do so only after the full mourning period had expired in July 1867.[73] On 19 November, the expected imperial order came and Tso's quest for a director-general finally ended.[74] Since Tso's request for Shen's appointment predated the edicts giving Wu T'ang a place in the Navy Yard's management, the impression that

1844 and rose to the post of director-general of grain transport (*ts'ao-yün tsung-tu*) in 1863, having twice held that office in an acting capacity earlier.
69 *TWHK*, 'Memorials', 19:26–8.
70 Tso to Tsungli Yamen, October 1866, in *TWHK*, 'Letters', 8:54b; Tso's memorial of 31 October 1866, in *TWHK*, 'Memorials', 19:26–28b.
71 This petition was cited at length in a joint memorial by Ying-kuei and Hsü Tsung-kan, dispatched at the end of October and reaching Peking on 17 November 1866. *YWYT*, vol. 5, pp. 13–14.
72 *HFT*, II, 17; *Shih-lu*, TC 186:17–18b.
73 *IWSM*, TC 45:26–9.
74 *HFT*, II, 20–21b; *Shih-lu*, TC 186:19b–20b.

a deliberate attempt was made to shut Wu T'ang out had been avoided. Wu had to wait for another day to vent his hostility.

In his memorial as well as his letter to the Tsungli Yamen, Tso argued convincingly for Shen's appointment. Because the Navy Yard was outside the regular administrative system, he asserted, Shen could direct its affairs while still in mourning, and because Ma-wei was close to Foochow, his ageing father need not suffer any neglect either. As regards the Navy Yard, Tso maintained that Shen was ideal because, unlike a regular official who would be transferred periodically, Shen could be expected to stay for a long tour of office. Besides, Shen was greatly respected both in the imperial capital and in the provinces and enjoyed the enthusiastic support of the officials and gentry of Fukien. In view of the difficulties Tso had had with the powers that be in Fukien, this last consideration was significant. But, above all else, Shen, Tso stressed, was careful and attentive to administrative details – qualities eminently suitable for the task.[75] What Tso had omitted were several other important factors: Shen's patriotism, high rank, excellent service record in Kiangsi, as well as certain political and personal considerations.

Shen's administrative skills and reputation have been analysed in preceding chapters. His patriotism has also been noted. More will be said about it in connection with his acceptance of the director-generalship. Regarding his reputation and standing in the Ch'ing hierarchy, it should be noted here that they were of great significance, for they would immediately give prestige and importance to the novel venture. With Shen in charge, the Foochow Navy Yard would appear superior even to the Kiangnan Arsenal, which was under a mere taotai,[76] a thought that could hardly have escaped Tso.[77]

Over the long haul, however, political considerations were far more important. Tso was himself an able administrator who had great plans for developing Fukien and Chekiang.[78] His labours had won him support

75 *HFT*, II, 18, 21.
76 Lü Shih-ch'iang, *Ting*, p. 52.
77 The thought was certainly important to d'Aiguebelle, who at first attached little significance to the navy yard since he expected it to be placed under a taotai and would end up wasting government money, just as the other arsenals had. Médard, 'Note confidentielle'.
78 William L. Bales writes: 'In the fall of 1866, he [Tso] was directed to go to the Northwest.... It was a heavy blow to him. He had set his heart on reorganizing and rehabilitating the coastal provinces of Fukien and Chekiang, and on promoting the Chinese navy. He had the greatest confidence in his capacity as a civil administrator and he had great plans in mind'. *Tso*, p. 194. See also the section 'Characteristics of the Foochow Naval Yard', this chapter.

from many quarters. When he was transferred to the North-West, a significant segment of the gentry and people were reluctant to let him go.[79] On the day of his scheduled departure, crowds of people, it was said, thronged the streets and demonstrated. He had to leave the following day unannounced.[80] Yet he was not without enemies in Fukien who later accused him of having organized the demonstration (see the next chapter). Therefore, it was a blow to him that he would soon be unable to protect his reform programme personally. To ensure the continuation of his reforms, he left behind a number of his close associates whom he had earlier placed in the provincial bureaucracy. In addition, in his last forty days at Foochow, he submitted no less than thirty memorials to the throne and wrote more than forty letters of instruction to his associates for implementing the reforms.[81] As with his other plans and projects, he wanted to see the Navy Yard passed on to trusted hands.[82] The appointment of Shen, who enjoyed the support of the local gentry, was thus a huge political coup for him.

To be sure, an element of chance did enter into Shen's appointment. Had this occurred at another point in his public life, it is doubtful whether Tso would have chosen him and, indeed, whether he would have accepted the post. It will be recalled that in 1859 and again in 1864–5 Shen, in the midst of a successful career, had repeatedly sought the emperor's permission to retire in order to take care of his ageing parents. After his mother's death, he felt an even greater urge to be with his ailing father. For a time, it appeared that only after his father's death and a proper mourning period had elapsed would he return to public life. However, Shen's service was in great demand in the post-Taiping era.[83] The leadership of the Navy Yard therefore came as a timely compromise for his Confucian sense of duty – a compromise between filial piety, on the one hand, and service and loyalty to the throne, on the other – since it was a service he could perform without having to leave his father.[84] The idea of such a compromise was used cogently by Tso to

---

79 Tso to Yang Ch'ang-chün, late November or early December 1866 in *TWHK*, 'Letters', 8:57b–58.
80 Bales, *Tso*, p. 195.
81 Ibid.
82 Tso to Yang Ch'ang-chün, late November or early December 1866 in *TWHK*, 'Letters', 8:57b.
83 *TWHK*, 'Letters', 7:57b; Kuo T'ing-i, *Chin-tai Chung-kuo shih-shih*, vol. 1, p. 468.
84 The rule of avoidance did not apply to Shen's case, for although the Navy Yard was theoretically an imperial institution, it was not part of the regular political or administrative structure. In these respects, the position of director-general was analogous to that of militia commissioner of the Taiping era.

assure all the parties concerned that Confucian protocol had not been violated.[85]

There is no doubt that the personal relationship between Tso and Shen, reinforced by shared political beliefs, also played an important role. Tso was an ardent admirer of Lin Tse-hsü, Shen's father-in-law, whose ideas he zealously embraced.[86] During the Taiping War, Tso and Shen were brought closer together as they co-operated in protecting the border regions between their provinces. The fact that both were ultimately estranged from Tseng Kuo-fan, their patron, may have contributed to a sense of comradeship. Nevertheless, before 1865, the relationship between the two was built entirely on correspondence.[87] Even after Shen had returned to Foochow, he had so assiduously avoided contact with public officials that it was questionable whether the two had met until Tso visited him at home in the middle of October 1866.[88] But then, given their concern for China's administrative and territorial integrity, it is certain that a strong bond quickly developed between the two. Besides, Shen's father-in-law was among the very first advocates of steamship building in 1840 and 1841.[89] Who else would have been more suitable for carrying out this family mission? Thus, from a personal and political point of view, Tso could not have chosen a better man.

Both Tso and Shen had risen to prominence in the Taiping era. Because of his gift as a military commander, Tso's service was given recognition much earlier. He was already a governor-general in mid-1863, whereas Shen was still a governor when he retired in 1865. Yet Shen was an able administrator with a *chin-shih* degree, which Tso had failed to obtain no less than three times.[90] For Shen to accept from Tso an appointment that was clearly below the dignity of a former governor of Shen's calibre was bound to invite comment, especially from those who had a cynical view of the Tso–Shen relationship. In late 1867, Tseng Kuo-fan told his close associate, Chao Lieh-wen, that by the

---

85 In addition to memorials cited earlier, see the one in *YWYT*, vol. 5, p. 18 (received in Peking on TC 5/10/27 [3 December 1866], not TC 5/10/8 [14 November 1866] as stated).
86 Gideon Ch'en, *Tso*, pp. 1–5; Li Shih-yüeh, 'Ts'ung yang-wu', p. 32; Shen Ch'uan-ching, *Fu-chou ch'uan-cheng*, pp. 33–4.
87 In the spring of 1862, when engaged in organizing the defence of the Kuang-hsin area, Shen had hoped to meet Tso, who was campaigning nearby. But they missed each other. *SWSK*, 1:16.
88 *TWHK*, 'Memorials', 19:27–8. Lin Ch'ung-yung, however, speculates that, because the two had so much in common, they must have seen a great deal of each other. See his *Shen*, pp. 203–4.
89 Gideon Ch'en, *Lin*, pp. 18–21.
90 Hummel, *Eminent Chinese*, vol. 2, p. 763.

mid-1860s these two had become 'sworn confederates' (*ssu-tang*) – a pejorative term. Tseng then continued:

As a person, Tso . . . is [quite] unapproachable, and yet Shen is drawn within his circle. [Despite the fact that their] achievements and reputation are equally prominent, [Shen], all of a sudden, became [his] 'vassal'. This is really beyond anybody's comprehension.[91]

Tseng went on to describe how Tso, after his arrival in Shensi, eased out the incumbent governor to make room for his protégé, Liu Tien, in 1868. In concurrence, Chao Lieh-wen exclaimed:

Alas! This is the precursor of the [rise of] regional power in T'ang times, and the [division of the country by the] eight kings in the Chin dynasty.[92]

Indisputably, this conversation exaggerated the insidious nature of Tso's political design and Shen's role in it.[93] The bond between Tso and Shen up to the mid-1860s was certainly not as strong as the remarks suggest, but the relationship was nonetheless special, in the sense described two paragraphs earlier. In the last analysis, Tso went to great lengths to secure Shen's appointment for a whole range of reasons, their personal relationship and Shen's high rank and reputation among them. Having secured Shen's acceptance, Tso left Foochow with peace of mind.[94]

Implications for Shen's political career

The acceptance of the director-generalship had major implications for Shen's career. The position was itself at least a step below his former

---

91 This conversation was recorded in Chao Lieh-wen's diary, *Neng-ching-chü jih-chi*, n.d, no pagination; see entry for TC 6/12/1 (26 December 1867). The passage is reprinted in Tseng Kuo-fan, *Tseng Kuo-fan wei-k'an hsin-kao*, p. 391. The date of this conversation is open to question since it later refers to Liu Tien's appointment in early 1868.

92 Ibid., p. 392.

93 The conversation was speculative and exaggerated on several counts. First, as noted, the Tso–Shen relationship was not as strong as Tseng would have us believe. Second, Tso's role in the removal of Governor Ch'iao Sung-nien in order to make room for Liu Tien is open to question. Liu, like Tso, was a Hunanese and had served as Tso's *mu-yu* (personal assistant). His rise to high positions owed much to Tso's patronage, but when he took over the governorship from Ch'iao, he did so only in an acting capacity. In less than a year he retired to his native Hunan to look after his parents. Tso certainly played a key role in making Liu acting governor, but whether he first removed Ch'iao remains unclear. *Ch'ing-shih*, vol. 6, pp. 4844–5, vol. 7, pp. 5002–3; *Shih-lu*, TC 224:14b; Hummel, *Eminent Chinese*, vol. 2, p. 764; Ch'ien Shih-fu, comp., *Ch'ing-chi chung-yao chih-kuan nien-piao* (Shanghai, 1959), p. 192.

94 Stanley Spector interprets Shen's appointment quite differently. He writes, 'In 1867 it [the Foochow Navy Yard] fell into the hands of Shen Pao-chen, a loyal follower of Tseng [Kuo-fan] and close colleague of Li [Hung-chang]'. In the light of the estrange-

office. Confucian teachings called for personal sacrifice in the service of the state, and Shen might well have been moved by such a notion, although given the Confucian demand for full mourning and care for an ailing father, the Navy Yard appointment was perhaps the best he could do at the time. If, at a personal level, the arrangement was agreeable, it could, at the political level, have put his career in jeopardy. Without territorial power, his administration of the Navy Yard had to depend on factors largely beyond his control. As we shall see in the following pages, the level of support from the central and provincial governments was to have a serious impact on his administration. Other factors, such as Tso Tsung-t'ang's continued involvement, relations with foreign employees and the Western powers, and China's financial health will be treated in later chapters.

At its inception, the Foochow Navy Yard, the product of Tso Tsung-t'ang's patriotic efforts, had the potential of becoming an interprovincial or even an imperial enterprise. However, it was quickly reduced to an essentially provincial undertaking. One of the reasons, as stated earlier, was the failure of the central government to grasp the meaning of a truly imperial institution and to make adjustments in its political system to accommodate such an enterprise. The court's ignorance was exacerbated by callousness. Nowhere was this more evident than in the appointment of the first director-general. It was only through Tso's wisdom and persistence that the Navy Yard eventually ended up with a full-time, high-ranking administrative head instead of an absentee 'committee' of high provincial officials directing its affairs part-time some twenty kilometres upstream.

The lack of concern at the centre is further demonstrated by the fact that, throughout the process, the Tsungli Yamen was by-passed. It is true that at the time three of the nine ministers at the Tsungli Yamen also sat on the Grand Council, the highest policy-making body under the throne. The Yamen was certainly aware of the goings-on. Tso and Ying-kuei also kept its ministers informed through correspondence. The fact remains that the Yamen was not formally consulted, which reinforces the impression that the central government fell short in grasping the signifi-cance of such an enterprise and in exploiting its potentially imperial character. Had there been closer co-operation at the centre and greater concern in appointing officials who were to manage the Navy Yard's

ment between Tseng and Shen since 1863, and in the face of the conversation just quoted, Spector's claim, which he left undocumented, is open to serious doubt. Spector, *Li*, pp. 173–4. Shen and Tseng eventually patched up their differences, probably after 1870.

affairs, the latter, Shen included, would not have had to depend as much on provincial personnel and resources.[95]

Even under the best of circumstances, the Foochow Navy Yard carried with it the stigma of a *yang-wu* enterprise. Now, dependent as it was on provincial resources and with direction from Peking uncertain, its position was precarious. To be associated with such an undertaking was to expose one's career to innumerable hazards, as Giquel so succinctly put it in his report:

> To establish an Arsenal such as that at Foochow, would be, in Europe or America, a very ordinary affair. But in China its promoter ran great risk; for, according to the system followed by the Government at Peking, which never takes the initiative in any new undertaking, but contents itself with vetoing or sanctioning what is proposed to it, the Viceroy Tso had to assume the entire responsibility of his project, and a failure of his experiment would have ruined one of the most successful careers that the mandarinate could present.[96]

Giquel was perhaps overstating the case a little, for the Navy Yard, important though it might have been, was only one among many of Tso's undertakings. Tso was a high territorial official whose main task, in the eyes of Peking, was to engage not in *yang-wu* but in internal administration. Besides, as governor-general, Tso could use his influence on the provincial government to the advantage of the Navy Yard.

In Shen's case, the risk was much greater. As a full-time director-general, and one who was to remain in this job for a longish period, his entire future depended on the success of the Navy Yard. In a later period, the post of director-general was perceived as a stepping-stone to a governorship or viceregal commission, although the post itself was not a lucrative one.[97] In Shen's time, however, no such pattern of promotion existed. Besides, Shen, with his high rank backed up by a successful career, had no need for a stepping-stone. As one of his critics observed, had he not occupied himself with driving out the barbarians but instead followed the regular path of a bureaucratic career, he would have become a governor-general by this time.[98] This, indeed, is no idle speculation. And to accuse Shen of being opportunistic in taking over the Navy Yard, as Li Huan and Wang K'ai-yün did, [99] is preposterous. As noted at the

---

95 It could be suggested that, in giving Wu T'ang part control over the Navy Yard, the court or the empress-dowager, with whom Wu was said to be in favour, was exerting its influence. If that were the case, the central authorities certainly did not try very hard, for they soon gave in to Tso's recommendation of Shen.
96 Giquel, *Foochow Arsenal*, p. 10.
97 *NCH*, 13 May 1876.
98 Wang K'ai-yün, cited in Chin Liang, *Chin-shih jen-wu*, p. 157.
99 Ibid.

beginning of this chapter, the throne did try to lure him from retirement with the prospect of a high-level appointment. Shen refused to be tempted then – why did he accept an inferior appointment now?

In this chapter, we have examined the factors that contributed to the founding of the Foochow Navy Yard, its character, and Tso's choice of Shen as director-general. They include personal relations, ambitions, rivalry, desire for regional power, provincialism, and patriotism. What moved Shen to accept Tso's invitation could have been one or several of these elements. But Shen, notwithstanding his service during the Taiping years, had never had his own army. Nor was his political power buttressed by a large network of patronage. He was an unlikely contender for regional power. Still, was it possible that he saw in the control of a modern navy yard and naval force the beginning of a power base? Here, we must once again emphasize the dependence of the Navy Yard on provincial resources, which, as later chapters reveal, significantly reduced its potential as a source of regional power. And, finally, although personal relations with Tso might have influenced his decision, the latter's departure to an opposite corner of the empire made an effective alliance difficult. It would appear that patriotism was the prime motive for his acceptance of the director-generalship.

We have come across Shen's patriotism on many occasions already. It was part of his education and an important element in his family life. The Opium Wars affected him deeply. They shaped his political consciousness and influenced his management of foreign affairs as governor of Kiangsi. By the early 1860s, there was no doubt in his mind that steamships, telegraphy, and railways were significant innovations, and as he sought to curb their use by foreigners, he might have also contemplated harnessing them for China's benefit. It is therefore of particular interest to note what he wrote to the throne in December 1867, five months after he formally assumed the direction of the Navy Yard:

To discuss and carry out *yang-wu* today is more difficult than in the past. . . . Why? Because when we began to implement *yang-wu* in the Tao-kuang period [1821–50], the empire was still prosperous. . . . It should have been easy. But the ministers of the day, seeking only superficial and immediate advantages, were careless and too accommodating. Blunder after blunder was made – hence the terrible situation in which we find ourselves today. . . . The only foolproof option open to us now is to strengthen ourselves (*tzu-ch'iang*). If we are strengthened, we can treat the foreigners as we wish. . . . Otherwise, even if they adhere faithfully to the letter of the treaties, our economic rights and administrative integrity, already under their control, will be in an unthinkable state in a few more years.[100]

100 *IWSM*, TC 53:1–2.

In October 1866, just before he was asked to head the Navy Yard, he said that the project was to build ships for China's benefit for 'ten thousand generations'.[101] One of the benefits, as shown in the preceding passage, was to recapture China's freedom and initiative in the new world order. Later, in 1872, he stated that the objective of the Navy Yard and other forms of military preparation was to protect the Chinese Empire and its people so that the humiliation inflicted by the British on the Chinese during the Opium War would not happen again.[102] But words are words. The greatest testimony to his patriotism still lies in the sacrifice he made in his career in order to bring China's naval development into a new age. As John Rawlinson has underscored, because of the tremendous appeal of the civil service 'it was difficult to find men to run China's arms establishments, and to keep them at it'.[103] Shen was an exception to the rule, and given his stature in the Ch'ing hierarchy, his willingness to take on the challenge was all the more impressive.

If there had ever been any regional design on the part of Tso Tsung-t'ang in founding the Navy Yard, that design was quickly subverted by his new assignment in the North-West, the court's vacillation in choosing someone to take charge of the Navy Yard, and the appointment of Wu T'ang as his successor. By the time Tso nominated Shen for the Navy Yard, there was little chance of Fukien becoming a power base under Tso. Nevertheless, can we see in Shen's appointment the emergence of a new 'coalition' between Tso and Shen? Was Tso able to retain control over the Navy Yard through Shen or his protégés after he had left Foochow? Did Shen direct the Navy Yard as though he were a 'vassal' of Tso's? Was his administration hamstrung by Tso's men? And, finally, did he try to restore the Navy Yard's imperial character and thus strengthen his position vis-à-vis the provincial authorities? We shall deal with these questions in the next several chapters.

---

101 *YWYT*, vol. 5, p. 14.   102 *HFT*, II, 346b–347, 350.
103 Rawlinson, *China's Struggle*, pp. 202–3.

6

The Foochow Navy Yard:
early developments,
1866–1867

The successful search for a director-general was a matter for self-congratulation. Shen was highly esteemed in Peking and at Foochow. As an imperial appointee bearing the title *ch'in-ming tsung-li ch'uan-cheng ta-ch'en* (lit., by imperial command the high minister for the general direction of the shipping administration), he reported directly to the throne, though certain restrictions applied. Initially, he was empowered to memorialize independently, without having to secure the imprimatur of the high provincial officials. Problems that could not be solved locally were therefore guaranteed a hearing at Peking. However, the privilege was withdrawn two weeks later; Shen would now have to memorialize jointly with the governor-general and the governor at Foochow. Then, realizing that Giquel and d'Aiguebelle's confidence in the Navy Yard had been undermined by this arrangement, Tso Tsung-t'ang had his name added to the list of joint memorialists as a constant reminder to potential critics and opponents that the Navy Yard was Tso's creation and Shen his chosen director-general.[1] But the arrangement did not restore Shen's independence.

Although Shen was often referred to as an imperial commissioner in Western sources, he was in fact a director-general by imperial appointment (*ch'in-ming*), not an imperial commissioner (*ch'in-ch'ai*). In official documents, he was simply addressed as the director-general of the shipping administration. His relationship with the regular bureaucracy bears comparison with that of the Tsungli Yamen, an organ that was also created by royal command; both suffered similar limitations in decision-

---

1 *HFT*, II, 21–22b, 45b–46; *IWSM*, TC 45:59a–b; *TWHK*, 'Memorials', 20:69a–b; Lin Ch'ung-yung, *Shen*, p. 267.

making powers. Institutionally, Shen enjoyed little authority outside the boundaries of the Navy Yard or beyond the decks of its vessels. Worse still, the name 'Fukien' was sometimes added to his title, as if the Navy Yard were merely a provincial enterprise, and this was done no less by agencies in Peking.[2] The cognomen was added perhaps to identify the Navy Yard's location, or to prevent the director-general from developing any illusions of grandeur. But there was no shipping administration anywhere else that might cause confusion, and given the institutional limitations, the fear that the director-general might assume unwarranted power was groundless. So much for the central government's understanding of the Navy Yard as a potentially imperial establishment.

Not being an imperial commissioner or a territorial official, Shen had no control over Fukien's resources, especially its financial resources. Nor did he have any restraining power over those high provincial officials whose actions, by virtue of the peculiar relationship between Fukien and the Navy Yard, could affect developments at Ma-wei. Shen's position regarding Fukien therefore makes Tseng Kuo-fan's in Kiangsi in the early 1860s look enviable. Both Tso Tsung-t'ang and Shen were aware of these institutional problems, and they did what they could to protect the Navy Yard's administrative integrity. Their efforts are examined in the first part of this chapter. In the second part, we analyse Shen's leadership and the Navy Yard's institutional strengths as it faced internal opposition and foreign threats.

Tso's legacy: a 'five-year plan' begun with a skeleton staff

The blueprint for the founding and execution of the Foochow Navy Yard was contained in four contracts and agreements reached by Tso Tsung-t'ang and Prosper Giquel on 3 September 1866. They were readily accepted by Paul d'Aiguebelle on his return from Annam in October. The two Frenchmen then signed the documents at Shanghai before the French consul-general, Vicomte Brenier de Montmorand.[3] Thereby, the two Frenchmen committed themselves to the construction of a naval dockyard, a metal-working forge for making the materials it needed, and

2 See, e.g., *HFT*, II, 219b.
3 *HFT*, II, 20–1; Henri Cordier, *Histoire des relations de la Chine avec les puissances occidentales, 1860–1902* (Paris, 1901–2), vol. 1, pp. 250–4. The documents were 'Un contrat général d'exécution', 'Des propositions d'exécution', 'Un devis', and 'Contrat d'engagement des ingénieurs, contre-maîtres et ouvriers Européens'. MM BB4 1555 17/5/2. Chinese text, *HFT*, II, 31–43.

schools for marine engineering and navigation. To achieve these goals, they were to employ from France and Britain thirty-seven foremen and mechanics, several instructors, an accountant, and a physician. The contracts were to last for five years, starting from the day the metalworking forge began operation. At the end of the period, the Navy Yard was to have produced eleven steamships of the 150-horsepower class and five of the 80-horsepower class. Only nine of the 150-horsepower engines were to be built in the Navy Yard; the rest were to be purchased from abroad. Also, at the conclusion of the contracts, the students of marine engineering should be capable of designing and constructing ships, marine engines, and other machines. Students of navigation should be capable of navigating in the open seas within sight of land. Other aspects of the contracts will be discussed in due course.

The Chinese, for their part, guaranteed a regular flow of funds and sufficient Chinese labourers and raw materials for the Europeans to carry out the terms of the contracts.[4] In short, they were solely responsible for the administration of the Navy Yard, creating a favourable working environment for the Europeans.

After the contracts were signed and Shen's appointment ensured, Tso Tsung-t'ang was ready to leave for the North-West. He had hoped that Shen, though still in mourning, would take over the Navy Yard project immediately. But Shen declined. Even an imperial injunction, which Tso requested, and the concession that he need not officially submit memorials before the mourning period expired were unavailing. Subsequent efforts by Ying-kuei and Acting Governor Chou K'ai-hsi, as well as repeated edicts from the throne, failed equally to change his mind. These officials finally yielded to Shen's wishes in February 1867. Given the slow speed of communications, and with his mourning ending in a mere five months, further attempts would not have had any real effect.[5]

Throughout, Shen had insisted that, at this stage, his presence was not essential: first, the Frenchmen had returned to Europe to recruit mechanics and secure the machinery; second, as for purchasing the land, erecting workshops, and opening the schools, Ying-kuei and Chou K'ai-hsi were already doing an excellent job.[6] Informal consultation was all Shen allowed himself even though his leadership was much needed. He did, however, play a decisive role in finalizing the regulations for the Navy Yard School, and when peasants protested against the government's buying up of their fields, beating up some yamen runners, he assumed

4 *HFT*, II, 32.
5 Ibid., 24b–25b, 59–63b; *YWYT*, vol. 5, pp. 47–8.
6 *HFT*, II, 60b–61.

personal authority and dealt with them severely.[7] Still, he concerned himself only with the most critical matters, leaving the rest to the already overburdened Ying-kuei and Chou K'ai-hsi. It is hard to imagine that the progress of the Navy Yard project did not suffer as a result.[8] But for Shen, filial piety was simply a concern of a higher order.

Meanwhile, work on the Navy Yard was left to a number of Tso's trusted subordinates whose expertise on 'foreign matters' was more useful to him in coastal China than in the North-West. Foremost among them were Chou K'ai-hsi, Wu Ta-t'ing, and Hu Kuang-yung; all had served him in Chekiang and were hand-picked to accompany him to Fukien in December 1864. While still at Foochow, Tso particularly relied on these men because, as he once lamented, 'the political environment in Fukien was so inhospitable that he contemplated suicide.... Chekiang was heavenly [by comparison]'.[9]

Chou K'ai-hsi (1827–71) was specially close to Tso. Both were Hunanese. Tso had been Chou's teacher and noticed his intelligence and accomplishment. His practical statecraft (*ching-shih*) bias, which his earlier career betrayed, may well have resulted from Tso's influence. During the Taiping years, he served successively under Tseng Kuo-fan, Hu Lin-i, and Li Shu-i, then governor of Anhwei (1862–1863), before joining Tso. Tso put him in charge of likin at Kuang-hsin, Kiangsi, during Shen's governorship. He was therefore known to Shen at least by reputation. When Tso became the governor-general of Fukien and Chekiang (1863), Wu Ta-t'ing, a close friend of Chou's, also entered Tso's service. Wu (1824–77) was a *chü-jen* and one-time secretary of the Grand Secretariat. He and Chou had been colleagues under Governor Li Shu-i. When Tso moved into Fukien in late 1864, he relied on both men to deal with the hostile political environment in that province. To ensure a steady flow of funds to his army, he had Chou appointed acting provincial treasurer and Wu the salt comptroller, a step reminiscent of Tseng Kuo-fan's placement of his men in Kiangsi's administration in 1862. On the death of Governor Hsü Tsung-kan in mid-December 1866

---

7 On School regulations, see Chapter 8, the section 'Training a New Naval Personnel'. On peasant protest, see Shen Ch'uan-ching, *Fu-chou ch'uan-cheng*, pp. 65–6. Shen at first tried to mollify the peasants but was himself hit by a stone in the ankle. Five war junks with three hundred soldiers were then sent in and warning cannon shots fired from the junks. Frightened, the village leaders surrendered eighteen trouble-makers. But for the pleas of the village elders, Shen would have had all of them summarily executed. In the end, two were beheaded, and the other sixteen detained until the land transactions were concluded.
8 Lin Ch'ung-yung claims that Shen was involved in practically every aspect of the Navy Yard's establishment during his period of mourning. *Shen*, pp. 271–4.
9 Tso to Yang Ch'ang-chün, salt comptroller of Chekiang, January–February 1865, in *TWHK*, 'Letters', 7:19.

(soon after Tso had left), Chou was made concurrently the acting governor, in which position he remained until the spring of 1867.[10]

Hu Kuang-yung (c. 1825–85) was a well-to-do merchant-banker, well known in official circles as a procuring agent of proven ingenuity. While campaigning in Chekiang, Tso made extensive use of him and his business connections for securing supplies and foreign arms. Hu was even more indispensable in Fukien, where Tso faced so many difficulties.[11]

Of the three, Wu Ta-t'ing was the only one not initially involved with the Navy Yard; he was appointed the military intendant of T'ai-wan in late 1866. Shen had him transferred to the Navy Yard in the spring of 1868.[12] As for Chou and Hu, Tso had intended an active part for them from the outset. Chou, as acting provincial treasurer, was to facilitate the remittance of funds to the Navy Yard. Hu, because of his business acumen, his knowledge of things Western, and, above all, the trust he commanded among foreigners, was given charge of purchasing, the reception of European mechanics, the employment of Chinese workmen, and the establishment of the Navy Yard School. Both he and Chou were empowered to submit memorials on matters related to the Navy Yard via the regular provincial authorities, a necessary measure while Shen was in mourning.[13]

Hu, however, was reluctant to take on such heavy responsibilities, partly because of his alleged corruption in handling military supplies several years earlier. Although the evidence against him was weak, he feared that an extension of his business activities would draw even more fire on himself. Still, he was prepared to render his services but, to forestall future accusations, he insisted on providing full documentation for all business transactions and guarantees for the people he recommended. In any event, because he was already in charge of the Procurement and Forwarding Office at Shanghai for Tso's campaign, he was unable

10 Li Ting-fang, *Tseng Kuo-fan*, pp. 17, 22, 23; Kuo Sung-tao, *Yang-chih shu-wu*, 19:19b–20b; Wu Ta-t'ing, *Hsiao-yu-yü shan-kuan wen-ch'ao* (n.p., n.d., prefaces dated 1863 and 1864, but the work was subsequently enlarged to include later writings), 6:7–10, 8:14, 9:14–16; *Hu-nan t'ung-chih* (n.p., 1885), 193:9b; Tso to Yang Ch'ang-chün, January–February 1865, in *TWHK*, 'Letters', 7:19; Ch'ien Shih-fu, *Ch'ing-chi chung-yao chih-kuan*, pp. 190–1; *T'ai-wan t'ung-chih* (hereafter, *TWTC*) (Taipei, 1962; compiled in manuscript form in 1894), p. 351; Shen Pao-chen's memorial of KH 4.2.25 (28 March 1878), in YCT KH 4/2, *ts'e* 4. Wu Ta-t'ing knew the Chou family well. He wrote congratulatory essays for Chou's mother on her sixty-fifth and seventieth birthdays. When Chou died, he composed a warm eulogy for his tombstone inscription.
11 For his services, Tso recommended him for the brevet of provincial treasurer. C. John Stanley, *Late Ch'ing Finance: Hu Kuang-yung as an Innovator* (Cambridge, Mass., 1961), 9–13; *TWHK*, 'Memorials', 19:12
12 *Hu-nan t'ung-chih*, 193:9b; *HFT*, II, 159a–b.
13 *HFT*, II, 21b; *YWYT*, vol. 5, p. 18.

to work at Ma-wei regularly, despite Tso's suggestion that he divide his time between the two places.[14]

Subsequently, Tso recommended four others to work at Ma-wei. The first was Yeh Wen-lan, a leading Fukien gentryman and an expectant taotai of Kwangtung. A former comprador, he was familiar with foreign affairs, apparently knew a little English, and was known among some foreign circles. Because of his background and skills, he served Tso in much the same way as Hu Kuang-yung did. His management of military supplies was essential to Tso's campaign in Kwangtung.[15]

Another 'barbarian expert' was Huang Wei-hsüan (1828–73), an expectant prefect from Ningpo. Huang began his career as a 'writer' in the British consulate at Ningpo in 1853–6 and was described by the *North-China Herald* as 'most reliable and talented'. Later, he became quite knowledgeable about foreign affairs as he took part in surveying the waters at Hong Kong, Shanghai, Ningpo, and the Pagoda Anchorage just below Ma-wei. He was an obvious choice to assist Hu Kuang-yung in negotiating with the Frenchmen in the summer of 1866. Tso naturally wanted him to stay at the Navy Yard.[16]

Third came Pei Chin-ch'üan, an officer of the fifth rank, who had acquired a knowledge of navigation through practical experience and had earned quite a reputation for suppressing piracy and smuggling. Already, he had been put in charge of the steamer purchased by Fukien province for patrolling its waters. Now Tso wanted him to recruit youths from his native Ningpo (Chekiang province) for training on his boat so that experienced sailors would be on hand for the Navy Yard's new vessels.[17]

The last of this second group was Hsü Wen-yüan, a Fukienese and an expectant commissary of a provincial treasurer. He was a resourceful man, particularly clever at making Western-style guns, and was said to be acquainted, however superficially, with a large number of foreign books.[18]

With the service of these 'barbarian experts' and the close connection with the province through some of its officials, work on the Navy Yard was ready to begin. After the land had been purchased, two expensive projects were undertaken: the construction of an embankment and the raising of the ground by five feet. Both were necessary because of the

---

14 Stanley, *Late Ch'ing Finance*, pp. 9–11, 13–14; *HFT*, II, 48b–49.
15 *HFT*, II, 50, 574b; FO 228/596, 'Intelligence Report', no. 1; *TWHK*, 'Memorials', 19:12a–b.
16 *NCH*, 18 January 1871; *HFT*, II, 50.
17 *HFT*, II, 50a–b.
18 Ibid., 50b.

tides and the need to provide firm support for the heavy machinery and structures. Since Shen stubbornly refused official involvement while still in mourning, and d'Aiguebelle and Giquel were still in France, the project was overseen by Chou K'ai-hsi, while work on the site was supervised by a certain Po-chin-ta, an otherwise unidentified Russian.[19]

Without an adequate staff, progress was slow. Further, the officials detailed by Tso to work in the Navy Yard were still occupied with their normal duties at Foochow, several hours' journey from Ma-wei. Then, in the spring of 1867 a number of them, for reasons to be explained, were forced into temporary inactivity. Under the circumstances, little construction work had been completed when Shen assumed office in July 1867 and when Giquel returned from France a month later.[20]

Shen's assumption of office at Ma-wei

Shen officially took up duties the day his mourning ended. As noted, his power was heavily circumscribed, and the edict that made him director-general further limited his power vis-à-vis the high provincial officials:

Regarding all the measures to be carried out and the funds needed, Ying-kuei, Wu T'ang, and Hsü Tsung-kan are instructed to manage them satisfactorily and to consult with Shen Pao-chen on every occasion. Let there be no delay or mistake.[21]

Clearly, the officials at Foochow were vested with certain powers, and Shen could hardly run the Navy Yard without their active co-operation.

Experienced in provincial politics, Shen had no illusions. In fact, he foresaw far more difficulties than the edict suggested. On the day he took office (18 July 1867), he, as was customary, reported to the throne his arrival at the work place and expressed his view of the new assignment. Unlike many such memorials, which tended to be formal and perfunctory, Shen's discussed at length the problem at hand. Here, in this oft-quoted document, we have more than a glimpse of how he saw the Navy Yard and his role in it.[22]

With uncanny foresight, Shen identified seven difficulties he expected the novel Navy Yard to encounter. They will be examined here under four categories. The first was related to the European employees, particularly the French directors d'Aiguebelle and Giquel. In Shen's opinion,

---

19 Giquel, *Foochow Arsenal*, p. 14; *SWSK*, 4:3b; *HFT*, II, 43b, 69b. The land was bought for 240,000 taels.
20 *SWSK*, 4:3b.
21 *Shih-lu*, TC 186:20a–b.
22 *SWSK*, 4:1–4b.

Westerners were by nature suspicious and trusted only those whose credibility had been established. The two Frenchmen had been with Tso Tsung-t'ang for a long time and were aware of his sense of justice, loyalty, and courage. Shen, by contrast, was entirely new to them; his future relationship with them was therefore unpredictable at best. Further, d'Aiguebelle and Giquel had been promised a cash reward of 24,000 taels each on the timely completion of the project.[23] Because of this huge reward, there would be many who, wishing a share of this wealth, would try to ruin their good names. If the Chinese failed to manage the Navy Yard with a firm hand, all would come to nought.

Financial matters and corruption were Shen's next concern. Speaking from past experience, he recognized that financing the Navy Yard would be different from funding military operations: whereas the traditional army had learned to cope with delays and shortfalls in remittances, a modern enterprise such as the Navy Yard could be seriously jeopardized even if only one part of its production were held up by tardy cash flows. The rough estimates of expenditure previously made would compound this problem since they had already been found to be inadequate after only a few months of operation. Worse still, they had left out altogether the maintenance cost for the steamships that were to be built. Shen therefore urged everyone to look beyond immediate needs, make overall plans, look for long-term results, and not grudge the expense. Besides, the budget, adequate or not, involved millions of taels, and there would certainly be many who would want to line their pockets. To keep corruption under control, he recommended heavy punishment.

Shen's third concern had to do with his peculiar position as a member of the gentry holding office near his home-town. As a gentryman, he was expected to be under official control, yet as director-general of the Navy Yard, he had to deal with the officials on an equal footing. The situation was certainly conducive to conflicts, just as the militia commissioners (*t'uan-lien ta-ch'en*) of the 1850s who, as high-ranking gentrymen, often found themselves at odds with the provincial officials. In consequence, many failed in their tasks while their differences, even when arising out of genuine difficulties, were scandalized. Minor disagreements were then blown out of proportion. His position in the Navy Yard, Shen warned, could generate similar problems.

The local people, too, were a source of complications. Shen's popularity among them plummeted as he turned away the tide of ill-qualified job seekers and the flood of letters of recommendation written on their

---

23 'Des propositions d'exécution', article 11; *HFT*, II, 35.

behalf. In an instant he became the target of much protest. All he could do was to lament this state of affairs.[24]

Finally, Shen worried about the Chinese attitude towards workmanship. Chinese artisans, he noted, took pride in cutting labour and materials, whereas foreigners were thorough and always seeking improvements. As he emphasized:

There are not too many things we can learn from foreign countries, yet their skill in manufacture is most ingenious. This is not because the foreigners are exceptionally intelligent but because they are thorough and are ever after greater improvements. [They] will not be daunted by difficulties and will not be content with small results. This is an attitude we can learn from them.[25]

Shen was therefore less concerned with the foreigners not being conscientious in their instruction than with the Chinese not being diligent in their learning. In his view, the way to deal with this problem was to control the Chinese workmen with discipline and entice them with material rewards.

Shen was clearly concerned with the successful transfer of technology so that China could quickly become technologically independent. This, too, was Tso Tsung-t'ang's intention when he proposed the Navy Yard School, but it was Shen who used the memorial to draw the throne's attention to its importance, calling it the 'foundation of the Navy Yard'.[26] Whether his progressive view on this matter could be realized by the application of discipline and material incentives remained to be seen.

Throughout the memorial, Shen stressed that, in ability and reputation, he could not measure up to Tso. Confucian modesty aside, it is true that Tso was a governor-general and he only a former governor and a gentry leader – hence his long list of worrisome concerns. Shen thus began his new job with considerable apprehension. Having first placed his career in jeopardy, he now faced the difficulties of the unknown. Seen from the vantage point of a Confucian administrator, who tended to stress the human factor in public affairs, his concerns were essentially human in origin. Yet as one who embraced the practical statecraft persuasion, he studied the issues in practical terms as he took note of the problems surrounding modern production and the attitude of the Chinese workmen. Again, thanks to his practical bent, he was aware of potential administrative and institutional problems, especially weaknesses in the budget and financial arrangements. His observations on these matters were

24 This difficulty was recognized by the throne in an edict of 24 February 1868: 'Directing the Foochow Navy Yard as a gentry member is certainly no easy matter for Shen Pao-chen.' *Shih-lu*, TC 224:7b.
25 *SWSK*, 4:2b.   26 Ibid., 4:3b.

sharp and, as it turned out, prophetic. All of this demonstrates that his insistence on Confucian protocol – observing a full mourning – had not prevented him from giving the Navy Yard considerable attention and thought.

We shall close this section with a personal statement by Shen on the reasons he, 'given these seven difficulties, dare not discharge his duties lightly'.[27] The passage is filled with protestations of loyalty, sense of sacrifice, and rational explanations to the question posed earlier – why did he accept the appointment?

Given these seven difficulties, how dare [I] discharge [my] duties lightly. but . . . these are troublesome times. The empress dowager and the emperor work strenuously . . . [until, by the] middle of the night, they are weary and worn. If those [of us] who are ministers perversely employ [our] intelligence selfishly to avoid slander and making mistakes, then how can we repay our rulers and fathers, and keep our place between heaven and earth? Therefore, despite repeated vacillations, I dare not decline the job. I can only leave my reputation to the decision of man, and let heaven determine my failure or success. [I shall] exhaust my simple sincerity to repay one-ten-thousandth the bountiful mercy and kindness [of the throne]. What I can truly depend on is the imperial injunction which was so emphatically made and from which I learn that the way of self-strengthening has decidedly come from imperial opinion. Since [the emperor himself] could not help but take such great pains in inaugurating the present project on which our future benefit depends, he will not be moved by frivolous talk. All I hope for is that my colleagues will embrace the court's intentions as their own, so that they will not fear difficulties simply because the project has no precedent, or distance themselves from it because the idea did not originate from them. [If my hopes are fulfilled], then I can wipe my eyes and wait for the success of this project.[28]

Shen undoubtedly gave too much credit to the throne; he literally put his own ideas on self-strengthening into the emperor's mouth. This was his device to inform the throne and to steer it in the right direction. As for the profusion of clichés, to which the mandarinate was prone, one need not summarily dismiss them in Shen's case. He was one of the few who could back up his protestations of loyalty, sacrifice, and dedication by action. On the day he assumed office, he arrived at Ma-wei by steamship, signalling his commitment to modern naval technology, and a few days afterwards took up residence at Ma-wei 'so that he could supervise the work at close quarters'.[29] For a former provincial governor to accept the director-generalship of the Navy Yard and then move his residence there (rather than direct the project from the political centre and the more

27 Ibid., 4:3.   28 Ibid., 4:3a–b.   29 Ibid., 4:4; *HFT*, II, 73.

congenial surroundings of Foochow) is certainly one of the most significant symbolic gestures in the history of the Restoration.[30] In the remaining months of 1867 there was even more evidence of Shen's dedication to the cause as he defended the Navy Yard against its opponents and predators.

Chinese opposition

When Tso Tsung-t'ang left Foochow, peace was only a few months old and his great plans for the reconstruction of Fukien and Chekiang had barely begun. To ensure that his efforts would be continued after his departure, he sought imperial approval of their adoption and implementation. Admirable though his intentions were, his tactics were bound to provoke opposition from a provincial administration that had not always been friendly. And short of a guarantee from his successor that his measures would be carried out, Tso's successor would in all likelihood adopt a different policy or approach. Because the reforms were closely identified with Tso, their modification or abandonment could easily result in personal conflicts.

Tso tried to smooth out these transitional problems by leaving behind a number of his associates, along with instructions on how to implement his reforms. But this stratagem would only increase the chances of factional struggle if Tso's successor upheld different policies. The situation looked even more unstable when Governor Hsü Tsung-kan died in December 1866. The province now expected not one but two new men of high rank, each with his own advisers and personal aides, and both could prove hostile to Tso's reforms.

Even without these personnel changes, Tso's men would face much hostility because they had been so blatantly brought in to increase Tso's control over the province. Tso himself, though able, benevolent, and incorruptible, was prone to being autocratic, boastful, inflexible, and excessively critical, flaws that had made him many a political enemy.[31] Troubles thus arose the moment he left Foochow. Although their nature remains cloudy, it was serious enough for Chou K'ai-hsi, the leader of Tso' men, to contemplate resignation. Tso advised strongly against the idea, insisting that Chou, occupying the key posts of acting provincial treasurer and acting governor, was extremely important if his measures

---

30 Shen's example was followed by his successor, Ting Jih-ch'ang, who was also a former governor, and by a number of later directors-general, all of whom were of a lesser rank and stature.
31 Hsiao I-shan, *Ch'ing-tai t'ung-shih*, vol. 3, pp. 807–14; *Ch'ing-shih*, vol. 6, pp. 4765–6.

were to be implemented and campaign funds assured.[32] Developments at Foochow, however, led Chou to think differently.

By early 1867, anti-Tso forces had gathered considerable momentum. In February, an expectant taotai produced an anonymous placard claimed to have been thrown into his sedan chair. Since misdemeanours by high officials were detailed in the placard, Tartar General Ying-kuei felt obliged to transmit it to Peking. The first to come under attack was Tso himself, who, it was said, had staffed the Fukien likin administration with a large number of Hunanese and then appropriated part of its revenue to defray illegitimate expenses at the Ao-feng Academy, which he patronized. Allegedly, he had also abused his power by having two officials to support his sedan chair and, when ordered to the North-West, by deliberately mobilizing the gentry to keep him at Foochow.[33]

The next target, Chou K'ai-hsi, was accused of having accepted as a gift a housemaid from Prefect Li Ch'ing-lin and having used a subordinate to arrange for the disposal of his divorced concubine. Li, it was claimed, also begged Ying-kuei to appoint Chou acting governor. Then, Chou, along with acting provincial treasurer Hsia Hisen-lun and T'ai-wan Taotai Wu Ta-t'ing, used his authority to cover up maladministration by Hunanese officials, and all three illicitly kept personal bodyguards.

Since all of the accused were close associates of Tso Tsung-t'ang's, these vitriolic attacks were clearly a campaign to dislodge Tso's men from power.[34] While the allegations were being looked into in the next several months, a ditty, penned by a frustrated local scholar and targeted at the leaders of the Tso group, began to circulate:

> Pull-Out-Sinew is Wu's name, Fleece-You is the alias of Chou,
> Scrape-Your-Bone so Hsia is called, even stranger to behold.
> The threesome on each other's might rely,
> Amassing wealth and fame ev'rywhere they ply.[35]

The pressure mounted; work at the Foochow Navy Yard suffered. Chou had already ceased having an interest in a public career in Fukien. Among the others, Hsia Hsien-lun and Li Ch'ing-lin had the closest ties with the Navy Yard. Hsia was Chou's successor as acting treasurer, on

---

32 Tso was particularly dependent on Chou and the funds from Fukien because he feared that remittances from Chekiang and Kwangtung might not be as reliable. Tso to Chou, January–February 1867, in *TWHK*, 'Letters', 8:65b.

33 *Shih-lu*, TC 196:14b–15, 205:19–21.

34 Two other persons were also accused. Their relationship with Tso is unclear. Given the context, however, it is probable that they had been his men. One of them had distinguished himself in mopping up the Taiping rump in the Amoy area in 1865. *IWSM*, TC 32:7a–b, 10b–13b, 16b–17b; *TWHK*, 'Letters', 7:48b–49.

35 Lin Ch'ing-yüan, *Fu-chien ch'uan-cheng*, p. 22.

whom the regular flow of funds to the Navy Yard depended. Li, however, was involved in the day-to-day work at Ma-wei. Having served several years in the Commerce Bureau (T'ung-shang chü) of Fukien, his experience was valuable. He had already played a key role in purchasing the grounds for the Navy Yard.[36] But while the cloud of corruption and misdemeanour hung over these men, their activities ground to a halt.

Meanwhile, in March 1867, a rancorous debate developed in Peking over the Tsungli Yamen's proposal to add to the T'ung-wen Kuan a department of astronomy and mathematics, two traditional subjects used by the Yamen to disguise the introduction of Western scientific studies to complement the modern defence industries at Shanghai and Foochow.[37] Though started by a junior official, leadership in the Confucian fundamentalist attack was soon assumed by Grand Secretary Wo-jen, the 'high priest of Ch'eng-Chu Neo-Confucianism'.[38] The objection focused mainly on the recruitment of successful civil service examination candidates for the study of astronomy and mathematics. Their concentration on techniques (*chi-ch'iao*), so the argument went, would ruin their moral courage. In the words of Wo-jen, 'The way to uphold the foundation of the state is to emphasize propriety and sense of duty . . . not expedient schemes. The basic polity of the state [is to cultivate] people's morale and not technique'.[39] Therefore, only artisans and intelligent soldiers should be selected to study these subjects. Further, the T'ung-wen Kuan should cease employing 'barbarians' as teachers. If the scholars followed the 'barbarians', in a few years all the people would also follow them. If astronomy and mathematics had to be studied, let Chinese experts be hired to teach them. In sum, the integrity of the Confucian scholar and the way of the sages must be preserved at all cost.

The throne, in no uncertain terms, condemned the initial attack as misguided. The Tsungli Yamen, for its part, also refuted Wo-jen's argument at length. No matter, Wo-jen repeated some of his arguments in a second memorial on 21 April 1867. Annoyed at his intransigence,

36 On Hsia, see *Shih-lu*, TC 196:14b. On Li, a prefect of Hupei bearing the brevet of the third rank, see *HFT*, II, 565b, and *YWYT*, vol. 5, p. 59.
37 Prince Kung's memorial of 11 December 1866, in *IWSM*, TC 46:3–4b. Kung referred to the armament and shipbuilding industries in Shanghai and Chekiang. Obviously, he meant Shanghai and Foochow. For a study of the controversy, see Kwang-ching Liu, 'Politics, Intellectual Outlook, and Reform: The T'ung-wen Kuan Controversy of 1867', in Paul A. Cohen and John E. Schrecker, eds., *Reform in Nineteenth-Century China* (Cambridge, Mass., 1976), pp. 87–100.
38 The junior official was Censor Chang Sheng-tsao. *IWSM*, TC 47:15–16b. For Wo-jen's memorial see ibid., 24–25b, translated in Teng and Fairbank, *China's Response*, pp. 76–7. On Wo-jen, see Chang Hao, 'The Anti-foreign Role of Wo-jen (1804–1871)', *Papers on China*, 14 (1960), 1–29.
39 Translation by Kwang-ching Liu, 'Politics, Intellectual Outlook', p. 93.

the throne now ordered him to recommend a few Chinese mathematicians and set up a rival school. But he could not find any Chinese mathematicians.[40] This was not the end of the matter, however, for on 28 April he was humiliated by an imperial instruction to join the Tsungli Yamen, ostensibly so that he could gain some exposure to foreign affairs and *yang-wu*.[41] Because ministers of the Yamen were prohibited from submitting separate memorials expressing a different opinion, the appointment was also an attempt to silence him.[42] Unwilling and embarrassed, Wo-jen declined the honour and, later, repeatedly pleaded ill-health.[43]

At this juncture, in June, a junior official from Szechwan entered the debate, blaming the T'ung-wen Kuan for having disturbed heaven and brought drought and plague upon the capital. He thus called for its abolition and that of the Foochow Navy Yard and other modernizing projects as well. His incoherent and often ridiculous arguments need not detain us, but they provided the throne an opportunity to denounce Wo-jen personally, alleging that he was the instigator of these absurd polemics, or at least, by his action, had inspired them. Wo-jen was then ordered to take up his post at the Tsungli Yamen at the end of his sick leave. But on the day in question he reportedly fell off his horse, injuring his foot. He then excused himself and relinquished all his posts except that of grand secretary.[44]

In dealing with this clamorous debate, the Tsungli Yamen enjoyed strong support from the throne and was itself able to stand firm. Even Wo-jen, an imperial tutor, chancellor of the Hanlin Academy, and grand secretary, was unable to avoid imperial reproach. He was criticized for lacking precisely the virtues he was known to represent: uprightness and high principles.[45] Why was the throne prepared to go to such lengths to defend the T'ung-wen Kuan, and thus benefit the other modernizing efforts as well? Political considerations were certainly important. A prolonged, highly charged debate would polarize opinion and lead to factionalism. Already, a metropolitan official had accused the throne of entrapping Wo-jen by ordering him to set up a rival institution.[46] Besides, Empress Dowager Tz'u-hsi was genuinely concerned about the

40 *IWSM*, TC 47:16b–17; 48:10b–12, 15b, 18b–19b; *Shih-lu*, TC 199:9a–b.
41 Hao Chang, 'Anti-Foreign Role of Wo-jen', p. 13.
42 S. M. Meng, *The Tsungli Yamen: Its Organization and Functions* (Cambridge, Mass., 1962), pp. 31–2, 52–3.
43 *Shih-lu*, TC 199:16b–17, 203:13.
44 The official was Yang T'ing-hsi. *IWSM*, TC 49:13–24b, 24b–25b; *Shih-lu*, 205:18b–19; Hao Chang, 'Anti-foreign Role of Wo-jen', pp. 13–14.
45 On the virtues Wo-jen represented, see Hummel, *Eminent Chinese*, vol. 2, pp. 861–2.
46 *IWSM*, TC 49:25; *Shih-lu*, TC 203:11b–13b; Hao Chang, 'Anti-foreign Role of Wo-jen', p. 13. The official was Chung P'ei-hsien, a candidate reader of the Grand Secretariat.

fate of the modernizing projects, for however distasteful they were to her, they and their promoters constituted a new political force which could be used to bolster her own power.[47] Yet having defended the T'ung-wen Kuan and condemned Wo-jen, she was not prepared to offend the conservatives too deeply. The conservatives, too, were a force to be reckoned with, and one she would use in her political manoeuvres. Thus, as she criticized Wo-jen she did not reissue the call for the recruitment of scholars for the T'ung-wen Kuan, a central feature of the reform.[48] Without her full support, scholar-official opposition was allowed to take its toll. As the Tsungli Yamen reported, 'Ever since Wo-jen raised his objection to it, the scholar-officials at the capital and in the provinces have been gathering in groups and engaging in secretive discussions, conspiring to obstruct [the T'ung-wen Kuan].... As a consequence, no one came to your humble ministers' Yamen to take the entrance examination'.[49]

Whatever the immediate results of the debate, the ideas so poignantly expressed by the eminent Neo-Confucianist Wo-jen quickly became an ideological arsenal for those who opposed *yang-wu*. They could not but rouse the feelings of the traditionalist majority, which had been largely silent since the T'ung-chih era began. Though it is improbable that Wo-jen and his supporters were linked to the anti-Tso and anti–Navy Yard forces at Foochow, a political climate favourable to the traditionalists had been created.

At Foochow, Tso's followers and the Navy Yard staff, already uncertain about their future, must have been doubly dispirited by the fundamentalist broadside. But their fortunes took an even worse turn after Wu T'ang and Li Fu-t'ai (1807–71) began their new jobs as governor-general and governor in April.[50] Wu, bent on winning instant popularity and gaining control over the provincial administration, tried to reduce likin charges and relax the likin regulations. To do this, he would have to break the power of the Tso group. A liaison with the anti-Tso elements was soon

47 My interpretation here is drawn from the analyses of Tzu-hsi's response to crises and controversial issues by Immanuel C. Y. Hsü, *China's Entrance into the Family of Nations: The Diplomatic Phase, 1858–1880* (Cambridge, Mass., 1960), pp. 203–6, and Lloyd E. Eastman, *Throne and Mandarins: China's Search for a Policy during the Sino-French Controversy, 1880–1885* (Cambridge, Mass., 1967), pp. 210–19.
48 Kwang-ching Liu, 'Politics, Intellectual Outlook', pp. 96–7.
49 *IWSM*, TC 48:14.
50 Charles Sinclair, British consul at Foochow, in his letter to Alcock described Wu and Li as 'taciturn and reserved'. Letter of 26 April 1867 in FO 228/430, no. 26. Though hostility towards foreigners cannot always be equated with opposition to *yang-wu*, in this case it can be.

forged. And since Tso' men were a closely knit group holding office in various branches of government, demolishing their grip over likin would require Wu's tackling the party en bloc – hence his scheme to repeal all of Tso's reforms.[51]

Was Wu really such a corrupt and conspiring person? Unfortunately, our information on his activities in Fukien, coming largely from Tso and his associates, casts him in an unfavourable light. However, perhaps we can get a better sense of his character by examining his earlier career. A *chü-jen* of 1835, Wu rose from a position of mere district magistrate in 1849 to become the acting director-general of grain transport in 1861 – after twelve years of public service and without a *chin-shih* degree. Then, in 1863, he was made actual director-general of grain transport. His rapid rise was attributed to his successes against the Nien rebels in northern Kiangsu, where he spent many years. His achievements were frequently reported to the throne, and he was more than once commended by Tseng Kuo-fan. Immediately after northern Kiangsu was cleared of rebels, he attempted to restore the shipping of tribute grain on the Grand Canal, a move that pleased the court. Knowing where the interests of the central government lay, Wu made the 'right' efforts and earned numerous titular awards and quick promotions.[52] However, less favourable sources point to his corruption, sycophancy, and pandering to local interests. The following story, unsubstantiated though it may be, reflects contemporary views of his character.

Around the year 1854, when Wu was magistrate of Ch'ing-ho, the father of a low-ranking imperial concubine died while serving as a colonel in Hunan, leaving the family in dire financial straits. On her way to mourn her father's death, the concubine stopped at Ch'ing-ho and moored her boat alongside that of a certain colonel, an old acquaintance of Wu's. Wu sent his friend a gift of 300 taels, which the messenger delivered by mistake to the boat of the imperial lady. Irate, Wu wanted the money back. But he was stopped by a personal aide who advised him that the lady was a Manchu beauty and probably a noble personage, and it behooved him to cultivate her goodwill. Thereupon, Wu paid the lady a visit of condolence. He was rewarded when the imperial concubine, who was none other than Yehonala, gave birth in 1856 to the future emperor Tsai-ch'un (reign title, T'ung-chih); Wu rose rapidly to power

---

51 Tso to Hsia Hsien-lun and to Chou K'ai-hsi, April–May, to Shen and Wu Ta-t'ing, May–June, and to Liu Chien-ch'ing and Yang Ch'ang-chün, June–July 1867, all in *TWHK*, 'Letters', 9:28b–30, 34b–40.
52 Ts'ai Kuan-lo, *Ch'ing-tai ch'i-pai ming-jen*, vol. 1, pp. 417–21.

from then on, despite his being an 'official of no particular talent'. It was said that frequent impeachments against him were never given a hearing at Peking.[53]

Stories of this kind are prone to exaggeration, but the account does reflect a contemporary perception of Wu as opportunistic and corrupt, which was corroborated by a subsequent event: in 1868 he was impeached by Governor-General Liu Yo-chao of Yün-Kuei for gross corruption and was acquitted under very dubious circumstances.[54] His tampering with Fukien's likin and Tso Tsung-t'ang's programmes for demobilization and military supplies can therefore be viewed in the context of a career marked by corruption. Within days of his arrival, he turned to the Navy Yard and volunteered to Tartar General Ying-kuei the opinion that it would not stand a chance of success; even if it did, what good would it do? On another occasion, he showed Shen Pao-chen a letter from the Tsungli Yamen and said, 'This letter shows concern over our misuse of funds [at the Navy Yard]'. Shen perused the letter and found no such statement. It was a confidence trick.[55]

Why did Wu wish to harm the Navy Yard? Robert Hart once described him as a 'feng shui-ist fogey'.[56] Conservatism apart, Wu probably saw in the Navy Yard, with its huge budget and staff, a chance for peculation and patronage if only Tso's men could be ousted. Or he saw in it a symbol and, even more important, a rather independent stronghold of Tso's influence which he must break if his other schemes were to succeed. But as Shen pointed out as well, he was prejudiced. Having spent more than a decade in northern Kiangsu and having directed the tribute grain transport on the Grand Canal, Wu's sympathies and vested interests rested with that region, now challenged by the Navy Yard and

53 *Ch'ing-ch'ao yeh-shih ta-kuan*, comp. Hsiao Heng-hsiang-shih chu-jen, pseud. (Taipei, 1959), vol. 1, p. 70. This work is a collection of picturesque anecdotes of the Ch'ing period, drawn from 150 sources ranging from the serious to the frivolous. Since sources are not given for individual entries, the truth of the story cannot be corroborated. It is certain that some details are inaccurate. For example, the last office held by Yehonala's father was the intendancy of the Circuit of Southern Anhwei (not as a colonel in Hunan). He was dismissed in 1853 for abandoning his post in the face of an imminent Taiping attack and died soon after. Hummel, *Eminent Chinese*, vol. 1, p. 295.

54 Wu was cleared of all charges by his former colleague Li Hung-chang. The two were natives of Anhwei. Apparently, the throne sent Li to investigate the case because of his close associations with the accused. Lin Ch'ung-yung, *Shen*, pp. 295–6.

55 Tso Tsung-t'ang to Chou K'ai-hsi, April 1867, in *TWHK*, 'Letters', 9:28b–29b, and Shen's memorial, 20 October 1867, in *HFT*, II, 88b.

56 Hart's journals quoted in Richard J. Smith, 'Robert Hart and China's Early Modernization, 1862–1874', Paper delivered at the First International Conference on the History of the Chinese Maritime Customs, Hong Kong, December 1988. Cited with permission.

the possible use of its steamships for grain transport.[57] Whatever his real intent, his opposition to the Navy Yard found a ready chorus at Foochow:

> Levying likin knows no stress,
> For one wants ships to impress.
> With small benefits come much harm,
> Millions wasted, yet unarmed.[58]

At first, neither Tso nor Shen worried too much about the Navy Yard; they were more troubled by Wu's nullification of Tso's other undertakings. After all, it was an institution outside the provincial government, it was under an imperially appointed director-general, and Tso's name was still attached to all memorials emanating from it.[59] However, the strength of the Navy Yard, built upon personnel holding key posts in the provincial government, was soon to become its weakness. Chou K'ai-hsi, because of the allegations made in the anonymous placard, had already taken a sick leave. Wu now ordered that it be extended and proceeded to appoint someone else. Then, Yeh Wen-lan, who had been acquitted in a recent trial, was ordered to attend a retrial. Under these circumstances, both declined service in the Navy Yard – a bad official record could only hinder the exercise of authority.[60]

Of the other men in the Tso group, Li Ch'ing-lin suffered the most. He was impeached by Wu, dismissed, and sent home. Wu Ta-t'ing, for his role in exposing a case of corruption involving more than 50,000 taels, also found it necessary to retire. Others previously recommended by Tso left office one after another. Hu Kuang-yung, then in Chekiang, saw the writing on the wall and excused himself from Foochow.[61] With these personnel problems, construction work at Ma-wei suffered.

Tso and Shen found Wu's underhanded machinations difficult to handle. To fight Wu on his own terms would only galvanize the factional character of the struggle for which they would surely be blamed. For Tso, this was a sensitive matter since he was no longer an official of the region. He thus hoped to draw Wu into the open, advising Hsia Hsien-

---

57 *HFT*, II, 88b. Tso Tsung-t'ang noted that Wu, years before he came to Foochow, had opposed the idea of steamships. Tso to Chou K'ai-hsi, April 1867, in *TWHK*, 'Letters', 9:29.
58 Lin Ch'ing-yüan, *Fu-chien ch'uan-cheng*, p. 22. At this stage, likin revenues had little to do with financing the Navy Yard, but the enemies of defence modernization did not bother with such fine distinctions.
59 Tso to Hisa Hsien-lun and Chou K'ai-hsi, April–May 1867, in *TWHK*, 'Letters', 9:28b–29.
60 *HFT*, II, 88b–89.
61 *HFT*, II, 88b–89, 96; *Shih-lu*, TC 210:17, 214:5b–6b; *TWHK*, 'Letters', 9:37b; Wu Ta-ting, *Hsiao-yu-yü shan-kuan*, 8:14b.

lun to impress upon Wu that his (Tso's) reforms had had to emperor's blessing – to change them, Wu would have to memorialize the throne. If Wu remained intransigent, however, Tso promised to fight to the bitter end. He now regretted his and Shen's optimism about Wu's appointment only a short while ago.[62]

Throughout the summer of 1867 Tso and Shen groped for an opening for a counterattack. They realized that to take the initiative would be to fall into Wu's trap, yet Wu's opposition must be confronted head-on, or else a future recurrence could not be forestalled. Finally, in October, frustrated by the fact that nearly all the key posts in the Navy Yard were still unfilled, Shen impeached Wu on his own, ignoring the requirement for a joint memorial which would have to include Wu's signature![63] At the same time Shen wrote to the Tsungli Yamen vehemently condemning Wu's underhanded methods:

If Wu T'ang, as governor-general, contends that [the Navy Yard] should not be established under any circumstance, he ought to have memorialized against it the day it was approved by the court. If, on arrival in Fukien, he found that it did not stand a chance of success, why did he not memorialize [on the matter]? Instead, during the past few months, he has maintained an equivocal posture [in public] while secretly hindering [our work] in every way. `...` He has intentionally reversed everything established by his predecessor. The Navy Yard is only one among many.[64]

As a result of Shen's efforts, the throne ordered Chou K'ai-hsi, Yeh Wen-lan, Li Ch'ing-lin, and Hu Kuang-yung to resume their duties at the Navy Yard; but they were not reinstated to their posts in the provincial bureaucracy.[65] Thus, while the staffing needs of the Navy Yard were met, Wu T'ang's control over Fukien's administration was ensured. If the story about Wu's relationship with the empress dowager contains a grain of truth, we can appreciate the reasons for this compromise. By not condemning Wu publicly, the court had avoided the need to inflict a punishment it might find embarrassing.

Now that Shen had opened the attack, Tso had no further apprehensions about undesirable political fall-out from a counterattack. Tso essentially repeated Shen's accusations, but because of his prestige,

---

62 Tso to Hsia and to Chou, April–May 1867, to Liu Chien-ch'ing and to Yang Ch'ang-chün, June–July 1867, in *TWHK*, 'Letters', 9:28b–30, 37b, 39b–40.
63 Tso to Shen, July 1867, in *TWHK*, 'Letters', 9:34b–35b; Shen's memorial of 20 October 1867 in *HFT*, II, 88–89b. On 13 July the throne denounced the allegations contained in the anonymous placard (*Shih-lu*, TC 205:19–21), but even that was not enough to deter Wu – hence Shen's frustration.
64 *HFT*, II, 94a–b.
65 Edict of 12 November 1867, in *Shih-lu*, TC 214:5b–6b.

his memorial evoked a stronger response from Peking. The Tsungli Yamen now denounced Wu's actions while promising Shen that it would henceforth take it upon itself to protect the Navy Yard. A policy change at the top had taken place, and on 12 January 1868 Wu was transferred to the governor-generalship of Szechwan, nine months after he had come to Foochow.[66] Since the new post was of lesser importance, it was in effect a form of demotion, though Wu was spared public disgrace.[67] Still, because of his actions and the encouragement he gave to the anti-Tso and anti–Navy Yard forces, he had done great, long-term damage to the Navy Yard in a short but stormy nine-month incumbency. The Navy Yard's personnel connection with the provincial administration was virtually broken, and construction work on Ma-wei had been seriously delayed.

Local British and French reactions

The Foochow Navy Yard was the product of Sino-foreign co-operation, a concrete example of the 'Co-operative Policy' believed to have been the basis for Chinese–Western relations in the decade after the Second Opium War. The assumption behind this policy was that the interests of China and the Western powers would be much better served if China could maintain its sovereignty, peace, and prosperity, with foreign assistance if necessary. As Mary Wright put it:

By 1864 the term had a single accepted meaning: co-operation on the part of Great Britain, the United States, France, Russia, *and* China to secure the peaceful settlement of disputes and the gradual modernization of China. . . . The Co-operative Policy of the 1860's provided China with a substantial international guarantee against aggression or undue pressure, and with international aid to restore and strengthen the central power.[68]

But Wright also pointed out that the policy did not always work. As Rutherford Alcock, British minister at Peking, was wont to complain, 'If only means can be found of keeping from them [the Chinese] all foreign meddling and attempts at dictation, there is yet ground of hope'.[69] Indeed, the degree of co-operation at Ma-wei depended much on local

---

66 *HFT*, II, 104; *YWYT*, vol. 5, pp. 64–5; *Shih-lu*, TC 219:25a–b. According to Li Yüan-tu, an old-time friend and relative of Shen's, Wu's removal was intended to avoid further trouble (*T'ien-yüeh shan-kuan*, 14:12b–13).

67 For example, the salary of the Min-Che governor-general was 18,000 taels per annum, whereas that of the Szechwan governor-general was only 13,000. *Ta-Ch'ing chin-shen ch'üan-shu*, KH3, Autumn, 2:72b, 87b, 4:1.

68 Wright, *Last Stand*, pp. 21–2.

69 Quoted in ibid., p. 23.

foreign interests and personnel. We shall examine here the initial British and French reactions to the Navy Yard in the context of the Co-operative Policy.

Strictly speaking, the British were not an interested party in the Navy Yard, yet their enormous interest in China inevitably led to a concern with the implications of a successful Chinese naval undertaking. So when details of the Navy Yard's creation became known in September 1866, the British acting vice-consul at Foochow, Charles Carroll, lost no time in expressing his reservations to Tso. While 'commending the vigorous nature of this scheme', especially because the steamers built were 'destined for the suppression of piracy', he emphasized the huge expenses involved and advised prudence. As success was uncertain, he reasoned, the Chinese should first experiment with shipbuilding by renting the dock facilities of the British-owned John Forster and Co. The dock, he claimed, was 'large and commodious', quite adequate for the kind of work the Chinese had in mind, and conveniently located at Pagoda Anchorage, abutting the projected site of the Navy Yard. 'If the project succeeds it would then be time enough to open other docks', he concluded.[70]

Tso's negative reply to this unsolicited advice was predictable. He argued that the dock of John Forster and Co. was too small for his purpose. (It was about a tenth the size of his projected Navy Yard.) But Tso's main concern was Chinese sovereignty,[71] for although he had stressed to the foreigners that the ships built were solely for piracy suppression, his real intention was to strengthen China's defence against foreign incursion. Total Chinese control over the shipbuilding facilities was thus imperative.

Carroll was obviously jealous of the French success and hoped to recapture the initiative for the British by moving the Chinese naval project to British facilities. And being contemptuous of the Chinese, he did not think they could succeed, even with French help. He felt that a smaller scheme in the spirit of a pilot project would be more judicious. Charles Sinclair, who arrived at Foochow in November as the British consul, had a similar opinion.[72] Since the views of local consular officials ran counter to his own, Alcock gave them no encouragement.[73] So as Tso Tsung-t'ang went doggedly ahead in pursuit of his modern navy, the British could only watch.

70 Carroll to Tso, quoted in Tso to Carroll, 10 September 1866, and enclosed in Carroll to Alcock, 15 September 1866, in FO 228/408, no. 38.
71 Ibid.
72 In his 'Annual Report' for the year 1866 he stated, 'There are serious doubts entertained as to the success of the undertaking, which is planned on a most extravagant scale of expenditure'. Sinclair to Alcock, 9 March 1867, in FO 228/430, no. 15.
73 For Alcocks's views, see Wright, *Last Stand*, pp. 29–30, 251–2, 280–1.

The French position was very different. Up to the founding of the Navy Yard, they had had no interest in Foochow. Not a single French resident was to be found there. So in September 1866, when the Navy Yard was created and it was felt necessary to have a vice-consul at the port, the French had to appoint a local British merchant.[74] In consequence, there was no local French reaction to the founding of the Navy Yard until January 1867, when Baron Eugène Herman de Méritens arrived as the commissioner of the Foochow customs. M. de Méritens had been the interpreter at the French legation at Peking when it was established in 1861. Later he became the commissioner of customs at Ningpo, where he met Tso Tsung-t'ang, and had competed unsuccessfully with Paul d'Aiguebelle for Tso's favours in the purchase of a minting machine. He also failed in his quest for the directorship of Tso's modern troop-training programme.[75] His ambitions thwarted, de Méritens came to Foochow, possibly in the hope that he could continue his rivalry with d'Aiguebelle, since he now enjoyed certain advantages. As a Frenchman and the commissioner of customs, on whose receipts the Navy Yard depended, he had a special relationship with that institution. Whatever he said had to be taken seriously by the Chinese.

On 21 February 1867, de Méritens delivered a memorandum to Tartar General Ying-kuei debunking the 'dream actions' of d'Aiguebelle and Giquel, accusing them of deceiving Tso into sinking huge sums of money into an impossible project. In his opinion, five years were barely enough for the Chinese to learn French and English, let alone build ships. He therefore recommended the programme adopted by Kwangtung province which limited its goal to teaching Chinese navigational skills on steamers purchased from abroad. This would cut expenses by two-thirds. Besides, he argued, the Chinese did not need as many as sixteen ships, whose maintenance costs alone would run to 120,000 taels a month. The whole arrangement was flawed; hence the French minister refused to have anything to do with it. The only guarantee the Chinese had was the signature of the French consul-general, but he had no authority from his government to be the guarantor. So in case of default, who was to be held responsible? De Méritens therefore urged the Chinese to bring the project to a halt, or at least trim it down to building four ships over a period of three years, with a European staff reduced from thirty-seven to fifteen. Then, in his capacity as the commissioner of customs, he offered to remit the funds directly to the Navy Yard, without going through the

74 Richard F. Hamilton, the local agent of Messrs. Jardine, Matheson & Co. Carroll to Alcock, 1 October 1866, in FO 228/408, no. 41.
75 Ibid.; *HFT*, II, 64b, 68; Cordier, *Histoire des relations*, vol. 1, p. 112; *TWHK*, 'Letters', 7:14–18, 19b–22, 26b–27b.

Tartar general, and, for auditing purposes, to make monthly reports to the inspector-general of the imperial customs (Robert Hart), who in turn would report to the Tsungli Yamen. In this way, financial matters could be properly supervised, presumably by him, and overspending avoided. The whole project, as revised, could be accomplished with about 800,000 taels, not 3 million.[76]

De Méritens's memorandum came at an unwelcome moment. The fate of the Navy Yard was at its gloomiest in the early months of 1867. Tso had just left and Shen was still in mourning. Meanwhile, anti-Tso forces were gathering momentum. Morale among those connected with the Navy Yard was low. Further, d'Aiguebelle and Giquel were still in Europe, unavailable to give advice on the more technical aspects of de Méritens's criticism, some of which might have been correct.

Ying-kuei, now practically the only high official left to deal with the matter, must have been flustered by de Méritens's argument. As Tartar general and superintendent of customs, his interests and authority were also threatened by the proposal to by-pass him in transmitting funds from customs to the Navy Yard. Besides, he believed that the project was correctly conceived and should not be altered. So without addressing the issues raised by de Méritens, which, as we shall see, were not entirely without merit, he decided that the Frenchman's intent was sinister: 'The moment he took over the post of commissioner of customs, he plotted to barge into the Navy Yard in order to make a profit for himself'.[77]

The Tsungli Yamen then lodged a complaint with the French minister, M. Henri de Bellonet, who, to his credit, lost no time in denouncing de Méritens for his machinations.[78] The latter countered by claiming that Robert Hart had secured for him authorization from the Tsungli Yamen to manage the Navy Yard jointly. Shen Pao-chen thought the claim ludicrous, but to prevent it from having an adverse effect on the project, he, through the Tsungli Yamen, had Hart deny its veracity.[79] Thus, unlike the drawn-out battle against Wu T'ang, the de Méritens episode fizzled out in a matter of months, but some of the issues he raised were perhaps no less significant.

The French minister, in fact, agreed with de Méritens on a number of points. He certainly felt that the Chinese could not reach their goals in less than twenty years. And, indeed, if the project failed, or any of the Frenchmen embezzled funds, who could be held responsible? Earlier,

76 *HFT*, II, 65–7.
77 Ying-kuei to Tsungli Yamen, 27 March 1867 (Peking), in *HFT*, II, 64b–5.
78 Bellonet to Tsungli Yamen, 1 April 1867, in *HFT*, II, 67b–68.
79 Shen to Tsungli Yamen, July 1867, and the Yamen's reply of 13 August, in *HFT*, II, 76b–77, 78b.

before the contracts with Giquel and d'Aiguebelle were signed, Tso Tsung-t'ang had tried to prevail upon the French consul-general at Shanghai, de Montmorand, to act as guarantor on behalf of the French government. But both de Montmorand and de Bellonet made it clear at the time that the two French officers were acting completely on their own; the French government was not a party to the enterprise. In fact, in an attempt to exonerate the French government from future failures and to avoid international rivalry, de Bellonet favoured a multinational navy yard modelled on the Imperial Maritime Customs Service. Still, he wished the project well and promised to help settle any difficulties that might arise in accordance with the provisions of the contracts.[80]

Because de Méritens's actions had been roundly denounced and the Chinese had concluded that his motives were dishonourable, the merit of his criticism was glossed over. Jurisdiction over misdemeanours or delinquency by European employees of the Navy Yard, a point highlighted by de Bellonet, was left unresolved. It was to haunt the Chinese authorities for years to come. Two other important issues concerning the allocation and maintenance of ships built at Ma-wei also proved to have serious long-term implications. Although Tso Tsung-t'ang once loosely referred to the deployment of ships by other provinces, no concrete plan was made. Without such a plan or an understanding with other provinces, four or five vessels would indeed suffice. As regards steamship maintenance costs, subsequent developments showed that de Méritens's estimates were far too high. But the problem was real, and Shen, perhaps alerted to it by de Méritens's memorandum, also alluded to this matter in his memorial of 18 July 1867. But he was unable to provide any solution in the absence of more informed advice from d'Aiguebelle and Giquel. The matter was left unattended until it was too late.

Meanwhile when Giquel arrived at Paris in February 1867, he was confronted by the naval minister with charges that the Navy Yard was created by a Chinese official without imperial approval and that the project, being doomed to failure, would only harm China and waste its money. According to Giquel, the allegations had originated from de Méritens and forwarded to Paris by de Bellonet. Previously, the latter had also questioned the advisability of French officers serving in an enterprise of uncertain status. So while the case was being investigated,

---

80 *HFT*, II, 13–14, 64–7, 67b–69. As de Méritens's memorandum reached Peking, however, de Bellonet was informed, erroneously, that the contracts contained a reference to d'Aiguebelle acting under orders from the French emperor. This immediately prompted a refutation from the French minister. For the exact wording of the reference, which appeared in a petition from Giquel and d'Aiguebelle to Tso and not in the contract, see ibid., 30a–b.

Giquel was asked to resign from the French navy and was prohibited from personnel recruitment. By the time he was cleared of the charges by a report from the French naval commander in China, it was already June. Valuable time had been lost and Giquel's return to China delayed by more than four months.[81]

Conclusions

In its first year of existence, the Navy Yard faced serious opposition and attempts to undermine its administrative integrity. Thanks to the combined efforts of the throne, the Tsungli Yamen, Tso Tsung-t'ang, Ying-kuei, and Shen, it weathered the storm. We have seen the Tsungli Yamen in one of its finer moments: it dealt firmly with the T'ung-wen Kuan controversy and Wu Tang's clandestine attack. By January 1868, Wu had been removed and all the officials appointed to the Navy Yard had taken up their jobs. Hu Kuang-yung's continued absence was not related to the situation at Foochow. Shen, however, because of his stubborn adherence to Confucian protocol, deprived the Navy Yard of vital and decisive leadership, which was so greatly needed in this turbulent interregnum. There is no question that he had participated unofficially in managing its affairs. Still, without assuming his full authority, he could not deal promptly and effectively with Wu and the anti-Tso elements, although, given the underhanded methods used, the opposition would have been difficult to handle.

In a sense, despite the outcome of the T'ung-wen Kuan controversy and the power struggle at Foochow, it was Wo-jen and Wu T'ang who had won the day. In the case of Wo-jen, this was so not because of any new light he might have shed on the antiforeign, anti-*yang-wu* position but because he, an eminent scholar and a powerful figure, was identified with that position in a noisy debate. His public stance changed the political climate of the time. As Kwang-ching Liu writes, 'In the T'ung-wen Kuan episode we see in fact the beginnings of the *ch'ing-i* politics that was to develop further in the following decade'.[82] In Wu T'ang's case, his 'victory' came from the permanent damage he inflicted on the Navy Yard personnel system. Without highly placed men holding office at both Foochow and Ma-wei, the Navy Yard's close link with the provincial government was effectively severed.

In the battle against Wu T'ang, the limitations of Shen's power were

---

81 Ibid., 68b, 97b–100b. For a narrative of what went on in Paris, see Leibo, *Transferring Technology*, pp. 79–82.
82 Liu 'Politics, Intellectual Outlook, and Reform', p. 98.

starkly exposed. Even as an imperial appointee, he was not able to ward off provincial intervention. The strong support of Tso Tsung-t'ang and the Tsungli Yamen was indispensable, at least in this instance.

The court itself, never intending to throw all its weight behind the *yang-wu* undertakings, was forever looking for a middle ground, sometimes even when ideology was not at stake. The mild treatment of Wu T'ang is a case in point. So even as the Tsungli Yamen pledged to defend the Foochow Navy Yard more vigorously in the future, the court continued to send to Fukien a succession of high officials who were not sympathetic to its needs.[83] But then should the court, when appointing provincial officials, have even considered the well-being of the Navy Yard, which supposedly was not part of Fukien's administration? The ambivalence of the Navy Yard's imperial status proved to be an even greater problem later on.

Sino-foreign understanding did not improve noticeably as a result of the Chinese pursuit of *yang-wu*. In fact, the establishment of the Foochow Navy Yard created a new source of tension. The attitude of the British consular officials and the behaviour of the French commissioner of customs tended to confirm Chinese fears. The foreigners' meddling and biased advice, both real and perceived, served only to heighten Chinese sensitivity to the problem of sovereignty. Consequently, they jealously guarded their own creation, the Foochow Navy Yard, even from criticism that might have had some merit.

The Co-operative Policy remained an ideal, too lofty and too vague. As such, it was easier to implement at Peking than at the local level. De Bellonet, though not without his reservations and certainly cautious in the extreme, was ultimately in favour of the Navy Yard because of the large French presence in it; Alcock, in view of his attitude towards the introduction of railways and telegraphy in China, could not have been opposed to it; Robert Hart was almost euphoric over it.[84] Though they

---

83 E.g., Tartar General Wen-yü (1868–76) and Governor-General Li Ho-nien (1871–6). In my earlier work, I stated that, after Wu T'ang, Peking did not appoint any more officials *overtly* hostile to the Navy Yard. I have since revised my view. David Pong, 'Modernization and Politics in China as Seen in the Career of Shen Pao-chen (1820–1879)', Ph.D. diss., University of London, 1969, p. 136.

84 Stanley F. Wright, *Hart and the Chinese Customs* (Belfast, 1950), p. 493. Hart's earlier reaction to the Navy Yard has been debated. Steven Leibo claims that Hart first wanted to put it under the Maritime Customs Service and, failing that, conspired with de Méritens to seize control of it. The claim lacks full documentation. Richard Smith, a specialist on Hart, finds no evidence of Hart's role in the plot, although he admits that the Irishman was not above conspiracy at times. Leibo, *Transferring Technology*, pp. 84, 87; Smith, 'Robert Hart'.

exercised a degree of moderation over their local representatives, they could not curb their excessive zeal or personal ambition. For the next few years, foreign, particularly French, interference continued to challenge Shen's authority and the interests of his establishment at Ma-wei.

7

The Foochow Navy Yard: administration and personnel

In the closing months of 1867, work at Ma-wei began to see substantial progress. The senior staff was now able to attend to the business at hand. The European engineers and mechanics also began to trickle in from October on. The tasks ahead were to assume far greater complexity than the realms of provincial politics, although relations with Fukien continued to be a major factor. This chapter focuses on Shen's organization and management of the Chinese administrative staff and the European engineers, mechanics, and instructors. Other developments will be dealt with later.

The administrative staff was drawn mainly from the local scholar-gentry class. As a leading gentryman, Shen was keenly aware that a staff composed of such men would be open to nepotism and corruption. But the gentry-scholars posed problems that were far more intricate and subtle. First, given their social and intellectual upbringing, they might prove wanting as managers of a modern enterprise. Second, there was the allure of better jobs elsewhere. It is true that the Navy Yard, headed by an imperial director-general, offered attractive new jobs for the growing number of unemployed or underemployed gentry in the post-Taiping era. But capable men who had acquired some expertise in a modernizing enterprise – the so-called *yang-wu* experts – were as much in demand elsewhere as at Ma-wei. Moving to another enterprise under a different patron might appeal to some of them. But the modern enterprises, not being organized under a single superstructure, offered little opportunity for upward mobility. The civil service still held the strongest attraction for the able and ambitious few. Although the chances of getting an appointment in the regular bureaucracy were slim, some gentrymen in the Navy Yard continued to regard officialdom as their ultimate career objective, thus sapping their dedication and self-esteem as managers of a modern enterprise.

Managing the European staff presented a different set of problems. The Chinese administrators and the Europeans, though total strangers, had to work closely together if the Navy Yard was to succeed. Mutual trust between them had to be quickly established. At the very least, contract obligations and the foreigners' rights had to be upheld, just as Chinese control had to be preserved. But the contracts did not provide for all contingencies; Shen had to define his authority as he went along. Beyond that, he also had to cultivate the goodwill of the foreigners. In these matters, as in managing the Chinese staff, there were factors beyond his control. A change of mood in Sino-French relations elsewhere in the empire, for example, could have repercussions at Ma-wei. These are the problems we shall examine in this chapter.

Shen and his Chinese staff

As an imperial appointee holding office outside the regular bureaucracy, Shen's charge was defined mainly in terms of the ultimate goals of the Navy Yard. The ways and means to realize these objectives were left largely to his ingenuity. Funds, of course, had been earmarked for the purpose, and they were to be funnelled through the provincial government. In exchange, Shen was to consult the provincial leadership whenever the need arose, but the manner in which he was to do this was not specified. In character, these arrangements were similar to those in which Tseng Kuo-fan found himself as imperial commissioner in the early 1860s; as we have seen, they were not always followed or possible to follow. Much of Shen's relationship with the powers that be at Foochow depended on the individuals and on the resources available. In the event of difficulties, Shen's only recourse was to seek further instructions from Peking. We shall return to this point later.

Within the Navy Yard, Shen enjoyed full decision-making and disciplinary powers. To be sure, when he took office, the goals of the Navy Yard had already been set by the contracts and most of the key staff positions filled by men recommended by Tso Tsung-t'ang; but in implementing the contracts and managing the staff, there was room for personal initiative. This was certainly true when it came to organizing and utilizing the Chinese personnel.

In not being a regular civil servant, Shen enjoyed additional advantages as well: in recruiting, deploying, and rewarding his staff, he was not always hamstrung by rigid bureaucratic rules. The wisdom with which he exercised this freedom was vital to the Navy Yard.

The role of the ranking Chinese staff was largely administrative and managerial. As spelled out in the contracts and summarized by Giquel, 'The Chinese are entrusted with the enforcement of discipline, the payment of their men, and, in the workshops, with the control of the materials which go in and come out; [whereas] the direction of the works and of the instruction belongs to the Europeans'.[1] The organization of the Chinese staff reflected this functional separation.

At the top of the Navy Yard administration, according to Giquel, was a 'high Committee of Supervision' made up of Shen, the Foochow Tartar general, the governor-general of Fukien and Chekiang, and the governor of Fukien.[2] Since all three provincial officials had been instructed by the throne to consult with Shen and the funds for the Navy Yard were managed by them, it is natural that they should take an interest in the works at Ma-wei. Whether they did so was entirely a matter of personal disposition. On critical issues, however, they could be ordered by the court to report to Peking. In either case, they acted as individuals rather than as a committee. The day-to-day supervision of the Navy Yard rested entirely with Shen and his assistants.

In fact, other than Shen, the highest officials directly involved in the management of the Navy Yard were the *t'i-tiao* (assistants to the director-general). There were usually two such officials. It will be recalled that, in the first instance, Tso recommended to Shen three persons – Chou K'ai-hsi, Hu Kuang-yung, and Yeh Wen-lan. After some deliberation, Shen picked Chou and Hu.[3] Since Chou was then the acting provincial treasurer, the financial interest of the Navy Yard was put in his hands. And Hu, because of his experience and connections, was put in charge of purchasing materials, receiving the Europeans, hiring Chinese work-

1 Giquel, *Foochow Arsenal*, p. 13; *HFT*, II, 31–32b; 'Contrat d'engagement des ingénieurs', in MM BB4 1555 17/5/2 (Chinese: *HFT*, II, 39–42b).
2 Giquel, *Foochow Arsenal*, p. 14. Captain Pierre Véron of the French navy, drawing his information from Giquel, stated in 1870 that this 'comité superieur' included Tso Tsung-t'ang ('Rapport de M. le Commandant Véron', BB4 1555 17/5/33). Though Tso's name, along with the other three, was invariably attached to Shen's memorials, his involvement was nominal.
3 Shen's memorial of 20 October 1867 (Foochow), in *HFT*, 88a–b. There were only two *t'i-tiao* at this point. As Shen wrote, 'Therefore, Tso ... discussed with me and appointed Chou K'ai-hsi and Hu Kuang-yung as *t'i-tiao*. Further, he memorialized that the services of Yeh Wen-lan ... be also made available to me'. Yeh became the general manager. John Rawlinson suggests that all three were made *t'i-tiao*. Lin Ch'ing-yüan also states that there were three *t'i-tiao*: Hsia Hsien-lun, Wu Ta-t'ing, and Hu Kuang-yung. Obviously, he refers to a later period. In any case, Hu never took office, and the only time there were three such officials was brief, in late 1869 and early 1870. Lin also errs in saying that Hu was replaced by Chou (instead of Hsia). Rawlinson, *China's Struggle*, p. 105; Lin, *Fu-chien ch'uan-cheng*, pp. 77–8.

men, and establishing the School.[4] Their function was therefore defined according to their special abilities.

Because of Wu T'ang's machinations, Chou did not report for duty until December 1867. Hu had arrived from Chekiang a little earlier, only to depart in less than a month, being preoccupied with Tso's Procurement and Forwarding Office at Shanghai. He was never mentioned again as having served at Ma-wei. To replace him, Shen, in February 1868, chose Hsia Hsien-lun (d. 1879), an expectant taotai and acting provincial treasurer of Fukien.[5] Hsia, too, was Tso's protégé, but he was no stranger to Shen, the one-time governor of his home province. Though himself a mere *chien-sheng*, a purchased title, he came from a distinguished lineage of Nanchang, which boasted numerous *chin-shih* degree holders and many more local leaders. Among them was Hsia T'ing-ch'ü, a key figure in the Nanchang antimissionary incident of 1862.[6]

Hsia was a worthy *t'i-tiao*. Shen valued him for his conscientiousness, and the British consular officials on Taiwan spoke of him as 'intelligent and energetic' and having a 'reputation of being a safe and cautious man, not eager for money, and considerate to his subordinates'.[7] As acting provincial treasurer during much of 1868 and 1869, he strengthened the Navy Yard's ties with Foochow, especially the financial ones. He thus performed the role originally intended for Chou K'ai-hsi. But as a replacement for Hu Kuang-yung, he was less adequate. Although he had served in the Commerce Bureau (T'ung-shang chü) of Fukien,[8] his strength lay in civil administration and he lacked the experience and connections Hu commanded.

In any event, before his tenure as acting provincial treasurer ended in mid-1869, Hsia could not spend much time at Ma-wei. Partly because of this and partly because an opportunity had arisen, Shen had Wu Ta-t'ing join the ranks of *t'i-tiao* in April 1868. Wu had been the T'ai-wan taotai on Tso Tsung-t'ang's recommendation. Tso had considered that island to be of great strategic value in China's defence, but Wu accepted the job with great reluctance because of its remoteness. So when pressured

4 *HFT*, II, 21b.
5 *Shih-lu*, TC 214:6a–b; *HFT*, II, 117a–b.
6 Tso's memorial of TC 2.8.2 (13 September 1863) in YCT, TC 23/8 *shang*; *Shih-lu*, KH 98:17; *Nan-ch'ang fu-chih*, 'chuan-shou': 3; *Ming Ch'ing li-k'o chin-shih t'i-ming pei-lu*, vol. 4, pp. 2534, 2547, 2570, 2575.
7 *HFT*, II, 117; Herbert J. Allen to Thomas Wade, 22 April 1875, and Thomas Watters to Wade, 8 August 1876, in FO 228/554, Tamsui: no. 7 and 228/570, Takow: no. 8, respectively.
8 Herbert J. Allen to Thomas Wade, 22 April 1875, and Thomas Watters to Wade, 8 August 1876, in FO 228/554, Tamsui: no. 7 and 228/570, Takow: no. 8, respectively.

by Wu T'ang and his own poor health, he resigned, offering Shen the chance to bring him to the Navy Yard. Wu did not report for duty until August 1869, however, after he had fully recovered from his illness.[9]

Wu was a scholar (a *chü-jen* of 1855) and an able administrator. But it was his dedication and patriotic sentiments that Shen most appreciated.[10] His previous career also revealed strong practical statecraft (*ching-shih*) leanings.[11] He was a valuable addition to the Navy Yard.

Thus, in mid-1869, with Wu and Hsia joining Chou K'ai-hsi, the Navy Yard enjoyed its heyday of administrative talents. But this was not to last. In early 1870, Chou was recruited by Tso Tsung-t'ang to assist him in his campaign.[12] Then, in November, Wu's fifteen-month incumbency also ended when he was asked by Tseng Kuo-fan to train the incipient squadron at the Kiangnan Arsenal. Tseng was well aware of Wu's ability when the latter was an officer in Anhwei in the early 1860s. When Wu was in Tientsin on Navy Yard business in 1870, Tseng discussed foreign affairs extensively with him and was greatly impressed – hence the request. For Wu, the move meant not only an advancement and a chance to serve perhaps the greatest statesman of the time but also a more challenging assignment. At Ma-wei, he had learned a great deal about naval construction and training, but the naval training programme had already been entrusted to d'Aiguebelle (see the next section). Wu was happy to go.[13]

During the next two and a half years, the Navy Yard's senior staff suffered further attrition. In October, just as Wu was about to leave, Shen was once again in mourning, this time after his father's death. Despite his long absence, which lasted till January 1873 (twenty-seven months), the posts vacated by Chou and Wu were not filled; the Navy Yard was simply put under the charge of Hsia Hsien-lun, although he was to consult with Shen regularly.[14]

Shen's return to office in early 1873 was soon followed by the depar-

---

9 Wu Ta-t'ing, *Hsiao-yu-yü shan-kuan*, 8:14–15; *TWTC*, vol. 2, p. 351; *YWYT*, vol. 5, pp. 73, 87; *HFT*, II, 159a–b.

10 On Wu's death, Shen wrote: '[In 1870, Wu] was transferred to take charge of the training programme at the Kiangnan Arsenal. From the outset, he used only Chinese'. Elsewhere, Shen reported that Wu gradually replaced foreign instructors with Chinese. *SWSK*, 7:54a–b; *HFT*, III, 147b.

11 *Hu-nan t'ung-chih*, 193:9b; *Ch'ing-ch'ao hsü wen-hsien t'ung-kao*, 224:9709b; Wu Ta-t'ing, *Hsiao-yu-yü shan-kuan*, 8:14–15.

12 Wu Ta-t'ing, *Hsiao-yu-yü shan-kuan*, 9:15; *TWHK*, 'Memorials', 33:38–39b, 43:94. Chou died two years later (2 July 1871), aged forty-three. *TWHK*, 'Letters', 11:36b.

13 *IWSM*, TC 77:8–9b; *Ch'ing-ch'ao hsü wen-hsien t'ung-kao*, 224:9709b; Memorials of Li Hung-chang and Shen Pao-chen, KH 3.8.10 (16 September 1877) and KH 4.2.25 (28 March 1878), in YCT, KH 3/8 *shang* and KH 4/2, *t'se* 4.

14 *YWYT*, vol. 5, pp. 94–5, 101.

ture of Hsia, who became the taotai of T'ai-wan. In the last two years of Shen's office, two other *t'i-tiao* were mentioned, but the dates of their appointment are uncertain. They were Wu Chung-hsiang (d. 1891) and Liang Ming-ch'ien (1826–77). Wu was a native of Foochow and Shen's brother-in-law. A *chü-jen* of 1855, he had acquired some local prominence as a militia leader in Taiping days. He had also held several positions as subdirector of schools in Fukien. In 1867 he was recruited by Shen to serve in the Navy Yard secretariat. In 1874–5, when Shen was preoccupied with the troubles on Taiwan, he was left in charge of the Navy Yard.[15]

Liang, also a Foochow gentrymen, had had a successful career before joining the Navy Yard. A *chin-shih* of 1859, he had served as a second-class secretary in the Board of Civil Appointments until his self-imposed retirement to look after his aged mother at Foochow. He taught for a living and was a tutor to Shen's fourth son, Yü-ch'ing. In 1867, he became Shen's personal assistant (*mu-yu*) at the Navy Yard and played an important role in its early stages. He spent his days with the European mechanics in the workshops studying the machines and rendering technical terms into Chinese. Without his contributions, Shen would not have been able to gain much technical knowledge or to write his detailed reports to Peking.[16]

The departure of Chou K'ai-hsi, Wu Ta-t'ing, and Hsia Hsien-lun in 1870 and 1873, and the rise of Wu Chung-hsiang and Liang Ming-ch'ien around 1874, symbolize the completion of the transition from Tso to Shen. The importance of this transition should not be overstressed. After all, the men introduced by Tso were not driven away by Shen; he valued them. They were simply lured away either by more powerful men with more to offer or by the civil service. That Shen should replace them with men of his choice was only natural.

In his report, Giquel spoke of a 'consultative committee' under Shen. John George Dunn, a Briton who had wide-ranging connections in the foreign commercial and diplomatic communities, also referred to a 'committee of four mandarins'.[17] The membership of this 'consultative committee' is not clear. Presumably designed to oversee day-to-day operations, it most likely included all the *t'i-tiao*, the general manager

15 Shen Tsan-ch'ing, 'Chia-p'u', p. 64; *MHHC*, 69:32a–b; *HFT*, II, 524.
16 *MHHC*, 43:13; *FCTC:LCH*, vol. 3, p. 291.
17 Giquel, *Foochow Arsenal*, p. 14; Dunn, 'Foochow Arsenal – description of the', FO 233/85, no. 3, p. 3. Dunn's report of 9 November 1873 drew heavily on Giquel's *Foochow Arsenal*, in either its draft form or its original French manuscript, but he also added his own observations.

(see later), and possibly one or two of Shen's top personal assistants (*mu-yu*).

Below the *t'i-tiao* was a general manager (*tsung-chien-kung*) in charge of daily operations. This office, created by Shen, was filled by Yeh Wen-lan, a Fukienese and a former comprador, who held the post from July 1867 to the autumn of 1876. Shen could not have made a better choice. Yeh had served Tso Tsung-t'ang earlier in arms supplies. Tso spoke of him as sincere, unaffected, and always expeditious in carrying out his duties. And thanks to his previous career as comprador, he had some command of English, was familiar with construction work, had wide business contacts, and, above all, favoured various types of modernization, including mechanized coal mining. At Ma-wei, Yeh's responsibility included the procurement of materials such as bricks and timber for both yard and ship construction. For this purpose, he took his men, some thirty of them, on buying trips up and down the Fukien coast, to Taiwan, and to far-away places like Singapore and Siam.[18] He was therefore doing what would have been Hu Kuang-yung's job had the latter stayed. Though he was introduced by Tso to the Navy Yard, it was Shen who made the best use of his talents. The record shows that he was an energetic official.

The thirty-some officers placed under Yeh were probably engaged in buying materials on a full-time basis. Seven were said to have travelled to Hong Kong regularly, and one spent extended periods of time on Taiwan to acquire coal and timber. Because of the constant demand for good-quality timber from Burma, the next logical step for Shen was to post a permanent timber agent at Rangoon.[19] For a government-run industry, this was a significant departure from past practice and a unique appointment in the 1870s.

The Secretariat, with a staff of at least eleven, was headed by two chief secretaries. Several were specially detailed to deal with 'foreign relations', presumably relations with the European staff. Two such officials were attached to Giquel's office. It is worth noting that one of them was Wang Pao-ch'en, a Fukien *chü-jen* of 1859, who, in 1867, if not earlier, favoured treaty revision and the sending of Chinese envoys abroad – ideas far ahead of his time. In addition, there was a bursary with two chief accountants and a small team of clerks serving in various departments.[20]

18 A. Frater to Hugh Fraser, 1 February 1877, 'Intelligence Report No. 1', in FO 228/596; *HFT*, II, 50, 117b, 157a–b; *IWSM*, TC 53:12–15b; *YWYT*, vol. 5, pp. 58–9; *TWHK*, 'Memorials', 19:12a–b; *NCH*, 1 December 1876.
19 *HFT*, II, 157a–b, 559–61; *Ch'uan-cheng tsou-yi hui-pien* (n.p., n.d.; last document dated 10 April 1902), 5:10.
20 *HFT*, II, 558–66; Giquel, *Foochow Arsenal*, p. 34. On Wang, see *FCTC:LCH*, vol. 3, p. 304; *MHHC*, 43:14; *IWSM*, TC 53:19b–22.

Among the junior ranks were more than thirty men in charge of the workshops, sawmills, storehouses, the three shipbuilding slips, and the famous Labat patent slip. In all, more than sixty staff members and foremen were given supervisory power at the work place. In 1875, about twenty of them were commended for having performed their disciplinary or inspectoral duties well. Another twenty or so were said to have acquired proficiency in Western methods of shipbuilding and marine engineering.[21] But the organization of these men left something to be desired. Their tasks were categorized according to the workshops to which they had been assigned (e.g., supervisor of the foundry), and not according to particular technical or scientific fields (e.g., metallurgy), an arrangement which would have encouraged them to pursue knowledge in these subjects as recognized, legitimate disciplines. The approach may well have reflected a preference for traditional practices or simply an inadequate understanding of the nature of modern science.

Finally, an unknown number of gentry-scholars were attached to the Navy Yard School either as instructors or administrators. Among these was Wang Yüan-chih (1843–1917), a lower gentryman, who took the opportunity to learn French, sat for an annual examination beside the regular students, and became sufficiently proficient to serve as translator. Between him and a certain Tseng Lan-sheng, books on mathematics and gunnery were rendered into Chinese.[22]

The scale of the Navy Yard project was such that by August 1868 the administrative staff numbered more than 100. By late 1873, if not earlier, the number reached 130.[23] The administrative structure and organization must have been more complex than presented here. Besides, many performed important functions but were not mentioned in connection with specific offices. For instance, Liang Ming-ch'ien, before he became a *t'i-tiao*, was never described as an office-holder. Similarly, Huang Wei-hsüan had participated in contract negotiations with the Frenchmen in 1866. He was also involved in labour recruitment and, in 1869, was

---

21 *HFT*, II, 563b–567b.
22 Wang was a native of Chekiang but had moved to Foochow at the age of fourteen. Liao Yü-wen, 'Wang Yüan-chih yü ch'i *"Yeh-yü teng-ch'ien lu hsü-lu"*', *T'ai-pei wen-hsien*, 11–12 (June 1970), 35–6; Lin Ch'ing-yüan, *Fu-chien ch'uan-cheng*, p. 86. Tseng Lan-sheng is probably an alias of Tseng Heng-chung (see note 135 below). According to Wang, the books translated were not published. Wang Yüan-chih, *Yeh-yü ch'iu-teng lu* (1917), reproduced in part in Lin Hsüan-chih, comp., *Fu-chou Ma-wei-kang t'u-chih* (Foochow, 1984), pp. 41–4.
23 The figure of 130 comes from Dunn, 'Foochow Arsenal', in FO 233/85, no. 3, p. 3. It seems to be fairly accurate, for in 1875 those commended by Shen numbered 149, among whom were a few who had left or died in office. *HFT*, II, 135, 556b–573b. According to Lin Ch'ing-yüan, there were 197 staff members, but he includes some students, military officers, and the like. Lin, *Fu-chien ch'uan-cheng*, p. 80.

among several assigned by Shen to sail on board the *Wan-nien Ch'ing*, Ma-wei's first steamer, for inspection by an imperial deputy at Tientsin. However, Huang was soon transferred to T'ai-wan prefecture as a first-class subprefect and died in 1873.[24] Then there were the Chang brothers, Ssu-kuei and Ssu-hsün, who were quite knowledgeable in Western science and were adept at making submarine mines and telegraphic instruments. The former, who had once been Tseng Kuo-fan's personal assistant (*mu-yu*), was particularly indispensable to Shen during the Taiwan crisis of 1874–5.[25] Finally, there were some, like Li Ch'ing-lin, who appeared to have served part-time in the Navy Yard (Li was also a member of the Commerce Bureau).[26] From these examples, it can be inferred that Shen preferred to use those with wide experience or special skills in a flexible manner, in the capacity of a deputy (*wei-yüan*), so that their many talents would not be restricted by a narrowly defined office.[27]

There was no shortage of talent at the Navy Yard. Apart from the lone *chin-shih*, Liang Ming-ch'ien, there were at least fifteen who possessed the *chü-jen* degree. Numerous others held lesser degrees, including one who topped the list in a prefectural examination, and virtually all had official ranks and brevets, some as high as that of provincial salt comptroller. Still more valuable was the administrative experience they brought with them. Two had been acting provincial treasurers, and one of these had also served as Fukien's acting governor. The number of high-ranking officials at Ma-wei was not equalled in any other modernizing enterprise. And there were many who had held junior civil service positions.[28] Others came with very different but equally valuable experience from the business and diplomatic worlds. Not a few embraced progressive views on China's modernization. In 1867, six senior staff members or advisers advocated a number of controlled modernization measures, including mechanized coal mining, the posting of envoys abroad, and the mobilization of overseas Chinese to promote China's commercial and political interests. They also saw the benefits that railways and telegraph lines could bring to China, but recognized that,

---

24 *IWSM*, TC 53:15b–17b; *HFT*, II, 122; *Yin hsien-chih* (1877), 44:38a–b. For more information on Huang, see Chapter 6.
25 *HFT*, II, 574b; Shen K'o, 'Hsien Wen-su kung', p. 70; Hummel, *Eminent Chinese*, vol. 1, p. 403. Chang Ssu-kuei was already well known for his knowledge of Western technology before coming to Ma-wei. Ch'en Chiang, 'Lun yang-wu-p'ai kung-yeh-chi-shu ti yin-chin huo-tung', *Chi-lin ta-hsüeh she-hui k'o-hsüeh lun-tsung*, 1980, no. 2: *Yang-wu yün-tung t'ao-lun chuan-chi*, p. 358.
26 *YWYT*, vol. 5, p. 104.
27 Huang wei-hsüan and Chang Ssu-kuei were referred to as *wei-yüan* on many occasions. *HFT*, II, 122; Shen K'o, 'Hsien Wen-su kung', p. 70.
28 *HFT*, II, 555b–556, 558–73, 574a–b; *MHHC*, 72:21a–b.

under the existing international situation, these new devices could bring more harm than good. Tempering their progressiveness with a concern for China's territorial and administrative integrity, they regarded the Foochow Navy Yard and the Peking T'ung-wen Kuan as the foundation of a controlled form of modernization.[29] Although some of these men of senior rank were brought in by Tso Tsung-t'ang, it was Shen who recruited the majority of them, and under his progressive and energetic leadership, they were a source of strength.

To make use of these men for their expertise was to encourage them. But beyond this, Shen also attempted to promote job specialization. On the institutional level, we have already noted, among others, the functional specialization of the Secretariat and the group of officers in charge of acquisitions. On the individual level, men with special skills, like Yeh Wen-lan and Huang Wei-hsüan, were encouraged to develop their interests. Over time, even some who had come from the most traditional backgrounds had acquired certain levels of competence in modern science and technology, or simply a deeper knowledge of the West. The outstanding examples among these were Liang Ming-ch'ien, Wang Pao-ch'en, and Wang Yüan-chih, all traditional scholars. In addition, four *chü-jen* degree holders assigned by Shen to the workshops became proficient in naval construction, and one, attached to the school, acquired a sound knowledge of French. Nevertheless, the results would have been more impressive had Shen taken fuller advantage of his powers and systematically institutionalized specialization among his staff, especially in the workshops and schools where the transfer of technological and scientific knowledge was to take place. As it was, too much was left to individual initiative, Shen's encouragement notwithstanding.

Unfortunately, the talents available to or cultivated by Shen were also much in demand elsewhere. Several of his staff had to serve periodically away from Ma-wei. In 1869 Huang Wei-hsüan and Hsia Hsien-lun were employed by Ying-kuei to negotiate with the British over an anti-missionary incident. In fact, from 1869 to 1872, Huang was concurrently an associate manager of the Fukien Arsenal at Foochow, a provincial enterprise set up by Ying-kuei.[30] Similarly, Li Ch'ing-lin had to devote a good part of his energy and time to the Commerce Bureau. Of course, there was Hu Kuang-yung, who left for good, though Shen continued to draw on his wisdom through correspondence from time to time.

---

29 *IWSM*, TC 53:7b–26.
30 *IWSM*, TC 65:3–5b; *NCH*, 18 January 1871; *HFT*, III, 81a–b, 127; Wang Erh-min, *Ch'ing-chi ping-kung-yeh*, p. 109.

In fact, those who left completely were few; the administrative staff enjoyed a remarkable degree of stability in Shen's time. Job opportunities elsewhere were limited. Only Wu Ta-t'ing moved to another *yang-wu* enterprise. Nor was there much movement in the opposite direction. Chang Ssu-kuei, once a member of Tseng Kuo-fan's staff, seems to have been an exception. After all, the modernizing sector, though expanding, was small and lacked a superstructure in which one could build a career. The traditional civil service could have been a more serious threat had entry been less competitive. During Shen's incumbency, this form of 'brain drain' claimed only two men, Hsia Hsien-lun and Huang Wei-hsüan, both of whom left for positions on less desirable Taiwan. Of the rest who were best qualified for civil service jobs, the single *chin-shih* and fifteen *chü-jen*, all but two stayed or died in office.[31] The exceptions were Chou K'ai-hsi and Wu Ta-t'ing. They were drafted by Tso Tsung-t'ang and Tseng Kuo-fan, as mentioned, not lured away by the civil service.

Nevertheless, a regular civil service appointment still had great allure. The Navy Yard men would readily accept such posts whenever the opportunity arose. Hsia Hsien-lun took an office that was below his former acting provincial treasurership, and Shen, for all his efforts, could detain him for only a year.[32] Furthermore, many members of Shen's staff continued to prepare themselves for the civil service examinations, although we can document only one case of success.[33] In this sense, the civil service was an important force in undermining the independence of the *yang-wu* enterprises, sapping the energy of those who served in them, and damaging their self-esteem.

To put things in proper perspective, it should be stressed that the Navy Yard began by drawing men from the traditional civil service. Provincial politics, as we have seen, partly contributed to this. But it should be noted also that not all civil service appointments were attractive. Qualified men traditionally shunned assignments in remote regions.[34] Wu Ta-t'ing, it will be recalled, reluctantly took up the intendancy on Taiwan and readily accepted Shen's invitation to come to Ma-wei. On balance, the Navy Yard was more successful in 'raiding' the civil service than the other way around. For all its institutional problems, it did

---

31 *HFT*, II, 558–73; *Shih-lu*, KH 15:13b.
32 *TWTC*, vol. 2, p 325; *Yin hsien-chih*, 44:38a–b; *YWYT*, vol. 5, p. 118.
33 This was Lin Ch'iung-shu, the grandson of Lin Tse-hsü and Shen's nephew, who obtained his *chü-jen* degree in 1875. *MHHC*, 72:21a–b. Wang Yüan-chih tried the local examinations twice, but did not succeed. Lin Hsüan-chih, *Fu-chou Ma-wei*, pp. 42–3.
34 James B. Parsons, *The Peasant Rebellions of the Late Ming Dynasty* (Tucson, Ariz., 1970), p. 2. Even today, the much stronger government of the People's Republic of China has difficulty placing able persons in remote areas such as Tibet. *New York Times*, 9 March 1988.

provide a career alternative, and the prestige of Tso Tsung-t'ang and Shen gave it additional appeal.

As for the few who did move on, they, having acquired valuable knowledge and skills, made notable contributions to *yang-wu* efforts elsewhere. Apart from Wu Ta-t'ing, who went to direct naval training at Kiangnan, all of them left after Shen's time. For instance, Wu Chung-hsiang, Shen's brother-in-law, stayed at Ma-wei until the 1880s before joining Li Hung-chang and Chang Chih-tung, helping them manage their naval academies and training programmes.[35] In 1884, Wang Pao-ch'en was also invited by Chang to operate his torpedo bureau in Canton.[36] Lin Ch'iung-shu, the grandson of Lin Tse-hsü and Shen's nephew, spent a short time on the Board of Works in 1876 before returning to supervise the Navy Yard School.[37] Yeh Wen-lan, too, continued as the general manager until he was dispatched by Ting Jih-ch'ang to direct modern coal mining on Taiwan in 1876.[38] The Chang brothers, Ssu-kuei and Ssu-hsün, eventually entered the Tsungli Yamen; the former ended up as an assistant envoy to Japan in 1877.[39] In that same year, Wang Yüan-chih of the Navy Yard School was recruited by Hsia Hsien-lun to help with the compilation of reference books on Taiwan.[40] Although their departure might have hurt the Navy Yard, they benefited the *yang-wu* 'movement' as a whole. Shen never begrudged the departure of Wu Ta-t'ing, who left during his incumbency; he had only good words to say about the man. Yeh Wen-lan's transfer to Taiwan's coal-mining project was also made with Shen's blessings, although Yeh, when left on his own, did not do well.[41]

As one who had sacrificed a successful career to come to Ma-wei, Shen was himself a powerful model for his subordinates and the scholar-gentry class. As if to emulate Shen, Wu Ta-t'ing, too, joined the Navy Yard after serving as the taotai of T'ai-wan, and he never sought another civil service job afterwards. Still, most of the Navy Yard men would have preferred a post in the civil service if given the chance. And Shen, for all his dedication to the cause, could not prevent his staff members from

---

35 *FCTC:LCH*, vol. 3, pp. 290–1; *MHHC*, 69:32a–b.
36 *MHHC*, 68:29.
37 Ibid., 72:21a–b.
38 *NCH*, 1 December 1876.
39 Ibid., 28 April 1877; *Shih-lu*, KH 44:3.
40 Liao Yü-wen, 'Wang Yüan-chih', pp. 35–6.
41 *HFT*, III, 147b; Shen's memorial of KH 4.2.25 (28 March 1878) in YCT, KH 4/2, *ts'e* 4; Lü Shih-ch'iang, *Ting*, p. 306. On Yeh and the coal mines, see Shannon R. Brown and Tim Wright, 'Technology, Economics and Politics in the Modernization of China's Coal Mining Industry: The First Phase, 1850–1895', *Explorations in Economic History*, 18.1 (January 1981), 60–83.

taking the civil service examinations; nor could he refuse them leave for this purpose.[42] Therefore, it is often alleged that when he rewarded the meritorious with civilian ranks and titles, he was abetting their desire to join the regular bureaucracy.[43] Shen indeed recommended an advancement in civil official ranks for more than 150 men on completion of the shipbuilding and training programmes in 1875.[44] But there was no other meaningful way to recognize their achievements. Besides, an advancement in the civil official ranks rarely facilitated entry into the congested civil service. The same can be said of the few who passed the lower civil service examinations. The real problem for these men lay in the future, when frustration mounted as upward mobility within the *yang-wu* sector declined. Shen foresaw the problem and tried to reform the system. We shall return to this subject in Chapter 10.

Nepotism and corruption are two factors that modern scholars often cite in the poor management and high production costs of late Ch'ing defence undertakings.[45] Insofar as the Navy Yard staff was drawn mainly from the local gentry, it was, as Shen had warned on his first day in office, most vulnerable to such evils. Since the number of men introduced by Tso Tsung-t'ang was small and Shen had a free hand in staffing, we may wonder whether the Navy Yard also fell victim to these entrenched bureaucratic vices or whether Shen, the 'foe of corruption',[46] was able to stave them off.

Shen's incorruptibility was legendary in his own time. Reportedly, so inflexibly upright was he that even influential personages of the Manchu court dared not ask favours of him. Once, a close friend and native of Foochow asked him for a letter of recommendation to the governor of Kiangsi in order to speed up his appointment. Shen, knowing that his friend had mishandled customs duties, upbraided him and sent him off with 400 taels, saying, 'If you have nothing to do, I shall pay you by the month!' If the truth of this anecdote, based on unofficial histories, is open to question, the veracity of the following incident, recorded in both the unofficial histories and a memorial accusing Shen of brutality, is beyond doubt. The incident concerned the beheading of a clerk from the provincial treasurer's yamen who lined his pockets with Navy Yard funds. Even though the clerk was related to Shen by marriage and despite the treasurer's supplication, Shen went ahead with the

---

42 Lin Hsüan-chih, *Fu-chou Ma-wei*, pp. 42–3.
43 See, e.g., Rawlinson, *China's Struggle*, pp. 104–6.
44 *HFT*, II, 556b–573b. The list includes some who had left the Navy Yard.
45 Wang Erh-min, *Ch'ing-chi ping-kung-yeh*, pp. 84–5; Kennedy, *Arms*, p. 158.
46 John K. Fairbank, Edwin O. Reischauer, and Albert M. Craig, *East Asia: The Modern Transformation* (Boston, 1965), p. 356.

execution. Yet another fully documented case shows that Shen adamantly denied office to a former subordinate of Tso Tsung-t'ang's. He was clearly impartial to friends and relatives alike.[47]

An examination of the Navy Yard staff turns up five persons bearing the surname of Shen, and those who bore the surname of Lin, suggesting a possible blood relation with his wife's family, numbered about twenty. Lin, however, was (and still is) such a common family name in Fukien, especially around Foochow, that this information is hardly helpful. We do know, however, that Shen had a brother-in-law (Wu Chung-hsiang) and a nephew (Lin Ch'iung-shu) on the staff, and a third man was married to his niece. There were, in addition, Liang Ming-ch'ien and Wang Yüan-chih, who had taught his fourth son, and the former might have been related to two other persons in the administration. None of them, it appears, had been given preferential treatment.[48]

In his diary, Chao Lieh-wen, a critic of Shen, quoted Tseng Kuo-fan as having said that many Hunanese, driven out of the provincial government by Wu T'ang, found refuge in the Navy Yard and thus contributed to its high salary expenditures.[49] In fact, Tso Tsung-t'ang had introduced altogether seven men to the Navy Yard, all before Wu arrived on the scene, and only two were Hunanese. Rather than expelled from the provincial government by Wu, they were prevented from assuming duties at the Navy Yard. Only Chou K'ai-hsi had to take a full-time job at Ma-wei because of Wu's machinations. Clearly, the Navy Yard had not been used as a receptacle for relatives and friends or for people not wanted elsewhere. The low expenditure for staff salary, amounting to a mere 1.66 per cent of the Navy Yard's total outlay,[50] confirms our finding. And this compares very favourably with the salary expenditures of Kiangnan Arsenal founded by Tseng, which spent 3.79 per cent on

---

47 Hsü I-t'ang, *Ch'ing-tai mi-shih*, p. 109; Li Ho-nien's memorial of KH 1/8/18 (17 September 1875) in YCT, KH 1/8; Lin Ch'ing-yüan, *Fu-chien ch'uan-cheng*, p. 81.

48 Lin was in charge of a warehouse or workshop. The possible relatives of Liang were Liang I-ch'ien, who had a similar job, and Liang Chi-ch'ien, a low-ranking supervisor. *HFT*, II, 562, 567b. Ch'en Shou-tsang, a *chü-jen*, married to Shen's niece, was a supervisor in the Navy Yard School, as was Wang Yüan-chih. *FCTC*, 'Ju-hsing chuan: Ch'ing', 28; *HFT*, II, 568–9. Shen Yü-ch'ing, *T'ao-yüan chi*, p. 169; Liao Yü-wen, 'Wang Yüan-chih', pp. 35–6; *HFT*, II, 563, 565; Lin Hsüan-chih, *Fu-chou Ma-wei*, pp. 42–3.

49 Chao Lieh-wen, *Neng-ching-chü*, unpaginated. Quoted in Tseng Wuo-fan, *Wei-k'an hsin-kao*, p. 391.

50 *HFT*, II, 536–547b. The percentage is arrived at by dividing the staff salary by the Navy Yard's total expenditure, less the steamship maintenance costs. The period covered is from 23 December 1866 to 11 August 1874, a total of ninety-four lunar months.

staff salary.[51] Whether nepotism was a serious problem in the Foochow Navy Yard, it was certainly more cost effective.

Writing in 1890, Pien Pao-ti, who was governor of Fukien in 1867–70, lauded Shen's careful selection of personnel and the firmness with which he turned away relatives and friends, thus corroborating the stories cited earlier. Pien lamented that this exemplary conduct was not followed by Shen's successors. Ch'en P'i, a native *chin-shih*, proudly added that the absence of corruption at the Foochow Navy Yard was not to be found in other arsenals.[52]

In fact, corruption existed. Peculation could well have been the cause for an entire shipment of poor-quality timber purchased from South-East Asia in 1868. Just as Shen had warned, the acquisition of huge quantities of raw materials inevitably invited peculation. A close watch was then kept over incoming materials, making sure they fit specifications. As for the bad timber, Giquel claimed that he had been duped by his French agent in Siam. Thereupon, Shen appointed his own permanent agent in South-East Asia. Chinese-led buying missions were also dispatched.[53] The problem seemed solved, and all the Navy Yard's vessels were built with excellent timber (see the next chapter).

Within the boundaries of the Navy Yard, corruption could be more easily detected and controlled. Shen certainly did not hesitate to impose strict discipline, heavy punishment, and dismissals, methods he considered necessary in managing a staff made up of fellow gentrymen. His intolerance of bureaucratic irregularities was widely known and praised, but some criticized the harsh penalties he so freely, though impartially, meted out.[54] To stamp out all forms of delinquency was well-nigh

---

51 *YWYT*, vol. 4, pp. 28–34. Steamship maintenance costs have been excluded in both cases. If included, the contrast between Foochow and Kiangnan would be even more startling. It would appear that the salary figures in both places applied to *junior* administrative staff members only. Also worthy of note is the fact that the Foochow Navy Yard had a staff of about 130, whereas Kiangnan had one of 'over 100'. The average salary per man per lunar month at Ma-wei was 7 taels and, at Kiangnan, more than 10 taels. *HFT*, II, 536–547b; Tsungli Yamen's memorial of KH 2.3.19 (13 April 1876) in YCT, KH 2/3 *chung*. In an earlier attempt to compare the salary expenses of the two institutions, I arrived at different figures. They now seem erroneous. See Pong, 'Modernization and Politics', pp. 148–9.

52 Pien Pao-ti, *Pien chih-chün tsou-i* (1894), 12:22b–23. It should be added that Ting Jih-ch'ang, Shen's immediate successor, was equally vigorous in stamping out corruption. But he was concurrently the governor of Fukien and his four-month tenure was too short to achieve results. On Ch'en, see Ho Liang-tung, *Huang-ch'ao ching-shih-wen ssu-pien* (1902), 44:9b.

53 *HFT*, II, 139–140b, 157a–b; *SWSK*, 4:7a–b, 32–4.

54 Tseng Kuo-fan was one of the critics, but the throne supported Shen's approach. Hsü K'o, *Ch'ing-pai lei-ch'ao*, 22:42; Chao Lieh-wen, *Neng-ching-chü*, quoted in Tseng Kuo-fan, *Wei-k'an hsin-kao*, p. 391; *Ch'uan-cheng tsou-i*, 4:7b.

impossible. Thus, despite the Navy Yard's impressive achievements, a foreign observer questioned whether the huge sums of money spent were duly represented at Ma-wei.[55] Instances of corruption in the workshops were evident (see the next chapter), and a case of peculation and laziness on the part of the commander of the Navy Yard guards went undetected for some time.[56] By and large, though, Shen's disciplinarian approach was effective. So when he tendered his resignation following his father's death in October 1870, Tartar General Wen-yü, no ardent supporter of the Navy Yard, requested an imperial order to keep him in office. His departure, Wen-yü asserted, would cause serious disruptions.[57] Nevertheless, Shen left for a twenty-seven-month period of mourning during which the quality of administration suffered. Again, in 1874–5, when he spent a year on Taiwan, laxity crept in as Ting Jih-ch'ang soon found out on taking over the Navy Yard.[58]

The administration of the Foochow Navy Yard was blessed with a full-time, resident director-general of high rank who was also an energetic and strong administrator. In all these respects, it was superior to the Kiangnan Arsenal.[59] While favourable results were produced, effective administration depended far too heavily on one man. Of all the positions Shen had held, the one at Ma-wei gave him the widest latitude in managing its affairs. Yet he was unable to establish institutional or legal means to perpetuate the quality of administration which he himself had taken so many pains to build up.[60]

Discord between the French directors and consular interference

Because d'Aiguebelle and Giquel's mission was concerned primarily with modern technology, about which the Chinese were largely ignorant, they were given a degree of freedom in the choice and organization of their men. The initial agreement simply stipulated that they should hire from Europe thirty-seven engineers, foremen, and workers as well as an

---

55 Anon., 'The Chinese Arsenals', p. 698.

56 Most of the transgressions were perpetrated during Shen's absence, as explained later. They were uncovered by his successor, Ting Jih-ch'ang. Ting's memorial of KH 2.2.11 (6 March 1876) in YCT, KH 2/2 *chung*.

57 *YWYT*, vol. 5, pp. 94–5. Giquel later remarked, 'This man [Shen] is remarkable for his energy, his strength of will and the authority with which he is able to make himself obeyed'. *Foochow Arsenal*, p. 13.

58 *HFT*, II, 649; *Shen-pao*, 18 December 1875.

59 Lü Shih-ch'iang, *Ting*, pp. 180–1.

60 Another example of Shen's inability to introduce more institutional safeguards relates to the management of labour (see the next chapter).

accountant and a physician.[61] Unforeseen requirements and expansion boosted this number to fifty-five by the end of 1868, and to more than seventy soon after.[62] Attrition and dismissals eventually whittled the number down to fifty in February 1874, when the bulk of the men left at the expiration of their contracts.[63]

By design, the vast majority of the Europeans were French; only a handful were British. Tso Tsung-t'ang had thought that the French excelled in naval construction and the British in navigation.[64] He was correct on the first count and probably so on the second, although his hatred of the British and the influence of d'Aiguebelle and Giquel also favoured a large French presence.[65]

As expected, d'Aiguebelle and Giquel were placed at the top of the European staff, and both were given the title of director. Immediately below was the chief engineer, who sat with them on the Council of Works, a body constituted to deal with administrative and disciplinary matters internal to the European staff.[66]

The directorate was served by a secretary, an interpreter, an accountant, and a small office staff. The largest number of Europeans by far were employed in shipbuilding. There were a master carpenter, a chief of the metal-working forge, some thirteen foremen, and about thirty workmen. They reported to the directors weekly. Most of them were said to have had a good primary education in France. The teaching staff, by comparison, was small. Its number rose from six in 1868 to eight in

61 *HFT*, II, 31–36b, 39–42b. There was a provision for a coal- and iron-mining expert to exploit resources in nearby areas.

62 The number rose above seventy some time in 1870. According to Dunn's report (*NCH*, 21 April 1870) there were about sixty Europeans. Captain Véron listed seventy-four in the same year, which seems to agree with Giquel's own account. Some of the men, it must be noted, were temporary workers. By August 1872, only fifty-five were left, although the *Cornhill Magazine*, in its December 1872 issue (p. 698), still placed the number at between sixty and seventy. D. Thibaudier to Ministère de la Marine, 'Arsenal de Fou-tchéou', 8 June 1868, in MM BB4 1555 17/5/8; *Chinese Recorder*, 2 (January 1870), 216; Véron, 'Rapport'; Contenson, 'Rapport de M. le Capitaine d'Etat-major de Contenson attaché militaire à la légation de France en Chine sur l'arsenal de Fou-tchéou', 13 August 1872, in MM BB4 1382; Giquel, *Foochow Arsenal*, p. 14. On the flexibility in hiring, see *HFT*, II, 121.

63 Giquel, *Foochow Arsenal*, pp. 37–8. On p. 14 Giquel refers to fifty-two men, but that number includes himself and possibly d'Aiguebelle, who had left the Navy Yard earlier but remained on its payroll.

64 Wang Hsin-chung, 'Fu-chou ch'uan-ch'ang', p. 12.

65 In the first half of the nineteenth century, the French, less inhibited by a strong naval tradition, were pioneers in many aspects of marine engineering. They accepted the steam engine more readily and were the first to produce an armoured battleship towards the end of the Crimean War. Michael Lewis, *The History of the British Navy* (Harmondsworth, 1957), pp. 223–7.

66 Thibaudier, 'Arsenal'; article 4, 'Contrat d'engagement de Mr. Trasbot', MM BB4 1555 17/5/5.

1874. Some instruction, however, was conducted by foremen who taught in the School for Apprentices and the School of Design.[67]

Shen's management of the Europeans fell into two broad areas: his relations with the French directors and his management of the European staff in general. It is to the former that we shall now turn.

Of all the defence industries founded in the 1860s and 1870s, the Foochow Navy Yard was at once the largest, the most expensive, and equipped with the most modern machinery. It also had the single largest contingent of European employees and, as far as the French presence went, it employed more Frenchmen than the Imperial Maritime Customs Service. The French community at Ma-wei was second only to that at Shanghai.[68] All in all, it was a major centre of French interests. As such, it attracted support as well as intervention.

French interests, however, were by no means homogeneous. The French foreign and naval ministries in Paris, as well as naval, consular, and customs personnel in China, all eyed the Navy Yard from different vantage points and frequently worked at cross purposes. National and personal ambitions became entwined. All impinged on the awkward situation in which individual Frenchmen, with access to extraterritorial rights and consular protection, had to operate as servants of China. This situation invited consular interference, and the first opening was provided by the friction between the two French directors and the disputes concerning disciplinary power over the French employees.

The relative position of the two French directors was a sensitive issue from the start. Although both had served many years under Tso Tsung-t'ang, d'Aiguebelle and Giquel were not equals. In the early 1860s d'Aiguebelle, as the commander of the Franco-Chinese Corps, had rendered Tso valuable service, whereas Giquel, though no less valiant, could not give him undivided attention as he continued to serve as customs commissioner at Ningpo. D'Aiguebelle was also several years Giquel's senior, both in age and in service in the French Imperial Navy. His naval rank was also higher, and he was of aristocratic blood. So when the Franco-Chinese Corps was disbanded in 1864, d'Aiguebelle was awarded the brevet of *t'i-tu* (provincial commander-in-chief; rank 1b) and Giquel only that of *tsung-ping* (brigade general; rank 2a).[69]

---

67 Thibaudier, 'Arsenal'; *Chinese Recorder*, 2, (January 1870), 216; Véron, 'Rapport'; Contenson, 'Rapport', pp. 325–43; Shen's memorial and letter to the Tsungli Yamen, 25 December 1873, in *HFT*, II, 469a, 471b–472; Giquel, *Foochow Arsenal*, pp. 37–8. These sources do not agree as to the number of foremen and workmen, partly because they were compiled at different times, but mainly they used different categorizations.
68 There were twenty-six French customs officials in 1875. Stanley Wright, *Hart*, p. 897.
69 D'Aiguebelle (1831–75), born of a good Parisian family, studied at the Ecole navale (1846–8) before joining the navy as a second-class midshipman in 1848. Although his

Now, for the direction of the works at Ma-wei, Tso's evaluation of the two changed. Giquel's knowledge of the Chinese language and his understanding of China acquired through his years with the Customs Service were declared important assets – he was better able to communicate with the Chinese. His linguistic ability was also regarded as critical in both the teaching and manufacturing processes of the Navy Yard. D'Aiguebelle, though a better engineer, lacked similar facilities. Giquel was therefore appointed the first director and d'Aiguebelle the second.[70]

Thirty years later, Léon Médard, who taught for many years in the Navy Yard School, accused Giquel of having conspired with Hu Kuang-yung to secure the top position.[71] There is no question that Hu was often consulted by Tso on matters relating to the Europeans, but ultimately it was Tso's overriding concern with Chinese control over the Navy Yard that led to the decision. In Tso's eyes, d'Aiguebelle, despite his previous

school record was rather poor and his behaviour uniformly bad (he had to do many extra watches, etc.), he did well in the navy, enjoying regular promotions. In 1862 he was made a lieutenant of the first class, the highest rank he was to hold. In 1859 he was also awarded *chevalier de la Légion d'Honneur*, a noble rank of the lowest order. Then, for his success with the Franco-Chinese Corps, he was conferred the title of *officier de la Légion d'Honneur*. MM CC7 1850: Dossier individuel – d'Aiguebelle; Cordier, *Histoire des relations*, vol. 1, p. 251; Stanley Wright, *Hart*, p. 493; Morse, *International Relations*, vol. 2, p. 79; Kuo T'ing-i, *Chin-tai Chung-kuo shih-shih*, vol. 1, pp. 416, 419; *IWSM*, 37:29–30.

Giquel (1835–86) was born in provincial France (Lorient, Morihan, in Brittany). He studied at the Collège de Cherbourg, a preparatory school for the navy (1850–1), then entered the Ecole navale (1852–4) before joining the navy as a second-class midshipman in 1854. His school record was much better than d'Aiguebelle's, and his behaviour exemplary. His weakest subjects were drawing and English. However, his two-year studies at the Ecole were interrupted by the Crimean War. Later, Léon Médard, who disliked him intensely, claimed that he did only one year there, when in fact he did three semesters. At any rate, he was awarded *chevalier de la Légion d'Honneur* for his gallantry in the Crimean War in 1855. In 1857 he accompanied Baron Gros in the Second Opium War, and when the Anglo-French forces took Canton, he was detached as aide de camp to assist the French member of the Allied Commission in governing the city. There he became acquainted with Robert Hart, secretary to the Commission at the time, and learned Chinese. He then joined the Foreign Inspectorate of Chinese Customs and, in 1861, became the first commissioner of customs at Ningpo. It was here that he began his association with Tso Tsung-t'ang, who moved into Chekiang in late 1861. His organization of the Franco-Chinese Corps, which he briefly commanded in 1862, and his valour (he was wounded twice) in retaking key cities in Chekiang won him the lifelong support of Tso. The French government also recognized his bravery and promoted him to lieutenant in 1863. MM CC7 1020: Dossier individuel – Giquel; Médard, 'Note confidentielle'; Stanley Wright, *Hart*, p. 492; Hummel, *Eminent Chinese*, vol. 2, p. 764; Morse, *International Relations*, vol. 2, p. 78; Kuo T'ing-i, *Chin-tai Chung-kuo shih-shih*, vol. 1, p. 412; *Far East*, 2 (January–June 1877), 24–5.

70 *HFT*, II, 19; an additional article on 'Des propositions d'exécution' (article 19) in ibid., 42b–43b; *YWYT*, vol. 5, p. 46, and Cordier, *Histoire des relations*, vol. 1, p. 254.

71 Médard, 'Note confidentielle'. The association between Giquel and Hu went back to the early 1860s. Leibo, *Transferring Technology*, p. 84.

service, was more of a mercenary, having little sympathy for the Chinese. (His subsequent behaviour showed him to be arrogant, small-minded, and self-seeking.) Robert Hart also noted that he had 'no special ability', whereas Giquel was 'clever and able', though 'also attached to sycee'.[72] But what commended Giquel to Tso was his sympathy for the plight of China: he was one of the few Frenchmen who openly criticized the extensive privileges secured by the missionaries in 1860.[73] Privately, Tso also preferred Giquel for his good nature; he was less prone to insubordination. With him as the first director, Tso would have less fear of foreign domination.[74]

Nevertheless, in relegating d'Aiguebelle to the second position, the Chinese realized that they had a delicate matter on hand. So when the issue was first discussed, Tso offered the two Frenchmen exactly the same salary. For the sake of public appearance and to preserve d'Aiguebelle's dignity, the appointment of the first and second directors was announced as though the idea had come from Consul-General de Montmorand, presumably representing the French government. No matter, d'Aiguebelle grew increasingly disgruntled about the 'fictitious position of responsibility' to which he had been consigned.[75]

Soon after, the two directors left for France to recruit workers and purchase machinery. Giquel returned on 6 October 1867, but d'Aiguebelle did not do so until April 1868.[76] The latter was absent for a total of sixteen months. Shen, who had in the meantime assumed office, was thus given a chance to remedy the situation.

Counselled by Hu Kuang-yung, Shen tried a two-prong approach. First, he elevated Giquel's brevet to the rank of *t'i-tu*, bringing him on a par with d'Aiguebelle so as to enhance his dignity and authority. Second, as a compensation for d'Aiguebelle, he awarded both directors the One-Eyed Peacock Feather, an honour given for distinguished public

72 Stanley Wright, *Hart*, p. 493.
73 Mary Wright, *Last Stand*, p. 296n; Prosper Giquel, *La politique française en Chine depuis les traités de 1858 et de 1860* (Paris, 1872), pp. 26–47.
74 Tso to Tsungli Yamen, November 1866, in *TWHK*, 'Letters', 8:55a–b. Mary Wright once wrote: 'In Chinese eyes no skill the foreigners could offer was worth the slightest concession of sovereignty. They were employees of the Chinese government. . . . Neither Macartney [of the Kiangnan Arsenal] nor Giquel was a mere technician. Their influence on the high Chinese officials whom they served was pronounced. . . . These men and others like them were able to extend their influence because they did not claim it as a right'. *Last Stand*, p. 216. Since d'Aiguebelle's ability as an administrator and engineer was a matter of debate among his contemporaries, it is not certain that the Chinese, in by-passing him, were sacrificing quality for the sake of sovereignty.
75 *HFT*, II, 34b–35a; *YWYT*, vol. 5, p. 25; d'Aiguebelle to Commander of the French Naval Division of the Seas of China and Japan, 20 July 1869, in MM BB4 1555 17/5/13.
76 *HFT*, II, 85a–b; *YWYT*, vol. 5, p. 72.

service. The official inauguration of the Navy Yard in February 1868 provided the occasion.[77]

The move was largely cosmetic. It failed to deal with the substantive issue of who should get what power, a matter that became urgent when d'Aiguebelle returned. Shen's awkward solution was to give d'Aiguebelle some semblance of authority when, in effect, power was concentrated in Giquel's hands and, ultimately, in the hands of the Chinese.[78] D'Aiguebelle, now more disenchanted than ever, decided, even before he had time to settle down at Ma-wei, to take a two-month leave of absence to go to South-East Asia, ostensibly to purchase a clipper for transporting raw materials.[79] Since Adrien Trasbot, the chief engineer, had already been dispatched to that region to procure materials,[80] d'Aiguebelle's trip was quite unnecessary. Clearly, he was trying either to avoid working at the Navy Yard or to make a profit for himself, or both. As it turned out, he did have several commercial ventures in Saigon, including a partnership in a banking and transport company, which could have been the reason for his trip.[81]

From late 1868, relations between the two directors deteriorated rapidly. As d'Aiguebelle complained:

It is not difficult to understand how I suffered from the ambiguity of my position: unable to complain, since my legitimate complaints were considered to express the sufferings of my wounded pride, and everyone saw in my criticisms, not the true sentiment of a responsible person who considers that things are being mismanaged, and wishes to improve them, but the expression of a base envy of an inadequate person whose merit was inferior to his vanity.[82]

---

77 *YWYT*, vol. 5, pp. 69–70.
78 Joint circular by Giquel and d'Aiguebelle, 19 June 1868, in MM BB4 1555 17/5/1.
79 D'Aiguebelle arrived at Ma-wei in April 1868 and left for Saigon in August, if not before. The date of his return is not known. He was on leave again around May 1869, on grounds of health – another sign that he had lost interest working at Ma-wei. The length of his absence is unknown. *HFT*, II, 131b, 135b, 175b.
80 *HFT*, II, 138.
81 D'Aiguebelle may have been having difficulties with the banking and transport company, which was liquidated in November as a result of a breach of commercial law. He continued his other commercial activities, however, until ordered to stop by the ministère de la marine under threat of losing his rank. *Courrier de Saigon* of 5 January 1869, Contre-Amiral G. Otrier to Ministère de la Marine of 1 April 1869, and Commander of the Seas of China and Japan to Ministère de la Marine of 28 July 1869 – all in MM CC7 1850: Dossier individuel – d'Aiguebelle. Lin Ch'ung-yung (*Shen*, p. 320) considers d'Aiguebelle's buying trip to South-East Asia to have been a deliberate move by Shen to separate him from Giquel. My sources suggest otherwise. Besides, Shen, in a letter to the Tsungli Yamen, referred to the trip as a two-month leave of absence, not a 'business trip', despite its stated objective. *HFT*, II, 131b.
82 D'Aiguebelle to the French Naval Commander of the Seas of China and Japan, 20 July 1869, in MM BB4 1555 17/5/13.

He then claimed that all the achievements up to mid-1869 were due to him, and him alone. He omitted to mention that, since the establishment of the Navy Yard, he had spent no more than ten months at Ma-wei, and even that time was split into two short stints.

To resolve the matter once and for all, Shen, again advised by Hu Kuang-yung, decided to separate the two and transferred d'Aiguebelle to a new naval training programme in preparation for the launching of the first steamer in September. To prevent future difficulties between two almost equal directors, Shen abolished the second directorship, instituting a subdirectorship in its stead. This new post, vested with far less formal power and totally free of any legal obligation stated in the initial contracts, was filled by Louis Dunoyer de Segonzac (b. 1843), a sub-lieutenant on leave from the French navy.[83] Thus, Giquel, despite his wishes to the contrary, was now left with sole legal responsibility for the European part of the operation.[84] Meanwhile, d'Aiguebelle, with great foresight and a touch of malice, carefully filed the relevant documents at the newly created French consulate and dissociated himself from all administrative responsibilities.[85]

The collective leadership had been destroyed. Giquel was now exposed as the sole target of consular interference as disputes arose over who should have disciplinary powers over the French employees. The squabbles and consular trials fully illustrate the potential for abuse of extraterritorial rights and the vulnerability of the Navy Yard to the personal ambitions and whims of the French consul, now egged on by de Méritens, Giquel's nemesis, and abetted by d'Aiguebelle. At the same time, the litigations revealed the powerlessness of Shen, without the strong backing of the central government, to challenge legally or diplomatically the arbitrary nature of foreign political power in China. In the end, Giquel and the Navy Yard were saved not so much by the

---

83 MM CC7 2728: Dossier individuel – Marie Joseph Louis Philibert Dunoyer de Segonzac.
84 Shen to Tsungli Yamen, 25 December 1869, and Giquel to Shen, 14 July 1869, in *HFT*, II, 215, 206b–207; Shen to Giquel of 6 July 1869, d'Aiguebelle to Shen of 6 July 1869, Giquel's circular of 5 December 1869, Giquel to d'Aiguebelle of 2 August 1869, d'Aiguebelle to Giquel of 3 August 1868, in MM BB4 1555 17/5/1; d'Aiguebelle's circular of 24 June 1869, and d'Aiguebelle to the Commander of the French Naval Division of the Seas of China and Japan, dated 10 July 1869, in MM BB4 1555 17/5/13. D'Aiguebelle claimed that he surrendered his second directorship voluntarily and that his new title was 'Director of the Military Organization of the Fleet'. In fact, his new charge was for naval training on board one steamship only. Whether the crew of future steamships would be placed under his direction was conditional upon his success. In any case, he kept his high salary of 1,000 taels per month. On de Segonzac, see his Dossier individuel in MM BB4 CC7 2728.
85 D'Aiguebelle to Shen, 9 July 1869, in *HFT*, II, 205b–206.

good-intentioned promoters of the Co-operative Policy at Peking as by the intervention of the French Imperial Navy.

Shortly before the reshuffling of the French directorate, a dispute erupted over the dismissal of a blacksmith, Pierre Percebois. During April and May, Percebois repeatedly disobeyed the orders of Brossement, chief of the metal-working forge, abusing him with incredibly rude language. Still, recognizing the terrible work the blacksmith had to put up with, Brossement recommended a raise in salary for him. No matter, Percebois refused to change his attitude, and Giquel had no recourse but to dismiss him.[86]

Percebois took the matter to the French acting consul, Ernest-Jules Blancheton (1842–81), who, in an unannounced visit to the Navy Yard, asked Shen to rescind the dismissal order. Shen flatly refused, insisting that the contracts and regulations be observed. Blancheton then appealed to Ying-kuei, but to no avail.[87]

Seeing that efforts made on his behalf had failed, Percebois filed suit against Giquel and d'Aiguebelle for a breach of contract and demanded payment of travelling expenses for him and his family (600 taels) as well as his salary for the rest of the five-year term (3,360 taels). The employment contract, it may be noted, did give the directors power to dismiss any European employee without compensation should he be found remiss or delinquent. Giquel therefore regarded the whole affair as a farce and refused to appear in court. The hearings were held nonetheless and, despite witness accounts to the contrary, the court, presided by Blancheton and with de Méritens and a subordinate of his as assessors, had no difficulty in fining Giquel 2,100 taels while completely exonerating d'Aiguebelle. Since at the time of the dismissal d'Aiguebelle was still the second director, and therefore a responsible party, his exoneration lends weight to the Chinese contention that he was in league with de Méritens and Blancheton to dislodge Giquel.[88]

---

86 Brossement to Trasbot of 23 May 1869, Trasbot to Giquel of 26 May 1869, Brossement to Giquel of 28 May 1869, in MM BB4 1555 17/5/17; Giquel to Percebois, 27 May 1869, in *HFT*, II, 178b. The two disliked each other even before coming to China. Leibo, *Transferring Technology*, p. 95.

87 Shen to Tsungli Yamen, 3 September 1869, in *HFT*, II, 172a–b; Blancheton to Ying-kuei of 16 June and Ying-kuei's reply of 18 June 1869, in MM BB4 1555 17/5/17.

88 *HFT*, II, 171, 172b, 179, 181b, 201b; Blancheton to Ying-kuei, 27 June 1869, in MM BB4 1555 17/5/17. In the contracts, Giquel, because of his knowledge of Chinese, was empowered to issue notices, instructions, etc., on behalf of both directors, who were thus equally responsible for these actions. D'Aiguebelle argued that when the dismissal occurred, he was on sick leave. While reasonable, his argument had no legal standing. Joint circular by Giquel and d'Aiguebelle, 19 June 1868, in MM BB4 1555 17/5/1, and *HFT*, II, 175b; Giquel to Blancheton, 14 September 1869, in MM BB4 1555 17/5/17; 'Contrat d'engagement', ibid., 17/5/2.

The court's decision severely hurt both Giquel's purse and his authority. Though he continued to enjoy Shen's confidence, he tendered his resignation while appealing the case at Saigon. The Court of Appeal, totally unfamiliar with the situation at Ma-wei, took the words of its consular colleague, Blancheton, at face value and sustained the decision. While the fine on Giquel was slightly reduced, he was ordered to pay Percebois's expenses for having to appear in court at Saigon.[89] The unpleasant affair came to a fitting end with a heated correspondence between Blancheton and Giquel over the manner in which the expenses for Percebois's return passage was to be paid.[90]

The Percebois case was to have serious implications and repercussions for the future of the Navy Yard. In the Europeans' employment contracts, it was stated that final decisions on all matters rested with the Chinese authorities; the French directors were only their intermediaries. They also stipulated that the European workers would not be protected by the treaties if they committed a crime that was work-related, such as dereliction of duty, fraud, striking and insulting the Chinese, or causing a disturbance.[91] In short, the contracts excused the French directors from all responsibilities while retaining for the Chinese vast judicial powers over the Europeans. They created a grey area in which jurisdiction over the Europeans begged for definition. The legality of the contracts remained uncontested only for as long as the Europeans had no access to a nearby consular authority. This was the case before 1869.

In early 1869 the French moved their consulate at Ningpo to Foochow.[92] Since the French at Ma-wei were his only concern, the consul, Eugène Simon, immediately assumed an adversary posture towards the Navy Yard authorities. First, he studied the contracts; then, to assert his authority, he sought permission to have consular notices posted in the Navy Yard. Shen hastily refused, insisting that the Navy Yard was outside consular jurisdiction. Simon, as if to flaunt his judicial power,

---

89 Shen to Ying-kuei, 13 October 1869, and to the Tsungli Yamen, 25 December 1869, in *HFT*, II, 182b, 215b; Giquel to Blancheton, 14 September 1869, and Judgement of the Court of Appeal, Saigon, 3 December 1869, in MM BB4 1555, 17/5/17; and Giquel to the Commander of the French Naval Division of the Seas of China and Japan, 15 March 1870, in ibid., 17/5/19.

90 Blancheton to Giquel, 20 January 1870, and subsequent exchanges, in ibid., 17/5/19.

91 Articles 5, 10, 13, and 14 of 'Contrat d'engagement', in MM BB4 1555 17/5/2.

92 France, Ministère des Affaires Etrangères [MAE], *Annuaire diplomatique de l'empire français pour l'année 1869*, p. 25; FO 228/408, no. 41 and 228/472, no. 9; French Minister to Tsungli Yamen, 6 March 1869, in TY: Fa-kuo ko-k'ou ling-shih. On the lack of French commercial interests at Foochow before the establishment of the Navy Yard, see Charles Carroll to Alcock, 1 October 1866, in FO 228/408, no. 41, and Charles Sinclair's 'Annual Report for the Year 1866' to Alcock, 9 March 1867, in FO 228/430, no. 15, encl. 6.

then summoned Giquel before the consular court over a trivial dispute with the Navy Yard's physician. All of this occurred within eight days of his arrival.[93]

Simon soon left but, as we have seen, the acting consul, Blancheton, was no less hostile. In Shen's opinion, Blancheton's actions not only infringed upon the Navy Yard administration, but also had the effect of inciting the workers to intimidate their superiors. He therefore urged the Tsungli Yamen to do whatever it could to have the French move their consulate back to Ningpo. Then, de Méritens, left on his own, could do less harm to Giquel, whom he had tried to replace. And to clip his wings further, Shen also questioned whether he, an employee of the Imperial Maritime Customs Service, and thus a servant of the Chinese government, should sit as an assessor on the French consular tribunal. But the Tsungli Yamen, after consulting Robert Hart, found nothing improper in the matter. Worse still, the Yamen was so fearful of further complications if the issue were raised with the French minister that it decided to ask Shen to seek a local solution instead.[94]

As Shen feared, Percebois's victory showed how easy it was for a European employee to extract, without working, more than full compensation from Giquel by simply causing a dispute.[95] The first to grasp the message was Chief Engineer Adrien Trasbot. A naval engineer bearing the rank of sublieutenant, Trasbot had been enticed to leave the Rochefort Arsenal for China under very favourable terms. The expansion and modification of the technical facilities at Ma-wei owed a great deal to his knowledge and vision. As a bona fide naval engineer, however, he had a poor opinion of Giquel and had hoped one day to replace him as director.[96] Up to mid-1869, he had been an extremely conscientious worker, and after the first steamer was launched in June 1869, he tried so hard to have it fitted out that he even worked on Sundays. Impressed by his diligence, Giquel proposed a huge award of 3,000 taels for him on the completion of the vessel. Shen readily agreed.[97]

But in late summer, Trasbot turned truculent as he was passed over for the directorship vacated by d'Aiguebelle. Trasbot indeed had every right to be upset, for his employment contract strongly hinted that he was to succeed either director should one of them leave. It therefore

93 Shen to Prince Kung, 3 September 1869, in *HFT*, II, 172–3.
94 Ibid.; Tsungli Yamen to Ying-kuei, 13 October 1869, in ibid., 181b–182b.
95 Shen to Tsungli Yamen, 3 September 1869, in ibid., 172b.
96 'Contrat d'engagement de Mr. Trasbot' in MM BB4 1555 17/5/5; Médard, 'Note confidentielle'.
97 Shen's memorial, 2 February 1868, and Giquel to Shen, 25 October 1869, in *HFT*, II, 116, 209b–210; Giquel to Commander of the French Naval Division of the Seas of China and Japan, 4 March 1869, in MM BB4 1555 17/5/11.

provided extremely generous repatriation conditions if he was not offered the directorship or if he simply could not get along with Giquel.[98] So on the day the Navy Yard's first steamer was to have its maiden run (18 September 1869), he boycotted it and ordered his French assistants not to board the vessel on the ground that his request for a European pilot had been declined. Giquel also favoured a European pilot, just to facilitate communication. Shen, however, thought a Chinese pilot more desirable because of his familiarity with the Min River. In truth, he was eager to keep both the piloting and navigation of the Navy Yard's vessels in Chinese hands. The trial run thus went ahead without Trasbot, and its success only increased the aggravation. To resolve the dispute, Shen took the unusual step of apologizing to Trasbot, attributing the incident to a misunderstanding. He then asked him to consider the trial as never having taken place and proposed that another date be set for it.[99] Trasbot remained intractable, and the steamer eventually had to sail to Tientsin for inspection by an imperial deputy without help from him and his assistants. Shen then had Giquel dismiss the chief engineer, offering him four months' salary and his fare home – about 4,000 taels – as his engagement contract stipulated. Trasbot obviously considered the compensation inadequate because he proceeded to sue Giquel for 22,000 taels (183,663 francs).[100]

Both Shen and Giquel objected strongly to Trasbot's demand, insisting that in matters of discipline and dismissal, Giquel had acted with Shen's permission. Personally, therefore, he could not be sued for damages. In support, Shen also stressed that 'the [French] directorate was established for the Navy Yard, and the Navy Yard is a work of the Chinese government. . . . If the French consul can control [the Navy Yard] as he pleases, then it is a French navy yard, not a Chinese navy yard'.[101] At the heart of the problem was the ambiguous status of the European staff. As Giquel admitted, although he liked to think of himself and other Europeans as servants of China, they were nonetheless

---

98 Articles 5 and 6, 'Contrat d'engagement de Mr. Trasbot', in MM BB4 1555 17/5/5.
99 Giquel to Shen, 8 October 1869, and Shen to Tsungli Yamen, 25 December 1869, in *HFT*, II, 207a–b, 215; Shen to Trasbot, 20 September 1869, in MM BB4 1555 17/5/14.
100 Summary of the meeting of the Council of Works, 24 September 1869, and Giquel to Trasbot, 8 October 1869, in ibid., 17/5/14; Giquel to Shen, 8 October 1869, in *HFT*, II, 208a–b; Proceedings of Consular Tribunal, 3 and 13 November 1869, in MM BB4 1555 17/5/16.
101 Giquel to Shen, 1 November, and Shen to Giquel, 3 November 1869, in *HFT*, II, 211–13, 213–14. Shen had previously made a similar argument that the French directors were acting on behalf of the Chinese authorities when paying salaries to the European employees. Ibid., 175b.

amenable to the laws of their own countries.[102] Still, he argued, the Navy Yard could hold together only under 'strict military discipline'. If the directors could be taken to court over the slightest conflicts, then the whole project would fall apart.[103]

The acting consul could not have cared less. Nor would he countenance Chinese control over the French employees. As far as he was concerned, full responsibility rested with Giquel, who signed the contracts of employment. Thus, when the tribunal finished its hearings, again with Blancheton presiding and de Méritens as the first assessor, Giquel was ordered to meet Trasbot's full claim (22,000 taels). Partly because of the large amount involved, but mainly because Shen wanted to underline that the ultimate authority rested with the Chinese, the fine was paid out of the Navy Yard's coffer.[104]

Before the establishment of the French consulate, Shen and Giquel had had no difficulty in disciplining or dismissing foreign employees, although they rarely exercised such powers.[105] Now, all of a sudden, they found themselves in a totally untenable position. Litigations that would have been laughed out of court in France were repeatedly settled against them. Powerless against Blancheton, Shen and Ying-kuei once again pressed the Tsungli Yamen to approach the French minister at Peking for his removal. But with its hands tied by a couple of incidents perpetrated against French missionaries, the Yamen was in no position to press the matter.[106]

To protect himself and the Navy Yard, Giquel finally turned to Commander Maudet of the French Naval Division in the Seas of China and Japan. Maudet was quick to grasp the importance of the Navy Yard to French political and industrial interests; by late February 1870 he assured Giquel that both he and Comte Julien de Rochechouart, chargé d'affaires at Peking, would lend him their support. A naval captain, Pierre Véron, was then sent to conduct secret investigations at Mawei.[107]

Sensing that his fortune was about to change, d'Aiguebelle left the Navy Yard for good in March 1870. He went straight to Kansu to his

102 Giquel to Shen, 1 November 1869, in ibid., 211–13.
103 Giquel to Maudet, Commander of the French Naval Division of the Seas of China and Japan, 15 March 1870, in MM BB4 1555 17/5/19.
104 Proceedings of the Consular Tribunal for 3, 13, and 25 November 1869; Giquel to Blancheton, 25 November 1869, and Giquel to Trasbot, 27 November 1869, in MM BB4 1555 17/5/16 and 15.
105 *HFT*, II, 116. In late 1867 or early 1868, a foreman and a boiler maker were punished, one for his indolence and the other, who was dismissed, for mistreating the Chinese.
106 Shen to Giquel of 3 November, Ying-kuei to Tsungli Yamen of 3 December, Shen to Tsungli Yamen of 25 December, Tsungli Yamen to Shen of 10 December 1869, in *HFT*, II, 214, 202b, 215b, 204b, respectively.
107 Dupré to Giquel, 25 February 1870, in MM BB4 1555 17/5/18.

former patron, Tso Tsung-t'ang. The latter, in an attempt to save his face, commissioned him to buy Prussian firearms in Europe. For the assignment he was given a 'bonus' of 5,000 taels. Meanwhile, he continued to draw his monthly salary of 1,000 taels from the Navy Yard for the next four years, which he did not serve.[108]

At Ma-wei, d'Aiguebelle's departure was welcome news indeed. Giquel, who now utterly detested his former colleague, reported with satisfaction that much of the internal difficulties of the Navy Yard 'were terminated by the departure of M. d'Aiguebelle' and morale, once again, was high. The French consul, however, remained a major source of trouble, threatening the very work he was supposed to protect.[109]

When Captain Véron arrived at Ma-wei in early March, an old dispute between Giquel and the Navy Yard's physician, Jean Vidal, came to a head. Vidal had been a troublesome person ever since he had set foot on Chinese soil in 1867. Though required by contract to treat all patients, European and Chinese, he soon refused to see Chinese patients on the flimsiest excuses.[110] And in the early days when there was a housing shortage, he, alone among the Europeans, complained incessantly. Eventually, he took the matter to the consular court, which fined Giquel

108 Tso's letters to Ying-kuei, Shen, and Hsia Hsien-lun of 1870 in *TWHK*, 'Letters', 11:6b–7, 8, 9a–b, 14–15b, 18–19. For three years after he left Foochow, d'Aiguebelle vacationed in Paris, spending a little time in a Naval Veterans Hospital in 1872. On returning to China in February 1873 he went to Ma-wei and asked Shen to commission him to negotiate with the French chargé d'affaires and the bishop in Peking for lowering the cathedral spire there – the Chinese had been protesting against the height of the tower for some time. Shen refused. D'Aiguebelle went to Peking on his own and then appealed personally to Tso Tsung-t'ang at Lan-chou. Tso blessed his venture with a 'bonus' of 5,000 taels and granted his request for twenty-five months' salary for the period before the Foochow Navy Yard was founded. Tso had thought that the request referred to the period after d'Aiguebelle's departure from Foochow in early 1870. Later, Tso realized that he had been cheated; d'Aiguebelle had been paid by the Navy Yard all along. But not wishing further complications, he paid the 25,000 taels out of his own pocket. Tso's letters of 1873 and 1874 to Shen and Hu Kuang-yung in ibid., 13:35b–36, 14:1b–3, 6a–b, 15b–16b, 19b–20; Lemaire (Foochow Consul) to de Ramusat (French Foreign Minister), 30 April 1873, in MAE, Dépêches politiques des consuls, Chine, vol. 2 (1870–6), p. 192; MM CC7 1850: Dossier individuel – d'Aiguebelle. According to Theodore Meyer, consul at Foochow in the early 1880s, Tso gave d'Aiguebelle a sum of 10,000 taels, not 5,000. Meyer to Ministre de Freycinet, 16 August 1880, in MAE, Dépêches politiques des consuls, Chine, vol. 3 (1877–81), p. 407.
109 Giquel to Maudet, 15 March 1870, in MM BB4 1555 17/5/19. Giquel's feelings towards d'Aiguebelle are reflected in his report, *Foochow Arsenal*, in which the role of d'Aiguebelle was barely mentioned. Even the latter's residence was deleted from the map of the Navy Yard.
110 'Contrat d'engagement du Docteur Vidal', 13 August 1867, in MM BB4 1555 17/5/6. Vidal to Giquel (two letters), Shen to Giquel, and Vidal to Shen, all dated 6 August 1868, in ibid., 17/5/10.

an unknown sum of money. As Giquel said, he was hurt by the court's decision.[111]

Assured of consular support and encouraged by the consular judgement in the Percebois case, Vidal showed even less restraint. When he and his wife assaulted a native grocer and Giquel intervened, he, claiming that neither Shen nor Giquel could 'deprive me of the inherent advantages of my quality as a French subject', once again took the matter to the consul. Two vituperative communications from Blancheton followed. Without even hearing the case, Blancheton accused Giquel of unwarranted hostility towards the doctor and of opposing his authority to that of the French consul. Blancheton expressed surprise that Giquel, having had a year's experience of consular authority, had not learned to give it greater respect.[112]

For Giquel, the arrival of these communications in the midst of Véron's secret mission was a godsend. They showed the consul in a bad light and increased Véron's sympathy for Giquel. So when Véron reported his findings to Contre-Amiral Dupré, Maudet's successor, and Chargé d'Affaires de Rochechouart, the latter was so enthusiastic about the Navy Yard that he immediately told Blancheton to desist from any further interference that might damage the Navy Yard and French interests there.[113]

Even in the face of this reprobation, Blancheton persisted in his old ways. In mid-1870, another dispute came to a head over the complaint of Deguine, foreman of the foundry, that he had been asked to do jobs that were not required by his contract and that the weather in May and early June was too hot for working in the foundry. Since Deguine had never complained of the heat, which had been far worse in the preceding summers, Giquel simply told him to get on with his work, in the evening if desired. Nevertheless, Deguine, who had once been disciplined for his insolence and menacing behaviour, took the dispute to the consular court. Because Giquel's order was issued on the basis of Engineer Arnaudeau's report, the large monetary fine on him was withdrawn and a small one inflicted on Arnaudeau instead. But as Giquel claimed, this consular decision removed from him his last means of maintaining discipline.[114]

111 Simon to Giquel of 2 May, Giquel to Simon of 3 May, Blancheton to Giquel of 3 August, and Giquel to Blancheton of 4 August 1869, in MM BB4 1555 17/5/3.

112 Shen to Giquel of 18 February, Vidal to Giquel of 3 March, Giquel to Shen of 16 March, Blancheton to Giquel of 4 and 18 March 1870, in MM BB4 1555 17/5/21.

113 Véron to Blancheton of 20 March, Véron to de Rochechouart of 26 April, Véron to Dupré of 9 May 1870, in MM BB4 1555 17/5/22.

114 Giquel to Deguine of 24 and 25 January; Arnaudeau to Giquel and Giquel to Deguine

Meanwhile, Vidal, the physician, became utterly derelict in his duties: a French foreman was confined to bed for days without medical care, and another, in the critical last four days of his life, was left completely unattended. Giquel simply had to seek help from the British doctors in the foreign settlement. Finally, in late August, Giquel suspended him from service.[115]

Comte de Rochechouart now realized how Blancheton's presence had encouraged these endless disputes and, in the summer of 1870, recalled him. Blancheton refused to comply, however, pleading ill-health, and stayed until he could deal Giquel his last blow in the Vidal case. Ignoring the doctor's dereliction, he ordered Giquel to pay Vidal four months' salary and first-class passage for him and his family to Paris.[116]

By October 1870, Giquel's position had become utterly untenable. As he complained to Contre-Amiral Dupré, 'I know that I am losing control of the Arsenal, and that the Chinese are aware of this too, since I hear that there is talk of looking for some English who, at a given moment, could replace the present [French] personnel'.[117] This veiled threat was unfounded. In any event, as the French navy put growing pressure on de Rochechouart, Blancheton found himself leaving Foochow, thus preserving French influence on this Chinese establishment.[118]

Chinese and Europeans: harmony at all costs

From the very first, Tso, Shen, Giquel, and d'Aiguebelle understood that the primary goal of the Navy Yard was to teach the Chinese the art of naval construction and navigation. At a minimum, the success of this programme depended on a good working relationship between the Chinese and the Europeans. Yet as Giquel anticipated, 'in a staff . . . newly arrived from Europe, there would be some who would refuse to act in harmony with a race considered by them to be their inferiors'.[119] The employment contracts for the Europeans therefore reflected the

---

of 13 May; Proceedings, Council of Works, 8 June; Deguine to Giquel and the latter's reply of 10 June; Consular Tribunal, 'Summons and Conciliation', 22 June 1870, all in MM BB4 1555 17/5/26. Proceedings, Consular Court, 20 August 1870, in ibid., 17/5/28. Giquel to Dupré, 8 October 1870, in ibid., 17/5/29.

115 Proceedings, Consular Court, in *NCH*, 13 December 1870.

116 Ibid., and Giquel to Dupré, 8 October 1870, in MM BB4 1555 17/5/29.

117 Ibid.

118 De Méritens left Foochow soon after, in August 1871. The circumstances surrounding his departure are unclear. *Fu-chien wen-shih tzu-liao*, no. 10 (Foochow, 1985), p. 187.

119 Giquel, *Foochow Arsenal*, p. 15. On the emphasis Tso and Shen placed on learning, see the next chapter.

Chinese desire for heavy penalties for those who struck or abused a Chinese workman or official or otherwise caused a disturbance.[120]

In a positive vein, Tso tried to secure the Europeans' whole-hearted service by offering them extremely attractive financial rewards. The French directors were each paid 1,000 taels a month, nearly 170 taels above the salary of a provincial governor and 400 taels more than Shen's.[121] The chief engineer took home 500 taels a month, whereas the professors in the School, the master carpenter, and the chief of the metalworking forge each got 200 taels. As for the foremen, they were paid 120 taels each, and the workmen, 60.[122] They received much higher pay than European employees at other government enterprises. No one at the Soochow Arsenal received more than 300 taels a month, while an instructor at the Tientsin Arsenal was paid only 100, and the professors at the T'ung-wen Kuan received 25 per cent less than their colleagues at Ma-wei.[123] Compared with those of the Chinese in the Navy Yard, their salaries were heavenly: their foremen received between four to ten times as much, and the workmen, three to more than thirteen times (see the next chapter). Captain Contenson, military attaché of the French legation at Peking, was impressed by the generous emoluments and reported that the Europeans owed Giquel a rapid profit and were sending back to France at least Fr. 30,000 (3,660 taels) a month.[124]

Rewards were also promised for the future: two months' salary for those who served out the entire contract period, a bonus of 24,000 taels each for the directors, and 60,000 taels to be shared among the meritorious.[125] To boost morale, Shen also awarded brevet ranks from time to time. Thus, James Carroll, who taught theoretical navigation, was awarded a silver medal and a military rank of the fifth grade for excellence in teaching after only eight months of service.[126] Chief

---

120 Article 10, 'Contrat d'engagement des ingénieurs, contre-maîtres et ouvriers Européens', MM BB4 1555 17/5/2; *HFT*, II, 41b.
121 *HFT*, II, 34b. Shen's salary is not known; he was probably paid much the same as a successor of his in the 1880s, at 600 taels a month (*NCH*, 22 October 1884). In any event, he could not have been paid more than a provincial governor, his previous title.
122 'Contrat d'engagement de Mr. Trasbot', MM BB4 1555 17/5/5; Carroll's 'Contrat d'engagement', 1 July 1876, in his private papers; Contenson to Ministre de la Guerre, 13 August 1872, in MM BB4 1382, p. 333. Figures given by Contenson are in francs, converted here at the rate of Fr. 8.33 to the tael. The exchange rates are computed by using Paul Einzig, *The History of Foreign Exchange*, 2d ed. (London, 1970), p. 195, and Stanley, *Late Ch'ing Finance*, p. 62. The exchange rates in the period in question fluctuated between Fr. 8 and Fr. 8.43 to the tael. Hsiao Liang-lin, *China's Foreign Trade Statistics, 1864–1949* (Cambridge, Mass., 1974), p. 190.
123 *IWSM*, TC 25:7b; Kennedy, *Arms*, p. 73; Stanley Wright, *Hart*, p. 325.
124 Contenson to Ministre de la Guerre, 13 August 1872, in MM BB4 1382, p. 333.
125 *HFT*, II, 32, 35.
126 'Certificate of Merit', 16 January 1868, in Carroll's papers.

Engineer Trasbot, too, was given the third-grade military rank in 1868 for his good performance and, in the following year, promised a bonus of 3,000 taels pending the successful voyage of the first steamer to Tientsin for inspection by an imperial deputy. Owing to the altercations mentioned earlier, Shen withdrew the bonus, but the others, Europeans and Chinese, were duly rewarded.[127]

In addition, all were provided free and commodious living quarters (see Map 2). The directors had their own houses, built in the European style adapted for the warmer climes of colonial Asia. Both were large, solid, two-storeyed houses with broad verandahs and were as big as the school buildings. A similar house was shared by the secretary-interpreter and the doctor, while the professors and accountants lived in yet another building of the same class. The foremen were housed in apartments in large buildings, each having a front room, a drawing room, a dining room, a bedroom, and the usual amenities, with a garden in the front and back. The kitchen and servants' quarters were outside. The married workmen were given two-room flats and the single men large one-room apartments. All had a verandah, a small garden, and an outside kitchen. Basic furniture was supplied.[128] As Carroll entered in his diary, he was 'much pleased with [his] House' even though it was not quite ready when he arrived.[129] A reliable supply of clean water, fresh food from the morning market nearby, and a 'sufficient medical staff' (except when Dr. Vidal neglected his patients) contributed to a comfortable environment.[130]

Apart from the fourteen men who brought their families, this 'petite colonie' was made up of young, single men who, under any circumstances, could be troublesome. Facilities were therefore provided to relieve boredom and prevent mischief. These were described with a tone of Victorian approval by John Dunn:

A club house was built for the foreign workmen, and billiard tables set up for their use. The reading room is well supplied with newspapers. A savings bank has been established by Monsieur Giquel, and admirable results have followed, for it has created a passion for thrift which is found to be a specific against turbulence, drunkenness, waste, and other sinful ways which beset us in our

---

127 *YWYT*, vol. 5, p. 70; *HFT*, II, 209b–211, 229b–230.
128 Véron, 'Rapport'; 'Arsenal et Ville de Fou-Tchéou', 6 June 1872, MM BB4 1555. According to Véron, the professors lived in the schools. Neither source gives the residence of the chief engineer (Trasbot), who was dismissed in late 1869 and was not replaced. For the appearance of some of these buildings, see Plate 13 in Arnold Toynbee, ed., *Half the World: The History and Culture of China and Japan* (London, 1973), p. 326.
129 Carroll's papers: 'Notes and Diary', book 1, entry for 6 November 1867.
130 J. G. Dunn's report in *NCH*, 21 April 1870. Vidal was replaced by another French physician, Dr. Poujade. Giquel, *Foochow Arsenal*, p. 37.

fallen state . . . and the Catholic priest . . . labours with evident success, for order, morality, and religion.[131]

Not all of the facilities were provided by the Chinese, but they existed with Shen's blessings. The presence of a priest, and a chapel each for the Catholics and the Protestants, show just how far he was prepared to go to accommodate the needs of the Europeans, for not only had Shen shown a particular distaste for Catholic missionaries in his earlier career but Tso Tsung-t'ang had also specifically told the French directors not to bring a missionary to China.[132] The evidence is overwhelming that the Chinese treated the Europeans generously, even down to the minute detail of sending the workers coal for heating in winter, which was beyond the call of duty.[133]

To be sure, the Chinese perception of the greedy foreigners contributed in part to the use of material incentives,[134] but their attempts at cultivating the Europeans' goodwill were not entirely contrived. Carroll was kindly received by Shen 'and 2 other great mandarins' on arrival. He was immediately given a Chinese name, which, he was proud to note, meant 'much happiness and joy' (Chia-lo-erh). Eleven days later, he was invited to dine with Shen and the '2nd Mandarin', probably Chou K'ai-hsi, 'en famille at Mr. Lysan [Tseng Heng-chung]'. As he was 'very tired', Shen sent him home in his sampan. Then Tartar General Ying-kuei visited the Navy Yard and had a brief audience with the European staff. The latter returned the compliments by receiving the Tartar general at Giquel's. The Chinese authorities, in turn, reciprocated by sending two lots of presents in three days.[135]

The little that we can glean from the sparse entries in Carroll's diary shows that Shen, along with Ying-kuei, was serious in trying to establish a healthy relationship with the Europeans so that the Chinese could

---

131 *NCH*, 21 April 1870.
132 *IWSM*, TC 51:23. On the chapels, see Wang Wei-hsüan, *I-shan-t'ang sheng-kao* (1893), reprinted in part in Lin Hsüan-chih, *Fu-chien Ma-wei*, p. 40.
133 Giquel to Maudet, 15 March 1870, in MM BB4 1555 17/5/19.
134 *HFT*, II, 6b.
135 Carroll's papers: 'Notes and Diary', book 1, entries for 7 and 18 November, 7 and 9 December 1867. Mr. Lysan was probably Tseng Heng-chung, alias Tseng Lai-shun, an English-speaking Chinese from Singapore, whom Giquel hired from Shanghai in 1866 to teach the students before Carroll's arrival. Afterwards, he became Carroll's assistant. In the English-language press on the China coast, his name was sometimes rendered as Chan Laisun. He is probably the Tseng Lan-sheng referred to in the first section of this chapter. Huang Yin-p'u, 'Pa Shen Pao-chen t'iao-shih Fu-chien i-chü (ch'uan-cheng hsüeh-t'ang) chang-ch'eng shou-chien', in Chou K'ang-hsieh, ed., *Yang-wu yün-tung yen-chiu lun-chi* (Hong Kong), pp. 145–55; *Chinese Recorder*, January 1879, pp. 217–18.

learn from the West as expeditiously as possible and become independent of their European mentors (see the next chapter). In fact, the Chinese placed such a premium on good relations that potentially disruptive incidents were simply glossed over. As mentioned earlier, Giquel had once acquired a shipment of bad timber through a French agent in South-East Asia. Shen, while recognizing the problems of buying materials through foreign agents in distant lands, was careful not to let the situation affect his relations with Giquel and pursued the matter no further. Instead, he entrusted all future timber purchases to his Chinese staff.[136] Had the error been committed by a Chinese, he would certainly have meted out heavy punishment. Again, in the case of d'Aiguebelle, who, rightly or wrongly, had been such a source of discord and bitterness, Shen met all his requests made on the eve of his departure: deputies (*wei-yün*) were to accompany him to Kansu, authorities along the way were asked to protect him, while his family was allowed to stay in the spacious house at Ma-wei with Chinese protection against possible mistreatment.[137] Whatever Shen thought of these requests, he must have weighed the possibility of further complications had he rejected them.

Still, small irritants cropped up often. In a situation where the Europeans and the Chinese were placed in a teacher–student or master–apprentice relationship, language difficulties loomed large, especially at first, and especially when so many of the Chinese workmen were not educated or literate. Besides, as Shen was keenly aware, different perceptions of workmanship could cause serious disagreements,[138] as when the European mechanics demanded a refabrication of what the Chinese workmen considered perfectly good parts. And those who had learned their skills elsewhere, such as Hong Kong or Shanghai, objected to the methods adopted by the French. Shen understood the situation, and thanks to his good sense, such differences were not allowed to develop into major disputes.[139]

It would be only fair to say that the Chinese, too, harboured prejudices against the Europeans. Yet of the several conflicts our records

136 *HFT*, II, 139–140b, 348.
137 Ibid., 226b–227.
138 Shen's memorial of 18 July 1867, in *SWSK*, 4:2b–3.
139 In 1880 Li Chao-t'ang, director-general in 1879–1883, accused Giquel and his staff of intentionally slowing down production by demanding the remaking of good parts in order to extend their lucrative contract. The allegation enjoyed some currency at the time. Li, however, was not associated with the Navy Yard until more than four years after the Europeans had left. His charges were based on second-hand sources. *HFT*, II, 856b; Rawlinson, *China's Struggle*, p. 98. Shen's understanding of the issue (*HFT*, II, 193a–b, 347b) is probably correct since the huge bonuses promised the Europeans were predicated upon the timely completion of their mission. Stalling would not have done them any good.

reveal, only one arose from hostility between members of the two ethnic groups, and that had everything to do with the attitude and behaviour of a single person, Dr. Vidal. As Giquel testified in 1870, Vidal 'and his family, during a residence of 3 years in the Arsenal, have committed many hostile acts against the Chinese of the district, especially against workmen... striking and insulting them so as to cause, from incessant provocation, a real ill-feeling'.[140]

Vidal was a curse to Europeans and Chinese alike. Over the years, Chinese ill-treated by him and his wife had made several noisy protests in front of their house.[141] So in the summer of 1870, after the Tientsin Massacre, in which more than a dozen French men and women lost their lives, Vidal felt threatened. On 9 August, 'he complained of the bad treatment of his wife, and asserted that, since the Tientsin affair, the insolence and arrogance of the Chinese had passed all bounds, and that threats of murder were daily used against the French employed in the Arsenal; that if he did not get prompt and real satisfaction, he would move his family to a place of safety'.[142] In view of the seriousness of the charges, Giquel and Shen conducted a thorough investigation but found no evidence that would support the allegations. As Shen argued, had there been any change for the worse, the local Chinese would not have tried to vent their animosity on Vidal alone.[143]

The Tientsin Massacre was the supreme test of the relations between the Chinese and the Europeans, particularly the French, in the Navy Yard. Tardy news transmission had led to vicious rumours, adding tension to an already uneasy atmosphere that prevailed in all the treaty ports until at least early winter.[144] Some French consuls clamoured for war.[145] Meanwhile, Shen, as a gentry leader, had to make secret defence preparations.[146] Yet no untoward incident occurred. As the *North-China Herald* reported, 'The work... appears to go on in the same satisfactory manner as it has previously done'.[147] This must be considered a crowning success by all the parties concerned in maintaining a sober attitude

---

140 *NCH*, 13 December 1870.
141 *HFT*, II, 255b.
142 *NCH*, 13 December 1870.
143 Ibid.; *HFT*, II, 254a–b. The only sign of hostility at the time concerned a young apprentice who told a French worker that Foochow would gradually be turned into another Tientsin. The worker simply dismissed the remark, attributing it to the youth's ignorance.
144 *NCH*, 28 July, 15 September, and 4 October 1870.
145 Dabry (consul at Canton) to Duc de Gramont (Ministre des Affaires Etrangères), 12 and 20 July, and 23 August 1870; Simon to Duc de Gramont, 18 July 1870, in MAE, Dépêches politiques des consuls, Chine vol. 2, pp. 26–31, 50.
146 *IWSM*, TC 75:36a–b, 76:26b–27b.
147 *NCH*, 15 September 1870.

at a difficult time. Wen-yü, the new Tartar general, who was no friend of Shen's, nevertheless attributed this success to the spirit and fairness with which he dealt with the Europeans, making it a pleasure for the latter to work in the Navy Yard.[148] Equally important, this sentiment was reciprocated, as when the Chinese cadets spoke 'with much appreciation' of their English training officer.[149] Giquel, too, deserved a great deal of credit. Years later, the British consul at Foochow reported that the thousand-odd Chinese workmen were well disposed towards the foreigners, and regarded this rare phenomenon as one of his legacies.[150] Throughout his association with the Ch'ing government, Giquel had deliberately cultivated the goodwill and trust of the Chinese, even if that meant an occasional departure from the policies of his own government. He was a practitioner of the Co-operative Policy before it was formally conceived and continued to practise it long after it had vanished.[151] And in the larger context of modern Chinese history, Sino-foreign relations *within* the Navy Yard in the period 1867–74 represent an important example of successful co-operation in which the Chinese had no fear of foreign domination.

There is no question that the Chinese benefited much from this co-operation, the concrete results of which will be discussed in the following chapters. But the benefits came at a hefty price. The European staff was expensive; it received more than ten times the combined salary of the 130-odd Chinese administrators, and that did not include the cost of housing, rewards, and travelling expenses.[152] It should be stressed, however, that these salaries, though higher than those at the Soochow and Tientsin arsenals, were not exorbitant.[153] The Europeans of the Foochow Navy Yard, made up of bona fide engineers, foremen, and skilled workers directly and systematically recruited from France and England, were simply superior. Carroll had taught at the Greenwich Naval College

---

148 *YWYT*, vol. 5, pp. 94–5.

149 John N. Jordan's memorandum of 22 July 1879, enclosed in Wade to Foreign Office, 1 August 1879, in FO 228/622, no. 129, encl. 3 in no. 6.

150 Acting Vice-Consul R. W. Mansfield's report, enclosed in Sinclair to Parkes, 21 April 1884, in FO 228/752, no. 15. A criticism often levelled at the Kiangnan Arsenal was the absence of any rapport (*kan-ch'ing*) between the Chinese and the Europeans. Li Shou-k'ung, *Li*, p. 184.

151 David Pong, 'Western Technicians and Technical Aid in China's Early Developmental Experience: The Foochow Navy Yard, 1866–1875', *Papers on Far Eastern History*, 20 (September 1979), 96. On two very important issues, namely, missionary privileges and the Alcock Convention, Giquel opposed the French government's policy. Giquel, *La politique française*, pp. 14–47.

152 Wang Hsin-chung, 'Fu-chou ch'uan-ch'ang', pp. 18–20.

153 Earlier, I had described the Europeans' salary as 'exorbitant'; I have since revised my view. Pong, 'Western Technicians', p. 89.

before coming to China, and Trasbot was hired from a French arsenal, as were many others.[154] This is in direct contrast to the often haphazard manner in which many foreigners were recruited at other arsenals.[155]

In the last analysis, what hurt the Chinese most was the loss of control over sensitive information about the Navy Yard. Thanks to the large number of European employees and Giquel's connection with the French navy, a constant stream of foreign visitors wandered through the Navy Yard, browsing freely and taking notes in detail. Thus, a British reporter acknowledged that 'Mr. Giquel gave me every facility for examining the various departments of the Arsenal, and kindly furnished information'.[156] Giquel even had a fact sheet prepared and distributed it to the more important visitors.[157] But the most privileged information was reserved for the French government, the ministère de la marine in particular.[158] The French continued to enjoy excellent reports on the Navy Yard well into the Sino-French War of 1883–5.[159]

154 *Chinese Recorder*, January 1870, p. 216; Médard, 'Note confidentielle', pp. 1–7. Médard, however, was critical of some Europeans, especially Giquel and his colleagues in the Navy Yard School, Carroll and Borel.

155 On the foreign staff at the Tientsin Naval College, Sir Harry Parkes said, 'The Viceroy [Li Hung-chang] pursues the practice of picking up officers of various nationalities as may happen either to suit himself, or please those who vie for a share of his patronage'. Parkes to Granville, 7 October 1884, in FO 17/951, no. 112.

156 *Chinese Recorder*, 2 (January 1870), 216–18 (reprint of an *NCH* report of the preceding month).

157 M. M. Delano, U.S. Consul at Foochow, to J. C. B. Davis, Assistant Secretary of State, 5 December 1871, in 'Report for Year ending September 30, 1871', in U.S., Department of State, Consular Dispatches, Foochow, vol. 4, Record Group no. 59. Despite the effort of the staff at the National Archives, Giquel's fact sheet cannot be found. Another U.S. visitor in 1873 reported that he, 'having [had] everything there courteously shown to me by the Director, Mr. Giquel', was also given a plan of the Navy Yard accompanied by detailed descriptions. Ibid., MF 89/259, document 29 (reorganized no. 35).

158 The British, of course, were interested in the Navy Yard and had published the several important reports already cited. Of note are the two by J. G. Dunn; the first appeared in the *North-China Herald* (21 April 1870), and the second, a more detailed update, was prepared for the British government in November 1873 (FO 233/85, no. 3). The French, naturally, produced excellent reports. Already cited many times were the ones by Engineer Thibaudier (June 1868), Captain Véron (1870), Captain Contenson (13 August 1872), and Contre-Amiral Garnault (2 June 1873). As Contenson admitted, the fact that the director of the Navy Yard was a French naval officer enabled him to write a detailed report. Giquel himself also wrote frequently to the French naval authorities, especially the commander-in-chief of the Division navale des mers de Chine et du Japon. The French consuls after Blancheton also reported regularly to Peking and Paris, using information supplied by Giquel. For example, see letters and reports by Gabriel Lemaire and Theodore Meyer of 3 July 1873, 13 March 1875, and 16 August 1880, in MAE, Dépêches politiques des consuls, Chine, vol. 2, pp. 202–4, vol. 3, pp. 399–419.

159 See, e.g., Consul Frandon to le Ministre des Affaires Etrangères, 11 June 1883, 12 and 19 February 1884, in ibid., vol. 5, pp. 104, 106, 169.

Since the Navy Yard was intended to improve China's defence, it is curious that Shen and other Chinese, who were certainly aware of the threat of foreign intelligence, should permit intelligence work before their very eyes.[160] Perhaps they felt that, since the technology had come from the West, there was little to hide. If that was their thinking, they were both naïve and sadly mistaken, for details as to armament and munitions in stock, fleet movement, not to mention the Navy Yard's layout and fortification, were all crucial information for the future enemy. A plausible explanation is that Shen recognized the close ties between the European staff and the French and British navies and, therefore, the futility of keeping classified information from them. To protest was to disrupt the harmony he had taken so much care to cultivate. So although he was able to ward off immediate foreign domination of the Navy Yard, he was unable to forestall future disaster.[161] But then, the position of China after the Opium Wars was such that perhaps Shen could not have done better.

Conclusions

Administration was the most important area of Shen's responsibilities. During the first years of his incumbency, much of his energy was consumed in fending off Chinese opponents and French detractors. His success preserved the Navy Yard as an institution, but the fulfilment of its mission depended on factors that were far more fundamental. At the very least, the Navy Yard needed an efficient and reasonably honest administration. Looking back a quarter of a century later, Médard attributed Shen's achievement in this area to his 'somewhat savage energy' and 'scrupulous integrity'.[162] Shen's personal probity and disciplinarian approach had certainly reduced corruption to a minimum and had produced a responsive and responsible staff. Nevertheless, short of any fundamental change in the status of the gentry and its privilege in the society at large, he, as an individual, could do little to institute *permanent* deterrents against deep-seated bureaucratic vices. Thus, instances of lax discipline and corruption increased during his extended absences.

160 For Shen's view on the threat of foreign intelligence expressed in 1865, see *HFT*, IV, 10.
161 The disaster came during the battle of the Min in 1884 when the Foochow squadron and the Navy Yard sustained terrible losses. One of the many reasons for the Chinese defeat was the information the French were able to gather beforehand. Rawlinson, *China's Struggle*, pp. 109–20; James F. Roche and L. L. Cowen, *The French at Foochow* (Shanghai, 1884).
162 Médard, 'Note confidentielle', p. 2.

Among Shen's achievements, the organization and deployment of administrators and managers among the gentry had the greatest potential for China's modern transformation. Under him staff members were given tasks that exposed them to the world of machines, transport, and foreign affairs. Many rose through the ranks by virtue of their special talents. Some became career *yang-wu* men. That a number of them were his close associates or relatives testifies to his personal influence and contribution to the growing sense of pride and identity in the still nascent and uncertain modernizing sector. His fault lay in his failure to multiply these successes by a wholesale and systematic organization of his staff in specialized departments.

In discussing the failure of the *yang-wu* 'movement', a modern scholar blames the gentry, especially the lower gentry, who engaged in *yang-wu* only because they had failed the civil service examinations. Motivated by material gains, they were corrupt and their knowledge remained superficial.[163] To be sure, the bulk of the gentry administrators and managers at Ma-wei could never have made a career in the regular bureaucracy. For them the Navy Yard offered an attractive alternative. Yet there was in the Navy Yard a significant minority of upper gentry-men, former officials, and future civil servants. And those who acquired a level of proficiency in foreign affairs or technical matters hailed from a wide range of social backgrounds. Further, although greed may have motivated many to join the Navy Yard staff, Shen saw to it that extra-legal profit seeking was curbed. In any event, personal gain, ambition, conviction, and patriotism were not mutually exclusive character traits; they could reinforce each other. The last three may well have been the driving force behind Shen's own dedication to self-strengthening. Whether *yang-wu* men of a particular social origin were prone to stagnation at a low level of proficiency is a much broader question which shall be addressed later.

The organization of the European staff was determined largely by Tso and the French directors before Shen took office. A major flaw in that system was the absence of the right of European employees to appeal to the Chinese authorities against the judgement of Giquel or d'Aiguebelle. Thus, unresolved disputes, however trivial, invited consular intervention. Why did Shen embrace this old method of managing the 'barbarians' through their 'headman'? The answer is that the alternative would not have been very effective either. The right of appeal would have seriously undermined the authority of the French directors and exposed the Chinese to a constant barrage of minor complaints. Nor could it be

163 Li Shou-k'ung, *Li*, pp. 183–4.

assumed that the aggrieved would accept Shen's judgement more readily than Giquel's. Similar situations were encountered elsewhere; the challenge to Robert Hart's authority in 1867–9 by the notorious Baron Johannes von Gumpach of the T'ung-wen Kuan shows just how difficult it was for the Chinese authorities, in this case the Tsungli Yamen, to prevail upon von Gumpach to carry out his teaching duties. When von Gumpach took Hart to court, Sir Edmund Hornby, chief judge of Her Britannic Majesty's Supreme Court for China and Japan, a far more honorable man than Blancheton of Foochow, also ruled in the plaintiff's favour – and this in spite of Earl Russell's ruling some years earlier that a British subject employed by the Chinese government was not civilly answerable to a British consular court for acts done in his official capacity. On this principle, Hornby's verdict was eventually overturned, but only after Hart had appealed to the Privy Council in 1873. In essence, the disupte was settled by diplomacy, a long and cumbersome process, during which the foreign staff at the T'ung-wen Kuan became demoralized.[164] At Foochow, Shen also tried diplomacy, through the Tsungli Yamen, but the latter was hesitant. And there was no one to take the cases to Paris. The disputes were finally terminated by Giquel's bringing to bear the weight of the French navy. It was a more expeditious method, but at the expense of not pressing home an important legal argument with the French government.

Although the disputes at Ma-wei were less drawn out than the von Gumpach case, their impact was hardly less debilitating.[165] Giquel had threatened to resign, and Shen, on the death of his father (6 October 1870), also asked to be relieved of the director-generalship so that he could go into full mourning. When allowed only a hundred days of mourning, he repeatedly pleaded ill health. Eventually, the throne, while blocking his resignation, granted the full mourning period if he made himself available for consultation during his absence.[166]

Shen had never enjoyed good health, but his condition was not such as to warrant resignation. Why then did he wish to relinquish his post? Li Hung-chang ascribed it to his misgivings about the Navy Yard, but Li did not elaborate.[167] Several reasons can be posited, however. First, Shen must have been deeply disappointed by the weak-kneed policy of the Tsungli Yamen, which had twice failed to support his attempt to

---

164 Stanley Wright, *Hart*, chap. 12, esp. pp. 334–48. Lord John Russell (earl since 1861) was foreign secretary in 1859–65 and prime minister in 1865–6.
165 European personnel to Giquel, 7 February 1874, enclosed in Giquel to Garnault, 15 February 1874, in MM BB4 1555 17/5/41.
166 *YWYT*, vol. 5, pp. 94–5, 97–8; *HFT*, II, 292.
167 Li to Tseng Kuo-fan, 5 March 1872, in *LWCK*, 'Letters', 12:3–4b.

remove the French consul. Second, he may well have been affected by the apathy, if not opposition, of Tartar General Wen-yü. Because Wen-yü was in charge of customs revenues from which the Navy Yard drew its fund, he saw in its growing needs a threat to the very source that had contributed to his 'enormous wealth' (see Chapter 9).[168] Finally, Shen's filial piety was beyond question. He had insisted on a full mourning after his mother's death (1865); it was only right that he should remember his father in the same way. But fearing that his prolonged absence would do great harm to the Navy Yard, he asked for another director-general.

The disputes among the Europeans had led to several fundamental changes. Emerging out of these crises was a much stronger bond between Shen and Giquel. Structurally, d'Aiguebelle's departure allowed Shen and Giquel to appoint de Segonzac to the down-graded office of sub-director. After Trasbot's dismissal, the office of chief engineer was briefly held in an acting capacity by Arnaudeau and then abolished. The chief engineer's work was delegated to the handful of engineers and a larger number of workshop superintendents scattered around the Navy Yard.[169] These changes eliminated the potential for a power struggle at the top and strengthened Giquel's position. The Council of Works, which formerly comprised Giquel, d'Aiguebelle, and Trasbot, now became a meeting between Giquel and de Segonzac, who made up the much-reduced directorate. Whether these changes had other effects is difficult to ascertain. And whether the Navy Yard suffered from inferior technical leadership without a chief engineer remains a moot question. After all, the project was eventually completed, despite minor delays. We can be certain, however, that the absence of serious disputes among the Europeans after 1870 did not preclude some lingering personal bitterness – hence Médard's continuing campaign against Giquel well into the 1890s, long after Giquel had died.[170]

As for the Navy Yard, the stormy 1860s gave way to the more tranquil 1870s, during which work progressed more or less as expected. Peace

---

168 *NCH*, 23 June 1877.
169 Giquel, *Foochow Arsenal*, pp. 23, 37–8. The abolition of the post of chief engineer is inferred; no reference to it is found after 1870. One poorly documented account refers to Arnaudeau as acting chief engineer from 1870 to 1875 or 1876. Médard did indicate that Arnaudeau was hired to fill Trasbot's shoes, but without the title. In any case, he was found unsatisfactory and was replaced in 1872 by Jouvet, whose title was simply 'engineer'. Although the Chinese referred to Jouvet as well as Trasbot and Arnaudeau as *chung-chien-kung* (general foreman), Giquel listed him and another Frenchman equally as 'engineer'. Giquel's omission of Arnaudeau indicates that he had indeed left by 1873. Ch'en Chen, comp., *Chung-kuo chin-tai kung-yeh-shih tzu-liao, ti-san-chi* (Peking, 1961), vol. 1, p. 144; Médard, 'Note confidentielle', p. 3.
170 Médard's 'Note confidentielle' of 1898 is in part a deliberate attempt to denigrate Giquel, who died in 1886.

among the Europeans was also ensured by the arrival of the new French consul, Gabriel Lemaire, who could not have been more enthusiastic.[171] The fear that Shen's long absence would result in chaos proved unfounded. In part this was due to the organizational strength of the Navy Yard's administration and the fact that Shen was constantly consulted by Hsia Hsien-lun, who took over the day-to-day operation. Despite some administrative laxity, there was no serious sign of decline. The labours of Shen and Giquel, as well as the human and institutional foundations they had laid, ensured the ultimate fulfilment of their mission. The time has come to examine the work of the Navy Yard, the raison d'être of Shen and Giquel's administrative efforts.

171 Lemaire to Ministre des Affaires Etrangères, 3 July 1873, 18 June and 6 July 1874, in MAE, Dépêches politiques des consuls, Chine, vol. 2, pp. 202–4, 305, 316–17.

8

The Foochow Navy Yard: building and training programmes

The building of modern warships and the training of naval personnel to operate these vessels were the main objectives of the Navy Yard. The 'General Contract of Execution' thus provided for the construction of a modern dockyard, equipped with the best facilities, to build a specific number of steamships and to train Chinese to build and operate them, all within a five-year term.[1] In the thinking of Tso Tsung-t'ang and Shen Pao-chen, these time-specific goals were but a means to a higher end – a modern defence facility based on technological independence. Anything less, Shen insisted, would be inconsistent with the goals of self-strengthening.[2] This chapter focuses on the construction of the dockyard facilities, shipbuilding, and naval training.

In the overall scheme of things, 'the direction of the works and of the instruction belongs to the Europeans'.[3] Having been promised generous rewards on completion of the contract, the Europeans had strong incentives to succeed, regardless of Chinese input. Yet an active role by Shen and his staff could prove valuable in a project that developed with time and changing needs. Their contribution, which could well be a first step towards technological independence, would depend on their growing understanding of the works.

On his first day in office, Shen stressed the superiority of Western technology. The foreigners were indefatigable in seeking improvement, he said; hence, their technology never stood still. The Chinese must therefore embrace the same attitude towards technology and see the need to catch up in an ever-growing field. The learning process was to be

1 *HFT*, II, 31–32b; MM BB4 1555 17/5/2.
2 Tso's memorial of 25 June 1866 in *HFT*, II, 5–9b; Shen's of 18 July 1867 in *SWSK*, 4:2b–3b; *Ch'uan-cheng tsou-yi*, 11:1.
3 Giquel, *Foochow Arsenal*, p. 13.

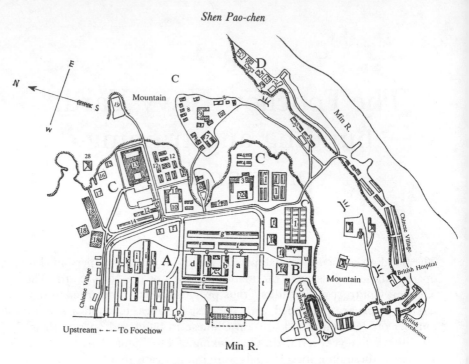

Map 2. Plan of the Foochow Navy Yard

conducted at both the work place and the Navy Yard School. The latter, Shen repeatedly emphasized, was the foundation of the whole enterprise.[4] The Navy Yard, in fact, was to be one big classroom. At the first gate to the grounds, he had this verse inscribed:

> Slow down your pace,
>> See what you have not before seen,
>> Hear what you have not before heard.
> This is the critical juncture,
>> The place, seriously
>> Where hands are put to science.
>
> How do we seek more refinement from refinement
>> And precision from what is already exact?
> From gods and demons, the inner secrets of a courtyard,
>> Make searching examinations![5]

Shen's own role was primarily administrative, but did he learn enough about the production process and its scientific bases to make him a

4 *SWSK*, 4:2b–3b, 6b.   5 Lin Hsüan-chih, *Fu-chou Ma-wei*, p. 342.

A. Navy Yard Proper

a	Boiler-house
b	Fitting shop
c	Setting-up shop
d	Foundry
e	Moulding hall
f	Stores
g	Rope and sail shop
h	Shops for chronometers, optical instruments, and compasses
i	Equipment forges
j	Small fitting and locksmith's shops
k	Mechanical sawmill
l	Model room and the joiners' shop
m	Shipbuilding slips
n	Wood-working sheds
o	Mast and small boats workshops
p	Wharf and caulking machine
q	Labat's patent slip
r	French Directors' Office
s	Office of the Chinese authorities
t	Moat

B. Annex: Metal-working Forge

u	Forging department
v	Rolling mill

C. Schools & Living Quarters

1	Chinese workers' dormitories
2	School of Navigation

3	Pupils' dormitories
4	Timber store-houses
5	European mechanics' quarters
6	French directors' residence
7	Deputies' (*wei-yüan*) residence
8	Barracks for the guards
9	Residence of the guards' commander
10	The School of Naval Construction
11	Pupils' dormitories
12	Timber store-houses
13	Yamen of the director-general and high officials
14	European mechanics' quarters
15	Theatre
16	Residence of secretary-interpreter and doctor
17	Residence of teachers and secretaries
18	Residence of European foremen
19	Temple to the Goddess of the Seas
20	Quarters for married workers
28	Second French director's residence

D. Brick & Coking Kilns

21	Overseers' and workers' quarters
22	Moulding shop
23	Brick kiln
24	Kiln for fire-proof bricks
25	Coking kiln
26	Shop for preparing fire-proof clay
27	Lime kiln

Legend to Map 2

better leader? Did he provide a better environment in which the Chinese could work and learn? What obstacles were to be overcome? Did Confucianism stand in the way? Or, in spite of his poem, did he share the mandarinate's disdain for technical matters?

Construction of the Navy Yard

Situated almost at the tip of the Ma-wei promontory where the Min River takes a 300-degree V-shaped turn from a southerly to a northerly direction, the main part of the Navy Yard, facing west, was protected on three sides by a range of hills rising to more than 200 feet. The grounds covered some 47 hectares and 77 ares (118 acres), and the compound, as it stood in early 1874, comprised four sections, each having a special function. The first section, to the west, along the river, contained all the shipbuilding facilities as they were originally conceived (Map 2, section A); this was the Navy Yard proper. To its south was the annex (section B), containing a large metal factory, which was added in 1871. The rest of the valley and the hillsides were given over to administrative, residential, and school buildings (section C). Over the hills, where the grounds rejoined the Min, were the brick factory and the living quarters for overseers and workers (section D).[6]

Construction began in early 1867. The most important task at this stage was to lay the foundation for the Navy Yard proper, which involved raising the soft alluvial ground by five feet, above the highest tides, to support the heavy machinery and structures. Work of this nature was necessarily slow, and despite Shen's concern – 1,200 men were employed for the job – it was only one-fifth complete when Giquel returned from Paris in October. The machines ordered from France had yet to arrive. Under pressure, Giquel had to make do with temporary workshops, using traditional Chinese tools to make iron nails and other building materials.[7]

The pressure from Shen was relentless. He was eager to start work on the hulls so that the seven marine engines (two 150-horsepower and five 80-horsepower) could be fitted the moment they arrived from France. Giquel, half-complaining, recalled, 'It was necessary to soothe the very natural impatience of the Chinese, who demanded to see results with the least possible delay'.[8] So with only makeshift workshops, work was begun on the first of three shipbuilding slips. It was finished in less than three months, ready for Shen to put the keel of the first steamer on the blocks and to lay the foundation stone of the metal-working forge on 18 January 1868. Part of the machinery, which had arrived on 31 December, was also set in motion for his inspection. The Navy Yard had been officially inaugurated.[9]

The Chinese mandarinate was not much given to technical matters. Even managers of arsenals seldom troubled themselves with such details. Shen, his high rank and strong Confucian values notwithstanding, showed an unusual interest in them. Soon after he assumed office, but before

6 Giquel, *Foochow Arsenal*, pp. 11–13; *HFT*, II, 305.
7 *Chinese Recorder*, 2 (January 1870), 216; *SWSK*, 4:3b–4, 5b–6b; Giquel, *Foochow Arsenal*, p. 11. Construction of offices and residences also began in early 1867.
8 Giquel, *Foochow Arsenal*, p. 11.
9 *SWSK*, 4:11; *HFT*, II, 94, 113b, 114b; *The Supreme Court and Consular Gazette*, 29 February 1868.

Giquel's return in October, he surveyed the Min River and familiarized himself with the Navy Yard's foundation work, the protection of its river front with wooden piles, and the construction of various buildings. An inspection tour of this kind, a formality in the eyes of most officials, was taken seriously by Shen; he described at length the work in progress, noting the many omissions in the original plans and, after consulting with the French directors, suggested remedial measures.[10] As aspects of the 'new' technology revealed themselves on a daily basis, Shen's knowledge expanded. The driving of 20- or 30-foot piles with a 700-catty weight for the shipbuilding slip fascinated him. The collapse of more than 20 feet of the foundation along the river also drove home the need for a stronger, stone-faced embankment; the wooden piles did not work. But what really caught his attention were the minute details on the blueprint of a hull as they were traced on the floor of the moulding hall:

The lines were drawn as if a thread of silk was being unwound from a cocoon. All the dovetail or mortice and tenon joints that are to be found on the ship's body were represented in drawing, all without confusion. Every curve, bend, and straight [piece] had its measurement clearly labelled and its name given in French. The Chinese carpenters could thus distinguish one from the other, build [the hull] according to the drawings and, at the same time, understand [the procedures] without laborious explanations.[11]

The key to modern shipbuilding, he concluded, lay not in the wielding of a hammer but in the principles of design and the art of making blueprints. On the basis of this new understanding, a School and Office of Design was created[12] – a major step forward for one with Shen's social and intellectual background.

As more machinery arrived and shipbuilding began in the summer of 1868, Shen's mind was stretched even more. Thanks to Giquel's linguistic ability and the staff who brought him knowledge from the shop floor, he was able to learn, in simple terms, the technical aspects of the project. He was now acquainted with the processes involved in iron casting and mould making. In the sawmills, he noted the transmission of energy from a steam engine through a series of cogwheels to power straight and circular saws, lathes, and drills. He marvelled at how this same engine could operate a fan which, through subterranean tunnels, supplied a strong enough draught for the furnaces in the small forge and the brass factory several hundred feet away. It would be tedious to dwell on his

10 *SWSK*, 4:5–8 (memorial of 5 September 1867).
11 *HFT*, II, 113a–b (memorial of 2 February 1868, Foochow).
12 Ibid., 113–115b. On the School, see later.

observations about the use of steam in wood bending, the uses of the chronometer or the wooden railway, the stages in constructing a ship's hull, and the like.[13] What is important is Shen's interest in mechanized production and his awareness of the interrelationship among the numerous workshops. And as he learned, he also tried to educate his colleagues in Peking: his reports to the throne and the Tsungli Yamen consistently contained more technical details than did those from other arsenals.[14]

Throughout 1868 yard construction was slow; there were shortages of timber, stone, bricks, and even earth (to fill the foundation). The failure to secure enough stone for the embankment soon led to another collapse of the foundation on the river front during a storm in June. Although instances like this were often left unreported in the Ch'ing bureaucracy, Shen, ever so conscientious, sought punishment for his 'negligence'. He was demoted one rank, though the penalty was cancelled as per regulation.[15]

High-quality timber, including a large number of 22-metre (72-foot) beams for workshops, curved and straight pieces for keels, and large teak planks for hulls, was hard to find. Lumber on Taiwan, the nearest source, proved hard to reach. The fear of foreign exploitation of the island's timber also prompted the Chinese to stop all lumbering activities there. Wood thus had to be imported, first via Ch'üan-chou, Hong Kong, and nearby ports, and then directly from the west coast of the United States, South-East Asia, and Ceylon. Chief Engineer Trasbot's trip to South-East Asia and the posting of a permanent Chinese agent there ensured a steady supply of wood from late 1868, enabling work on the yard and in the shipbuilding slips to proceed unimpeded.[16]

The recruitment, training, and organization of labour, too, presented difficulties at first. This was especially so with skilled labour: the foreign firms at Pagoda Anchorage had exhausted the supply. Consequently, most of the blacksmiths and certain types of carpenters had to be hired from Shanghai and Hong Kong. Even so, most had to be given further training and many were slow to learn. Shen therefore readily accepted Giquel's idea of creating a school for apprentices to train workmen and foremen. By late 1869 the supply of skilled labour was no longer a

---

13 *SWSK*, 4:27b–29, 32b–33.
14 This conclusion is based on a comparison of Shen's reports with those from other arsenals of the period found in *HFT*, IV and *YWYT*, vol. 4.
15 *SWSK*, 4:19, 23–5; *HFT*, II, 115b, 117b, 135a–b, 136b–137.
16 *YWYT*, vol. 5, p. 115; *SWSK*, 30b–31, 32–3; *HFT*, II, 114b, 117b, 121b, 138a–b; Contenson, 'Rapport'. Several more ship-loads of timber arrived in the spring of 1869. Timber supply ceased to be a problem from this time on. Giquel, *Foochow Arsenal*, p. 12; *SWSK*, 4:36–7.

problem, and when the works were finally in full swing, six hundred blacksmiths and five hundred wood workers were on hand.[17]

Of unskilled labour, and such tradesmen as builders and carpenters, supply was plentiful, thanks to the proximity of Foochow. Finding the thousand or more men to do the foundation work in 1867 was no problem. When construction materials began to arrive in quantity, more men, especially tradesmen, were engaged. Their number rose from 300 in mid-1868 to 500 in a little more than a year. At its peak, the Navy Yard employed nearly 3,000 workers all told. After the ground had been filled and the workshops completed, the labour force dropped to a normal level of 1,900, of whom 600 worked in the dockyard, 800 laboured in the workshops, and 500 were simply coolies. In addition, the 500 soldiers, whose primary duty was to guard the premises, also performed manual duties (ditching and hauling) when required.[18]

Shen's management of labour reflects a Confucian authoritarian approach, his high moral standard, and the scholar-gentry bias towards the lower classes. The workers were divided into categories – the skilled, unskilled, and manual labourers – with the last subjected to the most rigid control. They were organized into groups of fifty and subgroups of ten, each 'captained' by a reliable army officer. As Shen insisted from the very first, all workmen were subjected to 'military law', which for him was almost a corollary of efficiency. Pilfering, perhaps the most common offence among labourers in old China, was certainly made less attractive after a man was tried and executed for stealing brass in 1869. Even Shen's aides thought the punishment excessive.[19]

In each workshop, the workmen were placed under a deputy and two superintendents, whose disciplinary powers included the authority to withhold wages after conferring with the European overseers. Repeated offences were referred to Shen for punishment. Punctuality was imperative, and the hours were announced by a big clock on the clock tower in front of the directors' office. After work, the men were herded to their dormitories. Initial overcrowding, which abetted the spread of disease, was soon eliminated when Shen ordered the construction of more dormitories, which were arranged in rows of twos and threes in three large wards. Each ward was enclosed by a high wall, and to prevent

17 *Chung-Mei kuan-hsi*, p. 643; Thibaudier, 'Arsenal de Fou-tchéou'; *Chinese Recorder*, 2 (January 1870), 217; *HFT*, II, 117b, 122, 134b–135; Giquel, *Foochow Arsenal*, p. 14.
18 In February 1874, Giquel listed '500 workers in wood, – carpenters, cabinet-makers, modelers ... 600 workers in iron ... 500 labourers', some foremen and 130 apprentices – more than 1,730 in all. Ibid., pp. 10, 14; Thibaudier, 'Arsenal de Fou-tchéou', pp. 47–9; *Chinese Recorder*, 2 (January 1870), 217; *HFT*, II, 134b–135; *SWSK*, 4:26b, 35; FO 233/85, no. 3, p. III.
19 *HFT*, II, 135; *SWSK*, 4:2b–3; *MHHC*, 68:29.

disturbances, all movement between them was prohibited after dark. Within the wards, the disciplinary power of the officials continued to be felt, and gambling, drunkenness, opium smoking, and rowdiness were not tolerated. There was even an attempt to suppress prostitution outside the grounds of the Navy Yard. Opium use and prostitution remained two of Shen's concerns throughout his career.[20]

All the workers were indentured for a five-year period during which no unpaid leaves were allowed unless a worker's parents died or were gravely ill. In contrast to his own extended mourning observances and the hundred-day leaves he granted students of the Navy Yard School, Shen, betraying his dim view of the labouring masses, allowed the workers a mere twenty-one-day leave on the death of a parent. In practice, most poor people could ill afford long unpaid leaves, but this was not the reason for the regulation. Uninterrupted work was Shen's concern. Under normal circumstances, therefore, holidays were few: one day each for the spring and the autumn festivals and a week at New Year. Otherwise, the men worked a six-day week.[21]

If these conditions seem harsh, they were far less so in the context of nineteenth-century China or even industrial Europe. But discipline was only half of Shen's approach, the other half being material incentives.[22] All of the workers were relatively well paid and, even more important, paid regularly. Thus, since the unskilled labourers put in an eleven-hour day, they were paid 4.5 to 7 taels a month. The range at the Kiangnan Arsenal was 2.33 to 4.7 taels, and that for a Shanghai factory worker was 4 to 5 taels. The skilled labourers were treated better all round. They worked a shorter day: eight and a half hours in winter, nine in the spring and autumn, and ten during the four summer months. And they were paid 7 to 21 taels a month. Those recruited from Shanghai and Hong Kong received the higher wages because of their experience and the competition for their services in those cities. The lower-paid workers naturally begrudged this preferential treatment, although hard feelings did not result in open conflict. The best-paid men, of course, were the foremen, who brought home 21 to 49 taels a month, a very handsome wage for working men of the time.[23]

---

20 Lin Ch'ing-yüan, *Fu-chien ch'uan-cheng*, p. 46; *HFT*, II, 121; Thibaudier, 'Arsenal de Fou-tchéou', pp. 47–9; Shore, *Flight of the Lapwing*, pp. 101–2; biography of Lin Ping-hui in *MHHC*, 88:12.
21 Thibaudier, 'Arsenal de Fou-tchéou', pp. 47–9.
22 *SWSK*, 4:2b–3 (Shen's memorial of 18 July 1867).
23 Contenson, 'Rapport', 13 August 1872, p. 333; Thibaudier, 'Arsenal de Fou-tchéou', pp. 47–9; *Chinese Recorder*, January 1870, p. 218; Wu Tsan-ch'eng's memorial of 18 June 1877 (KH 3.5.8) in YCT, KH 3/5 *hsiang*. Giquel's *Foochow Arsenal* (p. 14) quotes a

Shen's two-pronged approach produced the desired results. As a French naval engineer pointed out, the workers, because they were paid well and regularly, 'worked marvels' under the direction of the mandarins. All other foreign visitors agreed that they were good workers. They were said to be intelligent, steady, persevering, and business-like, and 'would do credit to any European nation'. Although one visitor considered them less strong and energetic than their European brethren, the above-mentioned French naval engineer insisted that they were as good as and even quicker than European workers, they having so quickly learned the advantage of Western tools. As if to echo the moral concerns of a Confucian, he added that only the few – a mercifully small number – who had worked in the treaty ports tended to be less disciplined, even though they might have been more skilled.[24]

The balance between disciplinary control and productivity is a delicate one. Yet all foreign observers spoke approvingly of the Chinese approach and the results that it produced even as the more industrialized nations of the West were moving towards better treatment of labourers at the time. Captain Henry Shore of the British navy noted in particular the absence of labour disputes, which, he suggested, produced a tranquil environment conducive to good performance.[25] Shen did not have to worry, as he did earlier, about the workers' reluctance to learn new skills.

In fact, the threat to the work force came largely from the foremen and junior administrators, who abused their power. The root of the problem lay in the traditional practice whereby directors or managers delegated labour recruitment and control to midlevel officers. Tim Wright calls

much lower wage for skilled workers, starting from 4.5 taels a month, and a smaller range for the foremen, $40 to $50, or 26 to 33 taels. Shore, in *Flight of the Lapwing* (p. 102), mentions the high salary of $3 (2 taels) a day. A Chinese historian misread the per diem pay of the workers as a monthly salary and, on the basis of this, accused the Navy Yard administration of exploitation. Chiao Ching-i, 'Ts'ung Fu-chou ch'uan-cheng-chü k'an yang-wu-p'ai so pan chün-shih kung-yeh ti feng-chien chu-i hsing-chih', *Chi-lin ta-hsüeh she-hui k'o-hsüeh lun-tsung*, 1980, no. 2: *Yang-wu yün-tung t'ao-lun chuan-chi*, p. 240.

At the Kiangnan Arsenal, the range for the skilled workmen was 5.7 to 15 taels, and that for the foremen there as well as at the Soochow Arsenal (1864) was about 13 to 20 taels. Sun Yü-t'ang, comp., *Chung-kuo chin-tai kung-yeh-shih tzu-liao, ti-i-chi, 1840–1895 nien* (Peking, 1957), vol. 2, pp. 1208–10, 1212–13; Kennedy, *Arms*, p. 40. For comparison, all wages have been converted from the yüan to the tael.

24 Shore, *Flight of the Lapwing*, p. 102; Thibaudier, 'Arsenal de Fou-tchéou', pp. 47–8; Anon., 'Chinese Arsenals', p. 698 (the short quote comes from this source). Shen also reported that the Cantonese workers, presumably from Hong Kong, were often set in their ways and were reluctant to adopt the methods of their French masters. *HFT*, II, 193.
25 Shore, *Flight of the Lapwing*, p. 102.

this a 'method of evading management'.[26] How widespread this practice was at Ma-wei is not clear. But because the bulk of the men were recruited locally, the Navy Yard officials, mostly local gentrymen, could have had a special hold on the men they hired. The fact that the men were not necessarily assigned to workshops supervised by the gentrymen who hired them, and the fact that Shen's disciplinary measures were applied to persons of all ranks, might have had a mitigating effect. Still, the following example shows that problems existed.

Soon after Shen's incumbency, the foremen were found 'squeezing' the workmen, and Ting Jih-ch'ang, Shen's successor, had to have 'lists of the different rates of pay . . . posted . . . in order to check the "squeezing" '.[27] The practice was widespread in old China and, despite the lack of evidence, is likely to have existed in Shen's time. We know that discipline had become lax during the thirteen months in 1874 and 1875 when Shen was attending to the affairs of Taiwan.[28] The same was probably the case during his extended period of mourning.

What is remarkable, however, is the rapid progress that was made even in the face of some formidable obstacles. By early 1868, two small school buildings and one shipbuilding slip had been completed. With the steady arrival of machinery and timber, and the workmen's growing familiarity with their jobs, the machinery was quickly installed for operation in temporary workshops and open sheds until it was moved to the permanent buildings in 1870.[29] The Navy Yard's facilities, when completed, were impressive.[30]

Most of the shipbuilding facilities were located in the Navy Yard proper (Map 2, section A). Planning and design were done in the office

26 Tim Wright, ' "A Method of Evading Management" – Contract Labor in Chinese Coal Mines before 1937', *Comparative Studies in Society and History*, 23.4 (October 1981), 656–78. The methods used at the Foochow Navy Yard were not uniform but, as described, they possessed certain features of the contract labour (*pao-kung*) system which was widespread in China. The practice continued well into the 1950s. William Brugger, *Democracy and Organisation in the Chinese Industrial Enterprise (1948–1953)* (Cambridge, 1976), pp. 42, 171–5.
27 *NCH*, 13 January and 29 July 1876. The latter issue continues: 'Ting's reforms in this respect worked well, but we understand that the pay lists have been withdrawn, and that the Philistines are again plundering'.
28 Ting Jih-ch'ang, 'Ting chung-ch'eng cheng-shu', 'Fu-Min', 1:2. I am grateful to Professor Kwang-ching Liu for the opportunity to consult a photocopy of this manuscript.
29 *Supreme Court and Consular Gazette*, 2 February 1868; *HFT*, II, 132a–b, 138a–b, 161a–b; *Chinese Recorder*, 2 (January 1870), 217.
30 Unless otherwise stated, sources for the following paragraphs are Giquel, *Foochow Arsenal*, pp. 11–13, 24–9; Dunn's report, *NCH*, 21 April 1870; Pedder to Wade, 4 February 1876, in FO 371/568, no. 5, encl.; Anon., 'Chinese Arsenals', p. 699; Garnault to Ministre de la Marine, 2 June 1873, MM BB4 1395, pp. 616–20; Contenson, 'Rapport'; *HFT*, II, 113b.

of the engineer and the office of design, which were on top of the setting-up shop (section A, c) and next to the fitting shop (section A, b,b), where ship engines were manufactured and assembled. While the moulds for the engines and other equipment were made in the model room and the joiners' shop (section A, l), the parts for the engines (aside from the seven purchased in Europe) were produced at the foundry (section A, d) and the metal-working forge (section B, u,v), with the latter turning out the heavier pieces. The forging department (section B, u) of the metal-working forge was equipped with six large steam hammers, sixteen forge fires for heavy work, and six furnaces for reheating. The rolling mill (section B, v), also a department of the metal-working forge, had six furnaces for reheating, and four rollers, which were powered by a 100-horsepower engine. Together, these two departments manufactured parts for the 150-horsepower marine engines (e.g., straight and crank shafts), strong pieces for the equipment and gears of the ships (e.g., cat heads and anchors), as well as square and round bars. The rolling mill, it should be noted, was also intended to make use of the iron resources of China. Though not equipped to extract iron from the ore, it did process 400,000 kilogrammes of Chinese scrap iron annually. The last of the workshops designed for the manufacture of marine engines and heavy equipment was the boiler house (section A, a), which, aside from having assembled boilers purchased from Europe, produced fourteen boilers of its own.

All the workshops were solidly built with fine-quality bricks from Amoy on a deep granite foundation. In the workshops, cranes were used everywhere for lifting heavy objects. Much of the machinery was manufactured by Claparède et Cie, 'the excellence of whose work is well known. . . . The tools were heavier than those made by Whitworth, or Smith and Beacock'.[31] Referring to the metal-working forge, Rear-Admiral Garnault, commander of the French navy in the seas of China and Japan, called it 'a first-class establishment'.[32]

Precision instruments and small metal fittings that went into the construction, the masting, and the equipment of a ship were manufactured in a cluster of five workshops. They included those for making chronometers, optical instruments, and compasses (section A, h); the equipment forges (section A, i,i); and the small fitting and locksmith's shops (section A, j).

Hull construction began in the moulding hall (section A, e), on whose floor was traced in actual size the complete lines of a ship or its engines.

---

31 Dunn's report, *NCH*, 21 April 1870.
32 Garnault to Ministre de la Marine, 2 June 1873, in MM BB4 1395, pp. 616–20.

The hulls themselves were built in the four large sheds for wood working (section A, n,n,n,n) and the three shipbuilding slips (section A, m,m,m), whereas the parts were supplied by the mechanical sawmill (section A, k), and the mast and boats workshops (section A, o).

The pride of the Navy Yard's facilities was the patent slip on Labat's system for hull repairs and service (section A, q). It was the second ever to be built anywhere and was identical to the original at Bordeaux. This haulage system was designed to take a ship sideways on its cradle; its two sections could be used either separately or together, depending on the size of the ship. At high tide, a ship 122 metres long, with a displacement of 4,000 tons and drawing 7.32 metres of water, could be raised for repair in one to seven and a half hours, depending on the speed chosen. At Bordeaux, the Système Labat was used for the largest trans-Atlantic steamers. The Navy Yard therefore had no need for a wet or dry dock. The only drawback was the difficulty of repairing the lowest sections of the boat, although this problem could be obviated by raising the keel blocks.[33]

The rest of the facilities, displayed on Map 2, are self-explanatory. One should note, however, that the Navy Yard lacked its own fortification. Its defence was left to the provincial forts with their fixed battery positions, which, insofar as the Navy Yard was concerned, faced the wrong directions.[34]

The Navy Yard was built on a large scale and in a 'most substantial and permanent manner'.[35] With more than forty-five buildings for administrative, educational, and production activities, it compared favourably with the Kiangnan Arsenal, China's largest ordnance enterprise, which, in 1875, had thirty-two such buildings. The Navy Yard also was larger in area, covering 118 acres compared with about 73 acres at Kiangnan. The two establishments, built for different purposes, were not exactly comparable. Nonetheless, few would dispute *Shen-pao*'s claim that the Navy Yard was 'the leading industrial enterprise in China', and Li Hung-chang was filled with admiration.[36] Moreover, as J. G. Dunn

---

33 All foreign visitors were struck by the capabilities of this ingenious system. To my knowledge, the only criticism came from Contre-Amiral Garnault, who noted the difficulty in working on the lowest sections of the boat. Ibid., pp. 615–16; *HFT*, II, 262–265b.

34 Pedder to Wade, 4 February 1876, in FO 371/568, no. 5, encl.

35 DeLano to Hamilton Fish, 15 November 1870, U.S., Department of State, Consular Dispatches: Foochow, vol. 4.

36 *Shen-pao*, 16 December 1874 (TC 13.11.8); Li Hung-chang to Ting Jih-ch'ang, 18 June 1870, in *Feng-shun wen-shih*, no. 2 (April 1989), 59. A Western writer spoke of the Navy Yard as the 'most extensive and costly of the three existing arsenals' (Anon., 'Chinese Arsenals', p. 697). On the Navy Yard, see Giquel, *Foochow Arsenal*, p. 13. On the

noted, it had the capacity to build vessels much larger in size and power than those originally planned:

A steamer like the *Fire Queen*, 330 feet long and of 2500 tons cargo capacity could be built, engined, and in all respects constructed and completed in the dockyard . . . or a man-of-war like H.M.S. Favorite [*sic*] of 2300 tons and 400 H.P. could be built, her engines, boilers and screw manufactured, her armament, sails, cordage, iron masts, and anchors made, and her midship battery plated with heavy iron laminated plates rolled at the arsenal.[37]

Thus, by design, the Navy Yard was almost self-sufficient, yet another of its outstanding features.

Arguably, too, the Navy Yard was a truly modern enterprise: machines were used wherever feasible, and the whole plant was efficiently served by a tramway with turntables at important workshops and intersections.[38] Efficiency was also reflected in the method by which ships were equipped and provisioned: a hulk of three decks could, in twenty-four hours or less, 'receive systematically and without confusion, stores, rigging, cordage, armament and provisions, complete for a 3 years' commission'.[39] No wonder the Navy Yard soon came to serve the needs of other government agencies.[40] For its systematic and thorough planning, the Chinese had mainly Giquel and Trasbot to thank.[41]

However, one major flaw persisted: the foundation of filled earth, which was formed either improperly or too hastily. After about fifteen years, some of the heavier buildings appeared to have sunk considerably, and the Labat's patent slip was 'constantly getting out of order owing to the unstable nature of the ground and the enormous pressure brought to bear on it'.[42] Was Shen so impatient for results as to cause shoddy

Kiangnan Arsenal, see Sun Yü-t'ang, *Chung-kuo chin-tai kung-yeh*, vol. 1, p. 277; *HFT*, III, 41b; Spector, *Li*, p. 157; Kennedy, *Arms*, p. 63; Gideon Ch'en, *Tseng Kuo-fan, Pioneer Promoter of the Steamship in China* (Peiping, 1935), p. 49. Lin Ch'ung-yung (*Shen*, p. 365) categorically claims that the Foochow Navy Yard was far superior to the Kiangnan Arsenal.

37 *NCH*, 21 April 1870.
38 Anon., 'Chinese Arsenals', p. 699; Pedder to Wade, 2 June 1876, in FO 371/568, no. 5, incl.; Garnault to Ministre de la Marine, 2 June 1873, in MM BB4 1395, p. 618. The tramway superseded the earlier wooden tracks.
39 Dunn's report in *NCH*, 21 April 1870.
40 Once the Navy Yard cranes were used to unload the 18-ton Blakely guns bought by the province of Fukien. On another occasion, a vessel of the China Merchants' Steam Navigation Company had its damaged screw propeller repaired at Ma-wei. Pedder to Wade, 2 June 1876, in FO 371/568, no. 5, encl.; *Shen-pao*, 19 January 1875.
41 Médard, 'Note confidentielle', p. 3; Anon., 'Chinese Arsenals', p. 698; *NCH*, 21 April 1870.
42 Sinclair to Parkes, 21 April 1884, in FO 228/572, no. 15, encl.

workmanship?[43] Did Giquel or Trasbot's knowledge of civil engineering fall short? Whether the problem could have been avoided altogether is a question difficult to answer. Given the political considerations that went into the choice of the Ma-wei site, Tso Tsung-t'ang should bear the blame for inviting the problem.

Yet looking at the Navy Yard under Shen, one could see only evidence of progress. For this, credit must first go to Tso's foresight and Giquel's ambition. Shen's leadership, too, accounted for much, for it was he who presided over subsequent expansions and improvements. His understanding of Western technology, however crude, had led to flexibility and vision. No sooner had he assumed office in 1867 than he had issued an order prohibiting the sale of the adjacent Ma-wei Hill to the foreign community in order to curb its growth and allow room for the Navy Yard's future expansion.[44] But the most significant plant modification in his time was the removal of parts of the metal-forging and -rolling machines to the foot of the hill, where the ground could support these as well as new and heavier machinery. The addition of a rolling mill to this metal-working complex is particularly noteworthy.[45] Then, as the contract with the Europeans came to an end, Shen, on Giquel's advice, recommended further plant modernization in order to build the more efficient compound engine and iron frames for composite vessels. He even contemplated building ironclads at Ma-wei.[46] Having had a taste of the rudiments of Western naval technology, Shen wanted more. And in the course of pursuing his goal, he achieved admirable results. As J. G. Dunn reported to the British government after another visit in the autumn of 1873:

5 inverted 2 cylinder surface condenser screw engines have been built and fitted. Much of the boiler plate has been rolled in the arsenal, and all the forgings, shafting, cranks, screws, etc. have been made there. These engines are finely finished and their performance admirable. . . . All the sails are cut and made in the arsenal, all the blocks of iron, and wood, masts, yards, etc. are made in the arsenal.[47]

Shen would have been proud had he read the report.

---

43 In early 1868 Shen did report that the filling of the ground had to be done in three or four stages – more earth had to be added after the preceding layer had settled (*SWSK*, 4:19a–b). Nevertheless, Shen's impatience may have caused undue haste in foundation work.
44 Sinclair to Wade, 11 June 1870, in FO 228/491, no. 26.
45 *HFT*, II, 305.
46 Shen's memorials, 25 August 1874 and 8 January 1875, in *SWSK*, 4:68b, 70–1.
47 FO 233/85, no. 3, p. X.

Building a Chinese flotilla

The shipbuilding programme was, if anything, more ambitious. In the first place, eleven 150-horsepower vessels and all but the first two of their engines were to be built during the five-year contract. Since making the engines was expected to take much longer than it had taken to make the hulls, five 80-horsepower engines were bought from France to be mounted on Ma-wei-built hulls.[48] All the boats were to be of the screw-driven type with a strong but low hull, in the style of a warship. The choice was well made, for, as Tso Tsung-t'ang argued, although the screw-driven vessels drew more water than did the paddle boats, the loss of speed was more than compensated for by their stability in the high seas.[49] He could well have added that the low hulls would reduce exposure to gun-fire in battle.

Work on the first hull for a 150-horsepower steamer was slow. The workmen were unfamiliar with the job and even less so with their foreign masters. Supplies were often delayed. So the hull took more than a year to complete, and mounting the engine as well as work on the body, deck, and bridge took several more months. The boat was finally launched on 10 June 1869, even though it was not fully fitted out for almost another three months.[50]

The atmosphere on the day of the launching, chosen for its propitiousness, was one of excitement and anticipation. At about midday, Shen led his Chinese staff in a series of offerings to the deities of the seas, the rivers, the boats, and the earth. Then the stocks were removed from the boat, which, having been greased underneath, glided effortlessly into the Min amid firecrackers and rounds of applause. There was no champagne. Shen, true to his patriotic feelings, named this first ship the *Wan-nien Ch'ing*, the *Ten-Thousand-Year Ch'ing*.[51]

Even as Shen marvelled at the mechanism of the launching, he was impatient to see the boat in action. Giquel was ordered to press on with the fittings. Meanwhile Major Pei Chin-ch'üan, captain of a Fukien provincial steamer, was given command of the vessel. He was to train the eighty-odd crew members that he and Hu Kuang-yung had recruited from Ningpo. It was Shen's wish to keep the boat in Chinese hands. So when the crew was ready, the vessel was put to sea on 18 September. A week later, Shen took his Chinese staff and went along with Giquel for a

---

48 'Des propositions d'exécution', MM BB4 1555 17/5/2; *HFT*, II, 33–4.
49 *HFT*, II, 52b.
50 Ibid., 151, 160a–b, 183a–b.
51 Ibid., 160b, 161b. For a description of a similar ceremony when S.S. No. 14 was launched, see *NCH*, 29 January 1874.

two-day run on the open seas, sailing some twenty-five kilometres from the coast. The guns were also tested. The engine worked well, and Shen was impressed. He was also struck by the excellent co-ordination among the sailors, even in rough seas, especially when he was himself sea-sick. Nevertheless, he had to admit his inability to make an informed judgement as he lacked the technical knowledge, although he was proud to note the favourable comments from British and U.S. observers.[52]

To affirm the imperial nature of the Navy Yard, a detailed report and a set of drawings were presented to the Grand Council for imperial review. The boat was then presented for imperial inspection at Tientsin. Shen had intended to take the boat himself but was incapacitated by lumbago. Wu Ta-t'ing went in his stead. At Tientsin, the boat was examined both in port and at sea by Ch'ung-hou, imperial commissioner of trade for the northern ports, who represented the throne. Although his report was suspiciously similar to Shen's, the soundness of the vessel was later confirmed by J. G. Dunn.[53]

While the hull for the *Wan-nien Ch'ing* was still under construction, work on the first 80-horsepower *Mei-yün* had already begun in the second shipbuilding slip. With the earlier technical and logistical problems gradually sorted out, the hull and most of the fittings took only ten months to complete, while the finishing touches took another month, despite the vastly different dimensions of this smaller boat. By the time it was ready for service in January 1870, most of the Navy Yard's permanent structures and the three building slips had been finished; the entire establishment was ready for full production.[54]

The shipbuilding schedule for all the vessels built under Shen is shown in Table 3. After the *Wan-nien Ch'ing*, the time taken to build each boat was dictated by the supply of materials, available manpower, and the ability of the engine-building department to cope with a tight timetable. Under optimum conditions, a 150-horsepower vessel could be built in five months and a week (S.S. No. 11) and then fitted out in less than two months (S.S. No. 12). The slow delivery of the locally made 150-horsepower engines was the probable cause of the lengthy time taken to complete S.S. Nos. 12, 13, and 15, three of the last four to be built under Giquel's direction. The crammed construction schedule to beat the contract deadline may also have strained labour resources.[55] In fact, the launching of S.S. No. 15 came two and a half months after the contract had expired. In the next twenty months, from the departure of the

52 *HFT*, II, 160b–161, 183–4, 193a–b.
53 Ibid., 158b, 198b–199; *NCH*, 21 April 1870.
54 *HFT*, II, 153b, 161, 218; *Chinese Recorder*, 2 (January 1870), 217.
55 For more details, see Pong, 'Modernization and Politics', pp. 196–8.

Table 3. *Steamship construction schedule at the Foochow Navy Yard, 1868–77*

Official number	Name	Horse-power	Work begun	Launched	Trial run	Construction time (months)	Fitting-out time (months)
1	Wan-nien Ch'ing	150	18 Jan. 1868	10 June 1869	18 Sept. 1869	17	3
2	Mei-yün	80	8 Feb. 1869	6 Dec. 1869	9 Jan. 1870	10	1
3	Fu-hsing	80	6 Dec. 1869	30 May 1870	Sept./Oct. 1870[a]	6	4
4	Fu-po	150[b]	ca. June 1870	22 Dec. 1870	1 Apr. 1871	6	3
5	An-lan	150[b]	26 Nov. 1870	18 June 1871	ca. Dec. 1871	7	6
6	Chen-hai	80	29 Mar. 1871	28 Nov. 1871	July/Aug. 1872[a]	7	8
7	Yang-wu	250	12 July 1871	23 April 1872	Dec. 1872	9	8
8	Fei-yün	150[b]	Aug. 1871	3 June 1872	Oct. 1872	10	4
9	Ching-yüan	80	1 Dec. 1871	21 Aug. 1872	26 Mar. 1873	9	7
10	Chen-wei	80	24 June 1872	11 Dec. 1872	17 Aug. 1873	6	8
11	Chi-an	150[b]	25 July 1872	2 Jan. 1873	27 Sept. 1873	5	11
12	Yung-pao	150[b]	23 Oct. 1872	10 Aug. 1873	19 Oct. 1873	10	2
13	Hai-ching	150[b]	28 Feb. 1873	8 Nov. 1873	Jan./Feb. 1874[a]	8	3
14	Ch'en-hang	150[b]	3 July 1873	16 Jan. 1874	Mar./Apr. 1874[a]	6	3
15	Ta-ya	150[b]	16 Aug. 1873	16 May 1874	Aug./Sept. 1874[a]	9	4
16	Yüan-k'ai	150[b]	5 Dec. 1874	4 June 1875	July 1875	6	1
17	I-hsin	150[b]	4 June 1875	28 Mar. 1876	10 July 1876	10	3
18	Teng-ying-chou	150[b]	21 July 1875	June/July 1876[a]	15 Sept. 1876	11	2
19	T'ai-an	150[b]	12 July 1875	2 Dec. 1876	3 May 1877	5	5

Note: Construction includes setting up engines and boilers, and may include certain fittings.

[a] Double date indicates the lunar month overlapping the two months given.

[b] Engine and boiler fabricated in the Foochow Navy Yard.

Sources: Sun Yü-t'ang, *Chung-kuo chin-tai kung-yeh-shih*, pp. 405, 422–3; Giquel, *Foochow Arsenal*, p. 15; Wang Hsin-chung, 'Fu-chou ch'uan-ch'ang', table following p. 28; *HFT*, II, 114b, 153b, 160b, 183b, 217, 218b, 290, 291, 522b; *YWYT*, vol. 5, p. 140, vol. 8, pp. 518–19; *SWSK*, 4:51a–b, 59a–b, 62a–b, 64.

Table 4. *Steamships built at the Foochow Navy Yard during Shen Pao-chen's time*

Official number		Name	Date of launch	Class	Horsepower, nominal	Crew	Displacement (tons)	Armament
1	1869	Wan-nien Ch'ing	10 June	Transport	150	100	1,450	6 breechloading; 36-, 24-, and 18-pounders
2		Mei-yün	6 Dec.	Gunboat	80	70	515	1 7-in. Armstrong 2 23-pounders
3	1870	Fu-hsing	30 May	Gunboat	80	70	515	1 7-in. Armstrong 2 23-pounders
4	1871	Fu-po	22 Dec.	Transport	150	100	1,258	5 guns
5		An-lan (lost in a typhoon, Sept. 1874)	18 June	Transport	150	100	1,005	1 7-in. (French) 4 5⅝-in. (French) 2 4½-in. Blakeley
6		Chen-hai	28 Nov.	Gunboat dispatch	80	70	572	8 breechloading; 2 60-, 4 40-, 2 18-pounders,
7	1872	Yang-wu	23 Apr.	Corvette	250	200	1,393	1 7½-ton Whitworth 8 3½-ton Whitworth
8		Fei-yün	3 June	Transport	150	100	1,258	1 7-in. Armstrong 4 48-pounders 2 small brass guns
9		Ching-yüan	21 Aug.	Gunboat dispatch	80	70	572	6 guns
10		Chen-wei	11 Dec.	Gunboat dispatch	80	70	572	6 guns
11	1873	Chi-an	2 Jan.	Transport	150	100	1,258	1 64-pounders } rifled 4 48-pounders } breech- 2 36-pounders } loading
12		Yung-pao	10 Aug.	Transport	150	100	1,391	None
13		Hai-ching	8 Nov.	Transport	150	100	1,391	None
14	1874	Ch'en-hang	16 Jan.	Transport	150	100	1,391	None
15		Ta-ya (lost in typhoon, Sept. 1874)	May	Transport	150	100	1,391	None
16	1875	Yüan-k'ai	June	Transport	150	100	1,258	5 guns

Europeans to the end of Shen's tenure, another vessel was launched and work on three others had begun under circumstances to be discussed later and in the next chapter.

In all, fifteen vessels were built under the contract with the Europeans (Table 4). The original plan to build sixteen was revised in early 1871 when the decision was made to substitute two 150-horsepower transports with a 250-horsepower corvette. The engine and boiler, however, were to be purchased from France. Though Shen was in mourning (and also ill) at the time, such a major policy change could not have been made without his imprimatur.[56] In fact, the reasons given by Tartar General Wen-yü, who had never been very enthusiastic about the Navy Yard, reads very much like Shen's own:

Regarding steamships, the Westerners excel in having a large number of guns and great horsepower. Thus . . . they can be confident of victory. Now that the province of Fukien has unstintingly committed huge sums of money to build steamships, [we] should, as a matter of course, study [their principles so as] to learn their mystery. [We] then discussed the matter with Giquel. [As we put it to him,] because [we are] modelling [our ships] after foreign warships, the engines [we] make should have greater power. Giquel readily agrees.[57]

Ultimately, success should be measured not so much by the number or size of ships built, but by their quality and capabilities. On the latter, views varied but it is interesting that most of the favourable comments came from Western observers.

In Dunn's opinion, the first two vessels – a 150-horsepower transport and an 80-horsepower gunboat – were 'admirably fastened, and particularly well finished outside and inside. They could not be better finished in London or New York'. And the third, also an 80-horsepower gunboat, was 'good for speed under steam or canvas. The vessel seemed to us to be of too solid a construction and somewhat unnecessarily strong for the tonnage and weights, but the faults are good and unusual'.[58] S.S. Nos. 4, 6, 7, and 8 were also favourably reviewed by British and U.S. consular officials.[59]

---

56 During Shen's mourning, the Navy Yard was managed by Hsia Hsien-lun. For purposes of reporting to the throne, however, Hsia was to report to Tartar General Wen-yü and Governor-General Ying-kuei, who would then memorialize on his behalf. Hsia must have been critically involved in the new policy, although it is inconceivable that Shen did not have a major role in it as well. On the administration of the Navy Yard during Shen's absence, see *HFT*, II, 259, 260.

57 Ibid., 290–1.

58 *NCH*, 21 April 1870.

59 Gregory to Wade, 1 October 1874, in FO 228/542, no. 22, encl. 1; DeLano to J. C. B. Davis, 5 December 1871, 'Report for the year ending September 30, 1871', U.S. Department of State, Consular Dispatches, Foochow, vol. 4.

Dunn remained unshaken in his view after having seen the twelfth steamer in late 1873. He was particularly impressed by the structural engineering of the Ma-wei ships:

All the ships . . . are, frame, keel, planking exterior and interior, and decks, of the finest picked Bankok teak. The bows, sterns, and bottoms from keel to bilge are solid. The vessels have extra large scantling, are tied with iron diagonals, and of very great strength. They have deck basins and stauncheons strong enough to bear 10 ton guns amidship. The vessels steam fast and sail well without steam. The corvette and transports are most handy vessels under sail alone.[60]

The transports (150-horsepower), he continued, could carry some eight hundred tons of rice and three to four hundred soldiers. If need be, they could carry heavy armaments, either one 150-pounder and three 100-pounders or one 150-pounder and six 70-pounders. These vessels could steam twenty-four hours at 10 to 10½ knots in good weather on about twenty-two tons of Taiwan coal. The 80-horsepower gunboats, fitted with Penn's trunk engines horizontal with surface condensers, could do 11½ to 12 knots under steam. They were 'very strong[,] handsome, fast sailing boats, very much faster and superior to any new miserable double screw vessels like the Avon [*sic*], Hornet [*sic*], etc. . . . No navy has better vessels'.[61]

The show-piece was the 250-horsepower corvette, the *Yang-wu*, which was fitted with a new type of engine and boiler, both mounted below sea level for better protection. Its retractable, three-sectioned funnel was also designed to reduce exposure to gun-fire. Dunn maintained that, with a cruising speed of 12¼ to 12½ knots under steam and 11½ to 12 knots under sail, 'no European or United States ship of the class could do better'.[62] What made the *Yang-wu* formidable too was its battery consisting of eleven Whitworths: one 150-pounder, two 70-pounders, pivoted on Scotts iron carriages, and eight broadside 70-pounders. There were as well two brass, rifled 24-pounder Howitzers at foredeck.[63] Four years after its launching, however, the *Shen-pao* reported that the vessel was so run down that it had to undergo extensive repairs, the nature of which, to our regret, was not noted.[64] But in 1877, the year after the repairs

60 FO 233/85, no. 3, p. VIII.
61 Ibid., p. IX. According to Dunn, two of the five 80-horsepower engines were made by Claparède of Paris, one by Inglis of Glasgow, and the other two by Penn of London. Ibid., pp. IV–V.
62 Ibid., pp. VIII–IX.
63 Ibid.; *SWSK*, 4:51b–52.
64 *Shen-pao*, 17 March 1876. Just before the 'extensive repairs', however, the *North-China Daily News* (10 December 1875) insisted that 'the *Yang-woo* . . . will bear comparison with warships of any nation'.

were made, Captain Shore, not an uncritical observer, claimed that the ship was 'a very formidable vessel of her class' and 'was in very good order'.[65]

About the entire flotilla, the *North-China Daily News* had this to say:

Incomparably the best in every respect are the steamers built . . . at Foochow. . . . The Chinese have here . . . good ships; they are built throughout of teak, and so strongly that they will stand the wear and tear of gunnery and are fit to encounter any weather a ship can be expected to live through.[66]

Progress in the marine engineering department was also impressive. The first locally built 150-horsepower engine and boiler were ready by mid-1871, barely two years after the foundry began operation. Little is known about these early engines. Of the first three fabricated between 1871 and 1873, two were still in service in 1879 and the third was lost in a typhoon. The later products were all said to be of good quality.[67]

The favourable comments of foreign visitors are significant. But they were comparing Ma-wei vessels only with those of the same class in use in the West, not with the advanced types that were coming into service or were being developed there. Shore had good reason to admire the Chinese boats. His own vessel, the 774-ton, three-gun, 160-horsepower *Lapwing* was hardly superior.[68] But then it was not representative of the British or the French navy.

In learning to build modern warships, the Chinese understandably started with smaller vessels and simpler technology. Because the Navy Yard was also a teaching institution, it made sense to begin with the basics. But no sooner had the contract expired than Shen made arrangements to build larger and more advanced vessels.[69] The Chinese, at least those in the defence industry, had no illusions. Thus, Li Hung-chang realistically compared Ma-wei's steamers to second- and third-class vessels of the West. Li, however, did not intend this to be a criticism, for he conceded that those constructed at the Kiangnan Arsenal were even less adequate. The 80-horsepower *Chen-hai* from Ma-wei, he observed, was sturdy and well built, but none of the Chinese vessels was good enough for combat on the high seas.[70] Shen would have agreed.

65 Shore, *Flight of the Lapwing*, p. 233. By 1879, the Chinese themselves were beginning to question the seaworthiness of the *Yang-wu* because of its age. *YWYT*, vol. 2, p. 398.
66 *North-China Daily News*, 10 December 1875.
67 *YWYT*, vol. 2, p. 398, vol. 5, p. 102; *T'ung-chih chia-hsü Jih-ping ch'in-T'ai shih-mo* (hereafter, *CTSM*), comp. T'ai-wan yin-hang ching-chi yen-chiu shih (Taipei, 1959), pp. 169–70; *North-China Daily News*, 10 December 1875.
68 Shore, *Flight of the Lapwing*, p. 1. The *Lapwing* did have twin screws, however. Frater to Wade, 1 July 1876, in FO 228/570, Tamsui, no. 19.
69 *HFT*, II, 346b–350b: *SWSK*, 4:68–9, 70–1.
70 Li to Wang K'ai-t'ai, 22 June 1871 and 10 October 1872, in *LWCK*, 'Letters', 11:6b,

The fully rigged, wooden 'broadside' vessels of the Foochow Navy Yard were certainly years behind European developments. All the 150-horsepower transports, for example, had their perpendicular engines and boilers fitted well above water and were protected only by bunkers. Even as fine a ship as the *Yang-wu* could not measure up to its contemporaries in Europe.[71]

The third quarter of the nineteenth century saw dramatic and fundamental changes in naval engineering in the West. During the Crimean War, the French frustrated Russian guns by putting four-and-a-half-inch iron plates on their wooden steamers. With the arrival in 1858 of the modern gun, the Armstrong rifled cannon with its elongated shells, still stronger ships had to be built. The French responded with the 5,600-ton, heavily armoured, and powerful *La Gloire*, but it was the British 9,000-ton *Warrior*, the first capital ship built of iron throughout, that proved more revolutionary. The disappearance of the full-rig and broadside fixtures in the early 1870s, brought about by Armstrong and armour and no doubt inspired by the Union's *Monitor* in the U.S. Civil War, completed the first round of modern naval development.[72]

Meanwhile the compound engine was gaining favour in the West. Li Chao-t'ang, the Navy Yard's director-general in 1879–83, accused Giquel of having the Chinese build outmoded engines, and as a result the first Chinese compound engine was not built until 1877.[73] The accusation was groundless, since Giquel had offered to build a 300- to 400-horsepower compound engine as early as 1873. For reasons to be discussed in the next chapter, Shen rejected the proposal.[74]

Two modern Chinese historians also charge that Giquel, presumably with French interests in mind, deliberately 'dumped' on the Chinese obsolete engines from Europe.[75] This, too, seems unfounded, since none

---

12:25b; to Tseng Kuo-fan, 20 January 1872, in ibid., 31b; to Li Tsung-hsi (governor-general of Liang Kiang), 4 August 1873, in ibid., 13:14b. Later, in 1878, Li also said the Foochow ships were clumsy. *LWCK*, 'Letters to the Tsungli Yamen', 8:10b.

71 *HFT*, II, 626a–b; FO 233/85, no. 3, p. IX; Shore, *Flight of the Lapwing*, p. 97. For *Wan-nien Ch'ing*'s specifications, see *HFT*, II, 183b–184.

72 J. Dolby, *The Steel Navy* (London, 1862), pp. 12, 19–20; Lewis, *British Navy*, pp. 225–9.

73 *HFT*, II, 856b; Lin Ch'ung-yung, *Shen*, pp. 577–9; Rawlinson, *China's Struggle*, p. 98. For the first identification of *k'ang-pang* as compound engine, see Pong, 'Modernization and Politics', pp. 202, 275–6.

74 FO 233/85, no. 3, p. X.

75 Chang Chün-hua and Yü Su-yün, 'Yang-wu yün-tung chung chin-tai ch'i-yeh ching-ying kuan-li ti t'e-tien', in *Chi-lin ta-hsüeh she-hui k'o-hsüeh lun-ts'ung*, 1980, no. 2: *Yang-wu yün-tung t'ao-lun chuan-chi*, p. 286. These and some other Chinese scholars also assert that Giquel deliberately placed the ammunition hold next to the engine room to make sure

of the contemporary observers made a note of it. The fact of the matter is that Giquel was not a marine engineer. When he left the French naval service in the late 1850s, the fully rigged wooden ships still formed the backbone of the fleets of the major powers.[76] It was natural for him to introduce to the Chinese something with which he was familiar. Even then, he had to learn on the job, and from his own mistakes. As Shen recognized, those foreigners willing to come and teach the Chinese were not necessarily the best there were, but the Chinese had no choice.[77] Whatever Giquel's personal inadequacies, he did bring to China a group of fairly competent engineers and support personnel.[78]

On balance, the achievements of the construction programme after only six years of operation were impressive. As the *Shen-pao* categorically stated, the Ma-wei steamers were superior to those made at Kiangnan in design, workmanship, and material.[79] To say that they were the best in China might not mean very much but, as Shen emphasized, one must take the longer view. The superior Western naval technology was developed over decades, perhaps even a century. The Chinese could not catch up in a few years. The important thing, he insisted, was to learn the basics and then keep on learning and improving, unceasingly.[80]

Training new naval personnel

The Navy Yard owed its origins to a deliberate choice by Tso Tsung-t'ang to build instead of buy a naval service. Though a more costly option, he considered it the best way to acquire the technology.[81] Shen concurred. 'It is not so important to build ships as it is to learn [ship-

---

that the vessels would not survive if the ammunition area were hit in battle. In every instance, the source quoted is P'eng Yü-lin's memorial written in the acrimonious atmosphere following the destruction of the Ma-wei squadron in 1884. P'eng was opposed to most forms of Western technology and had rejected the steamship for his Yangtze River Fleet. Although an official of great probity, he spoke with ignorance and prejudice on this occasion. Wang Wen-hsien, 'Ch'ing-chi Ch'ang-chiang shui-shih chih ch'uang-chien chi ch'i ying-hsiang', *Li-shih hsüeh-pao*, 2 (February 1974), 261–99. Mou An-shih also claims that the engines purchased by Giquel were old and broken down (*Yang-wu yün-tung*, p. 76). Mou's belief seems to have been based on rumours circulating in early 1872 (see *HFT*, II, 328).

76 Richard Hough, *A History of Fighting Ships* (London, 1975), p. 102.
77 *HFT*, II, 347b, 359b.
78 Léon Médard, who bore a grudge against Giquel, also pointed to Giquel's lack of engineering knowledge, resulting in some confusion at first, though it was quickly dealt with by the engineers Giquel had hired. Médard, 'Note confidentielle', pp. 2–3.
79 *Shen-pao*, 18 December 1875.
80 *HFT*, II, 347a–b.
81 Ibid., 6b–7, 19; *IWSM*, TC 46:19–23, 86:7a–b.

building]',[82] he said, but cautioned that learning the skills on the job, though important, was merely scratching the surface, whereas the principles behind the skills should be the central concern. Shen stressed both learning and practice, and the Navy Yard School was his instrument for realizing this goal. He called it 'the root' of the entire establishment. His hope was that future men of talent to serve the dynasty would come from the School.[83] In his yamen, he inscribed this verse:

> With a basket of earth, our foundation laid;
> Nothing's too difficult since time began.
> Through nine translations, new methods obtained;
> Now there are sages in China.[84]

Among the earliest defence industries in China, the Foochow Navy Yard was unique in having a fully fledged school.

So strong was Tso and Shen's desire to cultivate China's new naval men that in February 1867, before the Ma-wei site was ready, the School was opened, though on a modest scale. As Yen Fu, one of the first students, recalled, it was housed in a temple in the southern part of Foochow city. Shortly thereafter, another building in the city and one outside were also turned into school-houses. For the time being, Anatole Borel, once a business clerk in Hankow, was hired to teach in the 'French division' and a Chinese from Singapore, Tseng Heng-chung, in the 'English division'.[85]

So important was the School to Shen that he attended to its business even during his mourning. On his first day in office, he interviewed the teachers and asked about the students. Two days later, he had the students examined and graded. The students were to write on the theme 'One must learn to become talented'. He was pleased to find many bright students of good character, but insisted that the stupid and the incorrigible be sent home.[86] Shen's reports on these visits betray a strong traditional emphasis on book learning at the expense of physical devel-

82 *HFT*, II, 461a–b, 463b.
83 Shen's memorials of 18 July and 5 September 1867, and 2 February 1868 in *SWSK*, 4:3b, 6b, 16–19b; Shen to Ting Jih-ch'ang, early 1876, in Shen Pao-chen, 'Shen Wen-su kung-tu', 3:36–7. I am grateful to Professor Lin Ch'ing-yüan of Foochow for the use of a mimeograph copy of the latter, which is a collection of Shen's official correspondence.
84 Lin Hsüan-chih, *Fu-chou Ma-wei*, p. 341.
85 Ch'ih Chung-hu, 'Hai-chün ta-shih chi', in Tso Shun-sheng, comp., *Chung-kuo chin-pai-nien shih tzu-liao hsü-pien* (Taipei, 1958), p. 323; *HFT*, II, 64a–b, 69b; Giquel, *Foochow Arsenal*, p. 17; Médard, 'Note confidentielle', p. 6. Borel was probably Giquel's subordinate at the Hankow customs. On Tseng, see the preceding chapter, note 135.
86 Huang Yin-p'u, 'Pa Shen Pao-chen', p. 145; *SWSK*, 4:3b, 6b; Lin Hsüan-chih, *Fu-chou Ma-wei*, p. 42.

opment, which he did not once mention. Later, some of the School's graduates proved physically unfit for active service.

The School's immediate problem was student recruitment. Tso Tsung-t'ang had envisaged that the students would come from a varied social background, selected on the basis of merit. But how could this new naval education be made attractive and the fear allayed that it might lead to an inferior career? His answer was the promise of material rewards, present and future. As he argued, 'If we do not pay them well, we cannot impose a strict curriculum; if we do not offer chances of promotion, we cannot give them sufficient encouragement'.[87] On the basis of this approach, students were to be paid, on top of their keep and medical care, 4 taels of silver a month. And when they graduated and became proficient as foremen and captains, they were to be paid on the same scale as their European counterparts – a very big promise indeed.[88]

The monthly stipend of 4 taels was intended to provide the students' parents with some support, which they might otherwise have obtained had their teenage sons been gainfully employed. The pay was comparable to that of a workman with a family to support.[89] Whether or not the emolument was in itself attractive, both the French and the English divisions were able to open with thirty students each. With a similar intake each year, the total enrollment reached three hundred by 1873. The majority were from places nearby, but a good many also came from Canton, Hong Kong, and Shanghai.[90]

Some students were indeed lured by the material incentives. For example, Ch'en Ching-k'ang, a native son, enrolled because his family needed the money. Yen Fu was also attracted by the liberal stipend, his father having recently died and his mother having to eke out a living as a seamstress. Then there was Lin T'ai-tseng, the impoverished grandson of Lin Tse-hsü who lost both parents at an early age. All three turned out to be good students and were given respectable positions upon graduation.[91] For those who were better off, financial reward could

---

87 *YWYT*, vol. 5, p. 28.
88 Ibid., 29.
89 A soldier in Tseng Kuo-fan's army, who was also expected to send part of his pay home, received 4.2 taels a month, which was considered ample (Wang Erh-min, *Huai-chün*, p. 9). Though students at the Navy Yard came from a different social background, some were poor (see later).
90 *NCH*, 14 July 1871; *HFT*, II, 419b; FO 233/85, no. 3, p. III.
91 After graduation, Ch'en became a first engineer and Lin a first mate on a Navy Yard boat. Yen went on to England for further studies and returned in 1879 as a professor in the Navy Yard School. *MHHC*, 87 ('Hsiao-i shang'): 21b–22; Chang Hsia et al., eds., *Ch'ing-mo hai-chün shih-liao* (Peking, 1982), p. 438; Y. C. Wang, *Chinese Intellectuals and the West, 1872–1949* (Durham, N.C., 1966), p. 194; *Fu-chou li-shih jen-wu* (Foochow, 1989), vol. 2, pp. 86–7, vol. 3, pp. 71–2.

not always compete with the promise of a brighter future, especially in the civil service. Thus, another local boy, who took first place in the entrance examinations at the age of twelve, was soon transferred to a more orthodox education when his father became aware of his potential. The youth got his first degree soon after.[92]

A few students from wealthy backgrounds did stay. Ch'en Chi-t'ung, who came from a Foochow scholar-gentry family, is one example. The majority were likely to have come from families of modest means, the kind that could give their children enough education to pass the entrance examinations. Of the three hundred pupils in 1873, Dunn observed that the majority were from good families and some were even sons of officials. They were said to have been 'apt and clever and anxious to learn'.[93] James Carroll, head of the English division, 'found some of them very intelligent, others just *so so*'.[94]

As always, the Chinese were eager to see results. The students were thus subjected to a rigorous academic life. Tso Tsung-t'ang had wanted a 'strict curriculum' and drew up a set of regulations to match. They betrayed a strong Confucian, disciplinarian bias. Classroom learning was emphasized and extracurricular activities discouraged. And when Giquel tried to introduce a more modern educational method, Shen accepted only a few of his ideas.[95] The old-fashioned approach certainly kept the student close to their books, but the prohibition against play (*hsi-yu*, lit., playing and sauntering) most likely inhibited creativity and physical development. If feeble-bodied men could still make good engineers, they made poor naval officers. But Giquel did not press his point. Nor did he provide reasons for his proposed revisions.

The regulations prescribed a long school year and a lengthy school day. Classes were held every day, including Sundays, except for a three-day holiday at the Dragon Boat Festival, the August Moon Festival, and a slightly longer vacation at New Year. On the students' entry, the parents had to sign an affidavit committing them to five years of

92 *FCTC*, 'Wen-yüan chuan, Ch'ing', 3:30b.
93 FO 233/85, no. 3, p. III. During an earlier visit in 1870, Dunn reported that the students in the French schools were 'young and intelligent'; *NCH*, 21 April 1879. On Ch'en, see *FCTC:LCH*, vol. 3, pp. 304–7 and *MHHC*, 69:38–39b, 72:18b–19; *FCTC*, 'Lieh-chuan', 5b:38–39b. For examples of students from educated but modest families, see *Fu-chou li-shih*, vol. 2, pp. 76–81, vol. 3, pp. 77–80.
94 Carroll, 'Note Book I', entry for 18 November 1867.
95 Tso's memorial of 11 December 1866 in *TWHK*, 'Memorials', 20:62–68b; Thibaudier, 'Arsenal de Fou-tchéou'; Shen to Hsia Hsien-lun in Huang Yin-p'u, 'Pa Shen Pao-chen', pp. 145–55. Giquel's proposed revisions were dated some time in early 1867. Steven Leibo errs in stating that the regulations originated from Giquel and were approved by Shen (*Transferring Technology*, pp. 110–11).

schooling; no long leaves were allowed, except for serious health problems. Giquel had tried to introduce a six-day week and a month-long summer holiday while shortening the traditional, extended mourning for a deceased parent. Shen turned down both suggestions, although, as a concession, he allowed parental visits on Sundays. The summer break, he argued, would only delay progress: 'Every additional day of study would produce results a day sooner'. On the hundred-day mourning, Shen, noted for his filial piety, remained adamant. As he reasoned, if a proper mourning period was denied, people would say that the students, once in the Navy Yard School, would have to abandon (in a Confucian sense) their parents. This kind of talk would only turn respectable people away. The quality of students would then suffer. Besides, who, upon a parent's death, could set his mind on his books? In any event, Shen insisted, the number of students so affected would be very small, and they could catch up with their studies later.[96]

The students' life was highly regimented. They were to rise, eat, and retire according to schedule. The rules were enforced by 'upright gentrymen', whose duties were also to prohibit frivolities, disrespect towards teachers, or bullying fellow students and to punish those who were lazy. Giquel's proposal that students who did poorly in the first two months be dismissed was in agreement with Shen's predilections and was adopted. To induce better performance, the students were subjected to quarterly examinations. Those with the highest score were awarded $10, and those with the lowest, a mark of laziness against them. Two successive marks of laziness would lead to a caution, and three to dismissal. In contrast, three successive top grades would be distinguished by an additional award of clothing materials, and each promotion would result in an extra silver tael added to the monthly stipend.[97]

The attitude and deportment of the students were of great importance to Shen. Therefore, the students were to be from 'good' families, young (twenty or under), and proficient in the Chinese language, so that they would be teachable. He would prefer them to be intelligent as well, but feared that their quick wit would all too readily lead to treachery and fickleness, and all the modern science they learned would be in vain. So their intelligence must be reined in by a sense of rectitude, instilled by a daily dose of simple Confucian works – the *Classic of Filial Piety* and the *Sacred Edicts* of the K'ang-hsi emperor – as well as essay writing on

---

96 Huang Yin-p'u, 'Pa Shen Pao-chen', pp. 145–55.
97 Ibid. Giquel's proposed increase in the students' stipend to 5 taels per month and an additional 3 to 5 taels for those who had mastered the English or French language was rejected by Shen.

related topics. As he asserted, 'It is permissible for a Chinese mind to master the skills of the foreigners, but it is not permissible for the bad habits of the foreign countries to contaminate the Chinese mind'.[98]

Shen's desire to produce a Confucian engineer or naval officer is understandable, but could it be realized? Did his emphasis on Confucian virtues and suspicion towards the students' native intelligence stand in the way of a technical or naval education? Available examples show that there were students, like the ones we have met (Ch'en Ching-k'ang, Yen Fu, and Ch'en Chi-t'ung), who had had a good Confucian education. They were also judged to be intelligent by the European teachers and many, having done well in the Navy Yard School, went on to careers in the *yang-wu* sector with various degrees of success. [99] They would have been more successful had they been given jobs that were more commensurate with their qualifications. But that is another question. In the School, the students were exposed to the European instructors most of the time, and the reward system was not based on Confucian virtues, although any flagrant infringement would surely invite punishment or expulsion. In practice, therefore, Shen's attitude and policy might not have been such great obstacles as they might at first appear to have been.

The Navy Yard School was divided into two divisions, the so-called French and English schools. The French schools were three in number: the School of Naval Construction, the School of Design, and the School for Apprentices. The object of the School of Naval Construction, headed by Léon Médard, was to teach the students the principles of hulls, engines, and sails and an understanding of the dimensions and functions of the parts involved. For this purpose, arithmetic, geometry, physics, trigonometry, calculus, and mechanics were taught. Naturally, these were preceded by a course in the French language, which was used in all the French schools, the workshops, and shipbuilding yards.[100] The initial language barrier must have caused problems since Giquel alone spoke Chinese, but the difficulty seemed to have been overcome soon enough.[101]

---

98 Ibid.; *SWSK*, 4:6b–7.
99 Another example is Yeh Po-yün, who later authored a literary work and a guide to navigation. *FCTC*, 'Lieh-chuan', 5b:40a–b.
100 Unless otherwise stated, the following paragraphs are based on Giquel's *Foochow Arsenal*, pp. 17–23, 29–32. The Navy Yard School has also been subjected to a detailed study by Knight Biggerstaff, although the perspective taken in the present study is slightly different. See his *Government Schools*, pp. 210–18.
101 There is no direct reference to language difficulties in the French schools, but in early 1868 Shen did point to the problem in the workshops. *HFT*, II, 115. Also in 1868, Giquel complained of the lack of French–Chinese teaching aids. Leibo suggests that this was a source of problems (*Transferring Technology*, p. 113). Modern language teaching tends to favour the exclusive use of the foreign language taught. The

The entire course lasted five years, with the last fourteen months given to practical work. As the contract expired in early 1874, only the first two of the four classes completed practical training. It included the study of the transmission of power from the engines to the machine tools, which, in turn, required an understanding of the mechanics of the pulleys and of the toothed and pinion wheels. The steam engines in the workshops and on board ships were closely studied. Students trained to build engines were taught the dynamics of steam engine operations, such as those of the cylinders, condensers, pistons, valves, crank shafts, and eccentrics. Those specializing in hull construction and ship equipment were taught to calculate the shape and size of a hull so as to meet the requirements for draught, carrying capacity, and so on. They were to know as well what sail spread a given ship ought to have and what scantling must be given to the wood of a timber so that it might have the requisite strength. Having thus made the plan of a ship, they were to trace it out in full size in the moulding hall in a manner that the workmen could follow in building the ship. During his visit in 1870, Dunn attended a geometry class and found that the students clearly understood the subject. 'The school', he wrote three years later, 'turns out admirable pupils'.[102]

The School of Design was created in January 1868. Proposed by Giquel, it was readily approved by Shen, who, having seen numerous drawings, immediately recognized the importance of the draughtsman.[103] The object was to train a staff with both theoretical and practical knowledge of different types of engines and parts of a ship so that they could, through calculation and design, render an engineer's general conception and rough sketch into a working plan. The curriculum included arithmetic, geometry, and French. Because the Navy Yard was to manufacture seven 150-horsepower engines for its ships, this engine was intensively studied. The engines and tools in the workshops were also examined. The course took three years to complete, and in April 1873 the ten students of the first class were sent to the School of Naval Construction for further studies, which now included algebra and physics. The second and third classes, each of eleven students, completed the course later.[104]

Frenchmen at Ma-wei might have stumbled upon a more effective teaching method by necessity.

102 *NCH*, 21 April 1870; Biggerstaff, *Government Schools*, p. 211, n. 27. The quotation comes from FO 233/85, no. 3, p. II.
103 *SWSK*, 4:18a–b.
104 According to Dunn, the pupils also investigated English and U.S. designs and went through a course of mathematics, dynamics, etc., similar to that proposed by Dupuy de Lorse. FO 233/85, no. 3, p. II.

The School for Apprentices was created in mid-1868, also as an afterthought, as older workmen could not be retrained in sufficient numbers to read and execute a plan.[105] The young men, aged fourteen to seventeen, were taught arithmetic, geometry, algebra, design, and the study of engines. They spent the day in the workshops and gathered for a ninety-minute lesson in the evening, but another hour and a half of study in the morning was soon added. The goal was to turn them into foremen and workshop superintendents who understood the mechanics of engines, gave the specifications for them, and calculated the weights and masses of each part. In 1870, the seventy-six apprentices were divided into four classes. Two of these completed the course when the contract period ended, the third class had yet to study algebra, and the pupils of the fourth, consisting of late-comers and slow learners, were simply returned to the workshops, where they, with their training, could at least make better workmen.

The English schools, so called because of the language of instruction, were also three in number: the School of Theoretical Navigation, the School of Practical Navigation, and the School for Engineers to train naval officers and engineers.

The School of Theoretical Navigation had a three-and-a-half-year curriculum, which embraced all the sciences essential to the navigator, namely, arithmetic, geometry, algebra, trigonometry, astronomy, the calculations of navigation, and geography. The School, headed by James Carroll, began in November 1867.[106] Language was a barrier at first, but Carroll, aided by his English-speaking Chinese assistant (probably Tseng Heng-chung), was able to carry on. By early 1870, if not before, the students had become proficient enough for instructional purposes, though some of them still did not speak the language as fluently as Carroll wished. Dunn was nonetheless impressed by 'the young Chinese [who] spoke correct and good English, and the jargon of pidgin English is [*sic*] not to be heard'.[107]

Twenty-three of the thirty students in the first class completed the course in May 1871. They were said to have mastered fractions, proportions, and percentages in arithmetic and quadratic equations of the second degree, with some slight knowledge of ratios, proportions, and progression, in algebra. Their command of world geography was elementary, but they could still calculate the position of their ship using the

---

105 *HFT*, II, 134b–135.
106 A detailed syllabus was published in *NCH*, 14 July 1871, quoted in Biggerstaff, *Government Schools*, p. 215. James Carroll, a fourth master at the Royal Naval College at Greenwich, was then twenty-five years of age. F. E. Elliott to author, 18 July 1966.
107 *NCH*, 14 July 1871 and 21 April 1870 (quotation from Dunn's report).

compass and the chronometer and their knowledge of geometry, trigonometry, and nautical astronomy. Before moving on to the School of Practical Navigation, they were given an examination by Lieutenant Swainson, R.N., then in charge of the training ship. The results were encouraging: the top pupil scored 392 marks out of 400, while seven went over 300, and only three fell below 200. The average grade was 273.85, or more than 68 per cent.[108] The second class of nine pupils also entered the School of Practical Navigation upon graduation in September 1873. Fifteen students were still in midcourse when the contract ended in early 1874. Those who had completed the course were said to have a 'fair theoretical knowledge of their work'.[109]

The School of Practical Navigation had a checkered beginning. As early as 1869 Shen had recognized the need for a training ship but could not find a suitable vessel. By mid-1870, with two ships launched, the matter had acquired an urgency of its own. So the Navy Yard's third vessel, the 80-horsepower gunboat *Fu-hsing* (*Lucky Star* or *Star of Fukien*), was temporarily used for training. A cruise to Hong Kong was then planned and quickly canncelled when a more suitable boat, a three-masted Prussian sailing ship, the *Mattadore*, was found. Shen liked the ship because more men (over thirty cadets with a crew of more than a hundred) could be trained on it.[110] After modification, the vessel, now renamed *Chien-wei* (*The Awe-Inspiring*), entered service in July 1871. Training, which also included gunnery, soon began. By early 1872, twenty pupils had taken part in a cruise to Newchwang, calling at Shanghai, Chefoo, and Tientsin along the way.[111]

Practical training gained momentum as Captain R. E. Tracey, R.N., took over from Swainson. An ambitious, seventy-five-day cruise to Singapore and Penang was then undertaken, with Tracey in charge on the outward journey and the students on the return voyage. The pupils'

---

108 Carroll to Giquel in *NCH*, 14 July 1871 (quoted at length in Biggerstaff, *Government Schools*, p. 215, n. 31). Seven students were discharged for unknown reasons. Of the twenty-three, two did not take the examination. Commander Tracey of H.M.'s gunboat *Avon* acted as 'external examiner'.
109 *North-China Daily News*, 10 December 1875.
110 Bought for $14,000, the *Mattadore* was 125 feet long, 27 feet wide, and 15 feet 8 inches high, with a cargo capacity of 475 tons. *HFT*, II, 266b–267b; *NCH*, 1 September 1870.
111 *HFT*, II, 267. Giquel reported that twenty students were on the cruise, whereas Ch'ih Chung-hu names only eighteen. Giquel, *Foochow Arsenal*, p. 30; Ch'ih, 'Hai-chün ta-shih chi', pp. 325–6. There was yet another slight delay apparently caused by a disagreement over the style of uniform for the students, 'the mandarins wishing to dress their men in the usual Chinese style, loose coats with red targets on either side, and the officer [Swainson] according to his own country's uniform'. The Chinese had their way. *NCH*, 14 July 1871 and 21 April 1870; Shore, *Flight of the Lapwing*, p. 234.

performance and their log were closely monitored, and individual ability was noted for future appointment. Navigating on the open seas, which this trip involved, was considered an impossibility in a five-year programme and was specifically excluded by contract. But Giquel, recognizing the intelligence and enthusiasm of the students, took the bold step and turned it into a success. Later, students from the second class were also put on the *Chien-wei* and were expected to have received adequate training after two years.[112]

Engine-room officers were trained in the School for Engineers. Its twenty-one students were recruited from Shanghai and Hong Kong, where they had had some factory experience. Still, they had to be taught the theoretical and practical aspects of steam engines, which included arithmetic, geometry, design, the description of engines, the use of various indicators and salinometer, and rules for engine management at sea. The students were said to produce good work, 'neat and exact'. A second part of the course involved practical work: setting up engines and boilers ashore and on board. Then a 'searching examination' followed, and the successful students were assigned to a ship. Thereafter, their log books were inspected at the end of every trip and the ships' engines examined annually. Reportedly, the training was thorough.[113]

In all the schools, the attrition rate was high. This was particularly true of the School of Naval Construction, which had the most demanding curriculum. James Carroll blamed the high failure rate on the students' frequent and long absences, some lasting six to eight weeks at a time. The Chinese were used to a much more informal educational environment. The traditional school, the *ssu-shu*, was usually housed on private property, and the 'school calendar' was flexible, as dictated by social usage and the needs of teachers and pupils alike. Since the teacher had both pedagogical and social functions, he was frequently involved in the familial affairs of the students, to whom he was often related.[114] The rigidity of the Navy Yard School thus challenged the traditional family system.

In applying a Confucian, disciplinarian approach to the Navy Yard School, Shen was not fully aware of the contradictions. For him, the new, formal education was an imperative, and hence he would make just one concession to time-honoured social customs, the hundred-day

112 *HFT*, II, 36, 467; Ch'ih, 'Hai-chün ta-shih chi', pp. 326–7.
113 Dunn's report, *NCH*, 21 April 1870.
114 Giquel, *Foochow Arsenal*, p. 20; Carroll to Giquel, in *NCH*, 14 July 1871; Biggerstaff, *Government Schools*, pp. 211–12 and note 28; and Sally Borthwick, 'Schooling and Society in Late Qing China', Ph.D. diss., Australian National University, 1978, pp. 49–50.

234

mourning period. But the School by neccessity had to recruit most of its students from at least moderately 'respectable' families, whose children had had some education and a healthy attitude towards learning. Yet these same youngsters were also brought up to respect social customs condoned by Confucian ideals, ones that Shen himself cherished and wanted the students to retain. Thus, though Shen deplored their absences, he could not condemn the customs to which they adhered.

Bookishness and disdain for physical work were yet another aspect of the upbringing of children in 'respectable' homes. Shen did not see these as impediments. His set of school regulations tended to reinforce these attitudes rather than modify them for a more effective technical and naval education. Only the nature of the education and the rigour of the curriculum served as a deterrent, though not necessarily an adequate corrective.

Yet among those who completed their studies, the results are impressive. Since scientific and technical training was conducted in the schools and at the work place, the following discussion includes the results of the training programmes for students, apprentices, workers, as well as foremen.

For Shen, the main goal of the Navy Yard was to provide a place of learning. It follows that the ultimate measure of success was to be Chinese technological independence. So six months before the Europeans left, all the Chinese from foremen down were tested: they were to manufacture objects from blueprints without help from their foreign mentors. Those who did not succeed at first were to try again and again until they did. On the basis of these tests and, in the case of students and apprentices, their school work as well, Giquel made his report and recommended them for appointments in the Chinese-run navy yard.[115]

In the manufacture of marine engines, seven students attained a high level of competence. One, Chang Ch'eng, was considered good enough to be given overall charge of engine building. Three qualified as superintendents, and two as assistants, in the foundry, the boiler shop, and the fitting and setting-up shop. These six men were to be assisted by twelve students. The seventh, because of a weak constitution, was made professor for lower classes. In addition, twenty-four students, some from the School of Design, had a sound knowledge of engine design. Eight of them, including several who could draw working plans from the engineer's rough sketch, had the potential to become heads of offices of design if they continued their studies. Further, eighty-seven apprentices

115 *SWSK*, 4:59b–60, 66a–b. Unless otherwise stated, the following paragraphs are drawn from Giquel, *Foochow Arsenal*, pp. 19–34.

who had attended school were able to work according to a plan. Of these, fifty-three could eventually become workshop superintendents or even engineers if they continued their studies and gained practical experience in Europe. Among the workmen and apprentices who did not attend school, one hundred and eighty-six were able to work according to a given plan.

In the hull, fittings, and equipment departments, nine pupils had mastered the calculations for all aspects of the kind of ship built at Mawei: from planning its hull and sails, and drawing it in full size in the moulding hall, to supervising its construction. Seven of them could eventually become engineers after further studies. However, in late 1873, one of them, Wei Han, was already qualified to take charge of hull construction and ship equipment, and three others in charge of the building yards, the wood-working and the chronometer shops. Of the apprentices who had studied carpentry, fourteen were able to sketch out a ship in the moulding hall. Half of them could become master carpenters with additional schooling. Finally, six foremen were likewise able to sketch out a ship in the moulding hall and oversee its construction, and fifty-eight workmen and apprentices were able to work a given plan.

From July 1873 Giquel began to withdraw the European engineers and foremen from the workshops. In consequence, the bulk of the last two vessels, hulls, engines, equipment and all, were manufactured, set up, and fitted out by the students and workers without European direction. The ultimate test, of course, was the Chinese ability to build, entirely on their own, a ship from scratch to finish. And this they did in building the two transports, S.S. Nos. 16 and 18, which were launched in 1875 and 1876, respectively. Captain Shore maintained that their 150-horsepower perpendicular marine engines were 'quite equal to anything turned out of our own engineering establishments'.[116] But what gave Shen the greatest joy was the 245-ton, 50-horsepower gunboat which was designed, from engine to hull, by four graduates of the School of Naval Construction. When it was launched in 1876, Shen named it the *I-hsin* – *Students' Creation*.[117]

In the navigation department, twenty-six pupils had received instruction adequate for commanding a warship, but only the fourteen who had the experience of an extended cruise were ready for a captaincy. In fact, several of them had gone beyond the syllabus and learned to sail on the high seas. Among them were Chang Ch'eng and Lü Han, both made captains in 1873 of the small vessels bought by the provincial govern-

116 Shore, *Flight of the Lapwing*, p. 97–8.
117 Ch'en Chen, *Chung-kuo chin-tai kung-yeh*, vol. 1, p. 414; *HFT*, II, 575.

ment.[118] By the time Shen left in late 1875, seven graduates had become captains (see Chapter 10). Two others, because of health, were respectively made an assistant professor and a translator of naval manuals. In addition, there were nine students whose studies had not gone far beyond theoretical navigation who served as junior officers. And among the fifteen still in the School, nine were said to be promising.

In the engine-room department, twenty-one students were deemed suitable for active service in late 1873, but only fourteen were given commissions on board ship because of limited openings. Another one, for reasons of health, was made an assistant professor instead.

Giquel, on whose report our assessment of the training programme largely depends, naturally wanted to highlight the successes. Still, it was widely recognized at the time that Ma-wei's students were much better trained than those at the Kiangnan Arsenal, thanks to the comprehensive curriculum, system of frequent examinations, and practical training. Only one British observer criticized the emphasis on applied science at the expense of basic science, but for what was actually taught, he had only praise. Ma-wei graduates also did better than their Kiangnan contemporaries on entering active service.[119] But Giquel did stress that the Chinese on their own were able to build, sail, and service only the kind of ships constructed at Ma-wei. To go beyond that, further studies, especially in Europe, would be necessary for all the graduates and the more intelligent workmen and apprentices. Of course, his contract did not ask for more. Shen himself, as early as May 1872, had also called for further studies in Europe for the Foochow graduates as something above and beyond what the contract stipulated.[120] Nonetheless, Giquel's claims came under scrutiny when charges were *subsequently* leveled at the quality of the training and the Chinese inability to work without foreign assistance.

In 1898 Médard blamed Giquel for deliberately setting low standards for the School and James Carroll of the School of Theoretical Navigation for an inability to teach mechanics. His own School of Naval Construction, however, was saved from mediocrity only because he insisted on an advanced curriculum, going beyond quadratic equations of the second degree and teaching calculus. His insubordination, he claimed, had

---

118 *HFT*, II, 467, 511b, 515b; *SWSK*, 4:63; Shen's memorial of 13 November 1875 (KH 1.10.16) in YCT, KH 1/10 *chung*.
119 *Shen-pao*, 18 December 1875; Anon., 'Chinese Arsenals', p. 698; Mary Wright, *Last Stand*, p. 213. For example, officers of the *Yang-wu* and the *Teng-ying-chou* – predominantly Foochow graduates – were much better at gunnery and marksmanship. Wu Tsan-ch'eng's memorial, 18 June 1877 (KH 3.5.8), in YCT, KH 3/5 *shang*.
120 *HFT*, II, 349b. Subsequently, Shen repeatedly reiterated the need for studies abroad. See, e.g., *YWYT*, vol. 5, pp. 140–1.

outraged Giquel, who had wanted to make further studies in Europe a necessity and thus extend his highly paid job. As we have seen, Médard had a low opinion of Giquel and his technical knowledge. The two disagreed on other major issues as well, from the treatment of Chief Engineer Trasbot to the equipment of the Navy Yard. Médard also felt strongly that the Navy Yard should have been purely French and deeply resented the high praise Giquel had piled on the English schools.[121] His were not the charges of a disinterested man.

Giquel was not averse to having a lucrative job, but to tie that to his pitching the School's instruction at a low level would require stronger evidence. After all, the contract was fulfilled and, at least in practical navigation, students were taught skills beyond the limits set by the contract. Whatever the quality of instruction, further studies in Europe would still have been necessary. To assert that that could have been dispensed with simply by adopting a more advanced curriculum at Ma-wei was foolhardy.

The other charge – that the Chinese were incapable of working without European help – was made by the *China Mail* in 1876 when it reported that some foreigners had been retained and new ones hired.[122] It would be well to remember that, at the founding of the Navy Yard, Tso Tsung-t'ang had considered the possibility of retaining 'one or two' foreigners to continue their instruction for several more years. But Shen, concerned with clearly marking the end of European tutelage so as to allay criticism, had once argued that, even if a few foreigners were kept after February 1874, the Navy Yard would have failed in its mission.[123] Yet he had no illusions about the Chinese having become technologically self-sufficient at this point.

The foreigners hired after the contract had expired were to help bring the Navy Yard to the next stage of development. Giquel and de Segonzac were kept, but not in their former elevated positions. Giquel was now put in charge of the School and naval training, and de Segonzac was to assist him. The main concerns were the students' education in Europe and the employment of new technicians to build the composite ships and compound engines. Subsequently, eight technicians and a secretary-translator arrived in 1875 and 1876, and they were gradually dismissed between 1877 and 1880.[124] Clearly, they were engaged only for

121 Médard, 'Note confidentielle', pp. 4–8.
122 Cited by Biggerstaff, *Government Schools*, p. 219, n. 37.
123 *HFT*, II, 36, 469b.
124 Those who can be identified are Jouvet, Cabouret, Robeson, Heim, and Meusburger. The first three had served in the Navy Yard under the initial contract. It appears that Borel, the secretary from the earlier period, was also retained until he left for Europe

as long as the Chinese needed to learn the new technology. Their presence had no bearing on the success of the initial programme.

Giquel was retained also for further naval training. In early 1874, three Ma-wei vessels were turned over to the China Merchants' Steam Navigation Company, but the company, having little faith in the Navy Yard's men, wanted them to be officered by Europeans. Thanks to Shen's insistence that Chinese vessels stay in Chinese hands, Navy Yard men were eventually given charge of the ships.[125] But if Shen could entrust them with commercial vessels, he had doubts about their battle-worthiness, especially after a near engagement with the Japanese on Taiwan (see Chapter 10). He thus accepted Giquel's suggestion that training be stepped up at Foochow, particularly in navigation, gunnery, and general on-deck drill. Captain Tracey was re-employed and he was joined by J. Harwood, a gunner, and F. Johnson, a boatswain. Training was to be conducted in six stages: (1) ports on the China coast; (2) Japanese ports, Manila, Singapore, and Penang; (3) San Francisco; (4) India and adjacent countries; (5) Europe; and (6) North America. Because the new programme required a larger vessel, the 250-horsepower corvette *Yang-wu* now replaced the *Chien-wei* as the training ship. By the time Shen left in late 1875, the first two stages had been completed.[126] Thus, although the Foochow students may have acquired the basics of navigation and engine-room operation under European tutelage, additional experience and training were needed to turn them into fully fledged naval officers.

Where the Navy Yard School had clearly failed was in the training of a Chinese teaching staff. The three graduates who were made professors did not live up to expectations, and they were ignorant of the new technology that the building of composite vessels and compound engines entailed. Recognizing the need for instructors in theoretical navigation and engine-room operations, Ting Jih-ch'ang, Shen's successor, recalled Carroll in 1876 for a three-year term and hired a certain A. Morton in 1878 to teach practical navigation on the *Wei-yüan*, Ma-wei's first composite vessel powered by a compound engine. Two former French

with Giquel in 1875. Giquel to Contre-Amiral Krantz of 10 March 1875, de Segonzac to Krantz of 26 November 1875 and to Commander Véron of 14 April 1876, in MM BB4 1555 17/5/43, 44, 45; *HFT*, II, 623a–b, 771a–b, 818b; Lin Ch'ing-yüan, 'Ma-wei ch'uan-cheng-chü p'ing-yung wai-kuo jen-yüan ti hsing-chih he tso-yung', in *Chi-lin ta-hsüeh she-hui k'o-hsüeh lun-ts'ung*, 1980, no. 2: *Yang-wu yün-tung t'ao-lun chuan-chi*, pp. 214–15; Biggerstaff, *Government Schools*, p. 219.

125 *NCH*, citing the *Foochow Herald*, 19 March 1874; *HFT*, II, 422, 502b.

126 *HFT*, II, 552b, 623–4; Ch'ih Chung-hu, 'Hai-chün ta-shih chi', pp. 326–7. Tracey was replaced by Captain Percy Luxmore, R.N., in 1876. Pedder to Wade, 1 August 1876, in FO 228/568, no. 43, encl.

staff members were also rehired for the School of Naval Construction: Dessaut, probably in 1876, and Médard, in early 1878.[127]

Part of the problem was that Shen, as much as Tso Tsung-t'ang, had set unrealistic goals; both wanted to free the Chinese from European tutelage at an early date. The spectre of conservative opposition also put great pressure on Shen to make a clean cut with the foreign staff, professors and all, at the end of the contract. Hence, young men with minimal experience were made captains or professors. To expect the Chinese to command their vessels or run a college of marine engineering or a naval academy after a few years of schooling was asking too much. Médard certainly thought that even his superior curriculum was not adequate for training professors.[128]

Conclusions

In discussing the Japanese success in the Meiji era, William G. Beasley observes that the Japanese had hired foreign instructors, advisers, and engineers to run a number of new concerns. The Japanese looked upon them as schoolmasters, but the official policy was to replace them as soon as possible. It was this approach, Beasley concludes, that eventually made Japan's industrial technology self-sustaining.[129] The reasons for Japan's success are many, but the point remains that Tso Tsung-t'ang created the Foochow Navy Yard for exactly the same purpose, and Shen never lost sight of it. As an individual institution, therefore, the Foochow Navy Yard had great potential, and Shen, with Giquel's help, went far towards realizing it.

In the Foochow Navy Yard the Chinese had a first-rate establishment. In magnitude, it compared favourably with the leading Japanese ship-building facilities at Yokosuka. The latter, begun in 1865, had a budget of $2,000,000 (around 1,300,000 taels) for a four-year period compared with 4,000,000 taels over five years at Ma-wei. The actual expenditure at Yokosuka eventually doubled the budget, but that at Ma-wei also went up to 5,360,000 taels (December 1866 to August 1874). The contingent

---

127 Carroll's contract was renewed for yet another three years in 1879, but he died the year following. 'Contracts of James Carroll' and letter of R. W. Mansfield, acting vice-consul of Foochow, to Mrs. Sophia Elliott, 8 June 1880 (both manuscripts are in the possession of, and were loaned to me by, Mr. F. E. Elliott, to whom I am grateful); John N. Jordan's memorandum, 22 July 1879, enclosed in Wade to Foreign Office, 1 August 1879, in FO 228/622, no. 129, encl. 3 in no. 6; Médard, 'Note confidentielle', p. 9; HFT, II, 675, 694b–695; Lin Ch'ing-yüan, 'Ma-wei ch'uan-cheng-chü', p. 215; Biggerstaff, Government Schools, p. 223.
128 Médard, 'Note confidentielle', p. 7.
129 William G. Beasley, The Modern History of Japan, 2d ed. (New York, 1974), p. 144.

of European (French) engineers and technicians at Yokosuka, too, was smaller, numbering between forty and fifty-five. And Ma-wei's shipbuilding and training programmes were more comprehensive and ambitious. The shipbuilding school at Yokosuka did not begin until about half-way through the contract. Under Shen's energetic leadership, the Chinese navy yard was also ready for full-scale operation much sooner, even when allowances are made for the political turmoil in Japan at the time. To be sure, the Japanese had several more Western-style dockyard facilities by the late 1860s, but when compared in isolation, the Foochow Navy Yard enjoyed many advantages over the Yokosuka works in the early 1870s.[130]

The Chinese, however, were beset with a number of difficulties, not the least of which was the lack of support, both political and financial, from the central government (see the next chapter). Here we focus on Shen's leadership as it pertains to the shipbuilding and training programmes.

Shen directed the Navy Yard with interest and vigour. Though his approach may at times have been reminiscent of the so-called method of evading management, he attended to administrative details, clamped down on corruption, and dealt personally even with cases of petty thievery. His authoritarian approach towards labour resulted in a well-organized and efficient work force. Marxist historians condemn him for oppression,[131] but the working conditions at Ma-wei were far better than those prevailing in early industrializing societies in Europe, Japan, or, later, China itself. By contemporary standards, workers at Ma-wei were well paid.

In dealing with technical matters, Shen made notable attempts to increase his knowledge. He familiarized himself with yard facilities and paid attention to the uses of materials. He recognized the importance of technical and naval architectural drawings, although his understanding remained superficial. His interest in machinery enabled him to appreciate the interrelationships among various machines and workshops.

130 Kodama Kota, *Sangyōshi* (Tokyo, 1965), vol. 2, pp. 428–32; Seymour Broadbridge, 'Shipbuilding and the State in Japan since the 1850s', *Modern Asian Studies*, 11.4 (1977), 602–3; Hazel J. Jones, 'The Meiji Government and Foreign Employees, 1868–1990', Ph.D. diss., University of Michigan, 1967, pp. 35–45. Jones points out that by 1868 Yokosuka had completed eight ships and eleven more were under way. But she does not go into the size and quality of the ships, or whether the engines, etc., were Japanese built. She does indicate that many of the materials used were purchased abroad or from foreign merchants in Japan. On the expenditure at Ma-wei, see Wang Hsin-chung, 'Fu-chou ch'uan-ch'ang', pp. 18–22. Total expenditure under Shen (up to October 1875) was higher (see the next chapter).
131 Chang Kuo-hui, *Yang-wu yün-tung*, pp. 73–4; Chiao Ching-i, 'Ts'ung Fu-chou ch'uan-cheng', pp. 239–40.

He could certainly describe their functions, though he was still ignorant of the principles behind them. For a mandarin of his rank and stature, this was no small step forward. And he was able to translate his limited knowledge into productive decisions. The expansion of the School and the addition of the heavy metal-working forge and rolling mill, for instance, would not have been possible without his say-so.

Yet Shen's approach somehow fell short, for although he encouraged and rewarded those members of his staff who had gained some knowledge of science and technology, he did not engage them more deeply in technical matters. At Yokosuka, Japanese were sent to Europe to coordinate the recruitment of technicians and the purchase of machinery.[132] At the founding of the Foochow Navy Yard, such an option was not even considered. It was to Shen's credit that in 1875 he took the opportunity to send five Navy Yard graduates with Giquel to Europe to buy iron frames and compound engines. Three returned with Giquel the following year; the other two stayed for further studies.[133] But these were young men who were years away from occupying any decision-making office. The sending of senior men abroad to study or even to observe would have had an untold impact on the Navy Yard's development. The idea was never contemplated.

Yet another flaw in Shen's approach was that, despite the years he spent with the Europeans, he never attempted to learn either French or English. Admittedly, no high official other than Tseng Chi-tse, the son of Tseng Kuo-fan and half a generation his junior, had acquired literacy in a Western language in this period,[134] but Shen's ignorance of a Western language exacerbated his other flaws. These flaws severely restricted Chinese access to technological and scientific knowledge. Thus, when charges were made that Giquel had held back technological secrets, Shen could not give a knowledgeable answer.[135] Nor was he able to judge the level of instruction at the Navy Yard School. There is little substance to the accusation that Giquel had set the standard low. What was taught could be explained as much by Giquel's limited knowledge, and his estimation of the Chinese capacity to learn, as by any chicanery on his part. Giquel did deliver in the end a more substantial navy yard and school system than planned. It was also he who proposed the building of compound engines before Shen was able to take advantage of that offer. The point remains that Shen and his staff, though able

---

132 Broadbridge, 'Shipbuilding', p. 603.
133 Ch'ih Chung-hu, 'Hai-chün ta-shih chi', p. 327.
134 Li En-han, *Tseng Chi-tse ti wai-chiao* (Taipei, 1966), pp. 18–25.
135 *HFT*, II, 318a–b.

to prevent administrative or political domination by the French, were vulnerable to 'technological domination'.

The Navy Yard had been criticized because it could produce only two types of warship. Outmoded to begin with, some of them were too large for China's rivers and all were too puny to cope with foreign threats.[136] Overlooked is the fact that the Navy Yard was meant to be both a shipbuilding and a teaching institution. It was to be a technological experience, one the Chinese could ill-afford to by-pass. Arguably, progress could have been quicker if two key conditions had been met. The first, already discussed, was the presence of a more technologically knowledgeable leadership. The second was the freedom of that leadership to make major policy changes. But this liberty was denied by external political forces. Without strong and constant imperial support, the Navy Yard was open to criticism on the slightest pretext. Any change of plan in midcourse would have been seized upon as a sign of failure. Shen's inability to introduce the composite vessel and the compound engine at an early date illustrates the point.

None of these problems were beyond remedy. A programme of advanced studies in Europe could, in time, have solved many of them. And the shipbuilding effort could easily have been supplemented by a judicious buying programme. Some of the reasons for the failure to bring these elements together became important only after Shen's incumbency. They lie beyond the scope of this volume; others will be discussed later.

Shen's Confucian approach to education has been discussed, and we have also noted that its adverse effects were to some degree neutralized by the nature of technical and naval training. However, as Dwight Perkins reminds us, no country in the early stages of industrialization was blessed with leaders who could clearly see the path ahead, Meiji Japan included. It was only through practice that one learned what was wrong and how to correct it.[137] Shen certainly learned from his experience and, from 1870 on, became one of the earliest advocates of sweeping educational change: modification of the civil service examinations and the large-scale creation of modern schools (see Chapter 10). China's problem was that there were not enough people practising or encouraged to practise *yang-wu* and learn from it.

Finally, the Navy Yard under Shen and Giquel was at the forefront of China's naval and technological development; it was truly the 'cradle of

---

136 *YWYT*, vol. 2, p. 393. Li Hung-chang once criticized the larger vessels from Ma-wei for drawing too much water in the region around Tientsin, but he found the 80-horsepower boats perfectly acceptable. *HFT*, II, 329a–b; Li to Wang K'ai-t'ai, 10 October 1872, in *LWCK*, 'Letters', 12:25b.

137 Perkins, 'Government as an Obstacle', pp. 491–2.

the Chinese navy'.[138] Evidence of their effort could still be seen years after they had left the establishment. Visitors to the Navy Yard and its vessels seldom failed to mention that the machines and engines were well kept. One noted:

Their machinery is . . . good, and what is more, is said to be well kept. Dirty as the Chinese are . . . they do keep the machinery of their gunboats in good order. . . . In this respect [they] are superior to the Japanese, who are unmistakably slovenly in their care of machinery, and come to frequent grief in consequence.[139]

Furthermore, despite the incompetent or indifferent directors-general in later years, the Navy Yard managed to maintain an unexpected level of competence, which E. Frandon, French vice-consul at Foochow, attributed to the quality of Giquel's students.[140] The School itself became a model institution in China. In 1884, even as the Foochow squadron was being wiped out by the French, J. G. Dunn advised Li Hung-chang, 'In Foochow you had a very good naval college. You want 4 colleges like that of Foochow'.[141] At the same time, the Navy Yard training departments became the main breeding ground of China's naval and technological personnel for years to come. When Li Hung-chang founded the naval academy at Tientsin and established the Peiyang fleet, he relied heavily on Foochow-trained men. Even when it came to the supply of skilled labour, the Foochow Navy Yard, which began as an importer of labour, had been transformed into a source. To this fact the construction of the Peking–Hankow Railway at the beginning of the twentieth century amply attests.[142]

138 Wang Chia-chien, 'Ch'ing-mo hai-chün liu-Ying hsüeh-sheng ti p'ai–ch'ien chi ch'i ying-hsiang (1876–1885)', *Li-shih hsüeh-pao*, no. 2 (February 1974), 162.
139 *North-China Daily News*, 10 December 1875, enclosed in FO 233/85, no. 5. The reporter then wondered whether the Chinese, in the event of a serious accident, could detect the source of trouble and make repairs. This remained a moot question since such an incident had not yet occurred.
140 Pedder to Wade, 4 February 1876, in FO 371/568, no. 5, encl.; Sinclair to Wade, 21 April 1884, in FO 228/752, no. 15, encl.; Frandon to Admiral Meyer, 22 October 1883, in MM BB4 1535 8/4/8.
141 Dunn to Li, 26 August 1884, in Dunn to Parkes, 23 September 1884, in FO 228/777, no. 110, encl. 2.
142 Biggerstaff, *Government Schools*, pp. 244–52; Rawlinson, *China's Struggle*, pp. 91–3; Hsiao I-shan, *Ch'ing-tai t'ung-shih*, vol. 3, p. 929; Jean Chesneaux, 'The Chinese Labour Force in the First Part of the Twentieth Century', in C. D. Cowan, ed., *The Economic Development of China and Japan* (London, 1964), p. 118. On the achievements of the Foochow Navy Yard, Lin Ch'ung-yung is singularly favourable. See his *Shen*, pp. 591–3.

9

The Foochow Navy Yard: financial crises

Financing a modern defence undertaking, and the most expensive one at that, required much greater governmental intervention than did traditional enterprises. It called priorities into question – political, ideological, and financial. Whether a Western-style military or naval establishment was necessary or desirable had been debated since the time of the Opium War. A hostile political climate had once prevented Shen's father-in-law from openly promoting defence modernization.[1] By the early 1860s, however, the situation had improved immeasurably. The Foochow Navy Yard experienced virtually no opposition from the gentry or the general population. On the contrary, it was Shen who led his fellow gentrymen in support of its creation. Then, in 1867, the first major political and ideological challenge (led by Wu T'ang and Wo-jen) had also been successfully overcome. And the qualified success portrayed in the preceding two chapters seems to suggest that not only had the political and ideological problems been resolved but the Navy Yard had also enjoyed adequate funding.

In a late-developing country, Dwight Perkins points out, the government must play an active part in promoting technological, industrial, and economic growth. But the Ch'ing government, whose revenue represented no more than 3 per cent of the country's gross national product, was an 'unbelievably weak instrument' for playing this role. Frances Moulder attributes this small revenue base to the weakness of Ch'ing economic policies, whose limited goal was to collect taxes for a static or slow-expanding state apparatus and to forestall social disorder by ensuring that the basic needs of the populace were satisfied. Both scholars thus agree that China's retarded development was a result more of the

1 Teng and Fairbank, *China's Response*, pp. 28–30.

sin of omission than of commission on the part of the central government. Where they differ is on the role of imperialism.[2] The impact of the first two factors – small revenue and weak central leadership – will be discussed in this chapter, that of imperialism in the Conclusion.

As Tso Tsung-t'ang had arranged, money for the Navy Yard, including contributions from Chekiang and Kwangtung, was to be handled by the province of Fukien. In Fukien, it was placed in the hands of his trusted associates, who were given key offices. But as they lost their positions, thanks to Wu T'ang's machinations, the Navy Yard had to compete with numerous other government undertakings for money. Politics thus became a major factor in its financial well-being. That being so, the capacity of the Ch'ing system to accommodate the requirements of a modern defence industry was critical.

If securing money from external sources was one problem, how finances were managed within the Navy Yard was another. We may ask whether Shen and his staff understood the differences between running a traditional enterprise and a modern one. Did they see the need for change? And did any change come about?

Initial financial arrangements

When the Navy Yard was founded, Tso Tsung-t'ang provided for it what he considered an ample budget. First, he set aside 400,000 taels for capital construction, equipment, and related expenses. This was to come from the Peking-bound portion of the Fukien maritime customs receipts, the so-called 40 per cent customs duties. Should this amount prove inadequate, it would be supplemented by Fukien's likin. Second, he budgeted 40,000 taels per month for operation expenses. This amount was to be appropriated from the remaining portion of the Fukien customs revenue, the '60 per cent customs duties', which supported various undertakings in Fukien and elsewhere. Unexpectedly large bills that came in from time to time were to be taken care of by an extra monthly appropriation of 10,000 taels from this source, increasing the monthly remittance from the 60 per cent duties to 50,000 taels, or 600,000 taels a year. In this way, adequate funds, which Tso promised the French directors, would be assured and the works would not be

2 Perkins, 'Government as an Obstacle'; Moulder, *Japan, China*; and Perkins's review of Moulder's book in the *Journal of Economic History*, 38.4 (December 1978), 591–2. The GNP for the 1880s was about 3,340 million taels and the revenue of the central government in the early 1890s around 89 million, or 2.67% of GNP. These figures are 'subject to a very wide margin of error'. Feuerwerker, 'Economic Trends', pp. 2, 61–5. According to Perkins, the revenue was only 1 to 2% of GNP.

subjected to delays.[3] In some ways, the extra sum of money could be considered an escrow account to take care of contingencies, although Tso never fully spelled out his intentions.

Since the European tutelage was to run for five years, the total operating cost would be in the area of 3 million taels, or 0.67 per cent of the central government's revenue.[4] This was truly a very large outlay, but Tso was quick to assure the court that the Navy Yard's success would not only strengthen China's defence but also greatly stimulate its economy. Its vessels would protect merchants from pirates, transport the government's tribute grain, and carry cargo. The monetary benefits to the government would be incalculable. The court was convinced, at least for the moment.[5]

Several aspects of Tso's financial arrangements deserve discussion. First, unlike the Kiangnan and Tientsin arsenals, both of which took a number of years to evolve,[6] the Foochow Navy Yard was planned on a grand scale from the start. Its founders were thus able to plan its budget systematically. Not the least important advantage of this was the ability to provide for the Navy Yard's operating funds from a single revenue source: the 60 per cent customs receipts. The pitfalls of funding an undertaking with monies from numerous sources were thus avoided. This latter practice, universal in Ch'ing public finance, had caused delays and shortfalls in remittances, and had invariably resulted in political rivalry and bickering among all parties concerned. Shen's dispute with Tseng Kuo-fan in the Taiping era was a classic example of this sort of disruptiveness, which Tso's arrangement promised to avoid.

Tso's scheme also drew a sharp distinction between capital and operation costs, again making it easier to administer the Navy Yard's finances. The inclusion in the operation account of an allowance of an extra 25 per cent for contingencies was also significant; it would help reduce the incidence of work slow-downs or stoppages that might result from shortages of supplies.

However farsighted these arrangements were, they had serious flaws. First, there was no guarantee that the funds would be remitted in full and on schedule. The Navy Yard's 600,000-tael operation budget represented a hefty chunk – 43 per cent – of the 60 per cent customs receipts, which averaged about 1,400,000 taels per year.[7] Against this amount

3 *HFT*, II, 6b, 29, 33–4, 46b–47; *TWHK*, 'Letters', 8:56b; Giquel, *Foochow Arsenal*, pp. 9–10.
4 The calculation is based on an annual revenue of around 89 million taels as estimated by Feuerwerker ('Economic Trends', p. 63).
5 *HFT*, II, 7a–b, 10, 53a–b.
6 Kennedy, *Arms*, pp. 34–57.
7 *YWYT*, vol. 5, pp. 167–8.

numerous funds were drawn, and the customs receipts had not grown fast enough to satisfy all demands. To ensure that the Navy Yard had the first call on funds, spending priorities would have to be rearranged by the central government and with strong backing from Fukien province. This, Tso was unable to accomplish.

Second, conceptually, Tso's arrangements did not provide for retooling, expansion, or new capital equipment, let alone depreciation. The so-called escrow account, which was never intended to cover these items, soon became in practice a part of the capital outlays and operation funds. Its original mission as a buffer against sudden surges in expenditure was never fulfilled.

The confusion between the various accounts occurred early in the Navy Yard's history. Tso himself became the first culprit when he agreed to underwrite another 30,000 taels for the Labat patent slip before the ink on the imperial approval of his original estimates had time to dry. Not long after, the 400,000 taels earmarked for capital construction and equipment were also found to be 30,000 to 40,000 taels short. Whence were these monies to come? Tso, following the scheme he had put in place, first tried the Fukien customs and then the provincial likin, but both were either fully committed or overcommitted for the year. He then appropriated some 70,000 taels from the operating funds on the grounds that work had not yet begun and that the two separate accounts – capital and operation – were really intended for a single purpose. Once again, he managed to convince the court of the wisdom of his solution.[8] We shall have occasion to look into this confusion between different accounts and its implications for the Navy Yard's financial administration under Shen.

Ever since the suppression of the Taiping Rebellion, Tso had commanded considerable influence at court, and his prestige continued to rise. This may well explain why he could manipulate the Navy Yard's finances with imperial approval or interpret other financial arrangements to the Navy Yard's advantage. For instance, his original proposal called for a monthly operation expense of 40,000 taels over a five-year period. It was not at all clear when this quinquennium was to begin. The contract with the French officers provided for their five-year term to begin on the day the metal-working forge commenced operation. Presumably, then, remittances to the operation account were also to start at that time, when shipbuilding could begin in earnest. But the metal-working forge began operation only in February 1869, twenty-six lunar months after Tso had started drawing funds from the operation

8 *HFT*, II, 27b–28b, 46b–47.

account. This devious, though well-intentioned move was to expose the Navy Yard to severe criticism in 1872, five years after Tso had started spending the monies.

Nevertheless, in 1867 Tso was confident that the 3 million tael operation fund was more than adequate. To the Tsungli Yamen he wrote: 'In the contract I have deliberately provided for a liberal estimate so that they [Giquel and d'Aiguebelle] may enjoy extra profits and will therefore be more disposed towards serving us. This will also forestall any additional demand in the future'.[9] In short, Tso expected some sort of surplus which could then be used to humour the two Frenchmen. Shen was soon to suffer the consequences of his naïveté.

As work got under way, Tso's claims were called into question. Shen did so the day he took office and expressed concern about the tardy delivery of funds, flaws in the original estimates, and ship maintenance expenses.[10] All three, and more, were to plague him at various times. The first problem to crop up concerned the expansion of the physical plant, notably the addition of a metal-working forge and the rolling mill, and the enlargement of the Navy Yard School; all came with an increase in European employees. Thanks to the practice Tso had introduced, the Navy Yard was able to build up considerable reserves by drawing the full operating funds more than two years before the quinquennium officially began. The crunch came only later, when ship maintenance costs had consumed the escrow. Shortly after, tardy and inadequate remittances from the province further hurt the Navy Yard's financial stability.

Steamship maintenance and financial crisis

The failure to provide for the steamships' operating expenses came under early criticism. De Méritens first pointed up this glaring budgetary omission in February 1867. When Shen assumed direction of the Navy Yard five months later, he also expressed concern about this problem, but being occupied by more pressing matters at the time, he offered no solution.

Tso's failure to tackle this issue stemmed from three shaky assumptions: first, the vessels would be used by all the coastal provinces, which would then pay for their upkeep; second, some of the ships could pay their way by carrying government tribute grain or cargo; finally, a separate fund would be found for ship maintenance.[11] But in 1866 there was no discussion as to which solution or set of solutions should be adopted; nor was consideration given as to how the second option might

9 Ibid., 53b.   10 *SWSK*, 4:1b–2.   11 *HFT*, II, 6–7.

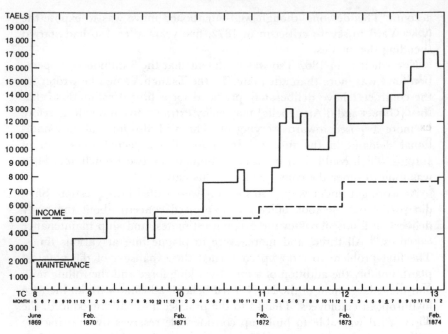

Figure 1. Comparison of the income and maintenance costs for steamships retained by the Foochow Navy Yard

change the naval character of the future squadron. The failure to deal with these issues proved to be extremely costly later on.

What Tso had failed to foresee was the reluctance of the other provinces to share a fleet and split the costs. With the creation of a new fund, however, the Navy Yard encountered some unexpected success. In late June 1869, soon after the first ship was launched, Shen managed to persuade the provincial authorities (Governor-General Ying-kuei and Governor Pien Pao-ti) to seek the court's permission to appropriate funds from the opium duties levied at Foochow and Amoy. The revenue had once been set aside for buying ships and guns, but no such purchase had been made since 24 March 1868. The money accumulated since that date could therefore be used for ship maintenance.[12] As the proposal did not entail additional calls on funds, it was readily approved, giving the Navy Yard a start of approximately 78,125 taels.[13]

12 Ibid., 166a–b; Pien, *Pien chih-chün*, 3:89.
13 The sum was accumulated over fifteen lunar months at 5,208.3 taels per month. For more details, see Pong, 'Keeping the Foochow Navy Yard Afloat', and idem, 'Modernization and Politics', pp. 226–9.

250

By the spring of 1870 (TC 9/4), three ships had been launched. Their upkeep rose to around 5,000 taels per month (Figure 1), close to what the Navy Yard received for that purpose. Fortunately, by the time the fourth steamer (the 150-horsepower *Fu-po*) was launched late that year, Chekiang province had already taken into its service one of the earlier vessels (S.S. No. 2, the 80-horsepower *Mei-Yün*), thus relieving the Navy Yard of some of its financial burden. But because the *Fu-po* cost more to keep, maintenance expenses exceeded the income from opium duties for the first time. After the completion of S.S. No. 5 (the *An-lan*) in June 1871 (TC 10/5), maintenance costs rose rapidly, and the money accumulated earlier had to be used. Tartar General Wen-yü, who had oversight of the Fukien customs (collected at Foochow, Amoy, and Taiwan), suggested to Peking that either the coastal provinces be ordered to take some of the vessels – one of Tso's solutions – or additional funds be found.[14]

Reluctant to grant new monies, Peking opted for the first solution. The provinces responded with silence. Part of the trouble was the Navy Yard's provincial image. To the other provinces, it was at best a joint venture by Fukien, Chekiang, and Kwangtung, the three southern provinces which funded it. But since Fukien monopolized all the decision-making power, not even Kwangtung felt obliged to help out. Chekiang took a Ma-wei vessel (the *Mei-yün*) mainly because it was part of the Min Che viceregal administration and its governor, Yang Ch'ang-chün, was one of Tso's protégés.[15] Unfortunately, the *Mei-yün* was soon reported to have developed engine troubles, and this immediately confirmed in the minds of all concerned that Ma-wei ships were inferior.

By the time *Mei-Yün*'s troubles had been satisfactorily explained, several months had elapsed, at considerable cost to the Navy Yard. Worse, before it could take advantage of the renewed confidence in its products, it came under severe criticism from Sung Chin (1802–74), a subchancellor of the Grand Secretariat, who, in January 1872, charged that both the Navy Yard and the Kiangnan Arsenal had overspent public funds in building ships that were inferior. He proposed that the two establishments be closed and their vessels hired out to merchants. The rent could then be used to defray the cost of repairs.[16] Sung's allegations sparked a controversy which lasted a good part of 1872 (see the next section), and for as long as the future of the Navy Yard remained in doubt, the reluctant provinces were even less inclined to

14 *HFT*, II, 257b, 306a–b, 311b–313.
15 Ibid., 257b. On Yang, see Ts'ai Kuan-lo, *Ch'ing-tai ch'i-pai ming-jen*, vol. 2, pp. 1397–9.
16 *HFT*, II, 327–328b; *YWYT*, vol. 5, pp. 105–6.

take a Ma-wei ship. Moreover, if they did take a vessel and then the Navy Yard were shut down, who would be responsible for repairs?

The leaders of China's defence industry rallied. Tseng Kuo-fan, the dean of the Restoration statesmen and co-founder of the Kiangnan Arsenal, wrote to the Tsungli Yamen supporting the shipbuilding efforts in no uncertain terms.[17] In April, Li Hung-chang, Kiangnan's other co-founder, showed his support by adopting the *Chen-hai*, the Navy Yard's sixth ship, though not before a close scrutiny of it at Tientsin. Jui-lin, the governor-general of Liang Kwang, followed suit and took a vessel.[18] The Tsungli Yamen then tried to cajole the two remaining coastal regions (Feng-t'ien and Shantung) into doing the same. (Kiangsu, already served by Kiangnan boats, was exempt.) But both Shantung and Feng-t'ien remained recalcitrant, either claiming a shortage of funds or using the additional expenditure as a pretext to keep part of the Peking-bound 40 per cent customs duties. After much correspondence and loss of time, the two finally yielded to the Yamen's wishes in May. But owing to some confusion as to who should get which boat, no vessel was sent to Shantung until February 1873 – the last to be dispatched to the provinces.[19]

Meanwhile, the situation at Ma-wei went from bad to worse. Already in May 1872 (TC 11/4), steamship maintenance expenses had soared to more than twice the revenue from opium duties (Figure 1), all in spite of an increase in opium duties to a monthly average of 5833.3 taels since the beginning of the year.[20] By the end of the year, the funds accumulated before June 1871, some 96,700 taels, had been depleted.

Earlier, Tso Tsung-t'ang, Li Hung-chang, and the Tsungli Yamen had each contemplated means to 'commercialize' some of the Navy Yard's vessels.[21] Sung Chin's charges compelled them to reconsider this option for both Foochow and Kiangnan. Thus, Tseng Kuo-fan proposed that the Kiangnan Arsenal, while continuing its warship building effort, should construct four or five merchant ships. Shen accepted a similar solution for the Foochow Navy Yard, although, faithful to the original intent of the Navy Yard, he insisted that the warship building pro-gramme not be allowed to suffer simply for lack of funds. But it was Li Hung-chang who had the boldest solution: the government should supply merchants with steamers and take the lead in forming a shipping

17 *HFT*, II, 325–326b.
18 Ibid., 329a–b, 338b–339b. Li had already taken one boat from the Kiangnan Arsenal. Li to Wang K'ai-t'ai, 1 January 1872, in *LWCK*, 'Letters', 11:30b–31.
19 *HFT*, II, 333–335b, 336, 341a–b, 397b–398; *IWSM*, TC 86:8b–10b; Pong 'Modernization and Politics', pp. 234–6.
20 *HFT*, II, 419b.
21 *LWCK*, 'Letters', 11:27b, 31b; *TWHK*, 'Letters', 11:54; *YWYT*, vol. 5, p. 456.

company. For the first time (June 1872) he broached the idea of *kuan-tu shang-pan* (official supervision and merchant management).[22]

On this idea was founded the China Merchants' Steam Navigation Company. In response, Shen had S.S. Nos. 13, 14, and 15 redesigned for service in the new company, but he was emphatic that warship building be resumed immediately thereafter. In any event, the company was slow in forming, and S.S. No. 13 would not be available until the autumn of 1873 (it was eventually taken over by the company in March 1874). Meanwhile the maintenance of S.S. Nos. 9, 10, 11, and 12 had to be provided for. The provinces, having each accepted a vessel, did not welcome the prospect of taking another, while Li Hung-chang's proposal to abolish the traditional water force in order to release money for the modern gunboats met with little enthusiasm.[23]

Thus, from the summer of 1873 expenses mounted sharply again until they passed the 17,000-tael mark in January and February 1874 (TC 12/12 and 13/1). Ma-wei was now supporting eight of the fourteen vessels launched.[24] Up to the beginning of 1873, thanks to the accumulated reserves, the maintenance account still had a small balance. After that, in spite of yet another rise in opium levies to an average of 7,812.3 taels per lunar month, a deficit rapidly built up. The corvette *Yang-wu*, Foochow's pride, could not afford a full complement of men. Despite drastic retrenchments, shipbuilding funds had to be used for ship maintenance.[25] Tso Tsung-t'ang had already set a precedent for such transfers of funds from the first days of the Navy Yard's history. At a time when shipbuilding had not yet begun, he could manipulate these accounts with immunity. Now, with four ships scheduled to be built in the year, such a stratagem could only have adverse consequences.

Then, in the spring of 1874, with an unexpected turn of events came temporary relief. The Japanese, in pursuit of an expansionist policy and to avert internal disorder, invaded Taiwan.[26] Nearly all the Foochow ships, including many of those adopted by other provinces, were called up for carrying troops, messages, and supplies. Expenses were to be met by a newly created Taiwan defence fund. But thanks to the foresight of Shen, now also in charge of maritime defence, the short-term defence mission was transformed into a broad, long-term programme for Taiwan's development. Fortifications, new roads, internal colonization

---

22 *HFT*, II, 325–326b, 350a–b, 371–372b.
23 Ibid., 422, 502, 371–372b, 386a–b.
24 Pong, 'Keeping the Foochow Navy Yard Afloat', Table 2.
25 *HFT*, II, 423–424b, 465b, 539–541.
26 Masakazu Iwata, *Okubo Toshimichi: The Bismarck of Japan* (Berkeley and Los Angeles, 1964), pp. 184–224.

projects, and a modern coal mine were to occupy the Chinese for several years. Consequently, the small defence fund could not reimburse in full the Navy Yard for its services. And since the fund was drawn from the same revenues which supported the Navy Yard, its creation meant yet another competitor for money. Steamship maintenance expenses at the Navy Yard thus remained high, as did the deficit. This condition persisted after Shen left Ma-wei in late 1875.[27]

Sung Chin and the debate on closing the Navy Yard

The Navy Yard's failure to cope with ship maintenance had unfortunately drawn unwanted attention to its overall financial problems. In early 1872, the 3 million taels Tso Tsung-t'ang budgeted for its operation had been spent, while capital construction and ship maintenance had added another 600,000 taels to the total. The fact that only six of the projected sixteen ships had been built, and with only two years left of the contract with the Europeans, further eroded its image. This set the stage for Sung Chin's criticism, which he submitted to the throne on 23 January 1872.

Sung's primary concern was priorities in government spending. In his view, the Navy Yard had spent 4 or 5 million taels on building ships that were inferior and useless against foreign aggression. And why were these ships necessary when there existed treaties of peace? As for piracy suppression and tribute grain transport, the traditional outer-sea water force (*wai-hai shui-shih*) and the sea-going junks (*sha-ch'uan*) were just as effective and far less costly. Besides producing expensive and useless boats, Navy Yard officials also inflicted endless hardship on the people by forcing upon them low prices for supplies. All these problems applied to the Kiangnan Arsenal as well. Therefore, the two enterprises should be closed, their steamships rented to merchants, and the fees used for repairs. The money saved should then be sent to Shantung for flood control and disaster relief.[28]

Sung is generally regarded as having been a conservative diehard.[29] That is not entirely correct, for he was not opposed to modern inventions. As early as 1856 he had advocated using steamships against the

---

27 *HFT*, II, 530; *CTSM*, vol. 1, p. 89; China, Tsungli Yamen Archives, 'O' (Russian file) (hereafter, TY: 'O'), 154, KH 1/8/29. In my article, 'Keeping the Foochow Navy Yard Afloat', I did not stress enough the adverse effects of the Taiwan crisis on the income of the Navy Yard.
28 *YWYT*, vol. 5, pp. 105–6; *IWSM*, TC 84:36.
29 See, e.g., Chung-kuo chin-tai-shi kao pien-hsieh-tsu, 'Yang-wu huo-tung: chin-tai chün-shih kung-yeh ti chien-li', *Chin-tai-shih yen-chiu*, 1981.2, 137.

Taipings, years before some of the leading modernizers had spoken publicly on such matters.[30] Nor had he any personal grudge against Shen, for it was he, among others, who recommended Shen for high office in 1861. He also thought highly of Tseng Kuo-fan and Tso Tsung-t'ang, founders of the institutions he now attacked. Personal ambitions, antiforeignism, or a desire to control Fukien's resources had motivated many a critic of the Navy Yard. Sung, however, was reputed for his out-spokenness on public policies; his attack on shipbuilding at Ma-wei and Kiangnan appears to have been moved by a genuine desire to change government spending priorities. In addition, because so much of his career had revolved around water control and government granaries, he was keenly aware of the damage caused by natural disasters in Chihli and Shantung.[31] His desire to direct more funds to that region is under-standable. Yet his failure to recognize the complex demands of modern industrial endeavours, to regard the inexperienced planners of the Navy Yard with a more sympathetic eye, or to appreciate the might of the modern means of war demonstrates intellectual rigidity. And he ex-aggerated the amount of money the Navy Yard had spent.

Still, it cannot be denied that there had been a sizeable cost overrun. Tso Tsung-t'ang's move to start drawing on the Navy Yard's operation fund before the commencement of the five-year contract now back-fired. What is surprising is that the Board of Revenue, which was usually tight-fisted about new expenditures, had overlooked the ramifications of Tso's manoeuvre at the time. Now, it was too late for recriminations. All the court could do was to seek remedies from those provincial leaders who were concerned.[32]

Tseng Kuo-fan responded almost immediately. In February 1872 he wrote the Tsungli Yamen defending the works at Ma-wei and Kiangnan. While admitting that their ships were both expensive and inferior, he maintained that the goal of the shipbuilding policy – to strengthen China's defence – was basically sound. His solution was to build a few cargo ships at the Kiangnan Arsenal and make them available to merchants under favourable terms. He promised to report formally to the throne after studying the matter further. It was a promise unfulfilled – he died on 12 March – but he had made himself clear.[33]

Tartar General Wen-yü was the first to memorialize, but he was not supportive. Counselled by his own political wisdom, he preferred to let

---

30 *Ch'ing-ch'ao hsü wen-hsien t'ung-kao*, 233:9779.
31 Chu Hsieh, *Chung-kuo yün-ho shih-liao hsüan-chi* (Peking, 1962), p. 138; *Ch'ing-shih*, vol. 6, p. 4824; Lin Ch'ung-yung, *Shen*, p. 421.
32 *YWYT*, vol. 5, pp. 105–6.
33 *HFT*, II, 325–326b.

the facts speak for themselves: the Navy Yard, having completed only six boats, had already overshot the budget. Although he doubted that the ships could prevent foreign aggression, he thought they were effective against pirates. It would be a pity, therefore, to turn them over to merchants. Instead, each coastal province should take a Foochow ship, leaving only two for Fukien. Having thus limited China's defence needs, he lay out before the throne the amount of money needed to wind down the Navy Yard: about 700,000 taels to send the Europeans home and pay for materials under order. Implicitly, he favoured closure.[34]

Known for his corruption and not much else, Wen-yü took little interest in the Navy Yard. Giquel, not an unbiased observer, spoke of him as 'utterly incompetent'. But as Tartar general, he controlled the Foochow customs and found the unremitting financial demands of the Navy Yard both an inconvenience and a threat to his interests. When he left the post with his chattel in 1877, his enormous wealth did not escape the public eye. Nevertheless, because of the relationship between his office and the Navy Yard, and the fact that he was the father-in-law of Prince Kung's eldest son, his word carried considerable weight.[35]

His memorial indeed put the court in a difficult spot. But the throne reacted quickly. On 7 April, within days of reading Wen-yü's representation, it issued a secret edict ordering Li Hung-chang, Tso Tsung-t'ang, and Shen Pao-chen to discuss the question of closure and possible means of retrenchment.[36] Since all three were deeply committed to the modernization of China's defence industry, the throne, without outwardly taking sides, was trying to rally support for the shipbuilding effort.

Despite the vast distances involved, Tso's memorial was the first to reach Peking (13 May), reflecting his eagerness to come to the Navy Yard's defence. Clearly, he was proud of his creation and employed an up-to-date enumeration of its successes as his defence. In plant facilities, ships built, the Navy Yard School, and its related training efforts, the Navy Yard had either acquired equipment or embarked on programmes far more sophisticated than originally planned. The corvette *Yang-wu*, for example, had capabilities not dreamed of at first. With regard to expenses, Tso was confident that shipbuilding costs would come down as more ships were built. But it was the training programme that was central to this investment in the future: in time, the Chinese would be able to develop new methods and to train other Chinese in naval construction and navigation. No one, therefore, should worry unduly about

34 Ibid., 330–331b; Pong, 'Modernization and Politics', pp. 245–6.
35 Giquel to Garnault, 29 November 1873, in MM BB4 1555 17/5/39; *NCH*, 23 June 1877.
36 *YWYT*, vol. 5, pp. 108–9.

present shortcomings.[37] One may indeed challenge Tso's optimism, some of his claims, or his glossing over of the ship maintenance problem. But his reiteration of the Navy Yard as an investment in the future brought things back into focus. His tone was assertive and, as we have seen, he had influence at court and would not be cowed into submission.

Shen's memorial, which followed a fortnight later, was even more strident. Still in mourning, he would not have been able to break his silence but for the specific imperial injunction ordering him to do so.[38] His basic premise was patriotism. The treaty of peace which concluded the Opium War, and to which Sung Chin referred, was the source of the country's present worries and sufferings. This was the sole reason for 'self-strengthening', the way to protect the empire and its people. To be sure, Chinese-built vessels were inferior but who, he asked, did not start from a modest position? The Westerners were able to produce superior vessels only after decades of development. Even then, some Western ships were better than others and, to keep up, they must learn from each other. Therefore, the Chinese, too, must learn from them; the nature of the Westerners' technology demanded so. Already, the Chinese had made considerable progress; the steamships coming out of Ma-wei were more effective against pirates and better for grain transport than traditional means.

Shen admitted to overspending, which he attributed partly to growing needs and partly to the French directors, who, unable to visualize the magnitude of the undertaking at first, had miscalculated. But all the added facilities and programmes were critical to the Navy Yard as a viable defence industry. And if it were to close now, existing ships could not be repaired; if the Europeans were dismissed, 700,000 to 800,000 taels would have to be found for their severance pay and repatriation. This was not the way to save money. Besides, if the Chinese terminated the contract at will, no foreigner would ever trust them again. The Navy Yard must not be closed, not now, not five years hence.

Finally, Shen firmly rejected the idea of cutting expenses. Even after the Europeans had left, their salary money should not be channelled elsewhere but used instead to send students abroad for further studies. Rather than retreat under pressure, Shen urged a more general programme of modernization. To create a truly naval unit out of the Ma-wei vessels now scattered among the provinces, he proposed a new expenditure of 500 taels a month to bring them together periodically for muster. Also, taking advantage of the occasion, he reiterated a previous proposal to replace the outdated traditional military examinations with

37 *IWSM*, TC 86:3b–8.　　38 *HFT*, II, 346b–350b.

ones on mathematics, which he and others considered the foundation of Western science (see Chapter 10).

Li Hung-chang's memorial came last, on 22 June. He, too, strongly defended the shipbuilding efforts at Kiangnan and Ma-wei. But privately, he was not so enthusiastic. As he confided to his friend, Wang K'ai-t'ai (governor of Fukien, 1870–5), the shipbuilding programmes at Kiangnan and Ma-wei were an 'unfruitful and wasteful use of funds'; he hoped that an early termination of the contract with the Europeans could be negotiated at Ma-wei.[39]

To Tseng Kuo-fan, Li was more circumspect, for it was on this issue of shipbuilding that he and the elder statesman held very divergent views.[40] His letter was nevertheless revealing. Unlike Tso and Shen, who would not give an inch, Li fenced about in a fashion worthy of a seasoned politician. His first concern was the political divisiveness of the shipbuilding programme. In his view, far too many officials wanted quick results and grudged the expense, and Sung Chin spoke for them. Hence, there would never be the kind of collective and sustained support that such a long and expensive venture as shipbuilding required. This, Li confessed, was why he opposed Tso Tsung-t'ang's founding of the Navy Yard. And then there was the discord between Tseng and Tso. If the promoters of China's defence industry could not agree among themselves now, what would happen a few decades hence? Li then cited Wu T'ang's departure from Foochow, Ying-kuei's request for a leave,[41] and Shen's refusal to resume office as evidence of the political problems caused by the Navy Yard. Li found the political price of shipbuilding too high. He thus focused his energies on the ordnance industry – an area where the Chinese could be more confident of success and which was politically less divisive.

As for ship maintenance, Li could see no solution. Even if the officials in the coastal provinces were changed a hundred times, he said, they would still be reluctant to use Chinese-built vessels. Thus, by way of explanation, Li had apologized to his former patron for his want of enthusiasm for the shipbuilding effort at Kiangnan. Recognizing Tseng's

39 Li to Wang, 29 February 1872, in *LWCK*, 'Letters', 12:2b. Earlier, Li, despite his admiration for the Foochow Navy Yard, said it was 'a big mistake'. Li to Ting Jih-ch'ang, 2 December 1870, in *Feng-shun wen-shih*, no. 2, p. 64.
40 Li to Tseng, 5 March 1872, in *LWCK*, 'Letters', 3–4b; *HFT*, II, 326.
41 I cannot document Ying-kuei's request for leave. He was summoned to Peking in March 1871 and stayed till late May or early June. He may have asked for leave at that time. Later, in October, he was made senior assistant chamberlain of the imperial body-guard (*nei ta-ch'en*, rank 1b) and then president of the Board of War in 1872. Ch'ien Shih-fu, *Ch'ing-chi chung-yao chih-kuan*, p. 139; *Ch'ing-shih*, vol. 6, p. 4918.

role as a pioneer promoter of modern shipbuilding, he urged Tseng to uphold his views.

In April, having read Tseng's letter to the Tsungli Yamen, Li changed his tune. To Wang K'ai-t'ai he now lauded Tseng's 'sincere and cogent argument', which, he thought, the Yamen could not ignore.[42] By June, he was apprised also of Tso and Shen's sentiments. He now felt the need to close ranks and presented to the throne an argument quite different from what he truly believed.

Li began with the premise that the Chinese needed to learn from the West to produce better guns and boats. But just as the superior military might of the West was achieved only after more than a century of development, China's defence capabilities would also need time to develop. When Tseng Kuo-fan and Tso Tsung-t'ang launched their shipbuilding projects, they were fully aware of the enormity of their undertakings. Increased production, however, would eventually lower costs, as in the West; the experience at the Kiangnan Arsenal also bore this out. He therefore pleaded for greater flexibility and patience in the government's policy towards the Foochow Navy Yard: 'It should not be tied down by the [rigid] regulations of the Board of Works'.[43]

Li then returned to a position that was more genuinely his own: China stood a much better chance of success if its resources were invested in its land forces. Nonetheless, the Western powers should not be given free rein on the high seas. Means should therefore be found to maintain the additional gunboats the Navy Yard produced – by scrapping the out-moded war junks of the water forces. As a concession to critics like Sung Chin, Li suggested that the shipbuilding policies at Kiangnan and Ma-wei be modified, alternating between merchantmen and men-of-war.

Li's solution, then, was a compromise between the staunch proponents of the warship-building industry and its critics. The former, as noted, had already come to accept the need for building some vessels for commercial purposes. The latter, while demanding closure, also advo-cated a commercial deployment of the vessels already built. So with the prospect of a Chinese shipping company coming into existence, Li's compromise gained acceptance.

Li had come to the shipbuilding industry's rescue reluctantly and only after months of canvassing his friends and colleagues. Later, he confided to Wang K'ai-t'ai that, since both Tso and Shen had made so much noise on the issue, he felt obliged to agree with them.[44] To my mind his

42 Li to Wang, 3 April 1872, in *LWCK*, 'Letters', 12:9b.
43 *HFT*, II, 367b–373. For a fuller representation of Li's argument, see Pong, 'Keeping the Foochow Navy Yard Afloat', pp. 140–1.
44 Li to Wang, 6 July 1872, in *LWCK*, 'Letters', 12:16b.

memorial was more an expression of his sense of *Realpolitik* than of conviction. Moreover, the debate sparked by Sung Chin also raised the possibility of ending the ordnance industry.[45] Li was simply too deeply committed to that industry to sacrifice it because of the shipbuilding industry.

The Tsungli Yamen did not submit its recommendations to the throne until 2 August, six weeks after Li's memorial reached the capital. The strong opposition to the shipbuilding programme, plus Li's personal views on the issue, which were certainly known to the Yamen, must have been the cause of some long and agonizing deliberations. Be that as it may, the Yamen once again pledged its support to the Foochow Navy Yard. But it was a qualified support: the shipbuilding programme was to continue with the proviso that some merchant ships be built to alleviate financial stringency.[46]

The months of debate and uncertainty caused considerable panic among the European staff at Ma-wei.[47] While the Yamen's decision eventually calmed things down, neither Shen nor Li could derive any satisfaction from its failure to provide long-term solutions. There was no reference to Shen's proposal to abolish the traditional military examinations, to institute examinations on mathematics, upgrade naval training, or send students abroad for further studies. As for Li's call for abolishing the war junks, the Yamen merely recommended further discussion in the provinces, where it would meet with certain rejection.[48] More important, because of the Yamen's timidity, the Navy Yard had to abandon its naval mission, albeit temporarily, in exchange for continued existence. A dangerous precedent had been set and the institutional integrity of the Navy Yard violated.

Continuing financial problems, 1873–5

During the Sung Chin debate, the leading modernizers of the empire achieved a level of rapport that had, by this time, become a rare phenomenon. Their unity, at least in public, had saved the shipbuilding programme. By the end of 1872, four of the Navy Yard's eight steamers had been taken over by other provinces. Still, the addition of S.S. Nos. 9 through 12, completed between August 1872 and August 1873, was to

45 Edict of 7 April 1872, in *HFT*, II, 332b.
46 Ibid., 385–386b.
47 Giquel to Garnault, 21 June 1872, in MM BB4 1555 17/5/37.
48 Li to Wang K'ai-t'ai and Ting Jih-ch'ang, 7 September and 12 October 1872, in *LWCK*, 'Letters', 12:21, 26b.

Table 5. *Cost of steamships produced at the Foochow Navy Yard*

150 horsepower		80 horsepower	
Ship	Cost (taels)	Ship	Cost (taels)
Wan-nien Ch'ing	163,000	*Mei-yün*	106,000
Fu-po	161,000	*Fu-hsing*	106,000
An-lan	165,000	*Chen-hai*	109,000
Fei-yün	163,000	*Ching-yüan*	110,000
Chi-an	163,000	*Chen-wei*	110,000
Yung-pao	167,000		
Hai-ching	165,000		
Ch'en-hang	164,000		
Ta-ya	162,000		

Note: Ships in each class are listed in order of construction. The 250-horsepower corvette, *Yang-wu*, cost 254,000 taels.
Source: *FCTC*, 'Ch'uan-cheng chih': 1–2b.

augment its maintenance expenses for years to come. While the creation of the China Merchants' Steam Navigation Company and its pledge to take the next three vessels (S.S. Nos. 13 through 15) temporarily removed the spectre of an ever-rising maintenance budget, Li Hung-chang had to warn Shen that the company, still in its infancy, would probably not have the capacity to absorb more cargo steamers from Ma-wei.[49]

In their rebuttal of Sung Chin's charges, both Li and Tso Tsung-t'ang, citing European experience, argued that shipbuilding costs would decrease over time. This was a reassuring thought, whose validity was predicated on the continued construction of very similar vessels. It ignored the cost of new technologies and new generations of warships. The critics of the shipbuilding programme had thus forced some of its proponents to take a defensive position at a time when they should have been pressing for expansion. Shen was the only one who asked for more money for technological progress.

Regarding the ships already built at Ma-wei, it may well be true that the cost of production had decreased over time. But Table 5 shows no clear pattern at all in the construction cost of the 150-horsepower vessels and a slight increase in cost of the 80-horsepower gunboats. Shen had emphasized that these figures were only approximations, it being impossible to break statistics down to the cost per boat, since a single piece

49 Li to Shen, 27 January 1874, in ibid., 13:28a–b.

of material would often end up partly in a workship and partly on a ship.[50] Book-keeping problems aside, the figures did not reflect capital investment, which, if included, would certainly have shown a downward trend in cost. But then the inclusion of capital outlays would also have revealed a much higher cost per ship, thus rendering the Navy Yard even more vulnerable to hostile criticism.

Should the Navy Yard be judged according to commercial standards? Shen, as much as anyone, knew that the cost per ship was high, much higher than what the Chinese could buy. But as he observed, 'No foreigners would ever sell us truly good ships'.[51] Thus, proponents of shipbuilding had all along justified the expense by pointing to the value of the learning experience and the political advantages of China having its own naval dockyard and academy. The Foochow Navy Yard, lest it be forgotten, was created to reap these benefits. Yet by the very manner in which it was funded, its 'financial success' had to be judged by the completion of a fixed number of vessels and other objectives in a given period of time on an inflexible *annual* budget. This was an impossible task, first, because the budget was not based on changing needs and, second, because its founders lacked the technical know-how to project its future needs or the sophisticated accounting methods that such projections required. We know only too well that even today very few military contracts are fulfilled without delays and cost inflation. During the first three years of the contract period (up to early 1872) the Navy Yard proper (i.e., excluding ship maintenance expenses) managed to keep within bounds of its budget. After that, expenditure soared. We can attribute this to two major causes.

The first was the expansion of capital equipment and the training programme. By early 1872, eight workshops and factories had been either created or added on to existing ones. At the same time, four more schools for design, practical navigation, engineers, and apprentices had been established and the number of students increased from the initial 60 to more than 300. With the new factories, the practical training programme, the purchase of a training ship, and the building of the 250-horsepower corvette *Yang-wu*, more European staff members had to be hired, while the labour force rose from 1,600 to more than 2,000.[52]

The second cause had to do with the shipbuilding timetable. In the early years, progress was slow, necessitating a crammed shipbuilding

50 *HFT*, II, 417b.
51 Shen K'o, 'Hsien Wen-su kung', p. 57.
52 *HFT*, II, 348a–b; *YWYT*, vol. 5, p. 112. Expansion of the building yard included two departments of the rolling mills, a chronometer shop, a sail and rigging shop, a brick factory, a sampan factory, two additional branches of the forge, and a fitting shop.

timetable for the last two years of the contract period. Eventually, four ships were launched in 1872, three in 1873, and the last two in the first half of 1874. Both material and labour costs were thus kept high. This conjunction of events was unfortunate, for just as the Navy Yard entered a phase of rapid construction, its steamship maintenance account was being depleted. As a result, up to May 1874, a total of 192,459 tasels had to be transferred from shipbuilding funds to maintenance, putting even greater pressure on the resources of the Navy Yard proper.[53]

Late in the summer of 1872, Shen appealed to Tso Tsung-t'ang for help. Tso responded generously. Noting that the Navy Yard's monthly expenses had soared to 70,000 to 80,000 taels, he requested imperial permission to transfer to it an additional 20,000 taels per month from Fukien's contribution to his campaign. Shen could not have been more grateful for what was a sacrifice on Tso's part and promised that this extra revenue would revert back to Tso the moment the expensive European staff had left. Meanwhile, he cut expenditures, starting with the miscellaneous expenses (*kung-fei*, lit. public expenses) for steamship operation. He also tried to prevent the revival of likin charges on Navy Yard and other government purchases, even though the exemption had been frequently abused.[54] Thus, despite his high moral principles, Shen, faced with imminent financial crisis, was for once compelled to come to terms with the forces of corruption.

Months passed before the Board of Revenue finally, in March 1873, decided against Tso's solution for fear that his campaign would suffer. Instead, the additional 20,000 taels per month were to be drawn from Fukien's tea revenue, with payment backdated to January 1873. It was the Board's distinct impression that the tea revenue had been on the rise for several years and could well cope with the added expenditure.[55] As it turned out, both the tea revenue and the tea likin were already over-committed. Governor-General Li Ho-nien (1828–90), who controlled these resources, was in any case ill-disposed towards the Navy Yard or anything foreign. And there was no love lost between him and Shen.[56]

---

53 *HFT*, II, 539a–b. For the shipbuilding schedule, see Chapter 8, Table 3.
54 *HFT*, II, 410b–412, 418–20, 430b–431b; Tso to Shen, late 1872, in *TWHK*, 'Letters', 12:59–60.
55 *HFT*, II, 445b–447b.
56 Li Hung-chang to Wang K'ai-t'ai, 10 October 1872, in *LWCK*, 'Letters', 12:25b; Giquel to Garnault, 29 November 1873, in MM BB4 1555 17/5/39; Frederick Mayers's report on his interview with Li Hung-chang, 10 April 1876, in FO 233/63, no. 4; Kuo T'ing-i, *Kuo-Sung-t'ao*, vol. 2, p. 499. Later, Li Ho-nien impeached Shen. Using the strongest language, which betrayed a personal hatred, Li accused him of brutality in the execution of a clerk of the provincial treasurer whom Shen found guilty of embezzling the Navy Yard's money. The impeachment was ignored in Peking. Li's memorial, 19 September 1875 (KH 1.8.18), in YCT, KH 1/8.

Unwilling to help with more of Fukien's money, he suggested to the court at Peking that Tso's original proposition, already rejected by the Board of Revenue, be given a second thought.[57]

The central government, unable to extract more monies from Fukien, reluctantly fell back on Tso's solution. Shen was pleased to announce soon after that work at the Navy Yard was progressing apace. However, declining revenue from opium duties forced him to dip once again into shipbuilding funds for ship maintenance. That was in the latter part of 1873. The candle was now burning at both ends. Then, after the Europeans had left in February 1874, the extra monthly remittance of 20,000 taels reverted to Tso's campaign. Nevertheless, in August 1874 Shen was still able to report a balance of 3,640 taels.[58] For an institution which, as it were, lived from hand to mouth, this was as best as could be expected.

With income cut back to its former level of 50,000 taels per lunar month, Shen had to tailor expenses to revenue and reluctantly limited construction to two ships a year. Still he ran into financial difficulties as remittances from the Foochow customs began to fall behind. By March 1875, payment from the 60 per cent customs duties was four months in arrears. Coming at a time when S.S. No. 16 was only half-finished and materials were already on order for a new generation of gunboats using iron frames and horizontal compound engines, this could not be tolerated. Shen therefore sought an injunction from Peking that would ensure prompt delivery of funds and bar further expenditures charged against the 60 per cent customs revenue. Earlier, on 27 January, an edict had already instructed Wen-yü to do his best to meet the needs of the Navy Yard and 'not to find any excuse' which might jeopardize its important mission.[59] But the Tartar general took no action until the middle of the year.

According to Wen-yü, he had been able to send funds to Ma-wei on all previous occasions when there was a shortfall in the 60 per cent customs receipts because he could take funds temporarily out of the 40 per cent account. But the practice had since been disallowed by the Board of Revenue. Then the Taiwan incident occurred, and all the customs duties levied on Taiwan were kept for that island's defence. Funds thus became even more scarce. Even so, Wen-yü claimed, he still had the Navy Yard's interests in mind and remitted to it 50,000 taels in June 1875 to take care of the instalment for October 1874. As for future

57 *HFT*, II, 459a–b.
58 Ibid., 465b, 537b–538.
59 Ibid., 472b–473b, 548–9, 550–2.

payments, however, he could not offer any assurances since the government of Fukien, to meet all its current commitments, had had to borrow from merchants.[60]

With its income several months in arrears, the Navy Yard could not pay for much-needed supplies. Previously, Shen had been able to tide over temporary shortages by securing advances from native banks against future revenue from the tea trade. But a slump in the tea trade in the summer of 1875 made it virtually impossible to raise loans from private sources. Shen thus repeatedly pressed Wen-yü for payment – 'three to four times a month' since April, when a second edict ordered him to deliver the funds. Subsequently, 200,000 taels were transmitted over a period of several months, but this was only enough to cover payments up to the beginning of February 1875, five instalments behind.[61]

The annual return from Fukien's 60 per cent customs duties amounted to some 1,400,000 taels. Out of this, 570,000 taels were remitted to Peking, 100,000 taels reserved for the upkeep of the imperial mausolea, a similar sum for Tso Tsung-t'ang's campaign, 120,000 taels for the salary of the customs officials, and 130,000 taels for various remittance charges. For the year 1875, another 130,000 taels were sent to Peking to make up for past arrears. Only 240,000 taels, instead of the budgeted 600,000, were left for the Navy Yard. Since the 40 per cent customs duties were expected to have a balance of 400,000 taels for the year, Wen-yü requested that this sum be forwarded to Ma-wei. This, of course, represented a call on funds which, by regulation, were reserved for Peking. Besides, an edict had distinctly prohibited the transfer of funds from the 40 per cent account only the year before. Shen nevertheless supported the request, arguing that after the Japanese invasion of Taiwan a special maritime defence fund had been created with money from the 40 per cent revenue, and since the Foochow Navy Yard was an important element of this new programme, it was a legitimate request.[62]

The Board of Revenue and the Tsungli Yamen were agreeable, but they emphasized that this was to be a makeshift arrangement only: the Navy Yard's future income should still be taken from the 60 per cent account. An edict was issued accordingly, and Wen-yü immediately delivered 150,000 taels to the Navy Yard. But because of shortfalls

60 Ibid., 554a–b. According to Ting Jih-ch'ang, who served a short term as the Navy Yard's director-general, Fukien had a revenue of 3,455,000 taels in 1875 against a scheduled outlay of more than 4,600,000 taels, and the modern defence sector was low in its spending priority. Ting Jih-ch'ang, *Ting Yü-sheng cheng-shu* (Hong Kong, 1987), vol. 2, pp. 580–1. See also his memorial of 6 March 1876 (KH 2.2.11), in YCT, KH 2/2 *chung*.

61 *HFT*, II, 615a–b; *YWYT*, vol. 5, pp. 166–7.

62 Ibid., pp. 166–8.

in customs receipts, only 50,000 taels of the remaining 250,000 were forwarded before the year was out.[63]

In utter frustration, Shen increased his pressure on Peking. In October he told the Tsungli Yamen that the Board must now draw up regulations stating in no uncertain terms that a fixed sum from a specific source had been earmarked for the Navy Yard and that the Fukien provincial authorities must abide by these regulations. Since Shen was about to leave for the viceregal post in Liang Kiang, he wanted a strong central government commitment to full and prompt delivery of funds. Otherwise, he warned, his successor (Ting Jih-ch'ang) would not be willing to stay.[64]

The court at Peking readily agreed with Shen but, typically, gave no instruction as to how the funds were to be secured. Wen-yü was thus caught in an awkward position. As he explained, from 1 July to early November, the 60 per cent customs receipts amounted to only 827,000 taels against a commitment of 1,070,000 taels. If the Navy Yard was to be given priority, then other undertakings would have to suffer. This he was not prepared to allow. So as he and Shen were at loggerheads, the Board of Revenue had to make a concession, opening Peking-bound funds from the 40 per cent account to the Navy Yard. Henceforth, 30,000 taels per month were to come from the 60 per cent customs duties and 20,000 from the 40 per cent account, and, the Board reiterated, no arrears, however small, were to be tolerated.[65]

No matter, four monthly instalments for 1875 remained unpaid. While the 20,000-tael instalments from the 40 per cent duties were remitted in full during 1876 and 1877, funds from the 60 per cent account were ten months in arrears in the same period.[66] By this time, however, the Navy Yard was well into a period of decline.[67]

Conclusions

Up to the end of Shen's incumbency in late October 1875, the Navy Yard had spent a total of 6,056,948 taels, of which 621,831 (10.27 per cent) went to ship maintenance.[68] Whether the Navy Yard was entitled to draw its monthly operation funds from December 1866 or February 1869, it had vastly exceeded its budget. Compared with the Kiangnan

63 *HFT*, II, 583–4, 615a–b, 616b. I misstated the situation somewhat in my article 'Keeping the Foochow Navy Yard Afloat', p. 147.
64 *HFT*, II, 595a–b, 621.
65 Ibid., 630b–632b, 644b–645.
66 Ibid., 824b–825.
67 Wang Hsin-chung, 'Fu-chou ch'uan-ch'ang', pp. 27–52.
68 *HFT*, II, 539–547b, 824b–825.

Arsenal, its expenditure was 2,042,925 taels, or some 50 per cent higher for roughly the same period.[69] While shipbuilding was a more expensive undertaking, the high expenditure nevertheless invited criticism, especially from those who also hated its foreignness, and created problems, particularly for those who gave it financial support.

Shen was aware that the financial requirements for managing a modern defence enterprise and a traditional one were different. 'It was not like financing a [traditional] military campaign', he said as he took over the Navy Yard in 1867. He had no illusions, only apprehensions – about the delivery of funds, the oversights in the original estimates, ship maintenance expenses, and the financial impact of imperial as well as provincial politics.[70] Indeed, as expenses rose above scheduled income, and when the Navy Yard had to draw its revenue from more than one source, the 60 per cent customs duties, its financial management became extremely complex.

As a rule, Ch'ing budgetary practices did not provide for inflation, growth, or retooling. Yet the financial requirements of running such modern enterprises as the Foochow Navy Yard failed to convince the imperial government that reforms were necessary. So new expenditures were accommodated only after the needs had become a pressing reality, and only if the officials concerned could pin-point a revenue source for them. This was how the ship maintenance account came about in mid-1869. Fortunately, the governor-general and governor at the time (Ying-kuei and Pien Pao-ti) were both supportive; they sacrificed the provincial arms-buying funds for ship maintenance. After 1871, however, provincial support diminished. Ying-kuei's successor, Li Ho-nien, was openly hostile, and Tartar General Wen-yü was less than enthusiastic. Under them, the more progressive, reform-minded Governor Wang K'ai-t'ai could not assert his independence. During the Sung Chin debate, when Wen-yü, then also acting as governor-general, suggested closing the Navy Yard, Wang had to attach his signature to the memorial. With little support from Fukien, the Navy Yard was compelled to look elsewhere for a solution to its problems. The answer was to impose Foochow vessels on other provinces, thus destroying what could have been the core of a modern squadron, and to build cargo steamers. Since neither

---

69 Kennedy, *Arms*, p. 163 (Table 2); Wang Erh-min, *Ch'ing-chi ping-kung-yeh*, Table 2 (following p. 82). For the period in question, these two sources provide identical information. The reader is once again reminded that the Foochow Navy Yard and the Kiangnan Arsenal were very different in nature and are not exactly comparable. A comparison is made nonetheless simply because these were the two largest defence industrial establishments at the time.

70 Shen's memorial of 18 July 1867, in *SWSK*, 4:1b–2b.

was a long-term solution, money had to be transferred from the ship-building account, forcing a cut in shipbuilding shortly thereafter.

With the delivery of funds, Shen encountered remarkably little tardiness until late summer 1874. The presence of the Europeans up to February was a deterrent to delinquency. Thereafter, with Shen's extended absences on Taiwan, Wen-yü began to take liberties. Apart from his personal greed, there was also his desire to please the throne.[71] Somewhat like the hoppo of the old Canton system, the position of the Foochow Tartar general, with its control over the customs, was a lucrative one. He who was favoured with this office must, first and foremost, satisfy the needs of the imperial establishment. Wen-yü would never have given funding priority to the Navy Yard at the expense of the imperial mausolea. His real feelings about the Navy Yard were difficult to decipher. He seemed to have accepted its existence despite his general agreement with Sung Chin's charges. Perhaps the fate of former governor-general Wu T'ang served as a reminder of what could happen to one who plotted its demise.

Still, the late delivery of funds became serious mainly because Fukien was facing real financial difficulties. Its resources were strained as the defence of Taiwan claimed an increasingly larger share of its funds from the spring of 1874.[72] Defence preparations also opened up a power struggle between Wen-yü and Li Ho-nien over arms purchases and the accompanying perquisites.[73] With the two contending for resources, the Navy Yard suffered.

The Japanese invasion of Taiwan and the strain it put on China's resources were a consequence of what Moulder calls China's incorporation into the world economy. China's inability to increase its tariff on foreign trade as a means to raise revenue also diminished its capacity to meet the rising costs of defence modernization. As regards the Navy Yard's finances, the only benefit imperialism brought was the revenue from the efficiently run Maritime Customs Service.

Erratic direction by the central government also added to the Navy Yard's financial woes. Whereas the government never denied Shen's requests for funds, it often failed to provide sound solutions or force the provinces to follow orders. The provinces dragged their feet when

---

71 Li Hung-chang to Shen, 20 November 1875, in *LWCK*, 'Letters', 15:30a–b.
72 Ting Jih-ch'ang's memorial of 6 March 1876 (KH 2.2.11), in YCT, KH 2/2 *chung*.
73 There was much bickering between the Tartar general and the governor-general over who should have the final say in foreign affairs. Wen-yü was particularly piqued by Li's monopoly on arms acquisition. Wen-yü's memorials, 11 December 1875 (KH 1.11.14) and 13 October 1876 (KH 2.8.26), in YCT, KH 1/11 *shang* and KH 2/8 *hsia*.

ordered to adopt Foochow ships. The Board of Revenue, ill-informed about Fukien's tea revenue, wasted months trying to locate additional monies for the Navy Yard. Meanwhile, it guarded the surplus in the 40 per cent customs jealously. It allowed Shen to claim a portion of it only after all the alternatives had been exhausted. It is important to note that it was this fund, directly controlled by Peking, that became the more reliable source of the Navy Yard's income from late 1875 on. The other source, the 60 per cent customs revenue, though nominally controlled by Peking, was more open to provincial manipulations and was far less dependable. Had the central government decided from the very beginning to fund the Navy Yard solely by monies in its control, the Navy Yard would have had less trouble. And the political gains would have been enormous: Ma-wei would then have become a truly imperial institution, one that would have been more amenable to the dictates of the central government. But the court was not prepared to pay the price.

The revenue of the Ch'ing empire was unquestionably small compared with its gross national product or even with the taxes it actually collected. But revenue did increase in the post-rebellion era, nearly doubling the midcentury figures by the 1880s. To be sure, some of the gains had been consumed by Tso Tsung-t'ang's campaign, but the large outlays for famine relief and foreign wars that eventually drained the government's resources still lay in the future.[74] China could well afford the Foochow Navy Yard and other modern defence enterprises. The question was one of priorities. As Kwang-ching Liu shows, the Ch'ing government was concerned with reasserting its control over the provinces in the Restoration era. It did so partly by adhering increasingly rigidly to regulations of the earlier periods. In financial matters, it tried to channel as much as possible the new revenues (likin and customs duties) to the center.[75] Funds available to modernizing enterprises thus became limited.

This being the case, the Foochow Navy Yard had to be financed in exactly the same manner as a large traditional enterprise: a single project funded by multifarious means drawn from numerous sources. When additional funds were needed, the central government, ignorant of the financial situation in the provinces, often produced unworkable solutions. While the agencies at Peking fumbled around for alternatives or negotiated with the provinces for an acceptable arrangement, much time was wasted. Shen's frustration with this haphazard system of public

74 Feuerwerker, 'Economic Trends', pp. 61–3.
75 Liu, 'The Ch'ing Restoration', pp. 480–2, 490.

finance eventually led to one of his more innovative proposals: central-ized budgeting. It fell on deaf ears.[76]

Chaotic at best, this system of financing also tended to generate and abet political discord and personal bickering. A huge amount of Shen's energy and time was consumed by the fight for money. The fact that he had a reputation for being difficult to work with did not help.[77] And the presence of hostile or unsympathetic officials at Foochow only made matters worse.

Shen was no stranger to provincial politics or the ins and outs of provincial finance. What made the present situation different from his earlier experience was this: he had no territorial power or control over financial resources. A man of less scruples might have exploited his position among the Fukien gentry and mobilized them against a hostile governor-general or Tartar general, but he did not. Though his local influence cannot be entirely discounted, his main sources of strength were his former high office, his reputation as an able administrator of great integrity, his prestige, qualified support from Peking, and, if need be, the intervention of Tso Tsung-t'ang.

To conclude, the Foochow Navy Yard did not enjoy financial stability. Meaningful long-term planning thus became impossible. Shen was energetic and, initially, successful in coping with expansion and in-creased funding, but he soon encountered resistance from Fukien and the coastal provinces. The Sung Chin debate, and the lack of stronger support from the central government during that debate, served as a reminder that economy was the key to the Navy Yard's survival. Retrenchment followed. So although he was aware that China's naval technology was many years behind that of the West, Shen could not adopt Giquel's suggestion of 1873 to build composite vessels with com-pound engines. The pressure to complete the existing contract with the Europeans was too great to jeopardize the future of the Navy Yard by engaging in yet another expensive venture. Once the contract expired, with an annual saving of around 80,000 taels from the Europeans' salary,[78] Shen embraced Giquel's proposal.

It has been said that the Foochow Navy Yard entered a period of decline after the Europeans left in early 1874.[79] From a purely financial standpoint, the decline began with the first tardy remittance of funds

76 Shen K'o, 'Hsien Wen-su kung', p. 61; Pong, 'The Vocabulary of Change: Reformist Ideas', p. 44.
77 Ting Jih-ch'ang's memorial, 14 June 1879, in *YWYT*, vol. 2, p. 391.
78 The Europeans' salary was nearly 120,000 taels per annum. But because Giquel and a few others were retained or hired, the actual saving would be closer to 80,000 or a little more.
79 Wang Hsin-chung, 'Fu-chou ch'uan-ch'ang', pp. 27–52.

from the provincial capital in late summer of that year. A combination of financial stringency, provincial politics, and weak direction from Peking led to further delays. And when Shen's imminent departure became known in June 1875,[80] his position vis-à-vis the Fukien authorities was weakened. Yet when Shen's incumbency is considered in its totality, the achievements were great and he managed efficiently whatever funds that came the Navy Yard's way. Corruption was reduced to a minimum. As a first-generation manager of a modern defence enterprise, he, despite his shortcomings (as analysed in the preceding two chapters), achieved more than Tso Tsung-t'ang had originally set out to do. Under him, the Navy Yard had become a naval establishment committed to further technological improvements. As for Shen himself, the experience of the director-generalship had awakened him to the need for a broad range of reforms and modernizing endeavours, the next and final subject of our study.

80 The edict appointing him governor-general of Liang Kiang was issued on 30 May 1875. *SWSK*, 5:69.

10

The next steps in defence modernization: Ma-wei and beyond

When Tso Tsung-t'ang founded the Navy Yard, his plan seemed grandiose, perhaps even impossible to achieve. In time, however, perceptions changed. Even as the Navy Yard came under heavy criticism in 1872, Shen Pao-chen felt positive about what had already been accomplished and argued that more, rather than less, should be done to modernize the country's defence. He then proposed the institution of a new civil service examination on mathematics, advanced studies in Europe for the students, and a programme for interprovincial naval training. Later, plans for building more advanced vessels were made. In his mind, Tso's original plan now represented the foundation, not the limits, of China's defence modernization.

It is hard to say when Shen began to see the Navy Yard as a germinal modernizing enterprise. It is clear to us that the Navy Yard, as a foreign implant, could not be efficiently run by traditional means, and as it expanded, it would demand changes in the milieu in which it operated. But it cannot be assumed that the nature of *yang-wu* enterprises would itself bring about a new understanding of their seminal role in China's modernization. Managers of some modern arsenals appeared not to have acquired such an understanding.[1] Shen, however, demonstrated a degree of awareness the day he took office as he accepted the inevitability of the Navy Yard's future expansion and the need to catch up with an ever-changing technology.

Shen's personal involvement in managing the Navy Yard greatly broadened his horizon and confronted him with many new questions. By what means could the Navy Yard best operate and expand in a tradition-bound milieu? What support industries ought to be developed to make it

1 Kennedy, *Arms*, p. 158.

272

more secure and efficient? As time passed, the Navy Yard as an institution had become inseparable from the interests of those who managed it or the men it trained. Therefore, with a growing number of young men trained in modern shipbuilding and naval affairs, the question arose as to how best they could be utilized for China's naval development. Was further training necessary? Should there be more incentives to entice a larger number of people to the modernizing defence industry and to keep those already in it? If so, what kind of incentives?

Shen's response to these questions fell into two categories: proposals for future development, to be examined in Chapter 11, and the changes he tried to implement before his departure from Ma-wei in late 1875, which we shall discuss here. They concerned the command of the modern warships, the promotion of scientific studies among the scholar-gentry class, the supply of good-quality coal, and the improvement of communication for defence operations. The last two resulted in the establishment of China's first modern coal mine and telegraph lines. All four were important for the defence potential of the Navy Yard.

The command of the Ma-wei vessels

Two issues arose as regards the command of the warships: who should be made captains, and how the boats should be organized so that they could operate as a unified force. In Shen's thinking, the ships should be commanded by officers versed in modern naval warfare. But this was not possible at first, for when the ships were launched, none of the students at the Navy Yard School was ready for a captaincy. Earlier, Tso Tsung-t'ang had anticipated the problem and introduced the practice of using men from the old water force or the treaty ports who, though lacking in formal training, had had experience with steam navigation. They were then given additional experience on small steamers belonging to Fukien province before service on a Navy Yard boat. Shen followed this practice. Thus, the captaincy of the first vessel, the *Wan-nien Ch'ing*, was given to Pei Chin-ch'üan, whom Tso had recruited in late 1866 to take charge of a small provincial steamer (the *Hua-fu-pao*) and its crew in preparation for service on a Ma-wei vessel. An officer of the traditional water force, he had previously commanded steamers in Chekiang province engaged in piracy suppression. In a similar fashion, a Major Wu Shih-chung was made captain of the second vessel, the *Mei-yün*. Wu was transferred from the 40-horsepower *Ch'ang-sheng*, also a Fukien steamer purchased in 1865 for coastal patrol.[2]

2 On Pei, see *HFT*, II, 19, 50, 161b–162; Shen Pao-chen to Giquel, 18 July 1869, in MM

By mid-1873, eight other captains had been commissioned, two – Pei San-ch'üan and Cheng Yü – in the manner just described.[3] The third, Shen Shun-fa, began as a chief officer (*ta-fu*) on a Fukien steamer and then on the Navy Yard's *Wan-nien Ch'ing* before taking over the captaincy from Pei Chin-ch'üan. Pei had moved on to a newly built corvette, the *Yang-wu*.[4] Of the remaining five, two – Lü Wen-ching and Lu Lun-hua – had been officers on foreign bottoms. The former, according to the *North-China Herald*, had distinguished himself in piracy suppression and rice transport and was 'capable' and 'well known to Europeans from his length of service in Hong Kong waters'.[5] The latter was said to be very familiar with China's coastal waters.[6] We have no background information on the other three.

Of the ten captains, only two had definitely come from the old water force, two others may have had a similar background, two were certainly recruited from the treaty ports, and the origin of the other four is not known. All but one were said to have been worthy captains. For example, Lü Wen-ching was referred to by the British consul on Taiwan, William Gregory, as the 'well-known and esteemed captain'.[7] Yang Yung-nien of the 80-horsepower *Fu-hsing*, about whose past we know little, was also warmly praised by the British for helping an English vessel in distress.[8] The captain of questionable quality was Lo Ch'ang-chih. He lost his boat, the 150-horsepower *Ta-ya* (S.S. No. 15), along with about ten men, in a typhoon in September 1874. He was dismissed and was heard of no more.[9] Lü Wen-ching, it should be said, also had his ship damaged during the same storm and lost his commission. He was soon reinstated owing to his creditable performance during the Japanese invasion of Taiwan.[10] The rest of these early captains, too,

BB4 1555 17/5/1. On Wu, see *YWYT*, vol. 5, p. 91; Wu Tsan-ch'eng's memorial of 18 August 1879 (KH 5.6.29), in YCT, KH 5/6 *chung*; Hewlett to Fraser, 12 August 1878, in FO 228/616, T'ai-wan fu, no. 7.

3 *HFT*, II, 161b–162. On Cheng, see Gregory to Wade, 10 January 1873, in FO 228/521, no. 2; *YWYT*, vol. 5, p. 137. On the *Ch'ang-sheng*, see Hewlett to Fraser, 12 August 1878, and Sinclair to Parkes, 14 March 1885, respectively, in FO 228/616, T'ai-wan fu, no. 7, and 228/796, no. 30.

4 *HFT*, II, 424b; Wu Tsan-ch'eng's memorial of 18 June 1877 (KH 3.5.8), in YCT, KH 3/5 *shang*.

5 *NCH*, 2 May 1874.

6 *HFT*, II, 375; *IWSM*, TC 88:6; Li Hung-chang to Wang K'ai-t'ai, 10 October 1872, in *LWCK*, 'Letters', 12:25b.

7 Gregory to Wade, 23 November 1874, in FO 228/542, no. 26.

8 Wade to Derby, 24 July 1875, in FO 17/699, no. 136; H. J. Allen to Wade, 26 June 1875, in FO 228/554, no. 11.

9 *Shih-lu*, KH 2:10b; Gregory to Wade, 5 October 1874, in FO 228/542, no. 23, encl. 1.

10 *Shih-lu*, KH 2:10b; Shen Pao-chen's memorial, 13 November 1875 (KH 1.10.16), in YCT, KH 1/10 *chung*.

carried out their assignment well during the Taiwan crisis and subsequently made steady progress in their naval career.[11]

Short of a real naval engagement, then, these men were equal to their
task. Their probationary service on the smaller provincial steamers may
have prepared them well for the command of the larger Navy Yard
vessels. But they had their limitations. As J. G. Dunn observed, they
'sail their vessels, in clear weather, by knowing the coast, and not by sun
observations'.[12] Shen had never intended simply to hand over Ma-wei's
modern vessels to men with no formal or theoretical training. So even as
he commissioned these men, he wanted to give them and their crew
additional training. His first attempt was aborted when d'Aiguebelle,
having been charged with naval training, left Ma-wei in 1870. Meanwhile, he made sure that the ships' officers acquired more experience by
engaging in piracy suppression or carrying shipwrecked sailors, examination candidates, officials, and the like between ports on Taiwan and
the mainland.[13] Meanwhile Shen eagerly waited for the students of the
Navy Yard School to take over.[14]

As noted in Chapter 8, the moment the students of the School of
Theoretical Navigation had completed their studies, they were transferred to the School of Practical Navigation for a two-year course on a
training ship. The course included two extensive cruises. The second
voyage was critical, because on the return journey (from South-East
Asia) two students were given sole command of the ship and another two
were assigned to assist them. Giquel, satisfied with their performance,
recommended in July 1873 the first two cadets for the captaincy and the
other two as 'also capable of commanding at sea'. Shen readily concurred, having personally gone on board the training ship and observed
the manoeuvring exercises under the students' command.[15] Thereupon,
Lü Han and Chang Ch'eng were appointed captains, but at first only on
the older and smaller provincial boats. The third student, Li Chia-pen,
was made chief officer, and the last, Li T'ien, was probably given a
similar job.[16]

---

11 Shen Pao-chen's memorial of 13 November 1875 (KH 1.10.16) in YCT, KH 1/10 *chung*.
   On the later career of some of them, see *HFT*, II, 569a–b, 700b–701b; *TWTC*, p. 336;
   NCH, 8 July 1881; *Shih-lu*, KH 37:8b–9. Shen Shun-fa died of illness on 7 July 1876.
   See Wu Tsan-ch'eng's memorial, 18 June 1877 (KH 3.5.8), in YCT, KH 3/5 *shang*.
12 Dunn's report of June 1875 in FO 233/85, no. 3, p. VIII.
13 *HFT*, II, 257b; Gregory to Wade, 10 January, 22 April, 31 July, and 8 October 1873, in
   FO 228/521, nos. 2, 11, 16, 18.
14 Shen to Giquel, 8 July 1869, in MM BB4 1555 17/5/1.
15 Giquel, *Foochow Arsenal*, pp. 30–1.
16 *HFT*, II, 551b; *SWSK*, 4:63; Shen Pao-chen's memorial, 13 November 1875 (KH
   1.10.16), in YCT, KH 1/10 *chung*; *Ch'uan-cheng tsou-yi*, 12:32. One of the provincial boats
   was the 40-horsepower *Chang-sheng*, and the other the 50-horsepower, three-gun *Hai-*

Following the same path of training, four more students from the first class qualified for active service in the latter part of 1873. Again, acting on Giquel's recommendation, Shen commissioned them in early 1874. Yeh Fu thus became the captain of a provincial steamer, replacing Chang Ch'eng, who was promoted to the captaincy of the 80-horsepower *Ching-yüan*. Chang was therefore the first Ma-wei graduate to command a Ma-wei vessel. At about the same time, a second cadet, Lin Kuo-hsiang, was given charge of the new, 150-horsepower *Ch'en-hang* (S.S. No. 14)[17] – the first Foochow graduate to command a boat of this class. As for the other two cadets, Teng Shih-ch'ang and Li Ho, we have no information at this point. They were probably made chief officers.

The period 1874–5 saw upward movement for numerous Foochow graduates. Lü Han, for example, was moved up from a small Fukien boat to become captain of the 80-horsepower *Chen-wei* in mid-1874. He underwent further training on the *Yang-wu* the following year, sailing to Japan and elsewhere before taking over the 150-horsepower *Fei-yün*, probably in 1876. Close behind was Li Chia-pen, who took over Lü's *Chen-wei* as captain in 1875 after having served a year each on a small provincial steamer and on the *Chen-wei* as chief officer.[18] Then, in either late 1874 or early 1875, Teng Shih-ch'ang and Li T'ien were promoted to the captaincy of a provincial steamer. Both had been recommended by Giquel for a chief officer's post a year or so earlier. Teng finally became the captain of a Ma-wei vessel, the *Chen-wei*, in late 1875.[19] Meanwhile, Yeh Fu moved up from a small steamer to succeed Chang Ch'eng as captain of the *Ch'ing-yüan*. What immediately happened to Chang is not clear; he was made captain of the Corvette *Yang-wu* in 1879,[20] probably still in his late twenties.

It has been said that Shen, in choosing captains, 'preferred the old water force men for the newer, bigger Foochow-built ships' even after Foochow graduates became fully qualified and that he was reluctant to adopt Giquel's recommendation of these young men.[21] The preceding analysis shows otherwise. First, the earliest captains (not all of them from the water force) were appointed before any of the Navy Yard cadets

tung-yün. YWYT, vol. 2, p. 398; *HFT*, I, 742b; Gregory to Wade, 13 August 1875, in FO 228/557, no. 12; Hewlett to Fraser, 12 August and 21 October 1878, in FO 228/616, T'ai-wan fu, nos. 7, 8.

17 Giquel, *Foochow Arsenal*, p. 31; *HFT*, II, 551b, 522b.
18 *Ch'uan-cheng tsou-yi*, 12:32; Lin Hsüan-chih, *Fu-chou Ma-wei*, p. 243; Wu Tsan-ch'eng's memorial, 21 May 1877 (KH 3.4.9), in YCT KH 3/4 *shang*; Shen Pao-chen's memorial, 13 November 1875 (KH 1.10.16), in YCT, KH 1/10 *chung*.
19 Shen Pao-chen's memorial, 13 November 1875 (KH 1.10.16), in YCT, KH 1/10 *chung*. Hewlett to Fraser, 12 August 1878, in FO 228/616, T'ai-wan fu, no, 7.
20 Shen Pao-chen's memorial, 29 July 1879 (KH 5.6.11), in YCT KH 5/6 *chung*.
21 Rawlinson, *China's Struggle*, pp. 58–9.

were adequately prepared. When they were ready, Shen followed Giquel's recommendations closely. Second, though the majority of the cadets were initially placed on board the older and smaller vessels, Shen did emphasize that their appointment was probationary. Once they had proved themselves, they were transferred to the larger, Ma-wei vessels.[22] In all cases, they were so promoted, within a year.

Where Shen can be faulted is in the haste with which he commissioned these young and inexperienced men, who were between the ages of twenty and twenty-six.[23] No Western navy would have given them such responsible positions so early. Shen was aware of the problem, but he was impatient to see results. He also considered these men, inexperienced though they were, better trained than the old hands. As he insisted, 'China's talents must come from the Navy Yard School'.[24] It was his hope that their probationary service on the smaller vessels would make them fit for the responsibilities ahead. Nevertheless, before they were ready, vessels were launched, and all except one had to be captained by men from either the old water force or the treaty ports.[25] Even so, by the time Shen left office, six Ma-wei graduates had been made captains of the Navy Yard's vessels, while another, still a captain of a small Fukien boat, was expected to be ready for a similar appointment later.[26]

As further proof of Shen's support for the younger, newly qualified cadets, he put them on the same pay scale as the older, 'experienced' men from the water force or treaty ports. And they were very well paid – 200 taels for the captain of a 150-horsepower boat, and 160 taels for that of an 80-horsepower vessel.[27] In offering such high salaries, Shen was making good a promise Tso Tsung-t'ang made at the founding of the Navy Yard: those who became proficient in the new skills were to be remunerated on the same scale as their European counterparts.

Two developments in the last years of Shen's incumbency directly

---

22 Shen's memorial, 15 September 1873, in *HFT*, II, 467.
23 For example, in 1874 Ch'en Chi-t'ung was twenty-two years old, Wei Han was twenty-four, and Yen Fu, twenty-two or twenty-four. *FCTC*, 'Lieh-chuan', 5b:38–39b; *MHHC*, 90:6. On Yen, see Hummel, *Eminent Chinese*, vol. 2, p. 643; Wang Shih, *Yen Fu chuan* (Shanghai, 1957), pp. 3–4, and the second edition (Shanghai, 1975), p. 1; Benjamin Schwartz, *In Search of Wealth and Power: Yen Fu and the West* (Cambridge, Mass., 1964), p. 22.
24 Shen to Ting Jih-ch'ang, early 1876, in 'Shen Wen-su kung-tu', 3:36–37; Lin Ch'ing-yüan, *Fu-chien ch'uan-cheng*, pp. 85–6; *SWSK*, 4:63.
25 Four new captains were appointed for S.S. Nos. 12 to 15 in 1874. One, Lin Kuo-hsiang, was a Navy Yard School graduate. The origins of the other three are not known.
26 This was Li T'ien, captain of the *Ch'ang-sheng* since late 1874. For unknown reasons, he was still in that position in 1878. Hewlett to Fraser, 12 August 1878, in FO 228/616, T'ai-wan fu, no. 7.
27 *HFT*, II, 425–8.

affected the training and employment of Foochow cadets as captains. First, Shen had realized by early 1872, if not before, that the next step towards technological independence must involve advanced studies in Europe for the Navy Yard graduates (see Chapter 8). And as he committed the Navy Yard to the building of composite vessels powered by compound engines in 1874 – he even contemplated the construction of ironclads at Ma-wei – it became even more urgent that Foochow graduates receive adequate training at home and abroad to build and officer these sophisticated vessels.[28] Here we are concerned only with his plan to train naval officers in Europe.

Extensive discussions with the Tsungli Yamen, Tso Tsung-t'ang, Li Hung-chang, and Giquel produced a plan in early 1874.[29] Worthy of note was Shen's particular concern that the principles of naval warfare should be part of the curriculum.[30] The plan, however, had to be shelved as the Japanese invaded Taiwan and the Navy Yard's financial situation worsened. Shen then resorted to two short-term solutions. First, taking advantage of Giquel's return to Europe to purchase hardware for the composite vessels, he sent five students, including two graduates of the School of Practical Navigation, to accompany him. They observed naval dockyards and warships in France and England. Three of them returned with Giquel after about half a year, while the other two stayed longer.[31] Second, the corvette *Yang-wu* was used for an extensive, six-stage programme of advanced training in seamanship and gunnery for the cadets of the first two classes (see Chapter 8).

The second development that affected the appointment of Foochow cadets as captains was the retrenchment of the shipbuilding programme. Thus, as more cadets became qualified, fewer new boats were available for their placement. Meanwhile those captains who had initially come from the old water force and the treaty ports were too entrenched to be dislodged. As advancement for the Foochow graduates became increasingly difficult, Shen had to consider means to deal with the problem. We shall return to this subject later.

The growing number of steam-powered naval vessels raised the question of fleet organization. Tseng Kuo-fan, who pioneered shipbuilding at the Kiangnan Arsenal, first discussed the issue in August 1870, suggesting that the Kiangnan and the Ma-wei vessels should each be trained as

28 Ibid., 349b, 472b–473b; *SWSK*, 4:68–9, 70–1.
29 See Pong, 'Modernization and Politics', pp. 355–8; Wang Chia-chien, 'Ch'ing-mo hai-chün liu-Ying hsüeh-sheng', pp. 161–6.
30 *HFT*, II, 473.
31 *YWYT*, vol. 5, p. 164; Ch'ih, 'Hai-chün ta-shih chi', pp. 326–7. Liu Pu-ch'an and Lin T'ai-tseng from the School of Practical Navigation returned with Giquel.

a naval squadron under a commander. The throne agreed and ordered Shen and Governor-General Ying-kuei to pick a commander for the Foochow boats.[32]

Shen readily embraced Tseng's idea but took pains to point out that the emerging naval force would pose unprecedented difficulties for the new commander. Whereas the traditional forces were made up of men from a common background, the new naval men, thanks to functional specialization, had diverse social and geographical origins. Discipline and unity in action would thus be hard to maintain. Would the Ningpo sailors be amenable to the orders of a Foochow-trained officer who had come from Hong Kong? Then there was the problem of the vessels being stationed at various ports, where training would have to be conducted in isolation, giving rise to regional idiosyncrasies. Periodic naval exercises under a commander would be absolutely necessary. So important was the role of this commander in Shen's eyes that he warned against the appointment of a territorial official, who would be unlikely to spend much time at sea. Yet he must be of high rank so as to command respect. He must, of course, be familiar with maritime affairs as well. Having defined the role of the new squadron commander, Shen refrained from nominating a candidate. The throne then named Li Ch'eng-mou, commander-in-chief of Fukien's water force.[33]

In all probability Shen did not make a recommendation because he saw no qualified person in sight. He could not have been overjoyed by Peking's choice. For one, it was not a full-time appointment, which Shen had wanted. To be sure, Li had the requisite high rank and, by virtue of his office, had oversight of the Fukien steamers used for coastal patrol – the same vessels on which Navy Yard graduates served as probationary officers. But a true commander of a modern naval service he was not. A little later, when looking for Li's successor, Shen emphasized that the commander should be familiar with modern naval affairs.[34] For the moment, however, he had to be content with Li.

To make the best of the situation, Shen had had regulations drawn up to ensure the squadron commander's involvement in the formation of a naval force. Naturally, the commander was to have control over all the Ma-wei boats. But since there was a distinct possibility that these vessels would be stationed in several provinces, provision was made for a division commander for every two, three, or four boats serving in the same province or viceroyalty. While the provincial authorities were to exercise

32 *IWSM*, TC 74:30–32b.
33 *HFT*, II, 251–252a, 252b.
34 Ibid., 50, 552b.

some control over these division commanders, the final say rested with the squadron commander.[35]

Twice a year, all the vessels were to gather for a joint exercise. The spring muster was to be directed by the squadron commander, whereas the autumnal review would be conducted in the presence of the Navy Yard's director-general and a high Min Che official. At other times, the commander was empowered to rotate the ships from one station to another on a regular basis so as to familiarize the officers and crew with different regions of China's coastal waters. To give new meaning to these changes, a 'national' navy ensign was adopted, the first such 'national' emblem in Chinese history.

Regular training was left in the hands of the captains and their officers. The captains were to conduct a drill of the entire crew once every ten days, while their lieutenants were responsible for the daily drills. The main objective was to improve co-ordination among the crew members.

The regulations left much to be desired, since numerous conflicting interests had to be catered to. Too much power was vested in the high officials of Fukien, Chekiang, and elsewhere, simply because it was their resources that supported the vessels. The squadron commander therefore enjoyed little independence. In spite of the regulations, he had no control over the movement of the vessels as a means to expose the captains and men to differing conditions. Nor did he have any say as to where the vessels were to be stationed, a matter that was determined by financial considerations and the wishes of the receiving provinces. As for drills on board, he was severely constrained by financial limitations and by the fact that he was, first and foremost, the commander-in-chief of Fukien's water force, which had first call on his time and energy. So even when Shen managed to secure in mid-1872 a budget item of 500 taels per month for him to travel to other provinces to conduct on-deck training, we have no evidence that Li carried out this aspect of his duties as Shen had intended.[36] The sources do not mention any semiannual muster as ever having taken place.

Whatever Li's limitations were as squadron commander, he must have done well as head of the provincial water force, for in early 1873 he was elevated to take command of the Yangtze Fleet, whereupon Governor-

---

35 Ibid., 279b–284b. The regulations were completed in early 1871 when Shen was already in mourning, but he definitely had a hand in drafting them, since his closest assistants, Hsia Hsien-lun and Huang Wei-hsüan, were in charge. Commander Li was also consulted. At the time, it should be noted, only one Ma-wei boat (the *Mei-yün*) was serving outside Fukien.

36 Ibid., 350.

General Li Ho-nien and Governor Wang K'ai-t'ai recommended that Lo Ta-ch'un, commander-in-chief of Fukien's Green Standard Army, take over the water force in an acting capacity. Then, after conferring with Shen, they made Lo the squadron commander of the Ma-wei ships as well. Lo's high rank and familiarity with local conditions were cited as important factors.[37] But Lo, his ability notwithstanding, had no experience outside the land forces. Shen would rather have seen someone versed in modern naval affairs be given the post.[38] His opportunity finally came in early 1875 when Lo returned to his army command.

But where could such a person be found in China in the mid-1870s? Shen saw a possibility in Ts'ai Kuo-hsiang, who, at the command of Tseng Kuo-fan, had constructed China's first steamboat in 1863. Tseng later named him commander of the ill-fated Lay–Osborn Flotilla. Since that never materialized, he stayed with the water force on the Yangtze. Thus, Ts'ai's qualifications also fell short of Shen's requirements. Shen therefore gave him the command of the squadron for a trial period of several months before actual appointment.[39]

In Ts'ai, Shen finally found the first full-time squadron commander. Whether Ts'ai lived up to expectations is difficult to tell, but at least he was energetic enough to take the *Yang-wu* to South-East Asia and Japan in 1876.[40] But as long as the constraints that had plagued his predecessors persisted, there could be no unified naval command.

In the absence of fleet organization, training on board individual ships had by default become the main activity on which the worthiness of the Foochow squadron depended. But even at this level there were serious problems. The diverse background of the captains and officers ensured that training would not be uniform. The lack of a full and independent command structure resulted in yet another type of confusion. In the squadron, under the commander, the captains were the highest officers. (No division commanders were appointed in Shen's time.) Yet the captaincy could be reached quite early in one's career. Service and merit thereafter could be recognized only by awards of ranks and titles in the traditional land and water forces. As a result, a captain could belong to

---

37 *IWSM*, TC 89:6b–7b.

38 *HFT*, II, 552b. See my biographical sketch of Lo in the Introduction, Lo Ta-ch'un, *Lo Ching-shan T'ai-wan k'ai-shan jih-chi* (Taipei, 1972), pp. i–iv.

39 *HFT*, II, 552b–553. On Ts'ai, see Gideon Ch'en, *Tseng*, p. 41; Wang Erh-min, *Ch'ing-chi ping-kung-yeh*, p. 43; Rawlinson, *China's Struggle*, p. 36; *TWCK*, 'Memorials', vol. 4, pp. 543–5.

40 J. D. Frodsham, trans., *The First Chinese Embassy to the West: The Journal of Kuo Sung-t'ao, Liu Hsi-hung and Chang Te-yi* (London, 1974), p. 13; *Kung-chung tang Kuang-hsü ch'ao chou-che*, comp. Kuo-li ku-kung po-wu-yüan, Ku-kung wen-hsien pien-chi wei-yüan-hui (Taipei, 1973), vol. 2, p. 217a–b.

one of several ranks, ranging from a lowly sublieutenant (*pa-tsung*, rank 7a) to a relatively elevated lieutenant-colonel (*ts'an-chiang*, 3a), while the chief officer of one boat could be of a higher rank than the captain of another.[41] Such a system tended to undermine the prestige and authority of captains with a lower rank. As for the cadets of the Navy Yard School, despite Shen's enthusiasm for them, there was no diploma conferred upon graduation to highlight their modern training or add to their prestige or self-esteem. Nor did their names appear on the active list in the Board of War.[42] And although Shen made sure that all, on taking command of a Navy Yard–built vessel, were awarded the respectable rank of second captain (*shou-pei*, 5b), they were still ranked below some of the older captains who lacked their modern training.[43]

Without a clear chain of command or a hierarchical structure among the officers, training and discipline suffered. The report by J. G. Dunn, possible exaggerations notwithstanding, points up this problem succinctly: 'The discipline is very bad, in fact scarcely exists, the cooks are as good as the captains[,] and the officers in some cases, or most, associate, and frequently mess with the sailors'.[44] Captain Noel Shore also noted that many officers did not command the respect of the crew. He 'saw them at gun drill one day, but they seem to treat the whole thing as a joke'.[45] The flaws in the system were exacerbated by the incompetence of at least some of the officers.[46]

Given this environment, Shen's warning that the diverse origins of the officers and crew would pose disciplinary problems became a self-fulfilling prophecy. Even Foochow men could not work well together because some of them were boatmen and others landsmen.[47] Shen's ambitious plan to transform the water force soldier into a modern naval man

---

41 For example, in 1874 Captain Pei Chin-ch'üan had the rank of a lieutenant-colonel (3a), Captain Lü Wen-ching that of a major (*yu-chi*, 3b), and Captain Lu Lun-hua that of a mere sublieutenant (7a), whereas First Officer Lin Wen-ho carried the rank of a second captain (*shou-pei*, 5b). *LWCK*, 'Letters', 12:25b; *HFT*, II, 162, 511b; *CTSM*, 2:275; *Shih-lu*, KH 2:10b; *NCH*, 2 May 1874; *YWYT*, vol. 5, p. 139.

42 Shen Yü-ch'ing, *T'ao-yüan chi*, p. 246.

43 Chang Cheng appeared to have been given the rank of first captain (4a) on reaching captaincy. Shen Pao-chen's memorial, 13 November 1875 (KH 1.10.16), in YCT KH 1/10 *chung*; *Ch'uan-cheng tsou-yi*, 12:32.

44 FO 233/85, no. 3, p. VIII. Captain Shore also wrote: 'The officers and men appear to live together on terms of easy familiarity, a condition of existence which . . . is hardly calculated to raise the tone of the service, or to bring about those habits of implicit obedience and respect which are generally considered essential to ensure success in battle'. *Flight of the Lapwing*, p. 105.

45 *Flight of the Lapwing*, p. 234.

46 Ibid., pp. 234–5; *NCH*, 1 March 1877.

47 Shore, *Flight of the Lapwing*, pp. 233–4. Whether the boatmen and the landsmen were identified with specific functional groups on board is not clear.

complicated matters further. In 1871 he detached groups of twenty to
fifty men from the water force to drill alongside the gunners and sailors
on Navy Yard steamers. But the water force men, fixed in their ways,
were slow to learn. Worse still, there was so much friction between the
ships' officers and the water force officers, and between the crew and the
soldiers, that Shen had to abandon the experiment.[48]

Training on board was quite dismal in any case, at least in the earlier
years. The old pitch captains were simply ignorant of modern naval
training. During his visit in 1873, Dunn had the men take up their
positions, and neither officers nor men knew how to work the expensive
modern guns. Reportedly, Giquel had offered to teach them but was
refused. So in Dunn's view, 'If the *Yang-wu* was boarded by a 60 horse
power gunboat, she would, being helpless[,] be carried away.... [Giquel]
builds ... fine ships and delivers them over in perfect order ... and is
allowed no further supervision'.[49]

Both Tso Tsung-t'ang and Shen were extremely sensitive to the danger
of foreign domination of the Navy Yard. Shen recognized the ignorance
of the Chinese and the need for foreigners to train them. But the British
officers hired as naval instructors were restricted to the training ship
only (the *Chien-wei* and, later, the *Yang-wu*). The idea was that, once the
young Chinese cadets became proficient, they would gradually replace
the older officers and spread the art of modern naval warfare to the other
boats. Meanwhile, as an imperial injunction stated, all Chinese vessels
must stay in Chinese hands.[50]

One question remains. Were the young cadets of the Navy Yard
School capable of fulfilling the historic task Shen assigned them? A full
answer would require an analysis of their performance well beyond
Shen's tenure, which we cannot attempt here. Our data yield a mixed
picture. Insofar as a good number of the young men came from well-to-
do families, we can expect that they had a traditional disdain for manual
work. And Shen's school regulations did little to change that attitude. As
Captain Shore testified:

The midshipmen were kept at the studies very regularly, but whether these
young gentlemen will ever make good practical sailors is another question. I
understand that they do not take kindly to manual labour, being afraid of soiling
their fingers.... Sometimes they were sent for a climb over the masthead, and

48 *HFT*, II, 286b; *YWYT*, vol. 2, p. 404.
49 FO 223/85, no. 3, pp. VIII–IX.
50 *IWSM*, TC 74:31b–32b. For Shen's ideas on training commanders and officers, see the
section on modernizing China's Defence capabilities.

cut a sorry figure, and a certain number were stationed aloft during the evolutions, but looked unhappy and out of their elements.[51]

Yet over the years, service and further training in Europe seem to have created a naval tradition and spirit, albeit slowly. During the Sino-French War of 1884–5, many officers, Foochow graduates, fought gallantly, and some died in action.[52] But in Shen's time, the disdain for physical work was a problem. He became more aware of it towards the end of his tenure and tried to correct the situation (see Chapter 11).

Fuel for Ma-wei and China's first modern coal mine

To use Chinese coal for a Chinese navy yard made economic and political sense. From the very start, Tso Tsung-t'ang had envisaged the use of local iron and coal. However, his initial interest was focused on the supply of iron. But because the metal extracted by traditional Chinese methods was poor, a metallurgist was included among the engineers hired from Europe. His job was to direct iron smelting and refining at nearby iron and coal mines and to impart his knowledge to the Chinese as well.[53]

The idea of the Navy Yard producing its own iron was soon abandoned, probably for financial reasons. Instead, steel and iron from Europe as well as recycled iron from local scraps and antiquated cannons were used. The latter was processed in the Navy Yard's metal-working forge. The search for coal, however, continued. Although the Navy Yard used coal from England, Australia, and Taiwan, English coal was expensive and was used sparingly. In contrast, Australian coal was reasonably priced at 7.12 to 8.30 taels per ton, and the quality good. It made excellent bunker coal as well as coke for the workshops. Taiwan coal, however, contained too much sulphur. While it could be used in some workshops, it did not make good coke and could shorten the life of the ships' boilers. But Formosan coal was potentially cheap and its quality might be improved by better mining methods.[54] It was a source worth exploring.

The search for Taiwan coal began as soon as Shen assumed office in July 1867, when he sent a resident agent to the island to procure coal and timber. Although the concern for timber supply was greater at this early stage, the decision to obtain coal from Taiwan had greater historical significance. Hitherto, coal mining on Taiwan had been pro-

51 Shore, *Flight of the Lapwing*, p. 234.
52 Rawlinson, *China's Struggle*, p. 119; Lin Ch'ung-yung, *Shen*, p. 551.
53 *HFT*, II, 36; *TWHK*, 'Memorials', 20:66a–b.
54 Contenson to Ministre de la Guerre, 13 August 1872, in MM BB4 1382, pp. 342–3.

hibited, even though the ban was often observed in the breach. By posting a government coal-buying agent there, Shen had in effect taken the first step towards legalization. In time, the demand for coal and timber increased, and Shen, on the death of the first agent, replaced him with two men. As more workshops entered production and the first steamships were launched, the demand for coal from Taiwan rose.[55]

The cost of Taiwan coal, however, was high. By the time one added the transport cost, the middleman's cut, and officials' peculation at the likin barriers, the price could exceed 4 taels a ton. And yet the supply was erratic. More direct Navy Yard intervention seemed desirable.[56]

Earlier, in November 1867, several high officials were ordered by the throne to discuss issues likely to arise in the impending negotiations for treaty revision. An item of concern was the Westerners' interest in mining coal in China. Shen jumped at the opportunity and proposed the employment of Western mining engineers to exploit China's coal deposits as long as the Chinese government maintained overall control. Of the six staff members whom Shen consulted, all were opposed to letting foreigners open coal mines in China, and three advocated Chinese-run modern mines (the other three were silent on the subject). The prevailing sentiment, then, was to modernize coal mining under some form of Chinese official control.[57]

In the summer of 1868 Shen sent the Navy Yard's metallurgist, Dupont, to survey coal reserves in northern Taiwan, around Keelung (Chi-lung). The report was encouraging: a 95-centimetre seam of good-quality bituminous coal was found which, according to Dupont, could be mined at a cost of $3.37 (approx. 2.25 taels) per ton, or 11.29 to 43.83 per cent less than the prevailing market price.[58] But Shen did not take the next logical step – that of establishing a modern mine.

It has been suggested that the Chinese stopped short of starting their own modern mines for fear that the British, in the course of treaty revision, would use their initiative as a wedge for introducing foreign mines in China.[59] The fear abated when the revised treaty – the Alcock Convention – was signed in October 1869. The Convention was even-

---

55 *Ch'uan-cheng tsou-yi*, 5:10; *HFT*, II, 560; *Tan-shui t'ing-chih* (1871; reprint ed., Taipei, 1963), vol. 1, p. 112. For a general history of coal mining in Taiwan, see Huang Chia-mo, *Chia-wu chan-ch'ien chih T'ai-wan mei-wu* (Taipei, 1961), pp. ii–v, 92–3.

56 *Tan-shui t'ing-chih*, vol. 1, pp. 112–13; Huang Chia-mo, *Chia-wu chan-ch'ien*, pp. 93–4; *SWSK*, 4:7a–b. Calculations of the price of Taiwan coal are based on data in Sun Yü-t'ang, *Chung-kuo chin-tai kung-yeh*, vol. 2, pp. 581–2.

57 *IWSM*, TC 50:34a–b, 53:6b, 11, 14b, 16b–17, 19, 20b, 21b, 25a–b.

58 Huang Chia-mo, *Chia-wu chan-ch'ien*, pp. 93–4, 103, n. 15; Sun Yü-t'ang, *Chung-kuo chin-tai kung-yeh*, vol. 2, p. 581.

59 Huang Chia-mo, *Chia-wu chan-ch'ien*, p. 94.

tually rejected by the British, but the Chinese did not learn of its rejection until the following summer.[60] Meanwhile they acted as if the Convention, which provided only for the opening of modern government mines, had been ratified. Availing himself of this new opportunity, Dupont again broached the matter with Shen. As a result, the T'ai-wan taotai, Li Chao-t'ang, was ordered to look into the situation.[61] Since Shen was the driving force behind this new initiative, the measures Li later introduced reflected his thinking on the matter. Li, it will be recalled, had also served under Shen in Kiangsi during the Taiping years.

Shen's strategy was first to regulate the privately owned mines on Taiwan in order to ensure a cheap and regular supply of coal for the Navy Yard and then prepare the ground for the establishment of a government-owned modern mine. Thus, Taotai Li's first step was to impose government control over the local mine owners in exchange for what amounted to legalization. By this measure, the number of pits was limited to seventy, one more than those in existence, and the number of miners was restricted to twenty per pit. Only local hands were to be hired. To preclude foreign interests, nonresidents and comprador types were barred from operating the mines. Further, the proprietors could sell their coal only through approved agents. Then, in a separate move, Shen secured likin exemption for all the Navy Yard's coal purchases.[62]

These measures greatly reduced the cost of Taiwan coal to the Navy Yard. And by limiting the number of pits and size of the labour force, Shen had also mollified traditional apprehensions about mines as breeding grounds for seditious elements.[63] More important, the restrictions forestalled the expansion of the local mines, making them less competitive for the future, government-owned modern mine. As Taotai Li reorganized the Taiwan mines, he also criticized traditional mining practices, giving Shen the ammunition to press once again for the creation of a modern mine on Taiwan in 1870.[64]

The proposal for a modern mine met with imperial approval,[65] but

---

60 Mary Wright, *Last Stand*, pp. 290–5; *IWSM*, TC 68:37.
61 Huang Chia-mo, *Chia-wu chan-ch'ien*, p. 95. It was Governor-General Ying-kuei who gave Taotai Li the instruction, but the initiative had probably come from Shen, who, having no authority over a provincial official, had to act through Ying-kuei. Ying-kuei was nevertheless an enthusiastic supporter of the Navy Yard. His role in this matter was not perfunctory.
62 Huang Chia-mo, *Chia-wu chan-ch'ien*, pp. 95–7; *Tan-shui t'ing-chih*, vol. 1, pp. 112–13.
63 For examples of this fear, see *YWYT*, vol. 1, pp. 116–18; Jonathan D. Spence, *Emperor of China: Self-portrait of K'ang-hsi* (New York, 1975), p. 49.
64 *Tan-shui t'ing-chih*, vol. 1, pp. 112–13.
65 Ibid.

no progress was made throughout the early 1870s, not even in 1872, when there was a severe shortage of British coal on the market. (The Australians, perhaps because of poor market intelligence, failed to take advantage of the situation.) So the Navy Yard had to rely on Taiwan coal more than ever before. An order for 5,000 tons at rather high prices was placed, but the inefficient native mines could not deliver the coal until the following year. In fact, Taiwan mines could not meet even a third of the Navy Yard's demand, and the issue of a mechanized government mine was raised again, but to no avail. In the meantime, to cut fuel costs, the Navy Yard used Taotai Li to extract from the Keelung coal dealers a 5 per cent price reduction on all future purchases.[66]

The reasons for the failure to establish a modern mine on Taiwan can only be conjectured. The most plausible explanation is the shortage of funds. In 1866 when Tso Tsung-t'ang pondered developing Fukien's iron and coal resources, he stated that the money would have to be found later.[67] As noted in Chapter 9, the Navy Yard had been feeling the pinch of a tight budget since 1870. By 1872, during the fuel crisis, it was even deeper into financial trouble. Shen's repeated proposal for a government mine was always approved by the court without a budgetary allowance. So to obtain coal at reasonable prices, he was forced to exert greater control over the native Taiwan mines and impose by fiat a purchasing mechanism favourable to the Navy Yard.

Politically, the year 1872 was bad for innovative changes as Sung Chin's accusations brought the Navy Yard's finances under close scrutiny. Similar proposals for modern mining from the Kiangnan Arsenal were quashed by Ho Ching, the conservative southern commissioner.[68] The empire was not in an expansive mood. Besides, back at Ma-wei, the contract with the Europeans was to end in a little more than a year. After that, new arrangements would have to be made. Meanwhile the Navy Yard would just have to put up with higher fuel costs.

The Japanese invasion of Taiwan brought unexpected changes, however. As Shen, now imperial commissioner in charge of defence, prepared for war, fuel consumption of his vessels shot up. The inefficiency of the Taiwan coal mines had to be confronted once more. As a first step, he tried to stimulate production by making Taiwanese coal more competitive with foreign coal, especially Japanese coal, which had been making significant inroads in the Chinese market. He therefore proposed reduc-

---

66 Huang Chia-mo, *Chia-wu chan-ch'ien*, pp. 102–3; Sun Yü-t'ang, *Chung-kuo chin-tai kung-yeh*, vol. 2, pp. 581–2.
67 *HFT*, II, 36.
68 Huang Chia-mo, *Chia-wu chan-ch'ien*, p. 99.

ing duties on Taiwan coal to at least the same level as that levied on foreign coal. In real terms, this meant a reduction of more than thirteen times, lowering the charges from 0.672 tael per ton to 0.05 tael. The prospect of losing revenue did not appeal to the central government, however, and a compromise was reached. The new rate was to be 0.1 tael per ton.[69] Though still twice as high as the duties on foreign coal, it was much more attractive than the old schedule. Shen's action had thus created a more hospitable environment for Taiwan's private coal industry.

Still, a government-owned modern mine remained his ultimate goal. Fortunately for him, the Chinese failure to repel even an Asian invader had jolted the Ch'ing government to re-examine the self-strengthening policy and its implementation. More than eight months of heated debate followed and, finally, in mid-1875 Shen's coal-mining proposal was accepted, this time with funds to match.[70] But he was too eager to wait for the outcome of the debate. In the autumn of 1874, having secured the blessing of the Tsungli Yamen and armed with greater power as imperial commissioner, he went ahead and engaged a British mining engineer through Robert Hart. The coal deposits in Keelung were then surveyed in the spring of 1875. That completed, Shen arranged for the hiring of eleven technicians and the purchase of machinery from Britain. By this time, in mid-July, imperial approval had already been received and the future of the undertaking was assured.[71]

As Shen looked to the future, he envisioned that eventually, after production was under way and demands by government enterprises satisfied, coal from the mine would become commercially available. More important, he also harboured a wish that the modern mine would stimulate the native mine owners to modernize their own operations.[72]

Work on the Keelung mine did not begin until May 1876.[73] By that

69 *IWSM*, TC 97:24b–25, 29b–30b; *SWSK*, 5:17–18; *Shih-lu*, KH 3:5b. On the import of Japanese coal, see Sugiyama Shinya, 'Bakumatsu Meiji shoki no sekitan yushutsu to Shanhai sekitan jijō', in Shinbo Hiroshi and Yasuba Yasukichi, eds., *Kindai ikōki no Nihon keizai* (Tokyo, 1979), p. 205. I am grateful to Dr. Tim Wright for drawing my attention to this work.

70 Pong, 'The Vocabulary of Change: Reformist Ideas', pp. 49–50; *YWYT*, vol. 1, pp. 153–4, 162–5. See also the next chapter.

71 *IWSM*, TC 97:24b, 30b; Sheng K'ang, *Huang-ch'ao ching-shih-wen hsü-pien*, 101:14; *SWSK*, 5:80a–b; Frater to Wade, 7 September 1876, in FO 228/570, Tamsui, no. 24.

72 Frater to Wade, 30 November 1875, in FO 228/554, Tamsui, no. 27, incl. Neither of Shen's wishes was realized. For the reasons for failure, see Shannon R. Brown and Tim Wright, 'Technology, Economics and Politics', pp. 60–83, and Tim Wright, *Coal Mining in China's Economy and Society, 1895–1937* (Cambridge, 1984), p. 140.

73 Frater to Wade, 9 May 1876, in FO 228/570, Tamsui, no. 17.

time, Shen had already been gone from Ma-wei for six months. But it was he who started it all, the first modern coal mine in China.

Promoting the study of science among China's elite

Shen's commitment to nurturing men capable of taking China to a higher stage of defence modernization led logically to an attempt to promote modern studies among China's educated. As he insisted, if an institution like the Foochow Navy Yard was to be truly successful and have a seminal effect, it must be able to draw its talent from a broader base. And to make *yang-wu* more appealing, prospects for upward mobility must be improved both within and beyond the modern defence sector. We alluded to these concerns earlier; here we shall examine the steps Shen took to bring them about.

In the 1860s and 1870s, a number of reformer-officials believed that mathematics was at the root of Western science.[74] This conception was not as erroneous as it appears – the systematic application of mathematicized science to technology had accounted for much of Western material progress since the Renaissance.[75] Whatever its merit, this idea was definitely progressive in the Chinese context. More important still, because mathematics was thought to be the heart of modern science, any attempt by the reformers to promote its study was in fact a move towards fundamental change. After three years at Ma-wei, Shen was ready to make that move.

By 1870 the first ships had been launched and the first groups of students had completed half their studies. It was a good time to reflect on past successes and failings and make changes for the future. The fact that the Navy Yard had to recruit men from the treaty ports and Hong Kong for the Navy Yard School, workshops, and steamers pointed up a major weakness in Chinese society: a shortage of men with even the most rudimentary knowledge of Western science or technology. And those who had acquired some knowledge did so through practical experience, not scientific understanding. So Shen and Governor-General Ying-kuei tried to rectify that situation.

In their opinion, the reason Westerners possessed superior ships and guns, and were able to improve them constantly, was that they excelled in mathematics. The Chinese, with the founding of government schools at Peking, the Kiangnan Arsenal, and the Foochow Navy Yard, had also

---

74 See, e.g., Feng Kuei-fen, *Chiao-pin-lu k'ang-i* (1898; reprint ed., Taipei, 1967), 2:68a–b.
75 Arnold Toynbee, *Mankind and Mother Earth: A Narrative History of the World* (London, 1976), p. 540.

begun to study mathematics. But they still had a long way to go. In order to make the study of mathematics appealing, especially to those from a respectable background, Shen and Ying-kuei proposed adding the subject to the civil service examinations. Those who could demonstrate their proficiency should be treated as people with an indispensable skill and given preferments in the Tsungli Yamen, other government offices, or arsenals and shipyards. As for those who possessed this special knowledge and had at the same time risen through the traditional civil service examinations, they should be even more highly rewarded so that they would be proud of their achievements and bear witness to the importance of the work undertaken at the arsenals and shipyards. When they were so encouraged, the number of experts and their knowledge would grow by the day.[76]

As its authors intended, the proposal, if adopted, would have widespread repercussions. People who entered the modern defence industry would have at least some knowledge of Western science and would appoach their tasks more scientifically. At the same time, those who were ambitious and eager to learn would find meaningful employment as they moved up the bureaucracy, beyond the confines of the small defence industry. In time this reform would successfully integrate the modernizing enterprises into the traditional system and alter the character of government officials and the scholar-gentry class.

The idea of using bureaucratic advancement to promote the study of mathematics was not new. In a treatise written in 1861, Feng Kuei-fen, when discussing the importance of mathematics to Western knowledge, proposed the award of a *chü-jen* degree to those who had mastered this knowledge and applied it.[77] In 1864 Li Hung-chang communicated to the Tsungli Yamen the idea of a new civil service examination for candidates specializing in technology so that more scholars would embrace the subject. The Yamen submitted his letter to the throne, but refrained from making any comment on changing the examination system.[78] Then, in 1867, Ting Jih-ch'ang, the treasurer of Kiangsu, also argued for adding mathematics and science to the civil service examinations. Li Hung-chang presented his memorandum to the throne, but nothing came of it.[79]

---

76 Shen K'o, 'Hsien Wen-su kung', pp. 37–8.
77 Feng Kuei-fen, *Chiao-pin-lu*, 2:68–9. For a partial translation of this essay, see Teng and Fairbank, *China's Response*, pp. 51–2.
78 *IWSM*, TC 25:10b; Liu Kwang-ching, 'The Confucian as Patriot and Pragmatist: Li Hung-chang's Formative Years, 1823–1866', *Harvard Journal of Asiatic Studies*, 30 (1970), 33–4.
79 *IWSM*, TC 55:6b–26.

The reform proposal by Ying-kuei and Shen, though not original, was nonetheless the first of its kind directly addressed to the throne. And in contrast to Li's and Ting's, it was specific and limited to mathematics – a tactic more likely to produce results. After all, mathematics, though scorned, had been an accepted discipline in China for more than two thousand years. Thus, the throne felt obliged to respond, whereas it did not in the other cases. Still, it found altering the examination system too drastic, but the reason it gave is as interesting as it is oblique: there was no one competent enough to conduct the examinations.[80] It is indeed ironic that this was precisely the excuse used by Wo-jen in 1867 for not establishing a school to teach mathematics, one the throne had itself rejected (see Chapter 6)!

This feeble, evasive imperial response may have encouraged Shen to renew his proposal in 1872. As if to meet the throne's challenge, he produced the names of two experts: Li Shan-lan and Yang Pao-ch'en, representing respectively the Western and the Chinese approach to mathematics. The examination on mathematics, he further proposed, should replace the outmoded military examination, which was still based on archery. If the study of mathematics was encouraged in this way, the Chinese could catch up with the West in a few decades.[81] Unwilling to give up, he repeated the proposal in 1874 and suggested also that those students of the T'ung-wen Kuan who excelled in mathematics be given junior positions in the Tsungli Yamen. If they did well, they should be promoted and treated as if they had risen through the regular civil service examinations. Again, the effort was in vain.[82]

Modernizing China's defence capabilities and erecting the first telegraph line

The Japanese invasion of Taiwan significantly affected Shen's overall effort at building a stronger China. Because of the expanded powers he was given during the incident, and the fact that his voice now carried greater weight in national affairs, he was able to introduce broad changes on Taiwan and in certain aspects of the empire's defence. The transformation of Taiwan, which he initiated, was of great importance. But it must be left to a future study. Here, we shall focus only on his actions that were directly related to *yang-wu*, matters that were an extension of his concerns as the director-general of a modern defence establishment.

80 *HFT*, II, 350.
81 Ibid., 349b–350.
82 Shen K'o, 'Hsien Wen-su kung', pp. 52–66.

The Japanese expedition to Taiwan was launched in late April 1874, ostensibly to punish the aborigines of the Botan (Mu-tan) tribe on Taiwan for killing fifty-four of the sixty-six shipwrecked Ryukyuan sailors in 1871. Since Japanese sovereignty over the Ryukyu Islands had never been recognized internationally and the landing of troops on Taiwan would constitute an act of war against China, the mission was prepared in utmost secrecy. The Chinese, hampered by slow communication and poor intelligence, were unable to take firm actions for some considerable time. Finally, acting on the advice of Li Hung-chang, the court sent Shen Pao-chen and a few ships to Taiwan under the guise of a routine patrol in order to keep an eye on Japanese movements.[83]

Shen's mission soon changed when it was learned that the expedition was a large one, thought to be 4,000 strong. On 29 May he was appointed imperial commissioner in charge of maritime defence and foreign affairs in relation to Taiwan. All the military and civil officials of Fukien from the brigade general and the taotai down were placed under his command, as were the steamships of the coastal provinces from Kiangsu to Kwangtung. The governors-general and the governors of these same provinces were to co-operate with him. Then, in response to his plan for defence, the court empowered him to use funds from Fukien and, if need be, raise foreign loans.[84]

Shen's plan was to settle the matter diplomatically and build up China's defences to take care of all contingencies. To the latter end, arms and munitions were bought, coal and gunpowder stockpiled, and spare-part production at the Navy Yard stepped up. To meet the Japanese navy boat for boat, Shen also recalled all but two of the Foochow vessels that had been stationed in other provinces. When he learned that the Japanese possessed two ironclads, he also began a search for ironclads. In addition, two steamships from the Kiangnan Arsenal were deployed, along with three of the Navy Yard's transports to bring troops from Li Hung-chang's Huai Army to Taiwan.[85]

83 Sophia Su-fei Yen, *Taiwan in China's Foreign Relations, 1836–1874* (Hamden, Conn., 1965), pp. 175–212; *CTSM*, vol. 1, pp. 1–4; *LWCK*, 'Letters', 13:33. On the international status of the Ryukyus, see Yen, *Taiwan*, pp. 157–8; Robert K. Sakai, 'The Ryukyu (Liu-ch'iu) Islands as a Fief of Satsuma', and Ta-tuan Ch'en, 'Investiture of Liu-ch'iu Kings in the Ch'ing Period', both in John K. Fairbank, ed., *The Chinese World Order* (Cambridge, Mass., 1968), pp. 112–34, 135–63, 311–20.

84 *CTSM*, vol. 1, pp. 5–8, 16–20.

85 Ibid., 13–14, 16–18, 24, 46–7, 121; Gabriel Lemaire to Ministère des Affaires Etrangères, 18 June 1874, in MAE, Dépêches politiques des consuls, Chine, vol. 2, p. 305; Li Hung-chang to Shen, 2 August 1874, in *LWCK*, 'Letters', 14:18a–b. Two Foochow vessels, the *Chen-hai* and the *Mei-yün*, remained at Tientsin and Newchwang respectively.

Among the measures Shen took, two deserve attention. First, he used the defence preparations to provide practical experience and training for the Navy Yard's personnel. Among the men he brought with him as he, Giquel, and de Segonzac set sail for Taiwan on 14 June were his right-hand man, Liang Ming-ch'ien, along with Chang Ssu-kuei and a dozen others. They were employed in defence planning and operations. Of course, Lo Ta-ch'un, the commander of the Ma-wei squadron, was sent for, but because his strength was on land, he was detailed to northern Taiwan to defend and open up the region. Instead, the British captain of a Maritime Customs Service steamer was hired to provide training in modern naval warfare for the six Navy Yard vessels stationed at the Pescadores. Meanwhile students of the Navy Yard School, six in marine engineering and four in practical navigation, were led by Chang Ssu-kuei and H. E. Hobson (commissioner of customs at Tamsui) to go to north-eastern Taiwan to survey and chart the land and nearby waters.[86] Our sources permit little more than a listing of these measures, but Shen's interest in extending the experience and training of his men is clearly evident. Lamentably, the practice of using students and cadets to chart coastal waters, which he pioneered, was not adopted by his successors at Ma-wei or their counterparts elsewhere.[87]

The second measure was even more innovative, for it involved the introduction of yet another type of modern technology to China, the telegraph. In managing the defence of Taiwan, Shen found that even the speed of the steamer was too slow for transmitting messages, where-upon he proposed a line linking Foochow, Ma-wei, Amoy, and Taiwan. Shen, in fact, had been aware of the advantages of the telegraph for some time and had wanted to see it introduced to China earlier. His thoughts on this matter over the years reflected an increasing commitment to the broader issues of modernization.

Shen's first known view on the telegraph became evident in 1865 when the Tsungli Yamen expressed concern about possible foreign requests to erect a line in China. Fearful that the speed of the telegraph, under foreign control, would undermine the empire's administrative integrity, Shen strongly opposed any such request. The speed with which the foreigners' steamships carried news had already tied the hands of the

---

86 *CTSM*, vol. 1, pp. 18, 27–8, 87; Pong, Introduction to Lo Ta-ch'un, *T'ai-wan*, pp. ii–iv; *SWSK*, 5:31; Shen's memorial, 13 November 1875 (KH 1.10.16), in YCT KH 1/10 *chung*; Gregory to Wade, 10 November 1874, in FO 228/542, no. 25, encl.: 'Official Record' dated 22 October 1874. In addition, thirteen Navy Yard officials were assigned to commissariats in various parts of the island, and fourteen others dispatched to Shanghai, Amoy, Hong Kong, etc., buying weapons and munitions (Shen's memorial of 13 November 1875).
87 Shen Yü-ch'ing, *T'ao-yüan chi*, p. 246.

Chinese government, he pointed out; the impact of a foreign-controlled telegraph line would be much worse. The Tsungli Yamen and all the high provincial officials concurred, except Li Hung-chang. Li, constantly pressed by foreigners to make the concession, suggested that, if the pressure became irresistible, the Chinese should meet the challenge by putting up their own lines.[88] His was the most advanced view in 1865.

By 1867 at the latest, Shen's position had changed. The Chinese, he now believed, could take advantage of the telegraph even if it were put up by foreigners. But means must be found to prevent damage to fields and graves. He likened the telegraph (and the railway) to the Great Wall of the Ch'in dynasty (221–206 B.C.), which, though considered a source of great calamity at the time of its construction, had benefited the Chinese ever since. Still, he had yet to think in terms of a Chinese line, as Li Hung-chang did.[89]

By 1870 Chinese resistance had collapsed and a foreign line was laid between Hong Kong and Shanghai. In retreat, the Tsungli Yamen and most of the provincial officials fought a rear-guard action against attempts to bring the line ashore. Shen rejected this negative policy and alone advocated hiring Western experts to build a line and to teach the Chinese all the essential skills. In this way, he said, 'control remains in our hands (*wo wo ch'i ch'üan*) and we can conduct our [official] business unhampered'.[90] The proposal fell on deaf ears in Peking.

Undaunted, Shen raised the matter with Li Hung-chang in early 1874, suggesting that Li, who had the territorial powers that he himself lacked, should start a line in Chihli. As he argued:

The foreigners have telegraphic lines linking Tientsin, Shanghai and Canton, and yet we have none. When something happens in the West, they all know about it while we remain ignorant. Though this can still be tolerated, how can we accept the fact that news about China are known to them and not to us?[91]

So when China urgently needed a telegraph line in mid-1874 he, now vested with territorial powers, reiterated his proposal and the throne approved.

Shen's plan was to run a line from Foochow to Ma-wei and Amoy, and then across the waters to T'ai-wan fu (modern Tainan). The history of its erection, however, is tortuous, replete with provincial politics, Peking diplomacy, officials at different locations working at cross purposes, and

88 *HFT*, IV, 5–20.
89 *IWSM*, TC 53:5a–b; 55:13–14.
90 *HFT*, IV, 88–96. Li Hung-chang was not consulted this time because he was then the governor-general of Hunan and Hupei, provinces not affected by the new line.
91 Shen to Li Hung-chang, 3 March 1874, in *HFT*, II, 504.

duplicity on the part of a nineteenth-century equivalent of a multinational corporation – the Danish Great Northern Company. The story has been told in great detail elsewhere.[92] Here we need only note that Shen's scheme eventually had to be abandoned, thanks to the Danish company's trickery and Governor-General Li Ho-nien's initial greed and subsequent opposition. Among the sections that survived was a short, 19-kilometre line from Nantai, the foreign settlement across the river from Foochow city, to Pagoda Anchorage, where foreign vessels were moored. Because it was designed to serve foreign commercial interests, the Danes assumed its entire cost. Li Ho-nien, greedy, took the bait and permitted its construction. It contributed little to China's defence needs, however, and was certainly not part of Shen's scheme. But since Li had given his approval, all Shen could do was to purchase it and use it partly for instructing Chinese youths in the art of telegraphy.[93]

Another section, forming part of the land line from Foochow to Amoy, had been partially completed at the time Shen left Ma-wei in late 1875 for his Liang Kiang governor-generalship. Again, its construction was undertaken with Li's approval without reference to Shen. The terms were extremely attractive but, in exchange, the Danish company was given the right to put up a second land line, parallel to the Chinese, and both were to be managed by the Danes. Hitherto, the Chinese had been vehemently opposed to any foreign-owned land lines (versus offshore lines with land terminals). Shen therefore bitterly protested and the Tsungli Yamen instructed Li to buy the line back. Li succumbed to the pressure, but secretly mobilized 'popular' opposition to the line, forcing its eventual removal. Subsequently, at Ting Jih-ch'ang's initiative and with Shen's blessing, the materials were salvaged and reassembled on Taiwan for two short lines connecting T'ai-wan fu with its defence outposts.[94] Despite the disappointing outcome, these were China's first telegraph lines, the results of Shen's effort.

Conclusions

Of the four areas in which Shen tried to broaden the base of China's defence modernization, the promotion of the new naval men and the

92 Huang Chia-mo, 'Chung-kuo tien-hsien ti ch'uang-chien', *Ta-lu tsa-chih*, 36.6–7 (April 1968), 171–87. Unless otherwise stated, my analysis, though quite different from Huang's, draws on the data in his article.
93 *NCH*, 27 June 1874; *HFT*, IV, 183, 195, 199–201.
94 Ibid., 123, 152, 191–3, 199–200, 203–4, 205, 211–13; Sinclair to Wade, 18 February 1875, in FO 228/554, Foochow, no. 2; *YWYT*, vol. 4, pp. 331–4, vol. 2, pp. 346–7; *Shih-lu*, KH 19:8; Wang Yen-wei and Wang Liang, comps., *Ch'ing-chi wai-chiao shih-liao* (Peiping, 1932–5), 10:12–13; Lü Shih-ch'iang, *Ting*, p. 303.

organization of the Foochow squadron can be regarded as a natural extension of the Navy Yard enterprise. Without a meaningful way to deploy the modern-trained young officers and organize their vessels in a single naval service, the Navy Yard could not have begun to fulfil its mission. Of the remaining three areas – the promotion of scientific learning, modern coal mining, and telegraphy – none was indispensable to the survival of the Navy Yard, but all were essential to its operational effectiveness and future development.

Shen's pursuit of each of these goals involved many years of effort. As regards the telegraph, it was his own attitude that had to change initially. Perhaps because the telegraph was not critical to the Navy Yard at first, he showed less insight on the matter until foreign-owned lines threatened Chinese administrative integrity in 1870. His view then took a sharp turn, calling for the erection of a Chinese line. The Japanese invasion of Taiwan then drove home the need for a telegraph network for the country's defence.

As for his other modernization efforts, he had little difficulty grasping their general significance or their particular relevance to the Navy Yard. But he pursued them with only various degrees of success. It comes as little surprise that the least innovative change – mechanized coal mining – met with the least resistance. After all, coal mining was a traditional occupation. And although modern coal mining was bound to effect drastic changes in the industry, not the least of which would be the congregation of a large labour force – a potential source of social disorder – its location in remote Taiwan mollified the opponents of *yang-wu*. Shen's proposals for modern coal mining consistently received imperial approval. The initial fear of foreign infiltration in the industry, the hostile political climate of the early 1870s, and the shortage of funds were the main causes of its tardy introduction.

By contrast, Shen's attempts to reform the examination system failed completely. The inclusion of mathematics in the examinations would have forced a revision of the philosophical foundation of the civil service system, modifying the qualities considered essential to the scholar-official since the rise of Neo-Confucianism nearly a thousand years earlier. It would also undermine the vested interests of the scholar-gentry class. An institutional change of this magnitude would require a strong, farsighted imperial leadership, which was conspicuously absent. Nonetheless, persistent imperial rejection does highlight the lengths to which Shen was willing to go in order to change the scholar-gentry class for the sake of a stronger China. His progressive ideas in this regard firmly place him alongside Li Hung-chang and Ting Jih-ch'ang as the most advanced *yang-wu* proponents among high officials of the early 1870s.

296

This chapter has shown that imperial approval was indispensable when significant departures from past practices were attempted. Then, as the changes were being implemented, the quality of central leadership assumed critical importance. The court's failure to grasp the nature of the squadron commander thus resulted in a poor choice of commander for the Foochow vessels. The eventual installation of a full-time commander who also had some knowledge of modern naval affairs was largely the product of Shen's perseverance.

In the mid-1870s the Navy Yard went through a critical transition. As modern-trained engineers and naval officers became available, their proper placement and deployment assumed great importance. Shen realized the weight of his responsibility and commissioned the young men as rapidly as possible. But he also had to avoid the disruptive measure of dislodging the old hands who had no modern training. So if he were to continue placing the new naval men at a steady pace, he would also have to expand the size of the Foochow squadron proportionately. This he was unable to do as funds started to dwindle.

In the mid-1870s, too, the Navy Yard had reached a point at which further growth would increasingly depend on changes elsewhere. Shen's grand scheme for change will be examined in the next chapter. Suffice it to note here that where he succeeded, his own power, in addition to central government support, was also an important factor. The eventual success in founding a mechanized coal mine was precisely the result of his appointment as imperial commissioner during the Taiwan crisis. But his appointment did not significantly diminish the authority of the high provincial officials at Foochow. If Governor-General Li Ho-nien felt threatened by Shen's new powers, he was no less responsible for the defences of his provinces. The situation was reminiscent of Tseng Kuo-fan's relationship with Shen during the early 1860s. But the analogy is somewhat misleading, for during the Taiping War Shen was placed by Tseng specifically to assist him, whereas in 1874 Shen's elevation was effected at Li's expense. Moreover, in the early 1860s Shen did not try to seize the initiative from Tseng by creating, for instance, his own army, whereas Li, as if to spite Shen, deliberately set out to establish a telegraph network under his own control in the full knowledge that negotiations were well under way between Shen, who was empowered to build the lines, and the Danish company. The fact that Li hitherto had not been a *yang-wu* advocate raises further questions about his motivation. His challenge to Shen was a power struggle, pure and simple. And when he accepted the terms of the Danish company, which disregarded all previous Chinese apprehensions about a foreign-controlled land line, Shen strenuously opposed them. In the end the whole scheme, including

Shen's own, had to be aborted. The struggle came to a fitting end as Li, upon Shen's promotion to the post of Liang Kiang governor-general, impeached Shen in the most intemperate terms. His protestations were ignored in Peking.[95]

In conclusion, we must stress that the Taiwan coal mine and the telegraph lines that Shen was able to salvage, despite their modest scale, were nonetheless the first of their kind in China. In a country that was slow to change, such innovations, even if they had little more than symbolic significance, were still milestones in the history of technology and industry in modern China. Their existence firmly established Shen as a pioneer and a promoter of innovative change.

95 Li's memorial, 17 September 1875 (KH 1.8.18), in YCT, KH 1/8.

11

Towards a plan for
self-strengthening

This study of Shen Pao-chen has reached a point where we can meaning-fully examine his grand scheme for building a stronger China. It has often been said that the Ch'ing Restoration failed because the reformers adopted aspects of Western technology and diplomatic methods (*yang-wu*) only to preserve the traditional order.[1] Therefore, to the extent that modernizers and their enterprises changed the world around them, they did so not so much by design, or even necessity, as by the inexorable seminal nature of the enterprises themselves. The issue is seldom seen from the perspective of those in charge of these undertakings, whose main concern may well have been to modify the outside world in order to make it more supportive of their labours. This chapter shows that Shen's plan for change was driven by this concern.

Shen was not given to discourses on comprehensive plans for change. Not that he was afraid of consequences. As a censor, he had been fearless in his criticism of the government. As the head of the Foochow Navy Yard, he had made numerous proposals for change. His proposals, however, were usually piecemeal, dealing with specific problems or needs as they arose. Indeed, he was known to his colleagues as a 'doer' rather than a 'theorist'. When comparing him with other reformers, Kuo Sung-tao spoke of him as the one who 'can put proposals into operation'.[2] Nevertheless, the ideas for reform and future development he put forward over the years did add up to a coherent programme, the backbone of which was highly apparent in his contributions to two major rounds of policy discussions in 1867 and 1874.

The policy discussions took place under very different circumstances.

---

1 Mary Wright, *Last Stand*, p. 312.
2 Kuo Sung-tao, *Yang-chih shu-wu wen-chi*, 11:10b; Frodsham, *First Chinese Embassy*, p. 109.

299

In 1867 the court, apprehensive of the upcoming negotiations on treaty revision with the Western powers, was concerned with defining China's interests beyond which no foreign demands could be entertained. The mood then was defensive. In 1874 the purpose was to generate ideas for defence modernization in the wake of the Japanese invasion. The mood, as the policy discussion opened, was expansive. Despite these differences in character and circumstance, Shen's ideas presented on these two occasions were largely consistent, a fact attributable to his growing awareness that foreign relations, internal affairs, and defence modernization were one indivisible whole.

Still, seven years separated the reform proposals, which virtually marked the beginning and the end of Shen's tenure at Ma-wei. It is to be expected that some of his ideas had changed in between. So to highlight the origins and the transformation of his more important ideas, reform proposals he presented at other times will also be discussed.

As we examine Shen's ideas, we shall see that his sentiments towards his country began to transcend patriotism, moving towards nationalism. Up to this point we have been describing his attitude and behaviour as patriotic, but without defining 'patriotism'. But as we oppose it to nationalism, a definition of both terms becomes necessary.

Patriotism and nationalism are largely compatible concepts and can be distinguished from each other only with difficulty.[3] Patriotism involves the love of one's country, including its laws, institutions, cultural heritage, and customs. Some scholars would insist that it is a higher feeling than that of allegiance and obligation to the sovereign. But in the case of traditional China, where the ruler could not be conceptually separated from the laws and institutions, loyalty and a sense of duty to the throne were a legitimate component of patriotism. When the term is understood in this way, we can say that Shen was patriotic.

Patriotism, like the love of one's parents, is largely a natural feeling. Nationalism, though it also involves the love of one's country, is more an acquired affection, a conscious awareness of the nation and its interests – territorial integrity, political independence, economic well-being, and so on. Above all, it is a state of mind in which the nation-state commands the supreme loyalty of the individual. Ch'ing China was not a nation-state, but if there arose a consciousness that put the interests and fate

---

3 The definitions of both terms, but particularly that of nationalism, are complex. Here the differences are emphasized for the sake of analytical clarity. The following passages, apart from references to Ch'ing China, are based on Hans Kohn, *Nationalism* (Princeton, N.J., 1955), pp. 9–15; Louis L. Snyder, *The New Nationalism* (Ithaca, N.Y., 1968), pp. 2–8; and Roger Scruton, *A Dictionary of Political Thought* (New York, 1982), pp. 315–16, 347–8.

of the country before its laws, intitutions, or heritage, it can be said that that consciousness approached nationalism. This, I submit, was increasingly Shen's state of mind from the late 1860s, one that led him to his bold reform proposals.

The way of self-strengthening

In late 1867 the Tsungli Yamen, in preparation for the forthcoming negotiations on treaty revision, solicited opinions from eighteen high provincial officials. To open up the discussion, it listed six areas where the Western powers were likely to make their demands for diplomatic, commercial, and missionary expansion. In response, Shen, combining his experience as a territorial official and his new exposure to a modernizing enterprise at Ma-wei, came forward with a powerful statement that wide-ranging reforms would be required to improve China's international position. Thus, as he called upon the throne to reject all major concessions, he volunteered a treatise on the meaning and the way of self-strengthening.[4]

He began with the proposition that, in the conduct of foreign affairs, as 'in managing the affairs of state, if we are in control, then even the difficult matters will become easy, whereas if everything is controlled by others, then even the easiest will become difficult'.[5] But the Chinese in their dealings with the West since the Opium War had no long-term plans, dealing with the crises only as they arose. They thus fumbled repeatedly, making concession after concession. So even if the foreigners made no further demands this time around, the Chinese had already lost control over their economic rights (*li-ch'üan*) and administrative integrity (*shih-ch'üan*). To increase China's options, the Chinese must seek new purpose (*pieh-ch'iu hsin-i*) in dealing with the West and, at the same time, strengthen themselves (*tzu-ch'iang*, lit., self-strengthening).

China's troubles were both internal and external. Self-strengthening, therefore, must be predicated upon the ability of the Chinese to govern themselves effectively (*tzu-chih*, lit., self-government). And since neither the outside threats could be removed in a single battle nor the internal problems rectified in a single day, both self-strengthening and effective government must involve sustained efforts. Shen thus implored the emperor to remind his ministers constantly of the catastrophe of 1860

---

4 *IWSM*, TC 50:24–35; 53:1–29b. On the policy disccusion, see Knight Biggerstaff, 'The Secret Correspondence of 1867–1868: Views of Leading Chinese Statesmen Regarding the Further Opening of China to Western Influence', *Journal of Modern History*, 22 (1950), 122–36; Mary Wright, *Last Stand*, pp. 271–7.
5 *IWSM*, TC 53:1.

and instruct them to shed all habits of window dressing and get down to the real substance of government.

In Shen's opinion, effective government depended on four broad areas of reform. First, the teachings of the sages should be studied and applied. These teachings, however, should not be confused with the scholarly pursuits of the literati, whose encyclopaedic knowledge and high-sounding philosophical discourses were hardly essential to self-cultivation or solving the larger problems of society. The emperor should therefore learn the moral principles of government from the interpretive histories of Confucius, Tso Ch'iu-ming, and the Sung Neo-Confucianists Ssu-ma Kuang and Chu Hsi.[6] He should then apply them to concrete political situations in his daily discussions with his ministers. A new trend would then be set and the officials would soon follow the imperial example.

This last suggestion betrays considerable Confucian idealism, but the idea of applying the more pragmatic Confucian works to concrete administrative matters was sound advice in the Ch'ing context. Shen himself derived much wisdom from these classics as he proposed sweeping changes in administrative practices and government structure – his second group of reform proposals. Thus, his call for the proper use of men – the Confucian key to good government – was in fact a means to return to a more pragmatic and better informed government. For example, the grand councillors should be assisted by an experienced provincial official such as Tseng Kuo-fan or Tso Tsung-t'ang so that they would be more aware of conditions outside the imperial capital. At the same time, officials with little administrative experience should be given practical training. And the Hanlin scholars, the cream of the Confucian elite, should be detailed to the Grand Council and the Tsungli Yamen to gain practical experience; they should not preoccupy themselves with literary refinement. Indeed, to steer the entire literati towards pragmatism in government, all examinations on literary art forms should be jettisoned.

Shen's concern with pragmatic government inevitably led to a proposal for greater specialization and the removal of wastefulness. The presidents and vice-presidents of the six boards should therefore be assigned specialized duties, and provincial capitals with both a governor-general and a governor should have the latter office abolished.[7] But Shen

6 The works were the *Ch'un-ch'iu* (Spring and autumn annals), the *Tso-chuan* (Commentary of Tso), the *Tzu-chih t'ung-chien* (General mirror for the aid of government), and the *T'ung-chien kang-mu* (Outline and digest of the general mirror).

7 The governorships of Fukien, Kwangtung, Hupei, and Yunnan. The last three were eventually abolished in 1904–5. That of Fukien had earlier been moved to the new province of Taiwan in 1885.

was even more concerned with streamlining the government structure to make it at once more efficient and more responsive to the needs of the people. The taotai, whom he considered an unnecessary barrier between the governor and the local officials, should be removed. At the same time, local government should extend further down, with new administrative units at the subvillage level and their officials partly appointed by the government and partly elected by the people, as in Han times. Then, to ensure that local conditions were represented and the emperor informed, only magistrates with a good record should be made censors. In this way, the rulers and the ruled would have common interests and become one.

Turning to military affairs Shen, curiously, barely touched upon military modernization, perhaps reflecting the defensive mood of the policy discussion in which modern inventions were seen as instruments of Western encroachment, or perhaps the creation of the new arsenals and shipyards convinced him that further discussion at this juncture would serve no purpose. At any rate, he focused on improving traditional methods: the mounting of cannons on war carriages and deploying them in formation, and the use of traditional warships, again mounted with cannons, to be reinforced by modern gunboats as they became available. As regards internal security – the Nien and the Muslim rebels were still a threat – Shen returned to a proposal he made as a censor back in 1854: for defence purposes, place local troops under local officials (prefects and magistrates), but deal with major rebel groups by means of a large, mobile army. In this way the tactic of clearing the countryside and protecting the people in fortified towns (*chien-pi ch'ing-yeh*) would become effective.

In the final group of proposals, Shen dealt with the problem of food supply in case of emergency, especially in the Peking region. Shipping grain to the north on the poorly maintained Grand Canal had proved expensive and unreliable. Shen's solution was to use the traditional water force to carry the grain by sea. In this way, the government could reap the triple benefit of economy, security of the imperial capital, and an alert and active water force.

A little more than four years later, in response to Sung Chin's criticism of the Foochow Navy Yard, Shen underlined that self-strengthening was concerned with defending the country and preventing future disasters.[8] Given the context in which the remark was made, Shen's focus on military matters was understandable. But in 1867 he was emphatic that internal reform was critical to the whole self-strengthening effort. The

---

8 Shen's memorial of 7 May 1872 in *YWYT*, vol. 5, p. 113.

Chinese must first put their house in order before they could deal effectively with *yang-wu*.

'It would be absurd if we did not strive for self-strengthening now', Shen proclaimed.[9] In his thinking, self-strengthening was not an option, for China's survival was at stake. It follows that if the traditional system could not function efficiently to deal with the problems of a new age, it would have to be changed. Making skilful use of historical precedents, he came up with a plan that included some very sweeping reforms. Only one other official, Ting Jih-ch'ang, proposed reforms that rivalled Shen's in breadth and audacity.[10]

Nevertheless, not all his proposals were forward-looking. His ideas on military affairs and granaries were the stock-in-trade of practical statecraft proponents a generation earlier. And there was another, more serious flaw in his thinking. Although he recognized the interdependence between *yang-wu* and effective civil government, his treatise implies that he still saw the two as separate components. In consequence, some of the administrative and structural changes in government he advocated were only marginally designed to accommodate or promote *yang-wu* modernization. It would take him several years of experience at Ma-wei before he realized that the continued growth of *yang-wu* modernization would require more than sound civil government; it would demand specific institutional changes. His proposal for changes in the civil service examinations to accommodate mathematics in 1870 was an example.

Towards a stronger and richer China

By the time of the great policy debate in late 1874, Shen had directed the Foochow Navy Yard for more than seven years; his ideas had progressed markedly. Recent events also coloured his views: the major rebellions had been quashed, and Tso Tsung-t'ang's campaign was beginning to bear fruit; only the foreign powers continued to threaten the empire's security. The fact that Japan had also become a threat compelled Shen to focus his discussions not only on military preparedness but also on military modernization. More important still, he was now firmly convinced that defence modernization must entail fundamental changes in the ways things were managed in the entire civil administration and that new institutions had to be created to accommodate new methods.

These ideas were spelled out in a memorial following the Tsungli Yamen's call for proposals on how to improve China's defence efforts.

9 *IWSM*, TC 53:26.
10 Pong, 'The Vocabulary of Change: Reformist Ideas', pp. 44–9.

Issued on 5 November 1874, the call was a direct reaction to the Peking Agreement, which settled the dispute with the Japanese over the Taiwan affair. In this agreement, the Chinese, acknowledging that the Japanese expedition was justified, agreed to pay an indemnity of 500,000 taels and take steps to control the savage tribes on Taiwan for the safety of international shipping.[11] Such a one-sided settlement in favour of a party whose justification for the expedition was at best dubious underscored China's weakness. The agreement was a disappointment to Shen, who blamed the diplomatic failure on his inadequate defence preparations, and to the Tsungli Yamen, which pointed its finger at all who had failed in fourteen years of self-strengthening.[12]

Shen's defence measures, in fact, were quite adequate: they held the Japanese at a standstill, enabling him to reject all Japanese demands for an indemnity during negotiations on Taiwan. It was only when the Japanese took the matter to Peking that the Chinese central government mistakenly took a 'disparaging view of her own power' and acceded to the Japanese demands.[13]

Clearly, slow communication and poor intelligence on the part of the central government had cost the Chinese dearly. Be that as it may, the object lesson learned by the Chinese was that their efforts at self-strengthening had fallen short. Shen accepted this conclusion and pressed for sweeping changes.

The Tsungli Yamen's call for proposals, addressed to fifteen high officials of the coastal and Yangtze provinces, sparked off a major policy debate that lasted more than eight months. The debate has been studied from various angles.[14] Here we shall focus on the Yamen's invitation and Shen's response: his assessment of past successes and failures and his vision of the future.

The Yamen's agenda contained six objectives which it considered critical to China's defence. They were laid out in detail and the respondents

11 Yen, *Taiwan*, pp. 281–4.
12 *YWYT*, vol. 1, pp 26–7.
13 Pong, 'Modernization and Politics', pp. 299–304. The quote comes from Parkes's letter to Wade, 16 February 1875, in FO 228/559.
14 See, e.g., Immanuel C. Y. Hsü, 'The Great Policy Debate in China, 1874: Maritime Defense vs. Frontier Defense', *Harvard Journal of Asiatic Studies*, 25 (1964–5), 212–28; Liu Kwang-ching, 'Li Hung-chang in Chihli: The Emergence of a Policy, 1870–1875', in Albert Feuerwerker, Rhoads Murphey, and Mary C. Wright, eds., *Approaches to Modern Chinese History* (Berkeley and Los Angeles, 1967), esp. pp. 92–103; Liu Shih-chi, 'Ch'ing-chi hai-fang yü sai-fang chih cheng ti yen-chiu', *Ku-kung wen-hsien*, 2.3 (June 1971), 37–59. Most studies tend to focus on the opposing views regarding maritime and frontier defence. Two exceptions are Kwang-ching Liu's and my own: 'Shen Pao-chen and the Great Policy Debate of 1874–1875', *Proceedings of the Conference on the Self-Strengthening Movement in Late Ch'ing China, 1860–1894* (Taipei: Institute of Modern History, Academia Sinica, 1988). My analysis here takes a different approach.

asked to discuss their content, suggest means for implementation, and make further suggestions. Hitherto unknown to scholars, the objectives were as follows:[15]

1. Military training should be stepped up and new units formed by selecting the best men from the old land and water forces. In particular, China must develop a naval force capable of attacking, intercepting, and giving chase to an enemy fleet.
2. The Chinese had been producing inferior weapons. They should purchase advanced and up-to-date weapons from the West and learn to make them.
3. The existing shipbuilding effort had to be upgraded and supplemented by the purchase of newer or larger vessels, ironclads, and the new heavy guns that could penetrate ironclads. Additional shipyard facilities thus had to be considered for building or repairing these new warships.
4. Large sums of money would be needed to finance these projects and the accompanying support or subsidiary industries. An overall plan must be made and spending prioritized. Beyond capital investment, new sources of income had to be developed and corruption curbed in order to provide funds for development and growth.
5. None of these goals could be achieved without the proper use of men. The Yamen therefore recommended the appointment of a commander-in-chief (*t'ung-shuai*), one familiar with foreign affairs, and he was to be assisted by a host of commanders. Candidates for these positions were to be nominated by the high officials and appointments made only after open and extensive consultation.
6. Once these self-strengthening undertakings were launched, every effort should be made to ensure their continuation. Since foreign threats represented China's greatest danger, those in responsible positions must hold fast to the objectives once they had been decided upon. These objectives should therefore be carefully arrived at, and only after opinions from all quarters had been considered. And if there were serious disagreements on particular goals, it would be better not to pursue them so as to avoid abandonment in midcourse.

Though narrowly focused on defence, the Yamen's suggestions indicated a willingness to change or abandon old practices in favour of a new military structure, improved training, as well as the upgrading of support facilities and defence industries. Learning from past failings, it was now prepared to face squarely the prickly problem of funding and spending priorities for the entire defence effort. And in the hope of producing a general defence modernization policy that was consistent and would enjoy sufficiently broad support, it also invited opinions on conflict resolution within the government.

15 *SCTI*, vol. 6, pp. 2610–14.

Following imperial instructions, Shen discussed in detail the Yamen's suggestions.[16] For the sake of clarity, his ideas will be analysed under the following heads: arms production, military training and organization, financial matters, and the politics of defence modernization.

First, on arms production, Shen recognized the inferiority of Chinese-made weapons and gunboats. To make matters worse, they were constantly rendered obsolete by Western advances. Although this technological gap could be somewhat narrowed by the purchase of Western weapons and ships, Shen doubted the foreigners' willingness to sell warships in good condition to the Chinese. So in addition to what could be judiciously bought, the Chinese must continue to make their own arms and warships. They might even have to contemplate building ironclads, which Shen considered the warship of the future. The Japanese, he noted, had already acquired dockyard facilities that could repair these vessels. The Chinese must therefore learn and master modern technology and try to catch up as much as possible, even in the knowledge that they would always be left behind by Western technological advances. Echoing his proposal of 1872, he strongly urged that young military and naval engineers be sent abroad for further studies.

Shen's most important contribution to the discussion of arms production was the idea of centralized planning and organization. As in the West, arms production should be based on a large number of complementary industrial plants, each manufacturing specialized, interchangeable parts that would be later assembled into a single weapon. In this way, the weapons would be of high quality and the empire's forces would be uniformly equipped.

Second, on military training and organization, Shen favoured Western-style drill and, departing from his earlier position, totally rejected the notion that men from the old land and water forces could be transformed into modern troops. His own attempt to train men from the water forces on Foochow Navy Yard vessels had failed utterly. For the land forces, he advocated modern training for the *yung* (mercenary) forces, which, as his personal experience showed, had proved their worth in the Taiping War. Since the *yung* had no naval counterparts, he favoured enlisting men

16 Shen's memorial of 23 December 1874. Three versions of the memorial exist: Shen K'o, 'Hsien Wen-su kung', pp. 50–68; Ko Shih-chün, *Huang-ch'ao ching-shih-wen*, 101: 8b–11; and Republic of China, Palace Museum, Taipei: 'Chün-chi ch'ü' [Grand Council Archives], no. 118328. The first, in manuscript form, differs slightly from the other two. Because we are as much concerned with Shen's ideas as his actual proposals, all versions will be used in this analysis. Only the last version gives the date of the memorial.

from the country's vast fishing population, who, he claimed, would be amenable to modern training.

Shen hastened to add that military effectiveness went far beyond individual training and valour. Rather, it came from a high degree of co-ordination among the men and, in the case of the artillery, a scientific approach to warfare. Commanders and officers must therefore be familiar with modern warfare. Concerning the army, Shen suggested that each province choose one or two commanders – those humble enough to learn – to train ten or twenty thousand *yung* troops with the help of a Western military expert. As for naval commanders and officers, he looked to the youths who were then studying in the United States and the Foochow Navy Yard School graduates after they had had several years of advanced training in Europe. Meanwhile, captains already in the service should be trained in naval manoeuvres by a British naval officer.

One of the Tsungli Yamen's proposals that had strong implications for modernization concerned the appointment of a commander-in-chief supported by a full hierarchy of commanders and officers. For the top military post, Shen recommended either Li Hung-chang or Tso Tsung-t'ang, but he skirted the issue of a centralized national military structure, at which the Yamen hinted. This is curious, for Shen generally favoured central control and planning, as in arms production and budgeting (see later). Perhaps Shen, as he looked around, could see no pool of officers from which a national military command could be created, the same problem he encountered earlier with the establishment of a navy.

In fact, Shen was deeply troubled by the shortage of men with modern training at every level of China's defence effort. In consequence, modernizing enterprises suffered from the lack of effective direction. Thus, at the Foochow Navy Yard, the foremen were not as well trained as the apprentices, the gentry administrators less knowledgeable than the foremen, and so on up to Shen himself. Were it directed by one with a sound knowledge of modern science and technology, how much greater would its achievements be! Therefore, the Chinese must lose no time in cultivating future talent.

Thus far, modern training had been localized and haphazard. To cultivate future leaders in sufficient numbers, Shen advocated the encouragement of 'true learning' (*shih-hsüeh*, lit. substantial learning), which combined Confucian principles with modern scientific knowledge. He called upon the scholar-gentry class to study science (*ke-chih*), 'learn what is useful, apply it, and become useful persons'. And in a remarkable statement two decades before his Navy Yard student Yen Fu introduced social Darwinism to China, he warned, 'Only those good at adapting themselves to the circumstances are destined to survive'. This, he proclaimed, was the prescription for self-strengthening.[17]

To provide incentives, Shen was prepared to see changes in established practices and institutions. In the West, he pointed out, whether in military affairs or in industry, everyone was given specialized training. In Prussia, schools were established for every vocation, and attendance was compulsory.[18] To move China in a similar direction, he proposed for the third time since 1870 the institution of an examination on mathematics, frankly admitting that this would be the quickest and most efficient way to encourage and cultivate China's men of talent. At the same time the government should make full use of the fruits of earlier reforms. Thus, the best graduates of the Peking T'ung-wen Kuan should be sent to the Tsungli Yamen for practical training and, on the basis of their performance, be given official preferment as if they had gone through the civil service examinations. And those who had successfully completed their studies abroad should be treated even better. In the new climate that would then prevail, many would take up the new learning. Soon there would be an ample supply of men of talent.

Third, on the question of funding, Shen, frustrated by the endless hassles for monies for the Foochow Navy Yard, called for central planning and budgeting. Like the Navy Yard, most of the modern defence projects were funded by the so-called 60 per cent receipts of the Maritime Customs Service, whereas the revenue from the 40 per cent account was to be remitted to the Board of Revenue in Peking. Over the years, as expenditures in the provinces grew, the receipts of the 60 per cent account became inadequate, and large amounts of money had to be 'temporarily shifted' to it from the 40 per cent account. Since the monies transferred were never returned, remittances to the Board diminished. Meanwhile, confusion reigned. The Board and the Tsungli Yamen, ignorant of the funds actually available at the various customs, were in no position to make overall planning. From now on, Shen proposed, the provinces should submit accurate and detailed reports on customs receipts, pin-pointing shortfalls in the 60 per cent account so as to facilitate prioritizing by the Board.

On developing new sources of revenue, Shen rejected a number of options: foreign loans which were simply a way of mortgaging the country's future income; the sale of examination degrees, which would lower the

17 The passage paraphrased in the last two sentences appears in Shen K'o, 'Hsien Wen-su kung', pp. 67–8, and not in Ko Shih-chün, *Huang-ch'ao ching-shih-wen*. On the introduction of social Darwinism, see Schwartz, *In Search of Wealth and Power*, pp. 42–7.
18 This passage appears in Shen K'o, 'Hsien Wen-su kung', p. 65, and not in Ko Shih-chün, *Huang-ch'ao ching-shih-wen*.

quality of the bureaucracy; and raising duties on foreign trade, which would surely face foreign opposition, inhibit trade, and encourage customs evasion. Turning the salt monopoly system into a completely government-run enterprise and tightening up land tax collection were also rejected, because the real gains in revenue would be small while too many officials would use the measures to line their pockets and harass the common folk. Instead, Shen advocated the exploitation of natural resources, such as coal, camphor, petroleum, and sulphur. To curtail wastefulness, he called for the abolition of the obsolete military examinations and, repeating proposals made in 1867, grain transport on the Grand Canal as well as provincial governorships in cities where there was already a governor-general. 'If we could cut wastefulness by 10 per cent', he said, 'we would gain just that much for truly worthwhile undertakings'.

Finally, Shen tackled the political problems of defence modernization: how to ensure its uninterrupted development in the face of deeply divided opinions. Here he proffered a new attitude towards conflict resolution. Because self-strengthening was a reality that could not be wished away, he appealed to those committed to its cause not to dispose of outside criticism lightly as frivolous talk, and he urged those not directly taking part in it to be more sympathetic. If everyone would speak his mind without the slightest reserve and not mindlessly agree with everyone else, there would be true harmony, and only then could all indifferent and heedless adherence to routine be excised.

As if to goad the empire's ruling elite into this novel kind of behaviour, he called for the awakening of a new spirit to combat the problems of the time:

When people are indignant, they will become aroused and exert themselves; when they are gratified, they will become lazy. But if those with whom the affairs of the state rest will always remind themselves of the humiliation of 1860, then who can for a single moment cast away the thought of self-strengthening?

To Shen's way of thinking, if those in government embraced this patriotic sentiment and the new approach to resolving differences, they could begin to work for the sustained development of all the self-strengthening efforts. Thus, as he closed his discussion, he amplified some of the important measures he recommended earlier. First, priorities must be set aright to ensure sufficient funds for self-strengthening projects. Otherwise, squabbles would emerge, inviting criticism from all sides. Second, if things were mismanaged, the responsible persons should by all means be criticized, but the projects themselves should not be jeopardized. Further, since the problems of self-strengthening were different from ordinary official matters, those engaged in it should be given wider latitude and discretion, and not be hamstrung by rigid rules and regulations. Only then could new things be learned and changes for the better be introduced. This, Shen emphasized, was the proper approach to self-strengthening. Quoting the *Book of Changes*, he said, 'When a system is exhausted, it must be modified; when modified, it will work; and if it works, it will endure'.

Space permits an evaluation of only the most important features of Shen's proposals in the context of the entire policy debate of 1874–5.[19] One quality which stands out is his pragmatic and utilitarian approach. As a rule the measures he recommended were feasible, especially from a budgetary standpoint. Moreover, the changes he proposed were almost always the first step towards a larger goal, to wit, the reform of the civil service examinations as the first stage of transforming the traditional elite.

In fact, cultivating a new modernizing elite and retraining scholar-officials were most central to Shen's concerns. Of the other fourteen officials who took part in the policy discussion, only Li Hung-chang urged a similarly fundamental and comprehensive reform.[20] In one respect Li went even further, proposing a 'bureau of Western studies' (*yang-hsüeh chü*) for each of the coastal provinces. Both he and Shen advocated changes in the examination system and in placing graduates of schools of Western learning in regular government posts after they had proved their worth. Shen was naturally interested in opening new channels for upward mobility for the young men trained at the Foochow Navy Yard, but this was no selfish move, for the new opportunities would be open to all. On the need to send students abroad, Shen was most emphatic, but he was supported only by Li Hung-chang and Li Tsung-hsi (governor-general of Liang Kiang).[21] Few, with the exception of Li Han-chang, the brother of Hung-chang, concerned themselves with the new learning at all, and only three others favoured rapid promotion for those who possessed special skills, irrespective of their educational background.[22]

By the 1870s, Western firearms and military drill were no longer a novelty. But in 1874 Shen was alone in identifying two other important remedies for China's military services: specialized training according to the weapons adopted, and the training of new, and retraining of

---

19 For a fuller analysis, see Pong, 'Shen'.
20 *YWYT*, vol. 1, pp. 40–54; Liu Kwang-ching, 'Li Hung-chang', pp. 96–7.
21 Li Tsung-hsi's memorial, *YWYT*, vol 1, pp. 69–76.
22 Li Han-chang's memorial, ibid., pp. 65–9. The three were Li Tsung-hsi, Ying-han, and Yü-lu. Ibid., 69–76, and *IWSM*, TC 99:2b–12b.

incumbent, commanders and officers. China's eventual failure to produce a competent officer corps, as Mary Wright pointed out, was a major reason for its military weakness.[23]

In the policy debate, Ting Jih-ch'ang proposed the creation of three regional fleets with a total of forty-eight ships. Li Hung-chang embraced the scheme emphatically, insisting that it represented the barest minimum. Shen, too, subscribed to the idea of three large regional fleets, but only as a future goal.[24] For the present he favoured a gradualistic approach, stressing the need for further introduction of Western military and naval technology, the construction of modern warships, progressing towards the larger and more advanced vessels and the training of naval officers and men.

Behind Shen's enthusiasm for naval development was the realization that the modern navy was designed more for intercepting and attacking an enemy fleet than just coastal and harbour defence. But this new strategic concept, spelled out by the Tsungli Yamen, found little support elsewhere. Most would follow Wei Yüan's advice expounded a generation earlier, arguing for port and riverine defence.[25] Even Li Hung-chang favoured a more positioned, shore-oriented defence. Thus, in terms of naval strategy, Shen's thinking was more expansive, whereas Li's was more immediately feasible.

Faithful to his utilitarian approach, Shen, like Li Hung-chang, did not hesitate to call for the replacement of useless practices and institutions. His proposal to end the transport of tribute grain on the Grand Canal was intended to cut expenses and boost the business of the China Merchants' Steam Navigation Company, itself a new vehicle for producing revenue. But in promoting mercantile interests, Li's ideas were more far-reaching. Already, he was speaking of 'commercial war' (*shang-chan*), which led him to suggest such an unorthodox option as legalizing opium cultivation in China. Shen, who tended to stay much closer to Confucian values, would never have gone this far.

There were flaws in Shen's proposals. His claim that Chinese fishermen could be transformed into modern naval men was too optimistic. And he addressed the traditional disdain for manual labour and physical exertions only obliquely even though he emphasized modern, specialized, and practical training for all, from the lowly mechanics and soldiers to the gentry or official administrators and commanders. But no one else dealt with this problem, either.

23 Mary Wright, *Last Stand*, p. 220.
24 *YWYT*, vol. 1, pp. 30–3, 40–54, 76–7.
25 Wang Chia-chien, *Wei Yüan*, p. 83.

All in all, Shen's proposals constituted a coherent and comprehensive programme for modernizing China. It was the fruit of almost eight years of practising *yang-wu* and, before that, several years of thinking about the matter. In 1867 he had already sensed the importance of practical training for Hanlin scholars and was fully aware of the advantages of sea transport for government grain as well as the opening of government coal mines. He also urged greater specialization in central and provincial administration, and pointed up the need to centralize coastal defence efforts. By 1874, his views on these topics had advanced considerably, betraying a willingness to use Western (modern) ideas and methods to solve both *yang-wu* and traditional problems. Not only did he advocate practical training for officials but now he also wanted to bring men with new skills into the bureaucracy and incumbents to retrain and undergo fundamental changes in attitude. On defence matters, his understanding that warfare had to be scientific and that technological progress was predicated upon efficient co-ordination of complementary industrial undertakings was also a step in the right direction. The antiquated ideas on military reforms he expounded in 1867 were no longer to be heard.

In both 1867 and 1874 he stressed that sociopolitical reforms of the traditional system and *yang-wu* modernization were mutually dependent and that all forms of change would have to be pragmatic. Efficiency and utility were his criteria. The government structure itself would have to be streamlined. In all cases, overall planning was essential, and that would require strong imperial and central leadership as well as open-minded policy discussions among officials. Everyone should feel that he had a stake in the empire.

Despite the threads that ran through both policy discussions, two features stood out in his 1874 deliberations. First, in the second part of the nineteenth century, the Chinese were faced with a daunting problem – the ever-widening technological gap between China and the West. Shen was keenly aware of the problem, yet he was not intimidated by it. Instead, he urged an unceasing effort to narrow that gap even without the prospect of closing it. As he had demonstrated through his repeated but failed attempts to introduce certain reforms, such as the incorporation of mathematics into the examination system, he was persistent and wanted to 'play catch-up' regardless.

The second, which was of even greater significance, was the drastic transformation in Shen's attitude towards some of the inherited institutions as well as the cultivation of a new elite. The latter, if implemented, would have irreversibly changed the character of the civil service and seriously undermined the enormous vested interests of the scholar-gentry class, the pillar of the old society. Shen was prepared to go so far because

313

he had become increasingly concerned with the fate of China, perhaps more so than with preserving the old order. Already, in 1867, he had advocated a restructuring of the political system to accommodate the lower strata of society, even to the extent of introducing local elections at the subvillage level. Administrative effectiveness was only part of the motive; the more important part was to create a sense of oneness and belonging, so that more and more people would support the government and the latter would be more capable of mobilizing the country's human and natural resources. By 1874 Shen had begun to see China as something larger than its inherited sociopolitical order. He had reached a higher stage of political consciousness, one that approached nationalism.

Conclusion

In the Introduction we identified four stages in the history of reform in the last hundred years or so of the Ch'ing. These stages often overlapped, and a reformer could easily graduate from one to the next, thus highlighting the continuity of that reform tradition. The first stage was ushered in by members of the School of Practical Statecraft, who diagnosed the dynastic decline. They expressed their concern by diligently attending to administrative details and public works and were not afraid to tamper with time-honoured but ineffective institutions. Theirs was a response to an internal crisis.

By the 1830s and 1840s, some of these scholar-officials, now joined by others, began to react to the new threat from the West. Patriotic sentiments emerged, as did the idea of adopting Western military technology to curb foreign encroachments. But it is often overlooked that they also advocated a selective renovation of inherited institutions in order to accommodate and maximize the benefits of the new technology. The civil service examination system, one of the most sacrosanct institutions of the state, was a main target of reform.[1] This willingness to modify traditional institutions and practices greatly adds to the significance of this second phase of reform.

When Shen began his education, he was exposed only to the practical statecraft ideas of the first stage. When he came of age, the reform ideas of the first two stages had already merged into a single tradition. At Canton, his father-in-law, Lin Tse-hsü, and his associates were putting these ideas into practice, trying to make Western-style warships and guns or seeking knowledge of Western countries and international law. Isolated and short-lived though these efforts were, they, because of

---

1 Wang Te-chao, *Ch'ing-tai k'o-chü chih-tu yen-chiu* (Hong Kong, 1982), p. 173.

his father-in-law's involvement, deeply influenced Shen. His growing patriotism might also have been fired by the conflicts surrounding the opening of his home-town as a treaty port. Be that as it may, the young Shen understandably channelled his energy towards passing the civil service examinations at this time. Then, for more than a decade after 1847 he was sheltered from China's 'Western problem', as an official first in Peking and then in the rebel-ridden provinces.

During his self-imposed retirement in 1859–61 at Foochow, now a treaty port, Shen might have become acquainted with the character of the Western presence. But on this our sources are silent. From early 1862 on, however, he was increasingly exposed to Western contact on all fronts. By this time, the third stage of reform – the Ch'ing Restoration – had already begun. The rehabilitation of areas recaptured from rebels, though spotty in many cases, was well under way. And with the founding of the Tsungli Yamen in 1861, *yang-wu* modernization was launched. Both these dimensions – reconstruction and *yang-wu* – can be traced to the earlier stages of reform. There was much ideological continuity. On the surface, therefore, it seemed that Shen, who had imbibed the earlier reformist ideas, should make his entry to the third stage of reform with ease.

In the sphere of internal reforms, this was indeed so. In Kiangsi, he worked closely with Tseng Kuo-fan to perfect a tax-reduction programme. He also restructured the province's financial administration and tried to raise the quality of government as well as the moral fibre of the scholar-gentry class. The province-wide Restoration in Kiangsi began with him.

In ideological terms, his involvement in *yang-wu* should not be difficult to explain either. But, politically and personally, his passage from traditional bureaucrat to modernizer was not an easy one. Recalling his early brushes with the French missionary and U.S. salt smugglers, it is understandable that he should find Westerners repugnant. Many who had had similar experiences were repelled by everything foreign. It took a 'higher' form of emotion – his patriotism – to open his eyes to the benefits of certain Western technological wonders.

If his 'conversion' to *yang-wu* was understandable, his total immersion in it as head of a navy yard utterly confounded his contemporaries. It quickly became a 'conversation piece', for no one of his rank and prestige had ever taken such a plunge or made such a radical break in his career. At the time he accepted the post, peace had been restored to most of the empire, and as soon as he had completed mourning his mother's death, he could have expected a high-level appointment, one that could now be enjoyed in an age of relative tranquillity. A governorship in an important province was certainly in order; a governor-generalship would not have been out of line. All was cast to the wind as he accepted a job that carried with it little prestige or power.

The reason for this remarkable, self-denying act is to be found in Shen's growing patriotism. While still governor of Kiangsi he had already found intolerable the threat of the steamship and telegraphy to China's administrative integrity. He tried using the treaties to curb further foreign encroachments then, but soon discovered by 1867 that even a strict enforcement of the treaties was not enough, for the Chinese had already conceded too much. Meanwhile, China's international position deteriorated. To recapture China's freedom of action in foreign affairs, self-strengthening was essential. Thus, in 1867 and again in 1874, he urged everyone to think constantly of the insult inflicted by the British and the French in the Second Opium War and devote themselves to self-strengthening. As his ideas became more refined in 1874, he stressed that self-strengthening must be predicated upon broad social and political changes so that China would have an efficient government and its people would have a sense of oneness and belonging. When that was achieved, the empire's human and material resources could be effectively mobilized. Shen's patriotism had now acquired the qualities of proto-nationalism. In 1866 the circumstances were such that the director-generalship of the Foochow Navy Yard seemed an appropriate expression of his growing political consciousness.

Still, the cause of patriotism could have been served in other ways. Tseng Kuo-fan, Tso Tsung-t'ang, and, from his own generation, Li Hung-chang had promoted *yang-wu* causes from their positions of power. Shen's acceptance of the Navy Yard post thus requires further explanation. Both he and his wife were unquestionably loyal to the throne, as their defence of Kuang-hsin in 1856 testified. Loyalty, in a Confucian bureaucratic context, meant service when called upon, no matter what the sacrifice. Shen's willingness to serve in a relatively lowly position might also have been inspired by his father-in-law's unswerving loyalty and dedicated service after his disgrace in 1840.[2]

Inasmuch as Shen's willingness to serve derived from his dedication, patriotism, and loyalty to the throne, he can be seen as Lin Tse-hsü's moral successor. But he had not always been ready to serve. In the late 1850s and towards the end of his governorship in the mid-1860s, he repeatedly expressed a desire to retire. During his first self-imposed retirement (1859–61), he also persistently declined office even when his service was much needed in the Taiping War. The reason was his ailing

2 On Lin Tse-Hsü, see Hummel, *Eminent Chinese*, vol. 1, p. 513.

and ageing parents. Loyalty and filial piety were competing demands in Confucianism, but when forced to make a choice, Confucius himself was partial to parents.[3] Shen's behaviour suggests that he felt the same way. His consent to take over the Navy Yard was predicated on a resolution of these competing principles: he could both serve his country and tend to his father near his home-town.

To these reasons we may add one other. From his earnest desire to change the civil service examinations and promote the study of science, we discern a strong wish to forge a new, modernizing elite out of the scholar-gentry class. It is entirely possible that Shen, by accepting the director-generalship, was trying to underscore the importance he thought the Navy Yard deserved and to set a personal example for the traditional educated elite. Whether this was so, he had, large as life, made the strongest personal statement on the need for the gentry-scholar to engage in *yang-wu*.

Once he was involved in the Navy Yard, Shen's entry into the third stage of late Ch'ing reform was complete. It may seem trite to say that what distinguishes the third stage from the second is more than a matter of scale. For although the arms production and modern diplomacy with which it began were an extension of efforts begun by the patriots of the Opium War generation, they soon gave way to changes and innovations that could have far-reaching consequences.

Current scholarship on the third stage, as it focuses on *yang-wu* under-takings, generally divides it into three periods. The first, 1861–72, was focused on the modernization of defence and diplomacy, and the training of personnel in these fields. The second, 1872–85, saw a growing recog-nition that power came from wealth and that the successes of the arma-ment industry would also require the development of support industries. A commercial shipping company (the China Merchants' Steam Naviga-tion Company) operating under official supervision, coal mines, a cotton mill, telegraph lines, and a railway were established or built. The last period, 1885–95, was marked by increasing centralization in defence efforts – the Board of Navy was created then – and the encouragement of light industry with less government interference to generate more wealth.[4]

In the *yang-wu* sector, Shen had made significant contributions in the first two periods (up to late 1875). His role in the Foochow Navy Yard was singularly important (more on this later). Further, he was respon-

---

3 The upright man in Confucius's eyes was one who would go so far as to shield his criminal father from the long arm of the law. De Bary, *Sources*, p. 30.
4 Mou An-shih, *Yang-wu yün-tung*, pp. 61–163; Immanuel C. Y. Hsü, *The Rise of Modern China*, 4th ed. (Oxford, 1990), pp. 282–7.

sible for China's first mechanized coal mine and telegraph lines and the first education mission to Europe. He also supported the China Merchants' Steam Navigation Company. But this focus on *yang-wu* enterprises conceals much that is significant about the Restoration or the self-strengthening movement and Shen's role in it.

I stressed in the Introduction that the Restoration and the self-strengthening movement encompassed a broad range of programmes to revitalize the dynasty. The Restoration contained a significant *yang-wu* component, and the self-strengthening movement, despite its apparent but misleading military connotations, had a strong emphasis on reforms in the civilian sector. Self-strengtheners like Shen and Ting Jih-ch'ang asserted that the success of the *yang-wu* undertakings was predicated upon the successful reform of the civil government and the skills as well as the moral fibre of its officials. To Shen's mind, self-strengthening meant both military modernization and administrative reform and re-vitalization, the regeneration of the individual as well as the collective.[5] Out of this conception emerged a reform programme far more dynamic and comprehensive than hitherto recognized.

The self-strengthening movement should be seen for what it was, an early step in China's modern state building, when measures were intro-duced to increase national strength, to improve internal security, and to provide better services. As the scope of government and the services it provided expanded, a larger and more efficient administrative system as well as a larger revenue was needed.[6] The tax-reduction scheme Shen introduced in Kiangsi was one such measure to increase state revenue without strangling the agrarian economy. It was designed to meet the Confucian requirement of *kuo-chi min-sheng*, satisfying both the needs of the state and the livelihood of the people. As defence modernization got under way in the 1860s, the reformers had to explore new ways to generate income, utilizing merchant skills and capital when appropriate.[7] Shen, without territorial power at the time, played only a marginal part in these discussions. Instead, his concern with the Foochow Navy Yard led him to consider other alternatives: the promotion of private coal industry and government-owned mechanized coal mining on Taiwan.

In the early 1860s there was talk of raising revenue through an empire-wide cadastral survey to tax unregistered land. Shen rejected the idea on the grounds that the bureaucracy, small and unreformed, would

---

5 Shen was very explicit on this point. *IWSM*, TC 53:1–3, 26–29b.
6 Susan Mann, *Local Merchants and the Chinese Bureaucracy, 1750–1950* (Stanford, Calif.,1987), p. 5.
7 Li Hung-chang and Ting Jih-ch'ang were particularly interested in this issue. Lü Shih-ch'iang, *Ting*, pp. 57–63.

only mismanage the reform and use it to further exploit the people. Here, Shen was caught in a vicious circle. To tax effectively, a larger and more efficient bureaucracy, not to mention a more costly one, was required.[8] The same went for the entire government: more services required more bureaucrats and revenue. Shen never directly discussed the merits of an enlarged bureaucracy, although his persistent call for cultivating a new modernizing elite and its incorporation in the government would have resulted in a larger civil service. Rather, he focused on the quality and training of officials, the retraining of incumbents, administrative specialization, and structural reforms of the government itself.

Shen's proposals have momentous implications. First, they would have reconstituted the scholar-official class. Second, a more hierarchical administrative structure would have emerged, with the centre enjoying much greater power based on a clearly defined chain of command and more information at its disposal. Third, with the administrative structure reaching far below the district level, a more interventionist yet responsive government, one more suited to mobilizing the empire's people and tapping its resources, would have arisen. All would have been enhanced by increased specialization, both administratively and technologically.

Shen's ideas were not the most advanced of his time. The honour belonged to a handful of reformer-writers from the treaty ports and Hong Kong.[9] But among high officials, who were not at liberty to engage in free-wheeling discourses, his reform programme was one of the boldest. While Li Hung-chang and Kuo Sung-tao were more progressive on specific issues, especially those concerning *yang-wu*, Shen and Ting Jih-ch'ang were more sweeping and comprehensive, particularly in their attack on the Ch'ing administrative system.[10] Thus, in response to Sung Chin's criticism of the Foochow Navy Yard, Li was more prepared to come to terms with the prevailing political forces and work within the existing administrative framework. In contrast, Shen, by advocating broad structural reforms of the government, took China a big step closer to the final stage of late Ch'ing reform. Returning to the questions raised in the Introduction, we can now say that the reforms advocated by Shen

---

8 Mann, *Local Merchants*, p. 5. On the efficacy of cadastral surveys in the early eighteenth century, Madeleine Zelin makes an observation that resonates with Shen's analysis: 'Gentry resistance and low government income combined to prevent the implementation of the thorough cadastral surveys that might have enabled the government to tap more fully the potential of the agrarian economy. But even had this been accomplished, the fluid land market in the areas of greatest tax evasion would have made such surveys useless within a short time'. *Magistrate's Tael*, p. 307.
9 Wang T'ao was an example. Cohen, *Between Tradition*, pp. 209–30.
10 Pong, 'Vocabulary of Change: Reformist Ideas', pp. 33–49.

and others in the 1860s and 1870s were more dynamic than those of the preceding era and had a more direct link with the reform movements of the 1890s than what Peter Mitchell and Mary Wright suggested.

Despite the radical implications of his ideas, Shen never departed from Confucian principles. As he searched for ways to build a stronger country, he insisted on a caring, though still autocratic, government. Many of his reform proposals were inspired by historical precedents and often justified by citations from Confucian classics. True, he embraced the goals of wealth and power, an idea that had a Legalist connotation, but this concept had already become a legitimate pursuit by the 1860s. Yet the Legalist term *pien-fa* (lit. changing the methods, but implying the laws and institutions), repeatedly used by Li Hung-chang and Ting Jih-ch'ang but vehemently denounced by Confucian fundamentalists, never appeared in his writings.[11]

Shen's career shows that it was possible to be a Confucian and advocate radical change. Whether his reforms went far enough must remain moot, since most of them were not tested when there was still time. By the 1890s, the international environment had become more inhospitable, while Chinese society had turned far more complex and pluralistic.[12] Sweeping institutional changes, first tried in 1898 and again in the mid-1900s, were thus easily transformed into a battle-ground for divergent interest groups. They unwittingly served to break up rather than unify or strengthen the country or its political system.

If Shen's Confucian mentality did not impede his developing radical ideas for large-scale reforms, did it help him as head of a modern defence industry? In his efforts to transfer Western science and technology to China, Shen believed that he had found a happy solution: those who had studied and practised Confucian moral principles were best suited to this task. Students of the Navy Yard School were thus given a Confucian education. His call on the literati to study science came from the same belief. It is entirely plausible that he saw in Western science and technology a new avenue to power and that this power would be best kept in the hands of the Confucian elite. But regardless of his motives, he still considered Confucian values and Western science compatible.

Historically, the so-called Confucian order and its Ch'ing manifestation had never been totally derived from Confucianism. This seemed to have been Shen's understanding, one that enabled him to propose sweeping reforms without feeling that he had betrayed Confucianism –

11 On Li and Ting's use of the term *pien-fa* in this period, see ibid., pp. 38–9.
12 Marianne Bastid-Bruguière, 'Currents of Social Change', in John Fairbank and Kwang-ching Liu, eds., *Late Ch'ing, 1800–1911*, part 2, pp. 535–602; Thomas, *Foreign Intervention*, pp. 109–59.

he was spared by Confucian ideologues during the polemical policy debate of 1874–5 (as discussed later). Of course, Shen's feelings and beliefs were not entirely in accord with reality. There were certain indisputably Confucian values that prevented him from being a more effective director-general. Filial piety, for one, required of him an extended period of mourning, which, together with his two tours of duty on Taiwan, contributed to administrative laxity in the Navy Yard. The disdain for physical labour was another. Although this bias was typical of a landed gentry in an agrarian society, Confucianism reinforced it, and it seriously impeded the practical application of science in the work place. Shen recognized that a knowledge of science and technology was important for the quality of leadership at the Navy Yard, and he encouraged his gentry-managers to acquire more of it. His attempts at modernizing the examination system and the scope of education for the scholar-gentry class had a similar intent. Some of his assistants did acquire a certain level of competency, but their knowledge appeared to have been derived from book learning and observation, not from physical involvement in the processes of marine design and construction. Shen himself never went beyond the superficial. The practical application of Western science was evident only at the lower levels, from the foremen down. Only the students of the Navy Yard School promised to bring this marriage of knowledge and application to a higher level in the future.

Shen was certainly more radical in his ideas on institutional change than in what he could put into practice. Why was it so difficult to implement change? Some historians attribute the failure of the Restoration to the fallacious Chinese belief that it was possible both to preserve the old order and to modernize. Their favourite example of one who tried and failed is the reformer Chang Chih-tung, who, as he opposed the sweeping reforms of the 1890s, insisted on using 'Chinese learning for the essential principles, Western learning for the practical application' (*Chung-hsüeh wei t'i, Hsi-hsüeh wei yung*, or *t'i-yung* for short).[13] In a similar vein, Shen had thought it 'permissible for a Chinese mind to master the skills of the foreigners, but not permissible for the bad habits of the foreign countries to contaminate the Chinese mind'. Were Shen's reform efforts therefore also doomed to failure?

The concept of *t'i-yung*, or principles-application, was central to Confucianism or, more accurately, Neo-Confucianism. It insisted that the practical application emanate from the principles; they were correlatives of a unifying whole (which the Chinese traditional order and

13 Levenson, *Confucian China*, vol. 1, pp. 59–78.

the nineteenth-century West were not). But what made up the essence of Confucianism(*t'i*) was not a closed issue. Thus, the reformers and their opponents espoused different solutions to the same problems because they understood basic Confucian principles differently. Though the difference was often one of emphasis, as in their interpretation of 'self-strengthening' (see the Introduction), the means by which the principles were to be realized could be worlds apart.

In the world of politics, means and ends are often confused. So the late Ch'ing conservative diehards defended the existing order as if it were the basic principles (*t'i*), when in fact it was merely the practical application (*yung*) of the principles, and a rather poor one at that. Shen had never expounded on the issue, but his reform proposals indicate that he indeed saw the ills of the Ch'ing state for what they were, a misguided application of the principles. He therefore insisted on a Confucian education, albeit abridged, for the future engineers and naval officers, while he himself, steeped in Confucian values, promoted defence modernization and set about reordering the Ch'ing state – to make the application worthy of the principles.

Shen's Confucianism was rooted in the School of Practical Statecraft, whose hallmark was a practical and utilitarian approach to government. From this vantage point, he, in words and in action, implied that the Ch'ing system had failed both in its traditional mission of preserving social order and in the modern need to defend the country against the West. But could the system that had been so changed to accomplish both tasks still be regarded as an application of Confucian principles? Shen never confronted the question squarely, for two reasons. First, historically, Confucianism had never been an immutable dogma, and Shen's pragmatic Confucianism was selective and adaptable.[14] He sought textual support for his ideas from a broad range of Confucian works, while antispecialist and antiutilitarian statements such as 'The gentleman is not a tool', which came from Confucius himself,[15] was nowhere to be found in his writings. Second, although it was Li Hung-chang who stated that science and technology were universal (and therefore could not harm the Chinese polity), neither did Shen see them as mere alien additions to be kept clinically apart from the Chinese body politic. Rather, he admired the Westerners' methods of and attitude towards manufacturing as worthy of adoption; only their 'bad habits' were to be

---

14 In this context, it is interesting to note how ideological adjustments were made to accommodate the likin, which called into question the purposes of taxation and the relative importance of the traditional class system. Mann, *Local Merchants*, pp. 96–103.
15 *Analects*, book 2, p. XII.

rejected. Western scientific studies were therefore to be fully incorporated into the education of the scholar-gentry class.

Joseph Levenson noted that a Confucian scholar who had studied Western science would never again read Confucian texts in the old way.[16] But Shen did not see Western science (*yung*) as a threat to Confucian principles (*t'i*), a view made possible by his pragmatic understanding of Confucianism. It gave him the confidence to pursue change without fearing its fate. The demise of Confucianism decades later can be explained either in the Levensonian vein or by the suggestion made in this study that those who held the reins of the Confucian state had long lost sight of Confucianism, with or without help from Western science.

On a more mundane level, one oft-cited reason for the eventual failure of China's modern defence enterprises is that the officials managed them as they would have managed a bureau of the traditional government. They paid little attention to cost effectiveness. Corruption and mismanagement were rife.[17] Until more is known about traditional government bureaus and how they operated, we cannot say for sure whether Shen ran the Navy Yard like a bureau. Some features of the 'method of evading management' were present, but by no means dominant. On the contrary, many aspects of the Navy Yard had a modern ring to them. The work force and the schools were organized and run according to publicized though rigid regulations. Punctuality and daily routines were emphasized. The workmen and foremen were trained in specialized skills, not as common labourers to be moved from task to task. Only the haulers and diggers were so deployed. Above them, the gentry-administrators were often given specialized tasks, which they performed on a regular basis. They did nevertheless retain characteristics of the generalist, and Shen should at least take part of the blame for not having institutionalized specialized positions. The reasons for his failure to do so are not clear, although they may have something to do with Confucian biases.

Cost effectiveness is a modern concept. Even in the modern West it often fails to produce the desired result. Scandals, cost overruns, delays are familiar stories in today's armament industry. To the extent that the Foochow Navy Yard was tied to a fixed budget and a rigid shipbuilding timetable, Shen was cost conscious. This was especially so when ship maintenance costs began to erode shipbuilding funds. But throughout Shen had directed the Navy Yard with an iron hand. Nepotism and corruption were kept under control. The work force was disciplined.

16 Levenson, *Confucian China*, pp. 63–4.
17 Kennedy, *Arms*, p. 158.

Though the methods he used were harsh and un-Confucian, in the context of his time they were not dysfunctional.

The achievements of the Navy Yard need no further elaboration. But how much can they be credited to Shen? Wang Hsin-chung attributes the success – the best period in the Navy Yard's entire history – primarily to the Europeans; decline set in the moment they left, fifteen months before the end of Shen's tenure. Wang's sole criterion was productivity: whereas fifteen ships were built in the first eight years, only twenty were completed in the next two decades. The reason was financial stringency, although he notes that the later ships were more advanced.[18]

Without doubt, the real cause of the Navy Yard's decline was financial, but our analysis shows that it occurred under European tutelage, in early 1873 when mounting ship maintenance costs produced a deficit. Neither the central nor the provincial government could devise a long-term solution. The shipbuilding programme was nonetheless completed because the Chinese government was bound by contract to supply the Europeans with sufficient funds. But in meeting this commitment, Shen had to cut expenses. Some ships did not have a full complement of men. The last three vessels were converted to merchantmen, and several gunboats had to be sent to other provinces. These measures helped ease the Navy Yard's financial burden but hurt its naval development.

The contract with the Europeans thus served to delay the Navy Yard's deepening financial crisis. Once the contract ended, the Chinese were free to make budget cuts. Shen was forced to build only two ships a year, far below the Navy Yard's capacity. Late payments and shortfalls in remittances from Foochow exacerbated its financial woes. The Navy Yard was now treated as one among many provincial agencies, each fighting for the delivery of its budgeted funds almost on a monthly basis. Shen was powerless, for all his prestige and his experience in battling for money. His main recourse was to appeal to the central government, calling (in vain) for centralized budgetary control.

Neither the Europeans' tutelage nor Shen's leadership was beyond criticism. But, together and separately, they contributed to the systematic and efficient operation of the Navy Yard. In fact, many ingredients for success were present during these early years. Shen's energetic direction and long tenure, the longest in the Navy Yard's history, provided administrative vigour and stability. And he enjoyed the continuing support of Tso Tsung-t'ang. The European engineers and technicians were capable of designing and constructing a modern naval dockyard and building the vessels the Chinese wanted. Yet, as noted, financial troubles

18 Wang Hsin-chung, 'Fu-chou ch'uan-chang', pp. 27–8.

had already appeared in early 1873. Shen tried his best to maintain the momentum he had set in motion. When he left, he insisted that his 'successor must be sought from among those who know and understand Western learning', and 'he must be familiar with [naval] construction or engineering and yet be strong, persevering, and trustworthy'.[19] His first choice was Kuo Sung-tao, once an acting governor of Kwangtung. Upon learning about Kuo's appointment as minister to London, he picked Ting Jih-ch'ang, a former governor of Kiangsu.[20] There is no doubt that Shen had chosen these men for their high rank and their commitment to *yang-wu* and reform in order to give the Navy Yard prestige, stability, as well as progressive leadership. But for all his efforts, the decline could not be arrested.

The study of the Ch'ing Restoration has yielded many reasons for China's failure to modernize in the second half of the nineteenth century. This study sheds further light on the many issues involved: financial administration, regionalism and provincialism, the reformers as a political group, and imperialism. Although each of these had a direct impact on the fate of modern China, I shall demonstrate that their adverse effects on the Restoration were closely related to the weaknesses of the throne and the central government.

Financial difficulties were the Navy Yard's first major problem, in magnitude and duration. China was poor, and modern defence enterprises like the Navy Yard strained the resources of the state. Dwight Perkins wonders what would have happened if central government revenues had been 5 or 10 per cent of gross national product (instead of less than 3 per cent).[21] The fact remains that Ch'ing tax rates were notoriously low; only corruption and inefficient tax collection methods made taxation oppressive. While these were important problems in themselves, they had limited bearing on the issue at hand, for central government revenue, with the addition of the likin and maritime customs, increased substantially in the second half of the century.[22] The question is, how was it handled?

Poorly. First, priority was not given to *yang-wu* enterprises despite the fact that taxes had increased and the central government was able to

---

19 Shen to Ting Jih-ch'ang, 1875, in 'Shen Wen-su kung-tu', 3:36–7; Lin Ch'ing-yüan, *Fuchien ch'uan-cheng*, p. 86; Shen's memorial of 17 September 1875, in *SWSK*, 4:77.
20 Ibid. On Shen's choice of his successor, see Shen Ch'uan-ching, *Fu-chou ch'uan-cheng-chü*, pp. 167–70; Lin Ch'ung-yung, *Shen*, 560–3.
21 Perkins, 'Government as an Obstacle', p. 487.
22 With between 17 and 20 million taels from likin and more than 20 million taels from maritime customs, central government revenues nearly doubled. Feuerwerker, 'Economic Trends', pp. 62–3. The likin figures (higher than Feuerwerker's) come from Mann, *Local Merchants*, p. 103.

disburse at least a portion of the provinces' new revenue. In the early 1860s the latter developments enabled the court to shift some 1.5 million taels a year from Kiangsi's taxes to support troops elsewhere, and this was from a province that had little customs revenue to speak of.[23] So one would expect that Fukien, though a province with a smaller tax base,[24] could have supported a navy yard that cost about 700,000 taels a year. But the Navy Yard was put near the bottom of the government's spending priorities, and the Foochow Tartar general, beholden to the throne for his lucrative job, usually followed its wishes. Looking across the empire we see a similar picture. The Yangtze River Fleet, a traditional water force created at the same time as the Foochow Navy Yard, had a larger budget and yet it never suffered financially in its entire history.[25]

Second, the central government could have exerted more control over the country's finances. Of course, the provinces would have resisted, but that should not have excused the lack of will at the centre. An aggressive use of censors could have secured for it financial data from the provinces. It was not done. Its occasional calls for more information thus sounded hollow. And without accurate information, confusion reigned. One result was late and inadequate delivery of funds. The other was that the Navy Yard, originally funded by a single revenue source, was compelled to rely on numerous sources. The lessons from the inefficient and chaotic management of military funds in the Taiping War was totally lost. Shen's call for central budgeting never got a hearing in Peking.

Mary Wright, however, laid the blame for the empire's financial problems squarely on the reformers:

The biggest difficulty was China's economy, which Restoration leaders did their best to keep stable, stagnant, and incapable of expansion.... The radical concepts of an expanding economy with expanding revenues, of a national military budget and a centralized administration, were as necessary to China as they were repugnant to China's leaders.[26]

This study yields a more complex picture. Some reformers were quite progressive. To be sure, they would have found it difficult to think in terms of an expanding economy, for it would have required a completely

---

23 See Chapter 2, esp. Tables 1 and 2.
24 Fukien's land tax was about half of Kiangsi's in 1908 (3 million taels as opposed to 6.84 million), but its likin was much higher in the late 1860s and 1870s (2 million taels to Kiangsi's 1.2 million). Also, Fukien had a customs revenue of 2.3 million taels in 1875, whereas Kiangsi's was negligible. Wang Yeh-chien, *Land Taxation*, p. 77; Lo Yü-tung, *Chung-kuo li-chin*, vol. 2, pp. 540, 562; *YWYT*, vol. 5, p. 167; *LKI* vol. 1, p. 205.
25 Wang Wen-hsien, 'Ch'ing-chi Ch'ang-chiang shui-shih'.
26 Mary Wright, *Last Stand*, pp. 207–8.

reordered society, particularly in the private sector. But as they sought new revenues, they opted for new and modern means. In 1867, Shen was already talking about retrieving economic rights (*li-ch'üan*) lost to the foreigners, while others were crying for commercial warfare(*shang-chan*), all in an effort to promote modern industrial or commercial enterprises. And Shen was not alone in seeking greater central budgetary control and financial administration in the 1870s.[27]

The Ch'ing decline has often been attributed to regionalism. As the argument goes, this centrifugal force was so powerful that 'there was no real T'ung-chih restoration'.[28] Recent scholarship has tended to refute this claim (see Introduction), as does our study of Shen's career. If Li Hung-chang was the father of regionalism (some would say Yüan Shih-k'ai was), then Tseng Kuo-fan was its grandfather or great-grandfather. But the immense power that Tseng enjoyed was brief, confined as it was to the last four years of the Taiping War. Tseng was nonetheless sensitive to the problems his power could bring. He repeatedly requested that the throne rescind his imperial commissionership, even as late as February 1862. In his memorial, he said:

The power that has been vested in your minister is so great that, one fears, it would start a trend for power struggles. [We should therefore] help prevent the growth of provincial power at the expense of the centre. Although [my appointment] is itself insignificant, it is bound to have dire consequences.[29]

Immediately after the Taiping War, Tseng disbanded most of his forces. Li Hung-chang then demobilized half of the Kiangsu troops; other provinces followed suit.[30] The few large forces that remained were needed for continuing rebel suppression or keeping the peace. (Some of Tseng's men were transferred to the Yangtze River Fleet to ensure government control of the region.)

This is not to say that Restoration officials did not want power, but even those who did knew their limitations. They owed their appointment and authority to the throne, and as they were moved about, at frequent intervals, they had to discharge some of their men or leave them behind. Li Hung-chang's troops were eventually scattered over several provinces over which he had little control.[31]

Even the political machines of the so-called regionalists were fragile.

27 Shen's memorial of 16 December 1867, *IWSM*, TC 53:2; Pong, 'Vocabulary of Change: Reformist Ideas', pp. 42–4; Pong, 'Shen'.
28 Michael, *Taiping Rebellion*, vol. 1, p. 198.
29 Tseng's memorial, TC 1.1.23 (PK 21.2.1862), in YCT, TC 1/1 *hsia*.
30 Mary Wright, *Last Stand*, pp. 208–10.
31 Kwang-ching Liu, 'The Limits of Regional Power'; Wang Erh-min, *Huai-chün*, pp. 339–70.

The men they implanted in their provinces were eventually torn apart by competing interests and loyalties: the 'regional leaders', their own official duties, and the throne. Shen Pao-chen, Tso Tsung-t'ang, Li Yüan-tu, and Li Huan were all close associates of Tseng Kuo-fan's at some point; all were either impeached by or alienated from him because of competing demands.

When Tso Tsung-t'ang moved into the Chekiang–Fukien region, he too had a strong following. But the moment he left, his associates were quickly removed from the provincial government. His influence in Fukien did not entirely disappear. Fukien remained his most reliable provider of military funds in the 1868–74 period. Two explanations have been proffered (without evidence): its high customs receipts and the fact that Tso was its former governor-general.[32] Tso also had some residual influence over the Navy Yard. He periodically received reports from Shen, Chou K'ai-hsi, and Hsia Hsien-lun, but time and distance prevented him from playing a significant role in its development. Under normal circumstances, the Tsungli Yamen ignored him on matters concerning the Navy Yard.[33] Shen managed it largely independent of him.

As regards Shen, he never had an army of his own, not even when he was a governor during the Taiping War. He came closest to having his own military command as head of the Foochow Navy Yard, but it did not turn out that way. His own political following (including personal assistants, *mu-yu*) was small. There was no Shen clique. His son once remarked that he, 'as an official . . . should not be mentioned in the same breath as members of the Hunan and Anhwei groups, who stick together and discriminate against each other'.[34] Personal bias notwithstanding, there is more than a grain of truth in this remark.

The power of the high provincial officials had its limits. The authority of Governor-General Tseng Kuo-fan over Governor Shen in the early 1860s and Shen's control over the officials and gentry of Kiangsi were circumscribed by both the Ch'ing administrative system and local, particularistic interests. It was the same everywhere in the empire. Even as the balance of power between the central government and the provinces shifted in favour of the latter in the second half of the nineteenth century,

---

32 Wang Hung-chih, 'Tso Tsung-t'ang p'ing hsi-pei Hui-luan chün-fei chi ch'ou-ts'u', *Shih-hsüeh chi-k'an*, 4 (May 1972), 231–50. Wang's claim deserves further analysis. One study points to Fukien's low customs revenue in the 1870s (Hsieh Sung, 'Min Hai-kuan shui-shou ch'ing-k'uang', in *Fu-chien wen-shih tzu-liao*, no. 10, p. 16). Also, Tso sometimes wondered about the dependability of Fukien's high officials. He had little faith in Li Ho-nien. Tso to Shen, 1872, in *TWHK*, 'Letters', 12:58–9.

33 Tso to Hsia Hsien-lun, 1872, in *TWHK*, 'Letters', 12:22; Tso's memorial of 13 May 1872, in *IWSM*, TC 86:3b–8.

34 Shen Yü-ch'ing, *T'ao-yüan chi*, p. 226.

the high provincial officials' control over men in their jurisdiction increased only marginally.[35] The system of appointment guaranteed that men of widely different stripes were posted in the same province, precluding any concentration of power. The dispute between Wu T'ang and Tso Tsung-t'ang's followers, and that between Wen-yü and Li Ho-nien, were only the more notable examples. As for the Foochow Navy Yard, which was neither claimed nor disowned by Fukien or Peking, it suffered as it was caught between these bureaucratic fall-outs. And Shen, without territorial power, could never have turned it into a real source of power. He did not even try.

If there was little regionalism in the third quarter of the nineteenth century, there was plenty of provincialism and subprovince localism. But even provincialism, which can be powerful at times, lacked purpose and focus until political participation became a possibility in the last years of the dynasty. Provincialism thus could not give the self-strengthening movement direction; it often acted as a negative force, attacking this or that enterprise, or withholding funds from them. Shen, directing a defence project as a gentry leader, might have deflected some of these negative effects. Still, he could not count on the province's consistent support. In this context his ideas about educational reforms made sense, for they would eventually lead to the emergence of a pro-*yang-wu* gentry. When that materialized, those provinces with a transformed gentry leadership could become the motivating force behind a strong self-strengthening movement, one worthy of its name.

Looking across the empire, it becomes even more evident that weakly organized provincial interests contributed little to self-strengthening, for money itself was not the problem. Perkins has shown that individual provinces like Szechwan or viceroyalties like Chekiang and Fukien had the capacity to raise an army to topple a dynasty,[36] not to mention the ability to support a naval dockyard and academy. But there was no common cause with which to mobilize the civic leaders – the gentry – and there were no durable institutions (such as 'regionalism') to impose their will on them.

The contrast between China and Japan in this era is striking. In late Tokugawa Japan (1850s and 1860s), there was also a weak central government, but some of the powerful feudal lords took matters into their own hands and built blast furnaces and shipyards in their domains, in defiance of the Tokugawa house. The latter was then forced to answer in kind. Their enterprises, crudely modern, then became the foundation of Japan's military and industrial strength when finally brought together

35 Kwang-ching Liu, 'The Limits of Regional Power'.
36 Perkins, *Agricultural Development*, pp. 174–82.

330

by a strong central government after 1868.[37] The ingredients for the rise of similarly powerful, nearly autonomous regional regimes in China were simply absent. This is why the central government's role was so critical to the self-strengthening effort in Ch'ing China.

In Japan, regional interests and factional disputes continued well into the Meiji era, despite its much stronger central government. The expedition to Taiwan was organized and sent by Saigo Tsugumichi without government approval. On the Chinese side, Shen was dispatched by the imperial court with the express instruction to settle the dispute diplomatically (although he was told to prepare for all eventualities). Shen followed Peking's order faithfully, though his forces were superior to the Japanese in number and equipment.[38] Had he, like Saigo, taken matters into his own hands and engaged the Japanese in battle, even a partial victory would have changed the course of China's defence modernization. As Perkins has suggested, if the self-strengtheners had been able to produce some relief from foreign domination, they could have gained greater support all round.[39] But Shen had to follow orders, and with forces that were not his own (they came from Li Hung-chang's Huai Army and Fukien's provincial troops), he could not take liberties.[40] Shen was not a regional leader, and his protonationalism had not reached a point where he could comfortably defy the court to save the country. Such a phenomenon did not occur until 1900 when some provincial officials declared neutrality in defiance of the Empress Dowager Tz'u-hsi's declaration of war against the foreign powers. In the defence of Taiwan, had the central government adopted a more aggressive policy,

---

37 Thomas C. Smith, *Political Change and Industrial Development in Japan: Government Enterprise, 1868-1880* (Stanford, Calif., 1965).

38 Yen, *Taiwan*, pp. 175–230; Iwata, *Ōkubo*, pp. 184–95; Pong, 'Modernization and Politics', pp. 295–313. The English press on the China coast was generally hostile to the Chinese. The *China Mail* (5 June 1874) maintained that 'ship for ship and gun for gun, we think that the Japanese will be the victors'. But the *North-China Herald* (16 May 1874) did point out that the overall situation did not favour the Japanese. Harry Parkes, British minister to Japan, also thought that the Japanese would prove unequal to the Chinese if hostilities occurred. Parkes to Wade, 4 April 1874, cited by Yen, *Taiwan*, pp. 214–15.

39 Perkins, 'Government as an Obstacle', pp. 487–8.

40 Shen was reported to have said to Saigo that, because both the Chinese and the Japanese navies were in their inception, they should avoid hostilities lest the Westerners detect their weaknesses. Shen Yü-ch'ing, *T'ao-yüan chi*, p. 171. There is no documentary evidence that such a conversation (or correspondence) actually took place. Even if it did, it should be interpreted as Shen's argument for a peace settlement, which was his order to follow. As pointed out earlier, the Chinese had numerical superiority and home-ground advantage. Further, any military confrontation would have to be conducted largely on land. Naval interception of Japanese reinforcements thereafter, even if only partially successful, would have cost the Japanese dearly and forced a withdrawal.

as it did in the largely conventional campaign in the North-West, a more favourable outcome could have been produced, greatly benefiting the cause of defence modernization.

The old imperial system, especially its Ch'ing manifestation, made radical reforms difficult. Reform begins when a few individuals see something wrong in their society and think they have a cure for it. But for any reform of significance to succeed, the reformers must transform their effort into a sustained movement. In his study of reformers in the pre–Civil War United States, Ronald Walters defines a reform movement as a 'collective, organized effort to improve society or individuals by achieving some well-articulated goal'.[41] Was there a reform movement in China up to 1875? Did it have a 'well-articulated goal'?

Most historians in the People's Republic of China speak of a *yang-wu p'ai* (clique or party), which was itself divided into factions, notably the Li Hung-chang (Huai or Anhwei) and Tso Tsung-t'ang (Hunanese) factions.[42] Whether the *yang-wu* advocates were a clique is debatable. My concern is whether a 'clique' or its 'factions' could function as a 'movement' for reform.

In the traditional state, it was the Confucian duty of an official to remonstrate with the emperor. But the state would not countenance any 'loyal opposition', which was branded as factionalism. The Ch'ing dynastic house, more than other traditional Chinese ruling clans, was so sensitive to the dangers of political movements that all organized causes were regarded with the greatest suspicion.[43] In practice, like-minded officials did form closely knit groups which met for poetry or literary sessions; sometimes they would cross the threshold into the realm of politics.[44] But such groups could exist only if they remained within acceptable bounds. Many simply disintegrated or lost vitality as their members were posted around the country. Dispersion rarely helped the groups spread their influence over a larger region. While former connections could be kept up to a degree through correspondence, different local concerns consumed the energy of these men, and to perform their jobs adequately, they had to maintain and improve their ties to the throne, the source of their power and legitimacy. For all practical

---

41 Ronald G. Walters, *American Reformers, 1815–1860* (New York, 1978), p. xiv.
42 Chung-kuo Chin-tai-shi kao pien-hsieh-tsu, 'Yang-wu huo-tung', pp. 127–44.
43 De Bary, *Sources*, pp. 446–8; David S. Nivison, 'Ho-shen and His Accusers: Ideology and Political Behavior in the Eighteenth Century', in David S. Nivison and Arthur F. Wright, eds., *Confucianism in Action* (Stanford, Calif., 1959), pp. 223–8.
44 Lin Tse-hsü belonged to a succession of literary groups. To illustrate the point made in the rest of this paragraph, it should be noted that the membership of these groups changed drastically over time because of the constant movement of these men, who were primarily officials. Lin Ch'ung-yung, *Lin Tse-hsü*, pp. 42–9, 86–92.

purposes, such group members, once dispersed, could not function collectively for long.

When in Peking, Shen enjoyed close relations with Li Hung-chang and Kuo Sung-tao; during his brief service under Tseng Kuo-fan, bonds with others were formed. But all were allowed to lapse until circumstances, largely because of imperial action, brought them closer again, but only ever so briefly. In any event, there were few such ties. In the case of the *yang-wu* officials, their numerical strength was insignificant: some forty in the provinces and around ten at the capital.[45] In this environment, to generate any 'well-articulated goal' was next to impossible. The *yang-wu* advocates rarely acted as a group. When they did, it was usually because their common concerns came under attack, as in the Sung Chin case. Their only opportunity to forge a genuinely broad programme for change came in the policy debate of 1874–5, which took place under the central government's auspices. But as we shall see, their efforts were frustrated by the throne and its machinations. We therefore cannot speak of a *yang-wu p'ai*, unless it is taken to mean a school of thought. There were reformers but no reform movement until the 1890s.

The impact of the West on the processes of change was wide-ranging. It also reflected the role of the Chinese central government. Our analysis here can benefit from Moulder's general approach: China's incorporation into the world economy affected more aspects of Chinese life than is usually assumed. The Western presence had not been peaceful or orderly. For all the high ideals of the proponents of the Co-operative Policy, who wanted to see the Chinese change at their own pace under their own steam,[46] merchants and missionaries, and even consular officials, seldom heeded its central message. Foremost in the minds of Chinese reformers like Shen, therefore, was not the new spirit under the Co-operative Policy, but the Opium Wars, which had made that policy necessary for mitigating imperialist-Chinese relations. This led to a serious distortion of Chinese development. Shen's preoccupation with curbing foreign inroads had retarded the emergence of a more benign attitude towards the telegraph and the railway, and thwarted the exploitation of natural resources on Taiwan,[47] just as it had predisposed Shen towards defence modernization. The Chinese thus had to seek power before they had the wealth to pursue it.

Wealth, in this case, meant what the central government earmarked for defence modernization (an internal problem), although the inability

---

45 The figures are Robert Hart's. Rawlinson, *China's Struggle*, p. 202.
46 Mary Wright, *Last Stand*, pp. 21–3.
47 Shen's memorial of 7 May 1872 in *YWYT*, vol. 5, p. 115.

to raise tariffs did adversely affect the financial stability of many defence efforts, the Foochow Navy Yard included. Antimissionary incidents also weakened the central government's capacity to deal with foreigners who subverted the operations of the Navy Yard. When the Navy Yard was finally free of foreign interference after 1870, it became a showcase for Sino-foreign co-operation and proof of how the fear of foreign domination could be dispelled.

Overall, the achievements of the self-strengtheners in the short fifteen years after the Second Sino-Foreign War were impressive, despite the generally unfavourable political milieu. Shen was a key actor in this vital though tortuous transition to modernity. To his colleagues, he was known as a 'doer', and by his doing, his ideas progressed. As David Apter observes, 'Action can be a way of creating new forms of consciousness'.[48] True, Shen's reform proposals were not all sound or practicable: his early, censorial memorials were rife with idealism. But by the mid-1860s, especially after his involvement with the Navy Yard, his ideas gained depth and his patriotism began to approximate nationalism. The proposals he made in 1867 and 1874 were a veritable coherent programme for reform, displaying a readiness to change the inherited system to accommodate modern demands and a willingness to use modern ideas to solve traditional problems. In this, he was not alone, and his ideas on some issues were not necessarily the most advanced, but fellow travellers were few.

Ultimately, the reason reformers like Shen could not have achieved more and why the foundation and momentum for change failed to bear fruit is to be found in the weaknesses of the central government. What constituted success in the context of the time is an open question. It would have been impossible for the Chinese to catch up with the West, but if they could have kept abreast of the Japanese and checked their aggression, it could be said that they had succeeded. In the Restoration era, however, central leadership often vacillated, and it cowered before foreign pressure. On the rare occasion when it took a decisive stance on behalf of the *yang-wu* enterprises, it invariably succeeded, but only to the extent that it quashed the opposition of the moment. Thus, Wo-jen was condemned and Wu T'ang removed, but officials of the same ilk soon succeeded them. The throne never considered improving the long-term political environment or climate. In Japan, right at the beginning of the Meiji Restoration, the boy-emperor proclaimed the Charter Oath, calling upon his subjects to seek knowledge throughout the world and

48 David E. Apter, *The Politics of Modernization* (Chicago, 1965), p. 8.

abandon the absurd customs of old so as to strengthen imperial rule.[49]
There was no Charter Oath in China.

Quite the reverse, the imperial message that brought the policy debate
of 1874–5 to a close was ambivalent. In the course of the debate, de-
fenders of Ch'ing orthodoxy – imperial princes and all – were unleashed
to lash out not only at the reforms but at the reformers themselves. A
severely trimmed programme resulted, providing for the creation of two
modern fleets with a 4 million tael budget, two modern coal mines
(including the one on Taiwan), greater power for the northern and the
southern imperial commissioners, and minor reorganization of the traditional armed forces. Though still the most comprehensive programme for
self-strengthening up to the mid-1880s, it was a far cry from what the
reformers had wanted. Worse still, since none of the institutional changes
regarding overall and long-term planning, budgeting, and governmental
restructure was adopted, it stood little chance of success.[50]

For years Shen had been frustrated by the lack of dependable provincial or central government support for his efforts. A major problem
lay in the administrative system. With virtually all officials given divided
yet overlapping responsibilities, the government was prone to move in
different directions at the same time, giving mixed signals to the rest of
the country. The promoters of *yang-wu* enterprises were then left to fight
endless petty political battles in the provinces in order to survive. One
can understand why Shen wanted a restructured system that would give
much greater power to the central government, for with increased power
came greater accountability and then decisive battles could be fought
and won in Peking. Shen thus repeatedly called for strong imperial
leadership and commitment to self-strengthening. Of course, conservative diehards, too, wanted strong imperial leadership, to oppose self-
strengthening.[51] But Shen was confident that the throne, when forced to
make a choice, would have to choose self-strengthening. After all, he
reasoned, only those who were adaptable could survive.[52]

Why did the central government reject more power in its hands? Of
the many reasons, only two are pertinent here. First, centralization, as

---

49 Ryusaku Tsunoda, William de Bary, and Donald Keene, comps., *Sources of Japanese
   Tradition* (New York, 1958), pp. 643–4.
50 The debate has been studied in some detail elsewhere. See Pong, 'Shen'.
51 These were Pao-t'ing (imperial clansman) and Pao Yüan-shen (governor of Shansi).
   See their memorials in *SCTI*, vol. 7, pp. 2742–4, 2764–5.
52 Shen's memorial of 23 December 1874, in Shen K'o, 'Hsien Wen-su Kung', pp. 67–8.
   The idea that the dynasty could not survive without broad changes appeared many
   times in Shen's memorials. See, e.g., his 'posthumous' memorial of 1879 in ibid., pp.
   97–8, and his earlier memorials in *IWSM*, TC 53:1–2b, 26–29b.

Shen and some self-strengtheners would have it, meant accountability, which in turn demanded administrative rationalization: specialization and clearly defined responsibilities in government. Such a change would require central government officials to be retrained to perform specialized functions, an idea abhorrent to the majority of Confucianists who still believed that government belonged to the generalists. More important, it would render untenable the existing system of patronage and privilege, especially for the idle or less able Manchus and imperial clansmen. That the empress dowager's position was largely propped up by patronage exacerbated the situation.

Second, the practice of divide and rule worked best under the traditional system, where officials of divergent persuasions and interests shared the same responsibilities. In this system, special interest groups could not easily be formed, whereas high officials could manipulate those below with ease, pitting them against one another. It was machinations of this kind that weakened the cause of the self-strengtheners and thwarted their reform efforts.

In early 1875, Empress Dowager Tz'u-hsi had just violated dynastic law by installing her three-year-old nephew as emperor to prolong her own rule. She badly needed support from the conservative majority. At the same time, the co-operation between Li Hung-chang and Shen in the defence of Taiwan alarmed those who feared the rise of Li and the spectre of an alliance between the two. Li's subsequent effort to have Shen appointed to the viceroyalty of Liang Kiang made the situation look even more ominous. Thus, during the on-going policy debate, the throne manipulated the ultraconservatives against the *yang-wu* advocates.

But Tz'u-hsi needed both the conservatives and the *yang-wu* reformers. The result, therefore, was a curiously incoherent attack on the latter. While the conservative ideologues were given free reign to oppose the reformers' proposals, including some of Shen's, the personal polemics were directed only at Li and his close associate, Ting Jih-ch'ang. The two were rebuked for trying to change China with barbarian ways. Shen, however, was praised. 'Shen', they said, 'was the son-in-law of Lin Tse-hsü; in both scholarship and public affairs, he was solidly rooted in tradition.... His Confucian qualities – integrity, strength of character, sincerity and loyalty – were also praised by Tso Tsung-t'ang'.[53] He was not to be talked about in the same vein as Li and Ting. Notice was thus served to Li and Ting that they should always be mindful of their

53 *YWYT*, vol. 1, p. 130. For Tso's original comment on Shen, see ibid., p. 115.

vulnerability, and to Shen that he had better keep his distance from these 'treacherous men'.[54]

The policy debate was conceived as a means to move the self-strengthening effort forward. The Tsungli Yamen, by setting the tone of the discussions with its bold suggestions, harboured high hopes. It was more than matched by the sweeping proposals of Shen and a few of the officials. The fact that Shen demanded drastic changes in the empire's internal administration, in the education of the scholar-gentry class, and in *yang-wu* modernization testifies to his intense patriotism. And despite the politics of the moment, the fact that he and his main ideas were acceptable to the ultraconservatives testifies to his faithfulness to Confucian ideals. But the changes he called for would require the abandonment of too much of the established bureaucratic practices and of the administrative system itself. Little wonder that the court finally settled on a mild programme, one that was restricted to *yang-wu* modernization. The throne and its conservative supporters still wanted to keep *yang-wu* sharply distinct from the traditional sphere of government. Only Shen, Ting Jih-ch'ang, and Li Hung-chang were prepared to argue for integration. Still, the programme that emerged was a step forward, but only a small step.

In conclusion, Shen was a truly transitional man. He reached out to the world beyond for a solution to China's ills while still firmly rooted in Confucianism. Because he understood Confucianism through a reformer's eyes, he saw the ills in his own society not as flaws in Confucianism itself, but as departures from it. This prognosis of the Ch'ing system was already evident in his censorial memorials; it was not a rationalization for his subsequent promotion of *yang-wu* modernization. But once engaged in *yang-wu*, he could see China's shortcomings with greater clarity and sought newer remedies for them. In the 1860s and 1870s, his approach made much greater sense than did that of those who worked only at *yang-wu* or internal reforms in isolation.

History belongs to those who bring changes to their own society. The transitional man is one such person. Shen was able to break with the past, yet without having to abandon it. But the problems facing the China of his time were immense. And if he was not able to change it to the extent he wanted, he had nonetheless brought China closer to the final stage of late Ching reform.

---

54 Both the motives and the nature of the conservatives' attacks on the reformers and their proposals were far more complex than this brief analysis can convey. For a fuller treatment, see Pong, 'Shen'.

Glossary of Chinese characters

(Common place names have not been included.)

An-lan	安瀾	Ch'i-ling	耆齡
Ao-feng Shu-yüan	鼇峯書院	Chia-lo-erh	嘉樂爾
Botan (Mu-tan)	牡丹	Chiang I-li	蔣益澧
Chang Ch'eng	張成	Chiang-nan tao	江南道
Chang Chih-tung	張之洞	chien-ch'a yü-shih	監察御史
Chang Kuo-ching	張國經	Chien-ch'ang	建昌
Chang Po-hsing	張伯行	*chien-pi ch'ing-yeh*	堅壁清野
Chang Ssu-hsün	張斯枸	*chien-sheng*	監生
Chang Ssu-kuei	張斯桂	*Chien-wei*	建威
Ch'ang-sheng	長勝	*ch'ien-tsung*	千總
ch'ang-shui	常稅	Chih-yüan t'ang	致遠堂
Chao Lieh-wen	趙烈文	Chin-ch'i	金谿
Chen-hai	鎮海	*chin-shih*	進士
Chen-wei	振威	*ch'in-ch'ai*	欽差
Ch'en Chi-t'ung	陳季同	*ch'in-ming*	欽命
Ch'en Ching-k'ang	陳景康	*ch'in-ming tsung-li*	欽命總理
Ch'en-hang	琛航	*ch'uan-cheng ta-ch'en*	船政大臣
Ch'en P'i	陳璧	*ch'in-ping*	親兵
Cheng Yü	鄭漁	*ching-shih*	經世
Ch'eng-Chu	程朱	Ching-te chen	景德鎮
Ch'eng Hao	程顥	*Ching-yüan*	靖遠
Ch'eng I	程頤	*Ch'ing-ch'e tu-yü*	輕車都尉
Chi-an	吉安	Ch'ing-chiang	清江
Chi-an	濟安	Ch'ing-ho	清河
chi-ch'iao	技考	*ch'ing-i*	清議
chi-chiu	祭酒	Chiu-chiang	九江
Chi-lung (*see* Keelung)		(prefecture)	
Chi-ts'ui ssu	積翠寺	Chou K'ai-hsi	周開錫

338

Chou T'eng-hu	周騰虎	Hung Hsiu-ch'üan	洪秀全
Chu Hsi	朱熹	*I-hsin*	藝新
chü-jen	舉人	Jao-chou	饒州
Chü-kuan kuei-nieh	居官圭臬	Jao T'ing-hsüan	饒廷選
ch'uan-ch'ang	船廠	*jen-ts'ai*	人才
Ch'üan-chou	泉州	Jui-lin	瑞麟
chün-tzu	君子	Kan-chou	贛州
chung	忠	K'ang-hsi	康熙
chung-hsiao	忠孝	*ke-chih*	格致
Chung-hsüeh wei t'i,	中學為體，	Keelung (Chi-lung)	基隆
Hsi-hsüeh wei yung	西學為用	Kiangnan (arsenal)	江南
Ch'ung-hou	崇厚	Kiukiang (city)	九江
Fang An-chih	方安之	Ku Yen-wu	顧炎武
Fei-yün	飛雲	K'uai-tzu hsiang	筷子巷
feng-shui	風水	*kuan-ping*	官兵
fu-ch'iang	富強	*kuan-tu shang-pan*	官督商辦
Fu-chou	撫州	Kuang-hsin	廣信
Fu-hsing	福星	Kuang-Jao-Chiu-Nan	廣饒九南
fu-piao	撫標	Kuei-ch'i	貴溪
Fu-po	伏波	Kung, Prince	恭（親王）
Hai-ching	海鏡	*kung-fei*	公費
Hanlin	翰林	Kung Tzu-chen	龔自珍
Ho Ching	何璟	*kuo-chi min-sheng*	國計民生
Ho-k'ou chen	河口鎮	Kuo K'un-tao	郭崑燾
Ho Kuei-ch'ing	何桂清	Kuo Sung-tao	郭嵩燾
Hou-kuan	候官	*kuo-t'i*	國體
hsi-yu	嬉遊	Lei Hai-tsung	雷海宗
Hsia Hsieh	夏燮	*li* (propriety)	禮
Hsia Hsien-lun	夏獻綸	*li* (profit)	利
Hsia T'ing-chü	夏廷榘	Li Chao-t'ang	黎兆棠
Hsia Yü	夏育	Li Ch'eng-mou	李成謀
hsiao	孝	Li Chia-pen	黎家本
Hsiao Kung-chuan	蕭公權	Li Ch'ing-lin	李慶霖
Hsin-chiang	信江	*li-ch'üan*	利權
Hsü Tsung-kan	徐宗幹	Li Fu-t'ai	李福泰
Hsü Wen-yüan	徐文淵	Li Han-chang	李翰章
Hu-k'ou	湖口	Li Ho	李和
Hu Kuang-yung	胡光墉	Li Ho-nien	李鶴年
Hu Lin-i	胡林翼	Li Hsiu-ch'eng	李秀成
Hua Chu-san	華祝三	Li Huan	李桓
Hua-fu-pao	華福寶	Li Hung-chang	李鴻章
Huai (army)	淮（軍）	Li Shan-lan	李善蘭
Huang T'i-fang	黃體芳	Li Shu-i	李續宜
Huang Wei-hsüan	黃維煊	Li T'ien	李田
Hung Fu	洪福	Li-tsung (Sung emperor)	理宗

Li Tsung-hsi	李宗羲	*pao-chia*	保甲
Li Yüan-tu	李元度	Pei Chin-ch'üan	貝錦泉
Liang Kiang	両江	Pei San-ch'üan	貝珊泉
Liang Kwang	両廣	Peiyang	北洋
Liang Ming-ch'ien	梁鳴謙	P'eng Yü-lin	彭玉麟
Lien Ch'ao-lun	廉兆綸	*pieh-ch'iu hsin-i*	別求新意
Lin Ch'ang-i	林昌彝	Pien-ch'ien Hui	邊錢會
Lin Ch'ing-t'ien	林青天	*pien-fa*	變法
Lin Ch'iung-shu	林泂淑	*pien-hsiu*	編修
Lin Kuo-hsiang	林國祥	Pien Pao-ti	卞寶第
Lin P'u-ch'ing	林普晴	Po-chin-ta	博錦達
Lin T'ai-tseng	林泰曾	Po-yang Lake	鄱陽湖
Lin Tse-hsü	林則徐	*sha-ch'uan*	沙船
ling-sheng	廩生	*shang-chan*	商戰
Liu K'un-i	劉坤一	Shen Chao-lin	沈兆霖
Liu Tien	劉典	*shen-ming ta-i*	申明大義
Liu Tsung-yüan	柳宗元	*Shen-pao*	申報
Liu Yo-chao	劉嶽昭	Shen Pao-chen	沈葆楨
Liu Yü-hsün	劉于潯	Shen Shun-fa	沈順發
Lo Ch'ang-chih	羅昌智	Shen Ta-ch'üan	沈大銓
Lo-p'ing	樂平	Shen T'ing-feng	沈廷楓
Lo Ta-ch'un	羅大春	Shen Yü-ch'ing	沈瑜慶
Lo Tse-nan	羅澤南	Shih Ching-fen	石景芬
Lu Hsiang-shan	陸象山	*shih-ch'üan*	事權
Lu Lun-hua	陸倫華	*shih-hsing*	實行
Lü Han	呂翰	*shih-hsüeh*	實學
Lü Wen-ching	呂文經	*shih-tu hsüeh-shih*	侍讀學士
Ma Hsin-i	馬新貽	*shou-pei*	守備
Ma-wei (Mamoi)	馬尾	*shu-ch'ang-kuan*	庶常館
Mei-yün	湄雲	*shu-chi-shih*	庶吉士
Meng Pen	孟賁	*shu-shih*	塾師
Miao hsiang	廟巷	Ssu-ma Kuang	司馬光
Min	閩	*ssu-shu*	私塾
Min Che	閩浙	*ssu-tang*	死黨
Mu-tan (*see* Botan)		Su-shun	肅順
mu-yu	幕友	Sun Chia-to	孫家鐸
Nanchang (city)	南昌	Sung Chin	宋晉
Nan-ch'ang (district or prefecture)	南昌	*ta-fu*	大副
		ta-shuai	大帥
Nan-k'ang	南康	*Ta-ya*	大雅
Nantai	南臺	Tainan (*see* T'ai-wan fu)	
Nien	捻	T'ai-wan	臺灣
nien-p'u	年譜	T'ai-wan fu (modern Tainan)	臺灣府
pa-tsung	把總		
Pao Ch'ao	鮑超	Tamsui	淡水

tan	石	Wang Pao-ch'en	王葆辰
Tao-kuang	道光	Wang Pi-ta	王必達
tao-k'u	道庫	Wang Yang-ming	王陽明
Teng Shih-ch'ang	鄧世昌	Wang Yüan-chih	王元稺
ti-ting	地丁	Wei Han	魏翰
t'i	體	Wei Yüan	魏源
t'i-tiao	提調	*Wei-yüan*	威遠
t'i-tu	提督	*wei-yüan*	委員
t'i-yung	體用	Wen-hsiang	文祥
Ting Jih-ch'ang	丁日昌	Wen-yü	文煜
tsa-shui	雜稅	Whampoa	黃浦
Tsai-ch'un	載淳	Wo-jen	倭仁
Ts'ai Kuo-hsiang	蔡國祥	*wo wo ch'i ch'üan*	我握其權
ts'an-chiang	參將	Wu (provinces)	吳
ts'ao-che	糟折	Wu-ch'eng	吳城
Tseng Chi-tse	曾紀澤	Wu Chung-hsiang	吳仲翔
Tseng Heng-chung	曾恒忠	Wu Lan-sun	吳蘭蓀
Tseng Kuo-fan	曾國藩	Wu Shih-chung	吳世忠
Tseng Lan-sheng	曾蘭生	Wu-shih shan	烏石山
Tso Ch'iu-ming	左丘明	Wu Ta-t'ing	吳大廷
Tso chuan	左傳	Wu T'ang	吳棠
Tso Tsung-t'ang	左宗棠	Wu-ying-tien	武英殿修書處
tsuan-hsiu	纂修	Hsiu-shu-ch'u	
tsung-chien-kung	總監工	Yang Ch'ang-chün	楊昌濬
tsung-li ch'uan-cheng	總理船政	*yang-hsüeh chü*	洋學局
Tsungli Yamen	總理衙門	Yang Pao-ch'en	楊寶臣
tsung-ping	總兵	*Yang-wu*	揚武
tu-ssu	都司	*yang-wu*	洋務
t'uan-lien	團練	*yang-wu p'ai*	洋務派
t'uan-lien ta-ch'en	團練大臣	Yang Yüeh-pin	楊岳斌
Tung Huai	董槐	Yang Yung-nien	楊永年
T'ung-chih	同治	Yeh Wen-lan	葉文瀾
t'ung-k'ao kuan	同考官	Yeh Fu	葉富
T'ung-shang chü	通商局	Yen Fu	嚴復
t'ung-shuai	統帥	Ying-kuei	英桂
T'ung-wen Kuan	同文館	*yu-yung chih hsüeh*	有用之學
tzu-ch'iang	自強	Yü-chang shu-yüan	豫章書院
tzu-ch'iang yün-tung	自強運動	Yü-k'o	毓科
tzu-chih	自治	Yü-shan	玉山
Tz'u-hsi	慈禧	*yung* (application)	用
wai-hai shui-shih	外海水師	*yung* (mercenaries)	勇
Wan-nien Ch'ing	萬年清	*Yung-pao*	永保
Wang K'ai-t'ai	王凱泰	*yung-ying*	勇營
Wang K'ai-yün	王闓運	Yün-Kuei	雲貴
Wang Mao-yin	王茂蔭		

341

Bibliography

Private papers

Carroll, James. Private papers, which include four small books of 'Notes and Diary', and miscellaneous papers, such as the 'Contrat d'engagement' of 1 July 1876. Possession of Mr. F. E. Elliott, Saltash, Cornwall, England.

Giquel, Prosper Marie. Diary. Covers the period from 21 April to 19 October 1864 and an odd entry for 14 January 1866. Possession of Giquel's granddaughter, Madame La Baronne d'Ussel, Château de Bois-Dauphin, Sable, France.

Shen K'o, comp. 'Hsien Wen-su kung cheng-shu hsü-pien' (The political works of Shen Pao-chen, a supplement). Manuscript (n.p., 1889). No pagination. Page numbers given for this work refer to my hand-copied manuscript. Original copy is in the hands of Mr. Shen Tsu-hsing of Taipei, Taiwan, Republic of China.

Shen Tsan-ch'ing, comp. 'Wu-lin Shen-shih ch'ien Min pen-chi chia-p'u' (Genealogy of the branch of the Shen lineage of Wu-lin [present-day Hang hsien, Chekiang] that had moved to Fukien). Manuscript (n.p., 1933). Possession of Mr. Shen Tsu-hsing, Taipei, Taiwan, Republic of China.

Ting Jih-ch'ang. 'Ting chung-ch'eng cheng-shu' (The political papers of Ting Jih-ch'ang). Manuscript at the Sterling Memorial Library, Yale University.

Newspapers and journals

Chinese Recorder and Missionary Journal, The, Foochow, 1869–73; Shanghai, 1873–1911

Far East, The, Shanghai, monthly, 1876–1878

North-China Daily News, Shanghai, 1864–1911

North-China Herald and Supreme Court and Consular Gazette, Shanghai, weekly, 1870–1911

Shen-pao, Shanghai, daily; est. 1872

Government archives and documents

China, National Palace Museum Archives, Taipei
  Kung-chung tang (Palace archives)
  Yüeh-che tang (Monthly compilation of memorials for the State History Office)
China, Tsungli Yamen Archives, Taipei
  Chiang-hsi chiao-wu (Missionary affairs in Kiangsi)
  'O' (Russian file)
France, Ministère de la Marine
  BB4 1382 Etat Major-General, 1ʳᵉ Section, Lettres de la Guerre, Années 1869–1887, which includes the following frequently cited report:
      Contenson (Captain), 'Rapport de M. le Capitaine d'Etat-major de Contenson attaché militaire à la légation de France en Chine sur l'arsenal de Fou-tchéou', 13 August 1872
      1395 Copie de la correspondance: Garnault avec M. le Ministre de la Marine et des colonies
      1426 Resources militaires des ports de la mer de Chine (1888)
      1535 Lettres des agents diplomatiques et consulaires (reçues par le commandant de la divisions, 1858–1883)
      1555 Arsenal de Foutchéou (1866–1877); correspondance et pièces diverses (1870–1895), which includes the following frequently cited reports:
        Thibaudier, D. (subengineer), 'Arsenal de Fou-tchéou', 8 June 1868; 17/5/8
        Véron, Pierre (Captain), 'Rapport de M. le Commandant Véron', 1870; 17/5/33
      1556 Arsenal de Foutchéou (1895–1896 et 1898–1900), which includes the following frequently cited report:
        Médard, Léon, 'Note confidentielle sur l'Arsenal', 1898; 17/5/54
  CC7 1020 Dossier individuel: Giquel, Prosper François Marie
      1850 Dossier individuel: Neveue d'Aiguebelle, Paul Alexandre
      2728 Dossier individuel: de Segonzac, Marie Joseph Louis Philibert Dunoyer
France, Ministère des Affaires Etrangères, Dépêches politiques des consuls, Chine Great Britain, *Parliamentary Papers of the House of Commons*
Great Britain, Foreign Office Archives
  FO 17   General Correspondence, China
  FO 228   Embassy and Consular Archives, China: Correspondence
  FO 233   Miscellanea
  FO 371   General Correspondence, Political
  FO 682   Miscellaneous Papers in Chinese
  FO 931   Kwangtung Provincial Archives (formerly a part of FO 682)
United States, Records of the Department of State, Consular Dispatches: Foochow, vol. 4 (Record Group 59, FM 105/4)

Books and articles

Adshead, S. A. M. *The Modernization of the Chinese Salt Administration, 1900–1920.* Cambridge, Mass., 1970.

Anon. 'The Chinese Arsenals and Armaments'. *Cornhill Magazine* (December 1872), 697–8.

Apter, David E. *The Politics of Modernization.* Chicago, 1965.

Balazs, Etienne. *Political Theory and Administrative Reality in Traditional China.* London, 1965.

Bales, W. L. *Tso Tsung-t'ang: Soldier and Statesman of Old China.* Shanghai, 1937.

Bastid-Bruguière, Marianne. 'Currents of Social Change'. In *Late Ch'ing, 1800–1911*, part 2. The Cambridge History of China, vol. 11, ed. John K. Fairbank and Kwang-ching Liu, pp. 535–402, Cambridge, 1980.

'Ch'ing-i and the Self-Strengthening Movement'. See *Ch'ing-chi tzu-ch'iang yün-tung yen-t'ao-hui lun-wen-chi*, vol. 2, pp. 873–93.

Beasley, William G. *The Modern History of Japan*, 2d ed. New York, 1974.

Bereznii, L. A. 'A Critique of American Bourgeois Historiography on China: Problems of Social Development in the Nineteenth and Early Twentieth Centuries'. An unauthorized digest of the book by the same title (in Russian; Leningrad, 1968). Cambridge, Mass., 1969.

Biggerstaff, Knight. 'The Secret Correspondence of 1867–1868: Views of Leading Chinese Statesmen Regarding the Further Opening of China to Western Influence'. *Journal of Modern History*, 22 (1950), 122–36.

The Earliest Modern Government Schools in China. Ithaca, N.Y., 1961.

Borthwick, Sally. 'Schooling and Society in Late Qing China'. Ph.D. diss., Australian National University, 1978.

Boulger, Demetrius. *The Life of Sir Halliday Macartney.* London, 1908.

Brandt, P. J. van den. *Les Lazaristes en Chine, 1697–1935: Notes biographiques.* Peiping, 1936.

Broadbridge, Seymour. 'Shipbuilding and the State in Japan since the 1850s'. *Modern Asian Studies*, 11.4 (1977), 601–13.

Brown, Shannon R. 'The Ewo Filature: A Study in the Transfer of Technology to China in the 19th Century'. *Technology and Culture*, 20.3 (July 1979), 550–68.

Brown, Shannon R., and Tim Wright. 'Technology, Economics and Politics in the Modernization of China's Coal Mining Industry: The First Phase, 1850–1895'. *Explorations in Economic History*, 18.1 (January 1981), 60–83.

Brugger, William. *Democracy and Organisation in the Chinese Industrial Enterprise (1948–1953).* Cambridge, 1976.

Brunnert, H. S., and V. V. Hagelstrom. *Present Day Political Organization of China.* Shanghai, 1912.

Chang Chin-chien. *Chung-kuo wen-kuan chih-tu shih* (A history of the Chinese civil bureauracy). Taipei, 1955.

Chang Chün-hua and Yü Su-yün. 'Yang-wu yün-tung chung chin-tai ch'i-yeh ching-ying kuan-li ti t'e-tien' (Special features in the management of modern enterprises in the *yang-wu* movement). See *Chi-lin ta-hsüeh she-hui k'o-hsüeh lun-ts'ung*, pp. 278–95.

Chang Chung-li. *The Chinese Gentry: Studies on Their Role in Nineteenth-Century Chinese Society*. Seattle Wash., 1955.

The Income of the Chinese Gentry. Seattle, Wash., 1962.

Chang Hao. 'The Anti-foreign Role of Wo-jen (1804–1871)'. *Papers on China*, 14 (1960), 1–29.

Liang Ch'i-ch'ao and Intellectual Transition in China, 1890–1907. Cambridge, Mass., 1971.

'On the *Ching-shih* Ideal in Neo-Confucianism'. *Ch'ing-shih wen-t'i*, 3.1 (November 1974), 36–61.

'Sung Ming i-lai Ju-chia ching-shih ssu-hsiang shih-shih' (An elucidation of Confucian statecraft ideas since Sung and Ming times). In *Chin-shih Chung-kuo ching-shih ssu-hsiang yen-t'ao-hui lun-wen-chi* (Proceedings of the Conference on the Theory of Statecraft of Modern China, 25–7 August 1983), comp. and ed. Institute of Modern History, Academia Sinica, pp. 3–19. Taipei, 1984.

Chang Hsia, Yang Chih-pen, Lo Shu-wei, Wang Su-po, and Chang Li-min, eds. *Ch'ing-mo hai-chün shih-liao* (Source materials on the navy in late Ch'ing). Peking, 1982.

Chang Hsin-pao. *Commissioner Lin and the Opium War*. Cambridge, Mass., 1964.

Chang Kuo-hui. *Yang-wu yün-tung yü Chung-kuo chin-tai ch'i-yeh* (The *yang-wu* movement and modern Chinese enterprises). Peking, 1979.

Chang Yü-fa. 'Fu-chou ch'uan-ch'ang chih k'ai-ch'ang chi ch'i ch'u-ch'i fa-chan (1866–1875)'. (The founding and early development of the Foochow Navy Yard, 1866–1875). *Chung-yang yen-chiu-yüan Chin-tai-shih yen-chiu-so chi-k'an* (Bulletin of the Institute of Modern History, Academia Sinica), 2 (1971), 177–225.

Chao Lieh-wen. *Neng-ching-chü jih-chi* (Chao Lieh-wen's diary). Taipei, 1964.

Ch'en Chen, comp. *Chung-kuo chin-tai kung-yeh-shih tzu-liao, ti-san-chi* (Source materials on the history of modern industry in China, 3rd collection). 2 vols. Peking, 1961.

Ch'en Chiang. 'Lun yang-wu-p'ai kung-yeh-chi-shu ti yin-chin huo-tung' (On the *yang-wu* group and their transfer of technology [to China]). See *Chi-lin ta-hsüeh she-hui k'o-hsüeh lun-ts'ung*, pp. 349–69.

Ch'en, Gideon. *Lin Tse-hsü: Pioneer Promoter of the Adoption of Western Means of Maritime Defense in China*. Peiping, 1934.

Tseng Kuo-fan: Pioneer Promoter of the Steamship in China. Peiping, 1935.

Tso Tsung-t'ang: Pioneer Promoter of the Modern Dockyard and the Woollen Mill in China. Peiping, 1938.

Ch'en, Jerome. 'The Hsien-feng Inflation'. *Bulletin of the School of Oriental and African Studies*, no. 21 (1958), 578–86.

Ch'en Ta-tuan. 'Investiture of Liu-ch'iu Kings in the Ch'ing Period'. In *The Chinese World Order*, ed. John K. Fairbank, pp. 135–63, 315–20. Cambridge, Mass., 1968.

Chesneaux, Jean. 'The Chinese Labour Force in the First Part of the Twentieth Century'. In *The Economic Development of China and Japan*, ed. C. D. Cowan, pp. 111–27. London, 1964.

Chi-lin ta-hsüeh she-hui k'o-hsüeh lun-ts'ung (Jilin University: Studies in social science), no. 2: *Yang-wu yün-tung t'ao-lun chuan-chi* (Special issue on the *yang-wu* movement), ed. Chi-lin ta-hsüeh she-hui k'o-hsüeh hsüeh-pao pien-chi-pu (Jilin University: Editorial Office of the Social Science Journal). Chi-lin, 1980.

Chiang-hsi t'ung-chih (Gazetteer of Kiangsi province). 180 *chüan*. 1880.

Chiang T'ing-fu (T. F. Tsiang), comp. *Chin-tai Chung-kuo wai-chiao shih-liao chi-yao* (Important materials on modern Chinese diplomatic history). 2 vols. Shanghai, 1932–4.

Chiao Ching-i. 'Ts'ung Fu-chou ch'uan-cheng-chü k'an yang-wu-p'ai so pan chün-shih kung-yeh ti feng-chien chu-i hsing-chih' (The feudal character of the military industry managed by the yang-wu group as seen in the Foochow Navy Yard). See *Chi-lin ta-hsüeh she-hui k'o-hsüeh lun-ts'ung*, pp. 229–43.

Chiao-wu chi-lüeh (An outline of Church affairs). Published by order of Chou Fu. Variétés sinologiques, no. 47. Shanghai, 1917.

Ch'ien Mu. *Chung-kuo chin-san-pai-nien hsüeh-shu-shih* (A history of Chinese scholarship in the last three hundred years). 2 vols. Shanghai, 1937.

Ch'ien Shih-fu, comp. *Ch'ing-chi chung-yao chih-kuan nien-piao* (Chronological tables of important officials of the late Ch'ing). Shanghai, 1959.

Ch'ing-chi hsin-she chih-kuan nien-piao (Chronological tables of occupants of new offices in late Ch'ing). Peking, 1961.

Chien Yu-wen. *T'ai-p'ing t'ien-kuo ch'üan-shih* (The complete history of the Taiping Kingdom). 3 vols. Hong Kong, 1962.

Ch'ih Chung-hu. 'Hai-chün ta-shih chi' (Major events in [Chinese] naval history). In *Chung-kuo chin-pai-nien shih tzu-liao hsü-pien* (Historical sources for the past hundred years, a preliminary compilation), comp. Tso Shun-sheng, pp. 323–63. Taipei, 1958.

Chin Liang, comp. *Chin-shih jen-wu chih* (Biographies of late Ch'ing and early Republican figures compiled from extracts from the works of Weng T'ung-ho, Li Tz'u-ming, Wang K'ai-yün, and Yeh Ch'eng-ch'ieh). Taipei, 1955.

Ch'ing-ch'ao hsü wen-hsien t'ung-kao (Encyclopaedia of Ch'ing administration, supplement), comp. Liu Chin-tsao et al. 400 *chüan*. Shanghai, 1936.

Ch'ing-ch'ao yeh-shih ta-kuan (A collection of anecdotal accounts of the Ch'ing dynasty), comp. Hsiao heng-hsiang-shih chu-jen (pseud.). 5 vols. Taipei, 1959.

Ch'ing-chi tzu-ch'iang yün-tung yen-t'ao-hui lun-wen-chi (Proceedings of the Conference on the Self-Strengthening Movement in Late Ch'ing China, 1860–1894), comp. and ed. Institute of Modern History, Academia Sinica. 2 vols. Taipei, 1988.

Ch'ing-shih (Dynastic history of the Ch'ing), comp. Ch'ing-shih pien-tsuan wei-yüan-hui (Committee for the compilation of the Ch'ing dynastic history). 8 vols. Taipei, 1961.

Ch'ing-shih lieh-chuan (Biographies of the Ch'ing dynasty), comp. Ch'ing-shih kuan (Office for the compilation of the dynastic history of the Ch'ing). 48 *chüan.* Shanghai, 1928.

Chiu-chiang fu-chih (Gazetteer of Chiu-chiang prefecture). n.p., 1873.

Chou Ku-ch'eng. *Chung-kuo shih-hsüeh lun-wen-chi* (Studies in Chinese historiography). Peking, 1983.

Ch'ou-pan i-wu shih-mo (The complete account of our management of barbarian affairs). Peiping, 1930.

Chu Hsieh. *Chung-kuo yün-ho shih-liao hsüan-chi* (Selected historical materials on the canals of China). Peking, 1962.

Ch'ü T'ung-tsu. *Local Government in China Under the Ch'ing.* Cambridge, Mass., 1962.

Ch'uan-cheng tsou-yi hui-pien (Memorials on the Foochow Navy Yard). 54 *chüan.* Last document dated 10 April 1902.

Chung-kuo chin-tai-shi kao pien-hsieh-tsu (Editorial group for the draft history of modern China). 'Yang-wu huo-tung: Chin-tai chün-shih kung-yeh ti chien-li' (Engaging in foreign matters: The establishment of modern military industries). *Chin-tai-shih yen-chiu,* 1981.2, 127–44.

Chung-kuo li-shih-hsüeh nien-chien (Chinese historical review, annual) ed. Chung-kuo shih-hsüeh-hui (Chinese historical association). Peking, 1979, 1981– .

Chung-Mei kuan-hsi shih-liao: T'ung-chih ch'ao (Documents on Sino-American relations during the T'ung-chih reign), comp. Kuo T'ing-i et al. 3 vols. Nankang, 1968.

Cohen, Paul A. 'The Hunan-Kiangsi Anti-Missionary Incidents of 1862'. *Papers on China,* 12 (1958), 1–27.

China and Christianity. Cambridge, Mass., 1963.

Between Tradition and Modernity: Wang T'ao and Reform in Late Ch'ing China. Cambridge, Mass., 1974.

Discovering History in China: American Historical Writing on the Recent Chinese Past. New York, 1984.

Cordier, Henri. *Histoire des relations de la Chine avec les puissances occidentales, 1860–1902.* 3 vols. Paris, 1901–2.

Dalby, Michael T. 'Court Politics in Late T'ang Times'. In *Sui and T'ang China, 589–906,* part 1. The Cambridge History of China, vol. 3, ed. Denis Twitchett, pp. 561–8. Cambridge, 1979.

Dean, Britten. *China and Great Britain: The Diplomacy of Commercial Relations, 1860–1864.* Cambridge, Mass., 1974.

DeBary, William Theodore, Wing-tsit Chan, and Burton Watson, eds. *Sources of Chinese Tradition.* New York, 1960.

Dolby, J. *The Steel Navy.* London, 1862.

Eastman, Lloyd E. *Throne and Mandarins: China's Search for a Policy during the Sino-French Controversy, 1880–1885.* Cambridge, Mass., 1967.

'Political Reformism in China before the Sino-Japanese War'. *Journal of Asian Studies,* 27.4 (August 1968), 695–710.

Fairbank, J. K., and Teng Ssu-yü. *Ch'ing Administration: Three Studies.* Cambridge, Mass., 1961.

Fairbank, John K., Edwin O. Reischauer, and Albert M. Craig. *East Asia: The Modern Transformation*. Boston, 1965.

Feifel, Eugene. *Po Chü-i as a Censor*. The Hague, 1961.

Feng Kuei-fen. *Chiao-pin-lu k'ang-i* (Straightforward words from the Lodge of Early Chou studies). 1898; reprint ed., Taipei, 1967.

Feng-shun wen-shih (Literary and historical materials on Feng-shun district, Kwangtung), no. 2. Feng-shun, April 1989.

Feng Yu-lan. 'Wei Yüan ti ssu-hsiang' (Wei Yüan's thought). In *Chung-kuo chin-tai ssu-hsiang-shih lun-wen-chi* (An anthology of modern Chinese thought), ed. Shang-hai Jen-min ch'u-pan-she (People's publishing house, Shanghai), pp. 11–25. Shanghai, 1958.

Feuerwerker, Albert. 'Economic Aspects of Reform'. In *Reform in Nineteenth-century China*, ed. Paul A. Cohen and John E. Schrecker, pp. 35–40. Cambridge, Mass., 1976.

'Economic Trends in the Late Ch'ing Empire, 1870–1911'. In *Late Ch'ing, 1800–1911*, part 2. The Cambridge History of China, vol. 11, ed. John K. Fairbank and Kwang-ching Liu, pp. 1–69. Cambridge, 1980.

Fogel, Joshua. *Politics and Sinology: The Case of Naito Konan (1866–1934)*. Cambridge, Mass., 1984.

Folsom, Kenneth E. *Friends, Guests, and Colleagues: The Mu-fu System in the Late Ch'ing Period*. Berkeley and Los Angeles, 1968.

Frodsham, J. D., trans. *The First Chinese Embassy to the West: The Journal of Kuo Sung-t'ao, Liu Hsi-hung and Chang Te-yi*. London, 1974.

Fu-chien li-tai ming-jen chuan-lüeh (Biographical sketches of famous people of Fukien), comp. Fu-chien shih-fan ta-hsüeh li-shih hsi (Department of History, Fuchien Normal University). Foochow, 1987.

Fu-chien t'ung-chih (General gazetteer of Fukien). n.p., 1922.

Fu-chien t'ung-chih lieh-chuan hsüan (Selections from the biographical section of *Fu-chien t'ung-chih*). 3 vols. Taipei, 1964.

Fu-chou li-shih jen-wu (Historical figures of Foochow). 3 vols. Foochow, 1989.

Fu Tsung-mou. *Ch'ing-tai tu-fu chih-tu* (The system of governors-general and governors in the Ch'ing period). Taipei, 1963.

Giquel, Prosper Marie. *La politique française en Chine depuis les traites de 1858 et de 1860*. Paris, 1872.

The Foochow Arsenal and Its Results: From the Commencement in 1867, to the end of the Foreign Directorate, on the 16th February, 1874, trans. H. Lang, Shanghai, 1874. This edition does not contain the plan of the Foochow Navy Yard found in the French original entitled, *L'Arsenal de Fou-tcheou, ses Resultats* (Shanghai, 1874).

Hai-fang tang (Facsimile of the maritime defence file), comp. Chung-yang yen-chiu-yüan chin-tai-shih yen-chiu-so (Institute of Modern History, Academia Sinica). 5 parts in 9 vols. Taipei, 1957.

Hail, W. J. *Tseng Kuo-fan and the Taiping Rebellion*. New Haven, Conn., 1927.

Hinton, Harold C. *The Grain Tribute System of China (1845–1911)*. Cambridge, Mass., 1956.

Ho Liang-tung. *Huang-ch'ao ching-shih-wen ssu-pien* (Collection of Ch'ing dynasty writings on statecraft, 4th suppl.). 1902.

Ho Ping-ti. *The Ladder of Success in Imperial China: Aspects of Social Mobility, 1368–1911.* New York, 1962.

Hough, Richard. *A History of Fighting Ships.* London, 1975.

Hsia Hsieh (pseud. Chiang-shang chien-sou). *Chung-Hsi chi-shih* (Accounts of Sino-Western relations). 1865.

Hsia Nai. 'T'ai-p'ing t'ien-kuo ch'ien-hou Ch'ang-chiang ko-sheng chih t'ien-fu wen-t'i' (The problem of land levies in the Yangtze provinces around the time of the Taiping Rebellion). *Tsing Hua hsüeh-pao,* 10.2 (April 1935), 409–74. See reprint in Li Ting-i, et al. eds., *Chung-kuo chin-tai-shi lun-ts'ung,* 2d ser., vol. 2, pp. 145–204.

Hsiao I-shan. *Ch'ing-tai t'ung-shih* (A general history of the Ch'ing period). 5 vols. Taipei, 1963.

Hsiao Kung-chuan. *A History of Chinese Political Thought,* vol. 1, trans. F. W. Mote. Princeton, N.J., 1979.

Hsiao Kung-chuan. *Rural China: Imperial Control in the Nineteenth Century.* Seattle, Wash., 1960.

Hsiao Liang-lin. *China's Foreign Trade Statistics, 1864–1949.* Cambridge, Mass., 1974.

Hsieh Sung, 'Min Hai-kuan shui-shou ch'ing-k'uang' (Revenue of the Fukien customs). *Fu-chien wen-shih tzu-liao* (Historical materials on Fukien), no. 10 (Foochow, 1985), 14–18.

Hsü I-t'ang. *Ch'ing-tai mi-shih, ch'u-chi* (Selections from notebooks, collections of anecdotes, etc., dealing with the Ch'ing period, a preliminary compilation). Taipei, 1953.

Hsü, Immanuel C. Y. *China's Entrance into the Family of Nations: The Diplomatic Phase, 1858–1880.* Cambridge, Mass., 1960.

'The Great Policy Debate in China, 1874: Maritime Defense vs. Frontier Defense'. *Harvard Journal of Asiatic Studies,* 25 (1964–5), 212–28.

The Ili Crisis: A Study of Sino-Russian Diplomacy, 1871–1881. London, 1965.

The Rise of Modern China, 4th ed. Oxford, 1990.

Hsü K'o, comp. *Ch'ing-pai lei-ch'ao* (A collection of anecdotes of the Ch'ing period). 12 vols. 1928.

Hsü T'ai-lai. 'Yeh p'ing yang-wu yün-tung' (Also a reappraisal of the *yang-wu* movement). *Li-shih yen-chiu* (Historical studies), 1980.4, 19–36.

Hsüeh Fu-ch'eng. 'Shu Ho-fei po-hsiang Li-kung yung Hu p'ing Wu' (How Li Hung-chang used Shanghai to pacify Kiangsu). In *Chung-kuo chin-pai-nien shih tzu-liao ch'u-pien* (Historical sources for the past hundred years, a preliminary compilation), comp. Tso Shun-sheng, pp. 163–7. Shanghai, 1931–3.

Hu Lin-i. *Hu Wen-chung kung i-chi* (The collected works of Hu Lin-i). 1867.

Hu Lin-i chi (The collected works of Hu Lin-i). Taipei, 1957.

Hu-nan t'ung-chih (Gazetteer of Hunan province). n.p., 1885.

Huang Chia-mo. *Chia-wu chan-ch'ien chih T'ai-wan mei-wu* (The coal industry in Taiwan before the Sino-Japanese War). Taipei, 1961.

'Chung-kuo tien-hsien ti ch'uang-chien' (The beginning of telegraph lines in China). *Ta-lu tsa-chih* (Continent magazine), 36.6–7 (April 1968), 171–87.

Huang Chun. *Hua-sui-jen-sheng an chih-i ch'üan-pien* (The recollections of Huang Chun), ed. Hsü Yen-p'ien and Su T'ung-ping. Hong Kong, 1979.

Huang I-feng. *Chung-kuo chin-tai ching-chi-shih lun-wen-chi* (Studies in modern Chinese economic history). Yangchow, 1981.

Huang I-feng and Chiang To. 'Ch'ung p'ing yang-wu yün-tung' (A reappraisal of the *yang-wu* movement). *Li-shih yen-chiu* (Historical studies), 1979.2, 58–70.

Huang Yin-p'u. 'Pa Shen Pao-chen t'iao-shih Fu-chien i-chü (ch'uan-cheng hsüeh-t'ang) chang-ch'eng shou-chien' (On Shen Pao-chen's instructions regarding the regulations for the Foochow Naval Academy). In *Yang-wu yün-tung yen-chiu lun-chi* (Studies on the *yang-wu* movement), ed. Chou K'ang-hsieh, pp. 145–55. Hong Kong, 1973.

Huc, Evariste-Regis. *The Chinese Empire: Forming a Sequel to the Work Entitled 'Recollections of a Journey through Tartary and Thibet'.* London, 1855.

Hucker, Charles O. *The Traditional Chinese State in Ming Times (1368–1644).* Tucson, Ariz., 1961.

The Censorial System of Ming China. Stanford, Calif., 1966.

Hummel, Arthur W., ed. *Eminent Chinese of the Ch'ing Period.* 2 vols. Washington, D.C., 1943.

I-wen ts'ung-chi (Anecdotes and jottings from the Ch'ing period). 16 vols. Taipei, 1978.

Iwata, Masakazu. *Okubo Toshimichi: The Bismarck of Japan.* Berkeley and Los Angeles, 1964.

Jones, Hazel J. 'The Meiji Government and Foreign Employees, 1868–1900'. Ph.D. diss., University of Michigan, 1967.

Kennedy, Thomas L. 'Industrial Metamorphosis in the Self-Strengthening Movement: Li Hung-chang and the Kiangnan Shipbuilding Program'. *Journal of the Institute of Chinese Studies* (Chinese University of Hong Kong), 4.1 (1971), 207–26.

'Self-strengthening: An Analysis Based on Some Recent Writings'. *Ch'ing-shih wen-t'i*, 3.1 (November 1974), 3–35.

The Arms of Kiangnan: Modernization in the Chinese Ordnance Industry, 1860–1895. Boulder, Colo., 1978.

King, Frank H. H. *Money and Monetary Policy in China, 1845–1895.* Cambridge, Mass., 1965.

Ko Hsü-ts'un. *Ch'ing-tai ming-jen i-shih* (Anecdotes of famous people of the Ch'ing period). Shanghai, 1933.

Ko Shih-chün, comp. *Huang-ch'ao ching-shih-wen hsü-pien* (Collection of Ch'ing dynasty writings on statecraft, continued). 120 *chüan*. Shanghai, 1888.

Kodama Kota. *Sangyōshi* (Industrial history [of Japan]), vol. 2. Tokyo, 1965.

Kuang-hsin fu-chih (Gazetteer of Kuang-hsin prefecture), comp. Li Shu-fan et al., 1873.

Kuhn, Philip A. *Rebellion and Its Enemies in Late Imperial China: Militarization and Social Structure, 1796–1864*. Cambridge, Mass, 1970.

'Local Self-Government under the Republic: Problems of Control, Autonomy, and Mobilization'. In *Conflict and Control in Late Imperial China*, ed. Frederic Wakeman, Jr., and Carolyn Grant, pp. 257–98. Berkeley and Los Angeles, 1975.

Kung-chung tang Kuang-hsü ch'ao chou-che (Secret palace memorials of the Kuang-hsü period), comp. Kuo-li ku-kung po-wu-yüan, Ku-kung wen-hsien pien-chi wei-yüan-hui. 26 vols. Taipei, 1973.

Kuo Sung-tao. *Yang-chih shu-wu i-chi* (The collected writings of Kuo Sung-tao). 55 *chüan*. 1892.

Kuo Ting-yee and Liu Kwang-ching. 'Self-strengthening: The Pursuit of Western Technology'. In *Late Ch'ing, 1800–1911*, part 1. The Cambridge History of China, vol. 10, ed. John K. Fairbank, pp. 491–542. Cambridge, 1978.

Kuo T'ing-i (Kuo Ting-yee), comp. *Chin-tai Chung-kuo shih-shih jih-chih* (A chronology of modern Chinese history, 1829–1911). 2 vols. Taipei, 1963.

Kuo T'ing-i (Kuo Ting-yee), K. Y. Yin, and Lu Pao-ch'ien, comps. *Kuo Sung-t'ao hsien-sheng nien-p'u* (A chronological biography of Kuo Sung-t'ao). 2 vols. Taipei, 1971.

Kuo-ying Chao-shang-chü ch'i-shih-wu chou-nien chi-nien-k'an (Volume to commemorate the seventy-fifth anniversary of the China Merchants' Steam Navigation Company). Shanghai, 1947.

Lary, Diana. *Region and Nation: The Kwangsi Clique in Chinese Politics, 1925–1937*. Cambridge, 1974.

Latourette, Kenneth S. *A History of Christian Missions in China*. London, 1929.

Lau, D. C. *Mencius*. Harmondsworth, 1970.

Lei Hai-tsung. 'Chung-kuo ti ping' (China's military). *She-hui k'o-hsüeh tsa-chih* (Social science journal), 1.1 (1935), 1–47.

'Wu-ping ti wen-hua' (An amilitary civilization). *She-hui k'o-hsüeh tsa-chih* (Social science journal), 1.4 (1936), 1005–39.

Leibo, Steven A. *Transferring Technology to China: Prosper Giquel and the Self-strengthening Movement*. China Research Monograph, Center for Chinese Studies, University of California, Berkeley, 1985.

Leonard, Jane Kate. *Wei Yuan and China's Rediscovery of the Maritime World*. Cambridge, Mass., 1984.

Levenson, Joseph R. *Confucian China and Its Modern Fate: A Trilogy*. Berkeley and Los Angeles, 1968.

Lewis, Michael. *The History of the British Navy*. Harmondsworth, 1957.

Li Chi (Book of rites), trans. James Legge; ed. with an introduction by Ch'u Chai and Winberg Chai. New York, 1967.

Li En-han. *Tseng Chi-tse ti wai-chiao* (The diplomacy of Tseng Chi-tse). Taipei, 1966.

Li Huan. *Pao-wei chai lei-kao* (The collected works of Li Huan). 1891.

Li Hung-chang. *Li Wen-chung kung ch'üan-chi* (The complete works of Li Hung-chang). 165 *chüan*. Nanking, 1905.

Li Kuo-ch'i. 'T'ung-chih chung-hsing shih-ch'i Liu K'un-i tsai Chiang-hsi hsün-fu jen-nei ti piao-hsien' (Liu K'un-i's governorship in Kiangsi during the T'ung-chih Restoration), *Li-shih hsüeh-pao* (Bulletin of historical research), 1 (January 1973), 241–69.

Li Shih-yüeh. 'Chia-wu chan-cheng ch'ien san-shih nien chien fan yang-chiao yün-tung' (The movement against Western religions during the thirty-year period before the Sino-Japanese War of 1894–1895). *Li-shih yen-chiu* (Historical studies), 6.5 (1958), 1–15.

'Ts'ung yang-wu, wei-hsin tao tzu-ch'an chieh-chi ke-ming' (From *yang-wu* and the Reform Movement of the 1890s to the Bourgeois Revolution of 1911). *Li-shih yen-chiu* (Historical studies), 1980.1, 31–40.

Li Shou-k'ung. *Li Hung-chang chuan* (A biography of Li Hung-chang). Taipei, 1978.

Li Ting-fang. *Tseng Kuo-fan chi-ch'i mu-fu jen-wu* (Tseng Kuo-fan and his personal assistants). Kwei-yang, 1946.

Li Ting-i, Pao Tsun-p'eng, and Wu Hsiang-hsiang, eds. *Chung-kuo chin-tai-shi lun-ts'ung* (Studies in modern Chinese history), 2nd ser. vol. 2: *She-hui ching-chi* (Society and economics) (Taipei, 1958); vol. 3: *Ts'ai-cheng ching-chi* (Finance and economics) (Taipei, 1958); vol. 5: *Cheng-chih* (Politics) (Taipei, 1963).

Li Yüan-tu. *T'ien-yüeh shan-kuan wen-ch'ao* (The collected writings of Li Yüan-tu). n.p., Kuang-hsü period.

Liang I-chen. *Ch'ing-tai fu-nü wen-hsüeh shih* (A history of literary works by women of the Ch'ing period). Taipei, 1958.

Liao Yü-wen. 'Wang Yüan-chih yü ch'i *Yeh-yü teng-ch'ien lu hsü-lu*' (Wang Yüan-chih and his autobiographical sketch, 1842–1917). *T'ai-pei wen-hsien* (Historical materials on T'ai-pei), 11–12 (June 1970), 35–42.

Lin Ch'ing-yüan. 'Ma-wei ch'uan-cheng-chü p'ing-yung wai-kuo jen-yüan ti hsing-chih he tso-yung' (The nature and impact of the employment of foreigners at the Ma-wei dockyard). See *Chi-lin ta-hsüeh she-hui k'o-hsüeh lun-ts'ung*, pp. 203–28.

Fu-chien ch'uan-cheng-chü shih-kao (History of the Foochow Navy Yard). Foochow, 1986.

Lin Ch'ung-yung. *Lin Tse-hsü chuan* (Biography of Lin Tse-hsü). Taipei, 1967.

'Lin Ching-jen yü ch'i-yüan hsüeh-shu' (Lin P'u-ch'ing's letter of blood begging for military help). *Chung-yang yen-chiu-yüan chin-tai-shih yen-chiu-so chi-k'an* (Bulletin of the Institute of Modern History, Academia Sinica), 7 (June 1978), 287–308.

Lin Ch'ung-yung. *Shen Pao-chen yü Fu-chou ch'uan-cheng* (Shen Pao-chen and the Foochow Navy Yard). Taipei, 1987.

Lin Hsüan-chih, comp. *Fu-chou Ma-wei-kang t'u-chih* (An illustrated gazetteer of Ma-wei harbour). Foochow, 1984.

Little, Alicia. *Li Hung-chang: His Life and Times*. London, 1903.

Liu, James T. C. 'The Variety of Political Reforms in Chinese History: A

Simplified Typology'. In *Reform in Nineteenth-Century China*, ed. Paul A. Cohen and John E. Schrecker, pp. 9–13. Cambridge, Mass., 1976.

Liu K'un-i. *Liu K'un-i i-chi* (Collected works of Liu K'un-i). 6 vols. Peking, 1959.

Liu Kwang-ching. 'Li Hung-chang in Chihli: The Emergence of a Policy, 1870–1875'. In *Approaches to Modern Chinese History*, ed. Albert Feuerwerker, Rhoads Murphey, and Mary C. Wright, pp. 68–104. Berkeley and Los Angeles, 1967.

'Nineteenth-Century China: The Disintegration of the Old Order and the Impact of the West'. In *China in Crisis*, ed. Ping-ti Ho and Tang Tsou, vol. 1, book 1, pp. 93–178. Chicago, 1968.

Liu Kwang-ching. 'The Confucian as Patriot and Pragmatist: Li Hung-chang's Formative Years, 1823–1866'. *Harvard Journal of Asiatic Studies*, 30 (1970), 5–45.

'The Limits of Regional Power in the Late Ch'ing Period: A Reappraisal'. *Tsing Hua hsüeh-pao*, new ser., 10.2 (July 1974), 176–207 (in Chinese), and 207–23 (in English).

'Politics, Intellectual Outlook, and Reform: The T'ung-wen Kuan Controversy of 1867'. In *Reform in Nineteenth-century China*, ed. Paul A. Cohen and John E. Schrecker, pp. 87–100. Cambridge, Mass., 1976.

'The Ch'ing Restoration'. In *Late Ch'ing, 1800–1911*, part 1. The Cambridge History of China, vol. 10, ed. John K. Fairbank, pp. 409–90. Cambridge, 1978.

Liu Shih-chi. 'Ch'ing-chi hai-fang yü sai-fang chih cheng ti yen-chiu' (A study of the dispute over maritime defence and Inner Asian frontier defence in late Ch'ing). *Ku-kung wen-hsien* (Journal of the National Palace Museum), 2.3 (June 1971), 37–59.

Liu T'ieh-leng, comp. *Ch'ing-tai erh-pai chia chün-cheng ming-tu hui-pien* (A collection of famous letters by two hundred military leaders and administrators in the Ch'ing period). Shanghai. 1926.

Lo Erh-kang. 'Ch'ing-chi ping wei chiang-yu ti ch'i-yüan' (The origin of personal armies in late Ch'ing times). *Chung-kuo she-hui ching-chi shih chi-k'an* (Chinese social and economic history quarterly), 5.2 (June 1937), 235–50.

Lo Ta-ch'un. *Lo Ching-shan T'ai-wan k'ai-shan jih-chi* (The diary of Lo Ta-ch'un on the opening up of Taiwan), ed. with an introduction by David Pong. Taipei, 1972.

Lo Yü-tung. *Chung-kuo li-chin shih* (The history of likin in China). 2 vols. Shanghai, 1936.

Lü Liang-hai. 'Wei Yüan hsiang Hsi-fang hsüeh-hsi wen-t'i ti t'an-t'ao' (An inquiry on Wei Yüan's idea of learning from the West). *Chin-tai-shih yen-chiu* (Studies on modern history), 1980.2, 239–55.

Lü Shih-ch'iang. *Chung-kuo tsao-ch'i ti lun-ch'uan ching-ying* (The early phase of steamship development in China). Nankang, 1962.

'Feng Kuei-fen ti cheng-chih ssu-hsiang' (Feng Kuei-fen's political ideas). *Chung-hua wen-hua fu-hsing yüeh-k'an* (Chinese culture revival monthly), 4.2 (February 1971), 1–8.

Ting Jih-ch'ang yü tzu-ch'iang yün-tung (Ting Jih-ch'ang and China's self-strengthening). Taipei, 1972.

Lui, Adam Yuen-chung. 'The Practical Training of Government Officials under the Early Ch'ing, 1644–1795'. *Asia Major*, 16.1–2 (1971), 82–95.

MacKinnon, Stephen R. *Power and Politics in Late Imperial China: Yuan Shi-kai in Beijing and Tianjin. 1901–1908*. Berkeley and Los Angeles, 1980.

Mann, Susan. *Local Merchants and the Chinese Bureaucracy*. Stanford, Calif. 1987.

Mayers, William F., N. B. Dennys, and Charles King. *The Treaty Ports of China and Japan*. London, 1867.

Meng, S. M. *The Tsungli Yamen: Its Organization and Functions*. Cambridge, Mass., 1962.

Meskill, John. *The Pattern of Chinese History: Cycles, Development, or Stagnation?* Boston, 1966.

Metzger, Thomas A. *The Internal Organization of Ch'ing Bureaucracy: Legal, Normative, and Communication Aspects*. Cambridge, Mass., 1973.

Escape from Predicament: Neo-Confucianism and China's Evolving Political Culture. New York, 1977.

Miao Ch'üan-sun, comp. *Hsü pei-chuan chi* (Collected memorial inscriptions, continued). 1893.

Michael, Franz, in collaboration with Chung-li Chang. *The Taiping Rebellion: History and Documents*. 3 vols. Seattle, Wash., 1966–71.

Michie, Alexander. *Missionaries in China*. London, 1891.

China and Christianity. Boston, 1900.

Min-Hou hsien-chih (Gazetteer of Min and Hou-kuan districts). Foochow, 1933.

Ming Ch'ing li-k'o chin-shih t'i-ming pei-lu (List of successful candidates in the *chin-shih* examinations during the Ming and Ching periods). 4 vols. Taipei, 1969.

Moidrey, Joseph de. *La hiérarchie Catholique en Chine, en Corée, et au Japon (1307–1914)*. Variétés sinologiques, no. 38. Shanghai, 1914.

Morohashi Tetsuji, comp. *Dai Kanwa jiten* (Chinese–Japanese dictionary). 13 vols. Tokyo, 1955.

Morse, Hosea Ballou. *The International Relations of the Chinese Empire*. 3 vols. London, 1910–18.

Mou An-shih. *Yang-wu yün-tung* (The *yang-wu* movement). Shanghai, 1961.

Moulder, Frances V. *Japan, China, and the Modern World Economy: Toward a Reinterpretation of East Asian Development, ca. 1600 to ca. 1918*. Cambridge, 1977.

Nan-ch'ang fu-chih (Gazetteer of Nan-ch'ang prefecture). 1873.

Nivison, David S. 'Ho-shen and His Accusers: Ideology and Political Behavior in the Eighteenth Century'. In *Confucianism in Action*, ed. David S. Nivison and Arthur F. Wright, pp. 209–43. Stanford, Calif., 1959.

'Protest Against Conventions and Conventions of Protest'. In *The Confucian Persuasion*, ed. Arthur F. Wright, pp. 177–201. Stanford, Calif., 1960.

Ocko, Jonathan K. *Bureaucratic Reform in Provincial China: Ting Jih-ch'ang in Restoration Kiangsu, 1867–1870*. Cambridge, Mass., 1983.

Pa hsien shou-cha (Letters of eight worthies). Shanghai, 1935.

Bibliography

P'eng Tse-i. *Shih-chiu-shih-chi hou-pan-ch'i ti Chung-kuo ts'ai-cheng yü ching-chi* (The economy and financial administration of China in the latter part of the nineteenth century). Peking, 1983.

P'eng Yü-hsin. 'Ch'ing-mo chung-yang yü ko-sheng ts'ai-cheng kuan-hsi' (The financial relationship between the central government and the provinces in late Ch'ing). *She-hui-k'o-hsüeh tsa-chih* (Social science journal), 9.1 (June 1947), 83–110.

Perkins, Dwight H. 'Government as an Obstacle to Industrialization: The Case of Nineteenth-Century China'. *Journal of Economic History*, 27.4 (December 1967), 478–92.

Agricultural Development in China (1368–1968). Chicago, 1969. Pien Pao-ti. *Pien chih-chün tsou-i*. 1894.

Polachek, James. 'Gentry Hegemony: Soochow in the T'ung-chih Restoration'. In *Conflict and Control in Late Imperial China*, ed. Frederic Wakeman, Jr., and Carolyn Grant, pp. 211–56. Berkeley and Los Angeles, 1975.

Pong, David. 'The Income and Military Expenditure of Kiangsi Province in the Last Years (1860–1864) of the Taiping Rebellion'. *Journal of Asian Studies*, 26.1 (November 1966), 49–66.

'Modernization and Politics in China as Seen in the Career of Shen Pao-chen (1820–1879)'. Ph.D. diss., University of London, 1969.

'Dynastic Crisis and Censorial Response: Shen Pao-chen in 1854'. *Journal of the Institute of Chinese Studies* (Chinese University of Hong Kong), 5.2 (1972), 455–76.

'Western Technicians and Technical Aid in China's Early Developmental Experience: The Foochow Navy Yard, 1866–1875'. *Papers on Far Eastern History*, 20 (September 1979), 83–104.

'The Vocabulary of Change: Reformism in the 1860s and 1870s'. Paper presented at the workshop 'China in Transformation, 1860–1949', Australian National University, 24–5 October 1981.

'The Vocabulary of Change: Reformist Ideas of the 1860s and 1870s'. In *Ideal and Reality*, ed. David Pong and Edmund S. K. Fung, pp. 25–61. Lanham, Md., 1985.

'Keeping the Foochow Navy Yard Afloat: Government Finance and China's Early Modern Defence Industry, 1866–75'. *Modern Asian Studies*, 21.1 (February 1987), 121–52.

'Shen Pao-chen and the Great Policy Debate of 1874–1875'. See *Ch'ing-chi tzu-ch'iang yün-tung yen-t'ao-hui lun-wen-chi*, pp. 189–225.

Pong, David, and Edmund S. K. Fung, eds. *Ideal and Reality: Social and Political Change in Modern China, 1860–1949*. Lanham, Md., 1985.

Porter, Jonathan. *Tseng Kuo-fan's Private Bureaucracy*. Berkeley and Los Angeles, 1972.

Rawlinson, John L. *China's Struggle for Naval Development, 1839–1895*. Cambridge, Mass., 1967.

Roche, James F., and L. L. Cowen. *The French at Foochow*. Shanghai, 1884.

Rowbotham, Arnold H. *Missionary and Mandarin: The Jesuits at the Court of China*. Berkeley and Los Angeles, 1942.

Sakai, Robert K. 'The Ryukyu (Liu-ch'iu) Islands as a Fief of Satsuma'. In *The Chinese World Order*, ed. John K. Fairbank, pp. 112–34, 311–14. Cambridge, Mass., 1968.

Schwartz, Benjamin. *In Search of Wealth and Power: Yen Fu and the West*. Cambridge, Mass., 1964.

Scruton, Roger. *A Dictionary of Political Thought*. New York, 1982.

Shen Chen Han-yin. 'Tseng Kuo-fan in Peking, 1840–1852: His Ideas on Statecraft and Reform'. *Journal of Asian Studies*, 27.1 (November 1967), 61–80.

Shen Pao-chen. *Shen Wen-su kung cheng-shu* (The political works of Shen Pao-chen), comp. Wu Yüan-ping. 7 *chüan*. Soochow, 1880.

Shen Sun-yü. 'Shen Wen-su kung i-shih k'ao-cheng' (Verification of anecdotes concerning Shen Pao-chen). *Tung-fang tsa-chih* (Eastern miscellany), 44.10 (October 1948), 39–40.

Shen Yü-ch'ing. *T'ao-yüan chi* (A collection of poems and essays by Shen Yü-ch'ing). n.p., 1920.

Sheng K'ang, comp. *Huang-ch'ao ching-shih-wen hsü-pien* (Statecraft writings of the reigning dynasty, continued). 120 *chüan*. Wu-chin, Kiangsu, 1897.

Sheridan, James, E. *Chinese Warlord: The Career of Feng Yü-hsiang*. Stanford, Calif., 1966.
    China in Disintegration: The Republican Era in Chinese History, 1912–1949. New York, 1975.

Shih Shu-i, comp. *Ch'ing-tai kuei-ko shih-jen cheng-lüeh* (A small collection of works by women poets of the Ch'ing period). Shanghai, 1922.

Shore, Henry N. *The Flight of the Lapwing: A Naval Officer's Jottings in China, Formosa, and Japan*. London, 1881.

Smith, Richard J. 'Robert Hart and China's Early Modernization, 1862–1874', Paper delivered at the First International Conference on the History of the Chinese Maritime Customs, Hong Kong, December 1988.

Smith, Thomas C. *Political Change and Industrial Development in Japan: Government Enterprise, 1868–1880*. Stanford, Calif., 1965.

Snyder, Louis L. *The New Nationalism*. Ithaca, N.Y., 1968.

Spector, Stanley. *Li Hung-chang and the Huai Army: A Study in Nineteenth-Century Chinese Regionalism*. Introduction, 'Regionalism in Nineteenth-Century China', by Franz Michael. Seattle, Wash., 1964.

Spence, Jonathan D. *Emperor of China: Self-portrait of K'ang-hsi*. New York, 1975.

Stanley, C. John. *Late Ch'ing Finance: Hu Kuang-yung as an Innovator*. Cambridge, Mass., 1961.

Sturdevant, Sandra. 'Imperialism, Sovereignty, and Self-strengthening: A Reassessment of the 1870s'. In *Reform in Nineteenth-century China*, ed. Paul A. Cohen and John E. Schrecker, pp. 63–70. Cambridge, Mass., 1976.

Sugiyama Shinya. 'Bakumatsu Meiji shoki no sekitan yushutsu to Shanhai sekitan jijō' (The Shanghai coal market and coal exports in the mid nineteenth century.) In *Kindai ikōki no Nihon keizai* (Japan's economy in the period of modern change), ed. Shinbo Hiroshi and Yasuba Yasukichi, pp. 199–218. Tokyo, 1979.

Sun Yü-t'ang, comp. *Chung-kuo chin-tai kung-yeh-shih tzu-liao, ti-i-chi, 1840–1895 nien* (Source materials on the history of modern industry in China, 1st collection, 1840–1895). 2 vols. Peking, 1957.

Sung-shih (Dynastic history of the Sung), comp. T'o-t'o, et al. Beijing, 1977.

Ta-Ch'ing chin-shen ch'üan-shu (The complete list of officials of the Ch'ing empire, quarterly).

Ta-Ch'ing li-ch'ao shih-lu (Veritable records of the successive reigns of the Ch'ing dynasty). Mukden, 1937.

T'ai-wan t'ung-chih (Gazetteer of T'ai-wan). 4 vols. Taipei, 1962. (Compiled in manuscript form in 1894.)

T'an Pi-an. 'Ch'ing chung-yeh chih huo-pi kai-ke yün-tung' (The currency reform movement of mid-Ch'ing). *Shuo-wen yüeh-k'an* (Shuo-wen monthly), no. 4 (May 1933). See reprint in Li Ting-i et al., eds., *Chung-kuo chin-tai-shi lun-ts'ung*, 2d ser., vol. 3, pp. 38–48.

Tan-shui t'ing-chih (Gazetteer of Tan-shui). 1871; reprint ed., 3 vols., Taipei, 1963.

T'ang Chi-ho. 'Ch'ing-tai k'o-tao-kuan chih kung-wu kuang-hsi' (The office of the censor in the Ch'ing period). *Hsin she-hui k'o-hsüeh chi-k'an* (New social science quarterly), 1.2 (1934), 207–13.

'Ch'ing-tai k'o-tao-kuan chih jen-yung' (The employment of Ch'ing censors). *She-hui k'o-hsüeh ts'ung-k'an* (Social science journal), 1.2 (November 1934), 153–62.

'Ch'ing-tai k'o-tao chih ch'eng-chi' (The performance of censors in the Ch'ing period). *Chung-shan wen-hua chiao-yü-kuan chi-k'an* (Quarterly of the Chung-shan Cultural and Educational Institute), no. 2 (1935), 517–25.

T'ao-feng-lou ts'ang ming-hsien shou-cha (A selection from Hsüeh Fu-ch'eng's collection of letters of famous people in the late Ch'ing period). 1930. Unpaginated.

Tao Hsien T'ung Kuang ming-jen shou-cha (Letters of prominent men of the Tao-kuang, Hsien-feng, T'ung-chih, and Kuang-hsü periods). Shanghai, 1924. Unpaginated.

Tao Hsien T'ung Kuang ssu-ch'ao tsou-i (Memorials from the Tao-kuang, Hsien-feng, T'ung-chih, and Kuang-hsü reigns). 12 vols. Taipei, 1970.

Teng Ssu-yü and John K. Fairbank. *China's Response to the West. A Documentary Survey, 1839–1923*. Cambridge, Mass., 1954.

Teng T'o. *Lun Chung-kuo li-shih ti chi-ko wen-t'i* (On certain problems in Chinese history), rev. ed. Peking, 1979.

Thomas, Stephen C. *Foreign Intervention and China's Industrial Development, 1870–1911*. Boulder Colo., 1984.

T'ien Pu-shan, comp. *K'un-ling Chou-shih chia chi* (Collected writings of the Chou family of K'un-ling). Ch'i-nan, 1924.

Ting Jih-ch'ang. *Ting Yü-sheng cheng-shu* (The political works of Ting Jih-ch'ang). 2 vols. Hong Kong, 1987.

Toynbee, Arnold. *Mankind and Mother Earth: A Narrative History of the World*. New York, 1976.

Ts'ai Kuan-lo. *Ch'ing-tai ch'i-pai ming-jen chuan* (Biographies of seven hundred eminent Chinese of the Ch'ing period). 3 vols. Shanghai, 1937.

Tseng Kuo-fan. *Tseng Wen-cheng kung ch'üan-chi* (The complete works of Tseng Kuo-fan). 10 vols. Taipei, 1952.

Tseng Kuo-fan wei-k'an hsin-kao (Tseng Kuo-fan's unpublished correspondence), comp. Chiang Shih-yung. Peking, 1959.

Tseng Kuo-fan et al. *Chin-tai shih-tai-chia ch'ih-tu* (Letters of ten great personages in modern times). Taipei, 1971.

Tso Tsung-t'ang. *Tso Wen-hsiang kung ch'üan-chi* (The complete works of Tso Tsung-t'ang). 109 *chüan*. 1890.

Tsunoda, Ryusaku, William de Bary, and Donald Keene, comps. *Sources of Japanese Tradition*. New York, 1958.

Tu Wei-ming. *Neo-Confucian Thought in Action: Wang Yang-ming's Youth (1472–1509)*. Berkeley and Los Angeles, 1976.

T'ung-chih chia-hsü Jih-ping ch'in-T'ai shih-mo (The complete account of the Japanese invasion of Taiwan in 1874 [documents selected from *Ch'ou-pan i-wu shih-mo*]), comp. T'ai-wan yin-hang ching-chi yen-chiu shih (Department of Economic Research, Bank of Taiwan). 2 vols. Taipei, 1959.

Tung Ts'ai-shih. *Tso Tsung-t'ang p'ing-chuan* (Biography of Tso Tsung-t'ang). Peking, 1984.

Twitchett, Denis. 'Problems of Chinese Biography'. In *Confucian Personalities*, ed. Arthur F. Wright and Denis Twitchett, pp. 24–39, Stanford, Calif., 1962.

Denis Twitchett and John K. Fairbank, gen. eds. The Cambridge History of China. Cambridge, 1978– .

Wakeman, Frederic, Jr. *Strangers at the Gate: Social Disorder in South China, 1839–1861*. Berkeley and Los Angeles, 1966.

History and Will: Philosophical Perspectives of Mao Tse-tung's Thought. Berkeley and Los Angeles, 1973.

Walters, Ronald G. *American Reformers, 1815–1860*. New York, 1978.

Wang Chia-chien. *Wei Yüan nien-p'u* (Wei Yüan: a chronological biography). Taipei, 1967.

'Ch'ing-mo hai-chün liu-Ying hsüeh-sheng ti p'ai-ch'ien chi ch'i ying-hsiang (1876–1885)' (Naval education of Chinese students in England and its influence in the late Ch'ing period). *Li-shih hsüeh-pao* (Bulletin of historical research), no. 2 (February 1974), 161–87.

Wang Erh-min. *Ch'ing-chi ping-kung-yeh ti hsing-ch'i* (The rise of the military industry in late Ch'ing). Nankang, 1963.

Huai-chün chih (A history of the Huai Army). Taipei, 1967.

'Tseng Kuo-fan yü Li Yüan-tu' (Tseng Kuo-fan and Li Yüan-tu). *Ku-kung wen-hsien* (Journal of the National Palace Museum), 3.3 (June 1972), 1–21.

'Ju-chia ch'uan-t'ung yü chin-tai Chung-Hsi ssu-ch'ao chih hui-t'ung' (The Confucian tradition and the understanding of Western ideas in modern times). *Hsin-ya hsüeh-shu chi-k'an* (New Asia academic quarterly), no. 2 (1979), 163–78.

Ch'ing-chih chün-shih shih lun-chi (Studies on late Ch'ing military history). Taipei, 1980.

Wang Hsin-chung. 'Fu-chou ch'uan-ch'ang chih yen-ko' (A history of the Foochow Shipyard). *Tsing Hua hsüeh-pao*, 8 (December 1932), 1–57.

Wang Hung-chih. 'Tso Tsung-t'ang p'ing hsi-pei Hui-luan chün-fei chi ch'ou-ts'u' (The problem of logistics in Tso Tsung-t'ang's suppression of the Moslem Rebellion). *Shih-hsüeh chi-k'an* (Bulletin of the Chinese historical association), 4 (May 1972), 231–50.

Wang K'ai-yün. *Hsiang-ch'i lou jih-chi* (Diary of Wang K'ai-yün, 1869–1916). 1928.

Wang Shih. *Yen Fu chuan* (A biography of Yen Fu). Shanghai, 1957 and 1975 (new edition).

Wang Te-chao. *Ch'ing-tai k'o-chü chih-tu yen-chiu* (A study of the civil service examination [system] of [the] Ch'ing dynasty). Hong Kong, 1982.

Wang Wen-hsien. 'Ch'ing-chi Ch'ang-chiang shui-shih chih ch'uang-chien chi ch'i ying-hsiang' (The establishment of the Yangtze River Fleet and its influence in late Ch'ing). *Li-shih hsüeh-pao* (Bulletin of historical research), 2 (February 1974), 261–99.

Wang, Y. C. *Chinese Intellectuals and the West, 1872–1949*. Durham, N. C., 1966.

Wang Yen-wei and Wang Liang, comps. *Ch'ing-chi wai-chiao shih-liao* (Historical materials concerning foreign relations in the late Ch'ing period, 1875–1911). 242 *chüan*. Peiping, 1932–5.

Watt, John R. *The District Magistrate in Late Imperial China*. New York, 1972.

Wright, Mary C. *The Last Stand of Chinese Conservatism: The T'ung-chih Restoration, 1862–1874*. 2d printing: Stanford, Calif. 1962; rev. ed.: New York, 1965.

Wright, Stanley F. *Hart and the Chinese Customs*. Belfast, 1950.

Wright, Tim. '"A Method of Evading Management" – Contract Labor in Chinese Coal Mines before 1937'. *Comparative Studies in Society and History*, 23.4 (October 1981), 656–78.

Coal Mining in China's Economy and Society, 1895–1937. Cambridge, 1984.

Wu Han. 'Wang Mao-yin yü Hsien-feng shi-tai ti hsin pi-chih' (Wang Mao-yin and the new currency system of the Hsien-feng period). *Chung-kuo she-hui ching-chi shih chi-k'an* (Chinese social and economic history quarterly), 6.1 (June 1939). See reprint in Li Ting-i et al., eds., *Chung-kuo chin-tai-shih lun-ts'ung*, 2d ser., vol. 3, pp. 49–70.

Wu Ju-lun. *Wu T'ung-ch'eng shih-wen chi* (The collected poems and literary writings of Wu Ju-lun). 1904.

Wu Ta-t'ing. *Hsiao-yu-yü shan-kuan wen-ch'ao* (The writings of Wu Ta-t'ing). n.p., n.d.; prefaces dated 1863 and 1864, but the work was subsequently enlarged to include later writings.

Yang Tuan-liu. *Ch'ing-tai huo-pi chin-yung shih-kao* (A draft history of money and finance in Ch'ing times). Peking, 1962.

Yang-wu yün-tung (The *yang-wu* movement), comp. Chung-kuo k'o-hsüeh-yüan chin-tai-shih yen-chiu-so shih-liao pien-chi-shih (Office of Archival Materials, Institute of Modern History, the Chinese Academy of Social Science). 8 vols. Shanghai, 1961.

Yang-wu yün-tung (The *yang-wu* movement), by the editorial group of Chung-kuo chin-tai-shih ts'ung-shu (modern Chinese history) series. Shanghai, 1973.

Yang Yen-chieh. 'Shen Pao-chen chia-shih jo-kan shih-shih k'ao-pien' (An examination of certain facts related to the family background of Shen Pao-chen). *Shih-hsüeh yüeh-k'an*, 158 (November 1985), 109–10.

Yen, Sophia Su-fei. *Taiwan in China's Foreign Relations, 1836–1874*. Hamden, Conn., 1965.

Yin hsien-chih (Gazetteer of Yin district). 1877.

Zelin, Madeleine. *The Magistrate's Tael: Rationalizing Fiscal Reform in Eighteenth-Century China*. Berkeley and Los Angeles, 1984.

Index

agrarian society, and modernization, 322

Aiguebelle, Paul-Alexandre Neveue, d', 110–11, 134, 165, 178–80, 249
  character, 180
  commercial interests in Saigon, 181
  departure from Foochow Navy Yard, 187–8, 201, 275
  involvement in establishing Foochow Navy Yard, 124, 135, 140, 156–7, 176–7, 190
  relations with Giquel, 182
  relations with Shen Pao-chen, 140–1
  relations with Tso Tsung-t'ang, 155, 178–9, 187–8
  second director of Foochow Navy Yard, 179–83, 199

Alcock, Rutherford
  and Co-operative Policy, 153
  and Foochow Navy Yard, 154, 159
  on introduction of railways and telegraphy in China, 159

Alcock Convention, 2, 21, 285–6

Americans, see United States

Amoy, 31

An-lan (S.S. No. 5), 223

Anhwei, 33, 54, 57, 59, 62, 74–5, 103

Anhwei group, 329

Anking, 41, 97

Anot, Antoine, 88–92, 94–9, 100, 101

anti-Catholicism, 88–96, 98–103; see also Tientsin Massacre

anti-Christian activities, see anti-Catholicism

antimissionary activities, 170, 187, 334; see also anti-Catholicism; Nanchang antimissionary incident

Ao-feng Shu-yüan, 28, 145

Apter, David, 334

arms (Western/modern)
  manufacture, 3, 109, 139, 306, 307, 318
  production of specialized and interchangeable parts, 307
  purchase and use of, 3, 138, 188

Armstrong rifled cannons, 224

army, 308; see also Green Standard army
  in Kiangsi, 71, 75

Arnaudeau, 201

arsenals, 7, 112, 114, 116, 131, 133, 175, 290, 303
  Chinese managers of, 206

artillery, 308

artisans; see also Western technicians
  Chinese, 110
  French, 111
  Western, 113

Australian coal, use in Foochow Navy Yard, 284, 287

Avon, H.M.S. 222

Bankok teak, 222
Banner army, 37, 39
Bellonet, Henri de, 156–7, 159
Bereznii, L. A., 7
Blancheton, Ernest-Jules, 183–5, 187, 189–90, 200
Book of Changes, 311
Book of Rites, *see Li chi*
Bordeaux, the original Labat system at, 214
Borel, Anatole, 226
Botan (Mu-tan), 292
Britain, 29, 31–2, 317
  British employees of the Chinese government, 200
  and Co-operative Policy, 153, 159
  government, 216
  interests in China, 154
  military assistance to the Chinese at Shanghai, 92
  observers' comments on Foochow Navy Yard, 218, 237
  Privy Council of, 200
  relations with Chinese, 100, 124, 133, 170
  tour of dockyards by Foochow Navy Yard graduates,
British consular court, 200
British consular officials, 221
British consulate at Ningpo, 139
British consuls:
  at Foochow, 159, 196
  at Kiukiang, 92
  on Taiwan, 164, 274
British coal, use in Foochow Navy Yard, 284, 287
British navy, 211, 223
Brossement, 183
Buddhism, 97, 101
bureaucracy, 1, 9, 30, 65, 161, 173, 199, 208, 290; *see also* officials
  local, 60
  provincial, 60–3
  quality and size, 310, 319–20
bureaucratic vices, 8, 14, 60, 173, 175, 198; *see also* officials

Burma, 167

Canton, 315
  linking by foreign telegraph lines, 294
  source of Foochow Navy Yard students, 227
capitalism
  bureaucratic, 9
  Chinese, 8–9
  Western, 8–9
Carroll, Charles, 154
Carroll, James, 191–3, 196, 228, 232, 234, 237, 239
Catholicism, 101–3
Catholics, 95, 98; *see also* Anot, Antoine; Chinese Christians/converts; Fang An-chih
  in Foochow Navy Yard, 193
censors, 33, 36–7, 42, 44, 48, 64, 146n, 327
  Shen Pao-chen's view on, 303
Ceylon timber for Foochow Navy Yard, 208
Chang Ch'eng, 235, 236, 275, 276
Chang Chih-tung, 172
  and *t'i-yung*, 322
Chang Hao, 43
Chang Kuo-ching, 89, 91
Chang Po-hsing, 28
Chang Sheng-tsao, 146n
Chang Ssu-hsün, 169, 172
Chang Ssu-kuei, 169, 171, 172
  on Taiwan, 293
Changsha, 102
Ch'ang-sheng (Fukien steamer), captain of, 273
ch'ang-shui ('regular' customs), 76–7, 79
Chao Lieh-wen, 81, 128–9, 174
Chefoo, 233
Chekiang, 48, 51, 57, 59, 65, 74–6, 78, 81, 87, 251
  officials and Foochow Navy Yard, 111, 118–19, 121–3
Chekiang-Fukien region, 329, 330

Chen-hai (S.S. No. 6), 221, 223, 252
Ch'en, Gideon, 114–15
Ch'en Chi-t'ung, 228, 230
Ch'en Ching-k'ang, 227, 230
Ch'en-hang (S.S. No. 14), 253
Ch'en P'i, 175
Cheng Yü, 274
Ch'eng Hao, 13
Ch'eng I, 13
Chi-an, 63
  prefect of, 64
chi-ch'iao (techniques), 146
Chi-lung, *see* Keelung
Ch'i Chün-tsao, 42
Ch'i-ling, 54
Chiang I-li, 111, 118–20, 122
Chien-ch'ang, 51
chien-pi ch'ing-yeh (tactic of clearing the
  countryside and protecting the
  people in fortified towns), 74, 303
Chien-wei (training ship), 233–4,
  239, 283
Chih-yüan t'ang (Hall for the
  Realization of Lofty Aspirations),
  107–8
Chihli, 252, 255
Chin-ch'i, 51
ch'in-ming tsung-li ch'uan-cheng ta-ch'en
  (by imperial command the high
  minister for the general direction
  of the shipping administration),
  124, 134
ch'in-ping (personal army), 39
Ch'in-she (Family Association), 108
China
  carrying trade, 105
  financial condition, 130
  foreign relations, 87, 153, 198
  incorporation into world economy,
    268, 333
  interests of, 153, 300
  international environment of, 2, 87,
    103, 170, 321
  labour conditions in, 241
  modernization of, 153, 169
  potential for change, 11–17

relations with Britain, 100, 124
relations with France, 92, 98, 101,
  162
relations with United States, 100,
  104–5
response to the West, 12, 14–15, 16,
  17
China Mail, 238
China Merchants' Steam Navigation
  Company, 318, 319
  accepance of Foochow Navy Yard
    vessels, 239, 253, 261
  shipping of tribute grain, 312
Chinese Christians/converts, 88, 90–3,
  96, 98, 103
Chinese envoys
  support for the despatch of, 167, 169
  to Japan, 172
Chinese sovereignty, 95, 153–4
Chinese tradition, 12
ching-shih, *see* practical statecraft
Ch'ing administrative system, 87, 320,
  335, 337; *see also* Ch'ing system
  antagonism towards self-
    strengtheners and reforms, 336
  capacity to accommodate
    modernizing enterprises, 123
  practice of divide and rule, 123, 336
Ch'ing court, *see* imperial court
Ch'ing dynastic house, 332
Ch'ing empire, 12, 82, 102, 269; *see also*
  Ch'ing government
  its defence, 291, 292
Ch'ing government; *see also* public
  finance
  approval of mechanized coal mining
    on Taiwan and elsewhere, 288,
    335
  capacity to play active role in
    modernization, 245
  economic policies, 245
  financial administration, 11, 326–7,
    335
  re-examination of the self-
    strengthening policy, 288
  small revenue base, 245, 269, 326

economic rights, *see li-ch'üan*
economy, 10–11, 16
    traditional, 3
emperor, *see* throne
Empirical Research, School of, 13–14
Europe, 239
    labour conditions in, 241
European workmen, comparison with
    Foochow Navy Yard workmen,
    211

factional politics, 147; *see also* Chou
    K'ai-hsi; Tso Tsung-t'ang
factionalism, 332
family system, traditional, impact on
    modernization, 234
famine relief, 28, 29
Fang An-chih, 89, 91, 95
Favorite, H.M.S., 215
Fei-yün (S.S. No. 8), 221
female infanticide, 66, 72
Feng Kuei-fen, 46
    view on importance of mathematics,
    290
feng-shui, 150
Feng-t'ien, 252
feudalism, 8–9, 11
Feuerwerker, Albert, 10
Fire Queen, 215
First Opium War, *see* Opium Wars
Foochow, 24, 30, 31, 32, 108, 110, 120,
    126, 174, 190, 200, 226, 316
    source of students for Foochow
    Navy Yard School, 228
    source of workers for Foochow Navy
    Yard, 209
Foochow Navy Yard, 17, 18, 46, 55,
    146, 178, 307
    achievements attributable to
    Europeans and to Shen Pao-chen,
    325
    administrative integrity, 135, 158,
    162, 170, 198
    anti–Navy Yard forces, *see*
    opposition, this entry

central government, role of, 119,
    130, 135, 182, 241, 245–6, 247,
    259, 264, 266, 267, 268–9, 325
characteristics, 112–23, 130, 226
China's defence, 113, 154, 198, 203,
    223–4, 247, 254, 255, 256
Chinese-owned defence
    establishment, 154, 262
coal supplies, 167, 284
composite vessels, 216, 242, 243,
    270; built at Ma-wei, 239, 264;
    technology required, 239
compound engines, 216, 224, 242,
    243; technology required, 239
condition after Shen Pao-chen's
    incumbency, 244
construction of, 136, 140, 145, 151,
    153, 167, 203, 206–9, 212, 213,
    215–16, 218
contracts with Europeans, 162–3,
    184, 216
criticism of, 249
debate on Sung Chin's proposal for
    closure, 254–60, 267, 270, 287
decline, 266, 270–1, 325–6
directors-general after Shen Pao-
    chen, 175, 176, 244, 326
establishment, 108–11, 135–6, 168
European tutelage, 238, 239, 240,
    325
French influence, 190
French interests, 178, 187, 224, 238
French presence, 177–8
Fukien province: dependence on,
    130–1, 132, 135, 248, 264–6;
    interference from, 159, 270;
    relations with, 135, 138, 139,
    140–1, 151, 153, 158, 161, 162,
    164, 221, 279–80; support from,
    267, 325, 327
'General Contract of Execution',
    203, 218, 237, 238
imperial character, 121, 123, 133,
    135, 159, 218, 269
instrument for transfer of

technology, 113–14, 223, 225–6, 243, 262, 271
interprovincial character, 118–23, 251
ironclads, 216
modern establishment, 215, 324
naval character, 114–16, 217, 221, 250, 252–3, 260, 325
objectives, 203, 240, 256–7, 262; *see also* characteristics, this entry
official inauguration, 181, 206
opposition to, 112; British, 154, 159; Chinese, 134, 135, 144–6, 147, 148–9, 150–3, 198, 201, 240, 245, 251–2; foreign, 135, 160; French, 154–8, 159–60, 198
place in Ch'ing bureaucracy, 134
protection of merchants, 247
provincial character, 121, 123, 133, 135, 251
regional character, 116–19, 121, 123
role in China's naval and technical development, 243–4
self-sufficiency and scale, 214–15, 247, 284
seminal role, 272, 289
service rendered to other government agencies, 215
Shen Pao-chen's successors, *see* directors-general after Shen Pao-chen, this entry
showcase of Sino-foreign co-operation, 334
site, 120–1, 205–6, 216, 226
support industries, 272
technological independence, 113, 117, 142, 194, 203, 235–8
vulnerability to criticism, 243, 262
Foochow Navy Yard, administration, 157, 198–9
administrative staff, 130, 133, 148, 152–3, 156, 158, 161–76, 172, 198–9, 211, 217, 324; concern for China's territorial and administrative integrity, 170;

financial administration, 246; from the civil service, 171, 199; qualifications, 169, 199; salary, 174; views on China's modernization, 169–70
Chinese authorities: control over sensitive information, 197–8; control over vessels, 217; fear and prevention of foreign domination, 196, 198, 242–3, 333–4; vis-à-vis French directors, 181, 199–200
Chinese role, 136, 163, 203
coal-buying agents on Taiwan, 285
'consultative committee', 166
corruption, 141, 161, 173–6; Shen Pao-chen's attempt to control, 141, 198–9, 241, 263, 271, 324
deputy (*wei-yüan*), 169, 209
director-general, 131, 140–1, 151, 176, 280; power of, 134–5, 140, 162, 176, 182, 325
disciplining Chinese employees, 163, 168, 175–6, 194, 198, 324
general manager (*tsung-chien-kung*), 166–7, 172
gentrymen on staff, 161–2, 173, 175, 198–9, 212, 308, 324
governance, 121–2, 124–6, 130
job specialization, 170
knowledge of foreign languages among staff, 167, 168, 170, 232
knowledge of Western science and technology among staff, 169, 170, 199, 207
laxity, 176, 202
luring away of staff by civil service, 166, 169, 171, 172–3
organization, 163, 166–8, 199, 201–2
Supervision, Committee of, 163
t'i-tiao (assistants to the director-general), 163–4, 166–8; *see also* Chou K'ai-hsi; Hsia Hsien-lun; Hu Kuang-yung; Liang Ming-ch'ien; Wu Chung-hsiang; Wu

Ta-t'ing
timber-buying agent at Rangoon,
167, 175, 194, 208
Foochow Navy Yard, European
employees, 136, 140–1, 155,
162–3, 176–8, 197–8, 201–2,
217, 225, 240, 249, 260, 263
adequacy for the Navy Yard, 325
British, 177, 196
chief engineer, 177, 181, 185–6, 191,
201
chief of the metal-working forge,
177, 191
Chinese authority over, 178, 184,
199–200
Chinese relations with, 167, 179,
188, 190, 194–6
contracts of employment, 184,
185–7, 188, 190
Council of Works, 177, 201
departure (February 1874), 264
directorate, 177, 182–3, 186, 201
disciplinary matters, 177, 182,
183–90, 190–1, 209–12
dismissal discussed, 256, 258
engine-room officers, training of, 234
engineers, 125, 161, 176, 201, 225
foremen, 136, 176, 177, 191, 201
French, 177, 182, 239–40
French directors, 140–1, 177,
178–82, 185–7, 191–3, 199, 201,
246; authority over European
employees, 183–4, 187–90; *see
also* directorate, this entry;
subdirectorship, this entry; and
individual directors
French 'technological domination',
243
hiring or retention of after initial
contract, 238
increase in numbers, 177, 262
instructors, 136, 177–8, 192, 194,
230, 240
living conditions, 188, 190, 192–3,
196

master carpenter, 177
material incentives, 191–2, 203
mechanics, 120, 136, 138, 161, 166,
176, 177, 180, 191, 192, 194
metallurgist, 284
misdeameanours and delinquency,
156–7, 183, 188–90
morale, 188
obligations, 162, 183, 184
organization, 176–8, 199
overseers (engineers, formen), 209
physician, 136, 185, 188, 190, 192;
see also Vidal, Dr. Jean
recruitment, 196–7
rights, 162, 178, 182, 183, 189
role, 163, 203
salary, 191, 196, 270
as servants of China, 178, 186
subdirectorship, 182, 201
technical leadership, 201, 225
Foochow Navy Yard, facilities,
Chinese workers, and the
workplace
artisans and workmen, 138, 163–4,
191, 196, 262; in construction of
Peking–Hankow Railway, 244;
instruction of, 142; job
performance, 211–12, 217, 241;
knowledge of modern
shipbuilding, 207, 236, 322;
labour disputes, 211; organization
of, 208–9, 324; recruitment, 168,
194, 208–9, 211–12; Shen Pao-
chen's methods of control, 142,
209–12, 241, 325; training, 208,
211, 232, 235–6, 237, 324; wages,
191, 210–11; working conditions,
209–12, 241; workmanship, 142,
194, 216
blacksmiths, 208–9
boiler house, 213
brass factory, 207
brick factory, 206
bricks, from Amoy, 213
builders, 209

carpenters, 207, 208–9
design, office of, 207, 213
dry dock, 214
engineer, office of the, 212–13
equipment, *see* facilities, this entry
equipment forges, 213
facilities, 135–6, 185, 203, 206,
    212–16, 238, 242, 256, 257;
    expansion of, 216, 262, 270;
    modernization of, 216, 238, 242
fitting shop, 213
foremen, 168, 191; organization of,
    168; proficiency in Western
    methods, 168, 235; training, 208,
    232, 235, 308, 324; treatment of
    labour, 211–12; wages, 210
forge (small), 207
forging department, 213
fortification, 198, 214
foundry, 213, 223
guards, 176, 209
joiners' shop, 213
Labat's system, 214, 215, 248
labour, 208–11, 218
labourers, 136
locksmith's shop, 213
machinery, 180, 206, 207, 212, 213,
    215, 216
maintenance of machinery, 244
metal factory, 206
metal-working forge, 206, 213, 216,
    242, 248, 249, 284
modernization of, 216, 238, 242
moulding hall, 207, 213
precision instruments workshops,
    213
rolling mill, 213, 216, 242, 249
sawmills, 207, 216
setting-up shop, 213
shipbuilding slips, 207, 208, 212
small fitting shop, 213
supervisors, 168
tramway and turntables, 215
wet dock, 214
workshop superintendents, 209;
    training, 232
Foochow Navy Yard, finances, 120–3,
    136, 140–1, 142, 154, 155, 156,
    162–3, 164, 174, 201, 221, 270,
    271, 324, 325
accounting methods and practices,
    261–2
administration, 122, 246, 253,
    254–5, 261–2, 263, 264
aid from Tso Tsung-t'ang (1872–4),
    263–4
budget by Tso Tsung-t'ang, 246–7,
    262, 324
capital construction funds, 246, 248
contributions from Chekiang and
    Kwangtung, 120, 122, 246
difficulties, 325–7
'escrow account', 247, 248, 249
expenditures, 240; compared with
    Kiangnan Arsenal, 266–7;
    increase after early 1872, 262; on
    plant facilities, 249; total, 266
flaws in, 247–9
funding, as a large traditional
    enterprise, 269
income: from Fukien maritime
    customs, 246–7, 264–6 (*see also*
    Fukien maritime customs); from
    opium duties for steamship
    maintenance, 250–1, 252, 253,
    264; from the special maritime
    defence fund, 265
operating funds, 246–8
and provincial politics, 246, 263–4,
    267, 271
requirements of a modern defence
    enterprise, 267
retrenchments, 253, 256, 257, 263,
    264, 270, 278, 325
ship allocation, 157, 249–52, 260,
    267
shipbuilding costs, 256, 261–2
spending priorities, 248
stability, 249, 264, 270, 334
steamship maintenance account and

expenses, 141, 155, 157, 249–54, 258, 260–1, 263–4, 267, 324, 325
tardy delivery of funds, 249, 264–6, 268, 327
total operating cost, 247
Foochow Navy Yard, school and training programmes, 111, 120, 136, 138, 142, 164, 170, 172, 179, 204, 210, 212, 226, 242, 256, 324
academic life, 228–9
achievements, 235–40
Apprentices, School for, 178, 208, 230; achievements, 235–6; curriculum, 232
apprentices (who did not attend school), training and results, 235–7, 308
book learning, emphasis on, 226, 228, 235
cadets, 196, 233
Chinese professors: failure to meet expectations, 239; training, 235, 237, 240
curriculum, 227–30, 237–8; Confucian elements, 228–30, 321, 323; counteracting of Confucian influence, 235, 243; criticism of, 237
Design, School of, 178, 207, 230, 231; achievements, 235; curriculum, 231
Engineers, School for, 232; achievements, 237, 307; curriculum, 234
'English division', 226–8, 230, 238
enrollment, 227
examinations, 229, 237
expansion of School, 249, 262
'French division', 226–7, 230
gentrymen in the School, 168
graduates, 227, 282; careers of, 230, 235–7; comparison with those from Kiangnan Arsenal, 237; design and building of gunboat, 236; difficulty of placement, 227;

further studies in Europe, 278, 284, 307, 311; promise of future careers, 227; recommendation of further studies in Europe 237–8, 243, 257, 260, 308; in Sino-French War, 284
instruction 113, 116, 163, 224
language difficulties, 194, 230, 232
marine engineering, 223; students of, 136
model for other naval academies, 244
Naval Construction, School of, 230– 1; achievements, 235–6; curriculum, 230–1, 234, 237, 240; professors, 240; role for future, 256
new technology after end of contract, 238–9
Practical Navigation, School of, 232, 233, 278; achievements, 236–7; curriculum, 233; training cruises and navigation on the open seas, 233–4, 236, 239, 275; uniform for cadets, 233 n111
purpose of, 225–6
regulations, 136, 228–9, 234–5; enforcement by 'upright gentrymen', 229
reward system, 229, 230
school calendar, 228–9, 234
students, 210, 226–7; attrition rate, 234; disdain for physical work, 235, 322; performance, 231–7; places of origin, 227; as potential modernizers, 322; practical training during the Japanese invasion of Taiwan, 293; promise of career in civil service, 228; quality of, 228, 229, 244; recruitment, 227, 234; social background, 227–9, 235; stipends for, 227; work in northeastern Taiwan, 293
teachers, 226; *see also* Chinese professors, this entry; Foochow

Navy Yard, European employees, instructors
technology, 223–5, 237–8, 243
Theoretical Navigation, School of, 232, 275; achievements, 236–7; curriculum, 232–3, 237
training programme, 173, 235, 237, 241, 256; expansion of, 262
Foochow Navy Yard, shipbuilding capacity, 215–16
cargo steamers, 251–3, 259, 267
costs, 256, 261–2
manpower, 218
marine engines, 218; bought from France, 206, 213, 217, 221; made at Ma-wei, 213, 217–18, 223, 231, 236
naval construction, 177, 190; proficiency of Chinese staff in, 165, 170
programme, 136, 167, 172, 177, 203, 206–7, 213, 217, 218, 221, 241, 325; debate over Sung Chin's criticism 254–9; political divisiveness of, 258; shortcomings of, 243; timetable, 262–3, 324; trimming of (1874), 264, 268
raw materials, 136, 167, 175, 181, 208–9, 217–18, 284
scrap iron, processing of, 213
spare parts production, 292
steamships, 122, 169, 182, 185, 186, 192, 217–18, 256; capabilities of, 221–2, 243; construction without European supervision, 236; quality of, 221–25, 251
timber supplies, 167, 175, 194, 208, 212, 284
Foochow Navy Yard, vessel deployment and naval training, 217, 244
armament, 218, 222
battle-worthiness, 223–4, 239, 275
captains trained at Navy Yard School: inadequate experience of,

240, 277; modern training of, 236–7, 239, 275; pay scale, 277; youthfulness, 277
chain of command, 281–2
Chinese control over vessels, 283
commander; appointment of, 279, 281, 298; definition of job by Shen Pao-chen, 279–80
crew, 217–18; recruitment of, 217; training, 233, 239, 273, 275, 280
disciplinary problems, 279, 282
'early' captains: background and experience, 273–5; lack of formal training, 275; performance, 274–5; probationary period, 273, 275
emergence of naval tradition and spirit, 284
engineers, 232
fleet movement, 198
fleet organization, 278–9, 296; and regulations, 279–80
gunnery, training in, 233, 239
mobilization of ships for defence of Taiwan (1874–5), 253
'national' naval ensign, 280
naval officers, training of, 232, 239
naval training, 113, 139, 165, 172, 182, 203, 239, 257, 279–80; after end of contract, 238–9, 278; counteracting of Confucian influences, 235, 243; during and after the Japanese invasion of Taiwan, 293, 239; obstacles to, 279, 281, 282; training ships, 283
navigation, 177; instruction in, 190, 238; students of, 136; training in, 239, 256; training on a composite vessel, 239
officers, 232; disdain for manual work, 283–4; incompetence of some, 282, 283; in Sino-French War, 284
piracy suppression, 247, 254
training ship, 233, 262; *see also Chien-wei; Fu-hsing; Yang-wu*

transport of government tribute
grain, 247, 249, 254, 257
undermining by steamships
stationed in different provinces,
267
Foochow Tartar general, 121, 156,
163, 193, 327; *see also* Wen-yü,
Ying-kuei
foreign affairs, management of, 2, 62;
Shen Pao-chen's proposal on, 301
foreign encroachments, 87, 100, 103,
109, 153–4; *see also* imperialism
modern inventions seen as
instruments of, 303
foreign inroads, *see* foreign
encroachments
foreign loans for defence
modernization, rejection of, 309
foreign merchants, 333
foreign technicians and engineers, 108
Forster, John, and Company, 154
France, 180, 187, 191, 317
and Foochow Navy Yard, 110
interest in Foochow, 155
military assistance at Ningpo, 92,
94–5, 99
relations with China or the Chinese,
91, 94–8, 98, 99, 101, 104, 162,
195
technical help from, 111
tour of dockyards by Foochow Navy
Yard graduates, 278
Franco-Chinese Corps, *see* Franco-
Chinese Ever-Triumphant Army
Franco-Chinese Ever-Triumphant
Army, 110, 178
Frandon, E., 244
French commissioners of customs, *see
also* Méritens, Baron Eugène
Herman de
in China, 178
at Foochow, 159
French consul at Foochow, 202; *see also*
Blancheton, Ernest-Jules;
Frandon, E.; Lemaire, Gabriel;

Simon, Eugène
Chinese ability to deal with
interference from, 334
interference with Foochow Navy
Yard, 182–90, 199, 201
French consular officials, 178, 195; *see
also* Montmorand, Vicomte
Brenier de
French consulates
at Foochow, 182, 184–5, 187, 188–9
at Ningpo, 184
French government, 180
and Co-operative Policy, 99 n43,
153, 159, 196
and Foochow Navy Yard, 197, 200
French Imperial Navy, *see* French
navy
French minister (chargé d'affaires) at
Peking, 93–5, 185, 187; *see also*
Bellonet, Henri de; Kleczkowski,
Count Michel; Rochechouart,
Comte Julien de
French Ministry of Foreign Affairs,
178
French Ministry of the Navy, 178, 197
French Naval Division in the Seas of
China and Japan, commander of,
158, 189; *see also* Maudet,
Commander; Dupré, Contre-
Amiral
French naval minister, 157
French naval officers, 108, 110, 178
in Chinese service, 157
French navy, 178, 182–3, 190, 200,
223
fu-ch'iang, see wealth and power
Fu-chou, 91
Fu-hsing (S.S. No. 3), 221, 233, 274
fu-piao (governor's brigade), 61
Fu-po (S.S. No. 4), 221, 251
Fukien, 31, 166, 174, 256
borrowing from merchants, 265
financial difficulties, 268
gentry support for Foochow Navy
Yard, 125, 245

gentrymen, 139, 141, 167, 173, 175
governor of, 121, 134, 163, 175
likin, 248
officials and Foochow Navy Yard,
    111, 118–19, 121–3, 131, 137–8,
    144–6, 159, 248, 270, 271, 327
provincial treasurer, 121
role during Japanese invasion of
    Taiwan, 292
steamships owned by, 139, 217,
    236–7, 273–4
tea likin and revenue, 263, 265, 269
vested interests, 123
Fukien Arsenal, 170
Fukien and Chekiang (Min Che),
    governor-general of, 121, 134, 163
Fukien maritime customs, 155, 248,
    251
low priority for Foochow Navy
    Yard, 265
provincial manipulations of 60 per
    cent account, 269
receipts and commitments, 265, 266
remittances to Tso Tsung-t'ang, 265
revenue from the 40 per cent
    account for Foochow Navy Yard's
    initial capital construction, 246
revenue from the 60 per cent
    account for Foochow Navy Yard's
    operating expenses, 246–7, 264–6
shortfalls in receipts, 265–6
tardy remittances to Ma-wei,
    264–266
temporary transfer of funds from 40
    per cent account for Foochow
    Navy Yard's operating expenses,
    264–6
use of funds from both 40 and 60 per
    cent accounts for Foochow Navy
    Yard's regular operating
    expenses, 266

Garnault, Admiral, 213
gentry, 3–5, 10, 18, 26, 31–2, 38,
    60, 63, 66–7, 90, 99, 103, 104

delinquency, 67, 68, 72, 104, 199
of Foochow, 125, 127, 165
ideology, 3
in Kiangsi, 48, 64, 66–8, 80, 83,
    89–90, 93, 95, 96
and modern enterprises, 139, 141,
    198–9
progressive elements, 125
public works, 66
self-interests, 3–4, 66, 73, 108
transformation into a pro-*yang-wu*
    elite, 330
gentry-led forces, 37, 39
Giquel, Prosper François Marie, 110,
    113, 115, 131, 134, 155, 163, 166,
    167, 178, 182, 191, 192, 193,
    206–7, 249
accusations against, by modern
    Chinese historians, 224
alleged holding back of
    technological knowledge from
    Chinese, 242
authority over European employees,
    182–90, 199–201
character, 180, 216
first director of Foochow Navy
    Yard, 175, 179–82, 188, 202, 207,
    216, 217–18, 221, 224, 240
involvement in establishing
    Foochow Navy Yard, 135, 140,
    156–8, 176–7, 190
knowledge of engineering, 216, 225,
    238, 242
management of Navy Yard affairs,
    194, 195–6, 208, 215–16, 236
proposal for building more
    advanced gunboats, 216, 242, 270
recommendation of graduates as
    captains and officers, 275–7
rejection of offer of naval training,
    283
relations with French navy, 197, 200
relations with Shen Pao-chen,
    140–1, 184, 201
relations with Tso tsung-t'ang,

178–80, 199

role in Foochow Navy Yard after 1874: building of composite vessels powered by compound engines, 238, 242, 278; direction of School and naval training, 238; further education in Europe for students, 238, 242, 278; recruitment of new technicians and staff, 238

shaping of the School curriculum, 228–9, 231, 233, 321

training programme, 237–8, 241

on Taiwan with Shen Pao-chen, 293

Gloire, La, 224

government, 3, 5, 10, 14, 16, 21–3, 33, 103, 106, 319; *see also* bureaucracy; provincialism; public finance; regionalism; revenue; throne

concern for the people, 96

local (subprovincial), 4, 21, 63–8, 303

provincial, 62, 119; support for *yang-wu* undertakings, 335

reform proposals on, 301–4, 319, 320

wastefulness, 302, 310

goverment, central, 5–6, 8, 31, 34, 37–8, 39, 40, 42, 53, 61, 64, 71, 72, 73, 78, 87, 92, 94–5, 104, 108, 119, 123, 130, 131, 135, 145, 150, 153, 162, 163, 166, 208, 251, 265, 266, 269, 270, 279, 284, 298, 330, 327; *see also* government, reform proposals on; Grand Council; imperial court; Peking; Six Boards and *individual boards*; throne; Tsungli Yamen

authority over the provinces, 264, 268–9, 328, 329

central budgetary control and financial administration, 328, 335

centralization of power, 335–6

control over revenue and spending

priorities, 269, 326, 327

Foochow Navy Yard, role in its development, 266, 270, 288, 325, 330

funds for modernizing enterprises, 269, 319, 326–7

inadequate reports on customs receipts from provinces to, 309

lack of accurate information, 327

leadership role, 135, 182, 245–6, 248, 264, 267, 268, 296, 297, 313, 327, 331–2, 333, 334

restructure proposed, 335

scope of, 319, 320

support for *yang-wu* enterprises, 131, 334, 335

underestimation of Chinese military strength on Taiwan (1875), 305

weaknesses, 334

Grain Tribute System, *see ts'ao-che*

granaries, 25, 33, 66

in Peking, 71, 105, 304

Grand Council, 92, 95, 302

and defence modernization, 117

and Foochow Navy Yard, 130, 218

grand secretary, 147

Great Wall of the Ch'in dynasty, 294

Green Standard army, 37, 39, 61, 306, 307

in Kiangsi, 75

minor reorganization of, 355

Greenwich Naval College, 196

Gregory, William, 274

Gumpach, Baron Johannes von, 200

gunboats, 110, 116

guns, *see* arms

Hai-ching (S.S. No. 13), 253

Hail, William J., 48

Han (dynasty), 39, 40

Han Learining, *see* Empirical Research, School of

Han-yang, 48

Hangchow, 110

Hankow, 41, 48, 226

Hanlin Academy, 32, 33, 93, 147
  practical training of scholars, 302,
    313
Hart, Robert, 200; *see also* Imperial
    Maritime Customs Service,
    inspector-general of
  and Foochow Navy Yard, 155, 156,
    159, 180, 185, 288
  memorandum on China's future
    policies, 109, 112, 117, 118
Harwood, J., 239
Ho Ching, 46
  opposition to modern mining for
    Kiangnan Arsenal, 287
Ho Kuei-ch'ing, 50
Hobson, H. E., 293
Hong Kong, 139, 167, 233, 274
  British fleet in, 112
  linking by foreign telegraph lines,
    293
  reformer-writers from, 320
  source of Foochow Navy Yard
    students, 227, 234, 289
  source of workmen for Foochow
    Navy Yard, 194, 208, 210, 289
hoppo of the Canton system, 268
Hornby, Sir Edmund, 200
Hornet, H.M.S., 222
Hou-kuan, 24, 25, 55, 58, 86, 103
howitzers on the *Yang-wu*, 222
Hsia Hsieh, 49, 89–91, 93–4
Hsia Hsien-lun, 93
  and factional struggles in Fukien,
    145, 151–2
  relations with Tso Tsung-t'ang, 329
  service in Foochow Navy Yard,
    164–6, 170, 202
  taotai of T'ai-wan, 166, 171, 172
Hsia T'ing-chü, 93, 164
Hsia Yü, 101
hsiao (filial piety), 27, 60, 90, 107, 127,
    137, 201, 229, 322
Hsiao Kung-chuan, 67
Hsien-feng emperor, 40, 41–2, 48
Hsien-feng inflation, 34–7, 42, 44

Hsin-chiang (river), 51–2
Hsü Tsung-kan, 125, 137, 140, 144
Hsü Wen-yüan, 139
Hu-k'ou, 41
Hu Kuang-yung, 167
  in charge of Tso Tsung-t'ang's
    Procurement and Forwarding
    Office, 138, 164
  and Foochow Navy Yard, 137–9,
    151–2, 158, 164, 170, 179–80,
    182, 217
Hu Lin-i, 39, 57–59, 137
Hua Chu-san, 65, 75
Hua-fu-pao (Fukien steamer), 273
Huang T'i-fang, 70
Huang Wei-hsüan, 139, 168–71,
Hunan, 53, 55, 78, 82, 88, 90, 97, 102
  anti-Christian literature, 93, 96
  governor of, 99
  Tseng Kuo-fan's main recruiting
    ground, 58, 62
Hunan Army, 38–9, 54, 57, 75
Hunanese in Fukien government, 145,
    174, 329
Hung Fu, 83–4
Hung Hsiu-ch'üan, 83
Hupei, 41, 53, 88

I-hsin (S.S. No. 17), 236
Idealistic School (in Confucianism),
    12–14, 28
imperial clansmen, 336
imperial court, 9, 41–2, 44, 50, 57, 59,
    71, 72, 95, 108, 109, 117, 119, 121,
    123, 124, 125, 133, 173, 264, 266,
    292, 337
  factional struggle at, 42
  and Foochow Navy Yard, 112, 117,
    120, 123, 124, 130, 152, 159, 163,
    243, 247, 250, 255, 263–4, 266,
    269, 297
imperial leadership, *see* throne
Imperial Maritime Customs Service,
    105, 109, 157, 178, 179, 185, 268,
    309; *see also* Hart, Robert

China's inability to raise tariff, 268, 310, 334
inspector-general of, 156
imperial princes, 335
imperial tutor, 147
imperialism, 1, 3, 7–11, 16, 17, 18, 100, 104, 182, 304; *see also* Co-operative Policy; foreign encroachments; semicolonialism
impact on China's modernization, 246, 268
India, 239
industrialization, 115
industry, modern, 8
Institutes of Chou, see Chou li
internal colonization, 16
iron-rolling plant, 113

Jao-chou, 53
Jao T'ing-hsüan, 51–2, 54, 56, 57–8
Japan, 244
aggression of, 334
invasion of Taiwan, *see* Taiwan
labour conditions in, 241
Meiji leaders, 243
modernization of, 7, 330–1
political environment compared with Restoration China, 334–5
ports, training cruise to, 239
proclamation of Charter Oath, 334
shipbuilding, 113, 240–1, 307; *see also* Yokosuka Naval Shipyard
success in the Meiji era, 240
threat to China, 304
training cruise to, 276, 281
Japanese coal, 287
jen-ts'ai (men of talent), 63, 306
Johnson, F., 239
judicial matters, 29
Jui-lin, 112, 118, 119, 252

Kan-chou, 76
ke-chih (science), 308
Keelung (Chi-lung)
coal reserves, 285

mechanized coal mine, 288–9
Kennedy, Thomas L., 7
Kiangnan Arsenal and Shipyard, 116, 146
comparison with Foochow Navy Yard, 126, 174, 176, 210, 214, 223, 225, 237, 247
construction of commercial vessels, proposal for, 252, 255, 259
deployment of steamships for defence of Taiwan, 292
modern mining, proposal for, 287
naval training, 165, 172
shipbuilding programme, 254–5, 258
squadron organization, 278
Kiangnan (circuit), 33
Kiangsi, 47, 48, 50–3, 54, 57, 59, 61, 62, 63, 71–2, 78, 84, 103, 105
bureaucracy, 54, 55, 64–5, 71, 87, 316; *see also* officials
financial affairs (including military expenditures), 68–83, 316, 327
foreign affairs, 87–9, 97, 99, 100
gentrymen, 64, 67, 72–3, 75, 78, 80–1, 83, 89–91, 93, 95, 316
governor, 57, 62, 84, 107, 173
Likin Bureau, 80
local elites, 55, 60, 73
military affairs, 74–6, 80–2, 86, 104
missionary case, *see* Nanchang antimissionary incident
Tseng Kuo-fan's source of revenue and supplies, 58–60, 68–83
Kiangsi Academy (Yü-chang shu-yüan), 93
Kiangsi-Anhwei supply line, 74
Kiangsi-Chekiang corridor, 50–1, 54, 55, 58, 74, 80
Kiangsu, 29, 33, 57, 59, 76, 81, 103
Nien rebels in, 150
service by Kiangnan boats, 252
Kiukiang (city), 47–8, 53, 54, 75, 76–7, 81, 88, 91, 94–5, 97–8, 100
Kiukiang customs, 77, 79, 81, 104

Kleczkowski, Count Michel, 91, 94–5, 97, 102
Ku Yen-wu, 29
kuan-ping, 38
kuan-tu shang-pan (official supervision and merchant management), 253
Kuang-hsin, 40, 48–9, 54, 58, 69, 70, 73, 80, 137
  gazetteer, 55
  Shen Pao-chen's administration and defence of, 49–53, 55–6, 74
Kuang-Jao-Chiu-Nan (circuit), 53
Kuei-ch'i, 51, 53
Kuhn, Philip A., 4
Kung, Prince, 3, 18, 23, 112
kung-fei (miscellaneous expenses for steamship operation), 263
Kung Tzu-chen, 14–15, 29, 112
kuo-chi min-sheng, 105, 319
Kuo K'un-tao, 49
Kuo Sung-tao, 46, 49
  appointment as minister to London, 326
  criticism of Shen Pao-chen, 102–3
  progressive ideas on *yang-wu* and Foochow Navy Yard, 118, 326
kuo-t'i (national polity), 96
Kwangsi, 48
Kwangtung, 48
  military aid to Tseng Kuo-fan, 78
  naval programme, 155
  navy yard, 122
  officials and Foochow Navy Yard, 111, 118–19, 121–3
Kweichow, 59

land forces, traditional, *see* Green Standard army
Lapwing, H.M.S., 223
Lay–Osborn Flotilla, 79, 81, 105, 106, 281
Legalist ideas, *see* Legalist School
Legalist School, 14, 18
Lei Hai-tsung, 40
Levenson, Joseph, 14, 324

li (benefits), 43
li (propriety), 102
li (profit), 16, 43
Li Chao-t'ang, 224, 286
Li Ch'eng-mou, 279, 280
Li chi (Book of Rites), 28, 29
Li Chia-pen, 275, 276
Li Ch'ing-lin
  factional struggles in Fukien, 145–6, 152
  service in Foochow Navy Yard, 169, 170
  vitimization by Wu T'ang, 151
li-ch'üan (economic rights), 132, 301
Li Fu-t'ai, 148
Li Han-chang, 49, 57, 74, 311
Li Ho, 276
Li Ho-nien
  advocacy of *yang-wu*, 297
  attitude to Foochow Navy Yard, 263, 267
  competition with Shen Pao-chen over telegraph lines in Fukien, 295, 297
  impeachment of Shen Pao-chen, 298
  political enemy of Shen Pao-chen, 263, 297–8
  power struggle with Wen-yü, 268
  role in appointing commander of Foochow Navy Yard squadron, 281
Li Hsiu-ch'eng, 75
Li Huan, 55, 65–6, 69, 72, 74, 78, 80–4, 90, 95–6, 99, 329
Li Hung-chang, 7, 18, 19, 23, 46, 57, 59, 74, 172
  abolition of traditional water force, proposal of, 253
  advocacy of integration of *yang-wu* and traditional government, 337
  advocacy of studies abroad, 278, 311
  and arsenals, 112, 116–17, 121
  bureau of Western studies proposed by, 311
  and 'commercial war' (*shang-chan*), 312

and conservatives, 336
criticism of shipbuilding at
　Kiangnan Arsenal, 258
disappointment with the Tsungli
　Yamen, 260
on elimination of war junks of the
　water forces, 259
faction, 332
favouring of ordnance industry over
　shipbuilding, 258, 260
and Foochow Navy Yard, 118, 200,
　214, 223, 244, 252, 258–9, 261,
　278
founding of China Merchants'
　Steam Navigation Co., 252–3
governor of Kiangsu, 59
legalization of opium cultivation,
　proposal of, 312
on modernization of the civil service
　examinations, 290
on naval development, 312
Peiyang fleet, 244
political style, 258–60, 320
position on telegraphy, 294
private and public views on
　shipbuilding, 256, 258–60, 261
promotion of mercantile interests,
　312
promotion of *yang-wu* causes, 317
public support for Foochow Navy
　Yard and the Kiangnan Arsenal,
　259
ranking among most advanced *yang-
　wu* proponents, 296, 320
regional power, 116–17, 119, 328
Shen Pao-chen, 292; observations
　about, 85, 99; relations with, 294,
　336
Tientsin naval academy, 244
and Tso Tsung-t'ang, 117
use of Legalist term *pien-fa*, 321
Li Shan-lan, 291
Li Shou-k'ung, 19
Li Shu-i, 137
Li T'ien, 275, 276

Li-tsung (Sung emperor), 23
Li Tsung-hsi, 46
Li Yüan-tu, 49, 54, 56, 57–8, 68, 84,
　329
Liang Kiang, 57, 102–3
　governor-general of, 57, 62, 82, 84
Liang Ming-ch'ien, 46, 174
　service in Foochow Navy Yard, 166,
　　168, 170
　on Taiwan, 293
Lien Ch'ao-lun, 50–3
likin, 4, 37, 73–4, 77–80, 82–3, 269,
　285, 326
　exemption for Foochow Navy Yard
　　purchases, 263, 286
　in Fukien, 145, 148, 150–1
　from Kwangtung, 78
Lin Ch'ang-i (Shen Pao-chen's
　teacher), 29–30, 31, 87
Lin Ch'iung-shu (Shen Pao-chen's
　nephew), 172, 174
Lin Kuo-hsiang, 276
Lin P'u-ch'ing (Shen Pao-chen's wife),
　30–1, 51–2, 104, 317
Lin T'ai-tseng (Lin Tse-hsü's
　grandson), 227
Lin Tse-hsü (Shen Pao-chen's father-
　in-law), 26, 28–32, 44–5, 56, 59,
　65, 87, 103, 108, 112, 128, 172,
　227, 315; *see also* Shen Pao-chen
　advocacy of defence modernization,
　　245
　advocacy of steamship building in
　　China, 128
　loyalty, 317
literati, *see* Confucian scholars
Liu K'un-i, 70, 72, 118
Liu Kwang-ching, 3, 5, 158, 269
Liu Tien, 76, 129
Liu Tsung-yüan, 28, 43
Liu Yo-chao, 150
Liu Yü-hsün, 73, 79–80, 93
Lo Ch'ang-chih, 274
Lo Ta-ch'un, 281, 293
Lo Tse-nan, 50

local elites, 5, 10, 25, 55, 67–8, 70, 73, 95, 311; *see also* gentry
loyal opposition, 332
loyalty (*chung*), 103, 107, 300; *see also* Shen Pao-chen
Lu Hsiang-shan, 13
Lu Lun-hua, 274
Lü Han, 236, 275, 276
Lü Wen-ching, 274

Ma Hsin-i, 46, 111, 118–19
Ma-wei (Mamoi), 120–1, 126, 139, 143, 151, 153, 158, 160, 161, 205, 216, 226, 294; *see also* Foochow Navy Yard
    French community at, 178
Ma-wei Hill, 216
Macartney, Halliday, 121
MacKinnon, Stephen, 5
Manchu court, *see* imperial court
Manchus, 336
Manila, 239
Mao Hung-pin, 99n
Margary Affair, 21
Marxist historians, 7, 9, 11, 241
mathematicized science, 289
mathematics
    accepted discipline in China, 291
    in Foochow Navy Yard School, 289
    in Kiangnan Arsenal school, 289–90
    proposed incorporation into civil service examinations, 290–1
    role in Western material progress, 289
    Shen Pao-chen's understanding of, 289
    threat to philosophical foundations of civil service, 296
    in T'ung-wen Kuan, 146–8, 289–90
Mattadore, see Chien-wei
Maudet, Commander, 187, 189
Médard, Léon, 110, 198, 240
    criticism of Giquel, 179, 201, 237–8
    teacher at Foochow Navy Yard School, 230

Mei-yün (S.S. No. 2), 218, 221, 251, 273
Mencius, 68
Meng Pen, 101
mercenaries (*yung* or *yung-ying*), 38–9, 50, 51, 71, 74–6, 307, 308
merchants, 35
    foreign, 114
    and government, 16, 99, 114–15, 138–9, 252, 254, 256, 265
Méritens, Baron Eugène Herman de; *see also* French commissioners of customs, at Foochow
    criticism of Foochow Navy Yard, 155–7, 249
    relations with Foochow Navy Yard, 182–3, 185, 187
metal-working forge, 113, 135–6
'method of evading management', 212, 241, 324
Michael, Franz, 4–6
military; *see also* Banner army; *ch'in-ping*; defence modernization; Green Standard army
    chain of command, 38–40, 51
    Ch'ing system, 38–9
    demoralization, 35
    finance, 34, 68, 71
    leadership, 62
    modernization, 303, 304
    officers' training, 308
    officials, relations with, *see* officials
    personnel, 35, 62
    possibility of centralized structure, 306, 308
    Shen Pao-chen's reform proposals on, 303, 304, 307–9
    training, 22, 23, 39, 307–8
militia (*t'uan-lien*), 37–40, 51, 71, 74–5, 165
militia commissioner (*t'uan-lien ta-ch'en*), 50, 108, 141
Min (district), 24
Min River, 108, 186, 205–7, 217
    conditions for a navy yard, 120–1

Ming Confucianism, *see* Idealistic
School
missionaries, 88–91, 104, 193
and Co-operative Policy, 333
French, 18, 187
Mitchell, Peter, 16
modern defence sector, *see* defence
industry; defence modernization
modern enterprises, 8, 17, 19, 87, 108,
141, 147–8, 161, 199; *see also*
defence industry; navy yard;
ordnance industry; *yang-wu*,
enterprises; *yang-wu* sector
integration into the traditional
system, 290
lack of superstructure, 161, 171
shortage of men with modern
training, 308
modernization, 32, *see also* Confucian
order; Confucianism; regionalism;
yang-wu
central government, role of, 8–9, 11,
109, 182, 245–6, 331
compatibility with the old order, 322
economy and, 9–11
regionalism and, 4, 7, 10, 118
throne, role of, 109, 112, 147, 152,
297
modernizers, 255
rapport among, 260
modernizing sector, *see* modern
enterprises
monetary system, *see* currency system
Montmorand, Vicomte Brenier de,
135, 157, 180
Morton, A., 239
Moulder, Frances V., 7, 245, 268, 333
mourning period, 229, 235; *see also*
Shen Pao-chen
Mu-tan, *see* Botan
mu-yu (personal assistants), 25, 47–8,
58, 59, 81, 144
Muslim rebels, 124, 303

Naito Konan, 11

Nan-ch'ang (district or prefecture),
89–90
Nan-k'ang, 47, 53
prefect of, 63
Nanchang (city), 48, 62, 73, 76,
88–90, 92, 93–5, 97–8, 100
center of gentry activism, 99
Nanchang antimissionary incident,
87–103, 104, 105, 164
Nanking, 41, 48, 57, 58, 62, 74, 83
Nanking Arsenal, 116
Nantai-Pagoda Anchorage telegraph
line, 295
national polity, *see kuo-t'i*
nationalism, definition, 300
naval academies, 172
naval dockyard, *see* navy yard
naval engineering in the West (French
and Russian), advances in, 224
naval training, 109, 172; *see also*
Foochow Navy Yard
naval warfare
study of, 278
thinking on, 113, 312
navy, 16, 17, 115
command structure, 306
manufacture and purchase of
warships, 306
national, 7, 9, 306
provincial squadrons, 7
Navy, Board of, 318
navy yard, 1, 18, 110, 111–12, 117,
118
and academy, 112–13
Neo-Confucianism, 43, 146, 148, 296;
see also t'i-yung
moral idealism, 43
practical statesmanship (*ching-shih*),
43
Neo-Confucianists, 302
new learning to promote
modernization, 311
New Text School, 14–15
Newchwang, 233
Nien (Rebellion), 124, 149

Ningpo, 110, 139
  customs at, 155
  source of sailors for Foochow Navy
    Yard, 139, 217
North America, 239
North-China Daily News, 223
North-China Herald, 117, 139, 195, 274
North-West, 108, 117

Ocko, Jonathan, 3–4
officials, 8–9, 29, 34, 43, 45, 56, 57, 86,
    94, 102, 103, 104, 207, 319; *see also*
    bureaucracy; bureaucratic vices;
    Confucian scholars
  central government, 42, 46, 92, 146,
    147
  clerks, 4, 65
  Confucian duty of, 332
  Confucian model, 40, 56, 63
  corruption/delinquency, 7, 53, 60,
    61, 63, 64, 66, 68, 70, 72, 104,
    146, 149–51, 285, 326, and land
    tax system 310
  divided and overlapping
    responsibilities, 335
  election of, 303
  evaluation of, 64
  incompetence/inefficiency, 7, 8, 53,
    64, 67, 100
  in Kiangsi, 48, 51–3, 55, 59–60, 64,
    73, 75, 81, 82, 83–5, 88, 96, 98
  local, 4, 6, 25, 40, 43, 47, 51, 60, 62,
    63, 64–6, 94, 303
  military, relations with, 38–40, 43
  and modern enterprises, 17, 106,
    109, 148
  and policy debate (1874), 305
  progressive, 109; *see also*
    progressives; reformers
  provincial, 4–7, 36, 60, 108, 117,
    118, 329
  runners, 4, 98
  special interest groups of, 332, 336;
    tendency to disperse over time,
    332–3

specialization, 302, 313, 320
  training and practical experience,
    302, 320
old order, *see* modernization
opium, 105
  proposed legalization of cultivation,
    312
  suppression, 29, 31, 32, 210
Opium Wars, 7, 132, 198, 333
  and distortion of Chinese
    development, 333
  First, 11, 17, 29, 31–2, 37, 109, 112,
    132, 257, 301, 318
  Second, 58, 93, 109, 153, 301, 310,
    317
ordnance industry, 7
overseas Chinese, mobilization of, 169

Pagoda Anchorage, 139, 154, 208
Pao Ch'ao, 76, 79
pao-chia (system of mutual
    responsibility), 39
Paris, 157, 200, 206
patriot, 29
patriotism, 30, 32, 315; *see also* Shen
    Pao-chen
  defined, 300
patronage and privilege, system of, 336
Pei Chin-ch'üan
  captain of Foochow Navy Yard
    vessels, 217, 273–4
  navigational experience, 139, 273
  service in Foochow Navy Yard, 139
Pei San-ch'üan, 274
Peking, 17, 18, 31, 36, 41, 44, 71, 80,
    91, 94, 97, 159, 183, 284, 303, 333;
    see also government, central;
    imperial court
  and Foochow Navy Yard, 119, 121,
    123, 124, 131, 135, 162, 163, 166,
    251, 264, 271, 330
  food supply in, 303, 304
Peking Agreement, *see* treaties
Peking – Hankow Railway, 244
Penang, training cruises to, 233, 239

P'eng Yü-lin, 73, 79–80
Penn's trunk engines, 222
People's Republic of China, historians
  in, 332
Percebois, Pierre, 183–5
Perkins, Dwight H., 9, 243, 245, 326,
  330
personal assistant or staff, *see mu-yu*
Personnel, Board of, 63, 67; *see also* Six
  Boards
Pescadores, 293
Pien-ch'ien Hui, 51
Pien Pao-ti, 250, 267
pien-t'ung (institutional adjustments),
  43
piracy, 110
  suppression of, 122, 139, 154, 254,
    257, 273, 274, 275
Po-chin-ta (unidentified Russian on
  Foochow Navy Yard staff), 140
Po-yang Lake, 76
Polachek, James, 4
policy debate (discussion) of 1874–5,
  299–300, 304, 322; *see also* defence
  modernization
  agenda, 305–6, 337

approval of limited self-
  strengthening programme, 335
attack on Li Hung-chang and Ting
  Jih-ch'ang, 336
conservatives' attack of reformers,
  336
conservatives' praise of Shen Pao-
  chen's Confucian qualities, 336
focus on defence, 306
imperial message at the close of, 334
Shen's proposals, 307–14
Tsungli Yamen's suggestions on
  new institutions and methods, 306
policy discussion of 1867, 299–300
political climate
  change in, by Wo-jen's attack on the
    T'ung-wen Kuan, 158
  in First Opium War era, 245
  in 1872, 287, 296

and throne, 334
political environment, 334
practical statecraft (*ching-shih*), 13,
  15–16, 17, 29, 43, 69, 87, 112,
  137, 304; *see also* Confucianism;
  Neo-Confucianism; Practical
  Statecraft, School of
Practical Statecraft, School of, 3,
  14–15, 39, 43, 44, 315; *see also*
  practical statecraft
private assistants, *see mu-yu*
progressives, 23; *see also* officials,
  progressive
Protestant religion, 101
Protestants, in Foochow Navy Yard, 193
provincialism, 3, 5–7, 10, 42, 330
  and self-strengthening, 330
Prussian schools, as inspiration for
  Shen Pao-chen, 309
public finance, 36, 247
  budgeting, 43, 72
  centralized budgeting, 270, 325, 327
  failure of budgetary practices to
    meet requirements of modern
    enterprises, 267
  tendency to generate discord, 270
  system of, 9, 269–70

railways and telegraph lines, 318
  Chinese view on, 169, 293–4
Rangoon, 167
Rawlinson, John, 6, 133
reconstruction, post-Taiping, 1, 22
reform, 3, 12, 15–16, 21–22, 32, 45,
  66, 127, 148, 267, 290, 320, 326,
  332; *see also* reform movement;
  reformers; self-strengthening
  civil service examinations, 257–8,
    273, 290–1, 296
  and disintegration of dynasty, 321
  educational, 243
  financial, 36, 68–73, 335
  four stages of, 17, 21, 314, 318, 337
  ideological continuity through the
    stages, 316, 320–1

institutional, 22, 39, 43, 304
local government, 3, 10
long-term planning, 335
military, 21, 22, 39–40
oppostition to, 3, 21, 45, 148, 335;
  see also conservatives
overall planning, 313, 335
prevention of, by administrative
  practices, 336
tradition, 18
reform movement, 333; *see also* reform;
  reformers; self-strengthening
defined, 332
frustration by the throne, 333
reformers, 3–4, 15, 28, 29, 30, 46, 289,
  333; *see also* reform; reform
  movement; self-strengthening
conservatives' attack of, 335
and failure of the economy to
  expand, 327
from treaty ports and Hong Kong,
  320
ideology and intellectual heritage, 4,
  323
inability to form a sustained
  movement, 332–3
progressiveness, 327
promotion of modern enterprises,
  328
reasons for limited achievements,
  334–7
retrieval of China's lost economic
  rights (*li-ch'üan*), 328
and search for new revenues by
  modern means, 328
self-interests, 4
regional leaders, *see* regionalism
regionalism, 3–8, 10, 19, 328
comparison of impact on
  modernization in China and
  Japan, 330–1
rehabilitation, post-Taiping, 21, 41
Restoration, *see* Ch'ing Restoration
revenue, 10, 35–6, 42, 319, 326; *see also*
  taxes

Revenue, Board of, 36–7, 255; *see also*
  Six Boards
decisions on use of 40 per cent
  customs revenue for Foochow
  Navy Yard, 264–6
response to needs of Foochow Navy
  Yard, 263–4, 269
shortcomings, 309
Rochechouart, Comte Julien de, 187,
  189–90
Rochefort Arsenal, 185
Roman Catholicism, *see* Catholicism
Russell, Earl, 200
Russia
and Co-operative Policy, 153
relations with China, 124
Ryukyu Islands, 292
Ryukyuans, 292

Sacred Edicts of the K'ang-hsi emperor,
  229
Saigo Tsugumichi, 331
Saigon, 181, 184
Court of Appeal at, 184
salt administration/monopoly, 25, 29,
  123, 310
salt smuggling, 100, 104, 316; *see also*
  smuggling
San Francisco, 239
San-li (*Three Ritual Classics*), 29
San-tai, *see* Three Ages
scholar-gentry, 3, 61, 68, 71, 73, 90,
  102, 145; *see also* gentry and
  management of modern
  enterprises, 161–2, 172, 209
social inequities, 3
vested interests and reform in the
  examination system, 296, 313
scholar-official
emerging patriotism of, 315
modification of qualities by potential
  modernization of examination
  system, 296, 311, 320
reaction to Western threat, 315
retraining of, 311

science, modern/Western, 18, 99, 204, 229; *see also* technology, modern
Chinese understanding of, 168
as a component of *shih-hsüeh*, 308
and Confucianism, 324
recognition by Li Hung-chang and Shen Pao-chen as universal, 323
T'ung-wen Kuan and the study of, 146
Second Opium War, *see* Opium Wars
Second Sino-Foreign War, *see* Opium Wars
secret societies, 51
self-strengthening, 117, 323; *see also* defence industry; defence modernization; modern enterprises; modernization; modernizers; reform; reform movement; reformers
definition, 22–3, 319
funding priorities, 310
limitation of achievements by political milieu, 334, 336
need for a new spirit of patriotism, 310
proper approach to, 310
Shen Pao-chen and, 117, 143, 199; his exposition on, 301–4
success in, 334
sustained development of, 310
Tso Tsung-t'ang and, 115, 117
Self-strengthening Movement, 2, 330
in state building, 319
Segonzac, Louis Dunoyer de, 182, 201, 293
semicolonialism, 7–9; *see also* imperialism
semifeudalism, 9
sha-ch'uan (sea-going junks), 254
Shanghai, 97, 104, 139, 178, 233
factory workers, 210
linking by foreign telegraph line, 293
source of Foochow Navy Yard students, 227, 234
source of workmen for Foochow

Navy Yard, 194, 208, 210
Shantung, 252, 254, 255
Shen Chao-lin, 105
Shen-pao, 214, 222, 225
Shen Pao-chen, 11, 17–20, 21, 23
benevolent government, concern with, 43, 63
career, 1, 17–19, 30, 31–2, 42–5, 46, 48 n7, 49–50, 53, 54–6, 57–60, 85–6, 103, 107–9, 128, 129–33, 142, 172, 200, 315–17
Catholic missionaries, distaste for, 193
character, 31, 43, 44, 55, 83, 85, 104, 126, 173, 196, 198, 206, 208, 209, 215, 263, 336
Confucian idealism, 36, 43, 45, 61, 68, 302
Confucianism, 18, 53, 56, 66, 96, 103, 106, 127, 142–3, 158, 209, 312, 321; *ching-shih* (practical statecraft) leanings, 39, 43, 69, 87, 103, 142, 323; idealism, 36, 40, 43, 45, 68, 302, 334; pragmatic application of, 63–4, 66, 104, 323–4, 337
education and upbringing, 27–9, 43, 44–5, 87, 132, 315
enemies of, 46; *see also* Li Ho-nien
family, 24–32, 44–5, 55, 58, 86, 103, 104, 107–8, 126–7, 130, 132, 165, 176, 201, 318
filial piety, 27, 127, 137, 140, 201
health, 27, 54, 85, 200, 218, 221
and Hu Lin-i, 57–9
and Kuo Sung-tao, 102–3, 333
and Li Hung-chang, 46, 57, 85–6, 99, 308, 333, 336
Liang Kiang, governor-general of, 1, 17, 295, 298
loyalty (*chung*), 27, 30, 44, 55, 71, 85, 95, 127, 143, 300, 317–18, 322, 336
loyalty and filial piety (*chung-hsiao*), 60, 318

on men of talents (*jen-ts'ai*), 63
as moral successor of Lin Tse-hsü,
    44–5, 56, 317, 336
Tseng Kuo-fan and his career, 49,
    52–3, 54, 55, 57–9
Tso Tsung-t'ang and his career, 57
t'ung-nien, 46
Shen Pao-chen, as civil official
antiforeignism, 95, 99, 106
censor, 33–44, 34 n30, 45, 55, 299,
    303, 334, 337
champion of the people, 99
financial administration in Kiangsi,
    69–73, 73–83
foreign affairs, management of, 87,
    90–102, 104, 105, 132; *see also*
    Nanchang antimissionary incident
and gentry of Kiangsi, 66–8, 71–3,
    99, 329
on government, 43, 60–1, 62–3,
    63–6, 83, 301–4
Kiangsi, governor of, 56, 57, 59–60,
    63, 65, 71–2, 78, 81, 83, 85–6, 93,
    329
and merchants, 99
military affairs in Kiangsi, 74–6, 80,
    83–4, 85, 104
people's will, use of, 102–3
popular well-being, 35–6, 39, 43,
    62–3, 66, 69–73, 83, 102, 104,
    105, 106
and Tseng Kuo-fan, 47–9, 49–56,
    65–6, 71–2, 73, 75, 78, 80–6, 99,
    104, 247, 297, 329
Shen Pao-chen, as director-general of
    Foochow Navy Yard, 121, 123,
    125–9, 130, 136, 139, 156, 170,
    190, 195, 198–202, 206, 215–16,
    217, 236, 299, 318, 329, 334
abolition of taditional military
    examinations, proposal for, 257,
    291, 310
advanced training in Europe, 242,
    273, 278, 319; call for, 237, 257,
    278; concern with curriculum,

278; delay, 278
agreement to build three
    commercial vessels, 252–3
assessment of technological self-
    sufficiency of the Navy Yard, 238,
    257
broadening the base of defence
    modernization, 271, 272–3,
    295–6
catching up with the West, 203, 225,
    257, 272, 291, 307, 313
central government, relations with,
    162
commission of captains and officers,
    273–7
dedication to, 144
defence of Navy Yard, 151–3, 158,
    200–1, 256, 257, 259
education mission to Europe, *see*
    advanced training in Europe, this
    entry
encouragement of staff to acquire
    knowledge of science and
    technology, 170, 199, 242, 322
European tutelage, view on, 238,
    240
expansion and improvements, 242
financial administration, 246, 248–
    50, 263–6, 267; appeal to Tso
    Tsung-t'ang for aid, 263
foreign domination, sensitivity to
    danger of, 283
foreign languages, 242
founding of Navy Yard, 108, 245
French directors, relations with,
    178, 180–2, 183, 194, 201, 207,
    208, 257
Fukien authorities, relations with,
    126, 128, 151–2, 158, 162, 297
on further modernization in 1872,
    257–8, 261
and gentry of Fukien, 125–7, 195,
    198–9, 270
goals, 240
job specialization, promotion of,

170, 199

leadership, 158, 203–4, 207, 215–
16, 217–18, 223–6, 233, 241–3,
270–1, 275, 308, 322, 325

leaves of absence and mourning
periods, 103, 107, 126, 130, 132,
140, 143, 165, 176, 198, 201–2,
210, 212, 221, 226, 257, 258, 268,
322

maintaining of Chinese control,
183–7, 196, 198, 239, 242–3

management of Chinese personnel,
162, 172–6, 198–9, 202

management of European staff, 178,
183–4, 186–7, 191–6, 199–200

management of labour, 209–212

mathematics examinations, proposal
for, 257–8, 273, 290, 291, 309

mechanized coal mining, promotion
of, 273, 285–8, 297, 313, 319

de Méritens's criticism, response to,
156–7

naval technology: commitment to,
143, 216, 312; early exposure to,
32; recognition of constant
change, 272, 307

naval training and organization,
257, 272, 278–84, 312

naval warfare, study of in Europe,
278

new generation of gunboats,
promotion of, 216, 242–3, 270,
272, 278, 312

nurturing of men for higher stage of
defence modernization, 289, 308

nurturing of new naval officers,
275–8, 295, 297

organization of the squadron,
279–81, 297

perception of the Navy Yard, 133,
140–1, 143, 225, 272

personal assistants (*mu-yu*), 166–7,
329

personnel, recruitment and use, 162,
164–70

plant modernization, 216

powers, 130, 134–5, 140–1, 158–60,
162–3, 182, 187, 297

School: importance of, 142, 203–4,
226, 235, 277; shaping of its
character, 226–31, 234–5, 243,
321

science and technology: attitude to,
229–32; knowledge of, 166, 168,
204, 206–8, 216, 217–18, 225,
226, 241–2, 322; understanding
of, 257–8, 272, 307

self-comparison to Tso Tsung-t'ang,
142

and self-strengthening, 199, 203;
view on, 257; *see also* Shen Pao-
chen, as reformer and modernizer

study of science among scholar-
gentry class, 273, 308, 318, 321,
324, 337

support industries, 272–3

Taiwan: attempt to match Japanese
with ironclads, 292; defence of,
292, 293, 305, 331; as imperial
commissioner for maritime
defence, 287, 291, 292, 297;
service on, 17, 166, 169, 176, 212;
use of defence preparations for
training Foochow Navy Yard
personnel, 293; use of students
and cadets to survey coastal
waters, 293

technological independence, concern
with, 142, 203, 235, 240, 278

territorial power, 270, 297

throne, relations with, 208

transfer of technology, 142, 170, 321

and Tseng Kuo-fan, 117, 128–9

and Tso Tsung-t'ang, 108, 128–9,
132–3, 134, 263, 270

Tsungli Yamen: relations with, 208;
disappointment with, 260

and Wen-yü, 265, 266, 270

and Wu T'ang's opposition, 150

Shen Pao-chen, as modernizer and

reformer
on arms production (modern
system), 307
on central planning in arms
production and budgeting, 308,
309
China's administrative autonomy
(or integrity), concern for, 105,
128, 132, 293–4, 296, 301, 317,
333
and China's control over
modernizing undertakings, 285,
294
China's territorial integrity, concern
for, 105, 128, 333
Ch'ing state, view of, 321
on close relationship among foreign
relations, internal affairs, and
defence modernization, 300,
301–2, 304
combination of Confucian values
and defence modernization,
321–2
Confucianism: impact on reform
ideas, 36, 302, 321–3; impact on
yang-wu modernization, 17–8,
205, 206–7, 211, 228, 229–30,
234–5, 243, 308, 321
education reforms, advocacy of ,
243, 309
fate of China, concern with, 314
governmental structure, reform
proposals on, 302–3, 304, 313,
320, 328, 335, 337; *see also* policy
dicussion of 1867, this entry
ideas: development of, 334;
similarity to social Darwinism,
308
inherited institutions, attitude to,
39, 312, 313–14, 334
integration of *yang-wu* and
traditional government, 337
and Japanese naval challenge, 307
military technology, early exposure
to, 32

modern science and technology,
promotion of, 99
on modern warfare, 308
and modernization, 106, 132, 296,
333; *see also yang-wu* modernization
modernization efforts, frustration by
shortage of funds, 296, 297
modernizing elite, cultivation of,
309, 311, 313, 318, 320
modernizing enterprises, plan to
create environment favourable to,
299, 309
patriotism, 29–30, 32, 44, 106, 126,
132–3, 199, 217, 257, 317, 326,
337; transformation into
protonationalism, 317, 331;
similarity to nationalism, 300–1,
314, 334
pioneer and promoter of innovative
change, 298
plan to build a stronger China, 299
policy debate of 1874–5, 334;
proposals on defence
modernization, 304, 307–14,
320–1
policy discussion of 1867, 301–4,
313–14, 334; proposals on
governmental reforms, 310–13,
320–1
promotion of study of mathematics
among elites, 289–91
on railway, steamships, and
telegraph, 106, 132, 293–4;
foreign ownership of, 132, 293–5,
317
reform, 17–18, 32, 34, 40, 44–5,
69–73, 103, 173, 270, 271, 290,
309; a family tradition, 28–30
regional power, 132–3, 329
relations with Li Hung-chang, 85,
99, 292, 336
reputation for implementing reform
proposals, 299, 334
and scholar-gentry class, 296, 337
and self-strengthening, 199, 203;

exposition on, 257, 301–4, 308, 317

substantial learning (*shih-hsüeh*), advocacy of, 308

Taiwan coal, legalization and regulation of, 284–8

telegraph lines, 273, 293–5, 319

telegraphy, changing views on, 293–5, 296

t'i-yung thinking, 322–3, 324

transitional man, 334, 337

treaties: observance of, 100–1; use of, to curb foreign encroachments, 93, 104–5, 317; view on, 301

Tso Tsung-t'ang, 308, 336

use of modern ideas and methods to solve both *yang-wu* and traditional problems, 313, 334

wealth and power as goal, 321

Western methods, attitude to, 323

yang-wu, contributions to, 318–9

and *yang-wu* modernization, 106, 289, 337

yang-wu proponent, 296

Shen Shun-fa, 274

Shen Ta-ch'üan (grandfather of Shen Pao-chen), 25, 69

Shen T'ing-feng (father of Shen Pao-chen), 25–8, 30, 32, 44, 55, 107, 126–7, 165, 200

Shen Yü-ch'ing (Shen Pao-chen's fourth son), 166

Shensi and Kansu, governor-general of, 105, 108

Shih Ching-fen, 53

shih-ch'üan (administrative integrity), 301, 317

shih-hsing (application of *shih-hsüeh*), 14

shih-hsüeh (substantial learning), 14, 28, 308

shipbuilding, as proposed by the Tsungli Yamen (1874), 306

shipping

  Chinese commercial, 114, 115

  foreign, 62, 114

shipyards, 290, 303

  additional facilities, proposal for (1874), 306

Shore, Captain Henry Noel

  comments on Foochow Navy Yard, 211

  on officers and crew of Navy Yard vessels, 282, 283–4

  and on Navy Yard vessels, 223, 236

Siam, 167

Simon, Eugène, 184–5

Sinclair, Charles, 154

Singapore, 167, 226

  training cruises to, 233, 239

Sino-French relations, *see* China, relations with France

Sino-French War (1883–5), 197

Sino-Japanese War (1894–5), 22

Six Boards, 33; *see also individual boards*

Smith and Beacock, 213

smuggling, 105, 139; *see also* salt smuggling

Soochow Arsenal, 191, 196

South-East Asia, 16, 105, 181

  source of timber for Foochow Navy Yard, 175, 181, 194, 208

  training cruises to, 275, 281

Spector, Stanley, 4–6, 8, 19, 119

Ssu-ma Kuang, 302

ssu-shu (traditional schools), 234

steam-powered warships, 116; *see also* gunboats

steamers/steamships, 104–5, 109–11, 114, 115, 118, 128, 139; *see also* Foochow Navy Yard

  first Chinese-built, 281

Su-shun, 99

subprovincial localism, 330

Sun Chia-to, 90

Sung Chin, 258

  advocacy of using steamships against Taipings, 254–5

  concern with government spending priorities, 254–5

  criticism of Foochow Navy Yard

and Kiangnan Arsenal, 251–2,
254, 260, 261, 303, 320, 333
intellectual rigidity, 255
recommendation of Shen Pao-chen
for office, 58–9, 255
regard for Tseng Kuo-fan and Tso
Tsung-t'ang, 255
reputation as conservative diehard,
254
Sung Learning, School of, 13–14, 28
superstition, 28
Swainson, Lieutenant, R. N., 233
Szechwan, 330

ta-fu (chief officer), 274, 275, 276
Ta-ya (S.S. No. 15), 218, 253, 274
Tainan, *see* T'ai-wan fu
Taiping Rebellion, 4, 16, 17, 33, 34,
37–8, 41–2, 47–8, 50–2, 53–4,
57–8, 74, 83–4, 86, 90, 92, 96, 99,
110, 117, 128, 248, 254, 296, 307,
317, 327, 328, 329
Taiping War, *see* Taiping Rebellion
Taipings, *see* Taiping Rebellion
Taiwan, 17, 164, 167, 171, 172
defence: funds from Foochow Navy
Yard, 253, 254, 264; strain on
Fukien's financial resources, 268
Japanese invasion of, 21, 166, 169,
239, 253, 265, 268, 274–5, 287,
291–2, 296, 300, 305, 331
long-term development introduced
by Shen Pao-chen, 253–4, 291
modern coal mining on, 172, 254,
288–9, 296, 297, 298
native coal mining on, 284–8
telegraph lines on, 295, 298
timber, 208
use of Taiwanese coal in Foochow
Navy Yard, 222, 284–8
T'ai-wan, 164, 166, 169, 172
T'ai-wan fu, 169, 294
tao-k'u (grain intendant's treasury), 80
Taoism, 101
taotai, elimination of, proposed by

Shen Pao-chen, 303
taxes, 3, 10, 35; *see also* likin; revenue;
taxpayers; *ti-ting*; *ts'ao-che*
collection, 35–7, 66, 69, 310, 326
reduction, 36, 68–71, 72, 73, 316,
319
reform, 22, 36, 68, 71, 319
surcharges, 68–70
taxpayers, 68–71; *see also* taxes
tea trade, slump (1875), 265
technology, 198; *see also* science,
modern
Chinese attitude to, 203, 205, 206
military (including naval), 1, 22, 32,
109
modern/Western, 2, 18, 32, 99, 106,
176, 307, 315
recognition by Li Hung-chang and
Shen Pao-chen as universal, 323
transfer of, 9, 116, 142, 166, 170,
199, 203, 223–5, 321
telegraphy; *see also* railways and
telegraph lines
Foochow-to-T'ai-wan fu line,
proposal by Shen Pao-chen, 294
erection of foreign lines, 294
introduction of, 293–5
popular opposition to, 295
Shen Pao-chen's views on, 293–4
threat to Chinese administrative
integrity, 293, 294
Temple Lane, church on, 89–91
Teng Shih-ch'ang, 276
Teng-ying-chou (S.S. No. 18), 236
Three Ages (San-tai), 43
Three Ritual Classics, see *San-li*
throne, 3, 18, 51–2, 58, 60, 72, 80, 82,
84, 85–6, 92, 97, 107, 118, 130,
132, 136, 143, 149, 152, 255, 332
commitment to self-strengthening,
355
director-general of Foochow Navy
Yard, role in appointment of,
124–6
leadership, 7, 9–11, 109, 285, 296,

300, 301, 302, 303, 313, 335, 337
and political environment, 334
subversion of reform efforts, 333
support for Foochow Navy Yard,
112, 152, 158, 218, 248, 279
support for steamship building, 256
support for *yang-wu* modernization,
143, 146–7, 286, 287, 290, 291,
294, 296, 297
ti-ting (land and poll tax), 36, 68–70,
76–9, 83
reform of, 310, 319–20
t'i (principles), 323
confusion with *yung*, 323
t'i-yung (principles-application), 322–
3, 324
Tientsin, 218, 233
linking by foreign telegraph lines,
294
Tientsin Arsenal, 191, 196
comparison with Foochow Navy
Yard, 247
Tientsin Massacre, 2, 21, 102, 195
Ting Jih-ch'ang, 19, 23, 172
addition of science and mathematics
to civil service examinations,
proposal for, 290
advocacy of integration of *yang-wu*
and traditional government, 337
conservatives, attack on, 336
director-general of Foochow Navy
Yard, 176, 212, 239, 326
erection of telegraph lines on
Taiwan, 295
reform proposals of 1867, 304, 320
three regional fleets, proposal for,
312
use of Legalist term *pien-fa*, 321
yang-wu proponent, 296
torpedo bureau in Canton, 172
Tracey, Captain R. E., 233, 239
trade, coastal and riverine, 105,
114–15; *see also* Yangtze, trade
traditionalists, *see* conservatives
transports, naval, 116

Trasbot, Adrien, 181, 185–6, 191, 197,
201, 208, 215–16, 238
ambitions, 185–6
knowledge of civil engineering, 216
opinion of Giquel, 185
treaties, 87, 91; *see also* Shen Pao-chen
implementation by Chinese, 91, 132
Nanking, Treaty of, 257
Peking Agreement, 305
Peking, Convention of, 87, 88 n5
revision of, 167; Chinese preparation
for, 285, 300, 301
Tientsin, Treaty of, 87
treaty ports, 12, 31, 100, 195, 274, 277
reformer-writers from, 320
source of students for Foochow
Navy Yard, 289
source of workmen for Foochow
Navy Yard, 211, 289
tribute grain, *see ts'ao-che*
tsa-shui (miscellaneous taxes), 76–7
Ts'ai-ch'un, *see* T'ung-chih emperor
Ts'ai Kuo-hsiang, 281
ts'ao-che (tribute grain), 33, 36, 68–72,
73, 76–81, 123
shipping of, 16, 71, 72, 105, 114–15,
151, 313
transport on the Grand Canal,
149–50, 303, 310, 312
Tseng Chi-tse, 242
Tseng Heng-chung, 168, 168n, 193,
193n
teacher at Foochow Navy Yard
School, 226, 232
Tseng Kuo-fan, 7, 13, 18, 23, 38–40,
41–2, 45, 62, 65, 78, 102, 137,
242, 281, 302
and arsenals, 112, 116–17
campaign in Kiangsi, 47–8, 50,
52–4, 57–8, 60, 73–6, 78, 81–3,
135, 137, 162
defence of Foochow Navy Yard and
Kiangnan Arsenal, 255
and Foochow Navy Yard, 118, 171
and the Kiangnan Arsenal, 252, 255

military revenue and supplies, 54,
  59, 68–70, 73–5, 78–83, 104
and Nanchang antimissionary
  incident, 94–5, 97, 99
personal assistants (*mu-yu*) of, 47–9,
  58–9, 81, 169, 171
promotion of fleet organization for
  Foochow Navy Yard and
  Kiangnan Arsenal, 278–9
promotion of *yang-wu* causes, 317
regional power, 42, 57, 62, 116–17,
  119, 328
relations with Tso Tsung-t'ang, 117,
  128–9, 258, 329
and Shen Pao-chen, 47–9, 49–53,
  55–6, 59, 65–6, 72–3, 78, 81–5,
  102, 104, 128–9, 174, 316, 329
support for shipbuilding, 252, 258–9
and Wu T'ang, 149
Tseng Lan-sheng, *see* Tseng Heng-
  chung
Tso Ch'iu-ming, 28, 302
Tso chuan, 28, 102
Tso Tsung-t'ang, 18, 19, 23, 62, 64,
  108, 110, 111, 174, 251, 302
anti-Tso forces in Fukien, 145, 148,
  153, 156, 158
benevolent government, ideal of, 115
character, 144
Chekiang: relations with the
  administration of, 137; campaign
  in, 138
Chinese sovereignty, concern for,
  154
enemies of, 127
faction, 332
followers of, 149
and Foochow Navy Yard, 193;
  appointment of director-general,
  124–9; appointment of early
  captains, 273; appointment of
  French directors, 178–80;
  appointment of staff, 137–9, 162,
  164; Chinese control, concern
  with, 179–80; continued

involvement with after 1867, 252,
  270, 278, 325; defence of, 151–3,
  158–9, 256–7, 259, 261;
  definition of its character, 112–
  22, 190, 217, 225–6; finances of,
  120, 246–50, 253–5; financial aid
  to, 263–4; foreign domination,
  sensitivity to danger of, 283;
  founding of, 109–11, 118–21,
  124, 131, 135, 142, 203, 216, 238,
  273, 277; goals, 240; relations
  with, 134–5, 137, 171, 188;
  School, 225–7; technological
  independence, concern with, 240;
  use of local iron and coal, 284
and Fukien: factional struggles in,
  144–6, 151–3; relations with the
  administration of, 126–7, 137,
  144–5; relations with the gentry
  of, 145
Fukien and Chekiang: as governor-
  general of, 131; reforms in, 126–7,
  144, 149–50, 152
hatred of the British, 112, 177
Hunanese troops, 74–6
influence at court, 248
influence in Fukien and on Foochow
  Navy Yard after 1867, 329
military revenue and supplies, 73,
  80
modern troop-training programme
  at Ningpo, 155
North-West campaign, 108, 117,
  124, 129, 133, 136, 145, 304
patriotism, 112–13, 117, 118
prestige, 248
promotion of *yang-wu* causes, 317
and regional power, 118, 129, 133,
  329
response to British meddling, 154
and Shen Pao-chen, 74–5, 80,
  128–9, 133, 329
on strategic importance of Taiwan,
  164
relations with Tseng Kuo-fan, 74,

83–4, 124, 128–9, 258, 329

tsung-li ch'uan-cheng, see ch'in-ming tsung-li ch'uan-cheng ta-ch'en

Tsungli Yamen, 134, 147, 150, 156, 172, 200, 249, 291, 302, 315, 316
    defence and promotion of modern enterprises, 146–7, 200, 294, 304–6, 312
    and Foochow Navy Yard, 130, 252, 278
    and founding of Foochow Navy Yard, 110, 112, 119, 122, 126
    leadership in policy debate of 1874–5, 304–6, 308
    and the Nanchang antimissionary incident, 92–5, 97
    position on erection of telegraph lines, 293–5
    role in treaty revision, 301
    support for Foochow Navy Yard, 152–3, 156, 158–9, 185, 187, 200–1, 252, 260, 265–6, 290, 329

t'uan-lien, see militia

t'uan-lien ta-ch'en, see militia commissioner

Tung Huai, 23

T'ung-chih emperor, 21, 59, 143, 149

T'ung-chih Restoration, *see* Ch'ing Restoration

t'ung-shuai (commander-in-chief), 306, 308
    Shen Pao-chen's recommendations for, 308

T'ung-wen Kuan, 191, 200, 289, 291
    debate over curriculum, 146–8, 158
    discussion of practical training and official preferment for graduates, 309

Twitchett, Denis, 20

tzu-ch'iang, 22, 132; *see also* self-strengthening

tzu-ch'iang yün-tung see Self-strengthening Movement

tzu-chih (lit., self-government), 301

Tz'u-hsi, empress dowager, 4; *see also*
    throne
    and conservatives, 148, 336
    declaration of war on the foreign powers, 331
    and modern enterprises, 143, 147–8
    and patronage, 336
    political manipulations in 1875, 336–7
    and Wu T'ang, 149, 152
    and *yang-wu* reformers, 336

United States
    Civil War, 224
    consul at Kiukiang, 100
    consular officials, 221
    and Co-operative Policy, 153
    merchants, 104
    observers' comments on Foochow Navy Yard, 218
    relations with the Chinese, 100
    source of timber for Foochow Navy Yard, 208
    students studying in, 308

Véron, Pierre, Captain, 187–9

Vidal, Dr. Jean, 188–90, 192, 194

Wade, Thomas, memorandum on China's future policies, 109, 112, 117, 118

wai-hai shui-shih (outer-sea water force), 254

Walters, Ronald, 332

Wan-nien Ch'ing (S.S. No. 1), 169, 217, 218, 221, 273–4

Wang Erh-min, 2, 5

Wang Hsin-chung, 114–15

Wang K'ai-t'ai, 258, 259, 267, 281

Wang K'ai-yün, 99–100

Wang Mao-yin, 36–7, 37n

Wang Pao-ch'en
    service in Foochow Navy Yard, 167, 170
    service under Chang Chih-tung, 172

Wang Pi-ta, 90

Wang Yang-ming, 13
Wang Yüan-chih, 168, 170, 172, 174
War, Board of, 40, 41, 44, 282; *see also*
  Six Boards
Warrior, H.M.S., 224
water control, 28, 29
water force, traditional, 280, 306, 327
  abolition, proposal for, 253
  officers of Foochow Navy Yard
    squadron with previous service in,
    273–4, 276–7, 279, 281
  river fleets in Kiangsi, 73, 79–80, 93
  Shen Pao-ch'en's attempt to give its
    men modern naval training,
    282–3, 307
  Shen Pao-chen's proposal on
    keeping it active and alert, 303
wealth and power (*fu-ch'iang*), 14, 16,
  318, 321, 333
weapons, purchase and manufacture
  of, 306
Wei Han, 236
Wei Yüan, 14–16, 29, 87, 112–13, 312
Wei-yüan (S.S. No. 20), 239
Wen-hsiang, 18, 58–9
Wen-yü
  attitude to closing Foochow Navy
    Yard, 255
  control over Fukien customs, 256,
    268
  corruption, 256, 268
  desire to please the throne, 268
  inability to meet financial needs of
    Foochow Navy Yard, 264–6
  power struggle with Li Ho-nien,
    268, 330
  relation to Prince Kung by
    marriage, 256
  relations with Foochow Navy Yard,
    176, 196, 201, 221, 251, 267, 268
  relations with Shen Pao-chen, 265,
    266
West Lake, 110–11
Western encroachment, *see* foreign
  encroachments

Western expansion, *see* imperialism
Western navy, commission of captains,
  277
Western observers of Foochow Navy
  Yard, 221, 225, 244
Western political institutions, 2
Western powers, 300
  and Foochow Navy Yard, 130
  interests of, 153, 301
  naval development of, 113
Western presence, 333
Western science and technology, 2, 99;
  see also science, modern;
  technology
Western technicians, 7; *see also*
  artisans, Western
Whampoa, 120
Whitworth
  guns on the *Yang-wu*, 222
  tools, 213
Wittfogel, Karl A., 11
Wo-jen, 291
  attack of T'ung-wen Kuan, 146, 158
  denunciation by the throne, 147–8,
    334
  ideological challenge to modern
    enterprises, 245
working class, 8
Works, Board of, 58, 172; *see also* Six
  Boards
world-system approach, 7–8
Wright, Mary C., 2, 6, 12, 16, 21, 22,
  153, 312, 327
Wright, Tim, 211
Wu (provinces), *see* Liang Kiang
Wu Chung-hsiang (Shen Pao-chen's
  brother-in-law), 166, 174
  service under Li Hung-chang and
    Chang Chih-tung, 172
Wu Lan-sun, 25
Wu Shih-chung, 273
Wu Ta-t'ing
  direction of naval training at
    Kiangnan Arsenal, 165, 171, 172
  and factional struggles in Fukien, 145

in Foochow Navy Yard, 137, 138,
164–6, 172, 218
patriotism and *ching-shih* leanings,
165
victimization by Wu T'ang, 151,
164–5
Wu T'ang, 124–6, 133, 140, 258, 268
career, 149–50, 153, 334
character, 149–50
opposed Foochow Navy Yard,
150–3, 158, 245, 330
power struggle in Fukien, 148–53,
156, 158, 164–5, 175, 246, 330
Wuchang, 41, 47–8
Wuhan, 41

Yang Ch'ang-chün, 251
Yang Pao-ch'en, 291
Yang P'ei, 41
Yang-wu (S.S. No. 7), 221–2, 224, 239,
253, 256, 262, 274, 278, 283
yang-wu (Western matters or affairs), 2,
6–7, 10, 17–18, 87, 124, 132, 147,
243, 291, 304, 313, 316, 317, 318,
326, 332, 333, 336, 337; *see also*
defence modernization;
diplomatic practices, Western;
modern enterprises;
modernization; reform; *yang-wu*
modernization; *yang-wu* movement
advocacy of acting as a group, 333
definition, 22–3
effect on Sino-foreign relations, 159
enterprises, 131, 159, 171, 199, 334,
335; promoters, 335; seminal role,
272
experts, 49, 139, 161, 199; *see also*
Hu Kuang-yung; Huang Wei-
hsüan; Hsü Wen-yüan
increasing its appeal, 289
objective, 299
opposition to, 148, 296
proponents, 296
yang-wu modernization, 337; *see also*

defence modernization;
diplomatic practices, Western;
modern enterprises;
modernization; reform; *yang-wu*;
yang-wu movement
contribution made by former
Foochow Navy Yard men, 172
relationship with internal reforms,
304, 313, 319
yang-wu movement, 8–9, 23, 118, 172,
199; *see also yang-wu*; *yang-wu*
modernization; *yang-wu p'ai*
class origins of, 9
failure, 199
yang-wu p'ai (clique or party), 332, 333
yang-wu sector
careers for Foochow Navy Yard
School graduates, 230, 311
upward mobility in, 172, 311
Yang Yüeh-pin, 76
Yang Yung-nien, 274
Yangtze, 41, 48, 61, 76, 105
provinces, 71, 305
trade, 100
Yangtze River Fleet, 327, 328
Yeh Fu, 276
Yeh Wen-lan
director of modern coal mining on
Taiwan, 172
service in Foochow Navy Yard, 139,
167, 170
in Tso Tsung-t'ang's campaign in
Kwangtung, 139, 167
victimization by Wu T'ang, 151–2
Yehonala, *see* Tz'u-hsi
Yen Fu
introduction of social Darwinism,
308
student at Foochow Navy Yard
School, 226–7, 230
Yi li (*Chou Rituals*), 29
Ying-kuei
involvement with Foochow Navy
Yard, 111, 122, 136–7, 140, 145,
150, 155, 156, 158, 170, 183, 187,

250, 258, 267
promotion of the study of
    mathematics, 289–91
Yokosuka Naval Shipyard, comparison
    with Foochow Navy Yard, 240–1
yu-yung chih hsüeh (practical learning),
    32

Yü-k'o, 84–5, 89–90
Yü-shan, 51
Yüan-k'ai (S.S. No. 16), 221, 236, 264
yung, see mercenaries
Yung-pao (S.S. No. 12), 222
yung-ying, see mercenaries
Yunnan, 34